CW01310124

Woodrow Wilson, Josephus Daniels

The Collected Works of Woodrow Wilson

Madison & Adams Press 2019

Reading suggestions (available from Madison & Adams Press as Print & eBook)

Charles A. Eastman
CHARLES EASTMAN Premium Collection: Indian Boyhood, Indian Heroes and Great Chieftains, The Soul of the Indian & From the Deep Woods to Civilization

Woodrow Wilson
Essays of Woodrow Wilson

Woodrow Wilson
George Washington

Woodrow Wilson, Josephus Daniels
Woodrow Wilson: Speeches, Inaugural Addresses, State of the Union Addresses, Executive Decisions & Messages to Congress

Charles Eastman
The Life of Charles Eastman OhiyeS'a: Indian Boyhood & From the Deep Woods to Civilization (Volume 1&2)

James Madison Page
The True Story of Andersonville Prison

John Alexander Logan
The Great Conspiracy: Its Origin and History (Illustrated Edition)

Samuel R. Watkins
Co. Aytch: Maury Grays First Tennessee Regiment

John Singleton Mosby
Mosby's War Reminiscences - Stuart's Cavalry Campaigns

Thomas Wentworth Higginson
Army Life in a Black Regiment

Woodrow Wilson, Josephus Daniels
The Collected Works of Woodrow Wilson

Congressional Government, George Washington, The New Freedom, Essays, Inaugural Addresses, State of the Union Addresses, Presidential Decisions and Biography of Woodrow Wilson

Madison & Adams Press, 2019.
Contact: info@madisonadamspress.com

ISBN 978-80-273-3431-5

This is a publication of Madison & Adams Press. Our production consists of thoroughly prepared educational & informative editions: Advice & How-To Books, Encyclopedias, Law Anthologies, Declassified Documents, Legal & Criminal Files, Historical Books, Scientific & Medical Publications, Technical Handbooks and Manuals. All our publications are meticulously edited and formatted to the highest digital standard. The main goal of Madison & Adams Press is to make all informative books and records accessible to everyone in a high quality digital and print form.

Contents

Congressional Government	15
Preface	17
I. Introductory.	19
II. The House of Representatives.	35
III. The House of Representatives. Revenue and Supply.	57
IV. The Senate.	75
V. The Executive.	89
VI. Conclusion.	105
George Washington	117
Chapter I In Washington's Day	118
Chapter II A Virginian Breeding	135
Chapter III Colonel Washington	146
Chapter IV Mount Vernon Days	158
Chapter V The Heat of Politics	165
Chapter VI Piloting a Revolution	180
Chapter VII General Washington	190
Chapter VIII The Stress of Victory	203
Chapter IX First in Peace	211
Chapter X The First President of the United States	223
On Being Human	249
I	250
II	252
III	255
IV	257
V	259
VI	261
Essays	263
The New Freedom	265
Preface	267
I The Old Order Changeth	269
II What is Progress?	277
III Freemen Need No Guardians	283
IV Life Comes from the Soil	289
V The Parliament of the People	293
VI Let There Be Light	299
VII The Tariff—"Protection," or Special Privilege?	305

VIII Monopoly, or Opportunity?	313
IX Benevolence, or Justice?	321
X The Way to Resume is to Resume	329
XI The Emancipation of Business	337
XII The Liberation of a People's Vital Energies	343
When A Man Comes To Himself	349
I	350
II	351
III	353
IV	354
V	356
VI	358
The Study of Administration	359
I.	361
II.	367
III.	371
Leaders of Men	375
The New Democracy	391
Inaugural Addresses	399
First Inaugural Address	401
Second Inaugural Address	405
State of the Union Addresses	407
First State of the Union address	408
Second State of the Union address	413
Third State of the Union address	419
Fourth State of the Union address	429
Fifth State of the Union address	432
Sixth State of the Union address	437
Seventh State of the Union address	444
Eighth State of the Union address	451
Speeches & Addresses	455
First Address to Congress	457
Address on the Banking System	459
Address at Gettysburg	461
Address on Mexican Affairs	463
Understanding America	467
Address Before the Southern Commercial Congress	471
Trusts and Monopolies	475

Panama Canal Tolls	479
14 Tampico Incident	481
In the Firmament of Memory	483
Memorial Day Address at Arlington	485
Closing a Chapter	486
Annapolis Commencement Address	489
The Meaning of Liberty	493
American Neutrality	497
Appeal for Additional Revenue	499
The Opinion of the World	501
The Power of Christian Young Men	503
A Message	509
Address Before the United States Chamber of Commerce	511
To Naturalized Citizens	517
Address at Milwaukee	519
The Submarine Question	525
American Principles	529
The Demands of Railway Employees	533
Speech of Acceptance	537
Lincoln's Beginnings	545
The Triumph of Women's Suffrage	547
The Terms of Peace	549
Meeting Germany's Challenge	553
Request for Authority	557
The Call to War	561
To the Country	567
The German Plot	571
Reply to the Pope	575
Labor Must be Free	577
The Call for War with Austria-Hungary	587
Government Administration of Railways	593
The Conditions of Peace	595
Force to the Utmost	599
Presidential Decisions	603
The State of War: The President's Proclamation of April 6, 1917.	605
Formal U.S. Declaration of War with Germany, 6 April 1917	609
Biography of Woodrow Wilson	611

Footnotes

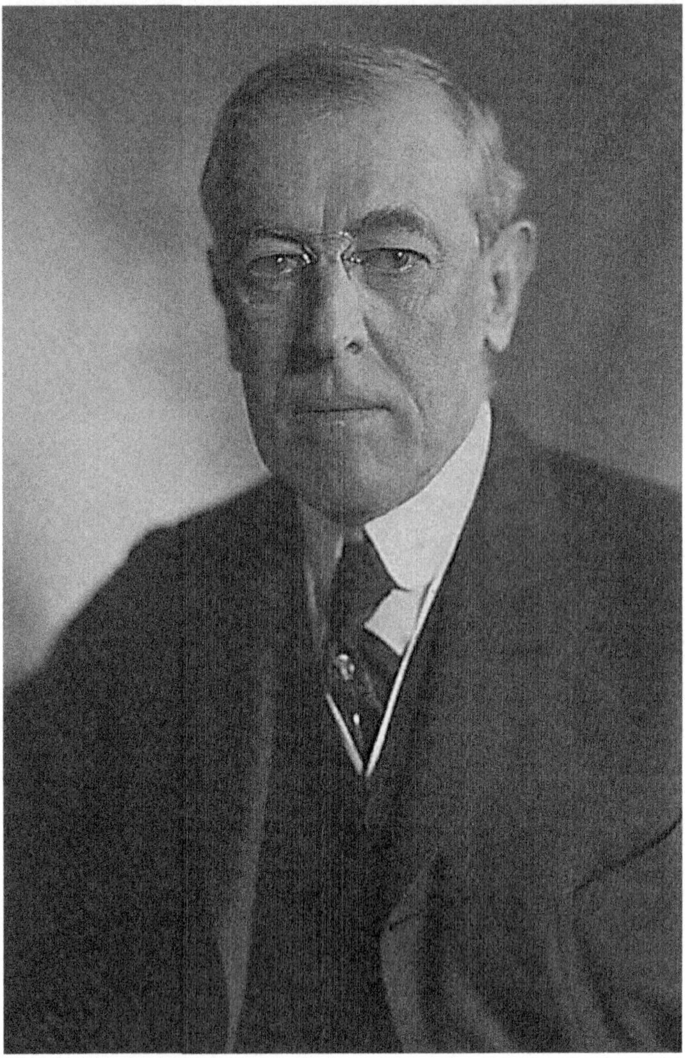

Congressional Government

Preface

The object of these essays is not to exhaust criticism of the government of the United States, but only to point out the most characteristic practical features of the federal system. Taking Congress as the central and predominant power of the system, their object is to illustrate everything Congressional. Everybody has seen, and critics without number have said, that our form of national government is singular, possessing a character altogether its own; but there is abundant evidence that very few have seen just wherein it differs most essentially from the other governments of the world. There have been and are other federal systems quite similar, and scarcely any legislative or administrative principle of our Constitution was young even when that Constitution was framed. It is our legislative and administrative *machinery* which makes our government essentially different from all other great governmental systems. The most striking contrast in modern politics is not between presidential and monarchical governments, but between Congressional and Parliamentary governments. Congressional government is Committee government; Parliamentary government is government by a responsible Cabinet Ministry. These are the two principal types which present themselves for the instruction of the modern student of the practical in politics: administration by semi-independent executive agents who obey the dictation of a legislature to which they are not responsible, and administration by executive agents who are the accredited leaders and accountable servants of a legislature virtually supreme in all things. My chief aim in these essays has been, therefore, an adequate illustrative contrast of these two types of government, with a view to making as plain as possible the actual conditions of federal administration. In short, I offer, not a commentary, but an outspoken presentation of such cardinal facts as may be sources of practical suggestion.

WOODROW WILSON
JOHNS HOPKINS UNIVERSITY, *October* 7, 1884.

I
Introductory.

> The laws reach but a very little way. Constitute government how you please, infinitely the greater part of it must depend upon the exercise of powers, which are left at large to the prudence and uprightness of ministers of state. Even all the use and potency of the laws depends upon them. Without them your commonwealth is no better than a scheme upon paper; and not a living, active, effective organization. —BURKE.
>
> The great fault of political writers is their too close adherence to the forms of the system of state which they happen to be expounding or examining. They stop short at the anatomy of institutions, and do not penetrate to the secret of their functions. —JOHN MORLEY.

IT would seem as if a very wayward fortune had presided over the history of the Constitution of the United States, inasmuch as that great federal charter has been alternately violated by its friends and defended by its enemies. It came hard by its establishment in the first place, prevailing with difficulty over the strenuous forces of dissent which were banded against it. While its adoption was under discussion the voices of criticism were many and authoritative, the voices of opposition loud in tone and ominous in volume, and the Federalists finally triumphed only by dint of hard battle against foes, formidable both in numbers and in skill. But the victory was complete,—astonishingly complete. Once established, the new government had only the zeal of its friends to fear. Indeed, after its organization very little more is heard of the party of opposition; they disappear so entirely from politics that one is inclined to think, in looking back at the party history of that time, that they must have been not only conquered but converted as well. There was well-nigh universal acquiescence in the new order of things. Not everybody, indeed, professed himself a Federalist, but everybody conformed to federalist practice. There were jealousies and bickerings, of course, in the new Congress of the Union, but no party lines, and the differences which caused the constant brewing and breaking of storms in Washington's first cabinet were of personal rather than of political import. Hamilton and Jefferson did not draw apart because the one had been an ardent and the other only a lukewarm friend of the Constitution, so much as because they were so different in natural bent and temper that they would have been like to disagree and come to drawn points wherever or however brought into contact. The one had inherited warm blood and a bold sagacity, while in the other a negative philosophy ran suitably through cool veins. They had not been meant for yoke-fellows.

There was less antagonism in Congress, however, than in the cabinet; and in none of the controversies that did arise was there shown any serious disposition to quarrel with the Constitution itself; the contention was as to the obedience to be rendered to its provisions. No one threatened to withhold his allegiance, though there soon began to be some exhibition of a disposition to confine obedience to the letter of the new commandments, and to discountenance all attempts to do what was not plainly written in the tables of the law. It was recognized as no longer fashionable to say aught against the principles of the Constitution; but all men could not be of one mind, and political parties began to take form in antagonistic schools of constitutional construction. There straightway arose two rival sects of political Pharisees, each professing a more perfect conformity and affecting greater "ceremonial cleanliness" than the other. The very men who had resisted with might and main the adoption of the Constitution became, under the new division of parties, its champions, as sticklers for a strict, a rigid, and literal construction.

They were consistent enough in this, because it was quite natural that their one-time fear of a strong central government should pass into a dread of the still further expansion of the power of that government, by a too loose construction of its charter; but what I would emphasize here is not the motives or the policy of the conduct of parties in our early national politics, but

19

the fact that opposition to the Constitution as a constitution, and even hostile criticism of its provisions, ceased almost immediately upon its adoption; and not only ceased, but gave place to an undiscriminating and almost blind worship of its principles, and of that delicate dual system of sovereignty, and that complicated scheme of double administration which it established. Admiration of that one-time so much traversed body of law became suddenly all the vogue, and criticism was estopped. From the first, even down to the time immediately preceding the war, the general scheme of the Constitution went unchallenged; nullification itself did not always wear its true garb of independent state sovereignty, but often masqueraded as a constitutional right; and the most violent policies took care to make show of at least formal deference to the worshipful fundamental law. The divine right of kings never ran a more prosperous course than did this unquestioned prerogative of the Constitution to receive universal homage. The conviction that our institutions were the best in the world, nay more, the model to which all civilized states must sooner or later conform, could not be laughed out of us by foreign critics, nor shaken out of us by the roughest jars of the system.

Now there is, of course, nothing in all this that is inexplicable, or even remarkable; any one can see the reasons for it and the benefits of it without going far out of his way; but the point which it is interesting to note is that we of the present generation are in the first season of free, outspoken, unrestrained constitutional criticism. We are the first Americans to hear our own countrymen ask whether the Constitution is still adapted to serve the purposes for which it was intended; the first to entertain any serious doubts about the superiority of our own institutions as compared with the systems of Europe; the first to think of remodeling the administrative machinery of the federal government, and of forcing new forms of responsibility upon Congress.

The evident explanation of this change of attitude towards the Constitution is that we have been made conscious by the rude shock of the war and by subsequent developments of policy, that there has been a vast alteration in the conditions of government; that the checks and balances which once obtained are no longer effective; and that we are really living under a constitution essentially different from that which we have been so long worshiping as our own peculiar and incomparable possession. In short, this model government is no longer conformable with its own original pattern. While we have been shielding it from criticism it has slipped away from us. The noble charter of fundamental law given us by the Convention of 1787 is still our Constitution; but it is now our *form of government* rather in name than in reality, the form of the Constitution being one of nicely adjusted, ideal balances, whilst the actual form of our present government is simply a scheme of congressional supremacy. National legislation, of course, takes force now as at first from the authority of the Constitution; but it would be easy to reckon by the score acts of Congress which can by no means be squared with that great instrument's evident theory. We continue to think, indeed, according to long-accepted constitutional formulae, and it is still politically unorthodox to depart from old-time phraseology in grave discussions of affairs; but it is plain to those who look about them that most of the commonly received opinions concerning federal constitutional balances and administrative arrangements are many years behind the actual practices of the government at Washington, and that we are farther than most of us realize from the times and the policy of the framers of the Constitution. It is a commonplace observation of historians that, in the development of constitutions, names are much more persistent than the functions upon which they were originally bestowed; that institutions constantly undergo essential alterations of character, whilst retaining the names conferred upon them in their first estate; and the history of our own Constitution is but another illustration of this universal principle of institutional change. There has been a constant growth of legislative and administrative practice, and a steady accretion of precedent in the management of federal affairs, which have broadened the sphere and altered the functions of the government without perceptibly affecting the vocabulary of our constitutional language. Ours is, scarcely less than the British, a living and fecund system. It does not, indeed, find its rootage so widely in the hidden soil of unwritten law; its tap-root at least is the Constitution; but the Constitution is now, like Magna Carta and the Bill of Rights, only the sap-centre of a system of government vastly larger than the stock from which it has branched, —a system some of whose forms have only very indistinct and rudimental beginnings in the simple substance of the Constitution, and which exercises many functions apparently quite foreign to the primitive properties contained in the fundamental law.

The Constitution itself is not a complete system; it takes none but the first steps in organization. It does little more than lay a foundation of principles. It provides with all possible brevity for the establishment of a government having, in several distinct branches, executive, legislative, and judicial powers. It vests executive power in a single chief magistrate, for whose election and inauguration it makes carefully definite provision, and whose privileges and prerogatives it defines with succinct clearness; it grants specifically enumerated powers of legislation to a representative Congress, outlining the organization of the two houses of that body and definitely providing for the election of its members, whose number it regulates and the conditions of whose choice it names; and it establishes a Supreme Court with ample authority of constitutional interpretation, prescribing the manner in which its judges shall be appointed and the conditions of their official tenure. Here the Constitution's work of organization ends, and the fact that it attempts nothing more is its chief strength. For it to go beyond elementary provisions would be to lose elasticity and adaptability. The growth of the nation and the consequent development of the governmental system would snap asunder a constitution which could not adapt itself to the new conditions of an advancing society. If it could not stretch itself to the measure of the times, it must be thrown off and left behind, as a by-gone device; and there can, therefore, be no question that our Constitution has proved lasting because of its simplicity. It is a corner-stone, not a complete building; or, rather, to return to the old figure, it is a root, not a perfect vine.

The chief fact, therefore, of our national history is that from this vigorous tap-root has grown a vast constitutional system, —a system branching and expanding in statutes and judicial decisions, as well as in unwritten precedent; and one of the most striking facts, as it seems to me, in the history of our politics is, that that system has never received complete and competent critical treatment at the hands of any, even the most acute, of our constitutional writers. They view it, as it were, from behind. Their thoughts are dominated, it would seem, by those incomparable papers of the "Federalist," which, though they were written to influence only the voters of 1788, still, with a strange, persistent longevity of power, shape the constitutional criticism of the present day, obscuring much of that development of constitutional practice which has since taken place. The Constitution in operation is manifestly a very different thing from the Constitution of the books. "An observer who looks at the living reality will wonder at the contrast to the paper description. He will see in the life much which is not in the books; and he will not find in the rough practice many refinements of the literary theory."[1] It is, therefore, the difficult task of one who would now write at once practically and critically of our national government to escape from theories and attach himself to facts, not allowing himself to be confused by a knowledge of what that government was intended to be, or led away into conjectures as to what it may one day become, but striving to catch its present phases and to photograph the delicate organism in all its characteristic parts exactly as it is to-day; an undertaking all the more arduous and doubtful of issue because it has to be entered upon without guidance from writers of acknowledged authority.

The leading inquiry in the examination of any system of government must, of course, concern primarily the real depositaries and the essential machinery of power. There is always a centre of power: where in this system is that centre? in whose hands is self-sufficient authority lodged, and through what agencies does that authority speak and act? The answers one gets to these and kindred questions from authoritative manuals of constitutional exposition are not satisfactory, chiefly because they are contradicted by self-evident facts. It is said that there is no single or central force in our federal *scheme*; and so there is not in the federal scheme, but only a balance of powers and a nice adjustment of interactive checks, as all the books say. How is it, however, in the practical conduct of the federal government? In that, unquestionably, the predominant and controlling force, the centre and source of all motive and of all regulative power, is Congress. All niceties of constitutional restriction and even many broad principles of constitutional limitation have been overridden, and a thoroughly organized system of congressional control set up which gives a very rude negative to some theories of balance and some schemes for distributed powers, but which suits well with convenience, and does violence to none of the principles of self-government contained in the Constitution.

This fact, however, though evident enough, is not on the surface. It does not obtrude itself upon the observation of the world. It runs through the undercurrents of government, and takes shape only in the inner channels of legislation and administration which are not open to the common view. It can be discerned most readily by comparing the "literary theory" of the Constitution with the actual machinery of legislation, especially at those points where that machinery regulates the relations of Congress with the executive departments, and with the attitude of the houses towards the Supreme Court on those occasions, happily not numerous, when legislature and judiciary have come face to face in direct antagonism. The "literary theory" is distinct enough; every American is familiar with the paper pictures of the Constitution. Most prominent in such pictures are the ideal checks and balances of the federal system, which may be found described, even in the most recent books, in terms substantially the same as those used in 1814 by John Adams in his letter to John Taylor. "Is there," says Mr. Adams, "a constitution upon record more complicated with balances than ours? In the first place, eighteen states and some territories are balanced against the national government....In the second place, the House of Representatives is balanced against the Senate, the Senate against the House. In the third place, the executive authority is, in some degree, balanced against the legislative. In the fourth place, the judicial power is balanced against the House, the Senate, the executive power, and the state governments. In the fifth place, the Senate is balanced against the President in all appointments to office, and in all treaties....In the sixth place, the people hold in their hands the balance against their own representatives, by biennial ...elections. In the seventh place, the legislatures of the several states are balanced against the Senate by sextennial elections. In the eighth place, the electors are balanced against the people in the choice of the President. Here is a complicated refinement of balances, which, for anything I recollect, is an invention of our own and peculiar to us."[2]

All of these balances are reckoned essential in the theory of the Constitution; but none is so quintessential as that between the national and the state governments; it is the pivotal quality of the system, indicating its principal, which is its federal characteristic. The object of this balance of thirty-eight States "and some territories" against the powers of the federal government, as also of several of the other balances enumerated, is not, it should be observed, to prevent the invasion by the national authorities of those provinces of legislation by plain expression or implication reserved to the States, —such as the regulation of municipal institutions, the punishment of ordinary crimes, the enactment of laws of inheritance and of contract, the erection and maintenance of the common machinery of education, and the control of other such like matters of social economy and every-day administration, —but to check and trim national policy on national questions, to turn Congress back from paths of dangerous encroachment on middle or doubtful grounds of jurisdiction, to keep sharp, when it was like to become dim, the line of demarcation between state and federal privilege, to readjust the weights of jurisdiction whenever either state or federal scale threatened to kick the beam. There never was any great likelihood that the national government would care to take from the States their plainer prerogatives, but there was always a violent probability that it would here and there steal a march over the borders where territory like its own invited it to appropriation; and it was for a mutual defense of such border-land that the two governments were given the right to call a halt upon one another. It was purposed to guard not against revolution, but against unrestrained exercise of questionable powers.

The extent to which the restraining power of the States was relied upon in the days of the Convention, and of the adoption of the Constitution, is strikingly illustrated in several of the best known papers of the "Federalist;" and there is no better means of realizing the difference between the actual and the ideal constitutions than this of placing one's self at the point of view of the public men of 1787-89. They were disgusted with the impotent and pitiable Confederation, which could do nothing but beg and deliberate; they longed to get away from the selfish feuds of "States dissevered, discordant, belligerent," and their hopes were centred in the establishment of a strong and lasting union, such as could secure that concert and facility of common action in which alone there could be security and amity. They were, however, by no means sure of being able to realize their hopes, contrive how they might to bring the States together into a more perfect confederation. The late colonies had but recently become compactly organized, self-governing States, and were standing somewhat stiffly apart, a group of consequential sovereignties, jealous to maintain their blood-bought prerogatives, and quick to distrust any power set above them, or arrogating to itself the control of their restive wills. It was not to be expected that the sturdy, self-reliant, masterful men who had won independence for their native colonies, by passing through the flames of battle, and through the equally fierce fires of bereavement and financial ruin, would readily transfer their affection and allegiance from the new-made States, which were their homes, to the federal government, which was to be a mere artificial creation, and which could be to no man as his home government. As things looked then, it seemed idle to apprehend a too great diminution of state rights: there was every reason, on the contrary, to fear that any union that could be agreed upon would lack both vitality and the ability to hold its ground against the jealous self-assertion of the sovereign commonwealths of its membership. Hamilton but spoke the common belief of all thinking men of the time when he said: "It will always be far more easy for the state governments to encroach upon the national authorities than for the national government to encroach upon the state authorities;" and he seemed to furnish abundant support for the opinion, when he added, that "the proof of this proposition turns upon the greater degree of influence which the state governments, if they administer their affairs uprightly and prudently, will generally possess over the people; a circumstance which, at the same time, teaches us that there is an inherent and intrinsic weakness in all federal constitutions, and that too much pains cannot be taken in their organization to give them all the force that is compatible with the principles of liberty."[3]

Read in the light of the present day, such views constitute the most striking of all commentaries upon our constitutional history. Manifestly the powers reserved to the States were expected to serve as a very real and potent check upon the federal government; and yet we can see plainly enough now that this balance of state against national authorities has proved, of all constitutional checks, the least effectual. The proof of the pudding is the eating thereof, and we can nowadays detect in it none of that strong flavor of state sovereignty which its cooks thought they were giving it. It smacks, rather, of federal omnipotence, which they thought to mix in only in very small and judicious quantities. "From the nature of the case," as Judge Cooley says, "it was impossible that the powers reserved to the States should constitute a restraint upon the increase of federal power, to the extent that was at first expected. The federal government was necessarily made the final judge of its own authority, and the executor of its own will, and any effectual check to the gradual amplification of its jurisdiction must therefore be found in the construction put by those administering it upon the grants of the Constitution, and in their own sense of constitutional obligation. And as the true line of division between federal and state powers has, from the very beginning, been the subject of contention and of honest differences of opinion, it must often happen that to advance and occupy some disputed ground will seem to the party having the power to do so a mere matter of constitutional duty."[4]

During the early years of the new national government there was, doubtless, much potency in state will; and had federal and state powers then come face to face, before Congress and the President had had time to overcome their first awkwardness and timidity, and to discover the safest walks of their authority and the most effectual means of exercising their power, it is probable that state prerogatives would have prevailed. The central government, as every one remembers, did not at first give promise of a very great career. It had inherited some of the contempt which had attached to the weak Congress of the Confederation. Two of the thirteen States held aloof from the Union until they could be assured of its stability and success; many of the other States had come into it reluctantly, all with a keen sense of sacrifice, and there could not be said to be any very wide-spread or undoubting belief in its ultimate survival. The members of the first Congress, too, came together very tardily, and in no very cordial or confident spirit of coöperation; and after they had assembled they were for many months painfully embarrassed, how and upon what subjects to exercise their new and untried functions. The President was denied formal precedence in dignity by the Governor of New York, and must himself have felt inclined to question the consequence of his official station, when he found that amongst the principal questions with which he had to deal were some which concerned no greater things than petty points of etiquette and ceremonial; as, for example, whether one day in the week would be sufficient to receive visits of compliment, "and what would be said if he were sometimes to be seen at quiet tea-parties."[5] But this first weakness of the new government was only a transient phase in its history, and the federal authorities did not invite a direct issue with the States until they had had time to reckon their resources and to learn facility of action. Before Washington left the presidential chair the federal government had been thoroughly organized, and it fast gathered strength and confidence as it addressed itself year after year to the adjustment of foreign relations, to the defense of the western frontiers, and to the maintenance of domestic peace. For twenty-five years it had no chance to think of those questions of internal policy which, in later days, were to tempt it to stretch its constitutional jurisdiction. The establishment of the public credit, the revival of commerce, and the encouragement of industry; the conduct, first, of a heated controversy, and finally of an unequal war with England; the avoidance, first, of too much love, and afterwards of too violent hatred of France; these and other like questions of great pith and moment gave it too much to do to leave it time to think of nice points of constitutional theory affecting its relations with the States.

But still, even in those busy times of international controversy, when the lurid light of the French Revolution outshone all others, and when men's minds were full of those ghosts of '76, which took the shape of British aggressions, and could not be laid by any charm known to diplomacy, —even in those times, busy about other things, there had been premonitions of the unequal contest between state and federal authorities. The purchase of Louisiana had given new form and startling significance to the assertion of national sovereignty, the Alien and Sedition Laws had provoked the plain-spoken and emphatic protests of Kentucky and Virginia, and the Embargo had exasperated New England to threats of secession.

Nor were these open assumptions of questionable prerogatives on the part of the national government the most significant or unequivocal indications of an assured increase of federal power. Hamilton, as Secretary of the Treasury, had taken care at the very beginning to set the national policy in ways which would unavoidably lead to an almost indefinite expansion of the sphere of federal legislation. Sensible of its need of guidance in those matters of financial administration which evidently demanded its immediate attention, the first Congress of the Union promptly put itself under the direction of Hamilton. "It is not a little amusing," says Mr. Lodge, "to note how eagerly Congress, which had been ably and honestly struggling with the revenue, with commerce, and with a thousand details, fettered in all things by the awkwardness inherent in a legislative body, turned for relief to the new secretary."[6] His advice was asked and taken in almost everything, and his skill as a party leader made easy many of the more difficult paths of the new government. But no sooner had the powers of that government begun to be exercised under his guidance than they began to grow. In his famous Report on Manufactures were laid the foundations of that system of protective duties which was destined to hang all the industries of the country upon the skirts of the federal power, and to make every trade and craft in the land sensitive to every wind of party that might blow at Washington; and in his equally celebrated Report in favor of the establishment of a National Bank, there was called into requisition, for the first time, that puissant doctrine of the "implied powers" of the Constitution which has ever since been the chief dynamic principle in our constitutional history. "This great doctrine, embodying the principle of liberal construction, was," in the language of Mr. Lodge, "the most formidable weapon in the armory of the Constitution; and when Hamilton grasped it he knew, and his opponents felt, that here was something capable of conferring on the federal government powers of almost any extent."[7] It served first as a sanction for the charter of the United States Bank, —an institution which was the central pillar of Hamilton's wonderful financial administration, and around which afterwards, as then, played so many of the lightnings of party strife. But the Bank of the United States, though great, was not the greatest of the creations of that lusty and seductive doctrine. Given out, at length, with the sanction of the federal Supreme Court,[8] and containing, as it did, in its manifest character as a doctrine of legislative prerogative, a very vigorous principle of constitutional growth, it quickly constituted Congress the dominant, nay, the irresistible, power of the federal system, relegating some of the chief balances of the Constitution to an insignificant rôle in the "literary theory" of our institutions.

Its effect upon the status of the States in the federal system was several-fold. In the first place, it clearly put the constitutions of the States at a great disadvantage, inasmuch as there was in them no like principle of growth. Their stationary sovereignty could by no means keep pace with the nimble progress of federal influence in the new spheres thus opened up to it. The doctrine of implied powers was evidently both facile and irresistible. It concerned the political discretion of the national legislative power, and could, therefore, elude all obstacles of judicial interference; for the Supreme Court very early declared itself without authority to question the legislature's privilege of determining the nature and extent of its own powers in the choice of means for giving effect to its constitutional prerogatives, and it has long stood as an accepted canon of judicial action, that judges should be very slow to oppose their opinions to the legislative will in cases in which it is not made demonstrably clear that there has been a plain violation of some unquestionable constitutional principle, or some explicit constitutional provision. Of encroachments upon state as well as of encroachments upon federal powers, the federal authorities are, however, in most cases the only, and in all cases the final, judges. The States are absolutely debarred even from any effective defense of their plain prerogatives, because not they, but the national authorities, are commissioned to determine with decisive and unchallenged authoritativeness what state powers shall be recognized in each case of contest or of conflict. In short, one of the privileges which the States have resigned into the hands of the federal government is the all-inclusive privilege of determining what they themselves can do. Federal courts can annul state action, but state courts cannot arrest the growth of congressional power.[9]

But this is only the doctrinal side of the case, simply its statement with an "if" and a "but." Its practical issue illustrates still more forcibly the altered and declining status of the States in the constitutional system. One very practical issue has been to bring the power of the federal government home to every man's door, as, no less than his own state government, his immediate over-lord. Of course every new province into which Congress has been allured by the principle of implied powers has required for its administration a greater or less enlargement of the national civil service, which now, through its hundred thousand officers, carries into every community of the land a sense of federal power, as the power of powers, and fixes the federal authority, as it were, in the very habits of society. That is not a foreign but a familiar and domestic government whose officer is your next-door neighbor, whose representatives you deal with every day at the post-office and the custom-house, whose courts sit in your own State, and send their own marshals into your own county to arrest your own fellow-townsman, or to call you yourself by writ to their witness-stands. And who can help respecting officials whom he knows to be backed by the authority and even, by the power of the whole nation, in the performance of the duties in which he sees them every day engaged? Who does not feel that the marshal represents a greater power than the sheriff does, and that it is more dangerous to molest a mail-carrier than to knock down a policeman? This personal contact of every citizen with the federal government, —a contact which makes him feel himself a citizen of a greater state than that which controls his every-day contracts and probates his father's will, —more than offsets his sense of dependent loyalty to local authorities by creating a sensible bond of allegiance to what presents itself unmistakably as the greater and more sovereign power.

In most things this bond of allegiance does not bind him oppressively nor chafe him distressingly; but in some things it is drawn rather painfully tight. Whilst federal postmasters are valued and federal judges unhesitatingly obeyed, and whilst very few people realize the weight of customs-duties, and as few, perhaps, begrudge license taxes on whiskey and tobacco, everybody eyes rather uneasily the federal supervisors at the polls. This is preëminently a country of frequent elections, and few States care to increase the frequency by separating elections of state from elections of national functionaries. The federal supervisor, consequently, who oversees the balloting for congressmen, practically superintends the election of state officers also; for state officers and congressmen are usually voted for at one and the same time and place, by ballots bearing in common an entire "party ticket;" and any authoritative scrutiny of these ballots after they have been cast, or any peremptory power of challenging those who offer to cast them, must operate as an interference with state no less than with federal elections. The authority of Congress to regulate the manner of choosing federal representatives pinches when it is made thus to include also the supervision of those state elections which are, by no implied power even, within the sphere of federal prerogative. The supervisor represents the very ugliest side of federal supremacy; he belongs to the least liked branch of the civil service; but his existence speaks very clearly as to the present balance of powers, and his rather hateful privileges must, under the present system of mixed elections, result in impairing the self-respect of state officers of election by bringing home to them a vivid sense of subordination to the powers at Washington.

A very different and much larger side of federal predominance is to be seen in the history of the policy of internal improvements. I need not expound that policy here. It has been often enough mooted and long enough understood to need no explanation. Its practice is plain and its persistence unquestionable. But its bearings upon the status and the policies of the States are not always clearly seen or often distinctly pointed out. Its chief results, of course, have been that expansion of national functions which was necessarily involved in the application of national funds by national employees to the clearing of inland water-courses and the improvement of harbors, and the establishment of the very questionable precedent of expending in favored localities moneys raised by taxation which bears with equal incidence upon the people of all sections of the country; but these chief results by no means constitute the sum of its influence. Hardly less significant and real, for instance, are its moral effects in rendering state administrations less self-reliant and efficient, less prudent and thrifty, by accustoming them to accepting subsidies for internal improvements from the federal coffers; to depending upon the national revenues, rather than upon their own energy and enterprise, for means of developing those resources which it should be the special province of state administration to make available and profitable. There can, I suppose, be little doubt that it is due to the moral influences of this policy that the States are now turning to the common government for aid in such things as education. Expecting to be helped, they will not help themselves. Certain it is that there is more than one State which, though abundantly able to pay for an educational system of the greatest efficiency, fails to do so, and contents itself with imperfect temporary makeshifts because there are immense surpluses every year in the national treasury which, rumor and unauthorized promises say, may be distributed amongst the States in aid of education. If the federal government were more careful to keep apart from every strictly local scheme of improvement, this culpable and demoralizing state policy could scarcely live. States would cease to wish, because they would cease to hope, to be stipendiaries of the government of the Union, and would address themselves with diligence to their proper duties, with much benefit both to themselves and to the federal system. This is not saying that the policy of internal improvements was either avoidable, unconstitutional, or unwise, but only that it has been carried too far; and that, whether carried too far or not, it must in any case have been what it is now seen to be, a big weight in the federal scale of the balance.

Still other powers of the federal government, which have so grown beyond their first proportions as to have marred very seriously the symmetry of the "literary theory" of our federal system, have strengthened under the shadow of the jurisdiction of Congress over commerce and the maintenance of the postal service. For instance, the Supreme Court of the United States has declared that the powers granted to Congress by the Constitution to regulate commerce and to establish post-offices and post-roads "keep pace with the progress of the country and adapt themselves to new developments of times and circumstances. They extend from the horse with its rider to the stage-coach, from the sailing vessel to the steamer, from the coach and the steamer to the railroad, and from the railroad to the telegraph, as these new agencies are successively brought into use to meet the demands of increasing population and wealth. They are intended for the government of the business to which they relate, at all times and under all circumstances. As they were intrusted to the general government for the good of the nation, it is not only the right but the duty of Congress to see to it that the intercourse between the States and the transmission of intelligence are not obstructed or unnecessarily encumbered by state legislation."[10] This emphatic decision was intended to sustain the right of a telegraph company chartered by one State to run its line along all post-roads in other States, without the consent of those States, and even against their will; but it is manifest that many other corporate companies might, under the sanction of this broad opinion, claim similar privileges in despite of state resistance, and that such decisions go far towards making state powers of incorporation of little worth as compared with federal powers of control.

Keeping pace, too, with this growth of federal activity, there has been from the first a steady and unmistakable growth of nationality of sentiment. It was, of course, the weight of war which finally and decisively disarranged the balance between state and federal powers; and it is obvious that many of the most striking manifestations of the tendency towards centralization have made themselves seen since the war. But the history of the war is only a record of the triumph of the principle of national sovereignty. The war was inevitable, because that principle grew apace; and the war ended as it did, because that principle had become predominant. Accepted at first simply because it was imperatively necessary, the union of form and of law had become a union of sentiment, and was destined to be a union of institutions. That sense of national unity and community of destiny which Hamilton had sought to foster, but which was feeble in his day of long distances and tardy inter-communication, when the nation's pulse was as slow as the stage-coach and the postman, had become strong enough to rule the continent when Webster died. The war between the States was the supreme and final struggle between those forces of disintegration which still remained in the blood of the body politic and those other forces of health, of union and amalgamation, which had been gradually building up that body in vigor and strength as the system passed from youth to maturity, and as its constitution hardened and ripened with advancing age.

The history of that trenchant policy of "reconstruction," which followed close upon the termination of the war, as at once its logical result and significant commentary, contains a vivid picture of the altered balances of the constitutional system which is a sort of exaggerated miniature, falling very little short of being a caricature, of previous constitutional tendencies and federal policies. The tide of federal aggression probably reached its highest shore in the legislation which put it into the power of the federal courts to punish a state judge for refusing, in the exercise of his official discretion, to impanel negroes in the juries of his court,[11] and in those statutes which gave the federal courts jurisdiction over offenses against state laws by state officers.[12] But that tide has often run very high, and, however fluctuating at times, has long been well-nigh irresistible by any dykes of constitutional state privilege; so that Judge Cooley can say without fear of contradiction that "The effectual checks upon the encroachments of federal upon state power must be looked for, not in state power of resistance, but in the choice of representatives, senators, and presidents holding just constitutional views, and in a federal supreme court with competent power to restrain all departments and all officers within the limits of their just authority, so far as their acts may become the subject of judicial cognizance."[13]

Indeed it is quite evident that if federal power be not altogether irresponsible, it is the federal judiciary which is the only effectual balance-wheel of the whole system. The federal judges hold in their hands the fate of state powers, and theirs is the only authority that can draw effective rein on the career of Congress. If their power, then, be not efficient, the time must seem sadly out of joint to those who hold to the "literary theory" of our Constitution. By the word of the Supreme Court must all legislation stand or fall, so long as law is respected. But, as I have already pointed out, there is at least one large province of jurisdiction upon which, though invited, and possibly privileged to appropriate it, the Supreme Court has, nevertheless, refused to enter, and by refusing to enter which it has given over all attempt to guard one of the principal, easiest, and most obvious roads to federal supremacy. It has declared itself without authority to interfere with the *political discretion* of either Congress or the President, and has declined all effort to constrain these its coördinate departments to the performance of any, even the most constitutionally imperative act.[14] "When, indeed, the President exceeds his authority, or usurps that which belongs to one of the other departments, his orders, commands, or warrants protect no one, and his agents become personally responsible for their acts. The check of the courts, therefore, consists in their ability to keep the executive within the sphere of his authority by refusing to give the sanction of law to whatever he may do beyond it, and by holding the agents or instruments of his unlawful action to strict accountability."[15] But such punishment, inflicted not directly upon the chief offender but vicariously upon his agents, can come only after all the harm has been done. The courts cannot forestall the President and prevent the doing of mischief. They have no power of initiative; they must wait until the law has been broken and voluntary litigants have made up their pleadings; must wait nowadays many months, often many years, until those pleadings are reached in the regular course of clearing a crowded docket.

Besides, in ordinary times it is not from the executive that the most dangerous encroachments are to be apprehended. The legislature is the aggressive spirit. It is the motive power of the government, and unless the judiciary can check it, the courts are of comparatively little worth as balance-wheels in the system. It is the subtile, stealthy, almost imperceptible encroachments of policy, of political action, which constitute the precedents upon which additional prerogatives are generally reared; and yet these are the very encroachments with which it is hardest for the courts to deal, and concerning which, accordingly, the federal courts have declared themselves unauthorized to hold any opinions. They have naught to say upon questions of policy. Congress must itself judge what measures may legitimately be used to supplement or make effectual its acknowledged jurisdiction, what are the laws "necessary and proper for carrying into execution" its own peculiar powers, "and all other powers vested by" the "Constitution in the government of the United States, or in any department or officer thereof." The courts are very quick and keen-eyed, too, to discern prerogatives of political discretion in legislative acts, and exceedingly slow to undertake to discriminate between what is and what is not a violation of the spirit of the Constitution. Congress must wantonly go very far outside of the plain and unquestionable meaning of the Constitution, must bump its head directly against all right and precedent, must kick against the very pricks of all well-established rulings and interpretations, before the Supreme Court will offer it any distinct rebuke.

Then, too, the Supreme Court itself, however upright and irreproachable its members, has generally had and will undoubtedly continue to have a distinct political complexion, taken from the color of the times during which its majority was chosen. The bench over which John Marshall presided was, as everybody knows, staunchly and avowedly federalist in its views; but during the ten years which followed 1835 federalist justices were rapidly displaced by Democrats, and the views of the Court changed accordingly. Indeed it may truthfully be said that, taking our political history "by and large," the constitutional interpretations of the Supreme Court have changed, slowly but none the less surely, with the altered relations of power between the national parties. The Federalists were backed by a federalist judiciary; the period of democratic supremacy witnessed the triumph of democratic principles in the courts; and republican predominance has driven from the highest tribunal of the land all but one representative of democratic doctrines. It has been only during comparatively short periods of transition, when public opinion was passing over from one political creed to another, that the decisions of the federal judiciary have been distinctly opposed to the principles of the ruling political party.

But, besides and above all this, the national courts are for the most part in the power of Congress. Even the Supreme Court is not beyond its control; for it is the legislative privilege to increase, whenever the legislative will so pleases, the number of the judges upon the supreme bench,—to "dilute the Constitution," as Webster once put it, "by creating a court which shall construe away its provisions;" and this on one memorable occasion it did choose to do. In December, 1869, the Supreme Court decided against the constitutionality of Congress's pet Legal Tender Acts; and in the following March a vacancy on the bench opportunely occurring, and a new justiceship having been created to meet the emergency, the Senate gave the President to understand that no nominee unfavorable to the debated acts would be confirmed, two justices of the predominant party's way of thinking were appointed, the hostile majority of the court was outvoted, and the obnoxious decision reversed.[16]

The creation of additional justiceships is not, however, the only means by which Congress can coerce and control the Supreme Court. It may forestall an adverse decision by summarily depriving the court of jurisdiction over the case in which such a decision was threatened,[17] and that even while the case is pending; for only a very small part of the jurisdiction of even the Supreme Court is derived directly from the Constitution. Most of it is founded upon the Judiciary Act of 1789, which, being a mere act of Congress, may be repealed at any time that Congress chooses to repeal it. Upon this Judiciary Act, too, depend not only the powers but also the very existence of the inferior courts of the United States, the Circuit and District Courts; and their possible fate, in case of a conflict with Congress, is significantly foreshadowed in that Act of 1802 by which a democratic Congress swept away, root and branch, the system of circuit courts which had been created in the previous year, but which was hateful to the newly-successful Democrats because it had been officered with Federalists in the last hours of John Adams's administration.

This balance of judiciary against legislature and executive would seem, therefore, to be another of those ideal balances which are to be found in the books rather than in the rough realities of actual practice; for manifestly the power of the courts is safe only during seasons of political peace, when parties are not aroused to passion or tempted by the command of irresistible majorities.

As for some of the other constitutional balances enumerated in that passage of the letter to John Taylor which I have taken as a text, their present inefficacy is quite too plain to need proof. The constituencies may have been balanced against their representatives in Mr. Adams's day, for that was not a day of primaries and of strict caucus discipline. The legislatures of the States, too, may have been able to exercise some appreciable influence upon the action of the Senate, if those were days when policy was the predominant consideration which determined elections to the Senate, and the legislative choice was not always a matter of astute management, of mere personal weight, or party expediency; and the presidential electors undoubtedly did have at one time some freedom of choice in naming the chief magistrate, but before the third presidential election some of them were pledged, before Adams wrote this letter the majority of them were wont to obey the dictates of a congressional caucus, and for the last fifty years they have simply registered the will of party conventions.

It is noteworthy that Mr. Adams, possibly because he had himself been President, describes the executive as constituting only *"in some degree"* a check upon Congress, though he puts no such limitation upon the other balances of the system. Independently of experience, however, it might reasonably have been expected that the prerogatives of the President would have been one of the most effectual restraints upon the power of Congress. He was constituted one of the three great coördinate branches of the government; his functions were made of the highest dignity; his privileges many and substantial-so great, indeed, that it has pleased the fancy of some writers to parade them as exceeding those of the British crown; and there can be little doubt that, had the presidential chair always been filled by men of commanding character, of acknowledged ability, and of thorough political training, it would have continued to be a seat of the highest authority and consideration, the true centre of the federal structure, the real throne of administration, and the frequent source of policies. Washington and his Cabinet commanded the ear of Congress, and gave shape to its deliberations; Adams, though often crossed and thwarted, gave character to the government; and Jefferson, as President no less than as Secretary of State, was the real leader of his party. But the prestige of the presidential office has declined with the character of the Presidents. And the character of the Presidents has declined as the perfection of selfish party tactics has advanced.

It was inevitable that it should be so. After independence of choice on the part of the presidential electors had given place to the choice of presidential candidates by party conventions, it became absolutely necessary, in the eyes of politicians, and more and more necessary as time went on, to make expediency and availability the only rules of selection. As each party, when in convention assembled, spoke only those opinions which seemed to have received the sanction of the general voice, carefully suppressing in its "platform" all unpopular political tenets, and scrupulously omitting mention of every doctrine that might be looked upon as characteristic and as part of a peculiar and original programme, so, when the presidential candidate came to be chosen, it was recognized as imperatively necessary that he should have as short a political record as possible, and that he should wear a clean and irreproachable insignificance. "Gentlemen," said a distinguished American public man, "I would make an excellent President, but a very poor candidate." A decisive career which gives a man a well-understood place in public estimation constitutes a positive disability for the presidency; because candidacy must precede election, and the shoals of candidacy can be passed only by a light boat which carries little freight and can be turned readily about to suit the intricacies of the passage.

I am disposed to think, however, that the decline in the character of the Presidents is not the cause, but only the accompanying manifestation, of the declining prestige of the presidential office. That high office has fallen from its first estate of dignity because its power has waned; and its power has waned because the power of Congress has become predominant. The early Presidents were, as I have said, men of such a stamp that they would under any circumstances have made their influence felt; but their opportunities were exceptional. What with quarreling and fighting with England, buying Louisiana and Florida, building dykes to keep out the flood of the French Revolution, and extricating the country from ceaseless broils with the South American Republics, the government was, as has been pointed out, constantly busy, during the first quarter century of its existence, with the adjustment of foreign relations; and with foreign relations, of course, the Presidents had everything to do, since theirs was the office of negotiation.

Moreover, as regards home policy also those times were not like ours. Congress was somewhat awkward in exercising its untried powers, and its machinery was new, and without that fine adjustment which has since made it perfect of its kind. Not having as yet learned the art of governing itself to the best advantage, and being without that facility of legislation which it afterwards acquired, the Legislature was glad to get guidance and suggestions of policy from the Executive.

But this state of things did not last long. Congress was very quick and apt in learning what it could do and in getting into thoroughly good trim to do it. It very early divided itself into standing committees which it equipped with very comprehensive and thorough-going privileges of legislative initiative and control, and set itself through these to administer the government. Congress is (to adopt Mr. Bagehot's description of Parliament) "nothing less than a big meeting of more or less idle people. In proportion as you give it power it will inquire into everything, settle everything, meddle in everything. In an ordinary despotism the powers of the despot are limited by his bodily capacity, and by the calls of pleasure; he is but one man; there are but twelve hours in his day, and he is not disposed to employ more than a small part in dull business: he keeps the rest for the court, or the harem, or for society." But Congress "is a despot who has unlimited time, —who has unlimited vanity, —who has, or believes he has, unlimited comprehension, —whose pleasure is in action, whose life is work." Accordingly it has entered more and more into the details of administration, until it has virtually taken into its own hands all the substantial powers of government. It does not domineer over the President himself, but it makes the Secretaries its humble servants. Not that it would hesitate, upon occasion, to deal directly with the chief magistrate himself; but it has few calls to do so, because our latter-day Presidents live by proxy; they are the executive in theory, but the Secretaries are the executive in fact. At the very first session of Congress steps were taken towards parceling out executive work amongst several departments, according to a then sufficiently thorough division of labor; and if the President of that day was not able to direct administrative details, of course the President of to-day is infinitely less able to do so, and must content himself with such general supervision as he may find time to exercise. He is in all every-day concerns shielded by the responsibility of his subordinates.

It cannot be said that this change has raised the cabinet in dignity or power; it has only altered their relations to the scheme of government. The members of the President's cabinet have always been prominent in administration; and certainly the early cabinets were no less strong in political influence than are the cabinets of our own day; but they were then only the President's advisers, whereas they are now rather the President's colleagues. The President is now scarcely the executive; he is the head of the administration; he appoints the executive. Of course this is not a legal principle; it is only a fact. In legal theory the President can control every operation of every department of the executive branch of the government; but in fact it is not practicable for him to do so, and a limitation of fact is as potent as a prohibition of law.

But, though the heads of the executive departments are thus no longer simply the counselors of the President, having become in a very real sense members of the executive, their guiding power in the conduct of affairs, instead of advancing, has steadily diminished; because while they were being made integral parts of the machinery of administration, Congress was extending its own sphere of activity, was getting into the habit of investigating and managing every thing. The executive was losing and Congress gaining weight; and the station to which cabinets finally attained was a station of diminished and diminishing power. There is no distincter tendency in congressional history than the tendency to subject even the details of administration to the constant supervision, and all policy to the watchful intervention, of the Standing Committees.

I am inclined to think, therefore, that the enlarged powers of Congress are the fruits rather of an immensely increased efficiency of organization, and of the redoubled activity consequent upon the facility of action secured by such organization, than of any definite and persistent scheme of conscious usurpation. It is safe to say that Congress always had the desire to have a hand in every affair of federal government; but it was only by degrees that it found means and opportunity to gratify that desire, and its activity, extending its bounds wherever perfected processes of congressional work offered favoring prospects, has been enlarged so naturally and so silently that it has almost always seemed of normal extent, and has never, except perhaps during one or two brief periods of extraordinary political disturbance, appeared to reach much beyond its acknowledged constitutional sphere.

It is only in the exercise of those functions of public and formal consultation and coöperation with the President which are the peculiar offices of the Senate, that the power of Congress has made itself offensive to popular conceptions of constitutional propriety, because it is only in the exercise of such functions that Congress is compelled to be overt and demonstrative in its claims of over-lordship. The House of Representatives has made very few noisy demonstrations of its usurped right of ascendency; not because it was diffident or unambitious, but because it could maintain and extend its prerogatives quite as satisfactorily without noise; whereas the aggressive policy of the Senate has, in the acts of its "executive sessions," necessarily been overt, in spite of the closing of the doors, because when acting as the President's council in the ratification of treaties and in appointments to office its competition for power has been more formally and directly a contest with the executive than were those really more significant legislative acts by which, in conjunction with the House, it has habitually forced the heads of the executive departments to observe the will of Congress at every important turn of policy. Hence it is that to the superficial view it appears that only the Senate has been outrageous in its encroachments upon executive privilege. It is not often easy to see the true constitutional bearing of strictly legislative action; but it is patent even to the least observant that in the matter of appointments to office, for instance, senators have often outrun their legal right to give or withhold their assent to appointments, by insisting upon being first consulted concerning nominations as well, and have thus made their constitutional assent to appointments dependent upon an unconstitutional control of nominations.

This particular usurpation has been put upon a very solid basis of law by that Tenure-of-Office Act, which took away from President Johnson, in an hour of party heat and passion, that independent power of removal from office with which the Constitution had invested him, but which he had used in a way that exasperated a Senate not of his own way of thinking. But though this teasing power of the Senate's in the matter of the federal patronage is repugnant enough to the original theory of the Constitution, it is likely to be quite nullified by that policy of civil-service reform which has gained so firm, and mayhap so lasting, a footing in our national legislation; and in no event would the control of the patronage by the Senate have unbalanced the federal system more seriously than it may some day be unbalanced by an irresponsible exertion of that body's semi-executive powers in regard to the foreign policy of the government. More than one passage in the history of our foreign relations illustrates the danger. During the single congressional session of 1868-9, for example, the treaty-*marring* power of the Senate was exerted in a way that made the comparative weakness of the executive very conspicuous, and was ominous of very serious results. It showed the executive in the right, but feeble and irresolute; the Senate masterful, though in the wrong. Denmark had been asked to part with the island of St. Thomas to the United States, and had at first refused all terms, not only because she cared little for the price, but also and principally because such a sale as that proposed was opposed to the established policy of the powers of Western Europe, in whose favor Denmark wished to stand; but finally, by stress of persistent and importunate negotiation, she had been induced to yield; a treaty had been signed and sent to the Senate; the people of St. Thomas had signified their consent to the cession by a formal vote; and the island had been actually transferred to an authorized agent of our government, upon the faith, on the part of the Danish ministers, that our representatives would not have trifled with them by entering upon an important business transaction which they were not assured of their ability to conclude. But the Senate let the treaty lie neglected in its committee-room; the limit of time agreed upon for confirmation passed; the Danish government, at last bent upon escaping the ridiculous humiliation that would follow a failure of the business at that stage, extended the time and even sent over one of its most eminent ministers of state to urge the negotiation by all dignified means; but the Senate cared nothing for Danish feelings and could afford, it thought, to despise President Grant and Mr. Fish, and at the next session rejected the treaty, and left the Danes to repossess themselves of the island, which we had concluded not to buy after all.

It was during this same session of 1868-9 that the Senate teased the executive by throwing every possible obstacle in the way of the confirmation of the much more important treaty with Great Britain relative to the Alabama claims, nearly marring for good and all one of the most satisfactory successes of our recent foreign policy;[18] but it is not necessary to dwell at length upon these well-known incidents of our later history, inasmuch as these are only two of innumerable instances which make it safe to say that from whatever point we view the relations of the executive and the legislature, it is evident that the power of the latter has steadily increased at the expense of the prerogatives of the former, and that the degree in which the one of these great branches of government is balanced against the other is a very insignificant degree indeed. For in the exercise of his power of veto, which is of course, beyond all comparison, his most formidable prerogative, the President acts not as the executive but as a third branch of the legislature. As Oliver Ellsworth said, at the first session of the Senate, the President is, as regards the passage of bills, but a part of Congress; and he can be an efficient, imperative member of the legislative system only in quiet times, when parties are pretty evenly balanced, and there are no indomitable majorities to tread obnoxious vetoes under foot.

Even this rapid outline sketch of the two pictures, of the theory and of the actual practices of the Constitution, has been sufficient, therefore, to show the most marked points of difference between the two, and to justify that careful study of congressional government, as the real government of the Union, which I am about to undertake. The balances of the Constitution are for the most part only ideal. For all practical purposes the national government is supreme over the state governments, and Congress predominant over its so-called coördinate branches. Whereas Congress at first overshadowed neither President nor federal judiciary, it now on occasion rules both with easy mastery and with a high hand; and whereas each State once guarded its sovereign prerogatives with jealous pride, and able men not a few preferred political advancement under the governments of the great commonwealths to office under the new federal Constitution, seats in state legislatures are now no longer coveted except as possible approaches to seats in Congress; and even governors of States seek election to the national Senate as a promotion, a reward for the humbler services they have rendered their local governments.

What makes it the more important to understand the present mechanism of national government, and to study the methods of congressional rule in a light unclouded by theory, is that there is plain evidence that the expansion of federal power is to continue, and that there exists, consequently, an evident necessity that it should be known just what to do and how to do it, when the time comes for public opinion to take control of the forces which are changing the character of our Constitution. There are voices in the air which cannot be misunderstood. The times seem to favor a centralization of governmental functions such as could not have suggested itself as a possibility to the framers of the Constitution. Since they gave their work to the world the whole face of that world has changed. The Constitution was adopted when it was six days' hard traveling from New York to Boston; when to cross East River was to venture a perilous voyage; when men were thankful for weekly mails; when the extent of the country's commerce was reckoned not in millions but in thousands of dollars; when the country knew few cities, and had but begun manufactures; when Indians were pressing upon near frontiers; when there were no telegraph lines, and no monster corporations. Unquestionably, the pressing problems of the present moment regard the regulation of our vast systems of commerce and manufacture, the control of giant corporations, the restraint of monopolies, the perfection of fiscal arrangements, the facilitating of economic exchanges, and many other like national concerns, amongst which may possibly be numbered the question of marriage and divorce; and the greatest of these problems do not fall within even the enlarged sphere of the federal government; some of them can be embraced within its jurisdiction by no possible stretch of construction, and the majority of them only by wresting the Constitution to strange and as yet unimagined uses. Still there is a distinct movement in favor of national control of all questions of policy which manifestly demand uniformity of treatment and power of administration such as cannot be realized by the separate, unconcerted action of the States; and it seems probable to many that, whether by constitutional amendment, or by still further flights of construction, yet broader territory will at no very distant day be assigned to the federal government. It becomes a matter of the utmost importance, therefore, both for those who would arrest this tendency, and for those who, because they look upon it with allowance if not with positive favor, would let it run its course, to examine critically the government upon which this new weight of responsibility and power seems likely to be cast, in order that its capacity both for the work it now does and for that which it may be called upon to do may be definitely estimated.

Judge Cooley, in his admirable work on "The Principles of American Constitutional Law," after quoting Mr. Adams's enumeration of the checks and balances of the federal system, adds this comment upon Mr. Adams's concluding statement that that system is an invention of our own. "The invention, nevertheless, was suggested by the British Constitution, in which a system almost equally elaborate was then in force. In its outward forms that system still remains; but there has been for more than a century a gradual change in the direction of a concentration of legislative and executive power in the popular house of Parliament, so that the government now is sometimes said, with no great departure from the fact, to be a government by the House of Commons." But Judge Cooley does not seem to see, or, if he sees, does not emphasize the fact, that our own system has been hardly less subject to "a gradual change in the direction of a concentration" of all the substantial powers of government in the hands of Congress; so that it is now, though a wide departure from the form of things, "no great departure from the fact" to describe ours as a government by the Standing Committees of Congress. This fact is, however, deducible from very many passages of Judge Cooley's own writings; for he is by no means insensible of that expansion of the powers of the federal government and that crystallization of its methods which have practically made obsolete the early constitutional theories, and even the modified theory which he himself seems to hold.

He has tested the nice adjustment of the theoretical balances by the actual facts, and has carefully set forth the results; but he has nowhere brought those results together into a single comprehensive view which might serve as a clear and satisfactory delineation of the Constitution of to-day; nor has he, or any other writer of capacity, examined minutely and at length that internal organization of Congress which determines its methods of legislation, which shapes its means of governing the executive departments, which contains in it the whole mechanism whereby the policy of the country is in all points directed, and which is therefore an essential branch of constitutional study. As the House of Commons is the central object of examination in every study of the English Constitution, so should Congress be in every study of our own. Any one who is unfamiliar with what Congress actually does and how it does it, with all its duties and all its occupations, with all its devices of management and resources of power, is very far from a knowledge of the constitutional system under which we live; and to every one who knows these things that knowledge is very near.

II
The House of Representatives.

> No more vital truth was ever uttered than that freedom and free institutions cannot long be maintained by any people who do not understand the nature of their own government.

Like a vast picture thronged with figures of equal prominence and crowded with elaborate and obtrusive details, Congress is hard to see satisfactorily and appreciatively at a single view and from a single stand-point. Its complicated forms and diversified structure confuse the vision, and conceal the system which underlies its composition. It is too complex to be understood without an effort, without a careful and systematic process of analysis. Consequently, very few people do understand it, and its doors are practically shut against the comprehension of the public at large. If Congress had a few authoritative leaders whose figures were very distinct and very conspicuous to the eye of the world, and who could represent and stand for the national legislature in the thoughts of that very numerous, and withal very respectable, class of persons who must think specifically and in concrete forms when they think at all, those persons who can make something out of men but very little out of intangible generalizations, it would be quite within the region of possibilities for the majority of the nation to follow the course of legislation without any very serious confusion of thought. I suppose that almost everybody who just now gives any heed to the policy of Great Britain, with regard even to the reform of the franchise and other like strictly legislative questions, thinks of Mr. Gladstone and his colleagues rather than of the House of Commons, whose servants they are. The question is not, What will Parliament do? but, What will Mr. Gladstone do? And there is even less doubt that it is easier and more natural to look upon the legislative designs of Germany as locked up behind Bismarck's heavy brows than to think of them as dependent upon the determinations of the Reichstag, although as a matter of fact its consent is indispensable even to the plans of the imperious and domineering Chancellor.

But there is no great minister or ministry to represent the will and being of Congress in the common thought. The Speaker of the House of Representatives stands as near to leadership as any one; but his will does not run as a formative and imperative power in legislation much beyond the appointment of the committees who are to lead the House and do its work for it, and it is, therefore, not entirely satisfactory to the public mind to trace all legislation to him. He may have a controlling hand in starting it; but he sits too still in his chair, and is too evidently not on the floor of the body over which he presides, to make it seem probable to the ordinary judgment that he has much immediate concern in legislation after it is once set afoot. Everybody knows that he is a staunch and avowed partisan, and that he likes to make smooth, whenever he can, the legislative paths of his party; but it does not seem likely that all important measures originate with him, or that he is the author of every distinct policy. And in fact he is not. He is a great party chief, but the hedging circumstances of his official position as presiding officer prevent his performing the part of active leadership. He appoints the leaders of the House, but he is not himself its leader.

The leaders of the House are the chairmen of the principal Standing Committees. Indeed, to be exactly accurate, the House has as many leaders as there are subjects of legislation; for there are as many Standing Committees as there are leading classes of legislation, and in the consideration of every topic of business the House is guided by a special leader in the person of the chairman of the Standing Committee, charged with the superintendence of measures of the particular class to which that topic belongs. It is this multiplicity of leaders, this many-headed leadership, which makes the organization of the House too complex to afford uninformed people and unskilled observers any easy clue to its methods of rule. For the chairmen of the Standing Committees do not constitute a coöperative body like a ministry. They do not consult and concur in the adoption of homogeneous and mutually helpful measures; there is no thought of acting in concert. Each Committee goes its own way at its own pace. It is impossible to discover any unity or method in the disconnected and therefore unsystematic, confused, and desultory action of the House, or any common purpose in the measures which its Committees from time to time recommend.

And it is not only to the unanalytic thought of the common observer who looks at the House from the outside that its doings seem helter-skelter, and without comprehensible rule; it is not at once easy to understand them when they are scrutinized in their daily headway through open session by one who is inside the House. The newly-elected member, entering its doors for the first time, and with no more knowledge of its rules and customs than the more intelligent of his constituents possess, always experiences great difficulty in adjusting his preconceived ideas of congressional life to the strange and unlooked-for conditions by which he finds himself surrounded after he has been sworn in and has become a part of the great legislative machine. Indeed there are generally many things connected with his career in Washington to disgust and dispirit, if not to aggrieve, the new member. In the first place, his local reputation does not follow him to the federal capital. Possibly the members from his own State know him, and receive him into full fellowship; but no one else knows him, except as an adherent of this or that party, or as a new-comer from this or that State. He finds his station insignificant, and his identity indistinct. But this social humiliation which he experiences in circles in which to be a congressman does not of itself confer distinction, because it is only to be one among many, is probably not to be compared with the chagrin and disappointment which come in company with the inevitable discovery that he is equally without weight or title to consideration in the House itself. No man, when chosen to the membership of a body possessing great powers and exalted prerogatives, likes to find his activity repressed, and himself suppressed, by imperative rules and precedents which seem to have been framed for the deliberate purpose of making usefulness unattainable by individual members. Yet such the new member finds the rules and precedents of the House to be. It matters not to him, because it is not apparent on the face of things, that those rules and precedents have grown, not out of set purpose to curtail the privileges of new members as such, but out of the plain necessities of business; it remains the fact that he suffers under their curb, and it is not until "custom hath made it in him a property of easiness" that he submits to them with anything like good grace.

Not all new members suffer alike, of course, under this trying discipline; because it is not every new member that comes to his seat with serious purposes of honest, earnest, and duteous work. There are numerous tricks and subterfuges, soon learned and easily used, by means of which the most idle and self-indulgent members may readily make such show of exemplary diligence as will quite satisfy, if it does not positively delight, constituents in Buncombe. But the number of congressmen who deliberately court uselessness and counterfeit well-doing is probably small. The great majority doubtless have a keen enough sense of their duty, and a sufficiently unhesitating desire to do it; and it may safely be taken for granted that the zeal of new members is generally hot and insistent. If it be not hot to begin with, it is like to become so by reason of friction with the rules, because such men must inevitably be chafed by the bonds of restraint drawn about them by the inexorable observances of the House.

Often the new member goes to Washington as the representative of a particular line of policy, having been elected, it may be, as an advocate of free trade, or as a champion of protection; and it is naturally his first care upon entering on his duties to seek immediate opportunity for the expression of his views and immediate means of giving them definite shape and thrusting them upon the attention of Congress. His disappointment is, therefore, very keen when he finds both opportunity and means denied him. He can introduce his bill; but that is all he can do, and he must do that at a particular time and in a particular manner. This he is likely to learn through rude experience, if he be not cautious to inquire beforehand the details of practice. He is likely to make a rash start, upon the supposition that Congress observes the ordinary rules of parliamentary practice to which he has become accustomed in the debating clubs familiar to his youth, and in the mass-meetings known to his later experience. His bill is doubtless ready for presentation early in the session, and some day, taking advantage of a pause in the proceedings, when there seems to be no business before the House, he rises to read it and move its adoption. But he finds getting the floor an arduous and precarious undertaking. There are certain to be others who want it as well as he; and his indignation is stirred by the fact that the Speaker does not so much as turn towards him, though he must have heard his call, but recognizes some one else readily and as a matter of course. If he be obstreperous and persistent in his cries of "Mr. Speaker," he may get that great functionary's attention for a moment, — only to be told, however, that he is out of order, and that his bill can be introduced at that stage only by unanimous consent: immediately there are mechanically-uttered but emphatic exclamations of objection, and he is forced to sit down confused and disgusted. He has, without knowing it, obtruded himself in the way of the "regular order of business," and been run over in consequence, without being quite clear as to how the accident occurred.

Moved by the pain and discomfiture of this first experience to respect, if not to fear, the rules, the new member casts about, by study or inquiry, to find out, if possible, the nature and occasion of his privileges. He learns that his only safe day is Monday. On that day the roll of the States is called, and members may introduce bills as their States are reached in the call. So on Monday he essays another bout with the rules, confident this time of being on their safe side, —but mayhap indiscreetly and unluckily over-confident. For if he supposes, as he naturally will, that after his bill has been sent up to be read by the clerk he may say a few words in its behalf, and in that belief sets out upon his long-considered remarks, he will be knocked down by the rules as surely as he was on the first occasion when he gained the floor for a brief moment. The rap of Mr. Speaker's gavel is sharp, immediate, and peremptory. He is curtly informed that no debate is in order; the bill can only be referred to the appropriate Committee.

This is, indeed, disheartening; it is his first lesson in committee government, and the master's rod smarts; but the sooner he learns the prerogatives and powers of the Standing Committees the sooner will he penetrate the mysteries of the rules and avoid the pain of further contact with their thorny side. The privileges of the Standing Committees are the beginning and the end of the rules. Both the House of Representatives and the Senate conduct their business by what may figuratively, but not inaccurately, be called an odd device of *disintegration*. The House virtually both deliberates and legislates in small sections. Time would fail it to discuss all the bills brought in, for they every session number thousands; and it is to be doubted whether, even if time allowed, the ordinary processes of debate and amendment would suffice to sift the chaff from the wheat in the bushels of bills every week piled upon the clerk's, desk. Accordingly, no futile attempt is made to do anything of the kind. The work is parceled out, most of it to the forty-seven Standing Committees which constitute the regular organization of the House, some of it to select committees appointed for special and temporary purposes. Each of the almost numberless bills that come pouring in on Mondays is "read a first and second time," —simply perfunctorily read, that is, by its title, by the clerk, and passed by silent assent through its first formal courses, for the purpose of bringing it to the proper stage for commitment, —and referred without debate to the appropriate Standing Committee. Practically, no bill escapes commitment-save, of course, bills introduced by committees, and a few which may now and then be crowded through under a suspension of the rules, granted by a two-thirds vote-though the exact disposition to be made of a bill is not always determined easily and as a matter of course. Besides the great Committee of Ways and Means and the equally great Committee on Appropriations, there are Standing Committees on Banking and Currency, on Claims, on Commerce, on the Public Lands, on Post-Offices and Post-Roads, on the Judiciary, on Public Expenditures, on Manufactures, on Agriculture, on Military Affairs, on Naval Affairs, on Mines and Mining, on Education and Labor, on Patents, and on a score of other branches of legislative concern; but careful and differential as is the topical division of the subjects of legislation which is represented in the titles of these Committees, it is not always evident to which Committee each particular bill should go. Many bills affect subjects which may be regarded as lying as properly within the jurisdiction of one as of another of the Committees; for no hard and fast lines separate the various classes of business which the Committees are commissioned to take in charge. Their jurisdictions overlap at many points, and it must frequently happen that bills are read which cover just this common ground. Over the commitment of such bills sharp and interesting skirmishes often take place. There is active competition for them, the ordinary, quiet routine of matter-of-course reference being interrupted by rival motions seeking to give very different directions to the disposition to be made of them. To which Committee should a bill "to fix and establish the maximum rates of fares of the Union Pacific and Central Pacific Railroads" be sent,—to the Committee on Commerce or to the Committee on the Pacific Railroads? Should a bill which prohibits the mailing of certain classes of letters and circulars go to the Committee on Post-Offices and Post-Roads, because it relates to the mails, or to the Committee on the Judiciary, because it proposes to make any transgression of its prohibition a crime? What is the proper disposition of any bill which thus seems to lie within two distinct committee jurisdictions?

The fate of bills committed is generally not uncertain. As a rule, a bill committed is a bill doomed. When it goes from the clerk's desk to a committee-room it crosses a parliamentary bridge of sighs to dim dungeons of silence whence it will never return. The means and time of its death are unknown, but its friends never see it again. Of course no Standing Committee is privileged to take upon itself the full powers of the House it represents, and formally and decisively reject a bill referred to it; its disapproval, if it disapproves, must be reported to the House in the form of a recommendation that the bill "do not pass." But it is easy, and therefore common, to let the session pass without making any report at all upon bills deemed objectionable or unimportant, and to substitute for reports upon them a few bills of the Committee's own drafting; so that thousands of bills expire with the expiration of each Congress, not having been rejected, but having been simply neglected. There was not time to report upon them.

Of course it goes without saying that the practical effect of this Committee organization of the House is to consign to each of the Standing Committees the entire direction of legislation upon those subjects which properly come to its consideration. As to those subjects it is entitled to the initiative, and all legislative action with regard to them is under its overruling guidance. It gives shape and course to the determinations of the House. In one respect, however, its initiative is limited. Even a Standing Committee cannot report a bill whose subject-matter has not been referred to it by the House, "by the rules or otherwise;" it cannot volunteer advice on questions upon which its advice has not been asked. But this is not a serious, not even an operative, limitation upon its functions of suggestion and leadership; for it is a very simple matter to get referred to it any subject it wishes to introduce to the attention of the House. Its chairman, or one of its leading members, frames a bill covering the point upon which the Committee wishes to suggest legislation; brings it in, in his capacity as a private member, on Monday, when the call of States is made; has it referred to his Committee; and thus secures an opportunity for the making of the desired report.

It is by this imperious authority of the Standing Committees that the new member is stayed and thwarted whenever he seeks to take an active part in the business of the House. Turn which way he may, some privilege of the Committees stands in his path. The rules are so framed as to put all business under their management; and one of the discoveries which the new member is sure to make, albeit after many trying experiences and sobering adventures and as his first session draws towards its close, is, that under their sway freedom of debate finds no place of allowance, and that his long-delayed speech must remain unspoken. For even a long congressional session is too short to afford time for a full consideration of all the reports of the forty-seven Committees, and debate upon them must be rigidly cut short, if not altogether excluded, if any considerable part of the necessary business is to be gotten through with before adjournment. There are some subjects to which the House must always give prompt attention; therefore reports from the Committees on Printing and on Elections are always in order; and there are some subjects to which careful consideration must always be accorded; therefore the Committee of Ways and Means and the Committee on Appropriations are clothed with extraordinary privileges; and revenue and supply bills may be reported, and will ordinarily be considered, at any time. But these four are the only specially licensed Committees. The rest must take their turns in fixed order as they are called on by the Speaker, contenting themselves with such crumbs of time as fall from the tables of the four Committees of highest prerogative.

Senator Hoar, of Massachusetts, whose long congressional experience entitles him to speak with authority, calculates[19] that, "supposing the two sessions which make up the life of the House to last ten months," most of the Committees have at their disposal during each Congress but two hours apiece in which "to report upon, debate, and dispose of all the subjects of general legislation committed to their charge." For of course much time is wasted. No Congress gets immediately to work upon its first assembling. It has its officers to elect, and after their election some time must elapse before its organization is finally completed by the appointment of the Committees. It adjourns for holidays, too, and generally spares itself long sittings. Besides, there are many things to interrupt the call of the Committees upon which most of the business waits. That call can proceed only during the morning hours,—the hours just after the reading of the "Journal,"—on Tuesdays, Wednesdays, and Thursdays; and even then it may suffer postponement because of the unfinished business of the previous day which is entitled to first consideration. The call cannot proceed on Mondays because the morning hour of Mondays is devoted invariably to the call of the States for the introduction of bills and resolutions; nor on Fridays, for Friday is "private bill day," and is always engrossed by the Committee on Claims, or by other fathers of bills which have gone upon the "private calendar." On Saturdays the House seldom sits.

The reports made during these scant morning hours are ordered to be printed, for future consideration in their turn, and the bills introduced by the Committees are assigned to the proper calendars, to be taken up in order at the proper time. When a morning hour has run out, the House hastens to proceed with the business on the Speaker's table.

These are some of the plainer points of the rules. They are full of complexity, and of confusion to the uninitiated, and the confusions of practice are greater than the confusions of the rules. For the regular order of business is constantly being interrupted by the introduction of resolutions offered "by unanimous consent," and of bills let in under a "suspension of the rules." Still, it is evident that there is one principle which runs through every stage of procedure, and which is never disallowed or abrogated,—the principle that the Committees shall rule without let or hindrance. And this is a principle of extraordinary formative power. It is the mould of all legislation. In the first place, the speeding of business under the direction of the Committees determines the character and the amount of the discussion to which legislation shall be subjected. The House is conscious that time presses. It knows that, hurry as it may, it will hardly get through with one eighth of the business laid out for the session, and that to pause for lengthy debate is to allow the arrears to accumulate. Besides, most of the members are individually anxious to expedite action on every pending measure, because each member of the House is a member of one or more of the Standing Committees, and is quite naturally desirous that the bills prepared by his Committees, and in which he is, of course, specially interested by reason of the particular attention which he has been compelled to give them, should reach a hearing and a vote as soon as possible. It must, therefore, invariably happen that the Committee holding the floor at any particular time is the Committee whose proposals the majority wish to dispose of as summarily as circumstances will allow, in order that the rest of the forty-two unprivileged Committees to which the majority belong may gain the earlier and the fairer chance of a hearing. A reporting Committee, besides, is generally as glad to be pushed as the majority are to push it. It probably has several bills matured, and wishes to see them disposed of before its brief hours of opportunity[20] are passed and gone.

Consequently, it is the established custom of the House to accord the floor for one hour to the member of the reporting Committee who has charge of the business under consideration; and that hour is made the chief hour of debate. The reporting committee-man seldom, if ever, uses the whole of the hour himself for his opening remarks; he uses part of it, and retains control of the rest of it; for by undisputed privilege it is his to dispose of, whether he himself be upon the floor or not. No amendment is in order during that hour, unless he consent to its presentation; and he does not, of course, yield his time indiscriminately to any one who wishes to speak. He gives way, indeed, as in fairness he should, to opponents as well as to friends of the measure under his charge; but generally no one is accorded a share of his time who has not obtained his previous promise of the floor; and those who do speak must not run beyond the number of minutes he has agreed to allow them. He keeps the course both of debate and of amendment thus carefully under his own supervision, as a good tactician, and before he finally yields the floor, at the expiration of his hour, he is sure to move the previous question. To neglect to do so would be to lose all control of the business in hand; for unless the previous question is ordered the debate may run on at will, and his Committee's chance for getting its measures through slip quite away; and that would be nothing less than his disgrace. He would be all the more blameworthy because he had but to ask for the previous question to get it. As I have said, the House is as eager to hurry business as he can be, and will consent to almost any limitation of discussion that he may demand; though, probably, if he were to throw the reins upon its neck, it would run at large from very wantonness, in scorn of such a driver. The previous question once ordered, all amendments are precluded, and one hour remains for the summing-up of this same privileged committee-man before the final vote is taken and the bill disposed of.

These are the customs which baffle and perplex and astound the new member. In these precedents and usages, when at length he comes to understand them, the novice spies out the explanation of the fact, once so confounding and seemingly inexplicable, that when he leaped to his feet to claim the floor other members who rose after him were coolly and unfeelingly preferred before him by the Speaker. Of course it is plain enough now that Mr. Speaker knew beforehand to whom the representative of the reporting Committee had agreed to yield the floor; and it was no use for any one else to cry out for recognition. Whoever wished to speak should, if possible, have made some arrangement with the Committee before the business came to a hearing, and should have taken care to notify Mr. Speaker that he was to be granted the floor for a few moments.

Unquestionably this, besides being a very interesting, is a very novel and significant method of restricting debate and expediting legislative action,—a method of very serious import, and obviously fraught with far-reaching constitutional effects. The practices of debate which prevail in its legislative assembly are manifestly of the utmost importance to a self-governing people; for that legislation which is not thoroughly discussed by the legislating body is practically done in a corner. It is impossible for Congress itself to do wisely what it does so hurriedly; and the constituencies cannot understand what Congress does not itself stop to consider. The prerogatives of the Committees represent something more than a mere convenient division of labor. There is only one part of its business to which Congress, as a whole, attends,—that part, namely, which is embraced under the privileged subjects of revenue and supply. The House never accepts the proposals of the Committee of Ways and Means, or of the Committee on Appropriations, without due deliberation; but it allows almost all of its other Standing Committees virtually to legislate for it. In form, the Committees only digest the various matter introduced by individual members, and prepare it, with care, and after thorough investigation, for the final consideration and action of the House; but, in reality, they dictate the course to be taken, prescribing the decisions of the House not only, but measuring out, according to their own wills, its opportunities for debate and deliberation as well. The House sits, not for serious discussion, but to sanction the conclusions of its Committees as rapidly as possible. It legislates in its committee-rooms; not by the determinations of majorities, but by the resolutions of specially-commissioned minorities; so that it is not far from the truth to say that Congress in session is Congress on public exhibition, whilst Congress in its committee-rooms is Congress at work.

Habit grows fast, even upon the unconventional American, and the nature of the House of Representatives has, by long custom, been shaped to the spirit of its rules. Representatives have attained, by rigorous self-discipline, to the perfect stature of the law under which they live, having purged their hearts, as completely as may be of all desire to do that which it is the chief object of that law to forbid by giving over a vain lust after public discussion. The entire absence of the instinct of debate amongst them, and their apparent unfamiliarity with the idea of combating a proposition by argument, was recently illustrated by an incident which was quite painfully amusing. The democratic majority of the House of the Forty-eighth Congress desired the immediate passage of a pension bill of rather portentous proportions; but the republican minority disapproved of the bill with great fervor, and, when it was moved by the Pension Committee, late one afternoon, in a thin House, that the rules be suspended, and an early day set for a consideration of the bill, the Republicans addressed themselves to determined and persistent "filibustering" to prevent action. First they refused to vote, leaving the Democrats without an acting quorum; then, all night long, they kept the House at roll-calling on dilatory and obstructive motions, the dreary dragging of the time being relieved occasionally by the amusement of hearing the excuses of members who had tried to slip off to bed, or by the excitement of an angry dispute between the leaders of the two parties as to the responsibility for the dead-lock. Not till the return of morning brought in the delinquents to recruit the democratic ranks did business advance a single step. Now, the noteworthy fact about this remarkable scene is, that the minority were not manœuvring to gain opportunity or time for debate, in order that the country might be informed of the true nature of the obnoxious bill, but were simply fighting a preliminary motion with silent, dogged obstruction. After the whole night had been spent in standing out against action, the House is said to have been "in no mood for the thirty-minutes' debate allowed by the rules," and a final vote was taken, with only a word or two said. It was easier and more natural, as everybody saw, to direct attention to the questionable character of what was being attempted by the majority by creating a somewhat scandalous "scene," of which every one would talk, than by making speeches which nobody would read. It was a notable commentary on the characteristic methods of our system of congressional government.

One very noteworthy result of this system is to shift the theatre of debate upon legislation from the floor of Congress to the privacy of the committee-rooms. Provincial gentlemen who read the Associated Press dispatches in their morning papers as they sit over their coffee at breakfast are doubtless often very sorely puzzled by certain of the items which sometimes appear in the brief telegraphic notes from Washington. What can they make of this for instance: "The House Committee on Commerce to-day heard arguments from the congressional delegation from" such and such States "in advocacy of appropriations for river and harbor improvements which the members desire incorporated in the River and Harbor Appropriations Bill"? They probably do not understand that it would have been useless for members not of the Committee on Commerce to wait for any opportunity to make their suggestions on the floor of Congress, where the measure to which they wish to make additions would be under the authoritative control of the Committee, and where, consequently, they could gain a hearing only by the courteous sufferance of the committee-man in charge of the report. Whatever is to be done must be done by or through the Committee.

It would seem, therefore, that practically Congress, or at any rate the House of Representatives, delegates not only its legislative but also its deliberative functions to its Standing Committees. The little public debate that arises under the stringent and urgent rules of the House is formal rather than effective, and it is the discussions which take place in the Committees that give form to legislation. Undoubtedly these siftings of legislative questions by the Committees are of great value in enabling the House to obtain "undarkened counsel" and intelligent suggestions from authoritative sources. All sober, purposeful, business-like talk upon questions of public policy, whether it take place in Congress or only before the Committees of Congress, is of great value; and the controversies which spring up in the committee-rooms, both amongst the committee-men themselves and between those who appear before the Committees as advocates of special measures, cannot but contribute to add clearness and definite consistency to the reports submitted to the House.

There are, however, several very obvious reasons why the most thorough canvass of business by the Committees, and the most exhaustive and discriminating discussion of all its details in their rooms, cannot take the place or fulfill the uses of amendment and debate by Congress in open session. In the first place, the proceedings of the Committees are private and their discussions unpublished. The chief, and unquestionably the most essential, object of all discussion of public business is the enlightenment of public opinion; and of course, since it cannot hear the debates of the Committees, the nation is not apt to be much instructed by them. Only the Committees are enlightened. There is a conclusive objection to the publication of the proceedings of the Committees, which is recognized as of course by all parliamentary lawyers, namely, that those proceedings are of no force till confirmed by the House. A Committee is commissioned, not to instruct the public, but to instruct and guide the House.

Indeed it is not usual for the Committees to open their sittings often to those who desire to be heard with regard to pending questions; and no one can demand a hearing as of right. On the contrary, they are privileged and accustomed to hold their sessions in absolute secrecy. It is made a breach of order for any member to allude on the floor of the House to anything that has taken place in committee, "unless by a written report sanctioned by a majority of the Committee;" and there is no place in the regular order of business for a motion instructing a Committee to conduct its investigations with open doors. Accordingly, it is only by the concession of the Committees that arguments are made before them.

When they do suffer themselves to be approached, moreover, they generally extend the leave to others besides their fellow-congressmen. The Committee on Commerce consents to listen to prominent railroad officials upon the subject of the regulation of freight charges and fares; and scores of interested persons telegraph inquiries to the chairman of the Committee of Ways and Means as to the time at which they are to be permitted to present to the Committee their views upon the revision of the tariff. The speeches made before the Committees at their open sessions are, therefore, scarcely of such a kind as would be instructive to the public, and on that account worth publishing. They are as a rule the pleas of special pleaders, the arguments of advocates. They have about them none of the searching, critical, illuminating character of the higher order of parliamentary debate, in which men are pitted against each other as equals, and urged to sharp contest and masterful strife by the inspiration of political principle and personal ambition, through the rivalry of parties and the competition of policies. They represent a joust between antagonistic interests, not a contest of principles. They could scarcely either inform or elevate public opinion, even if they were to obtain its heed.

For the instruction and elevation of public opinion, in regard to national affairs, there is needed something more than special pleas for special privileges. There is needed public discussion of a peculiar sort: a discussion by the sovereign legislative body itself, a discussion in which every feature of each mooted point of policy shall be distinctly brought out, and every argument of significance pushed to the farthest point of insistence, by recognized leaders in that body; and, above all, a discussion upon which something-something of interest or importance, some pressing question of administration or of law, the fate of a party or the success of a conspicuous politician-evidently depends. It is only a discussion of this sort that the public will heed; no other sort will impress it.

There could, therefore, be no more unwelcome revelation to one who has anything approaching a statesman-like appreciation of the essential conditions of intelligent self-government than just that which must inevitably be made to every one who candidly examines our congressional system; namely, that, under that system, such discussion is impossible. There are, to begin with, physical and *architectural* reasons why business-like debate of public affairs by the House of Representatives is out of the question. To those who visit the galleries of the representative chamber during a session of the House these reasons are as obvious as they are astonishing. It would be natural to expect that a body which meets ostensibly for consultation and deliberation should hold its sittings in a room small enough to admit of an easy interchange of views and a ready concert of action, where its members would be brought into close, sympathetic contact; and it is nothing less than astonishing to find it spread at large through the vast spaces of such a chamber as the hall of the House of Representatives, where there are no close ranks of coöperating parties, but each member has a roomy desk and an easy revolving chair; where broad aisles spread and stretch themselves; where ample, soft-carpeted areas lie about the spacious desks of the Speaker and clerks; where deep galleries reach back from the outer limits of the wide passages which lie beyond "the bar": an immense, capacious chamber, disposing its giant dimensions freely beneath the great level lacunar ceiling through whose glass panels the full light of day pours in. The most vivid impression the visitor gets in looking over that vast hall is the impression of space. A speaker must needs have a voice like O'Connell's, the practical visitor is apt to think, as he sits in the gallery, to fill even the silent spaces of that room; how much more to overcome the disorderly noises that buzz and rattle through it when the representatives are assembled, —a voice clear, sonorous, dominant, like the voice of a clarion. One who speaks there with the voice and lungs of the ordinary mortal must content himself with the audience of those members in his own immediate neighborhood, whose ears he rudely assails in vehement efforts to command the attention of those beyond them, and who, therefore, cannot choose but hear him.

It is of this magnitude of the hall of the representatives that those news telegrams are significant which speak of an interesting or witty speech in Congress as having drawn about the speaker listeners from all parts of the House. As one of our most noted wits would say, a member must needs take a Sabbath day's journey to get within easy hearing distance of a speaker who is addressing the House from the opposite side of the hall; for besides the space there are the noises intervening, the noises of loud talking and of the clapping of hands for the pages, making the task of the member who is speaking "very like trying to address the people in the omnibuses from the curbstone in front of the Astor House."[21]

But these physical limitations to debate, though serious and real, are amongst the least important, because they are amongst the least insuperable. If effective and business-like public discussions were considered indispensable by Congress, or even desirable, the present chamber could readily be divided into two halls: the one a commodious reading-room where the members might chat and write at ease as they now do in the House itself; and the other a smaller room suitable for debate and earnest business. This, in fact, has been several times proposed, but the House does not feel that there is any urgency about providing facilities for debate, because it sees no reason to desire an increase of speech-making, in view of the fact that, notwithstanding all the limitations now put upon discussion, its business moves much too slowly. The early Congresses had time to talk; Congresses of to-day have not. Before that wing of the Capitol was built in which the representative chamber now is, the House used to sit in the much smaller room, now empty save for the statuary to whose exhibition it is devoted; and there much speech-making went on from day to day; there Calhoun and Randolph and Webster and Clay won their reputations as statesmen and orators. So earnest and interesting were the debates of those days, indeed, that the principal speeches delivered in Congress seem to have been usually printed at length in the metropolitan journals.[22] But the number and length of the speeches was even then very much deplored; and so early as 1828 a writer in the "North American Review" condemns what he calls "the habit of congressional debating," with the air of one who speaks against some abuse which every one acknowledges to be a nuisance.[23] Eleven years later a contributor to the "Democratic Review"[24] declared that it had "been gravely charged upon" Mr. Samuel Cushman, then a member of the Twenty-fifth Congress from New Hampshire, "that he moves the previous question. Truly," continues the essayist, "he does, and for that very service, if he had never done anything else, he deserves a monument as a public benefactor. One man who can arrest a tedious, long-winded, factious, time-killing debate, is worth forty who can provoke or keep one up. It requires some moral courage, some spirit, and some tact also, to move the previous question, and to move it, too, at precisely the right point of time."

This ardent and generous defense of Mr. Cushman against the odious accusation of moving the previous question would doubtless be exquisitely amusing to the chairman of one of the Standing Committees of the Forty-eighth Congress, to whom the previous question seems one of the commonest necessities of life. But, after all, he ought not to laugh at the ingenuous essayist, for that was not the heyday of the rules; they then simply served and did not tyrannize over the House. They did not then have the opportunity of empire afforded them by the scantiness of time which hurries the House, and the weight of business which oppresses it; and they were at a greater disadvantage in a room where oratory was possible than they are in a vast chamber where the orator's voice is drowned amidst the noises of disorderly inattention. Nowadays would-be debaters are easily thrust out of Congress and forced to resort to the printing-office; are compelled to content themselves with speaking from the pages of the "Record" instead of from their places in the House. Some people who live very far from Washington may imagine that the speeches which are spread at large in the columns of the "Congressional Record," or which their representative sends them in pamphlet form, were actually delivered in Congress; but every one else knows that they were not; that Congress is constantly granting leave to its members to insert in the official reports of the proceedings speeches which it never heard and does not care to hear, but which it is not averse from printing at the public expense, if it is desirable that constituents and the country at large should read them. It will not stand between a member and his constituents so long as it can indulge the one and satisfy the others without any inconvenience to itself or any serious drain upon the resources of the Treasury. The public printer does not object.

But there are other reasons still more organic than these why the debates of Congress cannot, under our present system, have that serious purpose of search into the merits of policies and that definite and determinate party-or, if you will, partisan-aim without which they can never be effective for the instruction of public opinion, or the cleansing of political action. The chief of these reasons, because the parent of all the rest, is that there are in Congress no authoritative leaders who are the recognized spokesmen of their parties. Power is nowhere concentrated; it is rather deliberately and of set policy scattered amongst many small chiefs. It is divided up, as it were, into forty-seven seigniories, in each of which a Standing Committee is the court-baron and its chairman lord-proprietor. These petty barons, some of them not a little powerful, but none of them within reach of the full powers of rule, may at will exercise an almost despotic sway within their own shires, and may sometimes threaten to convulse even the realm itself; but both their mutual jealousies and their brief and restricted opportunities forbid their combining, and each is very far from the office of common leader.

I know that to some this scheme of distributed power and disintegrated rule seems a very excellent device whereby we are enabled to escape a dangerous "one-man power" and an untoward concentration of functions; and it is very easy to see and appreciate the considerations which make this view of committee government so popular. It is based upon a very proper and salutary fear of *irresponsible* power; and those who most resolutely maintain it always fight from the position that all leadership in legislation is hard to restrain in proportion to its size and to the strength of its prerogatives, and that to divide it is to make it manageable. They aver, besides, that the less a man has to do-that is to say, the more he is confined to single departments and to definite details-the more intelligent and thorough will his work be. They like the Committees, therefore, just because they are many and weak, being quite willing to abide their being despotic within their narrow spheres.

It seems evident, however, when the question is looked at from another stand-point, that, as a matter of fact and experience, the more power is divided the more irresponsible it becomes. A mighty baron who can call half the country to arms is watched with greater jealousy, and, therefore, restrained with more vigilant care than is ever vouchsafed the feeble master of a single and solitary castle. The one cannot stir abroad upon an innocent pleasure jaunt without attracting the suspicious attention of the whole country-side; the other may vex and harry his entire neighborhood without fear of let or hindrance. It is ever the little foxes that spoil the grapes. At any rate, to turn back from illustration to the facts of the argument, it is plain enough that the petty character of the leadership of each Committee contributes towards making its despotism sure by making its duties uninteresting. The Senate almost always discusses its business with considerable thoroughness; and even the House, whether by common consent or by reason of such persistent "filibustering" on the part of the minority as compels the reporting Committee and the majority to grant time for talk, sometimes stops to debate committee reports at length; but nobody, except, perhaps, newspaper editors, finds these debates interesting reading.

Why is it that many intelligent and patriotic people throughout this country, from Virginia to California, —people who, beyond all question, love their State and the Union more than they love our cousin state over sea, —subscribe for the London papers in order to devour the parliamentary debates, and yet would never think of troubling themselves to make tedious progress through a single copy of the "Congressional Record"? Is it because they are captivated by the old-world dignity of royal England with its nobility and its court pageantry, or because of a vulgar desire to appear better versed than their neighbors in foreign affairs, and to affect familiarity with British statesmen? No; of course not. It is because the parliamentary debates are interesting and ours are not. In the British House of Commons the functions and privileges of our Standing Committees are all concentrated in the hands of the Ministry, who have, besides, some prerogatives of leadership which even our Committees do not possess, so that they carry all responsibility as well as great power, and all debate wears an intense personal and party interest. Every important discussion is an arraignment of the Ministry by the Opposition, —an arraignment of the majority by the minority; and every important vote is a party defeat and a party triumph. The whole conduct of the government turns upon what is said in the Commons, because the revelations of debate often change votes, and a Ministry loses hold upon power as it loses hold upon the confidence of the Commons. This great Standing Committee goes out whenever it crosses the will of the majority. It is, therefore, for these very simple and obvious reasons that the parliamentary debates are read on this side of the water in preference to the congressional debates. They affect the ministers, who are very conspicuous persons, and in whom, therefore, all the intelligent world is interested; and they determine the course of politics in a great empire. The season of a parliamentary debate is a great field day on which Liberals and Conservatives pit their full forces against each other, and people like to watch the issues of the contest.

Our congressional debates, on the contrary, have no tithe of this interest, because they have no tithe of such significance and importance. The committee reports, upon which the debates take place, are backed by neither party; they represent merely the recommendations of a small body of members belonging to both parties, and are quite as likely to divide the vote of the party to which the majority of the Committee belong as they are to meet with opposition from the other side of the chamber. If they are carried, it is no party triumph; if they are lost, it is no party discomfiture. They are no more than the proposals of a mixed Committee, and may be rejected without political inconvenience to either party or reproof to the Committee; just as they may be passed without compliment to the Committee or political advantage to either side of the House. Neither party has any great stake in the controversy. The only importance that can attach to the vote must hang upon its relation to the next general election. If the report concern a question which is at the time so much in the public eye that all action upon it is likely to be marked and remembered against the day of popular action, parties are careful to vote as solidly as possible on what they conceive to be the safe side; but all other reports are disposed of without much thought of their influence upon the fortunes of distant elections, because that influence is remote and problematical.

In a word, the national parties do not act in Congress under the restraint of a sense of immediate responsibility. Responsibility is spread thin; and no vote or debate can gather it. It rests not so much upon parties as upon individuals; and it rests upon individuals in no such way as would make it either just or efficacious to visit upon them the iniquity of any legislative act. Looking at government from a practical and business-like, rather than from a theoretical and abstractly-ethical point of view, —treating the business of government as a business,—it seems to be unquestionably and in a high degree desirable that all legislation should distinctly represent the action of parties as parties. I know that it has been proposed by enthusiastic, but not too practical, reformers to do away with parties by some legerdemain of governmental reconstruction, accompanied and supplemented by some rehabilitation, devoutly to be wished, of the virtues least commonly controlling in fallen human nature; but it seems to me that it would be more difficult and less desirable than these amiable persons suppose to conduct a government of the many by means of any other device than party organization, and that the great need is, not to get rid of parties, but to find and use some expedient by which they can be managed and made amenable from day to day to public opinion. Plainly this cannot be effected by punishing here and there a member of Congress who has voted for a flagrantly dishonest appropriation bill, or an obnoxious measure relating to the tariff. Unless the punishment can be extended to the party-if any such be recognizable-with which these members have voted, no advantage has been won for self-government, and no triumph has been gained by public opinion. It should be desired that parties should act in distinct organizations, in accordance with avowed principles, under easily recognized leaders, in order that the voters might be able to declare by their ballots, not only their condemnation of any past policy, by withdrawing all support from the party responsible for it; but also and particularly their will as to the future administration of the government, by bringing into power a party pledged to the adoption of an acceptable policy.

It is, therefore, a fact of the most serious consequence that by our system of congressional rule no such means of controlling legislation is afforded. Outside of Congress the organization of the national parties is exceedingly well-defined and tangible; no one could wish it, and few could imagine it, more so; but within Congress it is obscure and intangible. Our parties marshal their adherents with the strictest possible discipline for the purpose of carrying elections, but their discipline is very slack and indefinite in dealing with legislation. At least there is within Congress no *visible*, and therefore no *controllable* party organization. The only bond of cohesion is the caucus, which occasionally whips a party together for coöperative action against the time for casting its vote upon some critical question. There is always a majority and a minority, indeed, but the legislation of a session does not represent the policy of either; it is simply an aggregate of the bills recommended by Committees composed of members from both sides of the House, and it is known to be usually, not the work of the majority men upon the Committees, but compromise conclusions bearing some shade or tinge of each of the variously-colored opinions and wishes of the committee-men of both parties.

It is plainly the representation of both parties on the Committees that makes party responsibility indistinct and organized party action almost impossible. If the Committees were composed entirely of members of the majority, and were thus constituted representatives of the party in power, the whole course of congressional proceedings would unquestionably take on a very different aspect. There would then certainly be a compact opposition to face the organized majority. Committee reports would be taken to represent the views of the party in power, and, instead of the scattered, unconcerted opposition, without plan or leaders, which now sometimes subjects the propositions of the Committees to vexatious hindrances and delays, there would spring up debate under skillful masters of opposition, who could drill their partisans for effective warfare and give shape and meaning to the purposes of the minority. But of course there can be no such definite division of forces so long as the efficient machinery of legislation is in the hands of both parties at once; so long as the parties are mingled and harnessed together in a common organization.

It may be said, therefore, that very few of the measures which come before Congress are party measures. They are, at any rate, not brought in as party measures. They are indorsed by select bodies of members chosen with a view to constituting an impartial board of examination for the judicial and thorough consideration of each subject of legislation; no member of one of these Committees is warranted in revealing any of the disagreements of the committee-room or the proportions of the votes there taken; and no color is meant to be given to the supposition that the reports made are intended to advance any party interest. Indeed, only a very slight examination of the measures which originate with the Committees is necessary to show that most of them are framed with a view to securing their easy passage by giving them as neutral and inoffensive a character as possible. The manifest object is to dress them to the liking of all factions.

Under such circumstances, neither the failure nor the success of any policy inaugurated by one of the Committees can fairly be charged to the account of either party. The Committee acted honestly, no doubt, and as they thought best; and there can, of course, be no assurance that, by taking away its congressional majority from the party to which the greater number of the committee-men belong, a Committee could be secured which would act better or differently.

The conclusion of the whole matter is, then, that public opinion cannot be instructed or elevated by the debates of Congress, not only because there are few debates seriously undertaken by Congress, but principally because no one not professionally interested in the daily course of legislation cares to read what is said by the debaters when Congress does stop to talk, inasmuch as nothing depends upon the issue of the discussion. The ordinary citizen cannot be induced to pay much heed to the details, or even to the main principles, of law-making, unless something else more interesting than the law itself be involved in the pending decision of the law-makers. If the fortunes of a party or the power of a great political leader are staked upon the final vote, he will listen with the keenest interest to all that the principal actors may have to say, and absorb much instruction in so doing; but if no such things hang in the balance, he will not turn from his business to listen; and if the true issues are not brought out in eager public contests which catch his ear because of their immediate personal interest, but must be sought amidst the information which can be made complete only by reading scores of newspapers, he will certainly never find them or care for them, and there is small use in printing a "Record" which he will not read.

I know not how better to describe our form of government in a single phrase than by calling it a government by the chairmen of the Standing Committees of Congress. This disintegrate ministry, as it figures on the floor of the House of Representatives, has many peculiarities. In the first place, it is made up of the elders of the assembly; for, by custom, seniority in congressional service determines the bestowal of the principal chairmanships; in the second place, it is constituted of selfish and warring elements; for chairman fights against chairman for use of the time of the assembly, though the most part of them are inferior to the chairman of Ways and Means, and all are subordinate to the chairman of the Committee on Appropriations; in the third place, instead of being composed of the associated leaders of Congress, it consists of the dissociated heads of forty-eight "little legislatures" (to borrow Senator Hoar's apt name for the Committees); and, in the fourth place, it is instituted by appointment from Mr. Speaker, who is, by intention, the chief judicial, rather than the chief political, officer of the House.

It is highly interesting to note the extraordinary power accruing to Mr. Speaker through this pregnant prerogative of appointing the Standing Committees of the House. That power is, as it were, the central and characteristic inconvenience and anomaly of our constitutional system, and on that account excites both the curiosity and the wonder of the student of institutions. The most esteemed writers upon our Constitution have failed to observe, not only that the Standing Committees are the most essential machinery of our governmental system, but also that the Speaker of the House of Representatives is the most powerful functionary of that system. So sovereign is he within the wide sphere of his influence that one could wish for accurate knowledge as to the actual extent of his power. But Mr. Speaker's powers cannot be known accurately, because they vary with the character of Mr. Speaker. All Speakers have, of late years especially, been potent factors in legislation, but some have, by reason of greater energy or less conscience, made more use of their opportunities than have others.

The Speaker's privilege of appointing the Standing Committees is nearly as old as Congress itself. At first the House tried the plan of balloting for its more important Committees, ordering, in April, 1789, that the Speaker should appoint only those Committees which should consist of not more than three members; but less than a year's experience of this method of organizing seems to have furnished satisfactory proof of its impracticability, and in January, 1790, the present rule was adopted: that "All committees shall be appointed by the Speaker, unless otherwise specially directed by the House." The rules of one House of Representatives are not, however, necessarily the rules of the next. No rule lives save by biennial readoption. Each newly-elected House meets without rules for its governance, and amongst the first acts of its first session is usually the adoption of the resolution that the rules of its predecessor shall be its own rules, subject, of course, to such revisions as it may, from time to time, see fit to make. Mr. Speaker's power of appointment, accordingly, always awaits the passage of this resolution; but it never waits in vain, for no House, however foolish in other respects, has yet been foolish enough to make fresh trial of electing its Committees. That mode may do well enough for the cool and leisurely Senate, but it is not for the hasty and turbulent House.

It must always, of course, have seemed eminently desirable to all thoughtful and experienced men that Mr. Speaker should be no more than the judicial guide and moderator of the proceedings of the House, keeping apart from the heated controversies of party warfare, and exercising none but an impartial influence upon the course of legislation; and probably when he was first invested with the power of appointment it was thought possible that he could exercise that great prerogative without allowing his personal views upon questions of public policy to control or even affect his choice. But it must very soon have appeared that it was too much to expect of a man who had it within his power to direct affairs that he should subdue all purpose to do so, and should make all appointments with an eye to regarding every preference but his own; and when that did become evident, the rule was undoubtedly retained only because none better could be devised. Besides, in the early years of the Constitution the Committees were very far from having the power they now possess. Business did not then hurry too fast for discussion, and the House was in the habit of scrutinizing the reports of the Committees much more critically than it now pretends to do. It deliberated in its open sessions as well as in its private committee-rooms, and the functionary who appointed its committees was simply the nominator of its advisers, not, as is the Speaker of to-day, the nominor of its rulers.

It is plain, therefore, that the office of Speaker of the House of Representatives is in its present estate a constitutional phenomenon of the first importance, deserving a very thorough and critical examination. If I have succeeded, in what I have already said, in making clear the extraordinary power of the Committees in directing legislation, it may now go without the saying that he who appoints those Committees is an autocrat of the first magnitude. There could be no clearer proof of the great political weight of the Speaker's high commission in this regard than the keen strife which every two years takes place over the election to the speakership, and the intense interest excited throughout the country as to the choice to be made. Of late years, the newspapers have had almost as much to say about the rival candidates for that office as about the candidates for the presidency itself, having come to look upon the selection made as a sure index of the policy to be expected in legislation.

The Speaker is of course chosen by the party which commands the majority in the House, and it has sometimes been the effort of scheming, self-seeking men of that majority to secure the elevation of some friend or tool of their own to that office, from which he can render them service of the most substantial and acceptable sort. But, although these intrigues have occasionally resulted in the election of a man of insignificant parts and doubtful character, the choice has usually fallen upon some representative party man of well-known antecedents and clearly-avowed opinions; for the House cannot, and will not willingly, put up with the intolerable inconvenience of a weak Speaker, and the majority are urged by self-respect and by all the weightiest considerations of expediency, as well as by a regard for the interests of the public business, to place one of their accredited leaders in the chair. If there be differences of opinion within the party, a choice between leaders becomes a choice between policies and assumes the greatest significance. The Speaker is expected to constitute the Committees in accordance with his own political views, and this or that candidate is preferred by his party, not at all because of any supposed superiority of knowledge of the precedents and laws of parliamentary usage, but because of his more popular opinions concerning the leading questions of the day.

Mr. Speaker, too, generally uses his powers as freely and imperatively as he is expected to use them. He unhesitatingly acts as the legislative chief of his party, organizing the Committees in the interest of this or that policy, not covertly and on the sly, as one who does something of which he is ashamed, but openly and confidently, as one who does his duty. Nor does his official connection with the Committees cease upon their appointment. It is his care to facilitate their control of the business of the House, by recognizing during the consideration of a report only those members with whom the reporting committee-man has agreed to share his time, and by keeping all who address the House within the strictest letter of the rules as to the length of their speeches, as well as by enforcing all those other restrictions which forbid independent action on the part of individual members. He must see to it that the Committees have their own way. In so doing he is not exercising arbitrary powers which circumstances and the habits of the assembly enable him safely to arrogate; he is simply enforcing the plain letter and satisfying the evident spirit of the rules.

A student of Roman law and institutions, looking at the Rules of the House of Representatives through glasses unaccustomed to search out aught but antiquities, might be excused for claiming that he found in the customs of the House a striking reproduction of Roman legislative methods. The Roman assembly, he would remind us, could not vote and debate at the same time; it had no privileges of amendment, but had to adopt every law as a whole or reject it as a whole; and no private member had a right to introduce a bill, that being the exclusive prerogative of the magistrates. But though he might establish a parallel satisfactory to himself between the magistrates of Rome and the Committees at Washington, and between the undebatable, unamendable laws of the ancient, and the undebated, unamended laws of the modern, republic, he could hardly find in the later system that compensating advantage which scholars have noted as giving to Roman legislation a clearness and technical perfection such as is to be found in none of the modern codes. Since Roman laws could not be amended in their passage, and must carry their meaning plainly to the comprehension of the commons, clear and brief drafting was cultivated as of the first necessity in drawing up measures which were first to gain popular approval and then to succeed or fail in accomplishing their ends according as they proved workable or impracticable.

No such comparison of our own with other systems can, however, find any favor in the eyes of a certain class of Americans who pride themselves upon being nothing if not patriotic, and who can consequently find no higher praise for the peculiar devices of committee government than that they are our own invention. "An ill-favored thing, sir, but mine own." No one will readily believe, however, that congressmen-even those of them who belong to this dutiful class-cherish a very loving admiration for the discipline to which they are nowadays subjected. As the accomplished librarian of Congress has declared, "the general conviction may be said to exist, that, under the great control over legislation and current business by the Speaker, and by the powerful Committee on Appropriations, combined with the rigor of the Rules of the House, there is less and less opportunity for individual members to make any influential mark in legislation. Independence and ability are repressed under the tyranny of the rules, and practically the power of the popular branch of Congress is concentrated in the Speaker and a few-very few-expert parliamentarians." And of course members of Congress see this. "We have but three forces in this House," exclaimed a jocose member from the Pacific coast, "the Brahmins of the Committee of Ways and Means-not the brains but the Brahmins of the House; the white-button mandarins of the Appropriations Committee; the dignified oligarchy called the Committee on Rules; the Speaker of the House; and the illustrious gentleman from Indiana." Naturally all men of independent spirit chafe under the arbitrary restraints of such a system, and it would be much more philosophical to conclude that they let it stand because they can devise nothing better, than that they adhere to its inconvenient practices because of their admiration for it as an American invention.

However that may be, the number of those who misuse the rules is greater than the number of those who strive to reform them. One of the most startling of the prevalent abuses is the hasty passage of bills under a suspension of the rules, a device "by means of which," says Senator Hoar, "a large proportion, perhaps the majority, of the bills which pass the House are carried through." This practice may be very clearly understood by following further Mr. Hoar's own words: "Every Monday after the morning hour, and at any time during the last ten days of a session, motions to suspend the rules are in order. At these times any member may move to suspend the rules and pass any proposed bill. It requires two thirds of the members voting to adopt such a motion. Upon it no debate or amendment is in order. In this way, if two thirds of the body agree, a bill is by a single vote, without discussion and without change, passed through all the necessary stages, and made a law, so far as the House of Representatives can accomplish it; and in this mode hundreds of measures of vital importance receive, near the close of an exhausting session, without being debated, amended, printed, or understood, the constitutional assent of the representatives of the American people."

One very obvious comment to be made upon habits of procedure so palpably pernicious is, that nothing could be more natural under rules which repress individual action with so much stringency. Then, too, the mills of the Committees are known to grind slowly, and a very quick and easy way of getting rid of minor items of business is to let particular bills, of apparently innocent meaning or laudable intent, run through without commitment. There must be some outlet, too, through which the waters of delayed and accumulated business may be drained off as the end of a session draws near. Members who know how to take the House at an indulgent moment, and can in a few words make out a *primâ facie* case for the action they urge, can almost always secure a suspension of the rules.

To speak very plainly, it is wonderful that under such a system of government legislation is not oftener at sixes and sevens than it actually is. The infinitely varied and various interests of fifty millions of active people would be hard enough to harmonize and serve, one would think, were parties efficiently organized in the pursuit of definite, steady, consistent policies; and it is therefore simply amazing to find how few outrageously and fatally foolish, how few bad or disastrous, things have been done by means of our disintegrate methods of legislation. The Committees of the House to whom the principal topics of legislation are allotted number more than thirty. We are ruled by a score and a half of "little legislatures." Our legislation is conglomerate, not homogeneous. The doings of one and the same Congress are foolish in pieces and wise in spots. They can never, except by accident, have any common features. Some of the Committees are made up of strong men, the majority of them of weak men; and the weak are as influential as the strong. The country can get the counsel and guidance of its ablest representatives only upon one or two subjects; upon the rest it must be content with the impotent service of the feeble. Only a very small part of its most important business can be done well; the system provides for having the rest of it done miserably, and the whole of it taken together done at haphazard. There could be no more interesting problem in the doctrine of chances than that of reckoning the probabilities of there being any common features of principle in the legislation of an opening session. It might lighten and divert the leisure of some ingenious mathematician to attempt the calculation.

It was probably some such reflections as these which suggested the proposal, made not long since in the House, that there should be appointed, along with the usual Standing Committees, a new committee which should be known as the Executive Committee of the House, and should be empowered to examine and sort all the bills reported favorably by the other Standing

Committees, and bring them forward in what might seem to it the order of their importance; a committee which should, in short, digest pending measures and guide the House in arranging its order of business. But it is seriously to be doubted whether such an addition to the present organization would do more than tighten the tyranny of committee rule and still further restrict freedom of debate and action. A committee to superintend committees would add very little to the efficiency of the House, and would certainly contribute nothing towards unifying legislation, unless the new committee were to be given the power, not yet thought of, of revising the work of the present Standing Committees. Such an executive committee is not quite the device needed.

Apparently committee government is but one of many experiments in the direction of the realization of an idea best expressed-so far as my reading shows-by John Stuart Mill; and is too much like other experiments to be quite as original and unique as some people would like to believe. There is, said Mr. Mill, a "distinction between the function of *making* laws, for which a numerous popular assembly is radically unfit, and that of *getting good laws made*, which is its proper duty, and cannot be satisfactorily fulfilled by any other authority;" and there is, consequently, "need of a legislative commission, as a permanent part of the constitution of a free country; consisting of a small number of highly-trained political minds, on whom, when parliament has determined that a law shall be made, the task of making it should be devolved; parliament retaining the power of passing or rejecting the bill when drawn up, but not of altering it otherwise than by sending proposed amendments to be dealt with by the commission."[25] It would seem, as I have said, that committee government is one form of the effort, now making by all self-governing peoples, to set up a satisfactory legislative commission somewhat after this order; and it might appear to some as if the proposed executive committee were a slight approximation to that form of the effort which is typified in the legislative functions of the British cabinet. It cannot, of course, be claimed that the forty-eight legislative commissions of the House of Representatives always answer the purpose when the House wants to get good laws made, or that each of them consists invariably of "a small number of highly-trained political minds;" but everybody sees that to say that they fall short of realizing the ideal would be nothing less than hypercritical.

In saying that our committee government has, germinally, some of the features of the British system, in which the ministers of the crown, the cabinet, are chosen from amongst the leaders of the parliamentary majority, and act not only as advisers of the sovereign but also as the great standing committee or "legislative commission" of the House of Commons, guiding its business and digesting its graver matters of legislation, I mean, of course, only that both systems represent the common necessity of setting apart some small body, or bodies, of legislative guides through whom a "big meeting" may get laws made. The difference between our device and the British is that we have a Standing Committee, drawn from both parties, for the consideration of each topic of legislation, whereas our English cousins have but a single standing committee that is charged with the origination of legislation, —a committee composed of the men who are recognized as the leaders of the party dominant in the state, and who serve at the same time as the political heads of the executive departments of the government.

The British system is perfected party government. No effort is made in the Commons, such as is made in the House of Representatives in the composition of the Committees, to give the minority a share in law-making. Our minorities are strongly represented on the Standing Committees; the minority in the Commons is not represented at all in the cabinet. It is this feature of closely organized party government, whereby the responsibility for legislation is saddled upon the majority, which, as I have already pointed out, gives to the debates and action of parliament an interest altogether denied to the proceedings of Congress. All legislation is made a contest for party supremacy, and if legislation goes wrong, or the majority becomes discontented with the course of policy, there is nothing for it but that the ministers should resign and give place to the leaders of the Opposition, unless a new election should procure for them a recruited following. Under such a system mere silent voting is out of the question; debate is a primary necessity. It brings the representatives of the people and the ministers of the Crown face to face. The principal measures of each session originate with the ministers, and embody the policy of the administration. Unlike the reports of our Standing Committees, which are intended to be simply the digested substance of the more sensible bills introduced by private members, the bills introduced into the House of Commons by the cabinet embody the definite schemes of the government; and the fact that the Ministry is made up of the leaders of the majority and represents always the principles of its party, makes the minority only the more anxious to have a chance to criticise its proposals. Cabinet government is a device for bringing the executive and legislative branches into harmony and coöperation without uniting or confusing their functions. It is as if the majority in the Commons deputized its leaders to act as the advisers of the Crown and the superintendents of the public business, in order that they might have the advantage of administrative knowledge and training in advising legislation and drafting laws to be submitted to parliament. This arrangement enlists the majority in behalf of successful administration without giving the ministers any power to coerce or arbitrarily influence legislative action. Each session of the Lords and Commons becomes a grand inquest into the affairs of the empire. The two estates sit as it were in committee on the management of the public business-sit with open doors, and spare themselves no fatigue in securing for every interest represented a full, fair, and impartial hearing.

It is evident why public debate is the very breath of life to such a system. The Ministry's tenure of office depends upon the success of the legislation they urge. If any of their proposals are negatived by parliament, they are bound to accept their defeat as an intimation that their administration is no longer acceptable to the party they represent, and are expected to resign, or to appeal, if they prefer, to the country for its verdict, by exercising their privilege of advising the sovereign to dissolve parliament and issue writs for a new election. It is, consequently, inevitable that the Ministry should be subjected to the most determined attacks and the keenest criticisms of the Opposition, and should be every day of the session put to the task of vindicating their course and establishing anew their claim to the confidence of their party. To shrink from discussion would be to confess weakness; to suffer themselves to be worsted in discussion would be seriously to imperil their power. They must look to it, therefore, not only that their policy be defensible, but that it be valiantly defended also.

As might be expected, then, the Ministry seldom find the task of leading the House an easy one. Their plans are kept under an unceasing fire of criticism from both sides of the House; for there are independent sharp-shooters behind the ministers as well as heavy batteries in front of them; and there are many amongst their professed followers who give aid and comfort to the enemy. There come ever and again showers of stinging questions, too, from friends and foes alike, —questions great and small, direct and indirect, pertinent and impertinent, concerning every detail of administration and every tendency of policy.

But, although the initiative in legislation and the general direction of the business of parliament are the undisputed prerogatives of "the government," as the Ministry is called, they have not, of course, all the time of the House at their disposal. During the session, certain days of each week are set apart for the introduction and debate of bills brought in by private members, who, at the opening of the session, draw lots to decide the precedence of their bills or motions on the orders of the day. If many draw, those who get last choice of time find the session near its end, and private members' days being absorbed by belated government measures, before their opportunity has come, and must content themselves with hoping for better fortune next year; but time is generally found for a very fair and full consideration of a large number of private members' bills, and no member is denied a chance to air his favorite opinions in the House or to try the patience of his fellow-members by annual repetitions of the same proposition. Private members generally find out by long experience, however, that they can exert a more telling influence upon legislation by pressing amendments to government schemes, and can effect more immediate and satisfactory results by keeping the Ministry constantly in mind of certain phases of public opinion, than they could hope to exert or effect by themselves introducing measures upon which their party might hesitate to unite. Living as he does under a system which makes it the minister's wisest policy to allow the utmost freedom of debate, each member can take as prominent a part in the proceedings of the House as his abilities give him title to take. If he have anything which is not merely frivolous to say, he will have repeated opportunities to say it; for the Commons cough down only the bores and the talkers for the sake of talk.

The House of Commons, as well as our House of Representatives, has its committees, even its standing committees, but they are of the old-fashioned sort which merely investigate and report, not of the new American type which originate and conduct legislation. Nor are they appointed by the Speaker. They are chosen with care by a "Committee of Selection" composed of members of both parties. The Speaker is kept carefully apart from politics in all his functions, acting as the impartial, judicial president of the body. "Dignity of presence, courtliness of manner, great physical endurance, courage and impartiality of judgment, a consummate tact, and familiarity, 'born of life-long experience,' with the written and unwritten laws of the House," —such are the qualities of the ideal Speaker. When he takes the chair he turns his back on partisan alliances and serves both parties alike with even hand. Such are the traditions of the office that its occupant feels himself as strictly bound to unbiased judgment as is the chiefest judge of the realm; and it has become no uncommon thing for a Speaker of tried ability to preside during several successive Parliaments, whether the party to whose suffrages he originally owed his elevation remains in power or no. His political principles do not affect his fitness for judicial functions.

The Commons in session present an interesting picture. Constrained by their habits of debate to sit in quarters suitable for the purpose, they crowd together in a hall of somewhat cramped proportions. It seems a place fit for hand to hand combats. The cushioned benches on which the members sit rise in close series on either side of a wide central aisle which they face. At one end of this aisle is raised the Speaker's chair, below and in front of which, invading the spaces of the aisle, are the desks of the wigged and gowned clerks. On the front benches nearest the Speaker and to his right sit the cabinet ministers, the leaders of the Government; opposite, on the front benches to the Speaker's left, sit the leaders of the Opposition. Behind and to the right of the ministers gather the majority; behind and to the left of their leaders, the minority. Above the rear benches and over the outer aisles of the House, beyond "the bar," hang deep galleries from which the outside world may look down upon the eager contests of the two parties which thus sit face to face with only the aisle between them. From these galleries the fortunate listen to the words of leaders whose names fill the ear of the world.

The organization of the French Assembly is in the main similar to that of the British Commons. Its leaders are the executive officers of the government, and are chosen from the ranks of the legislative majority by the President of the Republic, much as English cabinets are chosen by English sovereigns. They too are responsible for their policy and the acts of their administration to the Chamber which they lead. They, like their British prototypes, are the executive committee of the legislative body, and upon its will their tenure of office depends.

It cannot be said, however, that the proceedings of the French Assembly very closely resemble those of the British Commons. In the hall of the Deputies there are no close benches which face each other, and no two homogeneous parties to strive for the mastery. There are parties and parties, factions and factions, coteries and coteries. There are Bonapartists and Legitimatists, Republicans and Clericals, stubborn reactionists and headlong radicals, stolid conservatives and vindictive destructionists. One hears of the Centre, the Right Centre and the Left Centre, the Right, the Left, the Extreme Right and the Extreme Left. Some of these are, of course, mere factions, mere groups of irreconcilables; but several of them are, on the other hand, numerous and powerful parties upon whose mutual attractions and repulsions depend the formation, the authority, and the duration of cabinets.

Of course, too, there is in a body so made up a great deal of combustible material which the slightest circumstance suffices to kindle into a sudden blaze. The Assembly would not be French if it were not always excitable and sometimes uproarious. Absolute turbulence is so probable a contingency in its economy that a very simple and quickly applicable device is provided for its remedy. Should the deputies lose their heads altogether and become unmanageable, the

President may *put on his hat*, and by that sign, unless calm be immediately restored, the sitting is adjourned for one hour, at the expiration of which time it is to be expected that the members may resume the business of the day in a cooler frame of mind. There are other rules of procedure observed in the Chamber which seem to foreign eyes at first sight very novel; but which upon closer examination may be seen to differ from some of the practices of our own House of Representatives in form rather than in essence. In France greater freedom of speech is allowed individual members than is possible under committee government, but recognition is not given to just any one who first gets the floor and catches the presiding officer's eye, as it is in the House of Commons, where none but the ministers are accorded any right of precedence in gaining a hearing. Those who wish to speak upon any pending question "inscribe" their names beforehand on a list in the keeping of the President, and the discussion is usually confined to those members who have "inscribed." When this list has been exhausted, the President takes the sense of the Chamber as to whether the debate shall be closed. The Chamber need not wait, however, to hear all the gentlemen who have put their names upon the list. If *une portion notable* of it tires sooner of the discussion or thinks itself sufficiently informed before all who wish to inform it have spoken, it may demand that the debate be brought to an end. Of course such a demand will not be heeded if it come from only a few isolated members, and even *une portion notable* may not interrupt a speaker with this peremptory call for what we should denominate the previous question, but which the French parliamentarian knows as the *clôture*. A demand for the *clôture* is not debatable. One speech may be made against it, but none in its favor. Unless it meet with very powerful resistance, it is expected to go through of its own weight. Even the *clôture*, however, must give way if a member of the Ministry claims the right to speak; for a minister must always be heard, and after he has spoken, moreover, there must always be allowed one speech in reply. Neither can the *clôture* be pronounced unless a majority of the deputies are present; and in case of doubt as to the will of the Chamber in the matter, after two votes have been taken without eliciting a full-voiced and indubitable assent, the discussion is tacitly suffered to proceed.

These rules are not quite so compulsive and inexorable as are those which sustain the government of our Standing Committees, nor do they seem quite imperative enough for the effectual governance of rampant deputies in their moments of wildest excitement; but they are somewhat more rigid than one would expect to find under a system of ministerial responsibility, the purity of whose atmosphere depends so directly upon a free circulation of debate. They are meant for a body of peculiar habits and a fiery temperament, —a body which is often brought screaming to its feet by the words of a passionate speaker, which is time and again betrayed into stormy disquiet, and which is ever being blown about by every passing wind of excitement. Even in its minor points of observance, the Chamber is essentially un-English. Members do not speak from their seats, as we are accustomed to see members of our public assemblies do, but from the "tribune," which is a conspicuous structure erected near the desks of the President and secretaries, —a box-like stand, closely resembling those narrow, quaintly-fashioned pulpits which are still to be seen in some of the oldest of our American churches. And since deputies must gain its commanding top before they may speak, there are said to be many exciting races for this place of vantage. Sometimes, indeed, very unseemly scenes take place, when several deputies, all equally eager to mount the coveted stand, reach its narrow steps at the same moment and contest the privilege of precedence, —especially if their friends rally in numbers to their assistance.

The British House of Commons and the French Chamber, though so unlike in the elements which compose them, and so dissimilar in their modes of procedure, are easily seen to be alike in constitutional significance, being made close kin by the principle of cabinet government, which they both recognize and both apply in its fullest efficacy. In both England and France a ministry composed of the chief officers of the executive departments are constituted at once the leaders of legislation and the responsible heads of administration, —a binding link between the legislative and executive branches of the government. In this regard these two systems present a strong contrast to our own. They recognize and support simple, straightforward, inartificial party government, under a standing committee of responsible party leaders, bringing legislature and executive side by side in intimate but open coöperation; whilst we, preferring to keep Congress and the departments at arm's length, permit only a less direct government by party majorities, checking party action by a complex legislative machinery of two score and eight composite, semi-ministerial Committees. The English take their parties straight, —we take ours mixed.

There is another aspect, however, in which all three of these systems are alike. They are alike in their essential purpose, which is to enable a mass meeting of representatives to superintend administration and get good laws made. Congress does not deal so directly with our executive as do the French and English parliaments with theirs, and cannot, therefore, control it quite so effectually; there is a great deal of friction amongst the many wheels of committee government; but, in the long run, Congress is quite as omnipotent as either the Chamber of Deputies or the House of Commons; and, whether there be two score committees with functions mainly legislative, or only one with functions half legislative, half executive, we have one form or another of something like Mr. Mill's "legislative commission."

III
The House of Representatives Revenue and Supply.

> The highest works of statesmanship require these three things: Great power in the minister, genius to counsel and support him, enlightenment in parliament to weigh and decide upon his plans. —PROFESSOR SEELEY.
>
> When men are not acquainted with each other's principles, nor experienced in each other's talents, nor at all practiced in their mutual habitudes and dispositions by joint efforts of business; no personal confidence, no friendship, no common interest subsisting among them; it is evidently impossible that they can act a public part with uniformity, perseverance, or efficacy. —BURKE.

"It requires," says Mr. Bagehot, "a great deal of time to have opinions," and if one is to judge from the legislative experience of some very enlightened nations, it requires more time to have opinions about finance than about any other subject. At any rate, very few nations have found time to have correct opinions about it. Governments which never consult the governed are usually content with very shabby, short-sighted methods of taxation, —with any methods, indeed, which can be made to yield the desired revenues without much trouble; and the agents of a self-governing people are quite sure to be too busy with elections and party management to have leisure to improve much upon the practices of autocrats in regard to this important care of administration. And yet this subject of finance seems to be interesting enough in a way. It is one of the commonplaces of our history that, ever since long before we came westward across the ocean, we have been readier to fight about taxation than about any other one thing, —than about a good many other things put together, indeed. There are several sadly bloody spots in the financial history of our race. It could probably be shown, however, if one cared to take time to show it, that it is easy to get vexed about mismanagement of the finances without knowing how they might be better managed. What we do not like is that we are taxed, —not that we are stupidly taxed. We do not need to be political economists to get angry about it; and when we have gotten angry about it in the past our rulers have not troubled themselves to study political economy in order to find out the best means of appeasing us. Generally they have simply shifted the burden from the shoulders of those who complained, and were able to make things unpleasant, to the shoulders of those who might complain, but could not give much trouble.

Of course there are some taxes which are much more hateful than others, and have on that account to be laid more circumspectly. All direct taxes are heartily disliked by every one who has to pay them, and as heartily abused, except by those who have never owned an ounce or an inch of property, and have never seen a tax-bill. The heart of the ordinary citizen regards them with an inborn aversion. They are so straightforward and peremptory in their demands. They soften their exactions with not a grain of consideration. The tax-collector, consequently, is never esteemed a lovable man. His methods are too blunt, and his powers too obnoxious. He comes to us, not with a "please," but with a "must." His requisitions always leave our pockets lighter and our hearts heavier. We cannot, for the life of us, help thinking, as we fold up his receipt and put it away, that government is much too expensive a luxury as nowadays conducted, and that that receipt is incontestable documentary proof of unendurable extortion. What we do not realize is, that life would be robbed of one of its chief satisfactions if this occasion of grumbling were to be taken away.

Indirect taxes, on the other hand, offend scarcely anybody. It is one of the open secrets of finance that in almost every system of taxation the indirect overcrow the direct taxes by many millions, and have a knack for levying on the small resources of insignificant persons which direct taxes have never learned. They know how to coax pennies out of poor people whose names have never been on the tax-collector's books. But they are very sly, and have at command a thousand successful disguises. High or complicated tariffs afford them their most frequent and abundant opportunities. Most people have very short thoughts, which do not extend beyond the immediate phenomena of direct vision, and so do not recognize the hand of the government in the high prices charged them in the shops. Very few of us taste the tariff in our sugar; and I suppose that even very thoughtful topers do not perceive the license-tax in their whiskey. There is little wonder that financiers have always been nervous in dealing with direct, but confident and free of hand in laying indirect, taxes.

It may, therefore, be accounted one of the customary advantages which our federal government possesses over the governments of the States, that it has almost always, in ordinary times, derived its entire revenue from prompt and facile indirect taxes, whilst the States have had to live upon the tardy and begrudged income derivable from a direct levy. Since we have had to support two governments it has been wisely resolved to let us, as long as possible, feel the weight of only one of them, —and that the one which can get at us most readily, and, at the same time, be most easily and promptly controlled by our votes. It is a plain, convenient, and, on the whole, satisfactory division of domain, though the responsibility which it throws on state legislatures is more apt to pinch and prove vexatious than is that which it lays upon Congress. Mr. Gladstone, the greatest of English financiers, once playfully described direct and indirect taxes as two sisters, —daughters of Necessity and Invention, —"differing only as sisters may differ, ... the one being more free and open, the other somewhat more shy, retiring, and insinuating;" and frankly owned that, whether from "a lax sense of moral obligation or not," he, as Chancellor of the Exchequer, "thought it not only allowable, but even an act of duty, to pay his addresses to them both." But our chancellors of the exchequer, the chairmen of the Committee of Ways and Means, are bound by other traditions of courtship, and have, besides, usually shown no susceptibility to the charms of the blunt and forward elder of these two sisters. They have been constant, even if now and again a little wayward, in their devotion to the younger.

I suppose that no one ever found the paths of finance less thorny and arduous than have our national publicists. If their tasks be compared with those of European and English financiers, it is plain to see that their lines have fallen in pleasant places. From almost the very first they have had boundless resources to draw upon, and they have certainly of late days had free leave to spend limitless revenues in what extravagances they pleased. It has come to be infinitely more trouble to spend our enormous national income than to collect it. The chief embarrassments have arisen, not from deficits, but from surpluses. It is very fortunate that such has been the case, because for the best management of the finances of a nation, when revenue is scant and economy imperative, it is absolutely necessary to have financial administration in the hands of a few highly-trained and skillful men acting subject to a very strict responsibility, and this is just what our committee system does not allow. As in other matters of legislation, so in finance, we have many masters acting under a very dim and inoperative accountability. Of course under such ministration our financial policy has always been unstable, and has often strayed very far from the paths of wisdom and providence; for even when revenue is superabundant and extravagance easy, irresponsible, fast and loose methods of taxation and expenditure must work infinite harm. The only difference is that during such times the nation is not so sensitive to the ill effects wrought by careless policy. Mismanagement is not generally blamed until a great many people have discovered it by being hurt by it. Meantime, however, it is none the less interesting and important to study our government, with a view to gauging its qualities and measuring accurately its capabilities for good or bad service; and the study can doubtless be much more dispassionately conducted before we have been seriously hurt by foolish, unsteady administration than afterwards. The forces of the wind can be reckoned with much more readily while they are blowing only a gale than after they have thrown a hurricane upon us.

The national income is controlled by one Committee of the House and one of the Senate; the expenditures of the government are regulated by fifteen Committees of the House and five of the Senate; and the currency is cared for by two Committees of the House and one of the Senate; by all of which it appears that the financial administration of the country is in the hands of twenty-four Committees of Congress, —a mechanism of numerous small and great functions, quite complex enough to be worth careful study, perhaps too complex to be studied directly without an aiding knowledge of some simpler system with which it may be compared. Our own budget may be more readily followed through all the vicissitudes of committee scrutiny, and all the varied fortunes of committee action, after one has traced some other budget through the simpler processes of some other system of government.

The British system is, perhaps, in its main features, the simplest in existence. It is, besides, the pattern after which the financial systems of the chief governments of Europe have been modeled, and which we have ourselves in a measure copied; so that by prefacing the study of other systems by a careful examination of the British, in its present form, one may start with the great advantage of knowing the characteristics of what may fairly be called the parent stock. Parliament, then, in the first place, simply controls, it does not originate, measures of financial administration. It acts through the agency and under the guidance of the ministers of the Crown. Early in each annual session "the estimates" are submitted to the Commons, which, when hearing such statements, sits in Committee of the Whole House, known as Committee of Supply. The estimates come before the House in truly formidable shape. Each department presents its estimates in a huge quarto volume, "crammed with figures and minute entries of moneys wanted for the forthcoming year."[26] But the House itself does not have to digest this various and overwhelming mass of figures. The digesting is done in the first instance by the official leaders of the House. "The ministers in charge of the naval and military services lay before the Committee [of Supply] their respective statements of the sums which will be required for the maintenance of those services; and somewhat later in the session a common estimate for the various civil services is submitted also." Those statements are, as it were, condensed synopses of the details of the quartos, and are made with the object of rendering quite clear to the House, sitting under the informal rules of Committee, the policy of the expenditures proposed and the correctness of the calculations upon which they are based. Any member may ask what pertinent questions he pleases of the minister who is making the statement, so that nothing needing elucidation may be passed by without full explanation. After the statement has been completed to the satisfaction of the Committee, a vote is taken, at the motion of the minister, upon each item of expenditure, and the duties of the Committee of Supply have been performed.

The estimates are always submitted "on the collective responsibility of the whole cabinet." "The army and navy estimates have, as a rule, been considered and settled in cabinet council before being submitted to the House; and the collective responsibility of the Ministry is in this case, therefore, not technical merely, but substantial." If the estimates are resisted and rejected by the Committee, the ministers, of course, resign. They "cannot acquiesce in a refusal on the part of parliament to sanction the expenditure which" they "have assumed the responsibility of declaring necessary for the support of the civil government, and the maintenance of the public credit at home and abroad." The votes in Committee of Supply are, therefore, vital in the history of every administration, being taken as sure indexes of the amount of confidence placed by the House in the government.

But the votes in Committee of Supply are only the first steps in parliament's annual supervision of the public finances. They are simply the spending votes. In order to consider the means by which money is to be raised to meet the outlays sanctioned by the Committee of Supply, the House resolves itself into Committee of the Whole, under the name of the Committee of Ways and Means. It is to this Committee that the Chancellor of the Exchequer submits his budget every year, on or soon before the fifth of April, the date at which the national accounts are made up, the financial year closing on the thirty-first of March. In order to prepare his budget, the Chancellor must of course have early knowledge of the estimates made for the various services. Several months, therefore, before the estimates are laid before the House in Committee of Supply, the various departments are called upon by the Treasury to send in statements of the sums required to defray the expenses of the current year, and these estimates are carefully examined by the Chancellor, with a view not only to exercising his duty of keeping the expenditures within the limits of economy, but also to ascertaining how much revenue he will have to secure in order to meet the proper expenditure contemplated. He must balance estimated needs over against estimated resources, and advise the House in Committee of Ways and Means as to the measures by which taxation is to be made to afford sufficient revenue. Accordingly he calls in the aid of the permanent heads of the revenue departments who furnish him with "their estimates of the public revenue for the ensuing year, upon the hypothesis that taxation will remain unchanged."

Having with such aids made up his budget, the Chancellor goes before the Committee of Ways and Means prepared to give a clear history of the financial administration of the year just closed, and to submit definite plans for adjusting the taxation and providing for the expected outlays of the year just opening. The precedents of a wise policy of long standing forbid his proposing to raise any greater revenue than is absolutely necessary for the support of the government and the maintenance of the public credit. He therefore never asks the Committee to lay taxes which promise a considerable surplus. He seeks to obtain only such an over-plus of income as will secure the government against those slight errors of underestimation of probable expenses or of overestimation of probable revenue as the most prudent of administrations is liable to make. If the estimated revenue considerably exceed the estimated expenses, he proposes such remissions of taxation as will bring the balance as near equality as prudence will permit; if the anticipated expenses run beyond the figure of the hoped-for revenue, he asks that certain new taxes be laid, or that certain existing taxes be increased; if the balance between the two sides of the forecast account shows a pretty near approach to equilibrium, so the scale of revenue be but a little the heavier of the two, he contents himself with suggesting such a readjustment of existing taxes as will be likely to distribute the burden of taxation more equitably amongst the tax-paying classes, or facilitate hampered collections by simplifying the complex methods of assessment and imposition.

Such is the budget statement to which the House of Commons listens in Committee of Ways and Means. This Committee may deal with the proposals of the Chancellor of the Exchequer with somewhat freer hand than the Committee of Supply may use in passing upon the estimates. The Ministry is not so stiffly insistent upon having its budget sanctioned as it is upon having its proposed expenditures approved. It is understood to pledge itself to ask for no more money than it honestly needs; but it simply advises with the House as to the best way of raising that money. It is punctiliously particular about being supplied with the funds it asks for, but not quite so exacting as to the ways and means of supply. Still, no Ministry can stand if the budget be rejected out of hand, or if its demands for the means of meeting a deficiency be met with a flat refusal, no alternative means being suggested by the Opposition. Such votes would be distinct declarations of a want of confidence in the Ministry, and would of course force them to resign.

The Committee of Ways and Means, then, carries out, under the guidance of the Chancellor of the Exchequer, the resolutions of the Committee of Supply. The votes of the latter Committee, authorizing the expenditures mapped out in the estimates, are embodied in "a resolution proposed in Committee of Ways and Means for a general grant out of the Consolidated Fund 'towards making good the supply granted to Her Majesty;'" and that resolution, in order that it may be prepared for the consideration of the House of Lords and the Crown, is afterwards cast by the House into the form of a Bill, which passes through the regular stages and in due course becomes law. The proposals of the Chancellor of the Exchequer with reference to changes in taxation are in like manner embodied in resolutions in Committee of Ways and Means, and subsequently, upon the report of the Committee, passed by the House in the shape of Bills, "Ways and Means Bills" generally pass the Lords without trouble. The absolute control of the Commons over the subjects of revenue and supply has been so long established that the upper House would not now dream of disputing it; and as the power of the Lords is simply a privilege to accept or reject a money bill as a whole, including no right to amend, the peers are wont to let such bills go through without much scrutiny.

But so far I have spoken only of that part of parliament's control of the finances which concerns the future. The "Ways and Means Bills" provide for coming expenses and a prospective revenue. Past expenses are supervised in a different way. There is a double process of audit by means of a special Audit Department of the Civil Service, which is, of course, a part of the permanent organization of the administration, having it in charge "to examine the accounts and vouchers of the entire expenditure," and a special committee nominated each year by the House "to audit the Audit Department." This committee is usually made up of the most experienced business men in the Commons, and before it "all the accounts of the completed financial year are passed in review." "Minute inquiries are occasionally made by it into the reasons why certain items of expenditure have occurred; it discusses claims for compensation, grants, and special disbursements, in addition to the ordinary outgoings of the department, mainly, to be sure, upon the information and advice of the departments themselves, but still with a certain independence of view and judgment which must be valuable."

The strictness and explicitness with which the public accounts are kept of course greatly facilitate the process of audit. The balance which is struck on the thirty-first of every March is of the most definite sort. It deals only with the actual receipts and disbursements of the completed fiscal year. At that date all unexpended credits lapse. If the expenditure of certain sums has been sanctioned by parliamentary vote, but some of the granted moneys remain undrawn when April comes in, they can be used only after a regrant by the Commons. There are, therefore, no unclosed accounts to obscure the view of the auditing authorities. Taxes and credits have the same definite period, and there are no arrears or unexpended balances to confuse the book-keeping. The great advantages of such a system in the way of checking extravagances which would otherwise be possible, may be seen by comparing it with the system in vogue in France, in whose national balance-sheet "arrears of taxes in one year overlap with those of other years," and "credits old jostle credits new," so that it is said to be "always three or four years before the nation can know what the definitive expenditure of a given year is."

For the completion of this sketch of financial administration under the Commons it is of course necessary to add a very distinct statement of what I may call the *accessibility* of the financial officers of the government. They are always present to be questioned. The Treasury department is, as becomes its importance, exceptionally well represented in the House. The Chancellor of the Exchequer, the working chief of the department, is invariably a member of the Commons, "and can be called to account by interrogation or motion with respect to all matters of Treasury concern" —with respect, that is, to well-nigh "the whole sphere of the discipline and economy of the Executive Government;" for the Treasury has wide powers of supervision over the other departments in all matters which may in any way involve an outlay of public money. "And not only does the invariable presence of the Chancellor of the Exchequer in the House of Commons make the representation of that department peculiarly direct, but, through the Secretary of the Treasury, and, with respect to certain departmental matters, through the Junior Lords, the House possesses peculiar facilities for ascertaining and expressing its opinion upon the details of Treasury administration." It has its responsible servants always before it, and can obtain what glimpses it pleases into the inner workings of the departments which it wishes to control.

It is just at this point that our own system of financial administration differs most essentially from the systems of England, of the Continent, and of the British colonial possessions. Congress does not come into direct contact with the financial officers of the government. Executive and legislature are separated by a hard and fast line, which sets them apart in what was meant to be independence, but has come to amount to isolation. Correspondence between them is carried on by means of written communications, which, like all formal writings, are vague, or by means of private examinations of officials in committee-rooms to which the whole House cannot be audience. No one who has read official documents needs to be told how easy it is to conceal the essential truth under the apparently candid and all-disclosing phrases of a voluminous and particularizing report; how different those answers are which are given with the pen from a private office from those which are given with the tongue when the speaker is looking an assembly in the face. It is sufficiently plain, too, that resolutions which call upon officials to give testimony before a committee are a much clumsier and less efficient means of eliciting information than is a running fire of questions addressed to ministers who are always in their places in the House to reply publicly to all interrogations. It is reasonable to conclude, therefore, that the House of Representatives is much less intimately acquainted with the details of federal Treasury airs than is such a body as the House of Commons, with the particulars of management in the Treasury which it oversees by direct and constant communication with the chief Treasury officials.

This is the greater drawback in our system, because, as a further result of its complete separation from the executive, Congress has to originate and perfect the budget for itself. It does not hear the estimates translated and expounded in condensed statements by skilled officials who have made it their business, because it is to their interest, to know thoroughly what they are talking about; nor does it have the benefit of the guidance of a trained, practical financier when it has to determine questions of revenue. The Treasury is not consulted with reference to problems of taxation, and motions of supply are disposed of with no suggestions from the departments beyond an itemized statement of the amounts needed to meet the regular expenses of an opening fiscal year.

In federal book-keeping the fiscal year closes on the thirtieth of June. Several months before that year expires, however, the estimates for the twelve months which are to succeed are made ready for the use of Congress. In the autumn each department and bureau of the public service reckons its pecuniary needs for the fiscal year which is to begin on the following first of July (making explanatory notes, and here and there an interjected prayer for some unwonted expenditure, amongst the columns of figures), and sends the resulting document to the Secretary of the Treasury. These reports, including of course the estimates of the various bureaux of his own department, the Secretary has printed in a thin quarto volume of some three hundred and twenty-five pages, which for some reason or other, not quite apparent, is called a "Letter from the Secretary of the Treasury transmitting estimates of appropriations required for the fiscal year ending June 30," ...and which boasts a very distinct arrangement under the heads Civil Establishment, Military Establishment, Naval Establishment, Indian Affairs, Pensions, Public Works, Postal Service, etc., a convenient summary of the chief items, and a complete index.

In December this "Letter" is sent, as a part of the Secretary of the Treasury's annual report to Congress, to the Speaker of the House of Representatives, immediately after the convening of that body, and is referred to the Standing Committee on Appropriations. The House itself does not hear the estimates read; it simply passes the thin quartos over to the Committee; though, of course, copies of it may be procured and studied by any member who chooses to scrutinize the staring pages of columned figures with the dutiful purpose of keeping an eye upon the uses made of the public revenue. Taking these estimates into consideration, the Committee on Appropriations found upon them the "general appropriation bills," which the rules require them to report to the House "within thirty days after their appointment, at every session of Congress, commencing on the first Monday in December," unless they can give satisfactory reasons in writing for not doing so. The "general appropriation bills" provide separately for legislative, executive, and judicial expenses; for sundry civil expenses; for consular and diplomatic expenses; for the Army; for the Navy; for the expenses of the Indian department; for the payment of invalid and other pensions; for the support of the Military Academy; for fortifications; for the service of the Post-Office department, and for mail transportation by ocean steamers.

It was only through the efforts of a later-day spirit of vigilant economy that this practice of making the appropriations for each of the several branches of the public service in a separate bill was established. During the early years of the Constitution very loose methods of appropriation prevailed. All the moneys for the year were granted in a single bill, entitled "An Act making

Appropriations for the support of the Government;" and there was no attempt to specify the objects for which they were to be spent. The gross sum given could be applied at the discretion of the heads of the executive departments, and was always large enough to allow much freedom in the undertaking of new schemes of administration, and in the making of such additions to the clerical force of the different offices as might seem convenient to those in control. It was not until 1862 that the present practice of somewhat minutely specifying the uses to be made of the funds appropriated was reached, though Congress had for many years been by slow stages approaching such a policy. The history of appropriations shows that "there has been an increasing tendency to limit the discretion of the executive departments, and bring the details of expenditure more immediately under the annual supervision of Congress;" a tendency which has specially manifested itself since the close of the recent war between the States.[27] In this, as in other things, the appetite for government on the part of Congress has grown with that perfection of organization which has rendered the gratification of its desire for power easily attainable. In this matter of appropriations, however, increased care has unquestionably resulted in a very decided curtailment of extravagance in departmental expenditure, though Congress has often shown a blind ardor for retrenchment which has fallen little short of parsimony, and which could not have found place in its legislation had it had such adequate means of confidential communication with the executive departments as would have enabled it to understand their real needs, and to discriminate between true economy and those scant allowances which only give birth to deficiencies, and which, even under the luckiest conditions, serve only for a very brief season to create the impression which they are usually meant to beget,—that the party in power is the party of thrift and honesty, seeing in former appropriations too much that was corrupt and spendthrift, and desiring to turn to the good ways of wisdom and frugality.

There are some portions of the public expenditure which do not depend upon the annual gifts of Congress, but which are provided for by statutes which run without limit of date. These are what are known as the "permanent appropriations." They cover, on the one hand, such indeterminate charges as the interest on the public debt, the amounts annually paid into the sinking fund, the outlays of refunding, the interest on the bonds issued to the Pacific Railways; and, on the other hand, such specific charges as the maintenance of the militia service, the costs of the collection of the customs revenue, and the interest on the bequest to the Smithsonian Institution. Their aggregate sum constitutes no insignificant part of the entire public expense. In 1880, in a total appropriation of about $307,000,000, the permanent appropriations fell short of the annual grant by only about sixteen and a half millions. In later years, however, the proportion has been smaller, one of the principal items, the interest on the public debt, becoming, of course, continually less as the debt is paid off, and other items reaching less amounts, at the same time that the figures of the annual grants have risen rather than fallen.

With these permanent grants the Committee on Appropriations has, of course, nothing to do, except that estimates of the moneys to be drawn under authority of such grants are submitted to its examination in the Secretary of the Treasury's "Letter," along with the estimates for which special appropriations are asked. Upon these latter estimates the general appropriations are based. The Committee may report its bills at any stage of the House's business, provided only that it does not interrupt a member who is speaking; and these bills when reported may at any time, by a majority vote, be made a special order of the day. Of course their consideration is the most imperative business of the session. They must be passed before the end of June, else the departments will be left altogether without means of support. The chairman of the Committee on Appropriations is, consequently, a very masterful authority in the House. He can force it to a consideration of the business of his Committee at almost any time; and by withholding his reports until the session is well advanced can crowd all other topics from the docket. For much time is spent over each of the "general appropriation bills." The spending of money is one of the two things that Congress invariably stops to talk about; the other being the raising of money. The talk is made always in Committee of the Whole, into which the House at once resolves itself whenever appropriations are to be considered. While members of this, which may be called the House's Committee of Supply, representatives have the freest opportunity of the session for activity, for usefulness, or for meddling, outside the sphere of their own committee work. It is true that the "five-minutes' rule" gives each speaker in Committee of the Whole scant time for the expression of his views, and that the House can refuse to accord full freedom of debate to its other self, the Committee of the Whole, by limiting the time which it is to devote to the discussion of matters referred to it, or by providing for its discharge from the further consideration of any bill committed to it, after it shall have acted without debate on all amendments pending or that may be offered; but as a rule every member has a chance to offer what suggestions he pleases upon questions of appropriation, and many hours are spent in business-like debate and amendment of such bills, clause by clause and item by item. The House learns pretty thoroughly what is in each of its appropriation bills before it sends it to the Senate.

But, unfortunately, the dealings of the Senate with money bills generally render worthless the painstaking action of the House. The Senate has been established by precedent in the very freest possible privileges of amendment as regards these bills no less than as regards all others. The Constitution is silent as to the origination of bills appropriating money. It says simply that "all bills for *raising revenue* shall originate in the House of Representatives," and that in considering these "the Senate may propose or concur with amendments as on other bills" (Art. I., Sec. VII.); but, "by a practice as old as the Government itself, the constitutional prerogative of the House has been held to apply to all the general appropriation bills,"[28] and the Senate's right to amend these has been allowed the widest conceivable scope. The upper house may add to them what it pleases; may go altogether outside of their original provisions and tack to them entirely new features of legislation, altering not only the amounts but even the objects of expenditure, and making out of the materials sent them by the popular chamber measures of an almost totally new character. As passed by the House of Representatives, appropriation bills generally provide for an expenditure considerably less than that called for by the estimates; as returned from the Senate, they usually propose grants of many additional millions, having been brought by that less sensitive body up almost, if not quite, to the figures of the estimates.

After passing their ordeal of scrutiny and amendment in the Senate, the appropriation bills return with their new figures to the House. But when they return it is too late for the House to put them again into the crucible of Committee of the Whole. The session, it may be taken for granted, was well on towards its middle age before they were originally introduced by the House Committee on Appropriations; after they reached the Senate they were referred to its corresponding Committee; and the report of that Committee upon them was debated at the leisurely length characteristic of the weightier proceedings of the upper chamber; so that the last days of the session are fast approaching when they are sent down to the House with the work of the Senate's hand upon them. The House is naturally disinclined to consent to the radical alterations wrought by the Senate, but there is no time to quarrel with its colleague, unless it can make up its mind to sit through the heat of midsummer, or to throw out the bill and accept the discomforts of an extra session. If the session be the short one, which ends, by constitutional requirement, on the 4th of March, the alternative is the still more distasteful one of leaving the appropriations to be made by the next House.

The usual practice, therefore, is to adjust such differences by means of a conference between the two Houses. The House rejects the Senate's amendments without hearing them read; the Senate stoutly refuses to yield; a conference ensues, conducted by a committee of three members from each chamber; and a compromise is effected, by such a compounding of disagreeing propositions as gives neither party to the quarrel the victory, and commonly leaves the grants not a little below the amounts asked for by the departments. As a rule, the Conference Committee consists, on the part of the House, of the chairman of its Committee on Appropriations, some other well-posted member of that Committee, and a representative of the minority. Its reports are matters of highest prerogative. They may be brought in even while a member is speaking. It is much better to silence a speaker than to delay for a single moment, at this stage of the session, the pressing, imperious question of the supplies for the support of the government. The report is, therefore, acted upon immediately and in a mass, and is generally adopted without debate. So great is the haste that the report is passed upon before being printed, and without giving any one but the members of the Conference Committee time to understand what it really contains. There is no chance of remark or amendment. It receives at once sanction or rejection as a whole; and the chances are, of course, in favor of its being accepted, because to reject it would but force a new conference and bring fresh delays.

It is evident, therefore, that after all the careful and thorough-going debate and amendment of Committee of the Whole in the House, and all the grave deliberation of the Senate to which the general appropriations are subjected, they finally pass in a very chaotic state, full of provisions which neither the House nor the Senate likes, and utterly vague and unintelligible to every one save the members of the Conference Committee; so that it would seem almost as if the generous portions of time conscientiously given to their consideration in their earlier stages had been simply time thrown away.

The result of the under-appropriation to which Congress seems to have become addicted by long habit in dealing with the estimates, is, of course, the addition of another bill to the number of the regular annual grants. As regularly as the annual session opens there is a Deficiency Bill to be considered. Doubtless deficiencies frequently arise because of miscalculations or extravagance on the part of the departments; but the most serious deficiencies are those which result from the close-fistedness of the House Committee on Appropriations, and the compromise reductions which are wrung from the Senate by conference committees. Every December, consequently, along with the estimates for the next fiscal year, or at a later period of the session in special communications, come estimates of deficiencies in the appropriations for the current year, and the apparent economies of the grants of the preceding session have to be offset in the gifts of the inevitable Deficiency Bill. It is as if Congress had designedly established the plan of making semi-annual appropriations. At each session it grants part of the money to be spent after the first of July following, and such sums as are needed to supplement the expenditures previously authorized to be made after the first of July preceding. It doles out their allowances in installments to its wards, the departments.

It is usual for the Appropriations Committees of both Houses, when preparing the annual bills, to take the testimony of the directing officers of the departments as to the actual needs of the public service in regard to all the principal items of expenditure. Having no place upon the floor of the House, and being, in consequence, shut out from making complete public statements concerning the estimates, the heads of the several executive departments are forced to confine themselves to private communications with the House and Senate Committees. Appearing before those Committees in person, or addressing them more formally in writing, they explain and urge the appropriations asked in the "Letter" containing the estimates. Their written communications, though addressed only to the chairman of one of the Committees, frequently reach Congress itself, being read in open session by some member of the Committee in order to justify or interpret the items of appropriation proposed in a pending bill. Not infrequently the head of a department exerts himself to secure desired supplies by dint of negotiation with individual members of the Committee, and by repeated and insistent private appeals to their chairman.

Only a very small part of the relations between the Committees and the departments is a matter of rule. Each time that the estimates come under consideration the Committees must specially seek, or the departments newly volunteer, information and advice. It would seem, however, that it is now less usual for the Committees to ask than for the Secretaries to offer counsel and suggestion. In the early years of the government it was apparently not uncommon for the chairman of spending committees to seek out departmental officials in order to get necessary enlightenment concerning the mysteries of the estimates, though it was often easier to ask for than to get the information wanted. An amusing example of the difficulties which then beset a committee-man in search of such knowledge is to be found in the private correspondence of John Randolph of Roanoke. Until 1865 the House Committee of Ways and Means, which is one of the oldest of the Standing Committees, had charge of the appropriations; it was, therefore, Mr. Randolph's duty, as chairman of that Committee in 1807, to look into the estimates, and he thus recounts, in an interesting and exceedingly characteristic letter to his intimate friend and correspondent, Nicholson, this pitiful experience which he had had in performing that duty: "I called some time since at the navy office to ask an explanation of certain items of the estimate for this year. The Secretary called upon his chief clerk, who knew very little more of the business than his master. I propounded a question to the head of the department; he turned to the clerk like a boy who cannot say his lesson, and with imploring countenance beseeches aid; the clerk with much assurance gabbled out some commonplace jargon, which I could not take for sterling; an explanation was required, and both were dumb. This pantomime was repeated at every item, until, disgusted and ashamed for the degraded situation of the principal, I took leave without pursuing the subject, seeing that my object could not be attained. There was not one single question relating to the department that the Secretary could answer."[29] It is to be hoped that the Secretaries of to-day are somewhat better versed in the affairs of their departments than was respectable Robert Smith, or, at any rate, that they have chief clerks who can furnish inquiring chairmen with something better than commonplace jargon which no shrewd man can take for sterling information; and it is altogether probable that such a scene as the one just described would nowadays be quite impossible. The book-keeping of later years has been very much stricter and more thorough than it was in the infancy of the departments; the estimates are much more thoroughly differentiated and itemized; and a minute division of labor in each department amongst a numerous clerical force makes it comparatively easy for the chief executive officers to acquaint themselves quickly and accurately with the details of administration. They do not wait, therefore, as a general thing, to be sought out and questioned by the Committees, but bestir themselves to get at the ears of the committee-men, and especially to secure, if possible, the influence of the chairmen in the interest of adequate appropriations.

These irregular and generally informal communications between the Appropriations Committees and the heads of the departments, taking the form sometimes of pleas privately addressed by the Secretaries to individual members of the Committees, and again of careful letters which find their way into the reports laid before Congress, stand in our system in the place of the annual financial statements which are in British practice made by the ministers to parliament, under circumstances which constitute very full and satisfactory public explanations and the freest replies to all pertinent questions invariable features of the supervision of the finances by the Commons. Our ministers make their statements to both Houses indirectly and piecemeal, through the medium of the Committees. They are mere witnesses, and are in no definite way responsible for the annual appropriations. Their secure four-year tenure of office is not at all affected by the treatment the estimates receive at the hands of Congress. To see our cabinet officers resign because appropriations had been refused for the full amount asked for in the Secretary of the Treasury's "Letter" would be as novel in our eyes as would be, in the view of our English cousins, the sight of a Ministry of the Crown remaining in office under similar circumstances. Indeed, were our cabinets to stake their positions upon the fortunes of the estimates submitted to Congress, we should probably suffer the tiresome inconvenience of yearly resignations; for even when the heads of the departments tax all their energies and bring into requisition all their arts of persuasion to secure ample grants from the Committees, the House Committee cuts down the sums as usual, the Senate Committee adds to them as before, and the Conference Committee strikes a deficient compromise balance according to time-honored custom.

There is in the House another appropriations committee besides the Committee on Appropriations. This is the Committee on Rivers and Harbors, created in December, 1883, by the Forty-eighth Congress, as a sharer in the too great prerogatives till then enjoyed by the Committee on Commerce. The Committee on Rivers and Harbors represents, of course, the lately-acquired permanency of the policy of internal improvements. Until 1870 that policy had had a very precarious existence. Strenuously denied all tolerance by the severely constitutional

Presidents of the earlier days, it could not venture to declare itself openly in separate appropriations which offered an easy prey to the watchful veto, but skulked in the unobtrusive guise of items of the general grants, safe under the cover of respectable neighbor items. The veto has never been allowed to seek out single features in the acts submitted to the executive eye, and even such men as Madison and Monroe, stiff and peremptory as they were in the assertion of their conscientious opinions, and in the performance of what they conceived to be their constitutional duty, and much as they disapproved of stretching the Constitution to such uses as national aid to local and inland improvements, were fain to let an occasional gift of money for such purposes pass unforbidden rather than throw out the general appropriation bill to which it was tacked. Still, Congress did not make very frequent or very flagrant use of this trick, and schemes of internal improvement came altogether to a stand-still when faced by President Jackson's imperious disfavor. It was for many years the settled practice of Congress to grant the States upon the sea-board leave to lay duties at their ports for the improvement of the harbors, and itself to undertake the expense of no public works save those upon territory actually owned by the United States. But in later years the relaxation of presidential opposition and the admission of new States lying altogether away from the sea, and, therefore, quite unwilling to pay the tariffs which were building up the harbors of their eastern neighbors without any recompensing advantage to themselves who had no harbors, revived the plans which the vetoes of former times had rebuffed, and appropriations from the national coffers began freely to be made for the opening of the great water highways and the perfecting of the sea-gates of commerce. The inland States were silenced, because satisfied by a share in the benefits of national aid, which, being no longer indirect, was not confined to the sanctioning of state tariffs which none but the sea-board commonwealths could benefit by, but which consumers everywhere had to pay.

The greatest increase in appropriations of this class took place just after 1870. Since that date they have occupied a very prominent place in legislation, running from some twelve millions in the session of 1873-4 up and down through various figures to eighteen millions seven hundred thousand in the session of 1882-3, constituting during that decade the chief business of the Committee on Commerce, and finally having a special Standing Committee erected for their superintendence. They have thus culminated with the culmination of the protective tariff, and the so-called "American system" of protective tariffs and internal improvements has thus at last attained to its perfect work. The same prerogatives are accorded this new appropriations committee which have been secured to the greater Committee which deals with the estimates. Its reports may be made at any time when a member is not speaking, and stand in all respects upon the same footing as the bills proposing the annual grants. It is a special spending committee, with its own key to the Treasury.

But the Appropriation Committees of the two Houses, though, strictly speaking, the only committees of supply, have their work increased and supplemented by the numerous Committees which devote time and energy to creating demands upon the Treasury. There is a pension list in the estimates for whose payment the Committee on Appropriations has to provide every year; but the Committee on Pensions is constantly manufacturing new claims upon the public revenues.[30] There must be money forthcoming to build the new ships called for by the report of the Committee on Naval Affairs, and to meet the charges for the army equipment and reforms recommended by the Committee on Military Affairs. There are innumerable fingers in the budget pie.

It is principally in connection with appropriations that what has come to be known in our political slang as "log-rolling" takes place. Of course the chief scene of this sport is the private room of the Committee on Rivers and Harbors, and the season of its highest excitement, the hours spent in the passage of the River and Harbor Bill. "Log-rolling" is an exchange of favors. Representative A. is very anxious to secure a grant for the clearing of a small water-course in his district, and representative B. is equally solicitous about his plans for bringing money into the hands of the contractors of his own constituency, whilst representative C. comes from a sea-port town whose modest harbor is neglected because of the treacherous bar across its mouth, and representative D. has been blamed for not bestirring himself more in the interest of schemes of improvement afoot amongst the enterprising citizens of his native place; so it is perfectly feasible for these gentlemen to put their heads together and confirm a mutual understanding; that each will vote in Committee of the Whole for the grants desired by the others, in consideration of the promise that they will cry "aye" when his item comes on to be considered. It is not out of the question to gain the favoring ear of the reporting Committee, and a great deal of tinkering can be done with the bill after it has come into the hands of the House. Lobbying and log-rolling go hand in hand.

So much for estimates and appropriations. All questions of revenue are in their first stages in the hands of the House Committee of Ways and Means, and in their last, in charge of the Senate Committee on Finance. The name of the House Committee is evidently borrowed from the language of the British Parliament; the English Committee of Ways and Means is, however, the Commons itself sitting in Committee of the Whole to consider the statement and proposals of the Chancellor of the Exchequer, whilst ours is a Standing Committee of the House composed of eleven members, and charged with the preparation of all legislation relating to the raising of the revenue and to providing ways and means for the support of the government. We have, in English parliamentary phrase, put our Chancellorship of the Exchequer into commission. The chairman of the Committee figures as our minister of finance, but he really, of course, only represents the commission of eleven over which he presides.

All reports of the Treasury department are referred to this Committee of Ways and Means, which also, like the Committee on Appropriations, from time to time holds other more direct communications with the officers of revenue bureaux. The annual reports of the Secretary of the Treasury are generally quite full of minute information upon the points most immediately connected with the proper duties of the Committee. They are explicit with regard to the collection and disbursement of the revenues, with regard to the condition of the public debt, and with regard to the operation of all laws governing the financial policy of the departments. They are, in one aspect, the great yearly balance sheets, exhibiting the receipts and expenditures of the government, its liabilities and its credits; and, in another aspect, general views of the state of industry and of the financial machinery of the country, summarizing the information compiled by the bureau of statistics with reference to the condition of the manufactures and of domestic trade, as well as with regard to the plight of the currency and of the national banks. They are, of course, quite distinct from the "Letters" of the Secretary of the Treasury, which contain the estimates, and go, not to the Committee of Ways and Means, but to the Committee on Appropriations.

Though the duties of the Committee of Ways and Means in supervising the management of the revenues of the country are quite closely analogous to those of the British Chancellor of the Exchequer, the lines of policy in which they walk are very widely separated from those which he feels bound to follow. As I have said, the object which he holds constantly in view is to keep the annual balances as nearly as possible at an equilibrium. He plans to raise only just enough revenue to satisfy the grants made in Committee of Supply, and leave a modest surplus to cover possible errors in the estimates and probable fluctuations in the returns from taxation. Our Committee of Ways and Means, on the other hand, follow a very different policy. The revenues which they control are raised for a double object. They represent not only the income of the government, but also a carefully erected commercial policy to which the income of the government has for many years been incidental. They are intended to foster the manufactures of the country as well as to defray the expenses of federal administration. Were the maintenance of the government and the support of the public credit the chief objects of our national policy of taxation, it would undoubtedly be cast in a very different pattern. During a greater part of the lifetime of the present government, the principal feature of that policy has been a complex system of duties on imports, troublesome and expensive of collection, but nevertheless yielding, together with the license taxes of the internal revenue which later years have seen added to it, immense surpluses which no extravagances of the spending committees could exhaust. Duties few, small, and comparatively inexpensive of collection would afford abundant revenues for the efficient conduct of the government, besides comporting much more evidently with economy in financial administration. Of course, if vast revenues pour in over the barriers of an exacting and exorbitant tariff, amply sufficient revenues would flow in through the easy conduits of moderate and simple duties. The object of our financial policy, however, has not been to equalize receipts and expenditures, but to foster the industries of the country. The Committee of Ways and Means, therefore, do not concern themselves directly with regulating the income of the government-they know that that, in every probable event, will be more than sufficient-but with protecting the interests of the manufacturers as affected by the regulation of the tariff. The resources of the government are made incidental to the industrial investments of private citizens.

This evidently constitutes a very capital difference between the functions of the Chancellor of the Exchequer and those of our Committee of Ways and Means. In the policy of the former the support of the government is everything; with the latter the care of the industries of the country is the beginning and the end of duty. In the eyes of parliament enormous balances represent ignorant or improper management on the part of the ministers, and a succession of them is sure to cast a cabinet from office, to the lasting disgrace of the Chancellor of the Exchequer; but to the mind of Congress vast surpluses are indicative of nothing in particular. They indicate of course abundant returns from the duties, but the chief concern is, not whether the duties are fruitful, but whether they render the trades prosperous. Commercial interests are the essential consideration; excess of income is a matter of comparative indifference. The points of view characteristic of the two systems are thus quite opposite: the Committee of Ways and Means subordinates its housekeeping duties to its much wider extra-governmental business; the Chancellor of the Exchequer subordinates everything to economical administration.

This is evidently the meaning of the easy sovereignty, in the practice of the House, of questions of supply over questions of revenue. It is imperative to grant money for the support of the government, but questions of revenue revision may be postponed without inconvenience. The two things do not necessarily go hand in hand, as they do in the Commons. The reports of the Committee of Ways and Means are matters of quite as high privilege as the reports of the Committee on Appropriations, but they by no means stand an equal chance of gaining the consideration of the House and reaching a passage. They have no inseparable connection with the annual grants; the needed supplies will be forthcoming without any readjustments of taxation to meet the anticipated demands, because the taxes are not laid in the first instance with reference to the expenses which are to be paid out of their proceeds. If it were the function of the Committee of Ways and Means, as it is of the Chancellor of the Exchequer, to adjust the revenue to the expenditures, their reports would be as essential a part of the business of each session as are the reports of the Committee on Appropriations; but their proposals, occupying, as they do, a very different place in legislation, may go to the wall just as the proposals of the other Committees do at the demand of the chairman of the great spending Committee. The figures of the annual grants do not run near enough to the sum of the annual receipts to make them at all dependent on bills which concern the latter.

It would seem that the supervision exercised by Congress over expenditures is more thorough than that which is exercised by the Commons in England. In 1814 the House created a Standing Committee on Public Expenditures whose duty it should be "to examine into the state of the several public departments, and particularly into laws making appropriations of money, and to report whether the moneys have been disbursed conformably with such laws; and also to report from time to time such provisions and arrangements as may be necessary to add to the economy of the departments and the accountability of their officers;" but this Committee stood as the only committee of audit for but two years. It was not then abolished, but its jurisdiction was divided amongst six other Committees on Expenditures in the several departments, to which was added in 1860 a seventh, and in 1874 an eighth. There is thus a separate Committee for the audit of the accounts of each of the executive departments, beside which the original single Committee on Public Expenditures stands charged with such duties as may have been left it in the general distribution.[31] The duties of these eight Committees are specified with great minuteness in the rules. They are "to examine into the state of the accounts and expenditures respectively submitted to them, and to inquire and report particularly," whether the expenditures of the respective departments are warranted by law; "whether the claims from time to time satisfied and discharged by the respective departments are supported by sufficient vouchers, establishing their justness both as to their character and amount; whether such claims have been discharged out of funds appropriated therefor, and whether all moneys have been disbursed in conformity with appropriation laws; and whether any, or what, provisions are necessary to be adopted, to provide more perfectly for the proper application of the public moneys, and to secure the government from demands unjust in their character or extravagant in their amount." Besides exercising these functions of careful audit, they are, moreover, required to "report from time to time" any plans for retrenchment that may appear advisable in the interests of economy, or any measures that may be necessary to secure greater efficiency or to insure stricter accountability to Congress in the management of the departments; to ferret out all abuses that may make their appearance; and to see to it that no department has useless offices in its bureaux, or over or under-paid officers on its rolls.

But, though these Committees are so many and so completely armed with powers, indications are not wanting that more abuses run at large in the departments than they, with all their eyes, are able to detect. The Senate, though it has no similar permanent committees, has sometimes discovered dishonest dealings that had altogether escaped the vigilance of the eight House Committees; and even these eight occasionally, by a special effort, bring to light transactions which would never have been unearthed in the ordinary routine course of their usual procedure. It was a select committee of the Senate which, during the sessions of the Forty-seventh Congress, discovered that the "contingent fund" of the Treasury department had been spent in repairs on the Secretary's private residence, for expensive suppers spread before the Secretary's political friends, for lemonade for the delectation of the Secretary's private palate, for bouquets for the gratification of the Secretary's busiest allies, for carpets never delivered, "ice" never used, and services never rendered;[32] although these were secrets of which the honest faces of the vouchers submitted with the accounts gave not a hint.

It is hard to see how there could have been anything satisfactory or conclusive in the annual supervision of the public accounts during any but the latest years of this system of committee audit. Before 1870 our national book-keeping was much like that still in vogue in France. Credits once granted ran on without period until they were exhausted. There were always unexpended balances to confuse the accounts; and when the figures of the original grants had been on a too generous scale, as was often the case, these balances accumulated from year to year in immense surpluses, sometimes of many millions, of whose use no account was given, and which consequently afforded means for all sorts of extravagance and peculation. In 1870 this abuse was partially corrected by a law which limited such accumulations to a period of two years, and laid hands, on behalf of the Treasury, on the $174,000,000 of unexpended balances which had by that time been amassed in the several departments; but it was not till 1874 that such a rule of expenditure and accounting was established as would make intelligent audit by the Committees possible, by a proper circumscription of the time during which credits could be drawn upon without a regrant.[33]

Such is a general view, in brief and without technical detail, of the chief features of our financial system, of the dealings of Congress with the questions of revenue, expenditure, and supply. The contrast which this system offers to the old-world systems, of which the British is the most advanced type, is obviously a very striking one. The one is the very opposite of the others. On the one hand is a financial policy regulated by a compact, coöperative ministry under the direction of a representative chamber, and on the other hand a financial policy directed by the representative body itself, with only clerical aid from the executive. In our practice, in other words, the Committees are the ministers, and the titular ministers only confidential clerks. There is no concurrence, not even a nominal alliance, between the several sections of this committee-ministry, though their several duties are clearly very nearly akin and as clearly mutually dependent. This feature of disintegration in leadership runs, as I have already pointed out, through all our legislation; but it is manifestly of much more serious consequence in financial administration than in the direction of other concerns of government. There can be no doubt that, if it were not for the fact that our revenues are not regulated with any immediate reference to the expenditures of the government, this method of spending according to the suggestions of one body, and taxing in obedience to the suggestions of another entirely distinct, would very quickly bring us into distress; it would unquestionably break down under any attempt to treat revenue and expenditure as mutually adjustable parts of a single, uniform, self-consistent system. They can be so treated only when they are under the management of a single body; only when all financial arrangements are based upon schemes prepared by a few men of trained minds and accordant principles, who can act with easy agreement and with perfect confidence in each other. When taxation is regarded only as a source of revenue and the chief object of financial management is the graduation of outlays by income, the credit and debit sides of the account must come under a single eye to be properly balanced; or, at the least, those officers who raise the money must see and be guided by the books of those who spend it.

It cannot, therefore, be reasonably regarded as matter of surprise that our financial policy has been without consistency or coherency, without progressive continuity. The only evidences of design to be discovered in it appear in those few elementary features which were impressed upon it in the first days of the government, when Congress depended upon such men as Hamilton and Gallatin for guidance in putting the finances into shape. As far as it has any invariable characteristics, or any traceable heredity, it is the handiwork of the sagacious men who first presided over the Treasury department. Since it has been altogether in the hands of congressional Committees it has so waywardly shifted from one rôle to another, and has with such erratic facility changed its principles of action and its modes of speech, to suit the temper and tastes of the times, that one who studies it hardly becomes acquainted with it in one decade before he finds that that was a season quite apart from and unlike both those which went before and those which succeeded. At almost every session Congress has made some effort, more or less determined, towards changing the revenue system in some essential portion; and that system has never escaped radical alteration for ten years together. Had revenue been graduated by the comparatively steady standard of the expenditures, it must have been kept stable and calculable; but depending, as it has done, on a much-debated and constantly fluctuating industrial policy, it has been regulated in accordance with a scheme which has passed through as many phases as there have been vicissitudes and vagaries in the fortunes of commerce and the tactics of parties.

This is the more remarkable because upon all fiscal questions Congress acts with considerable deliberation and care. Financial legislation usually, if not always, occupies by far the most prominent place in the business of each session. Though other questions are often disposed of at odd moments, in haste and without thought, questions of revenue and supply are always given full measure of debate. The House of Representatives, under authority of the Rule before referred to, which enables it, as it were, to project the previous question into Committee of the Whole, by providing for the discharge of that Committee from the further consideration of any bill that is in its hands, or that may be about to be referred to it, after all amendments "pending and that may be offered" shall have been acted upon without debate, seldom hesitates, when any ordinary business is to be considered, to forbid to the proceedings of Committee of the Whole all freedom of discussion, and, consequently, almost all discretion as to the action to be taken; but this muzzle is seldom put upon the mouth of the Committee when appropriation or tariff bills are to be considered, unless the discussion in Committee wanders off into fields, quite apart from the proper matter of the measure in hand, in which case the House interposes to check the irrelevant talk. Appropriation bills have, however, as I have shown, a much higher privilege than have bills affecting the tariff, and instances are not wanting in which the chairman of the

Committee on Appropriations has managed to engross the time of the House in the disposal of measures prepared by his Committee, to the entire exclusion of any action whatever on important bills reported by the Committee of Ways and Means after the most careful and laborious deliberation. His prerogatives are never disputed in such a contest for consideration between a supply and a revenue bill, because these two subjects do not, under our system, necessarily go hand in hand. Ways and Means bills may and should be acted upon, but Supply bills must be.

It should be remarked in this connection, moreover, that much as Congress talks about fiscal questions, whenever permitted to do so by the selfish Appropriations Committee, its talk is very little heeded by the big world outside its halls. The noteworthy fact, to which I have already called attention, that even the most thorough debates in Congress fail to awaken any genuine or active interest in the minds of the people, has had its most striking illustrations in the course of our financial legislation; for, though the discussions which have taken place in Congress upon financial questions have been so frequent, so protracted, and so thorough, engrossing so large a part of the time of the House on their every recurrence, they seem, in almost every instance, to have made scarcely any impression at all upon the public mind. The Coinage Act of 1873, by which silver was demonetized, had been before the country many years, ere it reached adoption, having been time and again considered by Committees of Congress, time and again printed and discussed in one shape or another, and having finally gained acceptance apparently by sheer persistence and importunity. The Resumption Act of 1875, too, had had a like career of repeated considerations by Committees, repeated printings, and a full discussion by Congress; and yet when the "Bland Silver Bill" of 1878 was on its way through the mills of legislation, some of the most prominent newspapers of the country declared with confidence that the Resumption Act had been passed inconsiderately and in haste, almost secretly indeed; and several members of Congress had previously complained that the demonetization scheme of 1873 had been pushed surreptitiously through the courses of its passage, Congress having been tricked into accepting it, doing it scarcely knew what.

This indifference of the country to what is said in Congress, pointing, as it obviously does, to the fact that, though the Committees lead in legislation, they lead without concert or responsibility, and lead nobody in particular, that is, no compact and organized party force which can be made accountable for its policy, has also a further significance with regard to the opportunities and capacities of the constituencies. The doubt and confusion of thought which must necessarily exist in the minds of the vast majority of voters as to the best way of exerting their will in influencing the action of an assembly whose organization is so complex, whose acts are apparently so haphazard, and in which responsibility is spread so thin, throws constituencies into the hands of local politicians who are more visible and tangible than are the leaders of Congress, and generates, the while, a profound distrust of Congress as a body whose actions cannot be reckoned beforehand by any standard of promises made at elections or any programmes announced by conventions. Constituencies can watch and understand a few banded leaders who display plain purposes and act upon them with promptness; but they cannot watch or understand forty odd Standing Committees, each of which goes its own way in doing what it can without any special regard to the pledges of either of the parties from which its membership is drawn. In short, we lack in our political life the conditions most essential for the formation of an active and effective public opinion. "The characteristics of a nation capable of public opinion," says Mr. Bagehot, most sagacious of political critics, "is that ... parties will be *organized*; in each there will be a leader, in each there will be some looked up to, and many who look up to them; the opinion of the party will be formed and suggested by the few, it will be criticised and accepted by the many."[34] And this is just the sort of party organization which we have not. Our parties have titular leaders at the polls in the persons of candidates, and nominal creeds in the resolutions of conventions, but no select few in whom to trust for guidance in the general policy of legislation, or to whom to look for suggestions of opinion. What man, what group of men, can speak for the Republican party or for the Democratic party? When our most conspicuous and influential politicians say anything about future legislation, no one supposes that they are speaking for their party, as those who have authority; they are known to speak only for themselves and their small immediate following of colleagues and friends.

The present relations between Congress and public opinion remind us of that time, in the reign of George III., when "the bulk of the English people found itself powerless to control the course of English government," when the government was divorced from "that general mass of national sentiment on which a government can alone safely ground itself." Then it was that English public opinion, "robbed as it was of all practical power, and thus stripped of the feeling of responsibility which the consciousness of power carries with it," "became ignorant and indifferent to the general progress of the age, but at the same time ... hostile to Government because it was Government, disloyal to the Crown, averse from Parliament. For the first and last time ... Parliament was unpopular, and its opponents secure of popularity."[35] Congress has in our own day become divorced from the "general mass of national sentiment," simply because there is no means by which the movements of that national sentiment can readily be registered in legislation. Going about as it does to please all sorts of Committees composed of all sorts of men,—the dull and the acute, the able and the cunning, the honest and the careless,—Congress evades judgment by avoiding all coherency of plan in its action. The constituencies can hardly tell whether the works of any particular Congress have been good or bad; at the opening of its sessions there was no determinate policy to look forward to, and at their close no accomplished plans to look back upon. During its brief lifetime both parties may have vacillated and gone astray, policies may have shifted and wandered, and untold mischief, together with some good, may have been done; but when all is reviewed, it is next to impossible oftentimes to distribute justly the blame and the praise. A few stubborn committee-men may be at the bottom of much of the harm that has been wrought, but they do not represent their party, and it cannot be clear to the voter how his ballot is to change the habits of Congress for the better. He distrusts Congress because he feels that he cannot control it.

The voter, moreover, feels that his want of confidence in Congress is justified by what he hears of the power of corrupt lobbyists to turn legislation to their own uses. He hears of enormous subsidies begged and obtained; of pensions procured on commission by professional pension solicitors; of appropriations made in the interest of dishonest contractors; and he is not altogether unwarranted in the conclusion that these are evils inherent in the very nature of Congress, for there can be no doubt that the power of the lobbyist consists in great part, if not altogether, in the facility afforded him by the Committee system. He must, in the natural course of things, have many most favorable opportunities for approaching the great money-dispensing Committees. It would be impracticable to work up his schemes in the broad field of the whole House, but in the membership of a Committee he finds manageable numbers. If he can gain the ear of the Committee, or of any influential portion of it, he has practically gained the ear of the House itself; if his plans once get footing in a committee report, they may escape criticism altogether, and it will, in any case, be very difficult to dislodge them. This accessibility of the Committees by outsiders gives to illegitimate influences easy approach at all points of legislation, but no Committees are affected by it so often or so unfortunately as are the Committees which control the public moneys. They are naturally the ones whose favor is oftenest and most importunately, as well as most insidiously, sought; and no description of our system of revenue, appropriation, and supply would be complete without mention of the manufacturers who cultivate the favor of the Committee of Ways and Means, of the interested persons who walk attendance upon the Committee on Rivers and Harbors, and of the mail-contractors and subsidy-seekers who court the Committee on Appropriations.

My last point of critical comment upon our system of financial administration I shall borrow from a perspicacious critic of congressional methods who recently wrote thus to one of the best of American journals: "So long as the debit side of the national account is managed by one set of men, and the credit side by another set, both sets working separately and in secret, without any public responsibility, and without any intervention on the part of the executive official who is nominally responsible; so long as these sets, being composed largely of new men every two years, give no attention to business except when Congress is in session, *and thus spend in preparing plans the whole time which ought to be spent in public discussion of plans already matured*, so that an immense budget is rushed through without discussion in a week or ten days, —just so long the finances will go from bad to worse, no matter by what name you call the party in power. No other nation on earth attempts such a thing, or could attempt it without soon coming to grief, our salvation thus far consisting in an enormous income, with practically no drain for military expenditure."[36] Unquestionably this strikes a very vital point of criticism. Congress spends its time working, in sections, at preparing plans, instead of confining itself to what is for a numerous assembly manifestly the much more useful and proper function of debating and revising plans prepared beforehand for its consideration by a commission of skilled men, old in political practice and in legislative habit, whose official life is apart from its own, though dependent upon its will. Here, in other words, is another finger pointing to Mr. Mill's question as to the best "legislative commission." Our Committees fall short of being the best form of commission, not only in being too numerous but also in being integral parts of the body which they lead, having no life apart from it. Probably the best working commission would be one which should make plans for government independently of the representative body, and in immediate contact with the practical affairs of administration, but which should in all cases look to that body for the sanctioning of those plans, and should be immediately responsible to it for their success when put into operation.

IV
The Senate.

> This is a Senate, a Senate of equals, of men of individual honor and personal character, and of absolute independence. We know no masters, we acknowledge no dictators. This is a hall for mutual consultation and discussion, not an arena for the exhibition of champions. —DANIEL WEBSTER.

The Senate of the United States has been both extravagantly praised and unreasonably disparaged, according to the predisposition and temper of its various critics. In the eyes of some it has a stateliness of character, an eminency of prerogative, and, for the most part, a wisdom of practice such as no other deliberative body possesses; whilst in the estimation of others it is now, whatever it may have been formerly, but a somewhat select company of leisurely "bosses," in whose companionship the few men of character and high purpose who gain admission to its membership find little that is encouraging and nothing that is congenial. Now of course neither of these extreme opinions so much as resembles the uncolored truth, nor can that truth be obtained by a judicious mixture of their milder ingredients. The truth is, in this case as in so many others, something quite commonplace and practical. The Senate is just what the mode of its election and the conditions of public life in this country make it. Its members are chosen from the ranks of active politicians, in accordance with a law of natural selection to which the state legislatures are commonly obedient; and it is probable that it contains, consequently, the best men that our system calls into politics. If these best men are not good, it is because our system of government fails to attract better men by its prizes, not because the country affords or could afford no finer material.

It has been usual to suppose that the Senate was just what the Constitution intended it to be; that because its place in the federal system was exalted the aims and character of its members would naturally be found to be exalted as well; that because its term was long its foresight would be long also; or that because its election was not directly of the people demagogy would find no life possible in its halls. But the Senate is in fact, of course, nothing more than a part, though a considerable part, of the public service, and if the general conditions of that service be such as to starve statesmen and foster demagogues, the Senate itself will be full of the latter kind, simply because there are no others available. There cannot be a separate breed of public men reared specially for the Senate. It must be recruited from the lower branches of the representative system, of which it is only the topmost part. No stream can be purer than its sources. The Senate can have in it no better men than the best men of the House of Representatives; and if the House of Representatives attract to itself only inferior talent, the Senate must put up with the same sort. I think it safe to say, therefore, that, though it may not be as good as could be wished, the Senate is as good as it can be under the circumstances. It contains the most perfect product of our politics, whatever that product may be.

In order to understand and appreciate the Senate, therefore, one must know the conditions of public life in this country. What are those conditions? Well, in the first place, they are not what they were in the early years of the federal government; they are not what they were even twenty years ago; for in this, as in other things, the war between the States ends one distinct period and opens another. Between the great constructive statesmen of the revolutionary days and the reconstructing politicians of the sixties there came into public place and legislative influence a great race of constitutional lawyers. The questions which faced our statesmen while the Constitution was a-making were in the broadest sense questions of politics; but the questions which dominated our public life after the federal government had been successfully set up were questions of legal interpretation such as only lawyers could grapple with. All matters of policy, all doubts of legislation, even all difficulties of diplomacy, were measured by rules of constitutional construction. There was hardly a single affair of public concern which was not hung upon some peg of constitutional dogma in the testing-rooms of one or another of the contending schools of constitutional interpretation. Constitutional issues were ever the tides, questions of administrative policy seldom more than the eddies, of politics.

The Republicans under Jefferson drew their nourishment from constitutional belief no less than did the Federalists; the Whigs and Democrats of a later day lived on what was essentially the same diet, though it was served in slightly different forms; and the parties of to-day are themselves fain to go to these cooks of the olden time whenever they desire strong meat to fortify them against their present debility. The great questions attending the admission of new States to the Union and the annexation of foreign territory, as well as all the controversies which came in the train of the contest over slavery and the reserved powers of the States, were of the Constitution constitutional; and what other questions were then living-save those which found root in the great charter's implied powers, about which there was such constant noise of debate? It will be remembered that very few publicists opposed internal improvements, for instance, on the ground that they were unwise or uncalled for. No one who took a statesman-like view of the matter could fail to see that the opening up of the great water-ways of the country, the construction of roads, the cutting of canals, or any public work which might facilitate inter-State commerce by making intercourse between the various portions of the Union easy and rapid, was sanctioned by every consideration of wisdom, as being in conformity with a policy at once national in its spirit and universal in its benefits. The doubt was, not as to what it would be best and most provident to do, but as to what it would be lawful to do; and the chief opponents of schemes of internal improvement based their dissent upon a careful meditation of the language of the Constitution. Without its plain approval they would not move, even if they had to stand still all their days.

It was, too, with many professions of this spirit that the tariff was dealt with. It ran suddenly to the front as a militant party question in 1833, not as if a great free-trade movement had been set afoot which was to anticipate the mission of Cobden and Bright, but as an issue between federal taxation and the constitutional privileges of the States. The agricultural States were being, as they thought, very cruelly trodden down under the iron heel of that protectionist policy to whose enthronement they had themselves consented, and they fetched their hope of escape from the Constitution. The federal government unquestionably possessed, they admitted, and that by direct grant of the fundamental law, the right to impose duties on imports; but did that right carry with it the privilege of laying discriminating duties for other purposes than that of raising legitimate revenue? Could the Constitution have meant that South Carolina might be taxed to maintain the manufactures of New England?

Close upon the heels of the great tariff controversy of that time came the stupendous contest over the right of secession and the abolition of slavery; and again in this contest, as in all that had gone before, the party which was being hard driven sought refuge in the Constitution. This too was, in its first stages at least, a lawyer's question. It eventually slipped out of all lawyerly control, and was given over to be settled by the stern and savage processes of war; but it stayed with the constitutional lawyers as long as it could, and would have stayed with them to the end had it not itself been bigger than the Constitution and mixed with such interests and such passions as were beyond the control of legislatures or of law courts.

Such samples of the character which political questions have hitherto borne in this country are sufficient to remind all readers of our history of what have been the chief features of our politics, and may serve, without further elaboration, to illustrate the point I wish to emphasize. It is manifest how such a course of politics would affect statesmanship and political leadership. While questions affecting the proper construction of the Constitution were the chief and most imperative questions pressing for settlement, great lawyers were in demand; and great lawyers were, accordingly, forthcoming in satisfaction of the demand. In a land like ours, where litigation is facilitated by the establishment of many open and impartial courts, great lawyers are a much more plentiful product than great administrators, unless there be also some extraordinary means for the encouragement of administrative talents. We have, accordingly, always had plenty of excellent lawyers, though we have often had to do without even tolerable administrators, and seem destined to endure the inconvenience of hereafter doing without any constructive statesmen at all. The constitutional issues of former times were so big and so urgent that they brought great advocates into the field, despite all the tendencies there were in our system towards depriving leadership of all place of authority. In the presence of questions affecting the very structure and powers of the federal government, parties had to rally with definite purpose and espouse a distinct creed; and when the maintenance or overthrow of slavery had ceased to be a question of constitutional right, and had become a matter of contention between sentiment and vested rights, —between interest and passionate feeling, —there was of course a hot energy of contest between two compact hosts and a quick elevation of forceful leaders.

The three stages of national growth which preceded the war between the States were each of them creative of a distinct class of political leaders. In the period of erection there were great architects and master-builders; in the period of constitutional interpretation there were, at a distance from the people, great political schoolmen who pondered and expounded the letter of the law, and, nearer the people, great constitutional advocates who cast the doctrines of the schoolmen into policy; and in the period of abolitionist agitation there were great masters of feeling and leaders of public purpose. The publicists of the second period kept charge of the slavery question, as I have said, as long as they could, and gave place with bitter reluctance to the anti-slavery orators and pro-slavery champions who were to talk the war-feeling into a flame. But it was of course inevitable that the new movement should have new leaders. It was essentially revolutionary in its tone and in its designs, and so quite out of the reach of those principles of action which had governed the policy of the older school of politicians. Its aim was to change, not to vindicate, the Constitution. Its leaders spoke, not words of counsel, but words of passion and of command. It was a crusade, not a campaign; the impetuous movement of a cause, not the canvass of a mooted measure. And, like every big, stirring cause, it had its leaders-leaders whose authority rested upon the affections and sympathies of the people rather than upon any attested wisdom or success of statesmanship. The war was the work, mediately, of philanthropists; and the reconstructions which followed the war were the hasty strokes of these same unbalanced knights of the crusade, full of bold feeling, but not of steady or far-sighted judgment.

The anti-slavery movement called forth leaders who, from the very nature of their calling, were more picturesque than any who had figured on the national stage since the notable play of the Revolution had gone off the boards; but it was no better cast in leading parts than had been the drama which immediately preceded it. When the constitution of a self-governing people is being consciously moulded by the rapid formation of precedent during the earliest periods of its existence, there are sure to be antagonistic beliefs, distinct and strong and active enough to take shape in the creeds of energetic parties, each led by the greatest advocates of its cherished principles. The season of our constitutional development, consequently, saw as fine a race of statesmen at the front of national affairs as have ever directed the civil policy of the country; and they, in turn, gave place to men brave to encounter the struggles of changed times, and fit to solve the doubts of a new set of events.

Since the war, however, we have come into a fourth period of national life, and are perplexed at finding ourselves denied a new order of statesmanship to suit the altered conditions of government. The period of federal construction is long-passed; questions of constitutional interpretation are no longer regarded as of pressing urgency, the war has been fought, even the embers of its issues being now almost extinguished; and we are left to that unexciting but none the less capitally important business of every-day peaceful development and judicious administration to whose execution every nation in its middle age has to address itself with what sagacity, energy, and prudence it can command. It cannot be said that these new duties have as yet raised up any men eminently fit for their fulfillment. We have had no great administrators since the opening of this newest stage, and there is as yet no visible sign that any such will soon arise. The forms of government in this country have always been unfavorable to the easy elevation of talent to a station of paramount authority; and those forms in their present crystallization are more unfavorable than ever to the toleration of the leadership of the few, whilst the questions now most prominent in politics are not of such a nature as to compel skilled and trustworthy champions to come into the field, as did the constitutional issues and revolutionary agitations of other days. They are matters of a too quiet, business-like sort to enlist feeling or arouse enthusiasm.

It is, therefore, very unfortunate that only feeling or enthusiasm can create recognized leadership in our politics. There is no office set apart for the great party leader in our government. The powers of the Speakership of the House of Representatives are too cramped and covert; the privileges of the chairmanships of the chief Standing Committees are too limited in scope; the presidency is too silent and inactive, too little like a premiership and too much like a superintendency. If there be any one man to whom a whole party or a great national majority looks for guiding counsel, he must lead without office, as Daniel Webster did, or in spite of his office, as Jefferson and Jackson did. There must be something in the times or in the questions which are abroad to thrust great advocates or great masters of purpose into a non-official leadership, which is theirs because they represent in the greatest actions of their lives some principle at once vital and widely loved or hated, or because they possess in their unrivaled power of eloquent speech the ability to give voice to some such living theme. There must be a cause to be advanced which is greater than the trammels of governmental forms, and which, by authority of its own imperative voice, constitutes its advocates the leaders of the nation, though without giving them official title-without need of official title. No one is authorized to lead by reason of any official station known to our system. We call our real leaders by no names but their own: Mr. Webster was always Mr. Webster and never Prime Minister.

In a country which governs itself by means of a public meeting, a Congress or a Parliament, a country whose political life is representative, the only real leadership in governmental affairs must be legislative leadership-ascendency in the public meeting which decides everything. The leaders, if there be any, must be those who suggest the opinions and rule the actions of the representative body. We have in this country, therefore, no real leadership; because no man is allowed to direct the course of Congress, and there is no way of governing the country save through Congress, which is supreme. The chairman of a great Committee like the Committee of Ways and Means stands, indeed, at the sources of a very large and important stream of policy, and can turn that stream at his pleasure, or mix what he will with its waters; but there are whole provinces of policy in which he can have no authority at all. He neither directs, nor can often influence, those other chairmen who direct all the other important affairs of government. He, though the greatest of chairmen, and as great, it may be, as any other one man in the whole governmental system, is by no means at the head of the government. He is, as he feels every day, only a big wheel where there are many other wheels, some almost as big as he, and all driven, like himself, by fires which he does not kindle or tend.

In a word, we have no supreme executive ministry, like the great "Ministry of the Crown" over sea, in whose hands is the general management of legislation; and we have, consequently, no great prizes of leadership such as are calculated to stimulate men of strong talents to great and conspicuous public services. The Committee system is, as I have already pointed out, the very opposite of this. It makes all the prizes of leadership small, and nowhere gathers power into a few hands. It cannot be denied that this is in ordinary times, and in the absence of stirring themes, a great drawback, inasmuch as it makes legislative service unattractive to minds of the highest order, to whom the offer of really great place and power at the head of the governing assembly, the supreme council of the nation, would be of all things most attractive. If the presidency were competitive, —if it could be won by distinguished congressional service, —who can doubt that there would be a notable influx of talents into Congress and a significant elevation of tone and betterment of method in its proceedings; and yet the presidency is very far from being equal to a first-rate premiership.

There is, I know, one distinctive feature of legislative leadership which makes it seem to some not altogether to be desired; though it scarcely constitutes such an objection as to make no leadership at all seem preferable. It is the leadership of orators; it is the ascendency of those who have a genius for talking. In the eyes of those who do not like it, it seems a leadership of artful dialecticians, the success of tricks of phrase, the victory of rushing declamation-government, not by the advice of statesman-like counselors, but by the wagging of ready tongues. Macaulay pointed out with his accustomed force of statement just the fact which haunts those who hold to such objections. The power of speaking, he said, which is so highly prized by politicians in a popular government, "may exist in the highest degree without judgment, without fortitude, without skill in reading the characters of men or the signs of the times, without any knowledge, of the principles of legislation or of political economy, and without any skill in diplomacy or in the administration of war. Nay, it may well happen that those very intellectual qualities which give peculiar charm to the speeches of a public man may be incompatible with the qualities which would fit him to meet a pressing emergency with promptitude and firmness. It was thus with Charles Townshend. It was thus with Windham. It was a privilege to listen to those accomplished and ingenious orators. But in a perilous crisis they would be found inferior in all the qualities of rulers to such a man as Oliver Cromwell, who talked nonsense, or as William the Silent, who did not talk at all."

Nevertheless, it is to be observed that neither Windham nor Townshend rose to places of highest confidence in the assembly which they served, and which they charmed by their attractive powers of speech; and that Cromwell would have been as unfit to rule anything but an autocratic commonwealth as would have been William the Silent to be anything but a Dutch governor. The people really had no voice in Cromwell's government. It was absolute. He would have been as much out of place in a representative government as a bull in a china shop. We would not have a Bismarck if we could.

Every species of government has the defects of its own qualities. Representative government is government by advocacy, by discussion, by persuasion, and a great, miscellaneous voting population is often misled by deceitful pleas and swayed by unwise counsels. But if one were to make a somewhat freer choice of examples than Macaulay permitted himself, it would be easy to multiply the instances of ruling orators of our race who have added to their gifts of eloquence conspicuous sagacity in the administration of affairs. At any rate, the men who have led popular assemblies have often been, like Hampden, rarely endowed with judgment, foresight, and steadfastness of purpose; like Walpole, amazingly quick in "reading the characters of men and the signs of the times;" like Chatham, masterful in ordering the conquests and the policies of the world; like Burke, learned in the profoundest principles of statecraft; like Canning, adroit in diplomacy; like Pitt, safe in times of revolution; like Peel, sagacious in finance; or, like Gladstone, skilled in every branch of political knowledge and equal to any strain of emergency.

It is natural that orators should be the leaders of a self-governing people. Men may be clever and engaging speakers, such as are to be found, doubtless, at half the bars of the country, without being equipped even tolerably for any of the high duties of the statesman; but men can scarcely be orators without that force of character, that readiness of resource, that clearness of vision, that grasp of intellect, that courage of conviction, that earnestness of purpose, and that instinct and capacity for leadership which are the eight horses that draw the triumphal chariot of every leader and ruler of free men. We could not object to being ruled again by such men as Henry and Otis and Samuel Adams; but they were products of revolution. They were inspired by the great causes of the time; and the government which they set up has left us without any ordinary, peaceful means of bringing men like them into public life. We should like to have more like them, but the violent exercise of revolution is too big a price to pay for them. Some less pungent diet is to be desired for the purpose of giving health to our legislative service. There ought to be some quiet, effective tonic, some mild stimulant, such as the certain prospect of winning highest and most honorable office, to infuse the best talent of the nation into our public life.

These, then, are the conditions of public life which make the House of Representatives what it is, a disintegrate mass of jarring elements, and the Senate what it is, a small, select, and leisurely House of Representatives. Or perhaps it would be nearer the whole truth to say that these are the circumstances and this the frame of government of which the two Houses form a part. Were the Senate not supplied principally by promotions from the House, —if it had, that is, a membership made up of men specially trained for its peculiar duties, —it would probably be much more effective than it is in fulfilling the great function of instructive and business-like debate of public questions; for its duties are enough unlike those of the House to be called peculiar. Men who have acquired all their habits in the matter of dealing with legislative measures in the House of Representatives, where committee work is everything and public discussion nothing but "talking to the country," find themselves still mere declaimers when they get into the Senate, where no previous question utters its interrupting voice from the tongues of tyrannical committee-men, and where, consequently, talk is free to all.[37] Only superior talents, such as very few men possess, could enable a Representative of long training to change his spots upon entering the Senate. Most men will not fit more than one sphere in life; and after they have been stretched or compressed to the measure of that one they will rattle about loosely or stick too tight in any other into which they may be thrust. Still, more or less adjustment takes place in every case. If a new Senator knock about too loosely amidst the free spaces of the rules of that august body, he will assuredly have some of his biggest corners knocked off and his angularities thus made smoother; if he stick fast amongst the dignified courtesies and punctilious observances of the upper chamber, he will, if he stick long enough, finally wear down to such a size, by jostling, as to attain some motion more or less satisfactory. But it must be said, on the other hand, that even if the Senate were made up of something better than selections from the House, it would probably be able to do little more than it does in the way of giving efficiency to our system of legislation. For it has those same radical defects of organization which weaken the House. Its functions also, like those of the House, are segregated in the prerogatives of numerous Standing Committees.[38] In this regard Congress is all of a piece. There is in the Senate no more opportunity than exists in the House for gaining such recognized party leadership as would be likely to enlarge a man by giving him a sense of power, and to steady and sober him by filling him with a grave sense of responsibility. So far as its organization controls it, the Senate, notwithstanding the one or two special excellences which make it more temperate and often more rational than the House, has no virtue which marks it as of a different nature. Its proceedings bear most of the characteristic features of committee rule.[39] Its conclusions are suggested now by one set of its members, now by another set, and again by a third; an arrangement which is of course quite effective in its case, as in that of the House, in depriving it of that leadership which is valuable in more ways than in imparting distinct purpose to legislative action, because it concentrates party responsibility, attracts the best talents, and fixes public interest.

Some Senators are, indeed, seen to be of larger mental stature and built of stauncher moral stuff than their fellow-members, and it is not uncommon for individual members to become conspicuous figures in every great event in the Senate's deliberations. The public now and again picks out here and there a Senator who seems to act and to speak with true instinct of statesmanship and who unmistakably merits the confidence of colleagues and of people. But such a man, however eminent, is never more than *a* Senator. No one is *the* Senator. No one may speak for his party as well as for himself; no one exercises the special trust of acknowledged leadership. The Senate is merely a body of individual critics, representing most of the not very diversified types of a society substantially homogeneous; and the weight of every criticism uttered in its chamber depends upon the weight of the critic who utters it, deriving little if any addition to its specific gravity from connection with the designs of a purposeful party organization. I cannot insist too much upon this defect of congressional government, because it is evidently radical. Leadership with authority over a great ruling party is a prize to attract great competitors, and is in a free government the only prize that will attract great competitors. Its attractiveness is abundantly illustrated in the operations of the British system. In England, where members of the Cabinet, which is merely a Committee of the House of Commons, are the rulers of the empire, a career in the Commons is eagerly sought by men of the rarest gifts, because a career there is the best road, is indeed the only road, to membership of the great Committee. A part in the life of Congress, on the contrary, though the best career opened to men of ambition by our system, has no prize at its end greater than membership of some one of numerous Committees, between which there is some choice, to be sure, because some of them have great and others only small jurisdictions, but none of which has the distinction of supremacy in policy or of recognized authority to do more than suggest. And posts upon such Committees are the highest posts in the Senate just as they are in the House pf Representatives.

In an address delivered on a recent occasion,[40] in the capacity of President of the Birmingham and Midland Institute, Mr. Froude, having in mind, of course, British forms of government, but looking mediately at all popular systems, said very pointedly that "In party government party life becomes like a court of justice. The people are the judges, the politicians the advocates, who," he adds caustically rather than justly, "only occasionally and by accident speak their real opinions." "The truly great political orators," he exclaims, "are the ornaments of mankind, the most finished examples of noble feeling and perfect expression, but they rarely understand the circumstances of their time. They feel passionately, but for that reason they cannot judge calmly." If we are to accept these judgments from Mr. Froude in the face of his reputation for thinking somewhat too independently of evidence, we should congratulate ourselves that we have in this country hit upon a system which, now that it has reached its perfection, has left little or no place for politicians to make false declarations or for the orator to coin fine expression for views which are only feelings, except outside of the legislative halls of the nation, upon the platform, where talk is all that is expected. It would seem as if the seer had a much more favorable opportunity in the committee-room than the orator can have, and with us it is the committee-room which governs the legislative chamber. The speech-making in the latter neither makes nor often seriously affects the plans framed in the former; because the plans are made before the speeches are uttered. This is self-evident of the debates of the House; but even the speeches made in the Senate, free, full, and earnest as they seem, are made, so to speak, after the fact-not to determine the actions but to air the opinions of the body.

Still, it must be regarded as no inconsiderable addition to the usefulness of the Senate that it enjoys a much greater freedom of discussion than the House can allow itself. It permits itself a good deal of talk in public about what it is doing,[41] and it commonly talks a great deal of sense. It is small enough to make it safe to allow individual freedom to its members, and to have, at the same time, such order and sense of proportion in its proceedings as is characteristic of small bodies, like boards of college trustees or of commercial directors, who feel that their main object is business, not speech-making, and so say all that is necessary without being tedious, and do what they are called upon to do without need of driving themselves with hurrying rules. Such rules, they seem to feel, are meant only for big assemblies which have no power of self-control. Of course the Senate talks more than an average board of directors would, because the corporations which it represents are States, made up, politically speaking, of numerous popular constituencies to which Senators, no less than Representatives, must make speeches of a sort which, considering their fellow-members alone, would be unnecessary if not impertinent and out of taste, in the Senate chamber, but which will sound best in the ears of the people, for whose ears they are intended, if delivered there. Speeches which, so to say, run in the name of the Senate's business will generally be more effectual for campaign uses at home than any speech could be which should run in the name of the proper topics of the stump. There is an air of doing one's duty by one's party in speaking party platitudes or uttering party defiances on the floor of the Senate or of the House. Of course, however, there is less temptation to such speech-making in the Senate than in the House. The House knows the terrible possibilities of this sort in store for it, were it to give perfect freedom of debate to its three hundred and twenty-five members, in these days when frequent mails and tireless tongues of telegraphy bring every constituency within easy earshot of Washington; and it therefore seeks to confine what little discussion it indulges in to the few committee-men specially in charge of the business of each moment. But the Senate is small and of settled habits, and has no such bugbear to trouble it. It can afford to do without any *clôture* or previous question. No Senator is likely to want to speak on all the topics of the session, or to prepare more speeches than can conveniently be spoken before adjournment is imperatively at hand. The House can be counted upon to waste enough time to leave some leisure to the upper chamber.

And there can be no question that the debates which take place every session in the Senate are of a very high order of excellence. The average of the ability displayed in its discussions not infrequently rises quite to the level of those controversies of the past which we are wont to call great because they furnished occasion to men like Webster and Calhoun and Clay, whom we cannot now quite match in mastery of knowledge and of eloquence. If the debates of the present are smothered amongst the innumerable folios of the "Record," it is not because they do not contain utterances worthy to be heeded and to gain currency, but because they do not deal with questions of passion or of national existence, such as ran through all the earlier debates, or because our system so obscures and complicates party rule in legislation as to leave nothing very interesting to the public eye dependent upon the discussions of either House or Senate. What that is picturesque, or what that is vital in the esteem of the partisan, is there in these wordy contests about contemplated legislation? How does anybody know that either party's prospects will be much affected by what is said when Senators are debating, or, for that matter, by what is voted after their longest flights of controversy?

Still, though not much heeded, the debates of the Senate are of great value in scrutinizing and sifting matters which come up from the House. The Senate's opportunities for open and unrestricted discussion and its simple, comparatively unencumbered forms of procedure, unquestionably enable it to fulfill with very considerable success its high functions as a chamber of revision.

When this has been claimed and admitted, however, it still remains to be considered whether two chambers of equal power strengthen by steadying, or weaken by complicating, a system of representative government like our own. The utility and excellence of a bicameral system has never, I believe, been seriously questioned in this country; but M. Turgot smiles with something like contempt at our affectation in copying the House of Lords without having any lords to use for the purpose; and in our own day Mr. Bagehot, who is much more competent to speak on this head than was M. Turgot, has avowed very grave doubts as to the practical advantage of a two-headed legislature-each head having its own independent will. He finds much to recommend the House of Lords in the fact that it is not, as theory would have it, coördinate and coequal with the House of Commons, but merely "a revising and suspending House," altering what the Commons have done hastily or carelessly, and sometimes rejecting "Bills on which the House of Commons is not yet thoroughly in earnest, —upon which the nation is not yet determined."[42] He points out the fact that the House of Lords has never in modern times been, as a House, coequal in power with the House of Commons. Before the Reform Bill of 1832 the peers were all-powerful in legislation; not, however, because they were members of the House of Lords, but because they nominated most of the members of the House of Commons. Since that disturbing reform they have been thrown back upon the functions in which they never were strong, the functions of a deliberative assembly. These are the facts which seem to Mr. Bagehot to have made it possible for legislation to make easy and satisfactory progress under a system whose theory provided for fatal dead-locks between the two branches of the supreme legislature.

In his view "the evil of two coequal Houses of distinct natures is obvious." "Most constitutions," he declares, "have committed this blunder. The two most remarkable Republican institutions in the world commit it. In both the American and Swiss Constitutions the Upper House has as much authority as the second; it could produce the maximum of impediment —a dead-lock, if it liked; if it does not do so, it is owing not to the goodness of the legal constitution, but to the discreetness of the members of the Chamber. In both these constitutions this dangerous division is defended by a peculiar doctrine....It is said that there must be in a federal government some institution, some authority, some body possessing a veto in which the separate States comprising the Confederation are all equal. I confess this doctrine has to me no self-evidence, and it is assumed, but not proved. The State of Delaware is not equal in power or influence to the State of New York, and you cannot make it so by giving it an equal veto in an Upper Chamber. The history of such an institution is indeed most natural. A little State will like, and must like, to see some token, some memorial mark, of its old independence preserved in the Constitution by which that independence is extinguished. But it is one thing for an institution to be natural, and another for it to be expedient. If indeed it be that a federal government compels the erection of an Upper Chamber of conclusive and coördinate authority, it is one more in addition to the many other inherent defects of that kind of government. It may be necessary to have the blemish, but it is a blemish just as much."

It would be in the highest degree indiscreet to differ lightly with any conclusion to which Mr. Bagehot may have come in viewing that field of critical exposition in which he was supreme, the philosophical analysis, namely, of the English Constitution; and it must be apparent to any one who reads the passage I have just now quoted that his eye sees very keenly and truly even when he looks across sea at institutions which were repugnant to his own way of thinking. But it is safe to say that he did not see all in this instance, and that he was consequently in error concerning the true nature of our federal legislative system. His error, nevertheless, appears, not when we look only at the facts which he held up to view, but when we look at other facts which he ignored. It is true that the existence of two coequal Houses is an evil when those two Houses are of distinct natures, as was the case under the Victorian Constitution to which Mr. Bagehot refers by way of illustrative example. Under that Constitution all legislative business was sometimes to be seen quite suspended because of irreconcilable differences of opinion between the Upper House, which represented the rich wool-growers of the colony, and the Lower Assembly, which represented the lesser wool-growers, perhaps, and the people who were not wool-growers at all. The Upper House, in other words, was a class chamber, and thus stood quite apart from anything like the principle embodied in our own Senate, which is no more a class chamber than is the House of Representatives.

The prerogatives of the Senate do, indeed, render our legislative system more complex, and for that reason possibly more cumbersome, than the British; for our Senate can do more than the House of Lords. It can not only question and stay the judgment of the Commons, but may always with perfect safety act upon its own judgment and gainsay the more popular chamber to the end of the longest chapter of the bitterest controversy. It is quite as free to act as is any other branch of the government, and quite as sure to have its acts regarded. But there is safety and ease in the fact that the Senate never wishes to carry its resistance to the House to that point at which resistance must stay all progress in legislation; because there is really a "latent unity" between the Senate and the House which makes continued antagonism between them next to impossible-certainly in the highest degree improbable. The Senate and the House are of different origins, but virtually of the same nature. The Senate is less democratic than the House, and consequently less sensible to transient phases of public opinion; but it is no less sensible than the House of its ultimate accountability to the people, and is consequently quite as obedient to the more permanent and imperative judgments of the public mind. It cannot be carried so quickly by every new sentiment, but it can be carried quickly enough. There is a main chance of election time for it as well as for the House to think about.

By the mode of its election and the greater length of the term by which its seats are held, the Senate is almost altogether removed from that temptation to servile obedience to the whims of popular constituencies to which the House is constantly subject, without as much courage as the Senate has to guard its virtue. But the men who compose the Senate are of the same sort as the members of the House of Representatives, and represent quite as various classes. Nowadays many of the Senators are, indeed, very rich men, and there has come to be a great deal of talk about their vast wealth and the supposed aristocratic tendencies which it is imagined to breed. But even the rich Senators cannot be said to be representatives of a class, as if they were all opulent wool-growers or great land-owners. Their wealth is in all sorts of stocks, in all sorts of machinery, in all sorts of buildings, in possessions of all the sorts possible in a land of bustling commerce and money-making industries. They have made their money in a hundred different ways, or have inherited it from fathers who amassed it in enterprises too numerous to imagine; and they have it invested here, there, and everywhere, in this, that, and everything. Their wealth represents no class interests, but all the interests of the commercial world. It represents the majority of the nation, in a word; and so they can probably be trusted not to neglect one set of interests for another; not to despoil the trader for the sake of the farmer, or the farmer for the sake of the wool-grower, or the wool-grower for the behoof of the herder of short-horned cattle. At least the Senate is quite as trustworthy in this regard as is the House of Representatives.

Inasmuch as the Senate is thus separated from class interests and quite as representative of the nation at large as is the House of Representatives, the fact that it is less quickly sensitive to the hasty or impulsive movements of public opinion constitutes its value as a check, a steadying weight, in our very democratic system. Our English cousins have worked out for themselves a wonderfully perfect scheme of government by gradually making their monarchy unmonarchical. They have made of it a republic steadied by a reverenced aristocracy and pivoted upon a stable throne. And just as the English system is a limited monarchy because of Commons and Cabinet, ours may be said to be a limited democracy because of the Senate. This has in the trial of the scheme proved the chief value of that upper chamber which was instituted principally as an earnest of the abiding equality and sovereignty of the States. At any rate, this is the most conspicuous, and will prove to be the most lasting, use of the Senate in our system. It is valuable in our democracy in proportion as it is undemocratic. I think that a philosophical analysis of any successful and beneficent system of self-government will disclose the fact that its only effectual checks consist in a mixture of elements, in a combination of seemingly contradictory political principles; that the British government is perfect in proportion as it is unmonarchical, and ours safe in proportion as it is undemocratic; that the Senate saves us often from headlong popular tyranny.

"The value, spirit, and essence of the House of Commons," said Burke, "consists in its being the express image of the feelings of the nation;" but the image of the nation's feelings should not be the only thing reflected by the constitution of a free government. It is indispensable that, besides the House of Representatives which runs on all fours with popular sentiment, we should have a body like the Senate which may refuse to run with it at all when it seems to be wrong —a body which has time and security enough to keep its head, if only now and then and but for a little while, till other people have had time to think. The Senate is fitted to do deliberately and well the revising which is its properest function, because its position as a representative of state sovereignty is one of eminent dignity, securing for it ready and sincere respect, and because popular demands, ere they reach it with definite and authoritative suggestion, are diluted by passage through the feelings and conclusions of the state legislatures, which are the Senate's only immediate constituents. The Senate commonly feels with the House, but it does not, so to say, feel so fast. It at least has a chance to be the express image of those judgments of the nation which are slower and more temperate than its feelings.

This it is which makes the Senate "the most powerful and efficient second chamber that exists,"[43] and this it is which constitutes its functions one of the effectual checks, one of the real balances, of our system; though it is made to seem very insignificant in the literary theory of the Constitution, where the checks of state upon federal authorities, of executive prerogatives upon legislative powers, and of Judiciary upon President and Congress, though some of them in reality inoperative from the first and all of them weakened by many "ifs" and "buts," are made to figure in the leading rôles, as the characteristic Virtues, triumphing over the characteristic Vices, of our new and original political Morality-play.

It should, however, be accounted a deduction from the Senate's usefulness that it is seldom sure of more than two thirds of itself for more than four years at a time. In order that its life may be perpetual, one third of its membership is renewed or changed every two years, each third taking its turn at change or renewal in regular succession; and this device has, of course, an appreciably weakening effect on the legislative sinews of the Senate. Because the Senate mixes the parties in the composition of its Committees just as the House does, and those Committees must, consequently, be subjected to modification whenever the biennial senatorial elections bring in new men, freshly promoted from the House or from gubernatorial chairs. Places must be found for them at once in the working organization which busies itself in the committee-rooms. Six years is not the term of the Senate, but only of each Senator. Reckoning from any year in which one third of the Senate is elected, the term of the majority,—the two thirds not affected by the election,—is an average of the four and the two years which it has to live. There is never a time at which two thirds of the Senate have more than four years of appointed service before them. And this constant liability to change must, of course, materially affect the policy of the body. The time assured it in which to carry out any enterprise of policy upon which it may embark is seldom more than two years, the term of the House. It may be checked no less effectually than the lower House by the biennial elections, albeit the changes brought about in its membership are effected, not directly by the people, but indirectly and more slowly by the mediate operation of public opinion through the legislatures of the States.

In estimating the value of the Senate, therefore, as a branch of the national legislature, we should offset the committee organization, with its denial of leadership which disintegrates the Senate, and that liability to the biennial infusion of new elements which may at any time interrupt the policy and break the purpose of the Senate, against those habits of free and open debate which clear its mind, and to some extent the mind of the public, with regard to the nation's business, doing much towards making legislation definite and consistent, and against those great additions to its efficiency which spring from its observation of "slow and steady forms" of procedure, from the mediate election which gives it independence, and from its having a rational and august cause for existing.

When we turn to consider the Senate in its relations with the executive, we see it no longer as a legislative chamber, but as a consultative executive council. And just here there is to be noted an interesting difference between the relations of the Senate with the President and its relations with the departments, which are in constitutional theory one with the President. It deals directly with the President in acting upon nominations and upon treaties. It goes into "executive session" to handle without gloves the acts of the chief magistrate. Its dealings with the departments, on the other hand, are, like those of the House, only indirect. Its legislative, not its executive, function is the whip which coerces the Secretaries. Its will is the supreme law in the offices of the government; and yet it orders policy by no direct word to the departments. It does not consult and negotiate with them as it does with the President, their titular head. Its immediate agents, the Committees, are not the recognized constitutional superiors of Secretary A. or Comptroller B.; but these officials cannot move a finger or plan more than a paltry detail without looking to it that they render strict obedience to the wishes of these outside, uncommissioned, and irresponsible, but none the less authoritative and imperative masters.

This feature of the Senate's power over the executive does not, however, call for special emphasis here, because it is not a power peculiar to the Senate, this overlordship of the departments, but one which it possesses in common with the House of Representatives,—simply an innate and inseparable part of the absolutism of a supreme legislature. It is the Senate's position as the President's council in some great and many small matters which call for particular discussion. Its general tyranny over the departments belongs rather with what I am to say presently when looking at congressional government from the stand-point of the executive.

The greatest consultative privilege of the Senate,—the greatest in dignity, at least, if not in effect upon the interests of the country,—is its right to a ruling voice in the ratification of treaties with foreign powers. I have already alluded to this privilege, for the purpose of showing what weight it has had in many instances in disarranging the ideal balance supposed to exist between the powers of Congress and the constitutional prerogatives of the President; but I did not then stop to discuss the organic reasons which have made it impossible that there should be any real consultation between the President and the Senate upon such business, and which have, consequently, made disagreement and even antagonism between them probable outcomes of the system. I do not consult the auditor who scrutinizes my accounts when I submit to him my books, my vouchers, and a written report of the business I have negotiated. I do not take his advice and seek his consent; I simply ask his endorsement or invite his condemnation. I do not sue for his coöperation, but challenge his criticism. And the analogy between my relations with the auditor and the relations of the President with the Senate is by no means remote. The President really has no voice at all in the conclusions of the Senate with reference to his diplomatic transactions, or with reference to any of the matters upon which he consults it; and yet without a voice in the conclusion there is no consultation. Argument and an unobstructed interchange of views upon a ground of absolute equality are essential parts of the substance of genuine consultation. The Senate, when it closes its doors, upon going into "executive session," closes them upon the President as much as upon the rest of the world. He cannot meet their objections to his courses except through the clogged and inadequate channels of a written message or through the friendly but unauthoritative offices of some Senator who may volunteer his active support. Nay, in many cases the President may not even know what the Senate's objections were. He is made to approach that body as a servant conferring with his master, and of course deferring to that master. His only power of compelling compliance on the part of the Senate lies in his initiative in negotiation, which affords him a chance to get the country into such scrapes, so pledged in the view of the world to certain courses of action, that the Senate hesitates to bring about the appearance of dishonor which would follow its refusal to ratify the rash promises or to support the indiscreet threats of the Department of State.

The machinery of consultation between the Senate and the President is of course the committee machinery. The Senate sends treaties to its Standing Committee on Foreign Relations, which ponders the President's messages accompanying the treaties and sets itself to understand the situation in the light of all the information available. If the President wishes some more satisfactory mode of communication with the Senate than formal message-writing, his only door of approach is this Committee on Foreign Relations. The Secretary of State may confer with its chairman or with its more influential members. But such a mode of conference is manifestly much less than a voice in the deliberations of the Senate itself,—much less than meeting that body face to face in free consultation and equal debate. It is almost as distinctly dealing with a foreign power as were the negotiations preceding the proposed treaty. It must predispose the Senate to the temper of an overseer.[44]

Still, treaties are not every-day affairs with us, and exceptional business may create in Senators an exceptional sense of responsibility, and dispose them to an unwonted desire to be dispassionate and fair. The ratification of treaties is a much more serious matter than the consideration of nominations which every session constitutes so constant a diversion from the more ponderous business of legislation. It is in dealing with nominations, however, that there is the most friction in the contact between the President and his overlord, the Senate. One of the most noteworthy instances of the improper tactics which may arise out of these relations was the case of that Mr. Smythe, at the time Collector for the port of New York, whom, in 1869, President Grant nominated Minister to the Court of St. Petersburg. The nomination, as looking towards an appointment to diplomatic service, was referred to the Committee on Foreign Relations, of which Mr. Charles Sumner was then chairman. That Committee rejected the nomination; but Smythe had great influence at his back and was himself skilled beyond most men in the arts of the lobby. He accordingly succeeded in securing such support in the Senate as to become a very formidable dog in the manger, not himself gaining the appointment, but for a time blocking all other appointments and bringing the business of the Senate altogether to a stand-still, because he could not.[45] Smythe himself is forgotten; but no observer of the actual conditions of senatorial power can fail to see the grave import of the lesson which his case teaches, because his case was by no means an isolated one. There have been scores of others quite as bad; and we could have no assurance that there might not in the future be hundreds more, had not recent movements in the direction of a radical reform of the civil service begun to make nominations represent, not the personal preference of the President or the intrigues of other people, but honest, demonstrated worth, which the Senate is likely to feel forced to accept without question, when the reform reaches the highest grades of the service.

In discussing the Senate's connection with the civil service and the abuses surrounding that connection, one is, therefore, discussing a phase of congressional government which promises soon to become obsolete. A consummation devoutly to be wished!—and yet sure when it comes to rob our politics of a feature very conspicuous and very characteristic, and in a sense very entertaining. There are not many things in the proceedings of Congress which the people care to observe with any diligence, and it must be confessed that scandalous transactions in the Senate with reference to nominations were among the few things that the country watched and talked about with keen relish and interest. This was the personal element which always had spice in it. When Senator Conkling resigned in a huff because he could not have whom he liked in the collectorship of the port of New York, the country rubbed its hands; and when the same imperious politician sought reëlection as a vindication of that unconstitutional control of nominations which masqueraded as "the courtesy of the Senate," the country discussed his chances with real zest and chuckled over the whole affair in genuine glee. It was a big fight worth seeing. It would have been too bad to miss it.

Before the sentiment of reform had become strong enough to check it, this abuse of the consultative privileges of the Senate in the matter of nominations had assumed such proportions as to seem to some the ugliest deformity in our politics. It looked as if it were becoming at once the weakest and the most tried and strained joint of our federal system. If there was to be a break, would it not be there, where was the severest wear and tear? The evil practices seemed the more ineradicable because they had arisen in the most natural manner. The President was compelled, as in the case of treaties, to obtain the sanction of the Senate without being allowed any chance of consultation with it; and there soon grew up within the privacy of "executive session" an understanding that the wishes and opinions of each Senator who was of the President's own party should have more weight than even the inclinations of the majority in deciding upon the fitness or desirability of persons proposed to be appointed to offices in that Senator's State. There was the requisite privacy to shield from public condemnation the practice arising out of such an understanding; and the President himself was always quite out of earshot, hearing only of results, of final votes.

All through the direct dealings of the Senate with the President there runs this characteristic spirit of irresponsible dictation. The President may tire the Senate by dogged persistence, but he can never deal with it upon a ground of real equality. He has no real presence in the Senate. His power does not extend beyond the most general suggestion. The Senate always has the last word. No one would desire to see the President possessed of authority to overrule the decisions of the Senate, to treat with foreign powers, and appoint thousands of public officers, without any other than that shadowy responsibility which he owes to the people that elected him; but it is certainly an unfortunate feature of our government that Congress governs without being put into confidential relations with the agents through whom it governs. It dictates to another branch of the government which was intended to be coördinate and coequal with it, and over which it has no legalized authority as of a master, but only the authority of a bigger stockholder, of a monopolist indeed, of all the energetic prerogatives of the government. It is as if the Army and Navy Departments were to be made coördinate and coequal, but the absolute possession and control of all ammunition and other stores of war given to the one and denied the other. The executive is taken into partnership with the legislature upon a salary which may be withheld, and is allowed no voice in the management of the business. It is simply charged with the superintendence of the employees.

It was not essentially different in the early days when the President in person read his message to the Senate and the House together as an address, and the Senate in a body carried its reply to the executive mansion. The address was the formal communication of an outsider just as much as the message of to-day is, and the reply of the Senate was no less a formal document which it turned aside from its regular business to prepare. That meeting face to face was not consultation. The English Parliament does not consult with the sovereign when it assembles to hear the address from the throne.

It would, doubtless, be considered quite improper to omit from an essay on the Senate all mention of the Senate's President; and yet there is very little to be said about the Vice-President of the United States. His position is one of anomalous insignificance and curious uncertainty. Apparently he is not, strictly speaking, a part of the legislature,—he is clearly not a member,—yet neither is he an officer of the executive. It is one of the remarkable things about him, that it is hard to find in sketching the government any proper place to discuss him. He comes in most naturally along with the Senate to which he is tacked; but he does not come in there for any great consideration. He is simply a judicial officer set to moderate the proceedings of an assembly whose rules he has had no voice in framing and can have no voice in changing. His official stature is not to be compared with that of the Speaker of the House of Representatives. So long as he is Vice-President, he is inseparable officially from the Senate; his importance consists in the fact that he may cease to be Vice-President. His chief dignity, next to presiding over the Senate, lies in the circumstance that he is awaiting the death or disability of the President. And the chief embarrassment in discussing his office is, that in explaining how little there is to be said about it one has evidently said all there is to say.

V
The Executive.

> Every political constitution in which different bodies share the supreme power is only enabled to exist by the forbearance of those among whom this power is distributed. — LORD JOHN RUSSELL.
>
> Simplicity and logical neatness are not the good to be aimed at in politics, but freedom and order, with props against the pressure of time, and arbitrary will, and sudden crises. —THEO. WOOLSEY.
>
> Nothing, indeed, will appear more certain, on any tolerable consideration of this matter, than that *every sort of government ought to have its administration, correspondent to its legislature.* —BURKE.

IT is at once curious and instructive to note how we have been forced into practically amending the Constitution without constitutionally amending it. The legal processes of constitutional change are so slow and cumbersome that we have been constrained to adopt a serviceable framework of fictions which enables us easily to preserve the forms without laboriously obeying the spirit of the Constitution, which will stretch as the nation grows. It would seem that no impulse short of the impulse of self-preservation, no force less than the force of revolution, can nowadays be expected to move the cumbrous machinery of formal amendment erected in Article Five. That must be a tremendous movement of opinion which can sway two thirds of each House of Congress and the people of three fourths of the States. Mr. Bagehot has pointed out that one consequence of the existence of this next to immovable machinery "is that the most obvious evils cannot be quickly remedied," and "that a clumsy working and a curious technicality mark the politics of a rough-and-ready people. The practical arguments and legal disquisitions in America," continues he, "are often like those of trustees carrying out a misdrawn will, — the sense of what they mean is good, but it can never be worked out fully or defended simply, so hampered is it by the old words of an old testament."[46] But much the greater consequence is that we have resorted, almost unconscious of the political significance of what we did, to extra-constitutional means of modifying the federal system where it has proved to be too refined by balances of divided authority to suit practical uses, — to be out of square with the main principle of its foundation, namely, government by the people through their representatives in Congress.

Our method of choosing Presidents is a notable illustration of these remarks. The difference between the actual and the constitutional modes is the difference between an ideal non-partisan choice and a choice made under party whips; the difference between a choice made by independent, unpledged electors acting apart in the States and a choice made by a national party convention. Our Executive, no less than the English and French Executives, is selected by a representative, deliberative body, though in England and France the election is controlled by a permanent legislative chamber, and here by a transient assembly chosen for the purpose and dying with the execution of that purpose. In England the whole cabinet is practically elective. The French Chambers formally elect the President, the titular head of the government, and the President regards only the will of the Assembly in appointing the Prime Minister, who is the energetic head of the government, and who, in his turn, surrounds himself with colleagues who have the confidence of the legislature. And the French have but copied the English constitution, which makes the executive Ministry the representatives of the party majority in the Commons. With us, on the other hand, the President is elected by one representative body, which has nothing to do with him after his election, and the cabinet must be approved by another representative body, which has nothing directly to do with them after their appointment.

Of course I do not mean that the choice of a national convention is literally election. The convention only nominates a candidate. But that candidate is the only man for whom the electors of his party can vote; and so the expression of the preference of the convention of the dominant party is practically equivalent to election, and might as well be called election by any one who is writing of broad facts, and not of fine distinctions. The sovereign in England picks out the man who is to be Prime Minister, but he must pick where the Commons point; and so it is simpler, as well as perfectly true, to say that the Commons elect the Prime Minister. My agent does not select the particular horse I instruct him to buy. This is just the plain fact, —that the electors are the agents of the national conventions; and this fact constitutes more than an amendment of that original plan which would have had all the electors to be what the first electors actually were, trustworthy men given *carte blanche* to vote for whom they pleased, casting their ballots in thirteen state capitals in the hope that they would happen upon a majority agreement.

It is worth while, too, to notice another peculiarity of this elective system. There is a thorough-going minority representation in the assemblies which govern our elections. Across the ocean a Liberal Prime Minister is selected by the representatives only of those Liberals who live in Liberal constituencies; those who live elsewhere in a helpless minority, in a Conservative district, having of course no voice in the selection. A Conservative Premier, in like manner, owes nothing to those Conservatives who were unable to return a member to Parliament. So far as he is concerned, they count for Liberals, since their representative in the Commons is a Liberal. The parliaments which select our Presidents, on the contrary, are, each of them, all of a kind. No state district can have so few Republicans in it as not to be entitled to a representative in the national Republican convention equal to that of the most unanimously Republican district in the country; and a Republican State is accorded as full a representation in a Democratic convention as is the most Democratic of her sister States.

We had to pass through several stages of development before the present system of election by convention was reached. At the first two presidential elections the electors were left free to vote as their consciences and the Constitution bade them; for the Constitution bade them vote as they deemed best, and it did not require much discretion to vote for General Washington. But when General Washington was out of the race, and new parties began to dispute the field with the Federalists, party managers could not help feeling anxious about the votes of the electors, and some of those named to choose the second President were, accordingly, pledged beforehand to vote thus and so. After the third presidential election there began to be congressional oversight of the matter. From 1800 to 1824 there was an unbroken succession of caucuses of the Republican members of Congress to direct the action of the party electors; and nomination by caucus died only when the Republican party became virtually the only party worth reckoning with, —the only party for whom nomination was worth while, —and then public opinion began to cry out against such secret direction of the monopoly. In 1796 the Federalist congressmen had held an informal caucus to ascertain their minds as to the approaching election; but after that they refrained from further experiment in the same direction, and contented themselves with now and then a sort of convention until they had no party to convene. In 1828 there was a sort of dropping fire of nominations from state legislatures; and in 1832 sat the first of the great national nominating conventions.

There was, therefore, one form of congressional government which did not succeed. It was a very logical mode of party government, that of nominating the chief magistrate by congressional caucus, but it was not an open enough way. The French chamber does not select premiers by shutting up the members of its majority in caucus. Neither does the House of Commons. Their selection is made by long and open trial, in debate and in business management, of the men in whom they discover most tact for leading and most skill for planning, as well as most power for ruling. They do not say, by vote, give us M. Ferry, give us Mr. Gladstone; but Her Majesty knows as well as her subjects know that Mr. Gladstone is the only man whom the Liberal majority will obey; and President Grévy perceives that M. Ferry is the only man whom the

Chambers can be made to follow. Each has elected himself by winning the first place in his party. The election has openly progressed for years, and is quite different from the private vote of a caucus about an outsider who is to sit, not in Congress, but in the executive mansion; who is not their man, but the people's.

Nor would nominations by state legislatures answer any rational purpose. Of course every State had, or thought she had,—which is much the same thing,—some citizen worthy to become President; and it would have been confusion worse confounded to have had as many candidates as there might be States. So universal a competition between "favorite sons" would have thrown the election into the House of Representatives so regularly as to replace the nominating caucus by an electing caucus.

The virtual election of the cabinet, the real executive, or at least the Prime Minister, the real head of the executive, by the Commons in England, furnishes us with a contrast rather than with a parallel to the election of our premier, the head of our executive, by a deliberative, representative body, because of the difference of function and of tenure between our Presidents and English Prime Ministers. William Pitt was elected to rule the House of Commons, John Adams to hold a constitutional balance against the Houses of Congress. The one was the leader of the legislature; the other, so to say, the colleague of the legislature. Besides, the Commons can not only make but also unmake Ministries; whilst conventions can do nothing but bind their parties by nomination, and nothing short of a well-nigh impossible impeachment can unmake a President, except four successions of the seasons. As has been very happily said by a shrewd critic, our system is essentially astronomical. A President's usefulness is measured, not by efficiency, but by calendar months. It is reckoned that if he be good at all he will be good for four years. A Prime Minister must keep himself in favor with the majority, a President need only keep alive.

Once the functions of a presidential elector were very august. He was to speak for the people; they were to accept his judgment as theirs. He was to be as eminent in the qualities which win trust as was the greatest of the Imperial Electors in the power which inspires fear. But now he is merely a registering machine,—a sort of bell-punch to the hand of his party convention. It gives the pressure, and he rings. It is, therefore, patent to every one that that portion of the Constitution which prescribes his functions is as though it were not. A very simple and natural process of party organization, taking form first in congressional caucuses and later in nominating conventions, has radically altered a Constitution which declares that it can be amended only by the concurrence of two thirds of Congress and three fourths of the States. The sagacious men of the constitutional convention of 1787 certainly expected their work to be altered, but can hardly have expected it to be changed in so informal a manner.

The conditions which determine the choice of a nominating convention which names a President are radically different from the conditions which facilitate the choice of a representative chamber which selects for itself a Prime Minister. "Among the great purposes of a national parliament are these two," says Mr. Parton:[47] "first, to train men for practical statesmanship; and secondly, to exhibit them to the country, so that, when men of ability are wanted, they can be found without anxious search and perilous trial." In those governments which are administered by an executive committee of the legislative body, not only this training but also this exhibition is constant and complete. The career which leads to cabinet office is a career of self-exhibition. The self-revelation is made in debate, and so is made to the nation at large as well as to the Ministry of the day, who are looking out for able recruits, and to the Commons, whose ear is quick to tell a voice which it will consent to hear, a knowledge which it will pause to heed. But in governments like our own, in which legislative and executive services are altogether dissociated, this training is incomplete, and this exhibition almost entirely wanting. A nominating convention does not look over the rolls of Congress to pick a man to suit its purpose; and if it did it could not find him, because Congress is not a school for the preparation of administrators, and the convention is supposed to be searching not for an experienced committee-man, but for a tried statesman. The proper test for its application is not the test by which congressmen are assayed. They make laws, but they do not have to order the execution of the laws they make. They have a great deal of experience in directing, but none at all in being directed. Their care is to pass bills, not to keep them in running order after they have become statutes. They spend their lives without having anything to do directly with administration, though administration is dependent upon the measures which they enact.

A Presidential convention, therefore, when it nominates a man who is, or has been, a member of Congress, does not nominate him because of his congressional experience, but because it is thought that he has other abilities which were not called out in Congress. Andrew Jackson had been a member of Congress, but he was chosen President because he had won the battle of New Orleans and had driven the Indians from Florida. It was thought that his military genius evinced executive genius. The men whose fame rests altogether upon laurels won in Congress have seldom been more successful than Webster and Henry Clay in their candidacy for the chief magistracy. Washington was a soldier; Jefferson cut but a sorry figure in debate; Monroe was a diplomatist; it required diligent inquiry to find out what many of our Presidents had been before they became candidates; and eminency in legislative service has always been at best but an uncertain road to official preferment.

Of late years a tendency is observable which seems to be making the gubernatorial chairs of the greater States the nearest offices to the Presidency; and it cannot but be allowed that there is much that is rational in the tendency. The governorship of a State is very like a smaller Presidency; or, rather, the Presidency is very like a big governorship. Training in the duties of the one fits for the duties of the other. This is the only avenue of subordinate place through which the highest place can be naturally reached. Under the cabinet governments abroad a still more natural line of promotion is arranged. The Ministry is a legislative Ministry, and draws its life from the legislature, where strong talents always secure executive place. A long career in Parliament is at least a long contact with practical statesmanship, and at best a long schooling in the duties of the practical statesman. But with us there is no such intimate relationship between legislative and executive service. From experience in state administration to trial in the larger sphere of federal administration is the only natural order of promotion. We ought, therefore, to hail the recognition of this fact as in keeping with the general plan of the federal Constitution. The business of the President, occasionally great, is usually not much above routine. Most of the time it is *mere* administration, mere obedience of directions from the masters of policy, the Standing Committees. Except in so far as his power of veto constitutes him a part of the legislature, the President might, not inconveniently, be a permanent officer; the first official of a carefully-graded and impartially regulated civil service system, through whose sure series of merit-promotions the youngest clerk might rise even to the chief magistracy.[48] He is part of the official rather than of the political machinery of the government, and his duties call rather for training than for constructive genius. If there can be found in the official systems of the States a lower grade of service in which men may be advantageously drilled for Presidential functions, so much the better. The States will have better governors, the Union better Presidents, and there will have been supplied one of the most serious needs left unsupplied by the Constitution,—the need for a proper school in which to rear federal administrators.

Administration is something that men must learn, not something to skill in which they are born. Americans take to business of all kinds more naturally than any other nation ever did, and the executive duties of government constitute just an exalted kind of business; but even Americans are not Presidents in their cradles. One cannot have too much preparatory training and experience who is to fill so high a magistracy. It is difficult to perceive, therefore, upon what safe ground of reason are built the opinions of those persons who regard short terms of service as sacredly and peculiarly republican in principle. If republicanism is founded upon good sense, nothing so far removed from good sense can be part and parcel of it. Efficiency is the only just foundation for confidence in a public officer, under republican institutions no less than under monarchs; and short terms which cut off the efficient as surely and inexorably as the inefficient are quite as repugnant to republican as to monarchical rules of wisdom. Unhappily, however, this is not American doctrine. A President is dismissed almost as soon as he has learned the duties of his office, and a man who has served a dozen terms in Congress is a curiosity. We are too apt to think both the work of legislation and the work of administration easy enough to be done readily, with or without preparation, by any man of discretion and character. No one imagines that the dry-goods or the hardware trade, or even the cobbler's craft, can be successfully conducted except by those who have worked through a laborious and unremunerative apprenticeship, and who have devoted their lives to perfecting themselves as tradesmen or as menders of shoes. But legislation is esteemed a thing which may be taken up with success by any shrewd man of middle age, which a lawyer may now and again advantageously combine with his practice, or of which any intelligent youth may easily catch the knack; and administration is regarded as something which an old soldier, an ex-diplomatist, or a popular politician may be trusted to take to by instinct. No man of tolerable talents need despair of having been born a Presidential candidate.

These must be pronounced very extraordinary conclusions for an eminently practical people to have accepted; and it must be received as an awakening of good sense that there is nowadays a decided inclination manifested on the part of the nation to supply training-schools for the Presidency in like minor offices, such as the governorships of the greater States. For the sort of Presidents needed under the present arrangement of our federal government, it is best to choose amongst the ablest and most experienced state governors.

So much for nomination and election. But, after election, what then? The President is not all of the Executive. He cannot get along without the men whom he appoints, with and by the consent and advice of the Senate; and they are really integral parts of that branch of the government which he titularly contains in his one single person. The characters and training of the Secretaries are of almost as much importance as his own gifts and antecedents; so that his appointment and the Senate's confirmation must be added to the machinery of nomination by convention and election by automatic electors before the whole process of making up a working executive has been noted. The early Congresses seem to have regarded the Attorney-General and the four Secretaries[49] who constituted the first Cabinets as something more than the President's lieutenants. Before the republican reaction which followed the supremacy of the Federalists, the heads of the departments appeared in person before the Houses to impart desired information, and to make what suggestions they might have to venture, just as the President attended in person to read his "address." They were always recognized units in the system, never mere ciphers to the Presidential figure which led them. Their wills counted as independent wills.

The limits of this independence would seem, however, never to have been very clearly defined. Whether or not the President was to take the advice of his appointees and colleagues appears to have depended always upon the character and temper of the President. Here, for example, is what was reported in 1862. "We pretend to no state secrets," said the New York "Evening Post,"[50] "but we have been told, upon what we deem good authority, that no such thing as a combined, unitary, deliberative administration exists; that the President's brave willingness to take all responsibility has quite neutralized the idea of a joint responsibility; and that orders of the highest importance are issued, and movements commanded, which cabinet officers learn of as other people do, or, what is worse, which the cabinet officers disapprove and protest against. Each cabinet officer, again, controls his own department pretty much as he pleases, without consultation with the President or with his coadjutors, and often in the face of determinations which have been reached by the others." A picture this which forcibly reminds one of a certain imperious Prime Minister, in his last days created Earl of Chatham. These reports may have been true or they may have been mere rumors; but they depict a perfectly possible state of affairs. There is no influence except the ascendency or tact of the President himself to keep a Cabinet in harmony and to dispose it to coöperation; so that it would be very difficult to lay down any rules as to what elements really constitute an Executive. Those elements can be determined exactly of only one administration at a time, and of that only after it has closed, and some one who knows its secrets has come forward to tell them. We think of Mr. Lincoln rather than of his Secretaries when we look back to the policy of the war-time; but we think of Mr. Hamilton rather than of President Washington when we look back to the policy of the first administration. Daniel Webster was bigger than President Fillmore, and President Jackson was bigger than Mr. Secretary Van Buren. It depends for the most part upon the character and training, the previous station, of the cabinet officers, whether or not they act as governing factors in administration, just as it depends upon the President's talents and preparatory schooling whether or not he is a mere figure-head. A weak President may prove himself wiser than the convention which nominated him, by overshadowing himself with a Cabinet of notables.

From the necessity of the case, however, the President cannot often be really supreme in matters of administration, except as the Speaker of the House of Representatives is supreme in legislation, as appointer of those who are supreme in its several departments. The President is no greater than his prerogative of veto makes him; he is, in other words, powerful rather as a branch of the legislature than as the titular head of the Executive. Almost all distinctively executive functions are specifically bestowed upon the heads of the departments. No President, however earnest and industrious, can keep the Navy in a state of creditable efficiency if he have a corrupt or incapable Secretary in the Navy Department; he cannot prevent the army from suffering the damage of demoralization if the Secretary of War is without either ability, experience, or conscience; there will be corrupt jobs in the Department of Justice, do what he will to correct the methods of a deceived or deceitful Attorney-General; he cannot secure even-handed equity for the Indian tribes if the Secretary of the Interior chooses to thwart him; and the Secretary of State may do as much mischief behind his back as can the Secretary of the Treasury. He might master the details and so control the administration of some one of the departments, but he can scarcely oversee them all with any degree of strictness. His knowledge of what they have done or are doing comes, of course, from the Secretaries themselves, and his annual messages to Congress are in large part but a recapitulation of the chief contents of the detailed reports which the heads of the departments themselves submit at the same time to the Houses.

It is easy, however, to exaggerate the power of the Cabinet. After all has been said, it is evident that they differ from the permanent officials only in not being permanent. Their tenure of office is made to depend upon the supposition that their functions are political rather than simply ministerial, independent rather than merely instrumental. They are made party representatives because of the fiction that they direct policy. In reality the First Comptroller of the Treasury has almost, if not quite, as much weight in directing departmental business as has the Secretary of the Treasury himself, and it would practically be quite as useful to have his office, which is in intention permanent, vacated by every change of administration as to have that rule with regard to the office of his official chief. The permanent organization, the clerical forces of the departments, have in the Secretaries a sort of *sliding top*; though it would probably be just as convenient in practice to have this lid permanent as to have it movable. That the Secretaries are not in fact the directors of the executive policy of the government, I have shown in pointing out the thorough-going supervision of even the details of administration which it is the disposition of the Standing Committees of Congress to exercise. In the actual control of affairs no one can do very much without gaining the ears of the Committees. The heads of the departments could, of course, act much more wisely in many matters than the Committees can, because they have an intimacy with the workings and the wants of those departments which no Committee can possibly possess. But Committees prefer to govern in the dark rather than not to govern at all, and the Secretaries, as a matter of fact, find themselves bound in all things larger than routine details by laws which have been made for them and which they have no legitimate means of modifying.

Of course the Secretaries are in the leading-strings of statutes, and all their duties look towards a strict obedience to Congress. Congress made them and can unmake them. It is to Congress that they must render account for the conduct of administration. The head of each department must every year make a detailed report of the expenditures of the department, and a minute account of the facilities of work and the division of functions in the department, naming each clerk of its force. The chief duties of one cabinet officer will serve to illustrate the chief duties of his colleagues. It is the duty of the Secretary of the Treasury[51] "to prepare plans for the improvement and management of the revenue and for the support of the public credit; to prescribe forms of keeping and rendering all public accounts; to grant all warrants for moneys to be issued from the Treasury in pursuance of appropriations made by Congress; to report to the Senate or House, in person or in writing, information required by them pertaining to his office; and to perform all duties relating to finance that he shall be directed to perform." "He is required to report to Congress annually, on the first Monday in June, the results of the information compiled by the Bureau of Statistics, showing the condition of manufactures, domestic trade, currency, and banks in the several States and Territories." "He prescribes regulations for the killing in Alaska Territory and adjacent waters of minks, martens, sable, and other fur-bearing animals." "And he must lay before Congress each session the reports of the Auditors, showing the applications of the appropriations made for the War and Navy Departments, and also abstracts and tabulated forms showing separate accounts of the moneys received from internal duties."

Of course it is of the utmost importance that a Secretary who has within his choice some of the minor plans for the management of the revenue and for the maintenance of the public credit should be carefully chosen from amongst men skilled in financial administration and experienced in business regulation; but it is no more necessary that the man selected for such responsible duties should be an active politician, called to preside over his department only so long as the President who appointed him continues to hold office and to like him, than it is to have a strictly political officer to fulfill his other duty of prescribing game laws for Alaska and Alaskan waters. Fur-bearing animals can have no connection with political parties,—except, perhaps, as "spoils." Indeed, it is a positive disadvantage that Mr. Secretary should be chosen upon such a principle. He cannot have the knowledge, and must therefore lack the efficiency, of a permanent official separated from the partisan conflicts of politics and advanced to the highest office of his department by a regular series of promotions won by long service. The general policy of the government in matters of finance, everything that affects the greater operations of the Treasury, depends upon legislation, and is altogether in the hands of the Committees of Ways and Means and of Finance; so that it is entirely apart from good sense to make an essentially political office out of the post of that officer who controls only administrative details.

And this remark would seem to apply with still greater force to the offices of the other Secretaries. They have even less energetic scope than the Secretary of the Treasury has. There must under any system be considerable power in the hands of the officer who handles and dispenses vast revenues, even though he handle and dispense them as directed by his employers. Money in its goings to and fro makes various mares go by the way, so to speak. It cannot move in great quantities without moving a large part of the commercial world with it. Management even of financial details may be made instrumental in turning the money-markets upside down. The Secretary of the Treasury is, therefore, less a mere chief clerk than are his coadjutors; and if his duties are not properly political, theirs certainly are not.

In view of this peculiarity of the Secretaries, in being appointed as partisans and endowed as mere officials, it is interesting to inquire what and whom they represent. They are clearly meant to represent the political party to which they belong; but it very often happens that it is impossible for them to do so. They must sometimes obey the opposite party. It is our habit to speak of the party to which the President is known to adhere and which has control of appointments to the offices of the civil service as "the party in power;" but it is very evident that control of the executive machinery is not all or even a very large part of power in a country ruled as ours is. In so far as the President is an executive officer he is the servant of Congress; and the members of the Cabinet, being confined to executive functions, are altogether the servants of Congress. The President, however, besides being titular head of the executive service, is to the extent of his veto a third branch of the legislature, and the party which he represents is in power in the same sense that it would be in power if it had on its side a majority of the members of either of the other two branches of Congress. If the House and Senate are of one party and the President and his ministers of the opposite, the President's party can hardly be said to be in power beyond the hindering and thwarting faculty of the veto. The Democrats were in power during the sessions of the Twenty-fifth Congress because they had a majority in the Senate as well as Andrew Jackson in the White House; but later Presidents have had both House and Senate against them.[52]

It is this constant possibility of party diversity between the Executive and Congress which so much complicates our system of party government. The history of administrations is not necessarily the history of parties. Presidential elections may turn the scale of party ascendency one way, and the intermediate congressional elections may quite reverse the balance. A strong party administration, by which the energy of the State is concentrated in the hands of a single well-recognized political organization, which is by reason of its power saddled with all responsibility, may sometimes be possible, but it must often be impossible. We are thus shut out in part from real party government such as we desire, and such as it is unquestionably desirable to set up in every system like ours. Party government can exist only when the absolute control of administration, the appointment of its officers as well as the direction of its means and policy, is given immediately into the hands of that branch of the government whose power is paramount, the representative body. Roger Sherman, whose perception was amongst the keenest and whose sagacity was amongst the surest in the great Convention of 1787, was very bold and outspoken in declaring this fact and in proposing to give it candid recognition. Perceiving very clearly the omnipotence which must inevitably belong to a national Congress such as the convention was about to create, he avowed that "he considered the executive magistracy as nothing more than an institution for carrying the will of the legislature into effect; that the person or persons [who should constitute the executive] ought to be appointed by, and accountable to, the legislature only, which was the depository of the supreme will of the society." Indeed, the executive was in his view so entirely the servant of the legislative will that he saw good reason to think that the legislature should judge of the number of persons of which the executive should be composed; and there seem to have been others in the convention who went along with him in substantial agreement as to these matters. It would seem to have been only a desire for the creation of as many as possible of those balances of power which now decorate the "literary theory" of the Constitution which they made that prevented a universal acquiescence in these views.

The anomaly which has resulted is seen most clearly in the party relations of the President and his Cabinet. The President is a partisan, —is elected because he is a partisan, —and yet he not infrequently negatives the legislation passed by the party whom he represents; and it may be said to be nowadays a very rare thing to find a Cabinet made up of truly representative party men. They are the men of his party whom the President likes, but not necessarily or always the men whom that party relishes. So low, indeed, has the reputation of some of our later Cabinets fallen, even in the eyes of men of their own political connection, that writers in the best of our public prints feel at full liberty to speak of their members with open contempt. "When Mr. —— was made Secretary of the Navy," laughs the New York "Nation," "no one doubted that he would treat the Department as 'spoils,' and consequently nobody has been disappointed. He is one of the statesmen who can hardly conceive of a branch of the public Administration having no spoils in it." And that this separation of the Cabinet from real party influence, and from the party leadership which would seem properly to belong to its official station, is a natural result of our constitutional scheme is made patent in the fact that the Cabinet has advanced in party insignificance as the system has grown older. The connection between the early Cabinets and the early Congresses was very like the relations between leaders and their party. Both Hamilton and Gallatin led rather than obeyed the Houses; and it was many years before the suggestions of heads of departments ceased to be sure of respectful and acquiescent consideration from the legislative Committees. But as the Committees gained facility and power the leadership of the Cabinet lost ground. Congress took command of the government so soon as ever it got command of itself, and no Secretary of to-day can claim by virtue of his office recognition as a party authority. Congress looks upon advice offered to it by anybody but its own members as gratuitous impertinence.

At the same time it is quite evident that the means which Congress has of controlling the departments and of exercising the searching oversight at which it aims are limited and defective. Its intercourse with the President is restricted to the executive messages, and its intercourse with the departments has no easier channels than private consultations between executive officials and the Committees, informal interviews of the ministers with individual members of Congress, and the written correspondence which the cabinet officers from time to time address to the presiding officers of the two Houses, at stated intervals, or in response to formal resolutions of inquiry. Congress stands almost helplessly outside of the departments. Even the special, irksome, ungracious investigations which it from time to time institutes in its spasmodic endeavors to dispel or confirm suspicions of malfeasance or of wanton corruption do not afford it more than a glimpse of the inside of a small province of federal administration. Hostile or designing officials can always hold it at arm's length by dexterous evasions and concealments. It can violently disturb, but it cannot often fathom, the waters of the sea in which the bigger fish of the civil service swim and feed. Its dragnet stirs without cleansing the bottom. Unless it have at the head of the departments capable, fearless men, altogether in its confidence and entirely in sympathy with its designs, it is clearly helpless to do more than affright those officials whose consciences are their accusers.

And it is easy to see how the commands as well as the questions of Congress may be evaded, if not directly disobeyed, by the executive agents. Its Committees may command, but they cannot superintend the execution of their commands. The Secretaries, though not free enough to have any independent policy of their own, are free enough to be very poor, because very unmanageable, servants. Once installed, their hold upon their offices does not depend upon the will of Congress. If they please the President, and keep upon living terms with their colleagues, they need not seriously regard the displeasure of the Houses, unless, indeed, by actual crime, they rashly put themselves in the way of its judicial wrath. If their folly be not too overt and extravagant, their authority may continue theirs till the earth has four times made her annual journey round the sun. They may make daily blunders in administration and repeated mistakes in business, may thwart the plans of Congress in a hundred small, vexatious ways, and yet all the while snap their fingers at its dissatisfaction or displeasure. They are denied the gratification of possessing real power, but they have the satisfaction of being secure in a petty independence which gives them a chance to be tricky and scheming. There are ways and ways of obeying; and if Congress be not pleased, why need they care? Congress did not give them their places, and cannot easily take them away.

Still it remains true that all the big affairs of the departments are conducted in obedience to the direction of the Standing Committees. The President nominates, and with legislative approval appoints, to the more important offices of the government, and the members of the Cabinet have the privilege of advising him as to matters in most of which he has no power of final action without the concurrence of the Senate; but the gist of all policy is decided by legislative, not by executive, will. It can be no great satisfaction to any man to possess the barren privilege of suggesting the best means of managing the every-day routine business of the several bureaux so long as the larger plans which that business is meant to advance are made for him by others who are set over him. If one is commanded to go to this place or to that place, and must go, will he, nill he, it can be but small solace to him that he is left free to determine whether he will ride or walk in going the journey. The only serious questions are whether or not this so great and real control exerted by Congress can be exercised efficiently and with sufficient responsibility to those whom Congress represents, and whether good government is promoted by the arrangement.

No one, I take it for granted, is disposed to disallow the principle that the representatives of the people are the proper ultimate authority in all matters of government, and that administration is merely the clerical part of government. Legislation is the originating force. It determines what shall be done; and the President, if he cannot or will not stay legislation by the use of his extraordinary power as a branch of the legislature, is plainly bound in duty to render unquestioning obedience to Congress. And if it be his duty to obey, still more is obedience the bounden duty of his subordinates. The power of making laws is in its very nature and essence the power of directing, and that power is given to Congress. The principle is without drawback, and is inseparably of a piece with all Anglo-Saxon usage; the difficulty, if there be any, must lie in the choice of means whereby to energize the principle. The natural means would seem to be the right on the part of the representative body to have all the executive servants of its will under its close and constant supervision, and to hold them to a strict accountability: in other words, to have the privilege of dismissing them whenever their service became unsatisfactory. This is the matter-of-course privilege of every other master; and if Congress does not possess it, its mastery is hampered without being denied. The executive officials are its servants all the same; the only difference is that if they prove negligent, or incapable, or deceitful servants Congress must rest content with the best that can be got out of them until its chief administrative agent, the President, chooses to appoint better. It cannot make them docile, though it may compel them to be obedient in all greater matters. In authority of rule Congress is made master, but in means of rule it is made mere magistrate. It commands with absolute lordship, but it can discipline for disobedience only by slow and formal judicial process.

Upon Machiavelli's declaration that "nothing is more important to the stability of the state than that facility should be given by its constitution for the accusation of those who are supposed to have committed any public wrong," a writer in the "Westminster Review" makes this thoughtful comment: "The benefit of such a provision is twofold. First, the salutary fear of the probable coming of a day of account will restrain the evil practices of some bad men and self-seekers; secondly, the legal outlet of accusation gives vent to peccant humors in the body politic, which, if checked and driven inward, would work to the utter ruin of the constitution; ... the distinction is lost between accusation and calumny."[53] And of course it was these benefits which our federal Constitution was meant to secure by means of its machinery of impeachment. No servant of the state, not even the President himself, was to be beyond the reach of accusation by the House of Representatives and of trial by the Senate. But the processes of impeachment, like those of amendment, are ponderous and difficult to handle. It requires something like passion to set them a-going; and nothing short of the grossest offenses against the plain law of the land will suffice to give them speed and effectiveness. Indignation so great as to overcrow party interest may secure a conviction; nothing less can. Indeed, judging by our past experiences, impeachment may be said to be little more than an empty menace. The House of Representatives is a tardy grand jury, and the Senate an uncertain court.

Besides, great crimes such as might speed even impeachment are not ordinary things in the loosest public service. An open-eyed public opinion can generally give them effective check. That which usually and every day clogs and hampers good government is folly or incapacity on the part of the ministers of state. Even more necessary, therefore, than a power clothed with authority to accuse, try, and punish for public crime is some ultimate authority, whose privilege it shall be to dismiss for inefficiency. Impeachment is aimed altogether above the head of business management. A merchant would not think it fair, even if it were lawful, to shoot a clerk who could not learn the business. Dismissal is quite as effective for his purposes, and more merciful to the clerk. The crying inconvenience of our system is, therefore, that the constitutional authority whose prerogative it is to direct policy and oversee administration has fewer facilities for getting its work well done than has the humblest citizen for obtaining satisfactory aid in his own undertakings. The authority most interested in appointments and dismissals in the civil service has little to do with the one and less to do with the other. The President appoints with the sanction of the Senate, and cannot dismiss his advisers without legislative consent;[54] yet the ministers in reality serve, not the President, but Congress, and Congress can neither appoint nor dismiss. In other words, the President must in both acts take the initiative, though he is not the real master; and Congress, which is the real master, has in these vital matters only a consultative voice, which it may utter, through its upper chamber, only when its opinion is asked. I should regard my business as a hopeless undertaking if my chief agent had to be appointed by a third party, and, besides being himself put beyond my power of control, were charged with the choice and discipline of all his subordinates, subject not to my directions, but simply to my acquiescence!

The relations existing between Congress and the departments must be fatally demoralizing to both. There is and can be between them nothing like confidential and thorough coöperation. The departments may be excused for that attitude of hostility which they sometimes assume towards Congress, because it is quite human for the servant to fear and deceive the master whom he does not regard as his friend, but suspects of being a distrustful spy of his movements. Congress cannot control the officers of the executive without disgracing them. Its only whip is investigation, semi-judicial examination into corners suspected to be dirty. It must draw the public eye by openly avowing a suspicion of malfeasance, and must then magnify and intensify the scandal by setting its Committees to cross-examining scared subordinates and sulky ministers. And after all is over and the murder out, probably nothing is done. The offenders, if any one has offended, often remain in office, shamed before the world, and ruined in the estimation of all honest people, but still drawing their salaries and comfortably waiting for the short memory of the public mind to forget them. Why unearth the carcass if you cannot remove it?

Then, too, the departments frequently complain of the incessant exactions made upon them by Congress. They grumble that they are kept busy in satisfying its curiosity and in meeting the demands of its uneasy activity. The clerks have ordinarily as much as they can do in keeping afoot the usual routine business of their departments; but Congress is continually calling upon them for information which must be laboriously collected from all sorts of sources, remote and accessible. A great speech in the Senate may cost them hours of anxious toil: for the Senator who makes it is quite likely beforehand to introduce a resolution calling upon one of the Secretaries for full statistics with reference to this, that, or the other topic upon which he desires to speak. If it be finance, he must have comparative tables of taxation; if it be commerce or the tariff, he cannot dispense with any of the minutest figures of the Treasury accounts; whatever be his theme, he cannot lay his foundations more surely than upon official information, and the Senate is usually unhesitatingly ready with an easy assent to the resolution which puts the whole clerical force of the administration at his service. And of course the House too asks innumerable questions, which patient clerks and protesting Secretaries must answer to the last and most minute particular. This is what the departmental officials testily call the tyranny of Congress, and no impartial third person can reasonably forbid them the use of the word.

I know of few things harder to state clearly and within reasonable compass than just how the nation keeps control of policy in spite of these hide-and-seek vagaries of authority. Indeed, it is doubtful if it does keep control through all the roundabout paths which legislative and executive responsibility are permitted to take. It must follow Congress somewhat blindly; Congress is known to obey without altogether understanding its Committees: and the Committees must consign the execution of their plans to officials who have opportunities not a few to hoodwink them. At the end of these blind processes is it probable that the ultimate authority, the people, is quite clear in its mind as to what has been done or what may be done another time? Take, for example, financial policy,—a very fair example, because, as I have shown, the legislative stages of financial policy are more talked about than any other congressional business, though for that reason an extreme example. If, after appropriations and adjustments of taxation have been tardily and in much tribulation of scheming and argument agreed upon by the House, the imperative suggestions and stubborn insistence of the Senate confuse matters till hardly the Conference Committees themselves know clearly what the outcome of the disagreements has been; and if, when these compromise measures are launched as laws, the method of their execution is beyond the view of the Houses, in the semi-privacy of the departments, how is the comprehension-not to speak of the will-of the people to keep any sort of hold upon the course of affairs? There are no screws of responsibility which they can turn upon the consciences or upon the official thumbs of the congressional Committees principally concerned. Congressional Committees are nothing to the nation: they are only pieces of the interior mechanism of Congress. To Congress they stand or fall. And, since Congress itself can scarcely be sure of having its own way with them, the constituencies are manifestly unlikely to be able to govern them. As for the departments, the people can hardly do more in drilling them to unquestioning obedience and docile efficiency than Congress can. Congress is, and must be, in these matters the nation's eyes and voice. If it cannot see what goes wrong and cannot get itself heeded when it commands, the nation likewise is both blind and dumb.

This, plainly put, is the practical result of the piecing of authority, the cutting of it up into small bits, which is contrived in our constitutional system. Each branch of the government is fitted out with a small section of responsibility, whose limited opportunities afford to the conscience of each many easy escapes. Every suspected culprit may shift the responsibility upon his fellows. Is Congress rated for corrupt or imperfect or foolish legislation? It may urge that it has to follow hastily its Committees or do nothing at all but talk; how can it help it if a stupid Committee leads it unawares into unjust or fatuous enterprises? Does administration blunder and run itself into all sorts of straits? The Secretaries hasten to plead the unreasonable or unwise commands of Congress, and Congress falls to blaming the Secretaries. The Secretaries aver that the whole mischief might have been avoided if they had only been allowed to suggest the proper measures; and the men who framed the existing measures in their turn avow their despair of good government so long as they must intrust all their plans to the bungling incompetence of men who are appointed by and responsible to somebody else. How is the schoolmaster, the nation, to know which boy needs the whipping?

Moreover, it is impossible to deny that this division of authority and concealment of responsibility are calculated to subject the government to a very distressing paralysis in moments of emergency. There are few, if any, important steps that can be taken by any one branch of the government without the consent or coöperation of some other branch. Congress must act through the President and his Cabinet; the President and his Cabinet must wait upon the will of Congress. There is no one supreme, ultimate head-whether magistrate or representative body-which can decide at once and with conclusive authority what shall be done at those times when some decision there must be, and that immediately. Of course this lack is of a sort to be felt at all times, in seasons of tranquil rounds of business as well as at moments of sharp crisis; but in times of sudden exigency it might prove fatal, —fatal either in breaking down the system or in failing to meet the emergency.[55] Policy cannot be either prompt or straightforward when it must serve many masters. It must either equivocate, or hesitate, or fail altogether. It may set out with clear purpose from Congress, but get waylaid or maimed by the Executive.

If there be one principle clearer than another, it is this: that in any business, whether of government or of mere merchandising, *somebody must be trusted*, in order that when things go wrong it may be quite plain who should be punished. In order to drive trade at the speed and with the success you desire, you must confide without suspicion in your chief clerk, giving him the power to ruin you, because you thereby furnish him with a motive for serving you. His reputation, his own honor or disgrace, all his own commercial prospects, hang upon your success. And human nature is much the same in government as in the dry-goods trade. *Power and strict accountability for its use* are the essential constituents of good government. A sense of highest responsibility, a dignifying and elevating sense of being trusted, together with a consciousness of being in an official station so conspicuous that no faithful discharge of duty can go unacknowledged and unrewarded, and no breach of trust undiscovered and unpunished, — these are the influences, the only influences, which foster practical, energetic, and trustworthy statesmanship. The best rulers are always those to whom great power is intrusted in such a manner as to make them feel that they will surely be abundantly honored and recompensed for a just and patriotic use of it, and to make them know that nothing can shield them from full retribution for every abuse of it.

It is, therefore, manifestly a radical defect in our federal system that it parcels out power and confuses responsibility as it does. The main purpose of the Convention of 1787 seems to have been to accomplish this grievous mistake. The "literary theory" of checks and balances is simply a consistent account of what our constitution-makers tried to do; and those checks and balances have proved mischievous just to the extent to which they have succeeded in establishing themselves as realities. It is quite safe to say that were it possible to call together again the members of that wonderful Convention to view the work of their hands in the light of the century that has tested it, they would be the first to admit that the only fruit of dividing power had been to make it irresponsible. It is just this that has made civil service reform tarry in this country and that makes it still almost doubtful of issue. We are in just the case that England was in before she achieved the reform for which we are striving. The date of the reform in England is no less significant than the fact. It was not accomplished until a distinct responsibility of the Ministers of the Crown to one, and to only one, master had been established beyond all uncertainty. This is the most striking and suggestive lesson to be gathered from Mr. Eaton's interesting and valuable history of Civil Service in Great Britain. The Reform was originated in 1853 by the Cabinet of Lord Aberdeen. It sprang from the suggestion of the appointing officers, and was carried through in the face of opposition from the House of Commons, because, paradoxically enough, the Ministry had at last come to feel their responsibility to the Commons, or rather to the nation whom the Commons represented.

Those great improvements which have been made in the public service of the British empire since the days of Walpole and Newcastle have gone hand in hand with the perfecting of the system now known as responsible Cabinet government. That system was slow in coming to perfection. It was not till long after Walpole's day that unity of responsibility on the part of the Cabinet-and that singleness of responsibility which made them look only to the Commons for authority-came to be recognized as an established constitutional principle. "As a consequence of the earlier practice of constructing Cabinets of men of different political views, it followed that the members of such Cabinets did not and could not regard their responsibility to Parliament as one and indivisible. The resignation of an important member, or even of the Prime Minister, was not regarded as necessitating the simultaneous retirement of his colleagues. Even so late as the fall of Sir Robert Walpole, fifty years after the Revolution Settlement (and itself the first instance of resignation in deference to a hostile parliamentary vote) we find the King requesting Walpole's successor, Pulteney, 'not to distress the Government by making too many changes in the midst of a session;' and Pulteney replying that he would be satisfied, provided 'the main forts of the Government,' or, in other words, the principal offices of state, were placed in his hands. It was not till the displacement of Lord North's ministry by that of Lord Rockingham in 1782 that a whole administration, with the exception of the Lord Chancellor, was changed by a vote of want of confidence passed in the House of Commons. Thenceforth, however, the resignation of the head of a Government in deference to an adverse vote of the popular chamber has invariably been accompanied by the resignation of all his colleagues."[56] But, even after the establishment of that precedent, it was still many years before Cabinets were free to please none but the Commons,—free to follow their own policies without authoritative suggestion from the sovereign. Until the death of the fourth George they were made to feel that they owed a double allegiance: to the Commons and to the King. The composition of Ministries still depended largely on the royal whim, and their actions were hampered by the necessity of steering a careful middle course between the displeasure of parliament and the ill-will of His Majesty. The present century had run far on towards the reign of Victoria before they were free to pay undivided obedience to the representatives of the people. When once they had become responsible to the Commons alone, however, and almost as soon as they were assured of their new position as the servants of the nation, they were prompted to even hazardous efforts for the reform of the civil service. They were conscious that the entire weight and responsibility of government rested upon their shoulders, and, as men regardful of the interests of the party which they represented, jealous for the preservation of their own fair names, and anxious, consequently, for the promotion of wise rule, they were naturally and of course the first to advocate a better system of appointment to that service whose chiefs they were recognized to be. They were prompt to declare that it was the "duty of the executive to provide for the efficient and harmonious working of the civil service," and that they could not "transfer that duty to any other body far less competent than themselves without infringing a great and important constitutional principle, already too often infringed, to the great detriment of the public service." They therefore determined themselves to inaugurate the merit-system without waiting for the assent of parliament, by simply surrendering their power of appointment in the various departments to a non-partisan examining board, trusting to the power of public opinion to induce parliament, after the thing had been done, to vote sufficient money to put the scheme into successful operation. And they did not reckon without their host. Reluctant as the members of the House of Commons were to resign that control of the national patronage which they had from time immemorial been accustomed to exercise by means of various crooked indirections, and which it had been their pleasure and their power to possess, they had not the face to avow their suspicious unwillingness in answer to the honorable call of a trusted Ministry who were supported in their demand by all that was honest in public sentiment, and the world was afforded the gratifying but unwonted spectacle of party leaders sacrificing to the cause of good government, freely and altogether of their own accord, the "spoils" of office so long dear to the party and to the assembly which they represented and served.

In this country the course of the reform was quite the reverse. Neither the Executive nor Congress began it. The call for it came imperatively from the people; it was a formulated demand of public opinion made upon Congress, and it had to be made again and again, each time with more determined emphasis, before Congress heeded. It worked its way up from the convictions of the many to the purposes of the few. Amongst the chief difficulties that have stood in its way, and which still block its perfect realization, is that peculiarity of structure which I have just now pointed out as intrinsic in the scheme of divided power which runs through the Constitution. One of the conditions precedent to any real and lasting reform of the civil service, in a country whose public service is moulded by the conditions of self-government, is the drawing of a sharp line of distinction between those offices which are political and those which are *non*-political. The strictest rules of business discipline, of merit-tenure and earned promotion, must rule every office whose incumbent has naught to do with choosing between policies; but no rules except the choice of parties can or should make and unmake, reward or punish, those officers whose privilege it is to fix upon the political purposes which administration shall be made to serve. These latter are not many under any form of government. There are said to be but fifty such at most in the civil service of Great Britain; but these fifty go in or out as the balance of power shifts from party to party. In the case of our own civil service it would, I take it, be extremely hard to determine where the line should be drawn. In all the higher grades this particular distinction is quite obscured. A doubt exists as to the Cabinet itself. Are the Secretaries political or non-political officers? It would seem that they are exclusively neither. They are at least semi-political. They are, on the one hand, merely the servants of Congress, and yet, on the other hand, they have enough freedom of discretion to mar and color, if not to choose, political ends. They can wreck plans, if they cannot make them. Should they be made permanent officials because they are mere Secretaries, or should their tenure depend upon the fortunes of parties because they have many chances to render party services? And if the one rule or the other is to be applied to them, to how many, and to which of their chief subordinates, is it to be extended? If they are not properly or necessarily party men, let them pass the examinations and run the gauntlet of the usual tests of efficiency, let errand-boys work up to Secretary-ships; but if not, let their responsibility to their party be made strict and determinate. That is the cardinal point of practical civil service reform.

This doubt as to the exact *status* in the system of the chief ministers of state is a most striking commentary on the system itself. Its complete self is logical and simple. But its complete self exists only in theory. Its real self offers a surprise and presents a mystery at every change of view. The practical observer who seeks for facts and actual conditions of organization is often sorely puzzled to come at the real methods of government. Pitfalls await him on every side. If constitutional lawyers of strait-laced consciences filled Congress and officered the departments, every clause of the Constitution would be accorded a formal obedience, and it would be as easy to know beforehand just what the government will be like inside to-morrow as it is now to know what it was like outside yesterday. But neither the knowledge nor the consciences of politicians keep them very close to the Constitution; and it is with politicians that we have to deal nowadays in studying the government. Every government is largely what the men are who constitute it. If the character or opinions of legislators and administrators change from time to time, the nature of the government changes with them; and as both their characters and their opinions do change very often it is very hard to make a picture of the government which can be said to have been perfectly faithful yesterday, and can be confidently expected to be exactly accurate to-morrow. Add to these embarrassments, which may be called the embarrassments of human nature, other embarrassments such as our system affords, the embarrassments of subtle legal distinctions, a fine theoretical plan made in delicate hair-lines, requirements of law which can hardly be met and can easily and naturally be evaded or disregarded, and you have in full the conception of the difficulties which attend a practical exposition of the real facts of federal administration. It is not impossible to point out what the Executive was intended to be, what it has sometimes been, or what it might be; nor is it forbidden the diligent to discover the main conditions which mould it to the forms of congressional supremacy; but more than this is not to be expected.

VI
Conclusion.

> Political philosophy must analyze political history; it must distinguish what is due to the excellence of the people, and what to the excellence of the laws; it must carefully calculate the exact effect of each part of the constitution, though thus it may destroy many an idol of the multitude, and detect the secret of utility where but few imagined it to lie. —BAGEHOT.

Congress always makes what haste it can to legislate. It is the prime object of its rules to expedite law-making. Its customs are fruits of its characteristic diligence in enactment. Be the matters small or great, frivolous or grave, which busy it, its aim is to have laws always a-making. Its temper is strenuously legislative. That it cannot regulate all the questions to which its attention is weekly invited is its misfortune, not its fault; is due to the human limitation of its faculties, not to any narrow circumscription of its desires. If its committee machinery is inadequate to the task of bringing to action more than one out of every hundred of the bills introduced, it is not because the quick clearance of the docket is not the motive of its organic life. If legislation, therefore, were the only or the chief object for which it should live, it would not be possible to withhold admiration from those clever hurrying rules and those inexorable customs which seek to facilitate it. Nothing but a doubt as to whether or not Congress should confine itself to law-making can challenge with a question the utility of its organization as a facile statute-devising machine.

The political philosopher of these days of self-government has, however, something more than a doubt with which to gainsay the usefulness of a sovereign representative body which confines itself to legislation to the exclusion of all other functions. Buckle declared, indeed, that the chief use and value of legislation nowadays lay in its opportunity and power to remedy the mistakes of the legislation of the past; that it was beneficent only when it carried healing in its wings; that repeal was more blessed than enactment. And it is certainly true that the greater part of the labor of legislation consists in carrying the loads recklessly or bravely shouldered in times gone by, when the animal which is now a bull was only a calf, and in completing, if they may be completed, the tasks once undertaken in the shape of unambitious schemes which at the outset looked innocent enough. Having got his foot into it, the legislator finds it difficult, if not impossible, to get it out again. "The modern industrial organization, including banks, corporations, joint-stock companies, financial devices, national debts, paper currency, national systems of taxation, is largely the creation of legislation (not in its historical origin, but in the mode of its existence and in its authority), and is largely regulated by legislation. Capital is the breath of life to this organization, and every day, as the organization becomes more complex and delicate, the folly of assailing capital or credit becomes greater. At the same time it is evident that the task of the legislator to embrace in his view the whole system, to adjust his rules so that the play of the civil institutions shall not alter the play of the economic forces, requires more training and more acumen. Furthermore, the greater the complication and delicacy of the industrial system, the greater the chances for cupidity when backed by craft, and the task of the legislator to meet and defeat the attempts of this cupidity is one of constantly increasing difficulty."[57]

Legislation unquestionably generates legislation. Every statute may be said to have a long lineage of statutes behind it; and whether that lineage be honorable or of ill repute is as much a question as to each individual statute as it can be with regard to the ancestry of each individual legislator. Every statute in its turn has a numerous progeny, and only time and opportunity can decide whether its offspring will bring it honor or shame. Once begin the dance of legislation, and you must struggle through its mazes as best you can to its breathless end, —if any end there be.

It is not surprising, therefore, that the enacting, revising, tinkering, repealing of laws should engross the attention and engage the entire energy of such a body as Congress. It is, however, easy to see how it might be better employed; or, at least, how it might add others to this overshadowing function, to the infinite advantage of the government. Quite as important as legislation is vigilant oversight of administration; and even more important than legislation is the instruction and guidance in political affairs which the people might receive from a body which kept all national concerns suffused in a broad daylight of discussion. There is no similar legislature in existence which is so shut up to the one business of law-making as is our Congress. As I have said, it in a way superintends administration by the exercise of semi-judicial powers of investigation, whose limitations and insufficiency are manifest. But other national legislatures command administration and verify their name of "parliaments" by talking official acts into notoriety. Our extra-constitutional party conventions, short-lived and poor in power as they are, constitute our only machinery for that sort of control of the executive which consists in the award of personal rewards and punishments. This is the cardinal fact which differentiates Congress from the Chamber of Deputies and from Parliament, and which puts it beyond the reach of those eminently useful functions whose exercise would so raise it in usefulness and in dignity.

An effective representative body, gifted with the power to rule, ought, it would seem, not only to speak the will of the nation, which Congress does, but also to lead it to its conclusions, to utter the voice of its opinions, and to serve as its eyes in superintending all matters of government, —which Congress does not do. The discussions which take place in Congress are aimed at random. They now and again strike rather sharply the tender spots in this, that, or the other measure; but, as I have said, no two measures consciously join in purpose or agree in character, and so debate must wander as widely as the subjects of debate. Since there is little coherency about the legislation agreed upon, there can be little coherency about the debates. There is no one policy to be attacked or defended, but only a score or two of separate bills. To attend to such discussions is uninteresting; to be instructed by them is impossible. There is some scandal and discomfort, but infinite advantage, in having every affair of administration subjected to the test of constant examination on the part of the assembly which represents the nation. The chief use of such inquisition is, not the direction of those affairs in a way with which the country will be satisfied (though that itself is of course all-important), but the enlightenment of the people, which is always its sure consequence. Very few men are unequal to a danger which they see and understand; all men quail before a threatening which is dark and unintelligible, and suspect what is done behind a screen. If the people could have, through Congress, daily knowledge of all the more important transactions of the governmental offices, an insight into all that now seems withheld and private, their confidence in the executive, now so often shaken, would, I think, be very soon established. Because dishonesty can lurk under the privacies now vouchsafed our administrative agents, much that is upright and pure suffers unjust suspicion. Discoveries of guilt in a bureau cloud with doubts the trustworthiness of a department. As nothing is open enough for the quick and easy detection of peculation or fraud, so nothing is open enough for the due vindication and acknowledgment of honesty. The isolation and privacy which shield the one from discovery cheat the other of reward.

Inquisitiveness is never so forward, enterprising, and irrepressible as in a popular assembly which is given leave to ask questions and is afforded ready and abundant means of getting its questions answered. No cross-examination is more searching than that to which a minister of the Crown is subjected by the all-curious Commons. "Sir Robert Peel once asked to have a number of questions carefully written down which they asked him one day in succession in the House of Commons. They seemed a list of everything that could occur in the British empire or to the brain of a member of parliament."[58] If one considered only the wear and tear upon ministers of state, which the plague of constant interrogation must inflict, he could wish that their lives, if useful, might be spared this blight of unending explanation; but no one can overestimate the immense advantage of a facility so unlimited for knowing all that is going on in the places where authority lives. The conscience of every member of the representative body is at the service of the nation. All that he feels bound to know he can find out; and what he finds out goes to the ears of the country. The question is his, the answer the nation's. And the inquisitiveness of such bodies as Congress is the best conceivable source of information. Congress is the only body which has the proper motive for inquiry, and it is the only body which has the power to act effectively upon the knowledge which its inquiries secure. The Press is merely curious or merely partisan. The people are scattered and unorganized. But Congress is, as it were, the corporate people, the mouthpiece of its will. It is a sovereign delegation which could ask questions with dignity, because with authority and with power to act.

Congress is fast becoming the governing body of the nation, and yet the only power which it possesses in perfection is the power which is but a part of government, the power of legislation. Legislation is but the oil of government. It is that which lubricates its channels and speeds its wheels; that which lessens the friction and so eases the movement. Or perhaps I shall be admitted to have hit upon a closer and apter analogy if I say that legislation is like a foreman set over the forces of government. It issues the orders which others obey. It directs, it admonishes, but it does not do the actual heavy work of governing. A good foreman does, it is true, himself take a hand in the work which he guides; and so I suppose our legislation must be likened to a poor foreman, because it stands altogether apart from that work which it is set to see well done. Members of Congress ought not to be censured too severely, however, when they fail to check evil courses on the part of the executive. They have been denied the means of doing so promptly and with effect. Whatever intention may have controlled the compromises of constitution-making in 1787, their result was to give us, not government by discussion, which is the only tolerable sort of government for a people which tries to do its own governing, but only *legislation* by discussion, which is no more than a small part of government by discussion. What is quite as indispensable as the debate of problems of legislation is the debate of all matters of administration. It is even more important to know how the house is being built than to know how the plans of the architect were conceived and how his specifications were calculated. It is better to have skillful work-stout walls, reliable arches, unbending rafters, and windows sure to "expel the winter's flaw" —than a drawing on paper which is the admiration of all the practical artists in the country. The discipline of an army depends quite as much upon the temper of the troops as upon the orders of the day.

It is the proper duty of a representative body to look diligently into every affair of government and to talk much about what it sees. It is meant to be the eyes and the voice, and to embody the wisdom and will of its constituents. Unless Congress have and use every means of acquainting itself with the acts and the disposition of the administrative agents of the government, the country must be helpless to learn how it is being served; and unless Congress both scrutinize these things and sift them by every form of discussion, the country must remain in embarrassing, crippling ignorance of the very affairs which it is most important that it should understand and direct. The informing function of Congress should be preferred even to its legislative function. The argument is not only that discussed and interrogated administration is the only pure and efficient administration, but, more than that, that the only really self-governing people is that people which discusses and interrogates its administration. The talk on the part of Congress which we sometimes justly condemn is the profitless squabble of words over frivolous bills or selfish party issues. It would be hard to conceive of there being too much talk about the practical concerns and processes of government. Such talk it is which, when earnestly and purposefully conducted, clears the public mind and shapes the demands of public opinion.

Congress could not be too diligent about such talking; whereas it may easily be too diligent in legislation. It often overdoes that business. It already sends to its Committees bills too many by the thousand to be given even a hasty thought; but its immense committee facilities and the absence of all other duties but that of legislation make it omnivorous in its appetite for new subjects for consideration. It is greedy to have a taste of every possible dish that may be put upon its table, as an "extra" to the constitutional bill of fare. This disposition on its part is the more notable because there is certainly less need for it to hurry and overwork itself at law-making than exists in the case of most other great national legislatures. It is not state and national legislature combined, as are the Commons of England and the Chambers of France. Like the Reichstag of our cousin Germans, it is restricted to subjects of imperial scope. Its thoughts are meant to be kept for national interests. Its time is spared the waste of attention to local affairs. It is even forbidden the vast domain of the laws of property, of commercial dealing, and of ordinary crime. And even in the matter of caring for national interests the way has from the first been made plain and easy for it. There are no clogging feudal institutions to embarrass it. There is no long-continued practice of legal or of royal tyranny for it to cure, —no clearing away of old débris of any sort to delay it in its exercise of a common-sense dominion over a thoroughly modern and progressive nation. It is easy to believe that its legislative purposes might be most fortunately clarified and simplified, were it to square them by a conscientious attention to the paramount and controlling duty of understanding, discussing, and directing administration.

If the people's authorized representatives do not take upon themselves this duty, and by identifying themselves with the actual work of government stand between it and irresponsible, half-informed criticism, to what harassments is the executive not exposed? Led and checked by Congress, the prurient and fearless, because anonymous, animadversions of the Press, now so often premature and inconsiderate, might be disciplined into serviceable capacity to interpret and judge. Its energy and sagacity might be tempered by discretion, and strengthened by knowledge. One of our chief constitutional difficulties is that, in opportunities for informing and guiding public opinion, the freedom of the Press is greater than the freedom of Congress. It is as if newspapers, instead of the board of directors, were the sources of information for the stockholders of a corporation. We look into correspondents' letters instead of into the Congressional Record to find out what is a-doing and a-planning in the departments. Congress is altogether excluded from the arrangement by which the Press declares what the executive is, and conventions of the national parties decide what the executive shall be. Editors are self-constituted our guides, and caucus delegates our government directors.

Since all this curious scattering of functions and contrivance of frail, extra-constitutional machinery of government is the result of that entire separation of the legislative and executive branches of the system which is with us so characteristically and essentially constitutional, it is exceedingly interesting to inquire and important to understand how that separation came to be insisted upon in the making of the Constitution. Alexander Hamilton has in our own times, as well as before, been "severely reproached with having said that the British government was the 'best model in existence.' In 1787 this was a mere truism. However much the men of that day differed they were all agreed in despising and distrusting *a priori* constitutions and ideally perfect governments, fresh from the brains of visionary enthusiasts, such as sprang up rankly in the soil of the French revolution. The Convention of 1787 was composed of very able men of the English-speaking race. They took the system of government with which they had been familiar, improved it, adapted it to the circumstances with which they had to deal, and put it into successful operation. Hamilton's plan, then, like the others, was on the British model, and it did not differ essentially in details from that finally adopted."[59] It is needful, however, to remember in this connection what has already been alluded to, that when that convention was copying the English Constitution, that Constitution was in a stage of transition, and had by no means fully developed the features which are now recognized as most characteristic of it. Mr. Lodge is quite right in saying that the Convention, in adapting, improved upon the English Constitution with which its members were familiar, —the Constitution of George III. and Lord North, the Constitution which had failed to crush Bute. It could hardly be said with equal confidence, however, that our system as then made was an improvement upon that scheme of responsible cabinet government which challenges the admiration of the world to-day, though it was quite plainly a marked advance upon a parliament of royal nominees and pensionaries and a secret cabinet of "king's friends." The English constitution of that day had a great many features which did not invite republican imitation. It was suspected, if not known, that the ministers who sat in parliament were little more than the tools of a ministry of royal favorites who were kept out of sight behind the strictest confidences of the court. It was notorious that the subservient parliaments of the day represented the estates and the money of the peers and the influence of the King rather than the intelligence and purpose of the nation. The whole "form and pressure" of the time illustrated only too forcibly Lord Bute's sinister suggestion, that "the forms of a free and the ends of an arbitrary government are things not altogether incompatible." It was, therefore, perfectly natural that the warnings to be so easily drawn from the sight of a despotic monarch binding the usages and privileges of self-government to the service of his own intemperate purposes should be given grave heed by Americans, who were the very persons who had suffered most from the existing abuses. It was something more than natural that the Convention of 1787 should desire to erect a Congress which would not be subservient and an executive which could not be despotic. And it was equally to have been expected that they should regard an absolute separation of these two great branches of the system as the only effectual means for the accomplishment of that much desired end. It was impossible that they could believe that executive and legislature could be brought into close relations of coöperation and mutual confidence without being tempted, nay, even bidden, to collude. How could either maintain its independence of action unless each were to have the guaranty of the Constitution that its own domain should be absolutely safe from invasion, its own prerogatives absolutely free from challenge? "They shrank from placing sovereign power anywhere. They feared that it would generate tyranny; George III. had been a tyrant to them, and come what might they would not make a George III."[60] They would conquer, by dividing, the power they so much feared to see in any single hand.

"The English Constitution, in a word," says our most astute English critic, "is framed on the principle of choosing a single sovereign authority, and making it good; the American, upon the principle of having many sovereign authorities, and hoping that their multitude may atone for their inferiority. The Americans now extol their institutions, and so defraud themselves of their due praise. But if they had not a genius for politics, if they had not a moderation in action singularly curious where superficial speech is so violent, if they had not a regard for law, such as no great people have ever evinced, and infinitely surpassing ours, the multiplicity of authorities in the American Constitution would long ago have brought it to a bad end. Sensible shareholders, I have heard a shrewd attorney say, can work *any* deed of settlement; and so the men of Massachusetts could, I believe, work *any* constitution."[61] It is not necessary to assent to Mr. Bagehot's strictures; but it is not possible to deny the clear-sighted justice of this criticism. In order to be fair to the memory of our great constitution-makers, however, it is necessary to remember that when they sat in convention in Philadelphia the English Constitution, which they copied, was not the simple system which was before Mr. Bagehot's eyes when he wrote. Its single sovereign authority was not then a twice-reformed House of Commons truly representative of the nation and readily obeyed by a responsible Ministry. The sovereignty was at see-saw between the throne and the parliament,—and the throne-end of the beam was generally uppermost. Our device of separated, individualized powers was very much better than a nominal sovereignty of the Commons which was suffered to be overridden by force, fraud, or craft, by the real sovereignty of the King. The English Constitution was at that time in reality much worse than our own; and, if it is now superior, it is so because its growth has not been hindered or destroyed by the too tight ligaments of a written fundamental law.

The natural, the inevitable tendency of every system of self-government like our own and the British is to exalt the representative body, the people's parliament, to a position of absolute supremacy. That tendency has, I think, been quite as marked in our own constitutional history as in that of any other country, though its power has been to some extent neutralized, and its progress in great part stayed, by those denials of that supremacy which we respect because they are written in our law. The political law written in our hearts is here at variance with that which the Constitution sought to establish. A written constitution may and often will be violated in both letter and spirit by a people of energetic political talents and a keen instinct for progressive practical development; but so long as they adhere to the forms of such a constitution, so long as the machinery of government supplied by it is the only machinery which the legal and moral sense of such a people permits it to use, its political development must be in many directions narrowly restricted because of an insuperable lack of open or adequate channels. Our Constitution, like every other constitution which puts the authority to make laws and the duty of controlling the public expenditure into the hands of a popular assembly, practically sets that assembly to rule the affairs of the nation as supreme overlord. But, by separating it entirely from its executive agencies, it deprives it of the opportunity and means for making its authority complete and convenient. The constitutional machinery is left of such a pattern that other forces less than that of Congress may cross and compete with Congress, though they are too small to overcome or long offset it; and the result is simply an unpleasant, wearing friction which, with other adjustments, more felicitous and equally safe, might readily be avoided.

Congress, consequently, is still lingering and chafing under just such embarrassments as made the English Commons a nuisance both to themselves and to everybody else immediately after the Revolution Settlement had given them their first sure promise of supremacy. The parallel is startlingly exact. "In outer seeming the Revolution of 1688 had only transferred the sovereignty over England from James to William and Mary. In actual fact it had given a powerful and decisive impulse to the great constitutional progress which was transferring the sovereignty from the King to the House of Commons. From the moment when its sole right to tax the nation was established by the Bill of Rights, and when its own resolve settled the practice of granting none but annual supplies to the Crown, the House of Commons became the supreme power in the State....But though the constitutional change was complete, the machinery of government was far from having adapted itself to the new conditions of political life which such a change brought about. However powerful the will of the Commons might be, it had no means of bringing its will directly to bear on the control of public affairs. The ministers who had charge of them were not its servants but the servants of the Crown; it was from the King that they looked for direction, and to the King that they held themselves responsible. By impeachment or more indirect means the Commons could force a king to remove a minister who contradicted their will; but they had no constitutional power to replace the fallen statesman by a minister who would carry out their will.

"The result was the growth of a temper in the Lower House which drove William and his ministers to despair. It became as corrupt, as jealous of power, as fickle in its resolves and factious in its spirit as bodies always become whose consciousness of the possession of power is untempered by a corresponding consciousness of the practical difficulties or the moral responsibilities of the power which they possess. It grumbled ...and it blamed the Crown and its ministers for all at which it grumbled. But it was hard to find out what policy or measures it would have preferred. Its mood changed, as William bitterly complained, with every hour....The Houses were in fact without the guidance of recognized leaders, without adequate information, and destitute of that organization out of which alone a definite policy can come."[62]

The cure for this state of things which Sunderland had the sagacity to suggest, and William the wisdom to apply, was the mediation between King and Commons of a cabinet representative of the majority of the popular chamber, —a first but long and decisive step towards responsible cabinet government. Whether a similar remedy would be possible or desirable in our own case it is altogether aside from my present purpose to inquire. I am pointing out facts, —diagnosing, not prescribing remedies. My only point just now is, that no one can help being struck by the closeness of the likeness between the incipient distempers of the first parliaments of William and Mary and the developed disorders now so plainly discernible in the constitution of Congress. Though honest and diligent, it is meddlesome and inefficient; and it is meddlesome and inefficient for exactly the same reasons that made it natural that the post-Revolutionary parliaments should exhibit like clumsiness and like temper: namely, because it is "without the guidance of recognized leaders, without adequate information, and destitute of that organization out of which alone a definite policy can come."

The dangers of this serious imperfection in our governmental machinery have not been clearly demonstrated in our experience hitherto; but now their delayed fulfillment seems to be close at hand. The plain tendency is towards a centralization of all the greater powers of government in the hands of the federal authorities, and towards the practical confirmation of those prerogatives of supreme overlordship which Congress has been gradually arrogating to itself. The central government is constantly becoming stronger and more active, and Congress is establishing itself as the one sovereign authority in that government. In constitutional theory and in the broader features of past practice, ours has been what Mr. Bagehot has called a "composite" government. Besides state and federal authorities to dispute as to sovereignty, there have been within the federal system itself rival and irreconcilable powers. But gradually the strong are overcoming the weak. If the signs of the times are to be credited, we are fast approaching an adjustment of sovereignty quite as "simple" as need be. Congress is not only to retain the authority it already possesses, but is to be brought again and again face to face with still greater demands upon its energy, its wisdom, and its conscience, is to have ever-widening duties and responsibilities thrust upon it, without being granted a moment's opportunity to look back from the plough to which it has set its hands.

The sphere and influence of national administration and national legislation are widening rapidly. Our populations are growing at such a rate that one's reckoning staggers at counting the possible millions that may have a home and a work on this continent ere fifty more years shall have filled their short span. The East will not always be the centre of national life. The South is fast accumulating wealth, and will faster recover influence. The West has already achieved a greatness which no man can gainsay, and has in store a power of future growth which no man can estimate. Whether these sections are to be harmonious or dissentient depends almost entirely upon the methods and policy of the federal government. If that government be not careful to keep within its own proper sphere and prudent to square its policy by rules of national welfare, sectional lines must and will be known; citizens of one part of the country may look with jealousy and even with hatred upon their fellow-citizens of another part; and faction must tear and dissension distract a country which Providence would bless, but which man may curse. The government of a country so vast and various must be strong, prompt, wieldy, and efficient. Its strength must consist in the certainty and uniformity of its purposes, in its accord with national sentiment, in its unhesitating action, and in its honest aims. It must be steadied and approved by open administration diligently obedient to the more permanent judgments of public opinion; and its only active agency, its representative chambers, must be equipped with something besides abundant powers of legislation.

As at present constituted, the federal government lacks strength because its powers are divided, lacks promptness because its authorities are multiplied, lacks wieldiness because its processes are roundabout, lacks efficiency because its responsibility is indistinct and its action without competent direction. It is a government in which every officer may talk about every other officer's duty without having to render strict account for not doing his own, and in which the masters are held in check and offered contradiction by the servants. Mr. Lowell has called it "government by declamation." Talk is not sobered by any necessity imposed upon those who utter it to suit their actions to their words. There is no day of reckoning for words spoken. The speakers of a congressional majority may, without risk of incurring ridicule or discredit, condemn what their own Committees are doing; and the spokesmen of a minority may urge what contrary courses they please with a well-grounded assurance that what they say will be forgotten before they can be called upon to put it into practice. Nobody stands sponsor for the policy of the government. A dozen men originate it; a dozen compromises twist and alter it; a dozen offices whose names are scarcely known outside of Washington put it into execution.

This is the defect to which, it will be observed, I am constantly recurring; to which I recur again and again because every examination of the system, at whatsoever point begun, leads inevitably to it as to a central secret. It is the defect which interprets all the rest, because it is their common product. It is exemplified in the extraordinary fact that the utterances of the Press have greater weight and are accorded greater credit, though the Press speaks entirely without authority, than the utterances of Congress, though Congress possesses all authority. The gossip of the street is listened to rather than the words of the law-makers. The editor directs public opinion, the congressman obeys it. When a presidential election is at hand, indeed, the words of the political orator gain temporary heed. He is recognized as an authority in the arena, as a professional critic competent to discuss the good and bad points, and to forecast the fortunes of the contestants. There is something definite in hand, and he is known to have studied all its bearings. He is one of the managers, or is thought to be well acquainted with the management. He speaks "from the card." But let him talk, not about candidates, but about measures or about the policy of the government, and his observations sink at once to the level of a mere individual expression of opinion, to which his political occupations seem to add very little weight. It is universally recognized that he speaks without authority, about things which his vote may help to settle, but about which several hundred other men have votes quite as influential as his own. Legislation is not a thing to be known beforehand. It depends upon the conclusions of sundry Standing Committees. It is an aggregate, not a simple, production. It is impossible to tell how many persons' opinions and influences have entered into its composition. It is even impracticable to determine from this year's law-making what next year's will be like.

Speaking, therefore, without authority, the political orator speaks to little purpose when he speaks about legislation. The papers do not report him carefully; and their editorials seldom take any color from his arguments. The Press, being anonymous and representing a large force of inquisitive news-hunters, is much more powerful than he chiefly because it *is* impersonal and seems to represent a wider and more thorough range of information. At the worst, it can easily compete with any ordinary individual. Its individual opinion is quite sure to be esteemed as worthy of attention as any other individual opinion. And, besides, it is almost everywhere strong enough to deny currency to the speeches of individuals whom it does not care to report. It goes to its audience; the orator must depend upon his audience coming to him. It can be heard at every fireside; the orator can be heard only on the platform or the hustings. There is no imperative demand on the part of the reading public in this country that the newspapers should report political speeches in full. On the contrary, most readers would be disgusted at finding their favorite columns so filled up. By giving even a notice of more than an item's length to such a speech, an editor runs the risk of being denounced as dull. And I believe that the position of the American Press is in this regard quite singular. The English newspapers are so far from being thus independent and self-sufficient powers, —a law unto themselves, —in the politics of the empire that they are constrained to do homage to the political orator whether they will or no. Conservative editors must spread before their readers *verbatim* reports not only of the speeches of the leaders of their own party, but also of the principal speeches of the leading Liberal orators; and Liberal journals have no choice but to print every syllable of the more important public utterances of the Conservative leaders. The nation insists upon knowing what its public men have to say, even when it is not so well said as the newspapers which report them could have said it.

There are only two things which can give any man a right to expect that when he speaks the whole country will listen: namely, genius and authority. Probably no one will ever contend that Sir Stafford Northcote was an orator, or even a good speaker. But by proof of unblemished character, and by assiduous, conscientious, and able public service he rose to be the recognized leader of his party in the House of Commons; and it is simply because he speaks as one having authority, —and not as the scribes of the Press, —that he is as sure of a heedful hearing as is Mr. Gladstone, who adds genius and noble oratory to the authority of established leadership. The leaders of English public life have something besides weight of character, prestige of personal service and experience, and authority of individual opinion to exalt them above the anonymous Press. They have definite authority and power in the actual control of government.

They are directly commissioned to control the policy of the administration. They stand before the country, in parliament and out of it, as the responsible chiefs of their parties. It is their business to lead those parties, and it is the matter-of-course custom of the constituencies to visit upon the parties the punishment due for the mistakes made by these chiefs. They are at once the servants and scapegoats of their parties.

It is these well-established privileges and responsibilities of theirs which make their utterances considered worth hearing, —nay, necessary to be heard and pondered. Their public speeches are their parties' platforms. What the leader promises his party stands ready to do, should it be intrusted with office. This certainty of audience and of credit gives spice to what such leaders have to say, and lends elevation to the tone of all their public utterances. They for the most part avoid buncombe, which would be difficult to translate into Acts of Parliament. It is easy to see how great an advantage their station and influence give them over our own public men. We have no such responsible party leadership on this side the sea; we are very shy about conferring much authority on anybody, and the consequence is that it requires something very like genius to secure for any one of our statesmen a universally recognized right to be heard and to create an ever-active desire to hear him whenever he talks, not about candidates, but about measures. An extraordinary gift of eloquence, such as not every generation may hope to see, will always hold, because it will always captivate, the attention of the people. But genius and eloquence are too rare to be depended upon for the instruction and guidance of the masses; and since our politicians lack the credit of authority and responsibility, they must give place, except at election-time, to the Press, which is everywhere, generally well-informed, and always talking. It is necessarily "government by declamation" and editorial-writing.

It is probably also this lack of leadership which gives to our national parties their curious, conglomerate character. It would seem to be scarcely an exaggeration to say that they are homogeneous only in name. Neither of the two principal parties is of one mind with itself. Each tolerates all sorts of difference of creed and variety of aim within its own ranks. Each pretends to the same purposes and permits among its partisans the same contradictions to those purposes. They are grouped around no legislative leaders whose capacity has been tested and to whose opinions they loyally adhere. They are like armies without officers, engaged upon a campaign which has no great cause at its back. Their names and traditions, not their hopes and policy, keep them together.

It is to this fact, as well as to short terms which allow little time for differences to come to a head, that the easy agreement of congressional majorities should be attributed. In other like assemblies the harmony of majorities is constantly liable to disturbance. Ministers lose their following and find their friends falling away in the midst of a session. But not so in Congress. There, although the majority is frequently simply conglomerate, made up of factions not a few, and bearing in its elements every seed of discord, the harmony of party voting seldom, if ever, suffers an interruption. So far as outsiders can see, legislation generally flows placidly on, and the majority easily has its own way, acting with a sort of matter-of-course unanimity, with no suspicion of individual freedom of action. Whatever revolts may be threatened or accomplished in the ranks of the party outside the House at the polls, its power is never broken inside the House. This is doubtless due in part to the fact that there is no freedom of debate in the House; but there can be no question that it is principally due to the fact that debate is without aim, just because legislation is without consistency. Legislation is conglomerate. The absence of any concert of action amongst the Committees leaves legislation with scarcely any trace of determinate party courses. No two schemes pull together. If there is a coincidence of principle between several bills of the same session, it is generally accidental; and the confusion of policy which prevents intelligent coöperation also, of course, prevents intelligent differences and divisions. There is never a transfer of power from one party to the other during a session, because such a transfer would mean almost nothing. The majority remains of one mind so long as a Congress lives, because its mind is very vaguely ascertained, and its power of planning a split consequently very limited. It has no common mind, and if it had, has not the machinery for changing it. It is led by a score or two of Committees whose composition must remain the same to the end; and who are too numerous, as well as too disconnected, to fight against. It stays on one side because it hardly knows where the boundaries of that side are or how to cross them.

Moreover, there is a certain well-known piece of congressional machinery long ago invented and applied for the special purpose of keeping both majority and minority compact. The legislative caucus has almost as important a part in our system as have the Standing Committees, and deserves as close study as they. Its functions are much more easily understood in all their bearings than those of the Committees, however, because they are much simpler. The caucus is meant as an antidote to the Committees. It is designed to supply the cohesive principle which the multiplicity and mutual independence of the Committees so powerfully tend to destroy. Having no Prime Minister to confer with about the policy of the government, as they see members of parliament doing, our congressmen confer with each other in caucus. Rather than imprudently expose to the world the differences of opinion threatened or developed among its members, each party hastens to remove disrupting debate from the floor of Congress, where the speakers might too hastily commit themselves to insubordination, to quiet conferences behind closed doors, where frightened scruples may be reassured and every disagreement healed with a salve of compromise or subdued with the whip of political expediency. The caucus is the drilling-ground of the party. There its discipline is renewed and strengthened, its uniformity of step and gesture regained. The voting and speaking in the House are generally merely the movements of a sort of dress parade, for which the exercises of the caucus are designed to prepare. It is easy to see how difficult it would be for the party to keep its head amidst the confused cross-movements of the Committees without thus now and again pulling itself together in caucus, where it can ask itself its own mind and pledge itself anew to eternal agreement.

The credit of inventing this device is probably due to the Democrats. They appear to have used it so early as the second session of the eighth Congress. Speaking of that session, a reliable authority says: "During this session of Congress there was far less of free and independent discussion on the measures proposed by the friends of the administration than had been previously practiced in both branches of the national legislature. It appeared that on the most important subjects, the course adopted by the majority was the effect of caucus arrangement, or, in other words, had been previously agreed upon at meetings of the Democratic members held in private. Thus the legislation of Congress was constantly swayed by a party following feelings and pledges rather than according to sound reason or personal conviction."[63] The censure implied in this last sentence may have seemed righteous at the time when such caucus pledges were in disfavor as new-fangled shackles, but it would hardly be accepted as just by the intensely practical politicians of to-day. They would probably prefer to put it thus: That the silvern speech spent in caucus secures the golden silence maintained on the floor of Congress, making each party rich in concord and happy in coöperation.

The fact that makes this defense of the caucus not altogether conclusive is that it is shielded from all responsibility by its sneaking privacy. It has great power without any balancing weight of accountability. Probably its debates would constitute interesting and instructive reading for the public, were they published; but they never get out except in rumors often rehearsed and as often amended. They are, one may take it for granted, much more candid and go much nearer the political heart of the questions discussed than anything that is ever said openly in Congress to the reporters' gallery. They approach matters without masks and handle them without gloves. It might hurt, but it would enlighten us to hear them. As it is, however, there is unhappily no ground for denying their power to override sound reason and personal conviction. The caucus cannot always silence or subdue a large and influential minority of dissentients, but its whip seldom fails to reduce individual malcontents and mutineers into submission. There is no place in congressional jousts for the free lance. The man who disobeys his party caucus is understood to disavow his party allegiance altogether, and to assume that dangerous neutrality which is so apt to degenerate into mere caprice, and which is almost sure to destroy his influence by bringing him under the suspicion of being unreliable, —a suspicion always conclusively damning in practical life. Any individual, or any minority of weak numbers or small influence, who has the temerity to neglect the decisions of the caucus is sure, if the offense be often repeated, or even once committed upon an important issue, to be read out of the party, almost without chance of reinstatement. And every one knows that nothing can be accomplished in politics by mere disagreement. The only privilege such recalcitrants gain is the privilege of disagreement; they are forever shut out from the privilege of confidential coöperation. They have chosen the helplessness of a faction.

It must be admitted, however, that, unfortunate as the necessity is for the existence of such powers as those of the caucus, that necessity actually exists and cannot be neglected. Against the fatal action of so many elements of disintegration it would seem to be imperatively needful that some energetic element of cohesion should be provided. It is doubtful whether in any other nation, with a shorter inheritance of political instinct, parties could long successfully resist the centrifugal forces of the committee system with only the varying attraction of the caucus to detain them. The wonder is that, despite the forcible and unnatural divorcement of legislation and administration and the consequent distraction of legislation from all attention to anything like an intelligent planning and superintendence of policy, we are not cursed with as many factions as now almost hopelessly confuse French politics. That we have had, and continue to have, only two national parties of national importance or real power is fortunate rather than natural. Their names stand for a fact, but scarcely for a reason.

An intelligent observer of our politics[64] has declared that there is in the United States "a class, including thousands and tens of thousands of the best men in the country, who think it possible to enjoy the fruits of good government without working for them." Every one who has seen beyond the outside of our American life must recognize the truth of this; to explain it is to state the sum of all the most valid criticisms of congressional government. Public opinion has no easy vehicle for its judgments, no quick channels for its action. Nothing about the system is direct and simple. Authority is perplexingly subdivided and distributed, and responsibility has to be hunted down in out-of-the-way corners. So that the sum of the whole matter is that the means of working for the fruits of good government are not readily to be found. The average citizen may be excused for esteeming government at best but a haphazard affair, upon which his vote and all of his influence can have but little effect. How is his choice of a representative in Congress to affect the policy of the country as regards the questions in which he is most interested, if the man for whom he votes has no chance of getting on the Standing Committee which has virtual charge of those questions? How is it to make any difference who is chosen President? Has the President any very great authority in matters of vital policy? It seems almost a thing of despair to get any assurance that any vote he may cast will even in an infinitesimal degree affect the essential courses of administration. There are so many cooks mixing their ingredients in the national broth that it seems hopeless, this thing of changing one cook at a time.

The charm of our constitutional ideal has now been long enough wound up to enable sober men who do not believe in political witchcraft to judge what it has accomplished, and is likely still to accomplish, without further winding. The Constitution is not honored by blind worship. The more open-eyed we become, as a nation, to its defects, and the prompter we grow in applying with the unhesitating courage of conviction all thoroughly-tested or well-considered expedients necessary to make self-government among us a straightforward thing of simple method, single, unstinted power, and clear responsibility, the nearer will we approach to the sound sense and practical genius of the great and honorable statesmen of 1787. And the first step towards emancipation from the timidity and false pride which have led us to seek to thrive despite the defects of our national system rather than seem to deny its perfection is a fearless criticism of that system. When we shall have examined all its parts without sentiment, and ganged all its functions by the standards of practical common sense, we shall have established anew our right to the claim of political sagacity; and it will remain only to act intelligently upon what our opened eyes have seen in order to prove again the justice of our claim to political genius.

George Washington

Chapter I
In Washington's Day

George Washington was bred a gentleman and a man of honor in the free school of Virginian society, with the generation that first learned what it meant to maintain English communities in America in safety and a self-respecting independence. He was born in a season of quiet peace, when the plot of colonial history was thickening noiselessly and almost without observation. He came to his first manhood upon the first stir of revolutionary events; caught in their movement, he served a rough apprenticeship in arms at the thick of the French and Indian war; the Revolution found him a leader and veteran in affairs at forty-four; every turn of fortune confirmed him in his executive habit of foresight and mastery; death spared him, stalwart and commanding, until, his rising career rounded and complete, no man doubted him the first character of his age. "Virginia gave us this imperial man," and with him a companion race of statesmen and masters in affairs. It was her natural gift, the times and her character being what they were; and Washington's life showed the whole process of breeding by which she conceived so great a generosity in manliness and public spirit.

The English colonies in America lay very tranquil in 1732, the year in which Washington was born. It fell in a season between times, when affairs lingered, as if awaiting a change. The difficulties and anxieties of first settlement were long ago past and done with in all the principal colonies. They had been hardening to their "wilderness work," some of them, these hundred years and more. England could now reckon quite six hundred thousand subjects upon the long Atlantic seaboard of the great continent which had lain remote and undiscovered through so many busy ages, until daring sailors hit upon it at last amidst the stir of the adventurous fifteenth century; and there was no longer any thought that her colonists would draw back or falter in what they had undertaken. They had grown sedate even and self-poised, with somewhat of the air of old communities, as they extended their settlements upon the coasts and rivers and elaborated their means of self-government amidst the still forests, and each had already a bearing and character of its own. 'Twas easy to distinguish the New-Englander from the man of the southern colonies; and the busy middle provinces that stretched back from the great bay at New-York and from the waters of the spreading Delaware had also a breed of their own, like neither the men of the south nor the men of the northeast. Each region had bred for itself its characteristic communities, holding their own distinctive standards, knowing their own special purposes, living their own lives with a certain separateness and independence.

Virginia, the oldest of the colonies, was least to be distinguished by any private character of her own from the rural communities of England herself. Her population had come to her almost without selection throughout every stage of quick change and troubled fortune that England had seen during the fateful days since James Stuart became king; and Englishmen in Virginia were in no way radically distinguishable from Englishmen in England, except that they were provincials and frontiersmen. They had their own tasks and ways of life, indeed, living, as they did, within the old forests of a virgin continent, upon the confines of the world. But their tastes and temperament, spite of change and seclusion, they had in common with Englishmen at home. They gave leave to their opinions, too, with a like downright confidence and hardihood of belief, never doubting they knew how practical affairs should go. They had even kept the English character as they had received it, against the touch of time and social revolution, until Virginians seemed like elder Englishmen. England changed, but Virginia did not. There landed estates spread themselves with an ample acreage along the margins of the streams that everywhere threaded the virgin woodland; and the planter drew about him a body of dependants who knew no other master; to whom came, in their seclusion, none of that quick air of change that had so stirred in England throughout all her century of revolution. Some were his slaves, bound to him in perpetual subjection. Others were his tenants, and looked upon him as a sort of patron. In Maryland, where similar broad estates lay upon every shore, the law dubbed a great property here and there a "manor," and suffered it to boast its separate court baron and private jurisdiction. Virginian gentlemen enjoyed independence and authority without need of formal title.

There was but one centre of social life in Virginia: at Williamsburg, the village capital, where the Governor had his "palace," where stood the colonial college, where there were taverns and the town houses of sundry planters of the vicinage, and where there was much gay company and not a little formal ceremonial in the season. For the rest, the Old Dominion made shift to do without towns. There was no great mart to which all the trade of the colony was drawn. Ships came and went upon each broad river as upon a highway, taking and discharging freight at the private wharves of the several plantations. For every planter was his own merchant, shipping his tobacco to England, and importing thence in return his clothes, his tools, his household fittings, his knowledge of the London fashions and of the game of politics at home. His mechanics he found among his own slaves and dependants. Their "quarters" and the offices of his simple establishment showed almost like a village of themselves where they stood in irregular groups about his own square, broadgabled house, with its airy hall and homelike living-rooms. He might have good plate upon his sideboard and on his table, palatable old wine in his cellar, and on the walls about him portraits of the stately men and dames from whom he took his blood and breeding. But there was little luxury in his life. Plain comfort and a homely abundance sufficed him. He was a gentleman, owned all he saw around him, exercised authority, and enjoyed consideration throughout the colony; but he was no prince. He lived always in the style of a provincial and a gentleman commoner, as his neighbors and friends did.

Slaves, dependants, and planters, however, did not by any means make up the tale of Virginia's population. She had been peopled out of the common stock of Englishmen, and contained her own variety. Most of the good land that lay upon the lower courses of the James, the York, the Rappahannock, and the Potomac rivers, and upon the bay on either hand, had been absorbed into the estates of the wealthier planters, who began to conceive themselves a sort of aristocracy; but not a few plain men owned their own smaller tracts within the broad stretches of country that lay back from the rivers or above their navigable depth. Upon the western front of the colony lived sturdy frontiersmen; and no man was so poor that he might not hope by thrift to hold his own with the best in the country. Few could own slaves in any number, for the negroes counted less than a third in a reckoning of the whole population. There were hired servants besides, and servants bound for a term of years by indenture; even criminals who could be had of the colony for private service; but most men must needs work their own plots of ground and devise a domestic economy without servants. A wholesome democratic spirit pervaded the colony, which made even the greater planters hesitate to give themselves airs. A few families that had thriven best and longest, and had built up great properties for themselves, did indeed lay claim, as royal governors found to their great displeasure, to a right to be heard before all others in the management of the government. But they could of course show no title but that of pride and long practice. 'Twas only their social weight in the parish vestries, in the Council, and in the House of Burgesses that gave them ascendency.

It was the same in church as in state. Virginia prided herself upon having maintained the Establishment without schism or sour dissent; but she had maintained it in a way all her own, with a democratic constitution and practice hardly to be found in the canons. Nominally the Governor had the right of presentation to all livings; but the vestries took care he should seldom exercise it, and, after they had had their own way for a century, claimed he had lost it by prescription. They chose and dismissed and ruled their ministers as they would And the chief planters were nowhere greater figures than in the vestries of their own parishes, where so many neighborhood interests were passed upon-the care of the poor, the survey of estates, the correction of disorders, the tithe rates, and the maintenance of the church and minister. Sometimes the church building was itself the gift of the chief landowner of the parish; and the planters were always the chief rate-payers. Their leadership was natural and unchallenged. They enjoyed in their own neighborhood a sort of feudal preeminence, and the men about them easily returned in thought and estimation to that elder order of English life in which the chief proprietor of the country-side claimed as of course the homage of his neighbors. There were parishes, not a few, indeed, in which there was no such great planter to command consideration by a sort of social primacy. It was, after all, only here and there, and in the older parts of the colony, that affairs awaited the wish of privileged individuals. But it was the ascendency of the greater planters which most struck the imagination, and which gave to Virginia something of the same air and tone and turn of opinion that existed in England, with its veritable aristocracy, its lordly country gentlemen, its ancient distinctions of class and manners.

Those who took counsel in England concerning colonial affairs had constant occasion to mark the sharp contrast between the easy-going Virginians, who were no harder to govern than Englishmen everywhere, and the men of the northeastern colonies, with their dry reserve and their steadfast resolution not to be governed at all. These seemed unlike Englishmen elsewhere; a whit stiffer, shrewder, more self-contained and circumspect. They were, in fact, a peculiar people. Into New England had come a selected class, picked out of the general mass of Englishmen at home by test of creed. "God sifted the whole nation," one of their own preachers had told them, at election-time, in the far year 1668, "That he might send choice grain out into this wilderness." But the variety of the old life in England had been lost in the sifting. The Puritan, for all he was so strong and great a figure in his day, was but one man among a score in the quick and various English life. His single standard and manner of living, out of the many that strove for mastery in the old seats where the race was bred, had been transferred to New England; and he had had separate and undisputed ascendency there to build new commonwealths as he would. The Puritan Commonwealth in England had been the government of a minority. Cromwell had done his work of chastening with a might and fervor which he found, not in the nation, but in himself and in the stout men-at-arms and hardy reformers who stood with him while he purified England and brought upon all her foes a day of reckoning. The people had stood cowed and uneasy while he lived, and had broken into wild excess of joy at their release when he died. But in New England an entire community consented to the Puritan code and mastery with a hearty acquiescence. It was for this liberty they had come over sea.

And the thoughtful, strong-willed men who were their leaders had built, as they wished, a polity that should last. Time wrought its deep changes in New England, as elsewhere, but the stamp set upon these Puritan settlements by the generation that founded them was not effaced. Trade made its characteristic mark upon them. Their merchants had presently their own fleets and markets. Their hardy people took more and more to the sea, lived the rough life of the ocean ways with a relish, beat in their small craft up and down the whole coast of the continent, drove bargains everywhere, and everywhere added a touch to their reputation as doughty sea-dogs and shrewd traders. The population that after a while came to New England did not stay to be sifted before attempting the voyage out of the Old World, and the quaint sedateness of the settlements began to be broken by a novel variety. New men beset the old order; a rough democracy began to make itself felt; and new elements waxed bold amidst the new conditions that time had wrought. The authority of the crown at last made a place of command for itself, despite every stubborn protest and astute evasion. It became necessary to be a trifle less observant of sect and creed, to cultivate, as far as might be, a temper of tolerance and moderation. But it was a slow change at best. The old order might be modified, but it could not so soon be broken. New England, through all her jurisdictions, remained a body of churches, as well as a body of towns, submissive to the doctrine and discipline of her learned clergy, keeping the old traditions distinct, indubitable, alike in her schools and her meetinghouses. Even in Rhode Island, where there had from the first been such diversity of creed and license of individual belief, there was little variety of type among the people, for all they counted themselves so free to be what they would. There was here a singular assortment, no doubt, of the units of the stock, but it was of the Puritan stuff, none the less, through all its variety.

New England, indeed, easily kept her character, for she lived apart. Her people mustered a full hundred thousand strong before the seventeenth century was out; her towns numbered many score, both upon the margins of the sea and within the forests; but she still lay within a very near frontier, pushed back only a short journey from the coast. Except where the towns of Connecticut ran in broken line close to the westward strait of Long Island Sound, a broad wilderness of untouched woodland, of thicketed hills and valleys that no white man yet had seen, stretched between them and Hudson's river, where New York's settlements lay upon the edge of a vast domain, reaching all the way to the great lakes and the western rivers. Not till 1725 did adventurous settlers dare go so far as the Berkshire Hills. "Our country," exclaimed Colonel Byrd, of Virginia, who had seen its wild interior, " has now-been inhabited more than a hundred and thirty years, and still we hardly know anything of the Appalachian Mountains, which are nowhere above two hundred and fifty miles from the sea." A full century after the coming of the Pilgrims, New England, like Virginia, was still a frontier region, shut close about on every hand by thick forests beset by prowling bands of savages. She had as yet no intimate contact with the other colonies whose fortunes she was to share. Her simple life, quickened by adventure, but lacking the full pulse of old communities, kept, spite of slow change, to a single standard of conduct, made her one community from end to end, her people one people. She stood apart and compact, still soberly cultivating, as of old, a life and character all her own. Colonel Byrd noted how "New England improved much faster than Virginia," and was fain to think that " though these people may be ridiculed for some Pharisaical particularities in their worship and behavior, yet they were very useful subjects, as being frugal and industrious, giving no scandal or bad example." Public men in England, who had to face these "particularities in behavior," would hardly have agreed that the men of New England were good subjects, though they must have admitted their excellent example in thrift, and Virginia's need to imitate it. This contrast between the northern and southern settlements was as old as their establishment, for Virginia had from the first been resorted to by those who had no other purpose than to better their fortunes, while New England had been founded to be the home of a creed and discipline; but it was not until the Commonwealth was set up in England that the difference began to be marked, and to give promise of becoming permanent. The English in Virginia, like the bulk of their countrymen at home, ha!d stood aghast at a king's death upon the scaffold, and had spoken very hotly, in their loyalty, of the men who had dared do the impious deed of treason; but when the Guinea, frigate, brought the Commonwealth's commission into the river to demand their submission, even Sir William Berkeley, the redoubtable Cavalier Governor, who had meant stubbornly to keep his province for the second Charles, saw he must yield; perceived there was too nice a balance of parties in the colony to permit an execution of bis plans of resistance; heard too many plain men in his Council, and out of it, declare themselves very much of a mind with the Puritans for the nonce in politics — very willing to set up a democracy in Virginia which should call itself a part of the Puritan state in England. But a great change had been wrought in Virginia while the Commonwealth lasted. When the Commonwealth's frigate came in at the capes she counted scarcely fifteen thousand settlers upon her plantations, but the next twenty years saw her transformed. By 1670 quite twenty-five thousand people were added to the reckoning; and of the new-comers a great multitude had left England as much because they hated the Puritans as because they desired Virginia. They were drawn out of that great majority at home to whom Cromwell had not dared resort to get a new parliament in the stead of the one he had "purged." Many of them were of the hottest blood of the Cavaliers.

It was in these years Virginia got her character and received her leading gentry for the time to come-the years while the Commonwealth stood and royalists despaired, and the years immediately following the Restoration, when royalists took heart again and Englishmen turned with a new ardor to colonization as the times changed. Among the rest in the great migration came two brothers, John and Lawrence Washington, of a stock whose loyalty was as old as the Conquest. They came of a Norman family, the men of whose elder branch had for two hundred years helped the stout Bishops of Durham keep the border against the Scots; and in every branch of which men had sprung up to serve the king, the state, and the church with steadfastness and honor: dashing soldiers ready for the field at home or abroad, stout polemical priors, lawyers who knew the learning of their day and made their way to high posts in chancery, thrifty burghers, gallant courtiers, prosperous merchants-public-spirited gentlemen all. It was Colonel Henry Washington, cousin to the Virginian refugees, who had been with Rupert when he stormed Bristol, and who, with a handful of men, had made good an entrance into the town when all others were beaten back and baffled. It was he who had held Worcester for his master even after he knew Charles to be a prisoner in the hands of the parliamentary forces. "Procure his Majesty's commands for the disposal of this garrison," was all he would answer when Fairfax summoned him to surrender;" till then I shall make good the trust reposed in me. The worst I know and fear not; if I had, the profession of a soldier had not been begun." But it was an ill time to revive the traditions of the knights of Durham; loyalty only brought ruin. The Reverend Lawrence Washington, uncle to the gallant colonel who was the King's Governor at Worcester, had been cast out of his living at Purleigh in 1643 by order of Parliament, upon the false charge that he was a public tippler, oft drunk, and loud to rail against the Parliament and its armies; but really because, with all his race, he was a royalist, and his living one of the best in Essex. It was his sons who left off hoping to see things mend in England and betook themselves to Virginia. His ruin had come upon him while they were yet lads. He had been a brilliant university scholar, fellow and lector of Brasenose, and rector of Oxford; but he could give his sons neither a university career nor hope of fortune in the humble parish pitying friends bad found for him in an obscure village of Essex; and when he was dead they saw no reason why they should stay longer in England, where Cromwell was master.

John Washington, the oldest son of the unfortunate rector, reached Virginia in 1656, having made his way to the colony as "second man" to Edward Prescott, merchant and ship-owner, in whose company he had come; and his brother Lawrence, after passing to and fro between England and the colony several times upon errands of business, presently joined him in permanent residence upon the "northern neck" of rich land that lay between the Rappahannock and the Potomac rivers. It was a region where every settlement as yet was new. A few families had fixed themselves upon it when Maryland drove Captain Clayborne and his Virginian partisans forth from Kent Island in the years 1637 and 1638; and they had mustered numbers enough within a few years to send a representative to the House of Burgesses at Jamestown. But it was not till 1648 that the Assembly gave their lands a regular constitution as the County of Northumberland; for it was to this region the Indians had been driven by the encroachment of the settlements on the James and York, and for a while the Assembly had covenanted with the red men to keep it free from settlers. When once the ban was removed, however, in 1648, colonization set in apace-from the older counties of Virginia, from Maryland across the river and England over sea, from New England even, as if by a common impulse. In 1651 the Assembly found it necessary to create the two additional counties of Gloucester and Lancaster, and in 1653 still another, the County of Westmoreland, for the region's proper government, so quickly did it fill in; for the tide out of England already began to show its volume. The region was a natural seat of commerce, and merchants out of the trading ports of England particularly affected it. Rich land was abundant, and the Potomac ran strong and ample there, to carry the commerce alike of Virginia and Maryland to the bay, upon whose tributaries and inlets lay all the older settlements of both colonies. Lawrence Washington, though he still described himself, upon occasion, as "of Luton, County Bedford, merchant," found his chief profit where he made his home, with his brother John, in the new County of Westmoreland in Virginia. About them lived young men and old, come, like themselves, out of England, or drawn from the older settlements by the attractions of the goodly region, looking out, as it did, on either hand to a broad river and an easy trade. They felt it scarcely an expatriation to live there, so constantly did ships come and go between their wharves and the home ports at Bristol and London. It soon grew to be nothing singular to see well-to-do men go every year to England upon some errand of profit or pleasure.

It was with such a region and such stirring neighbors that the young Washingtons identified themselves while they were yet youths in their twenties; and there they prospered shrewdly with the rest. Prudent men and men of character readily accumulated estates in the untouched glades and forests of Westmoreland. The season of their coming, moreover, sadly as things seemed to go in 1656, turned out propitious. The Restoration opened a new era in the settlement of the country. Englishmen bestirred themselves to take actual possession of all the great coast-line they had so long claimed without occupying. "The Dutch had enjoyed New Netherland during the distractions of the reign of Charles I. without any other interruption" than the seizure of their post upon the Connecticut by the New-Englanders, and the aggressions alike of Swedes and English upon the Delaware; but the ministers of Charles II., though " for some time perplexed in what light to view them, whether as subjects or as aliens, determined at length that New Netherland ought in justice to be resumed," and the thing was presently accomplished in true sovereign fashion by force of arms. To the ducal province of New York, Penn presently added the thrifty Quaker colony which so promptly created a busy town and mart of trade at Philadelphia, and which pushed its rural settlements back so speedily into the fertile lands that lay towards the west. Then, while the new colonizing impulse still ran strong, New Jersey, too, was added, with her limits at one end upon the Hudson and the great bay at New York, where she depended upon one rival for a port of entry, and at the other upon the Delaware, where another rival presided over the trade of her southern highway to the sea. To the southward straggling settlements upon Albemarle Sound grew slowly into the colony of North Carolina; and still other settlements, upon the rivers that lay towards Florida, throve so bravely that Charleston presently boasted itself a substantial town, and South Carolina had risen to be a considerable colony, prosperous, well ordered, and showing a quick life and individuality of her own.

A new migration had come out of England to the colonies, and Englishmen looked with fresh confidence to see their countrymen build an empire in America. And yet perhaps not an empire of pure English blood. New York was for long scarcely the less a Dutch province, for all she had changed owners, and saw Englishmen crowd in to control her trade. There were Swedes still upon the Delaware; and Pennsylvania mustered among her colonists, besides a strange mixture out of many nations — Germans, French, Dutch, Finns, and English. Even in Virginia, which so steadily kept its English character, there were to be found groups of French Huguenots and Germans who had been given an ungrudging welcome; and South Carolina, though strongly English too, had taken some of her best blood out of France when Louis so generously gave the world fifty thousand families of the finest breed of his kingdom by the revocation of the Edict of Nantes (1685).

GEORGE WASHINGTON

The second quarter of the eighteenth century saw Scots-Irish enter Virginia and the middle colonies in hosts that for a time numbered ten thousand by the year. Pennsylvania alone, in the single year 1729, could reckon five thousand of these sturdy people who had come to multiply and strengthen her settlements.

It was to the middle colonies that most foreigners came, and their coming gave to the towns and farms of that region a variety of tongues and customs, of manners and trades and ways of life and worship, to be found nowhere else. Boston, with all its trade and seafaring, had no touch of that cosmopolitan character which New York had taken on quite inevitably in the course of her varying fortunes, and which Philadelphia had assumed by choice; and rural Virginia scarcely felt amidst her scattered plantations the presence of the few families who lived by standards that were not English. The common feature of the new time, with its novel enterprises and its general immigration, was that the colonies everywhere, whether young or old, felt a keen stimulation and a new interest in affairs beyond their borders. A partial exchange of population began, a noticeable intercolonial migration. Whole congregations came out of New England to found towns in New Jersey, and individuals out of every colony vent-tired more freely than before to exchange one region for another, in order to coax health or fortune. Population was thus not a little compacted, while the colonies were drawn by insensible degrees to feel a certain community of interest and cultivate a certain community of opinion.

An expanding life, widened fields of enterprise and adventure, quickened hopes, and the fair prospects of a growing empire everywhere heartened strong men in the colonies to steady endeavor when the new century opened-the scheming, calculating eighteenth century, so unimpassioned and conventional at first, so tempestuous at last. The men of the colonies were not so new as their continent in the ways of civilization. They were Old World men put upon fresh coasts and a forest frontier, to make the most of them, create markets, build a new trade, become masters of vast resources as yet untouched and incalculable; and they did their work for the most part with unmatched spirit and energy, notwithstanding they were checked and hampered by the statutes of the realm. The Navigation Acts forbade the use of any but English ships in trade; forbade all trade, besides, which did not run direct to and from the ports of England. The colonies must not pass England by even in their trade with one another. What they could not produce themselves they must bring straight from England; what they had to dispose of they mast send straight to England. If they would exchange among themselves they must make England by the way, so that English merchants should be their middlemen and factors; or else, if they must needs carry direct from port to port of their own coasts, they must pay such duties as they would have paid in English ports had they actually gone the intermediate voyage to England preferred by the statutes. 'Twas the "usage of other nations" besides England "to keep their plantation trade to themselves " in that day, as the Parliament itself said and no man could deny, and 'twas the purpose of such restrictions to maintain " a greater correspondence and kindness between " England and her subjects in America, "keeping them in a firmer dependence," and at the same time "rendering them yet more beneficial and advantageous" to English seamen, merchants, wool-growers, and manufacturers; but it cost the colonists pride and convenience and profit to obey.

Some, who felt the harness of such law too smartly, consoled themselves by inventing means to escape it. The coast was long; was opened by many an unused harbor, great and small; could not everywhere and always be watched by king's officers; was frequented by a tolerant people, who had no very nice conscience about withholding taxes from a sovereign whose messages and commands came quickly over sea only when the wind held fair for weeks together; and cargoes could be got both out and in at small expense of secrecy and no expense at all in duties. Iii short, smuggling was easy. 'Twas a time of frequent wars, moreover, and privateering commissions were to be had for the asking; so that French ships could be brought in with their lading, condemned, and handsomely sold, without the trouble of paying French prices or English port dues. Privateering, too, was cousin-german to something still better; 'twas but a sort of formal apprenticeship to piracy ; and the quiet, unused harbors of the coast showed many a place where the regular profession might be set up. Veritable pirates took the sea, hunted down what commerce they would —English no less than French and Dutch and Spanish —rendezvoused in lonely sounds, inlets, and rivers where king's officers never came, and kept very respectable company when they came at last to dispose of their plunder at New York or Charleston, being men very learned in subterfuges and very quick-fingered at bribing. And then there was "the Red Sea trade," whose merchants sent fleets to Madagascar in the season to exchange cargoes with rough men out of the Eastern seas, of whom they courteously asked no questions. The larger ports were full of sailors who waited to be engaged, not at regular wages but "on the grand account"; and it took many weary years of hangman's labor to bring enough pirates to the gallows to scotch the ugly business. In 1717 it was reported in the colonies that there were quite fifteen hundred pirates on the coast, full one-half of whom made their headquarters, very brazenly, at New Providence in the Bahamas; and there were merchants and mariners by the score who had pangs of keen regret to see the breezy trade go down, as the century drew on a decade or two, because of the steady vigilance and stem endeavor of Governors who had been straitly commanded to suppress it.

The Navigation Acts bred an irritation in the colonies which grew with their growth and strengthened with their consciousness of strength and capacity. Not because such restrictions were uncommon, but because the colonies were forward and exacting. There was, indeed, much to commend the legislation they resented. It attracted the capital of English merchants to the American trade, it went far towards securing English supremacy on the seas, and it was strictly within the powers of Parliament, as no man could deny. Parliament had an undoubted right to regulate imperial interests, of this or any other kind, even though it regulated them unreasonably. But colonies that reckoned their English population by the hundred thousand and lived by trade and adventure would not long have brooked such a policy of restraint had they had the leisure to fret over it. They did not as yet have the leisure. The French stood menacingly at their western gates, through which the great fur trade made its way; where the long rivers ran which threaded the central valleys of the continent; where the Mississippi stretched itself from north to south like a great body of dividing waters, flanking all the coast and its settlements—where alone a true mastery of the continent and its resources could be held. It would be time enough to reckon with Parliament touching the carrying trade when they had made good their title to what they were to trade withal.

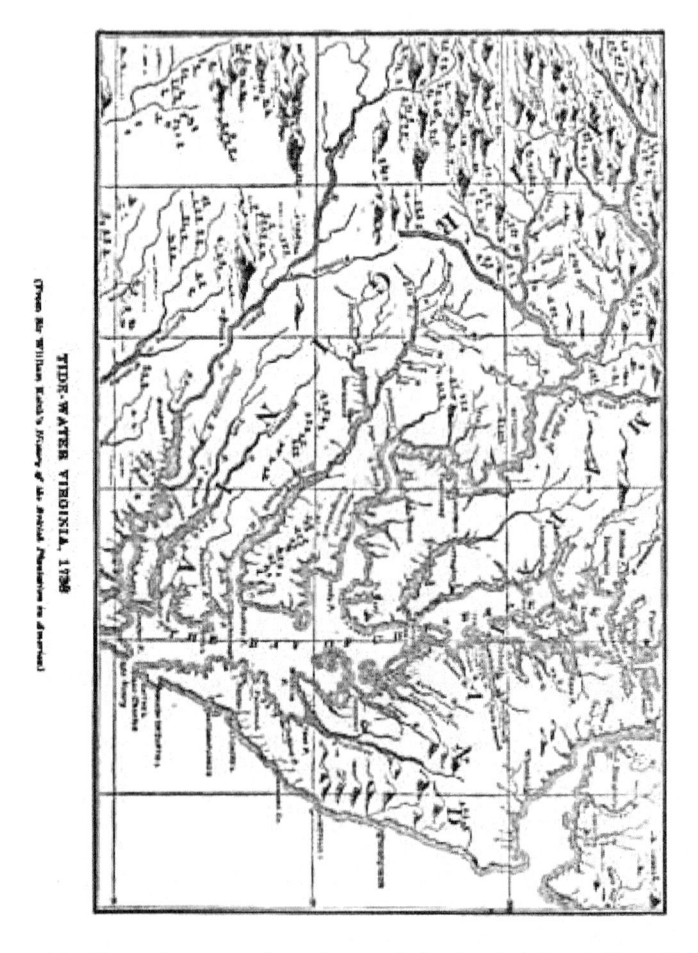

TIDE-WATER VIRGINIA, 1736
(From Sir William Kieth's *History of the British Plantations in America*)

The French had been a long time about their work, for they had done it like subjects, at the bidding of an ambitious king, rather than like free men striving as they pleased for themselves.

But what they had done they had done systematically. and with a fixed policy that did not vary, though ministers and even dynasties might come and go. The English had crowded to the coasts of the continent as they pleased, and had mustered their tens of thousands before the French reckoned more than a few hundreds. But the French had hit upon the mighty river St. Lawrence, whose waters came out of the great lakes and the heart of the continent; their posts were garrisons; what men they had they put forward, at each step of discovery, at some point of vantage upon lake or river, whence they were not easily dislodged. Their shrewd fur-traders and dauntless priests struck everywhere into the heart of the forests, leading forward both trade and conquest, until at last, through the country of the Illinois and out of far Lake Michigan, the streams had been found which ran down into the west to the flooding Mississippi. Colonists were sent to the mouth of the vast river, posts presently dotted its banks here and there throughout its length, trade passed up and down its spreading stream, and the English, their eyes at last caught by the stealthy movement, looked in a short space to see French settlements "running all along from our lakes by the back of Virginia and Carolina to the Bay of Mexico."

This was a business that touched the colonies to the quick. New York had her western frontiers upon the nearer lakes. Thence, time out of mind, had come the best furs to the markets at Albany, brought from tribe to tribe out of the farthest regions of the northwest. New England, with the French at her very doors, had to look constantly to her northern borders to keep them against the unquiet savage tribes the French every yeaj stirred up against her. Virginia felt the French power among her savage neighbors too, the moment her people ventured across the Blue Ridge into the valley where many an ancient war-path ran; and beyond the Alleghenies she perceived she must stand in the very presence almost of the French themselves. English frontiersmen and traders, though they had no advancing military posts behind them, were none the less quick to go themselves deep into the shadowed wilderness, there to meet the French face to face in their own haunts. The Carolinas were hardly settled before their more adventurous spirits went straight into the far valley of the Tennessee, and made trade for themselves there against the coming of the French. Out of Virginia, too, and out of Pennsylvania, as well as out of New York, traders pressed towards the West, and fixed their lonely huts here and there along the wild banks of the Ohio. 'Twas diamond cut diamond when they met their French rivals in the wigwams of the Indian villages, and their canoes knew the waterways of the wilderness as well as any man's. 'Twas they who learned at first hand what the French were doing. They were like scoots sent oat to view the ground to be fought for.

This hazardous meeting of rival nations at the heart of the continent meant many a deep change in the fortunes of the colonies. European politics straightway entered their counsels. Here was an end of their separateness and independence of England. Charles and James and William all showed that they meant to be veritable sovereigns, and had no thought but that the colonists in America, like all other Englishmen, should be their subjects; and here was their opportunity to be masters upon an imperial scale and with an imperial excuse. In Europe, England beheld France her most formidable foe; she must look to it that Louis and his ministers take no advantage in America. The colonies, no less than the Channel itself, were become the frontiers of an empire-and there must be no trespass upon English soil by the French. The colonists must be rallied to the common work, and, if used, they must be ruled and consolidated.

As it turned out, the thing was quite impossible. The colonies had too long been separate; their characters, their tempers, their interests, were too diverse and distinct; they were unused to co-operate, and unwilling; they were too slow to learn submission in anything. The plan of grouping several of them under a single governor was attempted, but they remained as separate under that arrangement as under any other. Massachusetts would interest herself in nothing beyond her own jurisdiction that did not immediately touch her safety or advantage; New York cared little what the French did, if only the Iroquois could be kept quiet and she could get her furs in the season, and find a market for them abroad or among the French themselves; Virginia had no eye for any movement upon the frontiers that did not menace her own fair valleys within the mountains with hostile occupation; the Carolinas were as yet too young to be serviceable, and New Jersey too remote from points of danger. Nowhere could either men or supplies be had for use against the French except by the vote of a colonial assembly. The law of the empire might be what it would in the mouths of English judges at home; it did not alter the practice of the colonies. The courts in England might say with what emphasis they liked that Virginia, "being a conquered country, their law is what the King pleases"; it was none the less necessary for the King's Governor to keep on terms with the people's representatives." Our government is so happily constituted," writes Colonel Byrd to his friend in the Barbadoes, "that a governor must first outwit us before he can oppress us. And if ever he squeeze money out of us, he must first take care to deserve it." Every colony held stoutly to a like practice, with a like stubborn temper, which it was mere folly to ignore. One and all they were even then "too proud to submit, too strong to be forced, too enlightened not to see all the consequences which must arise" should they tamely consent to be ruled by royal command or parliamentary enactment. Their obedience must be had on their own terms, or else not had at all. Governors saw this plainly enough, though the ministers at home could not. Many a governor had his temper sadly soured by the contentious obstinacy of the colonial assembly he was set to deal with. One or two died of sheer exasperation. But the situation was not altered a whit.

WILLIAM BYRD

When there is friction there must, sooner or later, be adjustment, if affairs are to go forward at all, and this contest between imperial system and colonial independence at last brought some things that had been vague to a very clear definition. 'Twas plain the colonies would not of themselves combine to meet and oust the French. They would supply neither men nor money, moreover. England must send her own armies to America, fight France there as she would have fought her in Europe, and pay the reckoning herself out of her own treasury, getting from the colonies, the while, only such wayward and niggardly aid as they chose to give. The colonies, meanwhile, might gather some of the fruits of experience; might learn how safe it was to be selfish, and how unsafe, if they hoped to prosper and be free; might perceive where their common interests lay, and their common power; might in some degree steady their lives and define their policy against the coming of more peaceful times. Two wars came and went which brought France and England to arms against each other in America, as in Europe, but they passed away without decisive incident in the New World, and there followed upon them thirty years of uneventful peace, during which affairs hung at a nice balance, and the colonies took counsel, each for itself, how they should prosper.

Virginia, meanwhile, had got the charter she was to keep. From the Potomac to the uncertain border of the Carolinas she had seen her counties fill with the men who were to decide her destiny. Her people, close upon a hundred thousand strong, had fallen into the order of life they were to maintain. They were no longer colonists merely, but citizens of a commonwealth of which they began to be very proud, not least because they saw a noble breed of public men spring out of their own loins to lead them. Though they were scattered, they were not divided. There was, after all, no real isolation for any man in Virginia, for all that he lived so much apart and was a sort of lord within his rustic barony. In that sunny land men were constantly abroad, looking to their tobacco and the labor of all kinds that must go forward, but would not unless they looked to it, or else for the sheer pleasure of bestriding a good horse, being quit of the house, and breathing free in the genial air. Bridle-paths everywhere threaded the forests; it was no great matter to ride from house to house among one's neighbors; there were county-court days, moreover, to draw the country-side together, whether there was much business or little to be seen to. Men did not thrive thereabouts by staying within doors, but by being much about, knowing their neighbors, observing what ships came and went upon the rivers, and what prices were got for the cargoes they carried away; learning what the news was from Williamsburg and London, what horses and cattle were to be had, and what dogs, of what breeds. It was a country in which news and opinions and friendships passed freely current; where men knew each other with a rare leisurely intimacy, and enjoyed their easy, unforced intercourse with a keen and lasting relish.

It was a country in which men kept their individuality very handsomely withal. If there was no town life, there were no town manners either, no village conventionalities to make all men of one carriage and pattern and manner of living. Every head of a family was head also of an establishment, and could live with a self-respect and freedom which were subject to no man's private scrutiny. He had leave, in his independence, to be himself quite naturally, and did not need to justify his liberty by excuses. And yet he had responsibilities too, and a position which steadied and righted him almost in spite of himself. It required executive capacity to make his estate pay, and an upright way of life to maintain his standing. If he was sometimes loud and hectoring, or over-careless what 'he said or did, 'twas commonly because he was young or but half come into his senses; for his very business, of getting good crops of tobacco and keeping on dealing terms with his neighbors, demanded prudence and a conduct touched with consideration. He had to build his character very carefully by the plumb to keep it at an equilibrium, though he might decorate it, if it were but upright, as freely, as whimsically even, as he chose, with chance traits and self-pleasing tastes, with the full consent and tolerance of the neighborhood. He was his own man, might have his own opinions if he held them but courteously enough, might live his own life if he but lived it cleanly and without offence. 'Twas by their living rather than by their creed or their livelihood that men were assessed and esteemed.

It was not a life that bred students, though it was a life that begot thoughtfulness and leadership in affairs. Those who fell in the way of getting them had not a few books upon their shelves, because they thought every gentleman should have such means of knowing what the world had said and done before his day. But they read only upon occasion, when the weather darkened, or long evenings dragged because there were no guests in the house. Not much systematic education was possible where the population was so dispersed and separate. A few country schools undertook what was absolutely necessary, and gave instruction in such practical branches as every man must know something of who was to take part in the management of private and public business. For the rest, those who chose could get the languages from private tutors, when they were to be had, and then go over sea to read at the universities, or to Williamsburg when at last the colony had its own college of William and Mary. More youths went from the Northern Neck to England for their education, no doubt, than from any other part of Virginia. The counties there were somewhat closer than the rest to the sea, bred more merchants and travellers, kept up a more intimate correspondence both by travel and by letter with Bristol and London and all the old English homes. And even those who stayed in Virginia had most of them the tradition of refinement, spoke the mother tongue purely and with a proper relish, and maintained themselves somehow, with perhaps an added touch of simplicity that was their own, in the practices of a cultivated race.

No one in Virginia thought that "becoming a mere scholar" was "a desirable education for a gentleman." He ought to "become acquainted with men and things rather than books." Books must serve only to deepen and widen the knowledge he should get by observation and a free intercourse with those about him. When Virginians wrote, therefore, you might look to find them using, not studied phrases, but a style that smacked fresh of all the free elements of good talk-not like scholars or professed students, but like gentlemen of leisure and cultivated men of affairs-with a subtle, not unpleasing flavor of egotism, and the racy directness of speech, withal, that men may use who are sure of their position. Such was the writing of Robert Beverley, whose History and Present State of Virginia, published in London in 1705, spoke at first hand and authoritatively of affairs of which the world had heard hitherto only by uncertain report. He did not write the manly book because he had a pricking ambition to be an author, but because he loved Virginia, and wished to give such an account of her affairs as would justify his pride in her. He came of an ancient English family, whose ample means were scarcely more considerable in Virginia than they had been in Beverley, in Yorkshire. He had himself been carefully educated in England, and had learned to feel very much at home there; but the attractions of the old home did not wean him from his love of the new, where he had been born-that quiet land where men dealt with one another so frankly, where Nature was so genial in all her moods, and men so without pretence. Official occupations gave him occasion while yet a very young man to handle familiarly the records of the colony, the intimate letters of its daily life, and he took a proud man's pleasure in extracting from them, and from the traditions of those who still carried much of the simple history in their own recollections of a stirring life, a frank and genial story of what had been done and seen in Virginia. And so his book became "the living testimony of a proud and generous Virginian" —too proud to conceal his opinions or withhold censure where it was merited, too generous not to set down very handsomely whatever was admirable and of good report in the life of his people. His own manly character, speaking out everywhere, as it does, in lively phrase and candid meaning, is itself evidence of the wholesome native air he so praises in Virginia.

He thought himself justified in loving a country where "plantations, orchards, and gardens constantly afford fragrant and delightful walks. In their woods and fields they have an unknown variety of vegetables and other rarities of nature to discover and observe. They have hunting, fishing, and fowling, with which they entertain themselves in a thousand ways. Here is the most good nature and hospitality practised in the world, both towards friends and strangers; but the worst of it is this generosity is attended now and then with a little too much intemperance. The neighborhood is at much the same distance as in the country in England, but with this advantage, that all the better sort of people have been abroad and seen the world, by which means they are free from that stiffness and formality which discover more civility than kindness. And besides, the goodness of the roads and the fairness of the weather bring people oftener together."

Of a like quality of genuineness and good breeding is the writing of Colonel William Byrd, the accomplished master of Westover, who was of the same generation. He may well have been the liveliest man in Virginia, so piquant and irrepressible is the humor that runs through almost every sentence he ever wrote. It must be he wrote for pastime. He never took the pains to publish anything. His manuscripts lay buried a hundred years or more in the decent sepulture of private possession ere they were printed, but were even then as quick as when they were written. Beverley had often a grave smile for what he recorded, or a quiet sarcasm of tone in the telling of it. "The militia are the only standing forces in Virginia," he says, very demurely, and "they are happy in the enjoyment of an everlasting peace." But Colonel Byrd is very merry, like a man of sense, not contriving the jest» but only letting it slip, revealing it; looks very shrewdly into things, and very wisely, too, but with an easy eye, a disengaged conscience, keeping tally of the score like one who attends but is not too deeply concerned. He was, in fact, very deeply engaged in all affairs of importance-no man more deeply or earnestly; but when he wrote 'twas not his chief business to speak of that. He was too much of a gentleman and too much of a wit to make grave boast of what he was doing.

No man born in Virginia had a greater property than he, a house more luxuriously appointed, or a part to play more princely; and no man knew the value of position and wealth and social consideration more appreciatively. His breeding had greatly quickened his perception of such things. He had had a long training abroad, had kept very noble company alike in England and on the Continent, had been called to the bar in the Middle Temple and chosen a Fellow of the Royal Society, and so had won his freedom of the world of letters and of affairs. Yet he had returned to Virginia, as all her sons did, with only an added zest to serve and enjoy her. Many designs for her development throve because of his interest and encouragement; he sought her advantage jealously in her Council, as her agent in England, as owner of great tracts of her fertile lands. 'Twas he who brought to her shores some of her best settlers, gave her promise of veritable towns at Richmond and Petersburg, fought arbitrary power wherever it showed itself in her government, and proved himself in every way " a true and worthy inheritor of the feelings and opinions of the old cavaliers of Virginia." But through all his busy life he carried himself like the handsome, fortunate man he was, with a touch of gayety, a gallant spirit of comradeship, a zest for good books, spirited men, and comely women-heartily, like a man who, along with honor, sought the right pleasures of the world.

Nothing daunted the spirits of this manly gentleman, not even rough work at the depths of the forest, upon the public business of determining the southern boundary-line of the colony, or upon the private business of seeing to his own distant properties in North Carolina. It gave him only the better chance to see the world; and he was never at a loss for something to do. There were stray books to be found even in the cabins of the remotest settlers; or, if not, there was the piquant literary gossip of those laughing times of Queen Anne, but just gone by, to rehearse and comment upon. Colonel Byrd was not at a loss to find interesting ways in which even a busy man might make shift to enjoy " the Carolina felicity of having nothing to do." A rough people lived upon that frontier in his day, who showed themselves very anxious to be put upon the southern side of the line; for, if taken into Virginia, " they must have submitted to some sort of order and government; whereas in North Carolina every one does what seems best in his own eyes." "They pay no tribute," he laughs, " either to God or to Caesar." It would not be amiss, he thinks, were the clergy in Virginia, once in two or three years-not to make the thing burdensome —to "take a turn among these gentiles." "'Twould look a little apostolical," he argues, with the characteristic twinkle in his eye, "and they might hope to be requited for it hereafter, if that be not thought too long to tarry for their reward." A stray parson was to be found once and again even at the depths of the forest — on the Virginian side-though to find his humble quarters you must needs thread "a path as narrow as that which leads to heaven, but much more dirty"; but a stray parson was no great evangel. Colonel Byrd was too sound a gentleman not to be a good churchman; but he accounted it no sin to see where the humor lurks even in church. " Mr. Betty, the parson of the parish, entertained us with a good, honest sermon," he chronicles upon occasion; "but whether he bought it, or borrowed it, would have been uncivil in us to inquire. Be that as it will, he is a decent man, with a double chin that fits gracefully over his band....When church was done we refreshed our teacher with a glass of wine, and then, receiving his blessing, took horse." 'Tis likely Colonel Byrd would have found small amusement in narrating the regular course of his life, his great errands and permanent concerns of weighty business. That he could as well leave to his biographer, should he chance to have one. For himself, he chose to tell the unusual things he had seen and heard and taken part in, and to make merry as well as he might by the way.

The Virginian writers were not all country gentlemen. There were austere and stately scholars, too, like the Reverend William Stith, who had held modest livings in more than one parish, had served the House of Burgesses as chaplain, and the college, first as instructor and then as president, until at length, having won "perfect leisure and retirement," he set himself in his last days to straighten into order the confusion of early Virginian history. "Such a work," he reflected,"will be a noble and elegant entertainment for my vacant hours, which it is not in my power to employ more to my own satisfaction, or the use and benefit of my country." What with his scholarly love of documents set forth at length, however, his painstaking recital of details, and his roundabout, pedantic style, his story of the first seventeen years of the colony lingered through a whole volume; and his friends' laggard subscriptions to that single prolix volume discouraged him from undertaking another. There was neither art nor quick movement enough in such work, much as scholars have prized it since, to take the taste of a generation that lived its life on horseback and spiced it with rough sport and direct speech. They could read with more patience the plain, business - like sentences of the Reverend Hugh Jones's Present State of Virginia and with more zest the downright, telling words in which the Reverend James Blair, "commissary" to the Bishop of London, spoke of their affairs.

James Blair, though born and bred in Scotland, educated at Edinburgh, and engaged as a minister at home till he was close upon thirty years of age, was as much a Virginian in his life and deeds as any man born in the Old Dominion. 'Twas he who had been the chief founder of the College of William and Mary, and who had served it as president through every vicissitude of fortune for fifty years. For fifty years he was a member, too, of the King's Council in the colony, and for fifty-eight the chief adviser of the mother Church in England concerning ecclesiastical affairs in Virginia. "Probably no other man in the colonial time did so much for the intellectual life of Virginia" as did this "sturdy and faithful" Scotsman. To the colonists, oftentimes, he seemed overbearing, dictatorial even, and, for all their "gentlemanly conformity to the Church of England," they did not mean to suffer any man to be set over them as bishop in Virginia; while to the royal governors he seemed sometimes a headstrong agitator -and demagogue, so stoutly did he stand up for the liberties of the people among whom he had cast his lot. He was in all things a doughty Scot. He made very straight for the ends he deemed desirable; dealt frankly, honestly, fearlessly with all men alike; confident of being in the right even when he was in the wrong; dealing with all as he thought he ought to deal, " whether they liked it or not"; incapable of discouragement, as he was also incapable of dishonor; a stalwart, formidable master of all work in church and college, piling up every day to his credit a great debt of gratitude from the colony, which honored him without quite liking him. It was very noteworthy that masterful men of many kinds took an irresistible liking to Virginia, though they were but sent upon an errand to it. There was Alexander Spotswood, for example, who, after he had been twelve years Lieutenant-Governor in the stead of his lordship the Earl of Orkney, spent eighteen more good years, all he had left, upon the forty-odd thousand acres of land he had acquired in the fair colony, as a country gentleman, very busy developing the manufacture of iron, and as busy as there was any need to be as Postmaster-General of the colonies. He came of a sturdy race of gentlemen, had seen service along with Marlborough and my uncle Toby " with the army in Flanders," had gone much about the world upon many errands and seen all manner of people, and then had found himself at last in Virginia when he was past forty. For all its rough life, he liked the Old Dominion well enough to adopt it as his home. There was there, he said, "less swearing, less profaneness, less drunkenness and debauchery, less uncharitable feuds and animosities, and less knavery and villany than in any part of the world " where his lot had been. Not all of his neighbors were gentlemen; not very many could afford to send their sons to England to be educated. Men of all sorts had crowded into Virginia: merchants and gentlemen not a few, but also commoner men a great many — mariners, artisans, tailors, and men without settled trades or handicrafts of any kind. Spotswood had found it no easy matter when he was Governor to deal patiently with a House of Burgesses to which so many men of "mean understandings" had been sent, and had allowed himself to wax very sarcastic when he found how ignorant some of them were. "I observe," he said, tartly, "that the grand ruling party in your House has not furnished chairmen of two of your standing committees who can spell English or write common - sense, as the grievances under their own handwriting will manifest." 'Twas not a country, either, where one could travel much at ease, for one must ford the streams for lack of bridges, and keep an eye sharply about him as he travelled the rude forest roads when the wind was high lest a rotten tree should fall upon him. Nature was so bountiful, yielded so easy a largess of food, that few men took pains to be thrifty, and some parts of the colony were little more advanced in the arts of life than North Carolina, where. Colonel Byrd said, nothing was dear " but law, physic, and strong drink." No doubt the average colonist in Virginia, when not sobered by important cares, was apt to be a fellow of coarse fibre, whose

"addiction was to courses vain;
His companies unlettered, rude, and shallow;
His hours fill'd up with riots, banquets, sports;
And never noted in him any study,
Any retirement, any sequestration
From open haunts and popularity."

ALEXANDER SPOTSWOOD

Bat to many a scapegrace had come "reformation in a flood, with such a heady current, scouring faults," as to make a notable man of him. There were at least the traditions of culture in the colony, and enough men of education and refinement to leaven the mass. Life ran generously, even if roughly, upon the scattered plantations, and strong, thinking, high-bred men had somehow a mastery and leadership in it all which made them feel Virginia their home and field of honor.

Change of time and of affairs, the stir of growing life in Virginia as she ceased from being a mere colony and became a sturdy commonwealth, boasting her own breed of gentlemen, merchants, scholars, and statesmen, laid upon the Washingtons, as upon other men, a touch of transformation. Seventy-six years had gone by since John Washington came out of Bedfordshire and took up lands on Bridges' Creek in Westmoreland in Virginia, and still his children were to be found in the old seats he had chosen at the first. They had become thorough Virginians with the rest, woven into the close fibre of the new life. Westmoreland and all the counties that lay about it on the Northern Neck were strictly of a piece with the rest of Virginia, for all they had waited long to be settled. There the Washingtons had become country gentlemen of comfortable estate upon the accepted model. John had begotten Lawrence, and Lawrence had begotten Augustine. John had thriftily taken care to see his offspring put in a way to prosper at the very first. He had acquired a substantial property of his own where the land lay very fertile upon the banks of the Potomac, and he had, besides, by three marriages, made good a very close connection with several families that had thriven thereabouts before him. He had become a notable figure, indeed, among his neighbors ere he had been many years in the colony—a colonel in their militia, and their representative in the House of Burgesses; and they had not waited for his death to call the parish in which he lived Washington Parish. His sons and grandsons, though they slackened a little the pace he had set them in his energy at the outset, throve none the less substantially upon the estates he had left them, abated nothing of the dignity and worth they had inherited, lived simply, and kept their place of respect in the parish and state. Wars came and went without disturbing incident for them, as the French moved upon the borders by impulse of politics from over sea; and then long peace set in, equally without incident, to stay a whole generation, while good farming went quietly forward, and politicians at home and in the colonies planned another move in their game. It was in the mid-season of this time of poise, preparation, and expectancy that George Washington was born, on the 22d of February, in the year 1732, " about ten in the morning," William Gooch, gentlest of Marlborough's captains, being Governor in Virginia. He came into the world at the plain but spacious homestead on Bridges' Creek, fourth son, fifth child, of Augustine Washington, and of the third generation from John Washington, son of the one-time rector of Purleigh. The homestead stood upon a green and gentle slope that fell away, at but a little distance, to the waters of the Potomac, and from it could be seen the broad reaches of the stream stretching wide to the Maryland shore beyond, and flooding with slow, full tide to the great bay below. The spot gave token of the quiet youth of the boy, of the years of grateful peace in which he was to learn the first lessons of life, ere war and the changing fortunes of bis country hurried him to the field and to the council.

Chapter II
A Virginian Breeding

George Washington was cast for his career by a very scant and homely training. Augustine Washington, his father, lacked neither the will nor the means to set him handsomely afoot, with as good a schooling, both in books and in affairs, as was to be had; he would have done all that a liberal and provident man should do to advance his boy in the world, had he lived to go with him through his youth. He owned land in four counties, more than five thousand acres all told, and lying upon both the rivers that refresh the fruitful Northern Neck; besides several plots of ground in the promising village of Fredericksburg, which lay opposite his lands upon the Rappahannock; and one-twelfth part of the stock of the Principio Iron Company, whose mines and furnaces in Maryland and Virginia yielded a better profit than any others in the two colonies. He had commanded a ship in his time, as so many of his neighbors had in that maritime province, carrying iron from the mines to England, and no doubt bringing convict laborers back upon his voyage home again. He himself raised the ore from the mines that lay upon his own land, close to the Potomac, and had it carried the easy six miles to the river. Matters were very well managed there. Colonel Byrd said, and no pains were spared to make the business profitable. Captain Washington had represented his home parish of Truro, too, in the House of Burgesses, where his athletic figure, his ruddy skin, and frank gray eyes must have made him as conspicuous as his constituents could have wished. He was a man of the world, every inch, generous, hardy, independent. He lived long enough, too, to see how stalwart and capable and of how noble a spirit his young son was to be, with how manly a bearing he was to carry himself in the world; and had loved him and made him his companion accordingly. But the end came for him before be could see the lad out of boyhood. He died April 12, 1743, when he was but forty-nine years of age, and before George was twelve; and in his will there was, of course, for George only a younger son's portion. The active gentleman had been twice married, and there were seven children to be provided for. Two sons of the first marriage survived. The bulk of the estate went, as Virginian custom dictated, to Lawrence, the eldest son. To Augustine, the second son, fell most of the rich lands in Westmoreland. George, the eldest born of the second marriage, left to the guardianship of his young mother, shared with the four younger children the residue of the estate. He was to inherit his father's farm upon the Rappahannock, to possess, and to cultivate if he would, when he should come of age; but for the rest his fortunes were to make. He must get such serviceable training as he could for a life of independent endeavor. The two older brothers had been sent to England to get their schooling and preparation for life, as their father before them had been to get his-Lawrence to make ready to take his father's place when the time should come; Augustine, it was at first planned, to fit himself for the law. George could now look for nothing of the kind. He must continue, as he had begun, to get such elementary and practical Instruction as was to be had of schoolmasters in Virginia, and the young mother's care must stand him in the stead of a father's pilotage and oversight.

Fortunately Mary Washington was a wise and provident mother, a woman of too firm a character and too steadfast a courage to be dismayed by responsibility. She had seemed only a fair and beautiful girl when Augustine Washington married her, and there was a romantic story told of how that gallant Virginian sailor and gentleman had literally been thrown at her feet out of a carriage in the London streets by way of introduction - where she, too, was a visiting stranger out of Virginia. But she had shown a singular capacity for business when the romantic days of courtship were over. Lawrence Washington, too, though but five-and-twenty when his father died and left him head of the family, proved himself such an elder brother as it could but better and elevate a boy to have. For all he was so young, he had seen something of the world, and had already made notable friends. He had not returned home out of England until he was turned of twenty-one, and he had been back scarcely a twelvemonth before he was off again, to seek service in the war against Spain. The colonies had responded with an unwonted willingness and spirit in 1740 to the home government's call for troops to go against the Spaniard in the West Indies; and Lawrence Washington had sought and obtained a commission as captain in the Virginian regiment which had Volunteered for the duty. He had seen those terrible days at Cartagena, with Vernon's fleet and Wentworth's army, when the deadly heat and blighting damps of the tropics wrought a work of death which drove the English forth as no fire from the Spanish cannon could. He had been one of that devoted force which threw itself twelve hundred strong upon Fort San Lazaro, and came away beaten with six hundred only. He had seen the raw provincials out of the colonies carry themselves as gallantly as any veterans through all the fiery trial; had seen the storm and the valor, the vacillation and the blundering, and the shame of all the rash affair; and had come away the friend and admirer of the gallant Vernon, despite his headstrong folly and sad miscarriage. He had reached home again, late in the year 1742, only to see his father presently snatched away by a sudden illness, and to find himself become head of the family in his stead. All thought of further service away from home was dismissed. He accepted a commission as major in the colonial militia, and an appointment as adjutant-general of the military district in which his lands lay; but he meant that for the future his duties should be civil rather than military in the life he set himself to live, and turned very quietly to the business and the social duty of a proprietor among his neighbors in Fairfax County, upon the broad estates to which he gave the name Mount Vernon, in compliment to the brave sailor whose friend he had become in the far, unhappy South.

Marriage was, of course, his first step towards domestication, and the woman he chose brought him into new connections which suited both his tastes and his training. Three months after his father's death he married Anne Fairfax, daughter to William Fairfax, his neighbor. 'Twas William Fairfax's granduncle Thomas, third Lord Fairfax, who had in that revolutionary year 1646 summoned Colonel Henry Washington to give into his hands the city of Worcester, and who had got so sharp an answer from the King's stout soldier. But the Fairfaxes had soon enough turned royalists again when they saw whither the Parliament men would carry them. A hundred healing years had gone by since those unhappy days when the nation was arrayed against the King. Anne Fairfax brought no alien tradition to the household of her young husband. Her father had served the King, as her lover had-with more hardship than reward, as behooved a soldier-in Spain and in the Bahamas; and was now, when turned of fifty, agent here in Virginia to his cousin Thomas, sixth Baron Fairfax, in the management of his great estates, lying upon the Northern Neck and in the fruitful valleys beyond. William Fairfax had been but nine years in the colony, but he was already a Virginian like his neighbors, and, as collector of his Majesty's customs for the South Potomac and President of the King's Council, no small figure in their affairs —a man who had seen the world and knew how to bear himself in this part of it.

THOMAS, SIXTH LORD FAIRFAX

In 1746 Thomas, Lord Fairfax, himself came to Virginia—a man strayed out of the world of fashion at fifty-five into the forests of a wild frontier. The better part of his ancestral estates in Yorkshire had been sold to satisfy the creditors of his spendthrift father. These untilled stretches of land in the Old Dominion were now become the chief part of his patrimony. 'Twas said, too, that he had suffered a cruel misadventure in love at the hands of a fair jilt in London, and so had become the austere, eccentric bachelor he showed himself to be in the free and quiet colony.

A man of taste and culture, he had written with Addison and Steele for the Spectator; a man of the world, be had acquired, for all his reserve, that easy touch and intimate mastery in dealing with men which come with the long practice of such men of fashion as are also men of sense. He brought with him to Virginia, though past fifty, the fresh vigor of a young man eager for the free pioneer life of such a province. lie tarried but two years with his cousin, where the colony had settled to an ordered way of living. Then he built himself a roomy lodge, shadowed by spreading piazzas, and fitted with such simple appointments as sufficed for comfort at the depths of the forest, close upon seventy miles away, within the valley of the Shenandoah, where a hardy frontier people had but begun to gather. The great manor-house he had meant to build was never begun. The plain comforts of "Green way Court" satisfied him more and more easily as the years passed, and the habits of a simple life grew increasingly pleasant and familiar, till thirty years and more had slipped away and he was dead, at ninety-one —broken-hearted, men said, because the King's government had fallen upon final defeat and was done with in America.

It was in the company of these men, and of those who naturally gathered about them in that hospitable country, that George Washington was bred. "A stranger had no more to do," says Beverley, " but to inquire upon the road where any gentleman or good housekeeper lived, and there he might depend upon being received with hospitality"; and 'twas certain many besides strangers would seek out the young major at Mount Vernon whom his neighbors had hastened to make their representative in the House of Burgesses, and the old soldier of the soldierly house of Fairfax who was President of the King's Council, and so next to the Governor himself. A boy who was much at Mount Vernon and at Mr. Fairfax's seat, Belvoir, might expect to see not a little that was worth seeing of the life of the colony. George was kept at school until he was close upon sixteen; but there was ample vacation-time for visiting. Mrs. Washington did not keep him at her apron-strings. He even lived, when it was necessary, with his brother Augustine, at the old home on Bridges' Creek, in order to be near the best school that was accessible, while the mother was far away on the farm that lay upon the Rappahannock. Mrs. Washington saw to it, nevertheless, that she should not lose sight of him altogether. When he was fourteen it was proposed that he should be sent to sea, as so many lads were, no doubt, from that maritime province; but the prudent mother preferred he should not leave Virginia, and the schooling went on as before-the schooling of books and manly sports. Every lad learned to ride-to ride colt or horse, regardless of training, gait, or temper —in that country, where no one went afoot except to catch his mount in the pasture. Every lad, black or white, bond or free, knew where to find and how to take the roving game in the forests. And young Washington, robust boy that he was, not to be daunted while that strong spirit sat in him which he got from his father and mother alike, took his apprenticeship on horseback and in the tangled woods with characteristic zest and ardor.

He was, above all things else, a capable, executive boy. He loved mastery, and he relished acquiring the most effective means of mastery in all practical affairs. His very exercise-books used at school gave proof of it.

They were filled, not only with the rules, formulae, diagrams, and exercises of surveying, which he was taking special pains to learn, at the advice of his friends, but also with careful copies of legal and mercantile papers, bills of exchange, bills of sale, bonds, indentures, land warrants, leases, deeds, and wills, as if he meant to be a lawyer's or a merchant's clerk. It would seem that, passionate and full of warm blood as he was, he conned these things as he studied the use and structure of his fowling-piece, the bridle he used for his colts, his saddle-girth, and the best ways of mounting. He copied these forms of business as he might have copied Beverley's account of the way fox or 'possum or beaver was to be taken or the wild turkey trapped. The men he most admired-his elder brothers, Mr. Fairfax, and the gentlemen planters who were so much at their houses-were most of them sound men of business, who valued good surveying as much as they admired good horsemanship and skill in sport. They were their own merchants, and looked upon forms of business paper as quite as useful as ploughs and hogsheads. Careful exercise in such matters might well enough accompany practice in the equally formal minuet in Virginia. And so this boy learned to show in almost everything he did the careful precision of the perfect marksman.

In the autumn of 1747, when he was not yet quite sixteen, George quit his formal schooling, and presently-joined his brother Lawrence at Mount Vernon, to seek counsel and companionship. Lawrence had conceived a strong affection for his manly younger brother. Himself a man of spirit and honor, he had a high-hearted man's liking for all that he saw that was indomitable and well-purposed in the lad, a generous man's tenderness in looking to the development of this thoroughbred boy; and he took him into his confidence as if he had been his own son. Not only upon his vacations now, but almost when he would, and as if he were already himself a man with the rest, he could live in the comradeship that obtained at Belvoir and Mount Vernon. Men of all sorts, it seemed, took pleasure in his company. Lads could be the companions of men in Virginia. Her outdoor life of journeying, sport, adventure, put them, as it were, upon equal terms with their elders, where spirit, audacity, invention, prudence, manliness, resource, told for success and comradeship. Young men and old can be companions in arms, in sport, in woodcraft, and on the trail of the fox. 'Twas not an indoor life of conference, but an outdoor life of affairs in this rural colony. One man, indeed, gave at least a touch of another quality to the life Washington saw. This was Lord Fairfax, who had been almost two years in Virginia when the boy quit school, and who was now determined, as soon as might be, to take up his residence at his forest lodge within the Blue Ridge. George greatly struck his lordship's fancy, as he did that of all capable men, as a daring lad in the hunt and a sober lad in counsel; and, drawn into such companionship, he learned a great deal that no one else in Virginia could have taught him so well — the scrupulous deportment of a high-bred and honorable man of the world; the use of books by those who preferred affairs; the way in which strength may be rendered gracious, and independence made generous. A touch of Old World address was to be learned at Belvoir.

His association with Lord Fairfax, moreover, put him in the way of making his first earnings as a surveyor.

Fairfax had not come to America merely to get away from the world of fashion in London and bury himself in the wilderness. His chief motive was one which did him much more credit, and bespoke him a man and a true colonist. It was his purpose, he declared, to open up, settle, and cultivate the vast tracts of beautiful and fertile land he had inherited in Virginia, and he proved his sincerity by immediately setting about the business. It was necessary as a first step that he should have surveys made, in order that he might know how his lands lay, how bounded and disposed through the glades and upon the streams of the untrodden forests; and in young Washington he had a surveyor ready to his hand. The lad was but sixteen, indeed; was largely self-taught in surveying; and had had no business yet that made test of his quality. But surveyors were scarce, and boys were not tender at sixteen in that robust, outdoor colony. Fairfax had an eye for capacity. He knew the athletic boy to be a fearless woodsman, with that odd, calm judgment looking forth at his steady gray eyes; perceived how seriously he took himself in all that he did, and how thorough he was at succeeding; and had no doubt he could run his lines through the thicketed forests as well as any man. At any rate, he commissioned him to undertake the task, and was not disappointed in the way he performed it. Within a very few weeks Washington conclusively showed his capacity. In March, 1748, with George Fairfax, William Fairfax's son, for company, he rode forth with his little band of assistants through the mountains to the wild country where his work lay, and within the month almost he was back again, with maps and figures which showed his lordship very clearly what lands he had upon the sparkling Shenandoah and the swollen upper waters of the Potomac. 'Twas all he wanted before making his home where his estate lay in the wilderness. Before the year was out he had established himself at Greenway Court; huntsmen and tenants and guests had found their way thither, and life was fairly begun upon the rough rural barony.

It had been wild and even perilous work for the young surveyor, but just out of school, to go in the wet springtime into that wilderness, when the rivers were swollen and ugly with the rains and melting snows from off the mountains, where there was scarcely a lodging to be had except in the stray, comfortless cabins of the scattered settlers, or on the ground about a fire in the open woods, and where a woodman's wits were needed to come even tolerably off. But there was a strong relish in such an experience for Washington, which did not wear off with the novelty of it. There is an unmistakable note of boyish satisfaction in the tone in which he speaks of it. "Since you received my letter in October last," he writes to a young comrade, "I have not sleep'd above three nights or four in a bed, but, after walking a good deal all the day, I lay down before the fire upon a little hay, straw, fodder, or bear-skin, whichever is to be had, with man, wife, and children, like a parcel of dogs and cats; and happy is he who gets the berth nearest the fire. ...I have never had my clothes off, but lay and sleep in them, except the few nights I have lay'n in Frederick Town." For three years he kept steadily at the trying business, without loss either of health or courage, now deep in the forests laboriously laying off the rich bottom lands and swelling hill-sides of that wild but goodly country between the mountains, now at Greenway Court with his lordship, intent upon the busy life there, — following the hounds, consorting with huntsmen and Indians and traders, waiting upon the ladies who now and again visited the lodge; when other occupations failed, reading up and down in his lordship's copy of the Spectator, or in the historians who told the great English story. His first success in surveying brought him frequent employment in the valley. Settlers were steadily making their way thither, who must needs have their holdings clearly bounded and defined. Upon his lordship's recommendation and his own showing of what he knew and could do, he obtained appointment at the hands of the President and Master of William and Mary, the colony's careful agent in the matter, as official surveyor for Culpeper County, "took the usual oaths to his Majesty's person and government," and so got for his work the privilege of authoritative public record.

Competent surveyors were much in demand, and, when once he had been officially accredited in his profession, Washington had as much to do both upon new lands and old as even a young man's energy and liking for an independent income could reasonably demand. His home he made with his brother at Mount Vernon, where he was always so welcome; and he was as often as possible with his mother at her place upon the Rappahannock, to lend the efficient lady such assistance as she needed in the business of the estate she held for herself and her children. At odd intervals he studied tactics, practised the manual of arms, or took a turn at the broadsword with the old soldiers who so easily found excuses for visiting Major Washington at Mount Vernon. But, except when winter weather forbade him the fields, he was abroad, far and near, busy with his surveying, and incidentally making trial of his neighbors up and down all the country-side round about, as his errands threw their open doors in his way. His pleasant bearing and his quiet satisfaction at being busy, his manly, efficient ways, his evident self-respect, and his frank enjoyment of life, the engaging mixture in him of man and boy, must have become familiar to everybody worth knowing throughout all the Northern Neck.

But three years put a term to his surveying. In 1751 he was called imperatively off, and had the whole course of his life changed, by the illness of his brother. Lawrence Washington had never been robust; those long months spent at the heart of the fiery South with Vernon's fever-stricken fleet had touched his sensitive constitution to the quick, and at last a fatal consumption fastened upon him. Neither a trip to England nor the waters of the warm springs at home brought him recuperation, and in the autumn of 1751 his physician ordered him to the Bahamas for the winter. George, whom he so loved and trusted, went with him, to nurse and cheer him. But even the gentle sea-air of the islands wrought no cure of the stubborn malady. The sterling, gifted, lovable gentleman, who had made his quiet seat at Mount Vernon the home of so much that was honorable and of good report, came back the next summer to die in his prime, at thirty-four. George found himself named executor in his brother's will, and looked to of a sudden to guard all the interests of the young widow and her little daughter in the management of a large estate. That trip to the Bahamas had been his last outing as a boy. He had enjoyed the novel journey with a very keen and natural relish while it promised his brother health. The radiant air of those summer isles had touched him with a new pleasure, and the cordial hospitality of the homesick colonists had added the satisfaction of a good welcome. He had braved the small-pox in one household with true Virginian punctilio rather than refuse an invitation to dinner, had taken the infection, and had come home at last bearing some permanent marks of a three weeks' sharp illness upon him. But he had had entertainment enough to strike the balance handsomely against such inconveniences, had borne whatever came in his way very cheerily, with that wholesome strength of mind which made older men like him, and would have come off remembering nothing but the pleasure of the trip had his noble brother only found his health again. As it was, Lawrence's death put a final term to his youth. Five other executors were named in the will; but George, as it turned out, was to be looked to to carry the burden of administration, and gave full proof of the qualities that had made his brother trust him with so generous a confidence.

His brother's death, in truth, changed everything for him. He seemed of a sudden to stand as Lawrence's representative. Before they set out for the Bahamas Lawrence had transferred to him his place in the militia, obtaining for him, though he was but nineteen, a commission as major and district adjutant in his stead; and after his return, in 1752, Lieutenant-Governor Dinwiddie, the crown's new representative in Virginia, added still further to his responsibilities as a soldier by reducing the military districts of the colony to four, and assigning to him one of the four, under a renewed commission as major and adjutant-general. His brother's will not only named him an executor, but also made him residuary legatee of the estate of Mount Vernon in case his child should die. He had to look to the discipline and accouterment of the militia of eleven counties, aid his mother in her business, administer his brother's estate, and assume on all hands the duties and responsibilities of a man of affairs when he was but just turned of twenty.

LAWRENCE WASHINGTON

The action of the colonial government in compacting the organization and discipline of the militia by redoing the number of military districts was significant of a sinister change in the posture of affairs beyond the borders. The movements of the French in the West had of late become more ominous than ever; 'twas possible the Virginian militia might any day see an end of that "everlasting peace" which good Mr. Beverley had smiled to see them complacently enjoy, and that the young major, who was now Adjutant-General of the Northern Division, might find duties abroad even more serious and responsible than his duties at home. Whoever should be commissioned to meet and deal with the French upon the western rivers would have to handle truly critical affairs, decisive of the fate of the continent, and it looked as if Virginia must undertake the fateful business. The northern borders, indeed, were sadly harried by the savage allies of the French; the brunt of the fighting hitherto had fallen upon the hardy militiamen of Massachusetts and Connecticut in the slow contest for English mastery upon the continent. But there was really nothing to be decided in that quarter. The French were not likely to attempt the mad task of driving out the thickly set English population, already established, hundreds of thousands strong, upon the eastern coasts. Their true lines of conquest ran within. Their strength lay in their command of the great watercourses which flanked the English colonies both north and west. 'Twas a long frontier to hold, that mazy line of lake and river that ran all the way from the Gulf of St. Lawrence to the wide months of the sluggish Mississippi. Throughout all the posts and settlements that lay upon it from end to end there were scarcely eighty thousand Frenchmen, while the English teemed upon the coasts more than a million strong. But the forces of New France could be handled like an army, while the English swarmed slowly westward, without discipline or direction, the headstrong subjects of a distant government they would not obey, the wayward constituents of a score of petty and jealous assemblies tardy at planning, clumsy at executing plans. They were still far away, too, from the mid-waters of the lakes and from the royal stream of the Mississippi itself, where lonely boats floated slowly down, with their cargoes of grain, meat, tallow, tobacco, oil, hides, and lead, out of the country of the Illinois, past the long, thin line of tiny isolated posts, to the growing village at New Orleans and the southern Gulf. But they were to be feared, none the less. If their tide once flowed in, the French well knew it could not be turned back again. It was not far away from the Ohio now; and if once settlers out of Pennsylvania and Virginia gained a foothold in any numbers on that river, they would control one of the great highways that led to the main basins of the continent. It was imperative they should be effectually forestalled, and that at once.

The Marquis Duquesne, with his quick soldier blood, at last took the decisive step for France. He had hardly come to his colony, to serve his royal master as Governor upon the St. Lawrence, when he determined to occupy the upper waters of the Ohio, and block the western passes against the English with a line of military posts. The matter did not seem urgent to the doubting ministers at Versailles. "Be on your guard against new undertakings," said official letters out of France; "private interests are generally at the bottom of them." But Buquesne knew that it was no mere private interest of fur trader or speculator that was at stake now. The rivalry between the two nations had gone too far to make it possible to draw back. Military posts had already been established by the bold energy of the French at Niagara, the key to the western lakes, and at Crown Point upon Champlain, where lake and river struck straight towards the heart of the English trading settlements upon the Hudson. The English, accepting the challenge, had planted themselves at Oswego, upon the very lake route itself, and had made a port there to take the furs that came out of the West, and, though very sluggish in the business, showed purpose of aggressive movement everywhere that advantage offered. English settlers by the hundred were pressing towards the western mountains in Pennsylvania, and down into that" Virginian Arcady," the sweet valley of the Shenandoah: thrifty Germans, a few; hardy Scots-Irish, a great many-the blood most to be feared and checked. It was said that quite three hundred English traders passed the mountains every year into the region of the Ohio.

Enterprising gentlemen in Virginia-Lawrence and Augustine Washington among the rest-had joined influential partners in London in the formation of an Ohio Company for the settlement of the western country and the absorption of the western trade; had sent out men who knew the region to make interest with the Indians and fix upon points of vantage for trading-posts and settlements; had already set out upon the business by erecting storehouses at Will's Creek, in the heart of the Alleghenies, and, farther westward still, upon Redstone Creek, a branch of the Monongahela itself.

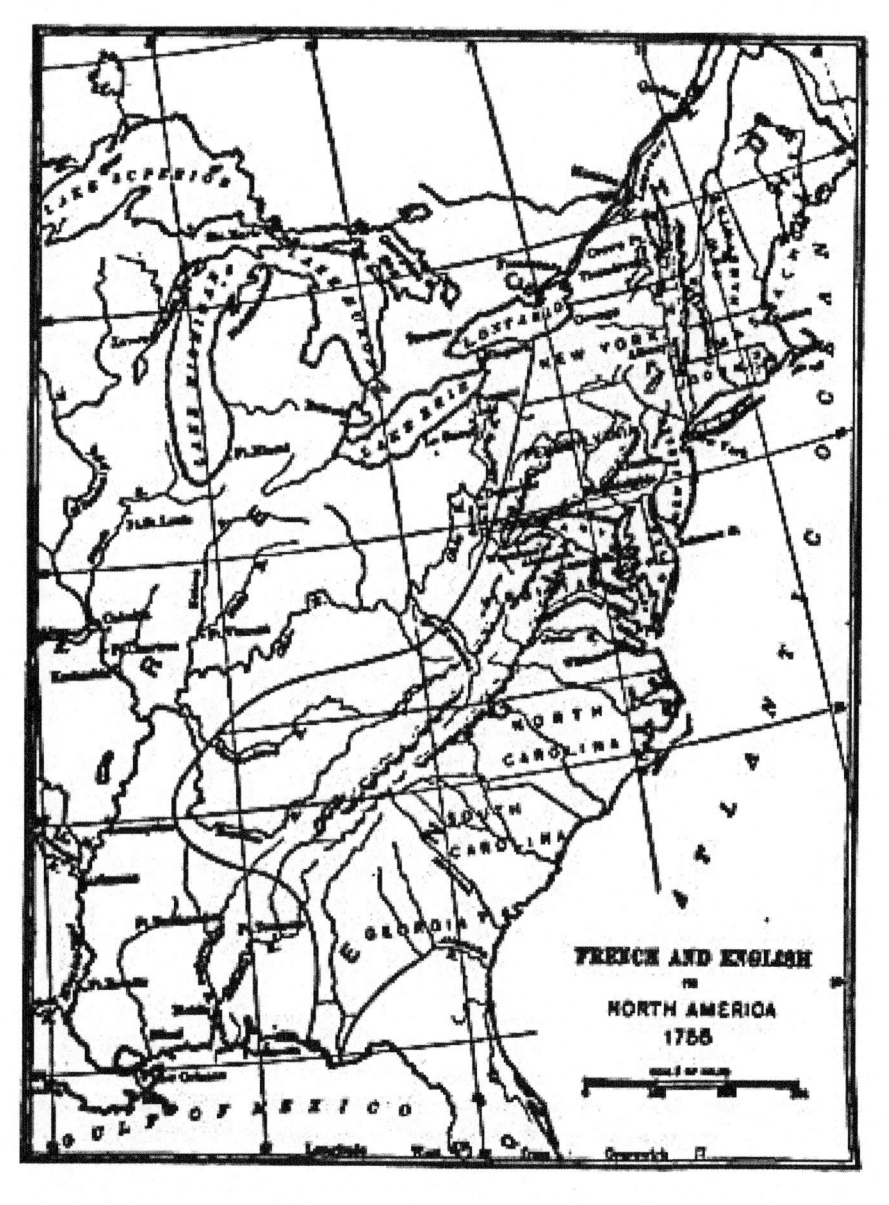

FRENCH AND ENGLISH IN NORTH AMERICA 1755

It was high time to act; and Duquesne, having no colonial assembly to hamper him, acted very promptly. When spring came, 1753, he sent fifteen hundred men into Lake Erie, to

Presque Isle, where a fort of squared logs was built, and a road cut through the forests to a little river whose waters, when at the flood, would carry boats direct to the Alleghany and the great waterway of the Ohio itself. An English lieutenant at Oswego had descried the multitudinous fleet of canoes upon Ontario carrying this levy to its place of landing in the lake beyond, and a vagrant Frenchman had told him plainly what it was. It was an army of six thousand men, he boasted, going to the Ohio, "to cause all the English to quit those parts." It was plain to every English Governor in the colonies who had his eyes open that the French would not stop with planting a fort upon an obscure branch of the Alleghany, but that they would indeed press forward to take possession of the Ohio, drive every English trader forth, draw all the native tribes to their interest by force or favor, and close alike the western lands and the western trade in very earnest against all the King's subjects.

Governor Dinwiddie was among the first to see the danger and the need for action, as, in truth, was very natural. In office and out, his study had been the colonial trade, and he had been merchant and official now a long time. He was one of the twenty stockholders of the Ohio Company, and had come to his governorship in Virginia with his eye upon the western country. He had but to look about him to perceive that Virginia would very likely be obliged to meet the crisis unaided, if, indeed, he could induce even her to meet it. Governor Hamilton, of Pennsylvania, also saw how critically affairs stood, it is true, and what ought to be done. His agents had met and acted with the agents of the Ohio Company already in seeking Indian alliances and fixing upon points of vantage beyond the Alleghanies. But the Pennsylvania Assembly could by no argument or device be induced to vote money or measures in the business. The placid Quaker traders were as stubborn as the stolid German farmers. They opposed warlike action on principle. The Germans opposed it because they could not for the life of them see the necessity of parting with their money to send troops upon so remote an errand. Dinwiddie did not wait or parley. He acted first, and consulted his legislature afterwards. It was in his Scots blood to take the business very strenuously, and in his trader's blood to take it very anxiously. He had kept himself advised from the first of the movements of the French. Their vanguard had scarcely reached Presque Isle ere he despatched letters to England apprising the government of the danger. Answer had come very promptly, too, authorizing him to build forts upon the Ohio, if he could get the money from the Burgesses; and meantime, should the French trespass further, " to require of them peaceably to depart." If they would not desist for a warning, said his Majesty, "we do hereby strictly charge and command you to drive them off by force of arms."

Even to send a warning to the French was no easy matter when the King's letter came and the chill autumn rains were at hand. The mountain streams, already swollen, presently to be full of ice, would be very dangerous for men and horses, and the forests were likely enough to teem with hostile savages, now the French were there. A proper messenger was found and despatched, nevertheless-young Major George Washington, of the Northern District. The errand lay in his quarter; his three years of surveying at the heart of the wilderness had made him an experienced woodsman and hardy traveller, had tested his pluck and made proof of his character; he was well known upon the frontier, and his friends were very influential, and very cordial in recommending him for this or any other manly service that called for steadiness, hardihood, and resource. Dinwiddie had been a correspondent of Lawrence Washington's ever since the presidency of the Ohio Company had fallen to the young Virginian upon the death of his neighbor Thomas Lee, writing to him upon terms of intimacy. He knew the stock of which George, the younger brother, came, and the interests in which he might be expected to embark with ardor; he could feel that he took small risk in selecting such an agent. Knowing him, too, thus through his family and like a friend, he did not hesitate in writing to Governor Hamilton, of Pennsylvania, to speak of this youth of twenty-one as " a person of distinction."

Washington performed his errand as Dinwiddie must have expected he would. He received his commission and the Governor's letter to the French commandant on the last day of October, and set out the same day for the mountains. Jacob Vanbraam, the Dutch soldier of fortune who had been his fencing-master at Mount Vernon, accompanied him as interpreter, and Christopher Gist, the hardy, self-reliant frontier trader, whom the Ohio Company had employed to make interest for them among the Indians of the far region upon the western rivers which he knew so well, was engaged to act as his guide and counsellor; and with a few servants and pack-horses he struck straight into the forests in the middle of bleak November. It was the 11th of December before the jaded party rode, in the cold dusk, into the drenched and miry clearing where the dreary little fort stood that held the French commander. Through two hundred and fifty miles and more of forest they had dragged themselves over swollen rivers, amidst an almost ceaseless fall of rain or snow, with not always an Indian trail, even, or the beaten track of the bison, to open the forest growth for their flagging horses, and on the watch always against savage treachery." It had become plain enough before they reached their destination what answer they should get from the French. Sixty miles nearer home than these lonely headquarters of the French commander at Fort Le Boeuf they had come upon an outpost where the French colors were to be seen flying from a house from which an English trader had been driven out, and the French officers there had uttered brutally frank avowal of their purpose in that wilderness as they sat at wine with the alert and temperate young Virginian. " It was their absolute design," they said, "to take possession of the Ohio, and, by G—, they would do it....They were sensible the English could raise two men for their one, yet they knew their motions were too slow and dilatory to prevent any undertaking of theirs." The commandant at Fort Le Boeuf received the wayworn ambassador very courteously, and even graciously—a thoughtful elderly man, Washington noted him,"with much the air of a soldier " —but would make no profession even that he would consider the English summons to withdraw; and the little party of Englishmen presently turned back amidst the winter's storms to carry through the frozen wilderness a letter which boasted the French lawful masters of all the continent beyond the Alleghanies. When Washington reached Williamsburg, in the middle of January, 1754, untouched by even the fearful fatigues and anxieties of that daring journey, he had accomplished nothing but the establishment of his own character in the eyes of the men who were to meet the crisis now at hand. He had been at infinite pains, at every stage of the dreary adventure, to win and hold the confidence of the Indians who were accounted friends of the English, and had displayed an older man's patience, address, and fortitude in meeting all their subtle shifts; and he had borne hardships that tried even the doughty Gist. When the horses gave out, he had left them to come by easier stages, while he made his way afoot, with only a single companion, across the weary leagues that lay upon his homeward way. Gist, his comrade in the hazard, had been solicitously "unwilling he should undertake such a travel, who had never been used to walking before this time," but the imperative young commander would not be stayed, and the journey was made, spite of sore feet and frosts and exhausting weariness. He at least knew what the French were about, with what strongholds and forces, and could afford to await orders what to do next.

Chapter III
Colonel Washington

Dinwiddie had not been idle while Washington went his perilous errand. He had gotten the Bargesses together by the 1st of November, before Washington had left the back settlements to cross the wilderness, and would have gotten a liberal grant of money from them had they not fallen in their debates upon the question of the new fee charged, since his coming, for every grant out of the public lands of the colony, and insisted that it should be done away with. "Subjects," they said, very stubbornly, "cannot be deprived of the least part of their property without their consent;" and such a fee, they thought, was too like a tax to be endured. They would withhold the grant, they declared, unless the fee was abolished, notwithstanding they saw plainly enough in how critical a case things stood in the West; and the testy Governor very indignantly sent them home again. He ordered a draft of two hundred men from the militia, nevertheless, with the purpose of assigning the command to Washington and seeing what might be done upon the Ohio, without vote of Assembly. A hard-headed Scotsman past sixty could not be expected to wait upon a body of wrangling and factious provincials for leave to perform his duty in a crisis, and, inasmuch as the object was to save their own lands, and perhaps their own persons, from the French, could hardly be blamed for proposing in his anger that they be taxed for the purpose by act of Parliament. "A Governor," he exclaimed, " is really to be pitied in the discharge of his duty to his King and country in haying to do with such obstinate, self-conceited people!" Some money he advanced out of his own pocket. When Washington came back from his fruitless mission, Dinwiddle ordered his journal printed and copies sent to all the colonial Governors. " As it was thought advisable by his Honour the Governor to have the following account of my proceedings to and from the French on Ohio committed to print," said the modest young major, "I think I can do no less than apologize, in some measure, for the numberless imperfections of it." But it was a very manly recital of noteworthy things, and touched the imagination and fears of every thoughtful man who read it quite as near the quick as the urgent and repeated letters of the troubled Dinwiddie.

Virginia, it turned out, was, after all, more forward than her neighbors when it came to action. The Pennsylvania Assembly very coolly declared they doubted his Majesty's claim to the lands on the Ohio, and the Assembly in New York followed suit. " It appears," they said, in high judicial tone, "that the French have built a fort at a place called French Creek, at a considerable distance from the river Ohio, which may, but does not by any evidence or information appear to us to be, an invasion of any of his Majesty's colonies." The Governors of the other colonies whose safety was most directly menaced by the movements of the French in the West were thus even less able to act than Dinwiddie. For the Virginian Burgesses, though they would not yield the point of the fee upon land grants, did not mean to leave Major Washington in the lurch, and before an expedition could be got afoot had come together again to vote a sum of money. It would be possible with the sum they appropriated to put three or four hundred men into the field; and as spring drew on, raw volunteers began to gather in some numbers at Alexandria —a ragged regiment, made up for the most part of idle and shiftless men, who did not always have shoes, or even shirts, of their own to wear; anxious to get their eightpence a day, but not anxious to work or submit to discipline. 'Twas astonishing how steady and how spirited they showed themselves when once they had shaken their lethargy off and were on the march or face to face with the enemy. A body of backwoodsmen had been hurried forward in February, ere spring had opened, to make a clearing and set to work upon a fort at the forks of the Ohio; but it was the 2d of April before men enough could be collected at Alexandria to begin the main movement towards the frontier, and by that time it was too late to checkmate the French. The little force sent forward to begin fortifications had set about their task very sluggishly and without skill, and their commander had turned back again with some of his men to rejoin the forces behind him before the petty works he should have stayed to finish were well begun. When, therefore, on the 17th of April, the river suddenly filled with canoes bearing an army of more than five hundred Frenchmen, who put cannon ashore, and summoned the forty men who held the place to surrender or be blown into the water, there was no choice but to comply. The young ensign who commanded the little garrison urged a truce till he could communicate with his superiors, but the French commander would brook no delay. The boy might either take his men off free and unhurt, or else fight and face sheer destruction; and the nearest succor was a little force of one hundred and fifty men under Colonel Washington, who had not yet topped the Alleghanies in their painful work of cutting a way through the forests for their field-pieces and wagons.

The Governor's plans had been altered by the Assembly's vote of money and the additional levy of men which it made possible. Colonel Joshua Fry, whom Dinwiddle deemed "a man of good sense, and one of our best mathematicians," had been given the command in chief, and Washington had been named his second in command, with the rank of lieutenant-colonel. " Dear George," wrote Mr. Corbin, of the Governor's Council, "I enclose you your commission. God prosper you with it!" and the brunt of the work in fact fell upon the younger man. But three hundred volunteers could be gotten together; and, all too late, half of the raw levy were sent forward under Washington to find or make a way for wagons and ordnance to the Ohio. The last days of May were almost at hand before they had crossed the main ridge of the Alleghanies, so inexperienced were they in the rough labor of cutting a road through the close-set growth and over the sharp slopes of the mountains, and so ill equipped; and by that time it was already too late by a full month and more to forestall the French, who had only to follow the open highway of the Alleghany to bring what force they would to the key of the West at the forks of the Ohio. As the spring advanced, the French force upon the river grew from five to fourteen hundred men, and work was pushed rapidly forward upon fortifications such as the little band of Englishmen they had ousted had not thought of attempting—a veritable fort, albeit of a rude frontier pattern, which its builders called Duquesne, in honor of their Governor. Washington could hit upon no watercourse that would afford him quick transport; 'twould have been folly, besides, to take his handful of ragged provincials into the presence of an intrenched army. He was fain to go into camp at Great Meadows, just across the ridge of the mountains, and there await his Colonel with supplies and an additional handful of men.

It was "a charming field for an encounter," the young commander thought, but it was to be hoped the enemy would not find their way to it in too great numbers. An "Independent Company" of provincials in the King's pay joined him out of South Carolina, whence they had been sent forward by express orders from England; and the rest of the Virginia volunteers at last came up to join their comrades at the Meadows-without good Colonel Fry, the doughty mathematician, who had sickened and died on the way-so that there were presently more than three hundred men at the camp, and Washington was now their commander-in-chief. The officers of the Independent Company from South Carolina, holding their commissions from the King, would not, indeed, take their orders from Washington, with his colonial commission merely; and, what was worse, their men would not work; but there was no doubt they would fight with proper dignity and spirit for his Majesty, their royal master. The first blood had already been drawn, on the 28th of May, before reinforcements had arrived, when Washington had but just come to camp. Upon the morning of that day Washington, with forty men, guided by friendly Indians, had come upon a party of some thirty Frenchmen where they larked deep within the thickets of the dripping forest, and, with thrust of bayonet when the wet guns failed, had brought them to a surrender within fifteen minutes of the first surprise. No one in the Virginian camp doubted that there was war already, or dreamed of awaiting the action of diplomats and cabinets over sea. The French had driven an English garrison from the forks of the Ohio with threats of force, which would certainly have been executed had there been need. These men hidden in the thickets at Great Meadows would have it, when the fight was over, that they had come as messengers merely to bear a peaceful summons; but did it need thirty odd armed men to bear a message? Why had they lurked for five days so stealthily in the forest; and why had they sent runners back posthaste to Fort Duquesne to obtain support for their diplomacy? Washington might regret that young M. Jumonville, their commander, had lost his life in the encounter, but he had no doubt he had done right to order his men to fire when he saw the French spring for their arms at the first surprise.

Now, at any rate, war was unquestionably begun. That sudden volley fired in the wet woods at the heart of the lonely Alleghanies had set the final struggle ablaze. It was now either French or English in America: it could no longer be both. Jumonville with his thirty Frenchmen was followed ere many weeks were out by Coulon de Villiers with seven hundred-some of them come all the way from Montreal at news of what had happened to France's lurking ambassadors in the far-away mountains of Virginia. On the 3d of July they closed to an encounter at "Fort Necessity," Washington's rude intrenchments upon the Great Meadows. There were three hundred and fifty Englishmen with him able to fight, spite of sickness and short rations; and as the enemy began to show themselves at the edges of the neighboring woods through the damp mists of that dreary morning, Washington drew his little force up outside their works upon the open meadow. He "thought the French would come up to him in open field," laughed a wily Indian, who gave him counsel freely, but no aid in the fight; but Villiers had no mind to meet the gallant young Virginian in that manly fashion. Once, indeed, they rushed to his trenches, but, finding hot reception there, kept their distance after-wards. Villiers brought them after that only "as near as possible without uselessly exposing the lives of the King's subjects," and poured his fire in from the cover of the woods. For nine hours the unequal fight dragged on, the French and their Indians hardly showing themselves outside the shelter of the forest, the English crouching knee-deep in water in their rude trenches, while the rain poured incessantly, reducing their breastworks to a mass of slimy mud, and filling all the air with a chill and pallid mist. Day insensibly darkened into night in such an air, and it was eight o'clock when the firing ceased and the French asked a parley. Their men were tired of the dreary fight, their Indian allies threatened to leave them when morning should come, and they were willing the English should withdraw, if they would, without further hurt or molestation. The terms they offered seemed very acceptable to Washington's officers as the interpreter read them out, standing there in the drenching downpour and the black night.

"It rained so hard we could hardly keep the candle lighted to read them by," said an officer; bat there was really no choice what to do. More than fifty men lay dead or wounded in the flooded camp; the ammunition was all but spent; the French strength had hardly been touched in the fight, and might at any moment be increased. Capitulation was inevitable, and Washington did not hesitate.

The next morning saw his wretched force making their way back again along the rude road they had cut through the forests. They had neither horses nor wagons to carry their baggage. What they could they burned; and then set out, sore stricken in heart and body, their wounded comrades and their scant store of food slung upon their backs, and dragged themselves very wearily all the fifty miles to the settlements at home. Two of the King's Independent Companies from New York ought to have joined them long ago, but had gotten no farther than Alexandria when the fatal day came at the Great Meadows. North Carolina had despatched three hundred and fifty of her militiamen, under an experienced officer, to aid them, but they also came too late. It had been expected that Maryland would raise two hundred and fifty men, and Pennsylvania had at last voted money, to be spent instead of blood, for she would levy no men; but no succor had come from any quarter when it should. The English were driven in, and all their plans were worse than undone.

It was a bitter trial for the young Virginian commander to have his first campaign end so disastrously — to be worsted in a petty fight, and driven back hopelessly outdone. No one he cared for in Virginia blamed him. His ragged troops had borne themselves like men in the fight; bis own gallantry no man could doubt. The House of Burgesses thanked him and voted money to his men. But it had been a rough apprenticeship, and Washington felt to the quick the lessons it had taught him. The discouraging work of recruiting at Alexandria, the ragged idlers to be governed there, the fruitless drilling of listless and insolent men, the two months' work with axe and spade cutting a way through the forests, the whole disheartening work of making ready for the fight, of seeking the enemy, and of choosing a field of encounter, he had borne as a stalwart young man can while his digestion holds good. He had at least himself done everything that was possible, and it had been no small relief to him to write plain-spoken letters to the men who were supposed to be helping him in Williamsburg, telling them exactly how things were going and who was to blame-letters which showed both how efficient and how proud he was. He had even shown a sort of boyish zest in the affair when it came to actual fighting with Jumonville and his scouts hidden in the forest. He had pressed to the thick of that hot and sudden skirmish, and had taken the French volleys with a lad's relish of the danger. "I heard the bullets whistle," he wrote his brother, "and believe me there is something charming in the sound." But after he had stood a day in the flooded trenches of his wretched "fort" at Great Meadows, and fought till evening in the open with an enemy he could not see, he knew that he had been taught a lesson; that he was very young at this terrible business of fighting; and that something more must be learned than could be read in the books at Mount Vernon. He kept a cheerful front in the dreary retreat, heartening his men bravely by word and example of steadfastness; but it was a sore blow to his pride and his hopes, and he must only have winced without protest could he have heard how Horace Walpole called him a "brave braggart" for his rodomontade about the music of deadly missiles.

He had no thought, however, of quitting his duty because his first campaign had miscarried. When he had made his report at Williamsburg he rejoined his demoralized regiment at Alexandria, where it lay but an hour's ride from Mount Vernon, and set about executing his orders to recruit once more, as if the business were only just begun. Captain Innes, who had brought three hundred and fifty men from North Carolina too late to be of assistance at the Meadows, and who had had the chagrin of seeing them take themselves off home again because there was no money forthcoming to pay them what had been promised, remained at Will's Creek, amidst the back settlements, to command the King's provincials from South Carolina who had been with Washington at the Meadows, and the two Independent Companies from New York, who had lingered so long on the way; and to build there a rough fortification, to be named Fort Cumberland, in honor of the far-away Duke who was commander-in-chief in England. Dinwiddie, having such hot Scots blood in him as pould brook no delays, and having been bred no soldier or frontiersman, but a merchant and man of business, would have had Washington's recruiting despatched at once, like a bill of goods, and a new force sent hot-foot to the Ohio again to catch the French while they were at ease over their victory and slackly upon their guard at Duquesne. When he was flatly told it was impossible, he turned to other plans, equally ill considered, though no doubt equally well meant. By October he had obtained of the Assembly twenty thousand pounds, and from the government at home ten thousand more in good specie, such as was scarce in the colony-for the sharp stir of actual fighting had had its effect alike upon King and Burgesses — and had ordered the formation and equipment of ten full companies for the frontier. But the new orders contained a sad civilian blunder. The ten companies should all be Independent Companies; there should be no officer higher than a captain amongst them. This, the good Scotsman thought, would accommodate all disputes about rank and precedence, such as had come near to making trouble between Washington and Captain Mackay, of the Independent Company from South Carolina, while they waited for the French at Great Meadows. Washington at once resigned, indignant to be so dealt with. Not only would he be reduced to a captaincy under such an arrangement, but every petty officer would outrank him who could show the King's commission. It was no tradition of his class to submit to degradation of rank thus by indirection and without fault committed, and his pride and sense of personal dignity, for all he was so young, were as high-strung as any man's in Virginia. He had shown his quality in such matters already, six months ago, while he lay in camp in the wilderness on his way towards the Ohio. The Burgesses had appointed a committee of their own to spend the money they had voted to put his expedition afoot in the spring, lest Dinwiddle should think, were they to give him the spending of it, that they had relented in the matter of the fees; and these gentlemen, in their careful parsimony, had cut the officers of the already straitened little force down to such pay and food as Washington deemed unworthy a gentleman's acceptance. He would not resign his commission there at the head of his men upon the march, but be asked to be considered a volunteer without pay, that be might be quit of the humiliation of being stinted like a beggar. Now that it was autumn, however, and wars stood still, he could resign without reproach, and he did so very promptly, in spite of protests and earnest solicitations from many quarters. "I am concerned to find Colonel Washington's conduct so imprudent," wrote Thomas Penn. But the high-spirited young officer deemed it no imprudence to insist upon a just consideration of his rank and services, and quietly withdrew to Mount Vernon, to go thence to his mother at the "ferry farm" upon the Rappahannock, and see again all the fields and friends he loved so well.

It was a very brief respite. He had been scarcely five months out of harness when he found himself again in camp, his plans and hopes once more turned towards the far wilderness where the French lay. He had set a great war ablaze that day he led his forty men into the thicket and bade them fire upon M. Jumonville and his scouts lurking there; and he could not, loving the deep business as he did, keep himself aloof from it when he saw how it was to be finished. Horace Walpole might laugh lightly at the affair, but French and English statesmen alike-even Newcastle, England's Prime-Minister, as busy about nothing as an old woman, and as thoroughly ignorant of affairs as a young man-knew that something must be done, politics hanging at so doubtful a balance between them, now that Frederick of Prussia had driven France, Austria, and Russia into league against him. The French Minister in London and the British Minister in Paris vowed their governments still loved and trusted one another, and there was no declaration of war. But in the spring of 1755 eighteen French ships of war put to sea from Brest and Rochefort, carrying six battalions and a new Governor to Canada, and as many ships got away under press of sail from English ports to intercept and destroy them. Transports carrying two English regiments had sailed for Virginia in January, and by the 20th of February had reached the Chesapeake. The French ships got safely in at the St. Lawrence despite pursuit, losing but two of their fleet, which had the ill luck to be found by the English befogged and bewildered off the coast. The colonies were to see fighting on a new scale.

The English ministers, with whom just then all things went either by favor or by accident, had made a sorry blunder in the choice of a commander. Major-General Edward Braddock, whom they had commissioned to take the two regiments out and act as commander-in-chief in America, was a brave roan, a veteran soldier, bred in a thorough school of action, a man quick with energy and indomitable in resolution; but every quality he had unfitted him to learn. Self-confident, brutal, headstrong, "a very Iroquois in disposition," he would take neither check nor suggestion. But energy, resolution, good soldiers, and a proper equipment might of themselves suffice to do much in the crisis that had come, whether wisdom held the reins or not; and it gave the Old Dominion a thrill of quickened hope and purpose to see Reppel's transports in the Potomac and Braddock's redcoats ashore at Alexandria.

The transports, as they made their way slowly up the river, passed beneath the very windows of Mount Vernon, to put the troops ashore only eight miles beyond.

Washington bad left off being soldier for Dinwiddie, bat be had resigned only to avoid an intolerable indignity, not to shun service, and he made no pretence of indifference when he saw the redcoats come to camp at Alexandria. Again and again was he early in the saddle to see the stir and order of the troops, make the acquaintance of the officers, and learn, if he might, what it was that fitted his Majesty's regulars for their stem business. The self-confident gentlemen who wore his Majesty's uniform and carried his Majesty's commissions in their pockets had scant regard, most of them, for the raw folk of the colony, who had never been in London or seen the set array of battle. They were not a little impatient that they must recruit among such a people. The transports had brought but a thousand men-two half-regiments of five hundred each, whose colonels had instructions to add two hundred men apiece to their force in the colony. Six companies of "rangers," too, the colonists were to furnish, and one company of light horse, besides carpenters and teamsters. By all these General Braddock's officers set small store, deeming it likely they must depend, not upon the provincials, but upon themselves for success. They were at small pains to conceal their hearty contempt for the people they had come to help.

But with Washington it was a different matter. There was that in his proud eyes and gentleman's bearing that marked him a man to be made friends with and respected. A good comrade he proved, without pretence or bravado, but an ill man to scorn, as he went his way among them, lithe and alert, full six feet in his boots, with that strong gait as of a backwoodsman, and that haughty carriage as of a man born to have his will.

GENERAL EDWARD BRADDOCK

He won their liking, and even their admiration, as a fellow of their own pride and purpose. General Braddock, knowing he desired to make the campaign if he might do so without sacrifice of self-respect, promptly invited him to go as a member of his staff, where there could be no question of rank, asking him, besides, to name any young gentlemen of his acquaintance he chose for several vacant ensigncies in the two regiments. The letter of invitation, written by Captain Orme, aide-de-camp, was couched in terms of unaffected cordiality. Washington very gladly accepted, in a letter that had just a touch of the young provincial in it, so elaborate and over-long was its explanation of its writer's delicate position and self-respecting motives, but with so much more of the proud gentleman and resolute man that the smile with which Captain Orme must have read it could have nothing of disrelish in it. The young aide-de-camp and all the other members of the General's military "family" found its author, at any rate, a man after their own hearts when it came to terms of intimacy among them.

By mid-April the commander-in-chief had brought five Governors together at Alexandria, in obedience to his call for an immediate conference-William Shirley, of Massachusetts, the stout-hearted old lawyer, every inch "a gentleman and politician," who had of a sudden turned soldier to face the French, for all he was past sixty; James De Lancey, of New York, astute man of the people; the brave and energetic Horatio Sharpe, of Maryland; Robert Hunter Morris, fresh from the latest wrangles with the headstrong Quakers and Germans of Pennsylvania; and Robert Dinwiddie, the busy merchant Governor of the Old Dominion, whose urgent letters to the government at home had brought Braddock and his regiments to the Potomac. Plans were promptly agreed upon. New York and New England, seeing war come on apace, were astir no less than Virginia, and in active correspondence with the ministers in London. Two regiments had already been raised and taken into the King's pay; the militia of all the threatened colonies were afoot; in all quarters action was expected and instant war. Governor Shirley, the council agreed, should strike at once at Niagara with the King's new provincial regiments, in the hope to cut the enemy's connections with their western posts; Colonel William Johnson, the cool-headed trader and borderer, who had lived and thriven so long in the forests where the dreaded Mohawks had their strength, should lead a levy from New England, New York, and New Jersey to an attack upon Crown Point, where for twenty-four years the French had held Champlain; and Lieutenant-Colonel Monckton, of the King's regulars, must take a similar force against Beausejour in Acadia, while General Brad-dock struck straight into the western wilderness to take Duquesne. 'Twere best to be prompt in every part of the hazardous business, and Braddock turned from the conference to push his own expedition forward at once. "After taking Fort Duquesne," he said to Franklin, "I am to proceed to Niagara; and after having taken that, to Frontenac, if the season will allow time; and I suppose it will, for Duquesne can hardly detain me above three or four days; and then I can see nothing that can obstruct my march to Niagara." " To be sure, sir," quietly replied the sagacious Franklin; " if you arrive well before Duquesne with these fine troops, so well provided with artillery, the fort...can probably make but a short resistance." Bat there was the trouble. 'Twould have been better, no doubt, had a route through Pennsylvania been chosen, where cultivated farms already stretched well into the West, with their own roads and grain and cattle and wagons to serve an army with; but the Virginia route had been selected (by intrigue of gentlemen interested in the Ohio Company, it was hinted), and must needs be made the best of. There was there, at the least, the rough track Washington's men had cut to the Great Meadows. This must be widened and levelled for an army with its cumbrous train of artillery, and its endless procession of wagons laden with baggage and provisions. To take two thousand men through the dense forests with all the military trappings and supplies of a European army would be to put, it might be, four miles of its rough trail between van and rear of the struggling Une, and it would be a clumsy enemy, as fighting went in the woods, who could not cut such a force into pieces —"like thread," as Franklin said.

The thing was to be attempted, nevertheless, with stubborn British resolution. It was the 19th of May before all the forces intended for the march were finally collected at Fort Cumberland, twenty-two hundred men in all-fourteen hundred regulars, now the recruits were in; nearly five hundred Virginians, horse and foot; two Independent Companies from New York; and a small force of sailors from the transports to rig tackle for the ordnance when there was need on the rough way. And it was the 10th of June when the advance began, straight into that "realm of forests ancient as the world" that lay without limit upon all the western ways. It was a thing of infinite difficulty to get that lumbering train through the tangled wilderness, and it kept the temper of the truculent Braddock very hot to see how it played havoc with every principle and practice of campaigning he had ever heard of. He charged the colonists with an utter want alike of honor and of honesty to have kept him so long awaiting the transportation and supplies they had promised, and to have done so little to end with, and so drew Washington into "frequent disputes, maintained with warmth on both sides"; but the difficulties of the march presently wrought a certain forest change upon him, and disposed him to take counsel of his young Virginian aide-the only man in all his company who could speak out of knowledge in that wild country. On the 19th, at Washington's advice, he took twelve hundred men and pressed forward with a lightened train to a quicker advance, leaving Colonel Dunbar to bring up the rest of the troops with the baggage. Even this lightened force halted "to level every mole-hill, and to erect bridges over every brook," as Washington chafed to see, and "were four days in getting twelve miles"; but the pace was better than before, and brought them at last almost to their destination.

On the 9th of July, at mid-day, they waded the shallow Monongahela, but eight miles from Duquesne, making a brave show as the sun struck upon their serried ranks, their bright uniforms, their fluttering banners, and their glittering arms, and went straight into the rough and shadowed forest path that led to the French post. Upon a sudden there came a man bounding along the path to meet them, wearing the gorget of a French officer, and the forest behind him swarmed with a great host of but half-discovered men. Upon signal given, these spread themselves to the right and left within the shelter of the forest, and from their covert poured a deadly fire upon Braddock's advancing lines. With good British pluck the steady regulars formed their accustomed ranks, crying, "God save the King!" to give grace to the volleys they sent back into the forest; the ordnance was brought up and swung to its work; all the force pressed forward to take what place it could in the fight; but where was the use? Washington besought General Braddock to scatter his men too, and meet the enemy under cover as they came, but he would not listen. They must stand in ranks, as they were bidden, and take the fire of their hidden foes like men, without breach of discipline. When they would have broken in spite of him, in their panic at being slaughtered there in the open glade without sight of the enemy, Braddock beat them back with his sword, and bitterly cursed them for cowards. He would have kept the Virginians, too, back from the covert if he could, when he saw them seek to close with the attacking party in true forest fashion. As it was, they were as often shot down by the terror-stricken regulars behind them as by their right foes in front. They alone made any head in the fight; but who could tell in such a place how the battle fared? No one could count the enemy where they sprang from covert to covert. They were, in fact, near a thousand strong at the first meeting in the way-more than six hundred Indians, a motley host gathered from far and near at the summons of the French, sevenscore Canadian rangers, seventy odd regulars from the fort, and thirty or forty French officers, come out of sheer eagerness to have a hand in the daring game. Contrecoeur could not spare more Frenchmen from his little garrison, his connections at the lakes being threatened, and he sorely straitened for men and stores. He was staking everything, as it was, upon this encounter on the way. If the English should shake the savages off, as he deemed they would, he must no doubt withdraw as he could ere the lines of siege were closed about him. He never dreamed of such largess of good fortune as came pouring in upon him. The English were not only checked, but beaten. They had never seen business like this. 'Twas a pitiful, shameful slaughter-men shot like beasts in a pen there where they cowered close in their scarlet ranks. Their first blazing volleys had sent the craven Canadians scampering back the way they had come; Beaujeu, who led the attack, was killed almost at the first onset; but the gallant youngsters who led the motley array wavered never an instant, and readily held the Indians to their easy work. Washington did all that furious energy and reckless courage could to keep the order of battle his commander had so madly chosen, to hold the regulars to their blind work and hearten the Virginians to stay the threatened rout, driving his horse everywhere into the thick of the murderous firing, and crying upon all alike to keep to it steadily like men. He had but yesterday rejoined the advance, having for almost two weeks lain stricken with a fever in Dunbar's camp. He could hardly sit his cushioned saddle for weakness when the fight began; but when the blaze of the battle burst, his eagerness was suddenly like that of one possessed, and his immunity from harm like that of one charmed. Thrice a horse was shot under him, many bullets cut his clothing, but he went without a wound. A like mad energy drove Braddock storming up and down the breaking lines; but he was mortally stricken at last and Washington alone remained to exercise such control as was possible when the inevitable rout came.

It was impossible to hold the ground in such fashion. The stubborn Braddock himself had ordered a retreat ere the fatal bullet found him. Sixty-three out of the eighty-six officers of his force were killed or disabled; less than five hundred men out of all the thirteen hundred who had but just now passed so gallantly through the ford remained unhurt; the deadly slaughter must have gone on to utter destruction. Retreat was inevitable —'twas blessed good fortune that it was still possible. When once it began it was headlong, reckless, frenzied. The men ran wildly, blindly, as if hunted by demons whom no man might hope to resist — haunted by the frightful cries, maddened by the searching and secret fire of their foes, now coming hot upon their heels. Wounded comrades, military stores, baggage, their very arms, they left upon the ground, abandoned. Far into the night they ran madly on, in frantic search for the camp of the rear division, crying, as they ran, for help; they even passed the camp, in their uncontrollable terror of pursuit, and went desperately on towards the settlements. Washington and the few officers and provincials who scorned the terror found the utmost difficulty in bringing off their stricken General, where he lay wishing to die. Upon the fourth day after the battle he died, loathing the sight of a redcoat, they said, and murmuring praises of "the blues," the once despised Virginians. They buried his body in the road, that the army wagons might pass over the place and obliterate every trace of a grave their savage enemies might rejoice to find and desecrate.

He had lived to reach Dunbar's camp, but not to see the end of the shameful rout. The terror mastered the rearguard too. They destroyed their artillery, burned their wagons and stores, emptied their powder into the streams, and themselves broke into a disordered, feverish retreat which was a mere flight, their craven commander shamefully acquiescing. He would not even hold or rally them at Fort Cumberland, but went on, as if upon a hurried errand, all the way to Philadelphia, leaving the fort, and all the frontier with it, "to be defended by invalids and a few Virginians," "I acknowledge," cried Dinwiddie, "I was not brought up to arms; but I think common-sense would have prevailed not to leave the frontier exposed after having opened a road over the mountains to the Ohio, by which the enemy can the more easily invade us. The whole conduct of Colonel Dunbar seems to be monstrous." And so, indeed, it was. But the colonies at large had little time to think of it. Governor Shirley had gone against Niagara only to find the French ready for him at every point, now that they had read Braddock's papers, taken at Duquesne, and to come back again without doing anything. Beausejour had been taken in Acadia, but it lay apart from the main field of struggle. Johnson beat the French off at Lake George when they attacked him, and took Dieskau, their commander ; but he contented himself with that, and left Crown Point untouched. There were other frontiers besides those of Virginia and Pennsylvania to be looked to and guarded. For three long years did the fortunes of the English settlements go steadily from danger to desperation, as the French and their savage allies advanced from victory to victory. In 1756 Oswego was taken; in 1757, Fort William Henry. Commander succeeded commander among the English, only to add blunder to blunder, failure to failure. And all the while it fell to Washington, Virginia's chief stay in her desperate trouble, to stand steadfastly to the hopeless work of keeping three hundred and fifty miles of frontier with a few hundred men against prowling bands of savages, masters of the craft of swift and secret attack, "dexterous at skulking," in a country "mountainous and full of swamps and hollow ways covered with woods."

THE BURIAL OP BRADDOCK

For twenty years now settlers had been coming steadily into this wilderness that lay up and down upon the nearer slopes of the great mountains-Germans, Scots-Irish, a hardy breed. Their settlements lay scattered far and near among the foot-hills and valleys. Their men were valiant and stout-hearted, quick with the rifle, hard as flint when they were once afoot to revenge themselves for murdered wives and children and comrades. But how could they, scattered as they were, meet these covert sallies in the dead of night —a sudden rush of men with torches, the keen knife, the quick rifle? The country filled with fugitives, for whom Washington's militiamen could find neither food nor shelter. " The supplicating tears of the women, and moving petitions of the men,"cried the young commander," melt me into such deadly sorrow that I solemnly declare, if I know my own mind, I could offer myself a willing sacrifice to the butchering enemy, provided that would contribute to the people's ease. ...I would be a willing offering to savage fury, and die by inches to save a people." It was a comfort to know, at the least, that he was trusted and believed in. The Burgesses had thanked him under the very stroke of Braddock's defeat, in terms which could not be doubted sincere. In the very thick of his deep troubles, when he would have guarded the helpless people of the border, but could not, Colonel Fairfax could send him word from "Williamsburg, "Your good health and fortune are the toast at every table." "Our Colonel," wrote a young comrade in arms, "is an example of fortitude in either danger or hardships, and by his easy, polite behavior has gained not only the regard but affection of both officers and soldiers." But it took all the steadiness that had been born or bred in him to endure the strain of the dis-heartening task, from which he could not in honor break away. His plans, he complained, were " to-day approved, to-morrow condemned." He was bidden do what was impossible. It would require fewer men to go against Duquesne again and remove the cause of danger than to prevent the effects while the cause remained. Many of his officers were careless and inefficient, many of his men mutinous. " Your Honor will, I hope, excuse my hanging instead of shooting them," he wrote to the Governor; " it conveyed much more terror to others, and it was for example' sake that we did it." It was a test as of fire for a young colonel in his twenties.

But a single light lies upon the picture. Early in 1756, ere the summer's terror had come upon the border, and while he could be spared, he took horse and made his way to Boston to see Governor Shirley, now acting as commander-in-chief in the colonies, and from him at first hand obtain settlement of that teasing question of rank that had already driven the young officer once from the service. He went very bravely dight in proper uniform of buff and blue, a white-and-scarlet cloak upon his shoulders, the sword at his side knotted with red and gold, his horse's fittings engraved with the Washington arms, and trimmed in the best style of the London saddlers. With him rode two aides in their uniforms, and two servants in their white-and-scarlet livery. Curious folk who looked upon the celebrated young officer upon the road saw him fare upon his way with all the pride of a Virginian gentleman, a handsome man, and an admirable horseman —a very gallant figure, no one could deny. Everywhere he was feted as he went; everywhere he showed himself the earnest, high-strung, achieving youth he was. In New York he fell into a new ambush, from which he did not come off without a wound. His friend Beverly Robinson must needs have Miss Mary Philipse at his house there, a beauty and an heiress, and Washington came away from her with a sharp rigor at his heart. But he could not leave that desolate frontier at home unprotected to stay for a siege upon a lady's heart; he had recovered from such wounds before, had before that left pleasure for duty; and in proper season was back at his post, with papers from Shirley which left no doubt who should command in Virginia.

WASHINGTON AND MARY PHILIPSE

At last, in 1758, the end came, when William Pitt thrust smaller men aside and became Prime-Minister in England. Amherst took Louisbourg, Wolfe came to Quebec, and General Forbes, that stout and steady soldier, was sent to Virginia to go again against Duquesne. The advance was slow to exasperation in the view of every ardent man like Washington, and cautious almost to timidity; but the very delay redounded to its success at last. 'Twas November before Duquesne was reached. The Indians gathered there, seeing winter come on, had not waited to meet them; and the French by that time knew themselves in danger of being cut off by the English operations in the North. When Forbes's forces, therefore, at last entered those fatal woods again, where Braddock's slaughtered men had lain to rot, the French had withdrawn; nothing remained bat to enter the smoking ruins of their abandoned fort, hoist the King's flag, and re-name the post Fort Pitt; and Washington turned homeward again to seek the rest he so much needed. It had been almost a bloodless campaign, but such danger as it had brought Washington had shared to the utmost. The French had not taken themselves off without at least one trial of the English strength. While yet Forbes lay within the mountains a large detachment had come from Duquesne to test and reconnoitre his force. Colonel Mercer, of the Virginian line, had been ordered forward with a party to meet them. He stayed so long, and the noise of the firing came back with so doubtful a meaning to the anxious ears at the camp, that Washington hastened with volunteers to his relief. In the dusk the two bodies of Englishmen met, mistook each other for enemies, exchanged a deadly fire, and were checked only because Washington, rushing between their lines, even while their pieces blazed, cried his hot commands to stop, and struck up the smoking muzzles with his sword. 'Twas through no prudence of his he was not shot.

For a long time his friends had felt a deep uneasiness about his health. They had very earnestly besought him not to attempt a new campaign. "You will in all probability bring on a relapse," George Mason had warned him, "and render yourself incapable of serving the public at a time when there may be the utmost occasion. There is nothing more certain than that a gentleman of your station owes the care of his health and his life not only to himself and his friends, bat to his country." Bat he had deemed the nearest duty the most imperative; and it was only after that duty was disposed of that he had turned from the field to seek home and new pleasures along with new duties. The winter brought news from Quebec of the fall of the French power in America, which made rest and home and pleasure the more grateful and full of zest.

Chapter IV
Mount Vernon Days

On a May day in 1758, as he spurred upon the way to Williamsburg, under orders from the frontier, Washington rode straight upon an adventure he had not looked for. He was within a few hours' ride of the little capital; old plantations lay close upon the way; neighborly homes began to multiply; and so striking a horseman, riding uniformed and attended, could not thereabouts go far unrecognized. He was waylaid and haled to dinner, despite excuses and protests of public business calling for despatch. There was a charming woman to be seen at the house, his friend told him, if a good dinner was not argument enough-and his business could not spoil for an hour's stay in agreeable company. And so, of a sudden, under constraint of Virginian hospitality, he was hurried into the presence of the gracious young matron who was at once, and as if of right, to make his heart safe against further quest or adventure. Martha Custis was but six-and-twenty. To the charm of youth and beauty were added that' touch of quiet sweetness and that winning grace of self-possession which come to a woman wived in her girlhood, and widowed before age or care has checked the first full tide of life. At seventeen she had married Daniel Parke Custis, a man more than twenty years her senior; but eight years of quiet love and duty as wife and mother had only made her youth the more gracious in that rural land of leisure and good neighborhood; and a year's widowhood had been but a suitable preparation for perceiving the charm of this stately young soldier who now came riding her way upon the public business. His age was her own; all the land knew him and loved him for gallantry and brave capacity; he carried himself like a prince-and he forgot his errand to linger in her company. Dinner was soon over, and his horses at the door; there was the drilled and dutiful Bishop, trained servant that he was, leading his restless and impatient charge back and forth within sight of the windows and of the terrace where his young Colonel tarried, absorbed and forgetful; man and beast alike had been in the service of the unhappy Braddock, and might seem to walk there lively memorials of duty done and undertaken. But dusk came; the horses were put up; and the next morning was well advanced before the abstracted young officer got at last to his saddle, and spurred on belated to Williamsburg. His business concerned the preparations then afoot for General Forbes's advance upon Duquesne. "I came here at this critical juncture," said Washington to the President of the Council, " by the express order of Sir John St. Clair, to represent in the fullest manner the posture of our affairs at Winchester" —lack of clothes, arms, and equipage, lack of money, lack of wise regulations touching rank and discipline. General Forbes had been in Philadelphia a month already, awaiting the formation of his army in Virginia; Sir John St. Clair, his quartermaster-general, had come into the province to see that proper plans were made and executed; it was necessary that matters should be pressed forward very diligently and at once; and Washington, when once at the seat of government, was not slack to urge and superintend official action. But, the troublesome business once in proper course, he turned back to seek Mrs. Custis again, this time at her own home, ere he went the long distance of the frontier. The onset was made with a soldier's promptness and audacity. He returned to his post, after a delay too slight to deserve any reasonable man's remark, and yet with a pledge given and taken which made him look forward to the end of the campaign with a new longing as to the winning of a real home and an unwonted happiness.

This was not his first adventure in love, but it was his last, and gave him a quiet joy which stood him in stead a whole lifetime. No young Virginian could live twenty-six years amidst fair women in that hale and sociable colony without being touched again and again by the quick passion; and this man had the blood of a lover beyond bis fellows. Despite the shyness of a raw lad who lived much in the open, he had relished the company of lively women from the first, meeting their gay sallies sometimes with a look from his frank blue eyes that revealed more than he knew. Love had first found him out in earnest six years ago, when he was but just turned of twenty; and it had taken all the long while since to forget his repulse at the hands of a fair young beauty in that day of passion. Mary Fillipse had but taken his fancy for a moment, because he could not pass such a woman by and deem himself still a true Virginian. It was more serious that he had been much in the company, these last years, of a fair neighbor of the vivacious house of Cary, whose wit and beauty had haunted him in the very thick of campaigns upon the frontier, and who still mastered his heart now and again, with a sort of imperious charm, in the midst of this very happy season when he knew Martha Custis his veritable heart's mistress for the future. It may well have made him glad of misadventures in the past to know his heart safe now.

The campaign dragged painfully, far into the drear autumn. December had come before the captured post on the Ohio could be left to the keeping of Colonel Mercer and a little garrison of provincials. But when at last he was free again there was no reason why Washington should wait longer to be happy, and he was married to Martha Custis on the 6th of January, 1759. The sun shone very bright that day, and there was the fine glitter of gold, the brave show of resplendent uniforms, in the little church where the marriage was solemnized. Officers of his Majesty's service crowded there, in their gold lace and scarlet coats, to see their comrade wedded; the new Governor, Francis Fauquier, himself came, clad as befitted his rank; and the bridegroom took the sun not less gallantly than the rest, as he rode, in blue and silver and scarlet, beside the coach and six that bore his bride homeward amidst the thronging friends of the country-side. The young soldier's love of a gallant array and a becoming ceremony was satisfied to the full, and he must have rejoiced to be so brave a horseman on such a day. For three months of deep content he lived with his bride at her own residence, the White House, by York River side, where their troth had been plighted, forgetting the fatigues of the frontier, and learning gratefully the new life of quiet love and homely duty. These peaceful, healing months gone by, he turned once more to public business. Six months before his marriage he had been chosen a member of the House of Burgesses for Frederick County-the county which had been his scene of adventure in the old days of surveying in the wilderness, and in which ever since Braddock's fatal rout he had maintained his headquarters; striving to keep the border against the savages. Small wonder that he led the poll taken there in Winchester, where through so many seasons men had seen him bear himself like a capable man and a gallant, indomitable soldier. 'Twas no unwelcome duty, either, to take his young wife to Williamsburg in "the season," when all Virginia was in town in the persons of the Burgesses and the country gentry come to enjoy the festivities and join in the business then sure to be afoot. The young soldier was unused to assemblies, however, and suffered a keen embarrassment to find himself for a space too conspicuous amidst the novel parliamentary scene. He had hardly taken his seat when the gracious and stately Robinson, Speaker of the House and Treasurer of the colony these twenty years, rose, at the bidding of the Burgesses, to thank him for the services of which all were speaking. This sudden praise, spoken with generous warmth there in a public place, was more than Washington knew how to meet. He got to his feet when Mr. Speaker was done, but he could not utter a syllable. He stood there, instead, hot with blushes, stammering, all a-tremble from head to foot. "Sit down, Mr. Washington," cried the Speaker; "your modesty is equal to your valor, and that surpasses the power of any language that I possess."

Again and again, as the years passed, Washington returned at each session to Williamsburg to take his place in the Assembly; and with custom came familiarity and the ease and firmness he at first had lacked upon the floor. His life broadened about him; all the uses of peace contributed to give him facility and knowledge and a wide comradeship in affairs. Along with quiet days as a citizen, a neighbor, and a country gentleman, came maturity and the wise lessons of a various experience. No man in Virginia lived more or with a greater zest henceforth than Colonel Washington. His marriage brought him great increase of wealth, as well as increase of responsibility. Mr. Custis had left many thousand acres of land, and forty-five thousand pounds sterling in money, a substantial fortune to the young wife and the two little children who survived him; and Washington had become, by special decree of the Governor and Council in General Court, trustee and manager of the whole. It needed capacity and knowledge and patience of no mean order to get good farming out of slaves, and profitable prices out of London merchants; to find prompt and trustworthy ship-masters by whom to send out cargoes, and induce correspondents over sea to ship the perishable goods sent in return by the right vessels, bound to the nearest river; and the bigger your estate the more difficult its proper conduct and economy, the more disastrous in scale the effects of mismanagement. No doubt the addition of Mrs. Custis's handsome property to his own broad and fertile acres at Mount Vernon made Colonel Washington one of the wealthiest men in Virginia. But Virginian wealth was not to be counted till crops were harvested and got to market. The current price of tobacco might leave you with or without a balance to your credit in London, your only clearing-house, as it chanced. Your principal purchases, too, must be made over sea and through factors. Both what you sold and what you bought must take the hazards of the sea voyage, the whims of sea captains, the chances of a foreign market. To be farmer and merchant at once, manage your own negroes and your own overseers, and conduct an international correspondence; to keep the run of prices current, duties, port dues, and commissions, and know the fluctuating rates of exchange; to understand and meet all changes, whether in merchants or in markets, three thousand miles away, required an amount of information, an alertness, a steady attention to detail, a sagacity in farming and a shrewdness in trade, such as made a great property a burden to idle or inefficient men. But Washington took pains to succeed. He had a great zest for business. The practical genius which had shone in him almost prematurely as a boy now grew heartily in him as a man of fortune. Messrs. Robert Gary & Company, his factors in London, must soon have learned to recognize his letters, in the mere handling, by their bulk. No detail escaped him when once he had gotten into the swing of the work. They must be as punctilious as he was, they found, in seeing to every part of the trade and accounting with which he intrusted them, or else look to lose his lucrative patronage. He was not many years in learning how to make the best tobacco in Virginia, and to get it recognized as such in England. Barrels of flour marked "George Washington, Mount Vernon," were ere long suffered to pass the inspectors at the ports of the British West Indies without scrutiny. It was worth while to serve so efficient a man to his satisfaction; worth while or not, he would not be served otherwise. He had emerged, as it were, after a tense and troubled youth, upon a peaceful tract of time, where his powers could stretch and form themselves without strain or hurry. He had robust health, to which he gave leave in unstinted work, athletic strength, and an insatiable relish for being much afoot and in the open, which he satisfied with early rounds of superintendence in the fields where the men were at their tasks, with many a tireless ride after the hounds, or steadfast wait at the haunts of the deer; a planning will that craved some practical achievement every day, which he indulged by finding tasks of betterment about the estate and keeping his men at them with unflagging discipline; a huge capacity for being useful and for understanding how to be so, which he suffered his neighbors, his parish, his county, the colony itself, to employ when there was need. To a young man, bred these ten years in the forests and in the struggle of warfare upon a far frontier, it had been intolerable to live tamely, without executive tasks big and various enough to keep his energy from rust. The clerical side of business he had learned very thoroughly in camp, as well as the exceeding stir and strain of individual effort-the incessant letter writing necessary to keep promised performance afoot, the reckoning of men and of stores, the nice calculations of time and ways and means; the scrutiny of individual men, too, which is so critical a part of management, and the slow organization of effort: he had been in a fine school for these things all his youth, and would have thought shame to himself not to have learned temperance, sagacity, thrift, and patience wherewith to use his energy. His happy marriage did him the service to keep him from restlessness. His love took his allegiance, and held him to his home as to a post of honor and reward.

"THE WHITE HOUSE" ON PAMUNKEY

He had never before had leave to be tender with children, or show with what a devotion he could preside over a household all his own. His home got strong hold upon him. His estates gave him scope of command and a life of action. 'Twas no wonder he kept his factors busy, and shipped goods authenticated by the brand.

The soldierly young planter gave those who knew him best, as well as those who met him but to pass, the impression of a singular restraint and self-command, which lent a peculiar dignity and charm to his speech and carriage. They deemed him deeply passionate, and yet could never remember to have seen him in a passion. The impression was often a wholesome check upon strangers, and even upon friends and neighbors, who would have sought to impose upon him. No doubt he had given way to bursts of passion often enough in camp and upon the march, when inefficiency, disobedience, or cowardice angered him hotly and of a sudden. There were stories to be heard of men who had reason to remember how terrible he could be in his wrath. But he had learned, in the very heat and discipline of such scenes, how he must curb and guard himself against surprise, and it was no doubt trials of command made in his youth that had given him the fine self-poise men noted in him now. He had been bred in a strict school of manners at Belvoir and Greenway Court, and here at his own Mount Vernon in the old days, and the place must have seemed to him full of the traditions of whatsoever was just and honest and lovely and of good report as he looked back to the time of his gentle brother. It was still dangerous to cross or thwart him, indeed. Poachers might look to be caught and soundly thrashed by the master himself if he chanced their way. Negligent overseers might expect sharp penalties, and unfaithful contractors a strict accounting, if necessary work went wrong by their fault. He was exacting almost to the point of harshness in every matter of just right or authority. But he was open and wholesome as the day, and reasonable to the point of pity in every affair of humanity, through it all. Now it was "my rascally overseer, Hard wick," in his diary, when certain mares were sent home "scarce able to highlone, much less to assist in the business of the plantations"; but not a month later it was "my worthy overseer. Hard wick, lying in Winchester of a broken leg." It was not in his way to add anything to the penalties of nature.

A quiet simplicity of life and a genuine love of real sport rid him of morbid humors. All up and down the English world, while the eighteenth century lasted, gentlemen were commonly to be found drunk after dinner —outside New England, where the efficient Puritan Church had fastened so singular a discipline in manners upon a whole society-and Virginian gentlemen had a reputation for deep drinking which they had been at some pains to deserve. A rural society craves excitement, and can get it very simply by such practices. There is always leisure to sleep afterwards, even though your dinner come in the middle of the day; and there is good reason you should be thirsty if you have been since daybreak in the saddle. To ride hard and to drink hard seemed to go together in Virginia as inevitably as the rhymes in a song; and 'twas famous hard riding after the fox over the rough fields and through the dense thickets. If Washington drank only small beer or cider and a couple of glasses of Madeira at dinner, it was no doubt because he bad found his quick blood tonic enough, and had set himself a hard regimen as a soldier. He did not scruple to supply drink enough for the thirstiest gathering when he presented himself to the voters of the country-side as a candidate for the House of Burgesses. "A hogshead and a barrel of punch, thirty - five gallons of wine, forty - three gallons of strong cider, and dinner for his friends," was what he cheerfully paid for at his first election, and the poll footed but a few hundred votes all told. Mount Vernon saw as much company and as constant merriment and good cheer as any house in Virginia; and the master was no martinet to his guests, even though they came upon professional errands. " Doctor Laurie came here, I may add drunk," says his quiet diary, without comment, though the doctor had come upon summons to attend Mrs. Washington, and was next morning suffered to use his lancet for her relief. No doubt a good fellow when sober, and not to be lightly chidden when drunk, like many a gallant horseman and gentleman who joined the meet of the country-side at the hospitable place to follow the hounds when the hunting was good. There was fox-hunting winter and summer, in season and out, but the sport was best in the frosty days of January and February, when the year was young and the gentlemen of the country round gathered at Belvoir or Gunston Hall or Mount Vernon two or three times a week to warm their blood in the hale, sport, and dine together after wards—a cordial company of neighbors, with as many topics of good talk as foxes to run to cover. The hunt went fastest and most incessantly when Lord Fairfax came down from his lodge in the Valley and joined them for days together in the field and at the table.

Washington loved horses and dogs with the heartiest sportsman of them all. He had a great gusto for stalking deer with George Mason on the broad forested tracts round Gunston Hall, and liked often to take gun or rod after lesser game when the days fell dull; but best of all he loved a horse's back, and the hard ride for hours together after the dogs and a crafty quarry —a horse it put a man to his points to ride, a country where the running was only for those who dared. His own mounts could nowhere be bettered in Virginia. There was full blood of Araby in his noble Magnolia, and as good hunting blood as was to be found in the colony in his Blueskin and Ajax, Valiant and Chinkling. His hounds he bred "so flew'd, so sanded," so matched in speed and habit, that they kept always tune and pace together in the field. "A cry more tuneable was never holla'd to, nor cheered with horn," than theirs when they were let " spend their mouths" till echo replied "as if another chase were in the skies." 'Twas first to the stables for him always in the morning, and then to the kennels.

It had been hard and anxious work to get his affairs into prosperous shape again when the war was over, and those long, hopeless summers on the stricken frontier. Stock, buildings, fences — everything had to be renewed, refitted, repaired. For the first two or three years there were even provisions to buy, so slow was the place to support itself once more. Not only all his own ready money, but all he got by his marriage too, and more besides, was swallowed up, and he found himself in debt before matters were finally set to rights and profitable crops made and marketed. But, the thing once done, affairs cleared and became easy as if of their own accord in the business of the estate. The men he had to deal with presently knew their master: the young planter had matured his plans and his discipline. Henceforth his affairs were well in hand, and he could take his wholesome pleasures both handsomely and with a free heart. There was little that was debonair about the disciplined and masterful young soldier. He had taken Pallas's gift: " Self-reverence, self-knowledge, self-control, these three alone lead life to sovereign power. And because right is right, to follow right were wisdom in the scorn of consequence." But he took heed of his life very genially, and was matured by pleasure no less than by duty done. He loved a game of cards in almost any company, and paid his stakes upon the rubber like every other well-conducted man of his century. He did not find Annapolis, or even Philadelphia, too far away to be visited for the pleasure of seeing a good horserace or enjoying a round of balls and evenings at the theatre, to shake the rustic dulness off of a too constant stay at home. Mrs. Washington enjoyed such outings, such little flings into the simple world of provincial fashion, as much as he did; and they could not sit waiting all the year for the short season at Williamsburg.

A young man at once so handsome, so famous, and so punctilious in point of dress as Colonel Washington could not but make a notable figure in any society. "I want neither lace nor embroidery," was the order he sent to London. " Plain clothes, with a gold or silver button (if worn in genteel dress), are all I desire. My stature is six feet; otherwise rather slender than corpulent." But he was careful the material, the color, and the fit should be of the best and most tasteful, and that very elegant stuffs should be provided from over sea for Mrs. Washington and her children, and very substantial for the servants who were to be in attendance upon the household — a livery of white and scarlet. 'Twas a point of pride with Virginians to know how to dress, both well and in the fashion; and the master of Mount Vernon would have deemed it an impropriety to be less careful than his neighbors, less well dressed than his station and fortune warranted. He watched the tradesmen sharply. "'Tis a custom, I have some reason to believe, with many shopkeepers and tradesmen in London," he wrote bluntly to the Messrs. Gary, " when they know goods are bespoken for exportation, to palm sometimes old, and sometimes very slight and indifferent, goods upon us, taking care at the same time to advance the price," and be wished them informed that their distant customers would not be so duped.

He longed once and again to be quit of the narrow life of the colony, and stretch himself for a little upon the broader English stage at home. "But I am tied by the leg," he told his friends there, "and must set inclination aside. My indulging myself in a trip to England depends upon so many contingencies, which, in all probability, may never occur, that I dare not even think of such a gratification." But the disappointment bred no real discontent. There could be no better air or company to come to maturity in than were to be had there in Virginia, if a young man were poised and master of himself. "We have few things here striking to European travellers (except our abundant woods)," he professed, when he wrote to his kinsman Richard Washington in England; "but little variety, a welcome reception among a few friends, and the open and prevalent hospitality of the country"; but it was a land that bred men, and men of affairs, in no common fashion.

Especially now, after the quickening of pulses that had come with the French war, and its sweep of continental, even of international, forces across the colonial stage, hitherto set only for petty and sectional affairs. The colonies had grown self-conscious and restless as the plot thickened and thrust them forward to a role of consequence in the empire such as they had never thought to play, and the events which succeeded hurried them to a quick maturity. It was a season a young man was sure to ripen in, and there was good company. The House of Burgesses was very quiet the year Washington first took his place in it and stood abashed to hear himself praised; but before Mr. Robinson, its already veteran Speaker, was dead, a notable change had set in. Within five years, before the country on the St. Lawrence and the lakes was well out of the hands of the French, the Parliament in England had entered upon measures of government which seemed meant of deliberate purpose to set the colonies agog, and every body of counsellors in America stood between anger and amazement to see their people in danger to be so put upon.

The threat and pressure of the French power upon the frontiers had made the colonies thoughtful always, so long as it lasted, of their dependence upon England for succor and defence should there come a time of need. Once and again — often enough to keep them sensible how they must stand or fall, succeed or fail, with the power at home — their own raw levies had taken part with the King's troops out of England in some clumsy stroke or other against a French stronghold in the North or a Spanish fortress in the South; and now at last they had gone with English troops into the field in a national cause. Provincials and redcoats had joined for a final grapple with the French, to settle once and for all who should be owners and masters on the coveted continent. The issue had been decisive. By the summer of 1760 Washington could write his kinsman in England that the French were so thoroughly drubbed and humbled that there remained little to do to reduce Canada from end to end to the British power. But the very thoroughness of the success wrought a revolution in the relations of the colonies to the mother-country. It rid them of their sense of dependence. English regiments had mustered their thousands, no doubt, upon the battle-fields of the war in order that the colonies might be free to possess the continent, and it was hard to see how the thing could have been accomplished without them. But it had been accomplished, and would not need to be done again. Moreover, it had shown the colonial militia how strong they were even in the presence of regulars. They had almost everywhere borne an equal part in the fighting, and, rank and file, they had felt with a keen resentment the open contempt for their rude equipment and rustic discipline which too many arrogant officers and insolent men among the regulars had shown. They knew that they had proved themselves the equals of any man in the King's pay in the fighting, and they had come out of the hot business confident that henceforth, at any rate, they could dispense with English troops and take care of themselves. They had lost both their fear of the French and their awe of the English.

Chapter V
The Heat of Politics

'Twas hardly an opportune time for statesmen in London to make a new and larger place for England's authority in America, and yet that was what they immediately attempted. Save Chatham and Burke and a few discerning men who had neither place nor power, there was no longer any one in England who knew, though it were never so vaguely, the real temper and character of the colonists. 'Twas matter of common knowledge and comment, it is true, that the men of Massachusetts were beyond all reason impatient of command or restraint, affecting an independence which was hardly to be distinguished from contumacy and insubordination; but what ground was there to suppose that a like haughty and ungovernable spirit lurked in the loyal and quiet South, or among the prudent traders and phlegmatic farmers who were making the middle colonies so rich, and so regardful of themselves in every point of gain or interest? Statesmen of an elder generation had had a sure instinct what must be the feeling of Englishmen in America, and had, with "a wise and salutary neglect," suffered them to take their own way in every matter of self-government. Though ministry after ministry had asserted a rigorous and exacting supremacy for the mother-country in every affair of commerce, and had determined as they pleased what the colonies should be suffered to manufacture, and how they should be allowed to trade-with what merchants, in what commodities, in what bottoms, within what limits — they had nevertheless withheld their hands hitherto from all direct exercise of authority in the handling of the internal affairs of the several settlements, had given them leave always to originate their own legislation and their own measures of finance, until self-government had become with them a thing as if of immemorial privilege. Sir William Keith, sometime Governor of Pennsylvania, had suggested to Sir Robert Walpole that he should raise revenue from the colonies. "What!" exclaimed that shrewd master of men. "I have Old England set against me, and do you think I will have New England likewise?"

But men had come into authority in England now who lacked this stout sagacity, and every element of sound discretion. English arms and English money, they could say, had swept the French power from America in order that the colonies might no longer suffer menace or rivalry. A great debt had been piled up in the process. Should not the colonies, who had reaped the chief benefit, bear part of the cost! They had themselves incurred burdensome debts, no doubt, in the struggle, and their assemblies would very likely profess themselves willing to vote what they could should his Majesty call upon them and press them. But an adequate and orderly system of taxation could not be wrought out by the separate measures of a dozen petty legislatures; 'twere best the taxation should be direct and by Parliament, whose authority, surely, no man outside turbulent Boston would be mad enough seriously to question or resist. It would, in any event, be wholesome, now the colonies were likely to grow lusty as kingdoms in their roomy continent, to assert a mother's power to use and restrain —a power by no means lost because too long unexercised and neglected. It was with such wisdom the first step was taken. In March, 1764, Parliament voted it "just and necessary that a revenue be raised m America," passed an act meant to secure duties on wines and sugars, and took measures to increase the efficiency of the revenue service in America.

George Grenville was Prime - Minister. He lacked neither official capacity nor acquaintance with affairs. He thought it just the colonists should pay their quota into the national treasury, seeing they were so served by the national power; and he declared that in the next session of Parliament he should propose certain direct taxes in addition to the indirect already in force. He saw no sufficient reason to doubt that the colonies would acquiesce, if not without protest, at least without tumult or dangerous resistance. It was a sad blunder. Virginia resented threat and execution alike in such a matter as deeply as did litigious Massachusetts. A long generation ago, in the quiet year 1732, when bluff Sir Eobert was Prime-Minister, there had been an incident which Governor Keith, maybe, had forgotten. The ministry had demanded of Massachusetts that she should establish a fixed salary for her governors by a standing grant; but she had refused, and the ministers had receded. The affair had not been lost upon the other colonies. That sturdy onetime royal Governor, Alexander Spotswood, in Virginia, had noted it very particularly, and spoken of it very bluntly, diligent servant of the crown as he was, to Colonel William Byrd, when he came his way on his "progress to the mines."

He declared "that if the Assembly in New England would stand bluff, be did not see how they could be forced to raise money against their will; for if they should direct it to be done by act of Parliament, which they have threatened to do (though it be against the right of Englishmen to be taxed but by their representatives), yet they would find it no easy matter to put such an act in execution." No observing man could so much as travel in Virginia without finding very promptly what it was that gave point and poignancy to such an opinion. That quiet gentleman the Rev. Andrew Burnaby, Vicar of Greenwich, was in Virginia in 1759, and saw plainly enough how matters stood. " The public or political character of the Virginians," he said, " corresponds with their private one; they are haughty and jealous of their liberties, impatient of restraint, and can scarcely bear the thought of being controlled by any superior power. Many of them consider the colonies as independent states, not connected with Great Britain otherwise than by having the same common King and being bound to her with natural affection."Not only so, but" they think it a hardship not to have an unlimited trade to every part of the world." All this, and more, Grenville might have learned by the simple pains of inquiry. One had but to open his eyes and look to see how imperious a race had been bred in the almost feudal South; and, for all they had never heard revolutionary talk thence, ministers ought to have dreaded the leisure men had there to think, the provocation to be proud, the necessity to be masterful and individual, quite as much as they had ever dreaded the stubborn temper and the quick capacity for united action they had once and again seen excited in New England.

TAZEWELL HALL, THE HOME OF THE RANDOLPHS

WILLIAM AND MARY COLLEGE

It was not necessary to try new laws to see what the colonies would do if provoked. The difficulty already encountered in enforcing the laws of trade was object-lesson enough; and the trouble in that matter had grown acute but yesterday. For long, indeed, no one in the colonies questioned the right of Parliament to regulate their trade; but it was notorious that the laws actually enacted in that matter had gone smoothly off in America only because they were not seriously enforced. "The trade hither is engrossed by the Saints of New England," laughed Colonel Byrd, "who carry off a great deal of tobacco without troubling themselves with paying that impertinent duty of a penny a pound." The Acts of Trade practically forbade direct commerce with foreign countries or their dependencies, especially in foreign bottoms; but ships from France, Spain, and the Canary Isles came and went very freely, not withstanding, in colonial ports; for royal officials liked to enjoy a comfortable peace, and the esteem of their neighbors, and very genially winked at such transgressions. Cargoes without number were sent to the Dutch and Spanish West Indies every year, and as many brought thence, which were undoubtedly forfeit under the navigation laws Parliament had been at such pains to elaborate and enforce; and privateering as well as smuggling had for long afforded the doughty seamen of Boston, Salem, Charleston, and New York a genteel career of profit. Things had come to such a pass that where business went briskly the people of the colonial ports demanded as of right "a full freedom of illegal trade," and broke sometimes into riot when it was denied them. The Boston News Letter had been known very courteously to mourn the death of a worthy collector of his Majesty's customs because, "with much humanity," be had been used to take "pleasure in directing masters of vessels how they ought to avoid the breach of the Acts of Trade." Sea captains grew accustomed to very confidential relations with owners and consignees, and knew very well, without official counsel, bow to take the advice "not to declare at the Custom-house"; and things went very easily and cordially with all parties to the understanding.

In 1761 that understanding was of a sadden rudely broken and the trouble began, which Grenville bad the folly to add to. The Board of Trade determined to collect the duties on sugar, molasses, and rum, so long and so systematically evaded in the trade between New England and the West Indies, at whatever cost of suit and scrutiny, and directed their agents in Boston to demand "writs of assistance" from the courts, giving them leave to enter what premises they would in search of smuggled goods. There were instant exasperation and resistance. General search - warrants, opening every man's door to the officers of the law, with or without just and explicit ground of suspicion against him, no English subject anywhere would submit to; and yet these writs authorized nothing less. Issued under a questionable extension to America of an exceptional power of the Court of Exchequer, they violated every precedent of the common law, no less than every principle of prudent administration; and the excitement which they provoked was at once deep and ominous. Sharp resistance was made in the courts, and no officer ever ventured to serve one of the obnoxious writs. Such challenge of the process was uttered by colonial counsel upon trial o the right, moreover, that ministers would be without excuse should they ignore the warning, so explicit and so eloquent of revolutionary purpose. It was James Otis who uttered it. He had but the other day carried the royal commission in his pocket as Advocate-General in his Majesty's Court of Admiralty; but he would not have scrupled, even as his Majesty's servant, he said, to oppose the exercise of a power which had already cost one King his head and another his throne. To oppose in such a case was to defend the very constitution under which the King wore his crown. That constitution secured to Englishmen everywhere the rights of freemen; the colonists had, besides, the plain guarantees of their own charters; if constitution and charter failed, or were gainsaid, the principles of natural reason sufficed for defence against measures so arrogant and so futile. No lawyer could justify these extraordinary writs; no King with an army at his back could ever force them to execution.

Protest not only, but defiance, rang very clear in these fearless words; and ministers must avow themselves very ignorant should they pretend they did not know how Mr. Otis had kindled fire from one end of the colonies to the other. But Grenville was resolute to take all risks and push his policy. He did not flinch from the enforcement of the measures of 1764, and in the session of 1765 calmly fulfilled his promise of further taxation. He proposed that the colonists should be required to use revenue stamps upon all their commercial paper, legal documents, pamphlets, and newspapers; and that, at once as a general measure of convenience and a salutary exhibition of authority, his Majesty's troops stationed in the plantations should be billeted on the people. Parliament readily acquiesced. It was thus Grenville purposed "defraying the expenses of defending, protecting, and securing" the colonies; but he came near losing them instead. The act was passed in March; it was not to go into effect until November; but the colonists did not keep him waiting until November for their protests. It was the voice of a veritable tempest that presently came over sea to the ear of the startled minister. And it was not the General Court of turbulent Massachusetts, but the House of Burgesses of loyal Virginia that first spoke the general indignation. Already in the autumn of 1764, upon the mere threat of what was to come, that House had spoken very urgently against the measures proposed, in a memorial to King and Parliament, which, amidst every proper phrase of loyalty and affection, had plainly declared it the opinion of his Majesty's subjects in Virginia that such acts would be in flat violation of their undoubted rights and liberties; and the committee by which that memorial was drawn up had contained almost every man of chief consequence in the counsels of the colony, the King's Attorney-General himself not excepted. But it was one thing to protest against measures to come and quite another to oppose their execution when enacted into laws. The one was constitutional agitation; the other, flat rebellion-little less. It was very ominous to read the words of the extraordinary resolutions passed by the Burgesses on the 30th of May, 1765, after the Stamp Act had become law, and note the tone of restrained passion that ran through them. They declared that from the first the settlers of "his Majesty's colony and dominion" of Virginia had possessed and enjoyed all the privileges, franchises, and immunities at any time enjoyed by the people of Great Britain itself; and that this, their freedom, had been explicitly secured to them by their charters," to all intents and purposes as if they had been abiding and born within the realm of England"; "that the taxation of the people by themselves or by persons chosen by themselves to represent them" was "a distinguishing characteristic of British freedom, without which the ancient constitution" of the realm itself could not subsist; "and that his Majesty's liege people of this most ancient colony" had "uninter-ruptedly enjoyed the right of being thus governed by their assemblies in the article of their taxes and internal police," had never forfeited or relinquished it, and had seen it "constantly recognized by the Kings and people of Great Britain."

Spoken as it was in protest against actual legislation already adopted by Parliament in direct despite of all such privileges and immunities, this declaration of rights seemed to lack its conclusion. The constitutional rights of Virginians had been invaded. What then? Resolved therefore, "that his Majesty's liege people, the inhabitants of this colony, are not bound to yield obedience to any law or ordinance whatever designed to impose any taxation whatsoever upon them, other than the laws or ordinances of the General Assembly aforesaid," and " that any person who shall, by speaking or writing, assert or maintain " the contrary "shall be deemed an enemy of his Majesty's colony." Such had been the uncompromising conclusion drawn by the mover of the resolutions. What other conclusion could any man draw if he deemed the colonists men, and proud men at that? But the Burgesses would not go so far or be so explicit. They feared to speak treason; they were content to protest of their rights, and let the issue bring conclusions to light. It had been hot fighting to get even that much said. The men hitherto accepted always as leaders in the House had wished to hold it back from rash and heated action, and there had been bitter debates before even those significant premises for a revolutionary conclusion had been forced to adoption. Old leaders and new, young men and old alike, had willingly united in the memorial of 1764; but now that the Stamp Act was law, conservative members shrank from doing what must look so like a flat defiance of Parliament. Only young men would have had the audacity to urge such action; only very extraordinary young men would have had the capacity to induce the House to take it. But such young men were at hand, their leader as veritable a democrat as had ever taken the floor in that assembly.

Patrick Henry was not of the aristocracy of the colony. Good Scots blood ran in his veins, quickened by the lively strain of an old Welsh stock. His father came of a race of scholars, and, good churchman though he was, knew his Livy and his Horace better than his Bible. His mother came of a vivacious line of easy-going wits and talkers, which but a touch more of steadiness and energy might any day have made famous. His father had served his county of Hanover very capably and acceptably as surveyor, colonel, magistrate, and his uncle had been beloved as the faithful pastor of quiet parishes. But they had been no long time in the colony; they lived back from the tide-water counties where the real aristocracy had its strength and supremacy; they were of that middle class of yeomen-gentlemen who love liberty but do not affect rank. "A vigorous aristocracy favors the growth of personal eminence even in those who are not of it, but only near it," and these plain men of the middle counties were the more excellent and individual in the cultivation of their powers by reason of the contact. But there was a touch of rusticity, a neglect of polish, a rough candor of speech, about them which set them apart and distinguished them sharply enough when they came into the presence of the courtly and formal gentlemen who practised the manners of London in the river counties. Patrick Henry, at any rate, must have seemed a very rustic figure to the Burgesses when he first came to take his seat amongst them on a May day in 1765. He was known, indeed, to many. This was the man, they must have known, who had won so strange a verdict from a jury two years ago in the celebrated parsons' case at Hanover court-house, against the law and the evidence. But his careless dress and manner, his loose, ungainly figure, his listless, absent bearing, must have set many a courtly member staring. For such men as Washington, indeed, there can have been nothing either strange or unattractive in the rough exterior and unstudied ways of the new member. Punctilious though he was himself in every point of dress and bearing, Washington's life had most of it been spent with men who looked thus, and yet were stuff of true courage and rich capacity within. The manner of a man could count as no test of quality with him. His experience had covered the whole variety of Virginian life. He was an aristocrat by taste, not by principle. And Patrick Henry had, in fact, come to the same growth as he in essential quality and principle, though by another way. Henry's life had been willful, capricious, a bit haphazard, Washington's all the while subject to discipline; but both men had touched and seen the whole energy of the commonwealth, knew its hope, could divine its destiny. There was but one Virginia, and they were her children. It could not take long to bring them to an understanding and comradeship in affairs.

It was characteristic of the new member that he should step at once and unhesitatingly to a place of leadership when debate of the Stamp Act stirred the House, and that he should instantly sweep the majority into his following with a charm and dash of eloquence that came like a revelation upon the quiet assembly. He was but twenty-nine years old, but he had spent all his life in learning how the world went, and by what manner of speech it was moved and governed. He had roamed the woods with no thought but for sport, or a quiet hour with a book or his fancy in the shade of the trees. He had kept a country store, and let gossip and talk of affairs of colony and country-side take precedence of business. Finally he had turned with a permanent relish to the law, and had set himself to plead causes for his neighbors in a way that made judges stare and juries surrender at discretion. In everything he had seemed to read the passions of men. Books no less than men, the chance company of an old author no less than the constant talk of the neighborly land he lived in, seemed to fill him with the quick principles of the people and polity to which he belonged, and to lend him as inevitably every living phrase in which to utter them. The universal sympathy and insight which made his pleasantry so engaging to men of every stamp rendered his power no less than terrible when he turned to play upon their passions. He was not conscious of any audacity when he sprang to his feet upon the instant he saw the House resolved into committee to consider the Stamp Act. It was of the ardor of his nature to speak when conviction moved him strongly, without thought of propriety or precedence; and it was like him to stand there absorbed, reading his resolutions from a fly-leaf torn from an old law-book.

It seemed no doubt a precious piece of audacity in the eyes of the prescriptive leaders of the House to hear this almost unknown man propose his high recital of Virginia's liberties and his express defiance of Parliament-in tones which rang no less clear and confident upon the clause which declared "his Majesty's liege people" of the colony in no way bound to yield obedience, than in the utterance of the accepted matter of his premises. Debate flamed up at once, hot, even passionate. The astounding, moving eloquence of the young advocate, his instant hold upon the House, the directness with which he purposed and executed action in so grave a matter, stirred the pulses of his opponents and his followers with an equal power, and roused those who would have checked him to a vehemence as great as his own. The old leaders of the House, with whom he now stood face to face in this critical business, were the more formidable because of the strong reason of their position. No one could justly doubt that they wished to see the Old Dominion keep and vindicate her liberty, but they deemed it folly to be thus intemperately beforehand with the issue. Almost to a man they were sprung of families who had come to Virginia with the great migration that had brought the Washingtons, in the evil day when so many were fleeing England to be quit of the Puritan tyranny-royalists all, and touched to the quick with the sentiment of loyalty. 'Twas now a long time since Cromwell's day, indeed; generations had passed, and a deep passion for Virginia had been added to that old reverence for the wearer of the crown in England. But these men prided themselves still upon their loyalty; made it a point of honor to show themselves no agitators, but constitutional statesmen. It made them grave and deeply anxious to see the privileges that were most dear to them thus violated and denied, but it did not make them hasty to quarrel with the Parliament of the realm. They had intended opposition, but they feared to throw their cause away by defiance. Twas as little wise as dignified to flout thus at the sovereign power before all means bad been exhausted to win it to forbearance.

It was not the least part of the difficulty to face the veteran Speaker, John Robinson, so old in affairs, so stately in his age, so gravely courteous, and yet with such a threat of good manners against those who should make breach of the decorous traditions of the place. But the men chiefly to be feared were on the floor. There was Richard Bland, "wary, old, experienced," with "something of the look," a Virginian wit said, "of old musty parchments, which he handleth and studieth much," author of a "treatise against the Quakers on water-baptism"; with none of the gifts of an orator, but a veritable antiquarian in law and the precedents of public business, a very formidable man in counsel. Quiet men trusted him, and thought his prudence very wise. George Wythe was no less learned, and no less influential. Men knew him a man of letters, bringing the knowledge of many wise books to the practice of affairs, and set great store by his sincerity, as artless as it was human, and sweetened with good feeling. It made Randolph and Pendleton and Nicholas, the elder orators of the House, seem the more redoubtable that they should have such men as these at their elbows to prompt and steady them. And yet they would have been formidable enough of themselves. Edmund Pendleton had not, indeed, the blood or the breeding that gave his colleagues prestige. He had won his way to leadership by his own steady genius for affairs. He read nothing but law-books, knew nothing but business, cared for nothing but to make practical test of his powers. But he took all his life and purpose with such a zest, made every stroke with so serene a self-possession, was so quick to see and act upon every advantage in his business of debate, and was withal so transparent, bore himself with such a grace and charm of manner, was so obviously right-minded and upright, that it meant a great deal to the House to hear him intervene in its discussions with his melodious voice, his cool, distinct, effective elocution. Robert Carter Nicholas added to like talents for business and debate a reverent piety, a title to be loved and trusted without question, which no man ever thought to gainsay. And Peyton Randolph, with his "knowledge, temper, experience, judgment, integrity " as of a true Roman spirit, was a sort of prince among the rest. No man could doubt he wished Virginia to have her liberties. He had gone over sea to speak for her in Dinwiddie's day, though he was the King's attorney, and had lost his office for his boldness. But there were traditions of loyalty and service in his breeding which no man might rightly ignore. His father before him had won knighthood and the royal favor by long and honorable service as his Majesty's attorney in the colony. Pride and loyalty had gone hand in hand in the annals of a proud race, and had won for the Randolphs a prestige which made it impossible Sir John's son should very long be kept from the office he had so honorably inherited. And so Peyton Randolph was now once again the King's attorney. It was not as the King's officer, however, but as an experienced Parliamentary tactician, a trained debater, a sound man of affairs, that he had set himself to check Henry in his revolutionary courses.

Henry found himself, in truth, passionately set upon. Even threats were uttered, and abuse such as proud men find ill to bear. They cried " Treason! treason!" upon him when he dared declare the King would do well to look to the fate of Caesar and Charles the First for profitable examples. But he was not daunted a whit. " If this be treason, make the most of it," was his defiance to them. One ally who might have stood with him, had he known, was absent. Richard Henry Lee would have brought to his support a name as ancient and as honorable as any in the colony and an eloquence scarcely less than his own. But, as it was, he was left almost alone, and won his battle with no other aid than very plain men could lend by vote and homely utterance. The vote was very close, but enough. Randolph flung out of the House, muttering in his heat that he " would have given five hundred guineas for a single vote." Henry, taking the triumph very simply, as was his wont, and knowing his work for the session done, quietly made his way homeward that very day, striding unconcernedly down Duke of Gloucester Street, chatting with a friend, his legs clad in buckskin as if for the frontier, his saddle-bags and the reins of his lean nag slung carelessly over his arm.

PEYTON RANDOLPH

The Assembly had adopted Henry's declaration of rights, not his resolution of disobedience, and had softened a little the language he would have used; but its action seemed seditious enough to Fauquier, the Governor, and he promptly dissolved them. It did little good to send Virginians home, however, if the object was to check agitation. The whole manner of their life bred thought and concert of action. Where men have leave to be individual, live separately and with a proud self-respect, and yet are much at each other's tables, often in vestry council together, constantly coming and going, talking and planning throughout all the country - side, accustomed to form their opinions in league, and yet express each man' his own with a dash and flavor of independence; where there is the leisure to reflect, the habit of joint efforts in business, the spirit to be social, and abundant opportunity to be frank withal, if you will-you may look to see public views form themselves very confidently, and as easily without assemblies as with them. Washington bad taken no part in the stormy scenes of the House, but had sat calmly apart rather, concerned and thoughtful. He was not easily caught by the excitement of a sudden agitation. He bad the soldier's steady habit of self-possession in the presence of a crisis, and his own way of holding things at arm's - length for scrutiny — "like a bishop at his prayers," a wag said. He had a soldier's loyalty, too, and slowness at rebellion. His thought, no doubt, was with the conservatives, whatever may have been the light that sprang into his quiet eye when Henry's voice rang out so like a clarion, calling Virginia to her standard; and he went home, upon the dissolution, to join and aid bis neighbors in the slow discussion which must shape affairs to an issue.

"The Virginia Resolutions" had run like a flame through the colonies-not as the Burgesses had adopted them, but as Henry had drawn them, with their express threat of disobedience. Nor was that all. October, 1765, saw delegates from nine colonies come together in New York, at the call of Massachusetts, to take counsel what should be done. Every one knew that Virginia, North Carolina, and Georgia, the only colonies absent from the "congress," would have sent delegates too had their Governors not prevented them by the dissolution of their Assemblies before they could act on the call. A deep excitement and concern had spread everywhere throughout the settlements. Not only did the impending enforcement of the act engross " the conversation of the speculative part of the colonists," as Washington wrote to Francis Dandridge in London; it promised to engross also the energies of very active, and it might be very violent, men in many quarters, and it began to grow evident that some part of government itself would be brought to a standstill by its processes. "Our courts of judicature," declared Washington,"must inevitably be shut up; for it is impossible (or next of kin to it), under our present circumstances, that the act of Parliament can be complied with . . .; and if a stop be put to our judicial proceedings, I fancy the merchants of Great Britain trading to the colonies will not be among the last to wish for a repeal of it." The congress at New York drew up nothing less than a bill of rights and immunities, and sent resolutions over sea which arrested the attention of the world. The Virginian Assembly despatched like papers for itself; and Richard Henry Lee, when he had assisted to draw its memorials, hastened home to form in his own Cavalier county a "Westmoreland Association," whose members (four Washingtons among the rest) bound themselves by a solemn covenant to "exert every faculty to prevent the execution of the said Stamp Act in any instance whatsoever within this colony." The ministry could not stand the pressure. They gave way to Lord Rockingham, and the act was repealed.

Meanwhile Washington, his calm temper unshaken, was slowly coming to a clear vision of affairs in all their significance. Fox-hunting did not cease. He was much in the saddle and at table with the Fairfaxes, whom nothing could shake from their allegiance, and who looked with sad forebodings upon the temper the colony was in. It was proper they should speak so if they deemed it just, and Washington had no intolerance for what they urged. But George Mason, the neighbor whom he most trusted, was of a very different mind, and strengthened and confirmed him in other counsels. Mason was six years his senior; a man, too, cast by nature to understand men and events, how they must go and how be guided. They conferred constantly, at every turn of their intimate life, in the field or in the library, mounted or afoot in the forests, and came very deliberately and soberly to their statesman's view. Randolph and Pendleton and Wythe and Bland had themselves turned, after the first hesitation, to act with ardent men like Lee in framing the memorials to King, Lords, and Commons which were to go from the Burgesses along with the resolutions of the Stamp Act Congress in New York; and Washington, who had never hesitated, but had only gone slowly and with his eyes open, with that self-poise men had found so striking in him from the first, came steadily with the rest to the at last common purpose of resolute opposition. The repeal of the act came to all like a great deliverance.

Governor Fauquier had deemed it his duty to dissolve the Assembly upon the passage of Henry's resolutions, but he had acted without passion in the matter, and had kept the respect of the men he dealt with. He was not a man, indeed, to take public business very seriously, having been bred a man of fashion and a courtier rather than a master of affairs. He loved gay company and the deep excitement of the gaming-table, not the round of official routine. Affable, generous, elegant, a scholar and real lover of letters, he vastly preferred the talk of vivacious women and accomplished men to the business of the General Court, and was a man to be liked rather than considted. Washington, always admitted to the intimacy of official circles at Williamsburg, very likely relished the gallant Fauquier better than the too officious Dinwiddie. It was, unhappily, no portent to see a man still devoted to dissipation at sixty-two, even though he were Governor of one of his Majesty's colonies and a trusted servant of the crown; and Fauquier's gifts as a man of wit and of instructed tastes made his companionship no less acceptable to Washington than to the other men of discernment who frequented the ballrooms and receptions, ate formal dinners, and played quiet games of cards during the brief season at the little capital. It did not seriously disturb life there that the (Governor upheld the power of Parliament to tax, while the Burgesses strenuously opposed it. Washington, for one, did not hesitate on that account to be seen often in friendly talk with the Governor, or to accept frequent invitations to the "palace." He was of the temper which has so distinguished the nobler sort of Englishmen in politics: he might regard opposition as a public duty, but he never made it a ground of personal feeling or private spite. In a sense, indeed, he had long been regarded as belonging to official circles in the colony, more intimately than any other man who did not hold office. He had been put forward by the Fairfaxes in his youth; men in the Council and at the head of affairs had been his sponsors and friends from the first; he had been always, like his brother before him, a member of one of the chief groups in the colony for influence and a confidential connection with the public business. It was even understood that he was himself destined for the Council, when it should be possible to put him in it without seeming to give too great a preponderance to the Fairfax interest, already so much regarded in its make-up.

GEORGE MASON

The first flurry of differing views and conflicting purposes among the Virginian leaders had passed off. The judgment of high-spirited men everywhere sustained Henry — gave him unmistakable authentication as a leader; put all public men in the way of understanding their constituents. Some were bold and some were timid, but all were animated by the same hope and purpose, and few were yet intemperate. " Sensible of the. importance of unanimity among our constituents," said Jefferson afterwards, looking back to that time when he was young and in the first flush of his radical sentiments, " although we often wished to have gone faster, we slackened our pace, that our less ardent colleagues might keep up with us; and they, on their part, differing nothing from us in principle, quickened their gait somewhat beyond that which their prudence might of itself have advised." Patrick Henry was received to the place be had earned; and although the older leaders resumed that away in counsel to which their tried skill and varied experience in affairs fairly entitled them, there was no longer any jealous exclusion of new men. Henry's fame crept through the colonies as the man who had first spoken the mind not of Virginians only, but of all just men, with regard to the liberties of Englishmen in America. Before a year was out Richard Bland himself, parchment man and conservative that he was, had written and published a pamphlet entitled " An Inquiry into the Rights of the British Colonies," which said nothing less than that in all that concerned her internal affairs Virginia was "a distinct, independent state," though " united with the parent state by the closest league and amity, and under the same allegiance." A colony "treated with injury and violence," he exclaimed, "is become an alien." When antiquarians and lawyers, fresh from poring upon old documents, spoke thus, there were surely signs of the times.

The government at home kept colonial sentiment very busy. Even Lord Rockingbam's government, with Burke to admonish it, coupled its repeal of the stamp duties with a "declaratory act" which sought to quiet controversy by giving the lie direct to every argument urged against its authority in the colonies. "Parliament has power to bind the colonies in all cases whatsoever," was its round assertion: "a resolution for England's right to do what the Treasury pleased with three mill ions of freemen," cried Chatham. Though Rockingham's government would not act on that right, its successors would without scruple; and they were soon about it, for Rockingham's ministry retained office scarcely a twelvemonth. Grenville was, indeed, discredited; but Grafton and Townshend were as bad, as stubborn in temper, as reckless in policy. The year 1767 saw taxes proposed and enacted on glass, paper, painters' colors, and tea imported into the colonies, with a purpose to pay fixed salaries to the crown's officers in the colonies out of the proceeds; and the contested ground was all to go over again. To show their temper, the new ministers suspended the legislative powers of the Colonial Assembly in New York for refusing to make provision for troops quartered upon the colony. To complete their fiscal arrangements they presently created a custom-house and board of revenue commissioners for America. It was an ominous year, and set opinion forward not a little in the colonies.

The House of Burgesses broke, at its next session (1768), into fresh protests and remonstrances, and there was no one to restrain or rebuke it. Fauquier was dead, and gone to his reckoning; the reins of government were in the hands of gentle John Blair, President of the Council, a Virginian every inch, and with never a thought of checking his fellow-colonists in the expression of their just opinions. The autumn brought Lord Botetourt, the new Governor - General, who came in showy state, and with genial display of courtly manners and good feeling; but his arrival made little difference. The Burgesses smiled to see him come to open their session of 1769 with pageant of coach and six, brave display of royal insignia, and the manner of a sovereign meeting Parliament; and turned from him almost in contempt to denounce once more the course of the ministers, argue again the rights of America, declare they would draw the colonies together in concerted opposition, and call upon the other colonies to concur with them alike in their principles and in their purpose. Botetourt came hot foot to dissolve them; but they only shifted their place of meeting, gathered again at the private house of Mr. Anthony Hay, and there resolved no longer to import the things which Parliament had taxed in despite of them. George Mason had drawn the resolutions, at Washington's request, and Washington himself presented them.

Mason's thought had hastened very far along the path of opposition under the whip of England's policy; and Washington's quite as far. The government had not only sent troops to Boston and dissolved every Assembly that protested, but had advised the King to press prosecutions for treason in the colonies, and, should there be deemed sufficient ground, transport the accused to England to be tried by special commission. It was this last measure that had provoked the Burgesses to their hottest outburst. "At a time when our lordly masters in Great Britain will be satisfied with nothing less than the deprivation of American freedom," wrote Washington to Mason, with a sudden burst of passion, "it seems highly necessary that something should be done to avert the stroke, and maintain the liberty which we have derived from our ancestors. . . . That no man should scruple, or hesitate a moment, to use a-ms in defence of so valuable a blessing, on which all the good and evil of life depends, is clearly my opinion. Yet a-ms, I would beg leave to add, should be the last resource." Addresses to the throne and remonstrances to

Parliament had failed: it remained to try "starving their trades and manufactures," to see if that at last would arrest their attention. No doubt even that would prove of little avail; but it was at least peaceable and worth the trial. The next month, accordingly, he got unhesitatingly to his feet in the private meeting of the Burgesses at Mr. Hay's and moved George Mason's resolutions; nor did he forget to subscribe his quota to the fund which was to defray the expenses of the "association" there formed.

The next evening he attended the "Queen's Birth-Night" at the palace with the same naturalness of demeanor and frankness of dealing towards the Governor as before. Botetourt was not all show and gallantry, but was a genuine man at bottom. He had come to Virginia thinking the colonists a pleasure-loving people who could be taken by display and cajoled by hospitality: he had been told they were such in London. But he knew his mistake almost as soon as he had made it; and was prompt, even while he upheld prerogative, to do what he could to deal with them in a liberal and manly spirit. He had acquiesced very heartily at the outset of bis administration in a decision of the Council that writs of assistance could not legally be issued in Virginia, —for the process had been tried there too. He made such representations with regard to the state of the colony to the ministers at home as were both just and wise; was assured in reply that the ministers were willing to make every necessary concession; pledged his word in Virginia that there should be a substantial change of policy; and died the sooner (October 15, 1770) because the government would not, after all, redeem his promises. " Your Governor is becoming very popular, as we are told here," wrote Arthur Lee to his brother, from London, "and I have the worst proof of it in the increased orders for fineries from the ladies." Virginians did not find it easy to break an immemorial habit in order to starve the English trades and manafactures; and it was more than once necessary to urge and renew the non-importation agreements alike among the Burgesses and merchants at Williamsburg and by means of local associations throughout the colony. But Washington was punctilious to observe to the letter the agreements he had himself proposed. Again and again he bade his mercantile agents in London assist him to guard against any inadvertent breach of them: not to send him the articles Parliament had picked out for taxation in the colonies.

Life still continued to go, it is true, with something of the old sumptuousness at Mount Vernon. It was in June, 1768, that Colonel Washington ordered a new chariot," made in the newest taste, handsome, genteel, and light, to be made of the best seasoned wood, and by a celebrated workman," which was to cost him, fittings and all, £133. For all he grew uneasy lest the colonies' disagreement with England should come at last to a conflict of arms, he pushed his private interests with no abatement of thoroughness or self-possession, as if there were no fear but that things would long enough stand as they were. lie had not run surveyor's lines for Lord Fairfax, or assisted to drive the French from the Ohio, without seeing what fair lands lay upon the western rivers awaiting an owner; and, though there was still doubt how titles were to be established in that wilderness, he took care, through the good offices of an old comrade in arms, at least to be quietly beforehand with other claimants in setting up such titles as might be where the land lay richest and most accessible. "A silent management" was what he advised, "snugly carried on under the guise of hunting other game," lest there should be a premature rush thither that would set rival interests a-clashing. A strange mixture of the shrewdness of the speculator and the honesty of the gentleman — claims pushed with privacy, but without trickery or chicane-ran through his letters to Captain Crawford, and drew as canny replies from the frontiered soldier. Business gave way often to sport and pleasure, too, as of old, when politics fell dull between sessions. Now it was the hunt; then a gunning party in the woods; and again a day or two aboard his schooner, dropping down the river, and drawing the seine for sheepsheads upon the bar at Cedar Point. Even politics was mixed with diversion. He must needs give a ball at Alexandria on the evening of his election to the House which was to meet Lord Botetourt, no less than on other like occasions, of whatever kind the business of the Assembly was likely to be. He did not lose his passion for fine horse-flesh, either, at the thickest of the plot. In 1770 he was with Governor Eden, of North Carolina, at the Jockey Club races in Philadelphia, no doubt relieved by the news that all but the tea tax had been repealed. The next year it was the races in Annapolis that claimed him; and in 1773 Jacky Custis held him again at Philadelphia on the same errand. It was wholesome to be thus calmly in pursuit of diversion in the intervals of trying business. It bespoke a hearty life and a fine balance in the man.

There was one matter to which Washington felt it his bounden duty as a soldier and a man of honor to devote his time and energies, whether politics pressed or not. A grant of two hundred thousand acres of the western lands bad been promised by the government of the colony to those who enlisted for the war against the French and Indians in 1754; but nothing had ever been done to fulfill the promise, and Washington undertook to act as agent for his comrades in the business. In the autumn of 1770, accordingly, he turned away for a space from the deepening trouble in the east to plunge once more into the western ways and search out proper tracts for the grant along the reaches of the Ohio. 'Twas a two-months journey, for he did not stop till he had gone close upon three hundred miles beyond Fort Pitt. And when he was home again no one in the government who could lend a hand in the matter got any peace from the stirring, thorough man until the business was put finally into shape. There was a tidy profit in the grant for himself; for his own share was large, and he providently bought, besides, the shares of others who were unwilling to spend or co-operate in the matter. But there were months upon months of weary, unrequited service for his comrades, too, given with hearty diligence and without grudging. Their portions were as well placed as his own, they were to find, when it came to the survey. He came off from the business very rich in western lands — buying the Great Meadows, among the rest, for memory's sake — but richer still in the gratitude and admiration of the men for whom he had labored.

Meanwhile events darkened ominously. A new administration had been formed in England under Lord North, and had begun its government by repealing all the taxes of 1769 except that on tea. But it was Parliament's right to tax them that the colonists were fighting, not the taxes themselves, and one tax was as hateful as a hundred. The year had been marked in sinister fashion, moreover, by a broil between townsmen and troops in the streets of Boston, in which arms had been used and men slain, and in the heated imaginations of the colonists the affair had taken on the ugly aspect of a massacre. The year 1771 went quietly enough for Virginians. Botetourt was dead, and that good merchant of York, William Nelson, President of the Council, sat in the place of authority throughout the year. Although the whole country refused the taxed tea, the attention of the ministers, as it happened, was fixed chiefly upon Massachusetts, where trade centred at a growing port and opposition had a local habitation. In Virginia there was no place to send troops to, unless the whole country were occupied, and so long as Mr. Nelson was acting Governor, Colonel Washington could go without preoccupation tp the races, and gentlemen everywhere follow their own devices in the quiet counties. There was rioting — rebellion, even — in North Carolina, so uneasily did affairs go there; but Governor Tryon was a soldier as well as a despot, and did not need to trouble his neighbors about that. It was not until the first months of 1772 that Virginians began to read plain signs of change in the face of their new Governor, John Murray, Earl Dunmore — a dark and distant man, who seemed to the Virginians to come like a satrap to his province, who brought a soldier with him for secretary and confidential adviser, set up a fixed etiquette to be observed by all who would approach him, spoke abruptly and without courtesy, displayed in all things an arbitrary temper, and took more interest, it presently appeared, in acquiring tracts of western land than in conducting the government of the colony.

The year of his coming was marked by the secret destruction of the revenue-schooner Gaspe in Rbode Island, and by many significant flaws of temper hero and there throughout the colonies; and 1773 saw affairs at last come to a crisis.

Dunmore had summoned the Burgesses to meet him upon bis first coming, but had liked their proud temper as little as they liked bis, and was careful not to call them together again till March, 1773, though he had promised to convene them earlier. There was instant trouble. In view of the affair of the Gaspe, Parliament had again resolved upon the trial of malcontents in England, and the Burgesses were hot at seeing the sentiments of the colonies so flouted. Conservative men would still have waited to try events, but their fellow-members of quicker pulse were diligent to disappoint them. Leadership fell to those who were bold enough to take it; and Patrick Henry, Richard Henry Lee, Dabney Carr, and Thomas Jefferson, radicals all, drew together, a self-constituted committee of guidance. Evening after evening they met in a private room at the Raleigh, with now and again one or two other like spirits called into counsel, to consult what should be done. Richard Henry Lee proposed that the colonies should be invited to join Virginia in appointing committees of correspondence, through which to devise steady concert of action, and that Virginia's committee, to be appointed at once, should be instructed to look into the character of the new court of trial lately established in Rhode Island. Dabney Carr was directed to move the resolutions, and the eloquence of Lee and Henry won for them an instant and hearty acceptance. Dunmore promptly dissolved the Assembly, and Wash-ington was free to set out for New York to place Jacky Castis at King's College, lingering on the way in Philadelphia to see the races, and pick up the talk of the hour during half a dozen evenings at the rooms of the Jockey Club, at the balls and assemblies of the gay town, and at the hospitable tables of his friends.

IN THE OLD RALEIGH TAVERN

The opening of the year had found Washington in a very genial humor, his letters touched with pleasantry and gossip. "Our celebrated fortune. Miss French, whom half the world was in pursuit of," he wrote, in February, to Colonel Bassett, "bestowed her hand on Wednesday last, being her birthday (you perceive, I think myself under a necessity of accounting for the choice), on Mr. Ben Dulany, who is to take her to Maryland Mentioning of one wedding puts me in mind of another" —and so through the news of Miss More, " remarkable for a very frizzled head and good singing," and the rest of the neighborhood talk. But the year turned out a very sad one for him. He had been scarcely ten days back from New York when Patsy Custis, whom he loved as his own daughter, died. It called forth all the latent Christian faith of the thoughtful, steadfast man to withstand the shock. And Master Jack Custis, the girl's wayward brother, gave him little but anxiety. He would not study, for all Washington was so solicitous he should have the liberalizing outlook of books, and be made " fit for more useful purposes than horse-racer," and though he was but twenty, could hardly be induced to see the year out at college before getting married.

It was no doubt very well that public affairs of the first consequence called Washington's mind imperatively off from these private anxieties, which could not but be dwarfed in the presence of transactions which threatened to shake the continent. As the year drew on, the government in England undertook to force cargoes of the East India Company's tea into the ports. When all resisted, and Boston, more forward even than the rest, threw three hundred and forty odd chests of tea into the harbor, acts passed Parliament giving dangerous increase of power to the Governor of Massachusetts, and directing that Boston port be closed to all commerce on and after the first day of June; and it became evident that vigorous action must be taken in response. The Burgesses in Virginia (May, 1774) resolved that June 1st should be set apart as a day of fasting and prayer — prayer that civil war might be averted and the people of America united in a common cause. Again Dun-more dissolved them; but they gathered in the long room of the Raleigh tavern, and there resolved to urge a congress of all the colonies, and to call a convention for Virginia to meet at that place on the first day of August to take action for the colony. They showed no spleen towards the Governor. Washington dined with him the very day of the dissolution, spent the evening at the palace, even rode out with him to his farm on the following morning and breakfasted there; and the Burgesses did not fail to give the ball they had planned in honor of Lady Dunmore and her daughters on the evening of the day they had held their meeting in the "Appolo room" at the Raleigh. But there were fasting and prayer on the 1st of June; the convention met on the first day of August; very outspoken resolutions were adopted; and Peyton Randolph, Richard Henry Lee, Patrick Henry, Richard Bland, Edmund Pendleton, George Washington, and Benjamin Harrison were directed to attend the congress of the colonies appointed to meet in Philadelphia on the fifth day of September. When the time came for the journey, Henry and Pendleton joined "Washington at Mont Vernon. It must have been with many grave thoughts that the three companions got to horse and turned to ride through the long August day towards the north.

Chapter VI
Piloting a Revolution

In the congress of 1774 the leaders of Virginia were for the first time brought into face-to-face conference with the men of the other colonies. In 1765 Fauquier had dissolved the Burgesses with such sharp despatch, upon the passage of Mr. Henry's resolutions, that they were all gone home before the call for a congress to act upon the stamp duties could reach them. But in 1774 they were not to be so cheated. They had themselves issued the call for a congress this time, and dissolution could not drive them home. Their leaders could at least linger at the Raleigh and concert means to have their way, House or no House. A convention took the place of the Assembly; and seven leading members of the House were sent to Philadelphia, with as full authority to speak and act for the colony as if the Burgesses themselves had commissioned them. Mr. Harrison declared in Philadelphia that "he would have come on foot rather than not come"; and quiet Richard Bland, that "he would have gone if it had been to Jericho." Colonel Harrison struck his new colleagues from the North as a bit rough in his free Southern speech and manner; and Mr. Bland seemed to them "a plain, sensible man," such as would be more given to study than to agitation. If such men, artless and steady as any downright country gentleman of old England, held so high a fancy for the business of the congress, it was easy to conclude what the hastier, younger men would be likely to plan and do; and the Massachusetts delegates found themselves greatly heartened.

John Adams, Thomas Gushing, Samuel Adams, and Robert Treat Paine were the representatives of Massachusetts. It was their people who had most provoked Parliament to be high-handed and aggressive. The struggle with the ministry at home had taken shape in Boston. It had come to actual riot there. All the continent and all England had seen how stubborn was the temper, how incorrigible the spirit of resistance, in that old seat of the Puritan power, always hard set and proud in its self-willed resolution to be independent; and all eyes were turned now upon Gushing and Paine and this "brace of Adamses," who had come, it was thought, to hurry the congress into radical courses. Kindness, applause, hospitality, "studied and expensive respect," had attended them at every stage of their long ride from Boston to Philadelphia. The country was much stirred by the prospect of a general " congress of committees" at Philadelphia; and the delegates from Massachusetts were greeted as they passed even more generously than the rest, because their people had been the first to suffer in this bad business; because their chief port at Boston was closed, and red-coated sentries were on their streets. It behooved the Massachusetts men, however, not to suffer themselves to be misled. Many looked upon them askance; some distrusted them heartily. Their own hot-headed mob had provoked the "massacre," of which they made so much. They had wantonly destroyed private property when they threw the tea into their harbor to show the government their spirit. There had been more than a touch of violence, more than a little turbulence, and a vast deal of radical and revolutionary talk in all that they had done; and the colonies were full yet of men who had no tolerance for anything that transgressed, were it never so little, the moderate limits of constitutional agitation. "There is an opinion which does in some degree obtain in the other colonies that the Massachusetts gentlemen, and especially of the town of Boston, do affect to dictate and take the lead in continental measures; that we are apt, from an inward vanity and self-conceit, to assume big and haughty airs," said Joseph Hawley, who, for all he had grown old as a quiet Massachusetts lawyer among his neighbors, had kept his shrewd eyes abroad. "It is highly probable," he told John Adams, with a wholesome bluntness, "that you will meet gentlemen from several of the other colonies fully equal to yourselves or any of you in their knowledge of Great Britain, the colonies, law, history, government, commerce.... By what we from time to time see in the public papers, and what our Assembly and committees have received from the Assemblies and committees of the more southern colonies, we must be satisfied that they have men of as much sense and literature as any we can, or ever could, boast of." It was mere counsel of prudence that they should play their part in the congress with modesty and discretion.

Not Cushing and Paine, but the Adamses, carried the strength of the Massachusetts delegation; and it was Samuel Adams, rather than John, who was just now the effective master in the great Bay Colony —"master of puppets," his enemies called him. Hale, bluff, adroit, plain, a man of the people, he had grown old in the business of agitation. Fifty-two years he had lived, planning always for others, never for himself. He had "never looked forward in his life," he frankly said; "never planned, laid a scheme, or framed a design of laying up anything for himself or others after him"; had let all his private business go neglected, and lived upon the petty salary of a small public office, the indulgence of fortune, and the good offices of the friends and neighbors who loved him. He was in Philadelphia now wearing the plain suit and spending the modest purse with which his friends and partisans had fitted him out —the very impersonation of the revolution men were beginning so to fear. 'No man had ever daunted him; neither could any corrupt him. He was possessed with the instinct of agitation: led the people, not the leaders; cared not for place, but only for power; showed a mastery of means, a self-containment, a capacity for timely and telling speech, that marked him a statesman, though he loved the rough ways of a people's government, and preferred the fierce democracy of the town meeting to the sober dignity of senates. Like an eagle in his high building and strength of audacious flight, but in instinct and habit a bird of the storm. Not over-nice what he did, not too scrupulous what he devised, he was yet not selfish, loved the principles he had given his life to, and spent himself without limit to see them triumph.

John Adams, his cousin, was of a very different mould: a younger man by thirteen years; no man of the people, but with a taste rather for the exclusive claims of education and breeding; self-regardful; a thought too calculating ; too quick-witted to be patient with dull men, too self-conscious to be at ease with great ones; and yet public-spirited withal, and generous in action if not in judgment; of great powers, if only he could manage to use them without jealousy. Samuel Adams thought only of his end, not of himself; seldom spoke of himself, indeed; seemed a sort of subtle engine for the people's business. John Adams thought of himself always, and yet mastered himself to play a great part with the nobility of a man of genius, if not with the grace of a man of modesty and self-forgetful devotion. For the time he could even hold back with his wily cousin, resign leadership in the congress to Virginia, and act in all things the wise part of those who follow.

It was a circumstance full of peril that the delegates of the several colonies should at such a juncture be strangers to one another, and provincials all, nowhere bred to continental affairs. Only since the passage of the Stamp Act had they taken any thought for each other. There was no assurance that even the best leaders of a colony could rise to the statesman's view and concert measures to insure the peace of an empire. Rising lawyers like John Adams, brusque planters like Colonel Harrison, well-to-do merchants like Thomas Mifflin, might bring all honesty and good intention to the task and yet miserably fail. A provincial law practice, the easy ascendency of a provincial country gentleman, the narrow round of provincial trade, might afford capable men opportunity to become enlightened citizens, but hardly fitted them to be statesmen. The real first business of the delegates was to become acquainted, and to learn how to live in the foreign parts to which most of them had come. There was a continual round of entertainment in the hospitable town, therefore, a universal exchange of courtesies, a rush of visiting and dining, a flow of excellent wine, a rich abundance of good cheer, such as for a while made the occasion seem one of festivity rather than of anxious counsel. Many of the delegates had come to town a week or more before the date set for the congress, and had settled to an acquaintance before it was time to effect an organization; but the gentlemen from Maryland and Virginia, more familiar with the journey, arrived almost upon the day. They made an instant impression upon their new colleagues. John Adams promptly declared them " the most spirited and consistent of any," and deemed Mr. Lee particularly "a masterly man." Joseph Hawley's prediction was fulfilled. "The Virginia and indeed all the Southern delegates appear like men of importance," said Silas Deane; "I never met, nor scarcely had an idea of meeting, with men of such firmness, sensibility, spirit, and thorough knowledge of the interests of America." Mr. Lynch of South

Carolina, though he wore " the manufacture of this country," and was in all things " plain, sensible, above ceremony," seemed to Mr. Deane to carry with him " more force in his very appearance than most powdered folks in their conversation."

The high bearing and capacity of the Southern delegates came upon the New England men like a great surprise: where they had expected to see rustic squires they found men of elegance and learning. But there was, in fact, no good reason to wonder at the natural leadership of these men. Their life had bred them more liberally than others. It required a much more various capacity and knowledge of the world to administer a great property and live the life of a local magnate in the South than sufficed to put a man at the front of trade or of legal practice in Boston or New York or Philadelphia.

WASHINGTON

The Southern colonies, besides, had lived more in sympathy with the life of the empire than had their North-em neighbors. Their life had depended directly upon that of England hitherto, and had partaken of it with a constant zest. They had no rival trade; they had wanted no rival government. The general air of the wide empire had blown in all ordinary seasons through their affairs, and they had cultivated none of that shrewd antagonism towards the home government which had so sharpened the wits and narrowed the political interests of the best men in New

England. They had read law because they were men of business, without caring too much about its niceties or meaning to practise it in litigation. They had read their English history without feeling that they were separate from it. Their passion for freedom was born not of local feeling so much as of personal pride and the spirit of those who love old practices and the just exemptions of an ancient constitution. It was the life they had lived, and the conceptions of personal dignity and immemorial privilege that had gone always with it, that gave them so striking an air of mastery. It was not simply because the Massachusetts delegates kept themselves prudently in the background and the rest yielded to her pretensions that Virginia was accorded primacy in the congress: it was also because her representatives were men to whom power naturally fell, and because she had won so honorable a place of leadership already in the common affairs of the continent.

Colonel Washington, striking and forceable man though he was, did not figure as a leader among the Virginian delegates. Peyton Randolph was elected president of the congress; Richard Henry Lee and Patrick Henry stood forth as the Virginian leaders on the floor. "If you speak of solid information and sound judgment, Colonel Washington is unquestionably the greatest man on that floor," was Henry's confident and generous verdict; but Washington was no politician, and did not stand in exactly the same class with the rest. He had headed committees and presided over popular meetings among his own neighbors in Fairfax, and had been prompt to join them in speaking with high spirit against the course of the ministry in Eng-land. He had been forward in urging and punctiliously careful in practising non-importation. He had declared Gage's conduct in Boston "more becoming a Turkish bashaw than an English governor." But he was a man of action rather than of parliaments. "I will raise one thousand men, enlist them at my own expense, and march myself at their head for the relief of Boston," had been his impetuous utterance in the Virginian convention — "the most eloquent speech that ever was made," Mr. Lynch declared. " I have heard he said," reported an admiring Philadelphian —" I have heard he said he wished to God the liberties of America were to be determined by a single combat between himself and George!" But his fellow Virginians understood him better. They had chosen him for force and sobriety; not as an orator, but as the first soldier and one of the first characters of the commonwealth; and he had made the impression they expected. He had not been put upon their committee of correspondence, or been appointed with Nicholas and Pendleton and Lee and Henry to draw resolutions and remonstrances; but when it came to choosing those who should represent the Old Dominion in the congress, but two names stood before his in the vote. Peyton Randolph, 104; Richard Henry Lee, 100; George Washington, 98; Patrick Henry, 89; Richard Bland, 79; Benjamin Harrison, 66; Edmund Pendleton, 62 —such had been the preference of the convention. The Northern delegates admired his easy, soldier like air and gesture" and his modest and "cool but determined" style and accent when he spoke; and wondered to see him look scarce forty, when they recalled how his name had gone through the colonies twenty years ago, when he had met the French so gallantly at Great Meadows, and with Braddock at the forks of the Ohio.

The Massachusetts delegates had reason to admire his manly openness, too, and straightforward candor. An old comrade in arms whom he esteemed —a Virginian now in regular commission, and stationed with the troops in Boston — had written him very damaging things about the "patriot" leaders of the beset town; of their "tyrannical oppression over one another," and "their fixed aim at total independence," and had charged them roundly with being no better than demagogues and rebels. Washington went at once to the men accused, to learn from their own lips their principles and intentions, taking Richard Henry Lee and discreet Dr. Shippen along with him as his sponsors and witnesses. " Spent the evening at home with Colonel Lee, Colonel Washington, and Dr. Shippen, who came in to consult us," was John Adams's entry in his diary for September 28th. No doubt Samuel Adams found the interview a trying one, and winced a little under the examination of the calm and steady soldier, going so straight to the point, for all his Virginian ceremony. There had been many outward signs of the demagogue in Adams's career.

He had been consciously and deliberately planning and scheming for independence ever since 1768, and had made public avowal of his purpose no longer ago than last year. It most have taxed even his adroit powers to convince these frank Virginians that his purpose was not rebellion, but liberty; that he venerated what they venerated, and wished only what they wished. But the truth somehow lay open before the evening was gone. There was frank cordiality in the parting: Washing-ton was convinced of their genuineness and sobriety. " Though you are led to believe by venal men," he replied to Captain Mackenzie, " that the people of Massachusetts are rebellious, setting up for independency, and what not, give me leave, my good friend, to tell you that you are abused, grossly abused. This I advance with a degree of confidence and boldness which may claim your belief, having better opportunities for knowing the real sentiments of the people you are among, from the leaders of them, in opposition to the present measures of the administration, than you have from those whose business it is not to disclose truths, but to misrepresent facts in order to justify as much as possible to the world their own conduct."

The Massachusetts men had come to a better understanding of the game-began to see how cautiously it must be played, how slowly and how wisely. It was a critical business, this of drawing all the colonies into a common congress, as if to create a directing body for the continent, without constitution or warrant. The establishment of committees of correspondence had seemed little short of seditious, for it was notorious the committees were formed to concert action against the government at home; but this "congress of committees" was an even more serious matter. Would the colonies venture a continental organization to defy Parliament? Dangerous differences of opinion were blown hot between neighbors by such measures. Some of the best men in America were opposed to the course which was now evidently to be taken. So long as it was merely a matter of protest by the colonies severally, they had no criticism to make — except perhaps that Mr. Otis and Mr. Henry had held unnecessarily high language, and had been bold and defiant beyond measure; but when they saw how the opposition gathered head, hastened from protest to concerted resistance, put popular conventions into the place of lawful legislative assemblies, and advanced at length to a continental organization, they deemed it high time to bestir themselves, vindicate their loyalty to his Majesty's government, and avert a revolution. They were not men to be trifled with. Had they been able to unite upon active measures, had they advanced from defence to aggressive action, they might have rendered themselves formidable beyond possibility of defeat. Everywhere men of substance and of influence were to be found by the score who were opposed to a revolutionary agitation, such as this that now seemed to be gathering head. Even in Massachusetts men who bore the best and the oldest names of the commonwealth were of this number; in New York and Pennsylvania, at the very heart of the continent, they could, it was believed, boast a majority, as well as to the far southward, in the low country of South Carolina and Georgia. No one, they declared, but designing politicians and men without property, those who had much to gain and nothing to lose by the upsetting of law and ordered government, wished to see this contest with the ministry pushed to extremes. They wished no less than others to see the colonies keep their lawful and chartered liberties, but the thing must be accomplished soberly, and without loss of things equally dear-of honor, and the maintenance of an unbroken English Empire.

The nice balance of parties was disclosed in the congress itself. The Pennsylvanian delegation was led by Joseph Galloway, a man in the prime of life, full of force and learning, who had been Speaker of the provincial House these eight years by the almost unanimous choice of his colleagues, and who now stood forth to utter the real voice of his colony in proposing measures of accommodation. He proposed that the home government be asked to sanction the establishment of a confederate parliament for America, composed of delegates to be chosen every third year by the legislatures of the several colonies, and acting under a governor-general to be appointed by the crown. Edward Rutledge, of South Carolina, hot orator for liberty though he was, declared it an "almost perfect plan," and was eager to see it adopted; influential members from almost every quarter gave it their hearty support, Mr. John Jay, of New York, among the rest; and it was defeated only by the narrow majority of a single colony's vote. Chatham might very justly commend the congress of 1774 as conspicuous among deliberative bodies for its " decency, firmness, and wisdom," its " solidity of reasoning, force of sagacity, and wisdom of conclusion, under such a complication of circumstances," for the complication of circumstances was such as even he did not fully comprehend. For seven weeks of almost continuous session did it hammer its stiff business into shape, never wearying of deliberation or debate, till it could put forth papers to the world-an address to the King, memorials to the people of Great Britain and to the people of British America, their fellow-subjects, and a solemn declaration of rights-which should mark it no revolutionary body, but a congress of just and thoughtful Englishmen, in love, not with license or rebellion, but with right and wholesome liberty. Their only act of aggression was the formation of an "American Association" pledged against trade with Great Britain till the legislation of which they complained should be repealed. Their only intimation of intention for the future was a resolution to meet again the next spring, should their prayers not meanwhile be heeded.

Washington turned homeward from the congress with thoughts and purposes every way deepened and matured. It had been a mere seven weeks' conference; no one had deemed the congress a government, or had spoken of any object save peace and accommodation; but no one could foresee the issue of what had been done. A spirit had run through those deliberations which gave thoughtful men, as they pondered it, a new idea of the colonies. It needed no prophet to discern beyond all this sober and anxious business a vision of America united, armed, belligerent for her rights. There was no telling what form of scornful rejection awaited that declaration of rights or the grave pleading of that urgent memorial to the crown. It behooved every man to hold himself in readiness for the worst; and Washington saw as clearly as any man at how nice a hazard things stood. He had too frank a judgment upon affairs to cheat himself with false hopes. "An innate spirit of freedom first told me that the measures which administration hath for some time been and now are most violently pursuing are repugnant to every principle of natural justice," had been his earnest language to Bryan Fairfax ere he set out for the congress; " whilst much abler heads than my own bath fully convinced me that it is not only repugnant to natural right, but subversive of the laws and constitution of Great Britain itself, in the establishment of which some of the best blood of the kingdom hath been split. ...I could wish, I own," he had added, "that this dispute had been left to posterity to determine"; but he knew more clearly than ever before, as he rode homeward from the congress through the autumn woods, that it had not been; that Lee and Henry and Mason were rightly of the same mind and purpose with the men from Massachusetts; that conference had only united and heartened those who stood for liberty in every colony; that there could be no compromise-perhaps no yielding either-and that every man must now take his soberest resolution for the times to come.

He turned steadily to his private business for the winter, nevertheless, as was bis wont-pushed forward the preparation and settlement of his western lands, and stood guard, as before, over the soldiers' grants upon the Ohio, against official bad faith and negligence. " For a year or two past there has been scarce a moment that I could properly call my own," he declared to a friend who solicited his promise to act as guardian to his son. " What with my own business, my present ward's, my mother's, which is wholly in my hands. Colonel Fairfax's, Colonel Mercer's, and the little assistance I have undertaken to give in the management of my brother Augustine's concerns, together with the share I take in public affairs, I have been constantly engaged in writing letters, settling accounts, and negotiating one piece of business or another; by which means I have really been deprived of every kind of enjoyment, and had almost fully resolved to engage in no fresh matter till I had entirely wound up the old." He promised to undertake the new charge, nevertheless. It was stuff of his nature to spend himself thus, and keep his powers stretched always to a great compass.

CARPENTER'S HALL, PHILADELPHIA

With the new year (1775) public affairs loomed big again, and ominous. The petitions of the congress at Philadelphia had been received in England almost with contempt. Chatham, indeed, with that broad and noble sagacity which made him so great a statesman, had proposed that America's demands should be met, to the utmost length of repeal and withdrawal of menace, and that she should be accorded to the full the self-government she demanded in respect of taxation and every domestic concern. "It is not cancelling a piece of parchment," he cried, that can win back America," the old fire burning hot within him; "you must respect her fears and her resentments." The merchants, too, in fear for their trade, urged very anxiously that there should be instant and ample concession. But the King's stubborn anger, the Parliament's indifference, the ministry's incapacity, made it impossible anything wise or generous should be done. Instead of real concession there was fresh menace. The ministry did, indeed, offer to exempt from taxation every colony that would promise that by its own vote it would make proper contribution to the expenses of public defence and imperial administration — in the hope thereby to disengage the lukewarm middle colonies from the plot now thickening against the government. But Massachusetts was at once proclaimed in rebellion, every port in New England was declared closed against trade, New England fishermen were denied access to the Newfoundland fisheries, and ten thousand fresh troops were ordered to Boston. Neither the pleas of their friends nor the threats of their enemies reached the ears of the colonists promptly from over sea that portentous spring; but they were not slow to perceive that they must look for no concessions; and they did not wait upon Parliament in their preparation for a doubtful future. Upon the very day the "congress of committees" at Philadelphia adjourned, a "provincial congress" in Massachusetts, formed of its own authority in the stead of the House of Delegates the Governor had but just now dissolved, had voted to organize and equip the militia of the colony and to collect stores and arms. Virginia had been equally bold, and almost equally prompt, far away as she seemed from the King's troops at Boston. By the end of January Charles Lee could write from Williamsburg:

"The whole country is full of soldiers, all furnished, all in arms. . . . Never was such vigor and concord heard of, not a single traitor, scarcely a silent dissentient."

"Every county is now arming a company of men for the avowed purpose of protecting their committees," Dunmore had reported to the ministry before the year 1774 was out, "and to be employed against government if occasion require. As to the power of government which your lordship directs should be exerted to counteract the dangerous measures pursuing here, I can assure your lordship that it is entirely disregarded, if not wholly overturned. There is not a justice of peace in Virginia that acts except as a committeeman; the abolishing of courts of justice was the first step taken, in which the men of fortune and preeminence joined equally with the lowest and meanest." Company after company, as it formed, asked Colonel Washington to assume command over it, not only in his own county of Fairfax, but in counties also at a distance-and he accepted the responsibility as often as it was offered to him. " It is my full intention," he said, simply, " to devote my life and fortune to the cause we are engaged in, if needful"; and he had little doubt any longer what was to come. He found time, even that stirring year, to quicken his blood once and again, nevertheless, while winter held, by a run with the hounds: for he was not turned politician so sternly even yet as to throw away his leisure upon anything less wholesome than the hale sport he loved.

On the 20th of May, 1775, the second Virginian convention met, not in Williamsburg, but at Richmond, and its chief business was the arming of the colony. Maryland bad furnished the ironical formula with which to justify what was to be done: "Resolved, unanimously, that a well-regulated militia, composed of the gentlemen freeholders and other freemen, is the natural strength and only stable security of a free government; and that such militia will relieve our mother-country from any expense in our protection and defence, will obviate the pretence of a necessity for taxing as on that account, and render it unnecessary to keep any standing army-ever dangerous to liberty — in this province." Mr. Henry accepted the formula with great relish, in the convention at Richmond, in his resolution "that the colony be immediately put into a posture of defence," but he broke with it in the speech with which he supported his measures of preparation. In that there was no plan or pretence of peace, but, instead, a plain declaration of war. Once more did Edmund Pendleton, Richard Bland, Mr. Nicholas, and Colonel Harrison spring to their feet to check him, as in the old days of the Stamp Act. Once more, nevertheless, did he have his way, completely, triumphantly. What he had proposed was done, and his very opponents served upon the committee charged with its accomplishment. It was not doing more than other colonies had done; it was only saying more; it was only dealing more fearlessly and frankly with fortune. Even slow, conservative men like John Dickinson, of Pennsylvania, shielded themselves behind only an " if." " The first act of violence on the part of administration in America," they knew, " or the attempt to reinforce General Gage this winter or next year, will put the whole continent in arms, from Nova Scotia to Georgia."

What they feared very speedily came to pass. 'Twas hardly four weeks from the day Mr. Henry proclaimed a state of war in the convention at Richmond before the King's regulars were set upon at Lexington and Concord and driven back in rout to their quarters by the swarming militia-men of Massachusetts. On the 19th of April they had set out across a peaceful country to seize the military stores placed at Concord. Before the day was out they had been fairly thrown back into Boston, close upon three hundred of their comrades gone to a last reckoning; and the next morning disclosed a rapidly growing provincial army drawn in threatened siege about them. In the darkness of that very night (April 20th), at the command of Dunmore, a force of marines was landed from an armed sloop that lay in James River, in Virginia, to seize the gunpowder stored at Williamsburg. The Virginians in their turn sprang to arms, and Dunmore was forced, ere he could rid himself of the business, to pay for the powder taken —pay Captain Patrick Henry, at the head of a body of militia under arms.

On the 10th of May the second Continental Congress met at Philadelphia, with business to transact vastly different from that to which the first "congress of committees" had addressed itself-not protests and resolves, but quick and efficient action. The very day it met, a body of daring provincials under Ethan Allen had walked into the open gates at Ticonderoga and taken possession of the stout fortress "in the name of the Great Jehovah and the Continental Congress "; and two days later a similar exploit secured Crown Point to the insurgents. Active war had begun; an army was set down before Boston —a rude army that had grown to be sixteen thousand strong within the first week of its rally; the country was united in a general resistance, and looked to the congress to give it organization and guidance. Colonel Washington had come to the congress in his provincial uniform, and found himself a great deal sought after in its committees. Not only the drawing of state papers which would once more justify their cause and their resort to arms in the eyes of the world, but the actual mustering and equipment of an army, quick fortification, the gathering of munitions and supplies, the raising of money and the organization of a commissariat, the restraint of the Indians upon the frontier, was the business in hand, and Washington's advice was invaluable when such matters were afoot. He showed no hesitation as to what should be done. His own mind had long ago been made up; and the sessions of the congress were not ended before Virginia was committed beyond all possibility of drawing back. The 1st of June saw her last House of Burgesses convene; for by the 8th of the month Dunmore was a fugitive — had seen the anger of a Williamsburg mob blaze hot against him, and had taken refuge upon a man-of-war lying in the river. The province was in revolution, and Washington was ready to go with it.

It meant more than he thought that he had come to Philadelphia habited like a soldier. It had not been his purpose to draw all eyes upon him: it was merely his instinctive expression of his own personal feeling with regard to the crisis that had come. But it was in its way a fulfillment of prophecy. When the first Virginian convention chose delegates to attend the congress of 1774, "some of the tickets on the ballot assigned reasons for the choice expressed in them. Randolph should preside in congress; Lee and Henry should display the different kinds of eloquence for which they were renowned; Washington should command the army, if an army should be raised; Bland should open the treasures of ancient colonial learning; Harrison should utter plain truths; and Pendleton should be the penman for business." No wonder the gentlemen from Virginia, coming with such confidence to the congress, made the instant impression they did for mastery and self-poise! "There are some fine fellows come from Virginia," Joseph Reed had reported, "but they are very high. We understand they are the capital men of the colony." Washington alone awaited his cue. Now he was to get it, without expecting it. The irregular army swarming before Boston was without standing or government. It had run hastily together out of four colonies; was subject to no common authority; hardly knew what allegiance it bore; might fall to pieces unless it were adequately commanded. The congress in Philadelphia was called upon to recognize and adopt it, give it leave and authority to act for all the colonies, give it a commander, and summon the whole country to recruit it. There was an obvious political necessity that the thing should be done, and done promptly. Massachusetts did not wish to stand alone; New England wanted the active assistance of the other colonies; something must be attempted to secure common action. The first thing to do was to choose an acceptable and efficient leader, and to choose him outside New England. To John Adams the choice seemed simple enough. There was no soldier in America, outside New England —nor inside either-to be compared, whether in experience or distinction, with Washington, the gallant, straightforward, earnest Virginian he had learned so to esteem and trust there in Philadelphia. He accordingly moved that congress "adopt the army at Cambridge," and declared that he had " but one gentleman in mind " for its command —"a gentleman from Virginia, who was among us," he said, " and very well known to all of us; a gentleman whose skill and experience as an officer, whose independent fortune, great talents, and excellent universal character, would command the approbation of all America, and unite the cordial exertions of all the colonies better than any other person in the union." Washington, taken unawares, rose and slipped in confusion from the room. Some of his own friends doubted the expediency of putting a. Virginian at the head of a New England army, but the more clear-sighted among the New-Englanders did not, and the selection was made, after a little hesitation, unanimously.

Washington accepted his commission with that mixture of modesty and pride that made men love and honor him. "You may believe me, my dear Patsy," were his simple words to his wife, "when I assure you in the most solemn manner, that, so far from seeking this appointment, I have used every endeavor in my power to avoid it, not only from my unwillingness to part with you and the family, but from a consciousness of its being a trust too great for my capacity. But as it has been a kind of destiny that has thrown me upon this service, I shall hope that my undertaking it is designed to answer some good purpose...It was utterly out of my power to refuse this appointment, without exposing my character to such censures as would have reflected dishonor upon myself and given pain to my friends." He spoke in the same tone to the congress. " I beg it may be remembered," he said, " by every gentleman in this room, that I this day declare with the utmost sincerity I do not think myself equal to the command I am honored with." His commission was signed on the 19th of June; on the 21st he was on the read to the north-the read he had travelled twenty years ago to consult with Governor Shirley in Boston upon questions of rank, and to fall into Mary Philipse's snare by the way; the road he had ridden after the races, but three years ago, to put Jacky Custis at college in New York. " There is something charming to me in the conduct of Washington," exclaimed John Adams; and it was wholesome for the whole country that such a man should be put at the head of affairs. Many ignoble things were being done in the name of liberty, and an ugly tyranny had been brought to every man's door —" the tyranny of his next-door neighbor." There were men by the score in the colonies who had no taste or sympathy for the rebellion they now saw afoot — common men who knew little or nothing of the mother-country, as well as gentlemen of culture who loved her traditions and revered her crown; farmers and village lawyers, as well as merchants at the ports who saw their living gone and ruin staring them in the face. But the local committees and the "Sons of Liberty" everywhere saw to it that such men should know and dread and fearfully submit to the views of the majority. Government was suspended: there was nowhere so much as a justice of the peace acting under the authority of the crown. There might have been universal license had the rabble not seen their leaders so noble, so bent upon high and honorable purposes. It was an object-lesson in the character of the revolution to see Washington ride through the colonies to take charge of an insurgent army. And no man or woman, or child even, was likely to miss the lesson. That noble figure drew all eyes to it; that mien as if the man were a prince; that sincere and open countenance, which every man could see was lighted by a good conscience; that cordial ease in salute, as of a man who felt himself brother to his friends. There was something about Washington that quickened the pulses of a crowd at the same time that it awed them, that drew cheers which were a sort of voice of worship. Children desired sight of him, and men felt lifted after he had passed. It was good to have such a man ride all the open way from Philadelphia to Cambridge in sight of the people to assume command of the people's army. It gave character to the thoughts of all who saw him.

Chapter VII
General Washington

Matters had not stood still before Boston to await a commander sent by congress. While Washington waited for his commission and made ready for his journey there had been fighting done which was to simplify his task. General William Howe had reached Boston with reinforcements on the 25th of May, and quite ten thousand troops held the city, while a strong fleet of men-of-war lay watchfully in the harbor. There was no hurry, it seemed, about attacking the sixteen thousand raw provincials, whose long lines were drawn loosely about the town from Charlestown Neck to Jamaica Plain. But commanding hills looked across the water on either hand-in Charlestown on the north and in Dorchester on the southeast-and it would be well, Howe saw, to secure them, lest they should be occupied by the insurgents. On the morning of the 17th of June, however, while leisurely preparations were a-making in Boston to occupy the hills of Charlestown, it was discovered that the provincials had been beforehand in the project. There they were in the clear sun, working diligently at redoubts of their own upon the height. Three thousand men were put across the water to drive them off. Though they mustered only seventeen hundred behind their unfinished works, three several assaults and the loss of a thousand men was the cost of dislodging them.

They withheld their fire till the redcoats were within fifty-nay, thirty-yards of them, and then poured out a deadly,blazing fire which no man could face and live. They were ousted only when they failed of powder and despaired of reinforcements. Veteran officers who had led the assault declared the regulars of France were not more formidable than these militia-men, whom they had despised as raw peasants. There was no desire to buy another American position at that price; and Washington had time enough for the complimentary receptions and addresses and the elaborate parade of escort and review that delayed his journey to headquarters.

He reached Cambridge on the 2d of July, and bore himself with so straightforward and engaging a courtesy in taking command that the officers he superseded could not but like him: jealousy was disarmed. But he found neither the preparations nor the spirit of the army to his liking. His soldierly sense of order was shocked by the loose discipline, and his instinct of command by the free and easy insolence of that irregular levy; and his authority grew stern as he labored to bring the motley host to order and effective organization. " The people of this government have obtained a character," his confidential letters declared," which they by no means deserved-their officers, generally speaking, are the most indifferent kind of people I ever saw. I dare say the men would fight very well (if properly officered), although they are an exceedingly dirty and nasty people. ...It is among the most difficult tasks I ever undertook in my life to induce these people to believe that there is, or can be, danger till the bayonet is pushed at their breasts. Not that it proceeds from any uncommon prowess, but rather from an unaccountable kind of stupidity in the lower class of these people, which, believe me, prevails but too generally among the officers of the Massachusetts part of the army, who are nearly of the same kidney with the privates." He had seen like demoralization and slackness in the old days at Winchester, on the wild frontier, but he had expected to find a better spirit and discipline in the New England levies.

His first disgust, however, soon wore off. He was not slow to see how shrewd and sturdy these uncouth, intractable ploughboys and farmers could prove themselves upon occasion. "I have a sincere pleasure in observing," he wrote to congress, " that there are materials for a good army, a great number of able-bodied men, active, zealous in the cause, and of unquestionable courage." There was time enough and to spare in which to learn his army's quality. " Our lines of defence are now completed," he could tell Lund Washington on the 20th of August, "as near so at least as can be-we now wish them to come out as soon as they please; but they discover no inclination to quit their own works of defence; and as it is almost impossible for us to get at them, we do nothing but watch each other's motions all day at the distance of about a mile." He could even turn away from military affairs to advise that "spinning should go forward with all possible despatch " on the estate at home, and to say, " I much approve of your sowing wheat in clean ground, although you should be late in doing it." Once more he settled to the old familiar work, this time upon a great scale, of carrying a difficult enterprise forward by correspondence. Letters to the Continental Congress at Philadelphia, letters to the provincial congresses of the New England colonies, letters to subordinate (sometimes insubordinate) officers at distant posts, letters to intimate friends and influential men everywhere, setting forth the needs and situation of the army, advising measures of organization, supply, and defence, pointing out means that might be used and mistakes that must be avoided, commanding, dissuading, guiding, forecasting, poured steadily forth from those busy headquarters, where the commander-in-chief was always to be found, intent, deeply employed, calmly imperative, never tiring, never hesitating, never storming, a leader and master of men and affairs. He was in his prime, and all the forty-three years of his strenuous life he had been at school to learn how such a task as this was to be performed. He had found the army not only without proper discipline and equipment, but actually without powder; and the winter had come and was passing away before even that primary and perilous need could be supplied. The men of that extemporized army had been enlisted but for a few months' service. When their brief terms of enlistment ran out they incontinently took themselves off; and Washington's most earnest appeals to the continental and provincial congresses to provide for longer enlistments and an adequate system of recruitment did not always suffice to prevent his force from perilously dwindling away under his very eyes. It was a merciful providence that disposed the British to lie quiet in Boston.

Such authority as he had, Washington used to the utmost, and with a diligence and foresight which showed all his old policy of Thorough. Under his orders a few fast vessels were fitted out and armed as privateers at the nearest safe ports. Marblehead volunteers in the army were put aboard them for crews, and the enemy's supplies were captured upon the seas and brought overland-the much-needed powder and all-into the American camp, while men-of-war which might have swept the coast lay just at hand in the harbor. No opportunity was missed either to disturb the British or to get what the army needed; and the ministers at home, as well as the commanders in Boston, grew uneasy and apprehensive in the presence of so active and watchful an opponent. He was playing the game boldly, even a bit desperately at times. More than once, as the slow months of siege dragged by, he would have hazarded a surprise and sought to take the city by storm, had not the counsel of his officers persistently restrained him.

Only in the north was there such fighting as he wished to see. Montgomery had pushed through the forests and taken Montreal (November 12th, 1775). At the same time Washington had sent a force of some twelve hundred men, under Benedict Arnold, to see what could be done against the little garrison at Quebec. The journey had cost Arnold four hundred men; but with what he had left he had climbed straight to the Heights of Abraham and summoned the British at their gates. When they would neither surrender nor fight, he had sat down to wait for Montgomery; and when he came, with barely five hundred men, had stormed the stout defences, in a driving snow-storm, in the black darkness that came just before the morning on the last day of the year. Had Montgomery not been killed in the assault, the surprise would have succeeded; and Arnold had no cause to be ashamed of the gallant affair. Failure though it was, it heartened the troops before Boston to think what might be done under such officers.

The monotony of the long, anxious season was broken at Cambridge by a touch now and again of such pleasures as spoke of home and gracious peace. In midwinter Mrs. Washington had driven into camp, come all the way from Virginia, with proper escort, in her coach and four, her horses bestridden by black postilions in their livery of scarlet and white; and she had seemed to bring with her to the homely place not only the ceremonious habit, but the genial and hospitable air of Virginia as well. Many a quiet entertainment at headquarters coaxed a little ease of mind out of the midst of even that grim and trying winter's work while she was there.

With the first month of spring Washington determined to cut inaction short and make a decisive stroke. He had been long enough with the army now to presume upon its confidence and obedience, though he followed his own counsels. Siege cannon had been dragged through the unwilling forests all the way from Ticonderoga; the supplies and the time had come; and on the morning of the 5th of March, 1776, the British stared to see ramparts and cannon on Dorchester Heights. "It was like the work of the genii of Aladdin's wonderful lamp," declared one of their astonished officers. Why they had themselves neglected to occupy the hills of Dorchester, and had waited so patiently till Washington should have time and such guns as he needed, was a question much pressed at home in England; and their stupidity was rewarded now. They had suffered, themselves to be amused all night by a furious cannonading out of Roxbury, Somerville, and East Cambridge, while two thousand men, a battery of heavy ordnance, and hundreds of wagons and ox-carts with timber, bales of hay, spades, crowbars, hatchets, hammers, and nails, had been gotten safely to the Dorchester hills. When they saw what had happened they thought of the assault upon Bunker's Hill, and hesitated what to do. A violent storm blew up while they waited, rendering an attack across the water impracticable, and when the calmer morning of the 6th dawned it was too late; the American position was too strong. Neither the town nor the harbor could safely be held under fire from Dorchester Heights. There was nothing for it but to evacuate the place, and no one gainsaid their departure. By the 17th they were all embarked, eight thousand troops and nine hundred loyalist citizens of Boston, and had set sail towards the north for Halifax. They were obliged to leave behind them more than two hundred cannon and a great quantity of military stores of every kind-powder, muskets, gun-carriages, small-arms — whatever an army might need. When Washington established himself in General Howe's headquarters, in Mrs. Edwards's comfortable lodging-house at the head of State Street, he could congratulate himself not only on a surprising victory brilliantly won, but on the possession, besides, of more powder and better stores and equipments than he could have dreamed of in his camp at Cambridge. He caught up his landlady's little granddaughter one day, set her on his knee, as he liked to do, and asked her, smiling, which she liked the better, the redcoats or the provincials.

"The redcoats," said the child.

"Ah, my dear," said the young general, a blithe light in his blue eyes, " they look better, but they don't fight. The ragged fellows are the boys for fighting."

But he did not linger at Boston. He knew that its capture did not end, but only deepened, the struggle.

Reinforcements would be poured out of England with the spring, and the next point of attack would unquestionably be New York, the key to the Hudson. Here again was a city flanked about on either hand by water, and commanded by heights-the heights of Brooklyn. A garrison must be left in Boston, and New York must be held for the most part by a new levy, as raw, as ill organized and equipped, as factious, as uncertain in capacity and purpose, as that which had awaited his discipline and guidance before Boston. It was an army always a-making and to be made. The sea was open, moreover. The British could enter the great harbor when they pleased. The insurgents had no naval force whatever with which to withstand them on the water. There were a score of points to be defended which were yet without defence on the long island where the town lay, and round about the spreading arms of the sea that enclosed it; and there were but eighteen thousand militia-men mustered for the formidable task, in the midst of an active loyalist population. The thing must be attempted, nevertheless. The command of the Hudson would very likely turn out to be the command of the continent, and the struggle was now to be to the death. It was too late to draw back. The royal authority had, in fact, been everywhere openly thrown off, even in the middle colonies, where allegiance and opinion hung still at so doubtful a balance. For Washington the whole situation must have seemed to be summed up in what had taken place in his own colony at home. Dunmore, when he fled to the men-of-war in the bay, had called upon all who were loyal to follow him; had even offered freedom to all slaves and servants who would enlist in the force he should collect for the purpose of "reducing the colony to a proper sense of its duty." Unable to do more, he had ravaged the coasts on either hand upon the Bay, and had put men ashore within the rivers to raid and burn, making Norfolk, with its loyalist merchants, his headquarters and rendezvous. Driven thence by the provincial militia, he had utterly destroyed the town by fire, and was now refuged upon Gwynn's Island, striking when he could, as before, at the unprotected hamlets and plantations that looked everywhere out upon the water. Virginia's only executive, these nine months and more, had been her Committee of Safety, of which Edmund Pendleton was president.

Washington had hardly begun his work of organization and defence at New York before North Carolina (April 12th, 1776) authorized her delegates in the congress at Philadelphia to join in a declaration of independence; and the next month (May 15th) the congress advised the colonies to give over all show and pretence of waiting for or desiring peace or accommodation: to form complete and independent governments of their own, and so put an end to " the exercise of every kind of authority under the crown." The next step was a joint Declaration of Independence, upon a motion made in congress by Richard Henry Lee, in eager obedience to the express bidding of a convention met in the hall of the Burgesses at Williamsburg to frame a constitution for Virginia. His motion was adopted by the votes of every colony except New York. It was a bitter thing to many a loyal man in the colonies to see such things done, and peace rendered impossible. Not even those who counted themselves among the warmest friends of the colonial cause were agreed that it was wise thus to throw off one government before another was put in its place-while there was as yet no better guidance in that distracted time than might be had from a body of gentlemen in Philadelphia who possessed no power but to advise. Bat the radicals were in the saddle. Washington himself came down from New York to urge that the step be taken. He deemed such radicalism wise; for he wished to see compromise abandoned, and all minds set as sternly as his own in the resolve to fight the fight out to the bitter end. "I have never entertained an idea of an accommodation," he said, "since I heard of the measures which were adopted in consequence of the Bunker's Hill fight; and his will hardened to the contest after the fashion that had always been characteristic of him when once the heat of action was upon him. He grew stern, and spoke sometimes with a touch of harshness, in the presence of his difficulties at New York; because he knew that they were made for him in no small part by Americans who were in the British interest, and whom he scorned even while scrupulous to be just in what he did to thwart and master them. "It requires more serenity of temper, a deeper understanding, and more courage than fell to the lot of Marlborough to ride in this whirlwind," said John Adams; and the young commander-in-chief had them all. But his quiet was often that of a metal at white heat, and he kindled a great fire with what he touched.

No strength of will, however, could suffice to hold New York and its open harbor against a powerful enemy with such troops as Washington could drill and make between April and July. On the 28th of June British transports began to gather in the lower bay. Within a few days they had brought thirty thousand men, armed and equipped as no other army had ever been in America. It was impossible to prevent their landing, and they were allowed to take possession of Staten Island unopposed. Men-of-war passed untouched through the Narrows, and made their way at will up the broad Hudson, unhurt by the batteries upon either shore. General Howe remembered Dorchester and Charlestown Heights, and directed his first movement against Washington's intrenched position on the hills of Brooklyn, where quite half the American army lay. For a little space he waited, till his brother, Admiral Lord Howe, should come to act with him in negotiation and command. Lord Howe was authorized to offer pardon for submission, and very honorably used a month and more of good fighting time in learning that the colonists had no desire to be pardoned. "No doubt we all need pardon from Heaven for our manifold sins and transgressions," was Governor Trumbull's Connecticut version of the general feeling, "but the American who needs the pardon of his Britannic Majesty is yet to be found." On the 22d of August, accordingly, General Howe put twenty thousand men ashore at Gravesend Bay. On the 27th, bis arrangements for an overwhelming attack succeeding at every point, he drove the five thousand Americans thrown out to oppose him back into their works upon the heights, with a loss of four hundred killed and wounded and a thousand taken. Still mindful of Bunker's Hill, he would not storm the intrenchments, to which Washington himself had brought reinforcements which swelled his strength upon the heights to ten thousand. He

193

determined, instead, to draw lines of siege about them, and at his leisure take army, position, stores, and all. Washington, seeing at once what Howe intended, and how possible it was, decided to withdraw immediately, before a fleet should be in the river and his retreat cut off. It was a masterly piece of work. The British commander was as much astounded to see Brooklyn Heights empty on the morning of August 30th as he had been to see Dorchester Heights occupied that memorable morning six months before. Washington had taken ten thousand men across that broad river, with all their stores and arms, in a single night, while a small guard kept up a sharp fire from the breastworks, and no sound of the retreat reached the dull ears of the British sentries.

But the sharp fighting and bitter defeat of the 27th had sadly, even shamefully, demoralized Washington's raw troops, and he knew he must withdraw from New York. All through September and a part of October he held what he could of the island, fighting for it almost mile by mile as he withdrew-now cut to the quick and aflame with almost uncontrollable anger to see what cowards his men could be; again heartened to see them stand and hold their ground like men, even in the open. The most that he could do was to check and thwart the powerful army pressing steadily upon his front and the free fleet threatening his flanks. He repulsed the enemy at Harlem Heights (September 16th); he kept his ground before them at White Plains, despite the loss of an outpost at Chatterton Hill (October 28th); he might possibly have foiled and harassed them the winter through had not General Greene suffered a garrison of three thousand of the best-trained men in the army to be penned up and taken, with a great store of artillery and small-arms besides, in Fort Washington, on the island (November 16th). After such a blow there was nothing for it but to abandon the Hudson and retreat through New Jersey. His generals growing insubordinate, Washington could not even collect his divisions and unite his forces in retreat. His men deserted by the score; whole companies took their way homeward as their terms of enlistment expired with the closing of the year; barely three thousand men remained with him by the time he had reached Princeton. Congress, in its fright, removed to Baltimore; hundreds of persons hurried to take the oath of allegiance upon Howe's offer of pardon; and the British commanders deemed the rebellion at an end.

They did not understand the man they were fighting. When he had put the broad Delaware between his dwindling regiments and the British at his heels, he stopped, undaunted, to collect force and give his opponents a taste of his quality. Such an exigency only stiffened his temper, and added a touch of daring to his spirit. Charles Lee, his second in command, hoping to make some stroke for himself upon the Hudson, had withheld full half the army in a safe post upon the river, in direct disobedience to orders, while the British drove Washington southward through New Jersey; but Lee was now happily in the hands of the enemy, taken at an unguarded tavern where he lodged, and most of the troops he had withheld found their way at last to Washington beyond the Delaware. Desperate efforts at recruiting were made. Washington strained his authority to the utmost to keep and equip his force, and excused himself to congress very nobly. " A character to lose," he said, "an estate to forfeit, the inestimable blessing of liberty at stake, and a life devoted must be my excuse." What he planned and did won him a character with his foes. Before the year was out he had collected six thousand men, and was ready to strike a blow at the weak, extended line-Hessian mercenaries for the most part-which Howe had left to hold the Delaware.

On Christmas Day he made his advance, and ordered a crossing to be made in three divisions, under cover of the night. Only his own division, twenty-five hundred strong, effected the passage. 'Twas ten hours' perilous work to cross the storm-swept river in the pitchy darkness, amidst the hazards of floating ice, but not a man or a gun was lost. There was a nine miles' march through driving snow and sleet after the landing before Trenton could be reached, the point of attack, and two men were frozen to death as they went. General Sullivan sent word that the guns were wet: " Tell him to use the bayonet," said Washington, " for the town must be taken." And it was taken-in the early morning, at the point of the bayonet, with a loss of but two or three men. The surprise was complete. Colonel Rahl, the commander of the place, was mortally wounded at the first onset, and nine hundred Hessians surrendered at discretion.

When he had gotten his prisoners safe on the south side of the river, Washington once more advanced to occupy the town. It was a perilous place to be, no doubt, with the great unbridged stream behind him; but the enemy's line was everywhere broken, now that its centre had been taken; had been withdrawn from the river in haste, abandoning its cannon even and its baggage at Burlington; and Washington calmly dared to play the game he had planned. It was not Howe who came to meet him, but the gallant Cornwallis, no mean adversary, bringing eight thousand men. Washington let him come all the way to the Delaware without himself stirring, except to put a small tributary stream between his men and the advancing columns; and the confident Englishman went to bed that night exclaiming, "At last we have run down the old fox, and we'll bag him in the morning." Then, while a small force kept the camp-fires burning and worked audibly at the ramparts the cold night through, the fox was up and away. He put the whole of his force upon the road to Princeton and New Brunswick, where he knew Cornwallis's stores must be. As the morning's light broadened into day (January 3d, 1777) he met the British detachment at Princeton in the way, and drove it back in decisive rout, a keen ardor coming into his blood as he saw the sharp work done. "An old-fashioned Virginia fox-hunt, gentlemen," he exclaimed, shouting the view-halloo. Had his troops been fresh and properly shod to outstrip Cornwallis at their heels, he would have pressed on to New Brunswick and taken the stores there; but he had done all that could be done with despatch, and withdrew straight to the heights of Morristown. Cornwallis could only hasten back to New York. By the end of the month the Americans were everywhere afoot; the British held no posts in New Jersey but Paulus Hook, Amboy, and New Brunswick; and Washington had issued a proclamation commanding all who had accepted General Howe's offer of pardon either to withdraw within the British lines or to take oath of allegiance to the United States. Men loved to tell afterwards how Frederick the Great had said that it was the most brilliant campaign of the century. Congress took steps before the winter was over to secure long enlistments, and substitute a veritable army for the three months' levies with which Washington had hitherto been struggling to make shift. After the affair at Trenton, Washington had been obliged to pledge his own private fortune for their pay to induce the men whose terms of enlistment were to expire on New Year's Day-more than half his force-to stay with him but a few weeks more, till his plan should be executed. Now he was authorized to raise regiments enlisted till the war should end, and to exercise almost dictatorial powers in everything that might affect the discipline, provisioning, and success of his army. There was need, for the year witnessed fighting of tremendous consequence. The British struck for nothing less than complete possession of the whole State of New York, throughout the valleys of the Hudson and the Mohawk. General Howe, who had above twenty thousand men in New York city, was to move up the Hudson; General Burgoyne, with eight thousand men, from Canada down Lake Champlain; Colonel St. Leger, with a small but sufficient force, down into the valley of the Mohawk, striking from Oswego, on Ontario; and the colonies were to be cut in twain. New England hopelessly separated from her confederates, by the converging sweep of three armies, aggregating more than thirty-three thousand men. But only the coast country, it turned out, was tenable ground for British troops. Sir Guy Carleton had attempted Champlain out of Canada the year before, and had gone back to Quebec without touching Ticonderoga, so disconcerted had he been by the price he had had to pay for his passage up the lake to a small force and an extemporized fleet under Benedict Arnold. This time Burgoyne, with his splendid army, made short work of Ticonderoga(July, 1777), and drove General Schuyler and his army back to their posts beyond the Hudson; but the farther he got from his base upon the lake into the vast forests of that wide frontier, the more certainly did he approach disaster. No succor came. St. Leger was baffled, and sent in panic back the way he had come. Howe did not ascend the river. The country swarmed with gathering militia. They would not volunteer for distant campaigns; but this invading host, marching by their very homes into the deep forest, roused and tempted them as they had been roused at Concord, and they gathered at its rear and upon its flanks as they had run together to invest Boston. A thousand men Burgoyne felt obliged to leave in garrison at Ticonderoga; a thousand more, sent to Bennington to seize the stores there, were overwhelmed and taken (August 16th). Quite twenty thousand provincials presently beset him, and he had but six thousand left wherewith to save himself. He crossed the river, for he still expected Howe; and there was stubborn fighting about Saratoga (September 19th, October 7th), in which Arnold once more made his name in battle. But the odds were too great; Burgoyne's supplies were cut off, his troops beaten; there was nothing for it but capitulation (October 17th). He had been trapped and taken by a rising of the country.

Howe had not succored him, partly because he lacked judgment and capacity, partly because Washington had thwarted him at every turn. From his position at Morristown, Washington could send reinforcements to the north or recall them at will, without serious delay; and Howe, in his hesitation, gave him abundant time to do what he would. It was Sir William's purpose to occupy the early summer, ere Burgoyne should need him, in an attack on Philadelphia. On the 12th of June, accordingly, he threw a force of eighteen thousand men into New Jersey. But Washington foiled him at each attempt to advance by hanging always upon his flank in such a position that he could neither be safely ignored nor forced to fight; and the prudent Howe, abandoning the march, withdrew once more to New York. But he did not abandon his project against Philadelphia. lie deemed it the "capital" of the insurgent confederacy, and wished to discredit congress and win men of doubtful allegiance to his standard by its capture; and he reckoned upon some advantage in drawing Washington after him to the southward, away from Burgoyne's field of operations in the north. Though July had come, therefore, and Burgoyne must need him presently, he put his eighteen thousand men aboard the fleet and carried them by sea to the Chesapeake. Washington was sorely puzzled. He had taken it for granted that Howe would go north, and he had gone south! "Howe's in a manner abandoning Burgoyne is so unaccountable," he said, "that I cannot help casting my eyes continually behind me;" and he followed very cautiously, ready upon the moment to turn back, lest the movement should prove a feint. But there was no mistake. Howe entered the Delaware, and, being frightened thence by reports of obstructions in the river, went all the long four hundred miles about the capes of Chesapeake, and put his army ashore at Elkton for its advance upon Philadelphia. It was then the 25th of August. Washington met him (September 11th) behind the fords of the Brandywine, and, unable to check Cornwallis on his flank, was defeated. But for him defeat was never rout: his army was still intact and steady; and he held his foe yet another fortnight on the road ere the "capital" could be entered (September 27th). Burgoyne was by that time deep within the net spread for him at Saratoga. On the morning of the 4th of October, in a thick mist, Washington threw himself upon Howe's main force encamped across the village street of Germantown, and would have overwhelmed it in the surprising onset had not two of his own columns gone astray in the fog, attacked each other, and so lost the moment's opportunity. General Howe knew very soon how barren a success he had had. The end of November came before he had made himself master of the forts upon the Delaware below the " capital" and removed the obstructions from the river to give access to his fleet; the British power was broken and made an end of in the north; and Washington was still at hand as menacing and dangerous as ever. Dr. Franklin was told in Paris that General Howe had taken Philadelphia. " Philadelphia has taken Howe," he laughed.

Philadelphia kept Howe safely through the winter, and his officers made themselves easy amidst a round of gayeties in the complacent town, while Washington went to Valley Forge to face the hardships and the intrigues of a bitter season. A deep demoralization fell that winter, like a blight, upon all the business of the struggling confederacy. The congress, in its exile at York, had lost its tone and its command in affairs. It would have lost it as completely in Philadelphia, no doubt, for it was no longer the body it had been. Its best members were withdrawn to serve their respective states in the critical business, now everywhere in hand, of reorganizing their governments; and it itself was no government at all, but simply a committee of advice, which the states heeded or ignored as they pleased. Oftentimes but ten or twelve members could be got together to transact its business. It suffered itself to fall into the hands of intriguers and sectional politicians. It gave commissions in the army not according to merit, but upon a plan carefully devised to advance no more officers from one section than from another- even men like John Adams approving. Adams denounced claims of seniority and service as involving " one of the most putrid corruptions of absolute monarchy," and suggested that the officers who did not relish the idea of seeing the several states given " a share of the general officers," proportioned to the number of troops they had sent to the army, had better take themselves off, and see how little they would be missed. Worst of all, an ugly plot was hatched to displace Washington; and the various distempers of different men for a brief season gave it a chance to succeed. Some were impatient of Washington's " Fabian policy," as they called it, and would have had him annihilate, instead of merely checking, these invading hosts. " My toast," cried John Adams, " is a short and violent war." Others envied Washington his power and his growing fame, resented their own subordination and his supremacy, and intrigued to put General Oates in his place. Had not Gates won at Saratoga, and Washington lost at the Brandywine and at Germantown? Schuyler had prepared the victory in the north; Arnold and Morgan had done the fighting that secured it; but Gates had obtained the command when all was ready, and was willing to receive the reward. With a political committee congress in charge of affairs, nothing was impossible.

WASHINGTON'S HEADQUARTER AT VALLEY FORGE

Washington and his army were starving the while at Valley Forge, in desperate straits to get anything to eat or anything to cover them in that bitter season — not because there were no supplies, but because congress had disorganized the commissary department, and the supplies seldom reached the camp. The country had not been too heavily stricken by the war. Abundant crops were everywhere sown and peacefully reaped, and t there were men enough to do the work of seed-time and harvest. It was only the army that was suffering for lack of food and lack of men. The naked fact was that the confederacy was falling apart for lack of a government.

Local selfishness had overmastered national feeling, and only a few men like Washington held the breaking structure together. Washington's steadfastness was never shaken; and Mrs. Washington, stanch lady that she was, joined him even at Valley Forge. The intrigue against him he watched in stem silence till it was ripe and evident, then he crushed it with sudden exposure, and turned away in contempt, hardly BO much as mentioning it in his letters to bis friends. "Their own artless zeal to advance their views has destroyed them," he said. His soldiers he succored and supplied as he could, himself sharing their privations, and earning their love as he served them. " Naked and starving as they are," he wrote, " we cannot sufficiently admire the incomparable patience and fidelity of the soldiers." And even out of that grievous winter some profit was wrung. Handsome sums of French money had begun of late to come slowly into the confederate treasury-for France, for the nonce, was quick with sympathy for America, and glad to lend secret aid against an old foe. Presently, she promised, she would recognize the independence of the United States, and herself grapple once more with England. Meanwhile French, German, and Polish officers hurried over sea to serve as volunteers with the raw armies of the confederacy — adventurers, some of them; others sober veterans, gentlemen of fortune, men of generous and noble quality-among the rest the boyish Lafayette and the distinguished Steuben. Baron von Steuben had won himself a place on the great Frederick's staff in the Seven Years' War, and was of that studious race of soldiers the world was presently to learn to fear. He joined Washington at Valley Forge, and turned the desolate camp into a training-school of arms, teaching, what these troops had never known before, promptness and precision in the manual of arms, in massed and ordered movement, in the use of the bayonet, the drill and mastery of the charge and of the open field. Neither Washington nor any of his officers had known how to give this training. The commander-in-chief had not even had a properly organized staff till this schooled and thorough German supplied it, and he was valued in the camp as he deserved. " You say to your soldier, 'Do this,' and he doeth it," he wrote to an old comrade in Prussia; "I am obliged to say to mine, 'This is the reason why you ought to do that,' and then he does it." But he learned to like and to admire his new comrades soon enough when he found what spirit and capacity there was in them for the field of action.

The army came out of its dismal winter quarters stronger than it had ever been before, alike in spirit and in discipline; more devoted to its commander than ever, and more fit to serve him. At last the change to a system of long enlistments had transformed it from a levy of militia into an army steadied by service, unafraid of the field. The year opened, besides, with a new hope and a new confidence. They were no longer a body of insurgents even to the eye of Europe. News came to the camp late in the night of the 4th of May (1778) that France had entered into open alliance with the United States, and would send fleets and an army to aid in securing their independence. Such an alliance changed the whole face of affairs. England would no longer have the undisputed freedom of the seas, and the conquest of her colonies in America might turn out the least part of her task in the presence of European enemies. She now knew the full significance of Saratoga and Germantown. Washington's splendid audacity and extraordinary command of his resources in throwing himself upon his victorious antagonist at Germantown as the closing move of a long retreat had touched the imagination and won the confidence of foreign soldiers and statesmen hardly less than the taking of Burgoyne at Saratoga. Parliament at last (February, 1778) came to its senses: resolved to renounce the right to tax the colonies, except for the regulation of trade, and sent commissioners to America to offer such terms for submission. But it was too late; neither congress nor the states would now hear of anything but independence.

With a French fleet about to take the sea, it was necessary that the British commanders in America should concentrate their forces. Philadelphia, they had at last found out, was a burden, not a prize. It had no strategic advantage of position; was hard to defend, and harder to provision; was too far from the sea, and not far enough from Washington's open lines of operation. Before the summer's campaign began, Sir William Howe resigned bis command and bade the town good-bye, amidst elaborate festivities (May 18th, 1778). General Clinton, who succeeded him, received orders from England to undo Howe's work at once, abandon Philadelphia, and concentrate his forces at New York. 'Twas easier said than done. There were not transports enough to move his fifteen thousand men by sea; only the three thousand loyalists who had put themselves under his protection could be sent in the ships, with a portion of his stores; he must cross the hostile country; and his march was scarcely begun (June 18th) before Washington was at his heels, with a force but little inferior to his own either in numbers or in discipline. He might never have reached New York at all had not Charles Lee been once more second in command in the American army. He had come out of captivity, exchanged, and now proved himself the insubordinate poltroon he was. He had never had any real heart in the cause. He owned estates in Virginia, but he was not of the great Virginian family of the Northern Neck. He was only a soldier of fortune, strayed out of the British service on half-pay to seek some profit in the colonies, and cared for no interest but his own. While a prisoner he had secretly directed Howe's movement against Philadelphia, and now he was to consummate his cowardly treachery. Washington outstripped his opponent in the movement upon New York, and determined to fall upon him at Monmouth Court House, where, on the night of the 27th of June, Clinton's divisions lay separate, offering a chance to cut them asunder. On the morning of the 28th, Lee was ordered forward with six thousand men to enfold Clinton's left wing-eight thousand men, the flower of the British force-by gaining its flank, while Washington held his main body ready to strike in his aid at the right moment. The movement was perfectly successful, and the fighting had begun, when, to the amazement and chagrin alike of officers and men, Lee began to withdraw. Lafayette sent a messenger hot-foot for Washington, who rode up to find his men, not attacking, but pursued. " What is the meaning of all this ?" he thundered, his wrath terrible to see. When Lee would have made some excuse, he hotly cursed him, in his fury, for a coward, himself rallied the willing troops, and led them forward again to a victory: won back the field Lee had abandoned, and drove the enemy to the cover of a morass. In the night that followed, Clinton hastily withdrew, leaving even his wounded behind him, and Washington's chance to crush him was gone.

"Clinton gained no advantage except to reach New York with the wreck of his army," commented the observant Frederick over sea; "America is probably lost for England." But a great opportunity had been treacherously thrown away, and the war dragged henceforth with every painful trial of hope deferred. A scant three weeks after Clinton had reached New York, the Count d'Estaing was off Sandy Hook, with a French fleet of twelve ships of the line and six frigates, bringing four thousand troops. The British fleet within the harbor was barely half as strong; but the pilots told the cautious Frenchman that his larger ships could not cross the bar, and he turned away from New York to strike at Newport, the only other point now held by the British in all the country. That place had hardly been invested, however, when Lord Howe appeared with a stronger fleet than the French. D'Estaing was obliged to draw off to meet him; a great storm sent both fleets into port to refit instead of to fight; and the disgusted militia-men and continentals, who had come to take the town with the French, withdrew in high choler to see the fleet, without which they could do nothing, taken off to Boston. When the autumn came Clinton felt free to send thirty-five hundred men to the Southern coast, and Savannah was taken (December 29th, 1778). Only in the far West, at the depths of the great wilderness beyond the mountains, was anything done that promised decisive advantage. George Rogers Clark, that daring Saxon frontiersman, who moved so like a king through the far forests, swept the whole country of the Illinois free from British soldiers and British authority that winter of 1778-9, annexing it to the states that meant to be independent; and a steady stream of immigration began to pour into the opened country, as if to prepare a still deeper task of conquest for the British at far New York.

But few noted in the East what gallant men were doing in the valley of the Mississippi. They saw only that the British, foiled in New England and the middle colonies, had changed their plans, and were now minded to try what could be done in the South. There at last their campaigns seemed about to yield them something. Savannah taken, they had little trouble in overrunning Georgia, and every effort to dislodge them failed; for Washington could not withdraw his army from before Clinton at New York. Spain joined France in offensive alliance in April, 1779; in August a combined French and Spanish fleet attempted an invasion of England; all Europe seemed about to turn upon the stout little kingdom in its unanimous fear and hatred of her arrogant supremacy upon the seas. Everywhere there was war upon the ocean highways-even America sending forth men of desperate valor, like John Paul Jones, to ravage and challenge Britain upon her very coasts. But England's spirit only rose with the danger, and Washington waited all the weary year through for his French allies. In 1780 it looked for a little as if the British were indeed turned victors. In the spring Clinton withdrew the force that had held Newport to New York, and, leaving General Knyphausen there with a powerful force to keep Washington and the city, carried eight thousand men southward to take Charleston. There were forces already in the South sufficient to swell his army to ten thousand ere he invested the fated town; and on the 12th of May (1780) it fell into his hands, with General Lincoln and three thousand prisoners. Washington had sent such succor as he could, but the British force was overwhelming, and South Carolina was lost. South Carolina teemed with loyalists. The whole country was swept and harried by partisan bands. The men who should have swelled General Lincoln's force knew not when their homes might be plundered and destroyed, if they were to leave them. The planters of the low country dared not stir for fear of an insurrection of their slaves. In June, Clinton could take half his force back to New York, deeming the work done. General Gates completed the disastrous record. On the 13th of June he was given chief command in the South, and was told that the country expected another "Burgoynade." His force was above three thousand, and he struck his blow, as he should, at Camden, where Cornwallis had but two thousand men, albeit trained and veteran troops; but the end was total, shameful rout (August 16th, 1780), and men knew at last the incapacity of their "hero of Saratoga." " We look on America as at our feet," said Horace Walpole.

Certainly things looked desperate enough that dark year. The congress was sinking into a more and more helpless inefficiency. Definitive articles of confederation had been submitted to the states nearly three years ago (November, 1777), but they had not been adopted yet, and the states had almost ceased to heed the requisitions of the congress at all. Unable to tax, it paid its bills and the wages of its troops in paper, which so rapidly fell in value that by the time the hopeless year 1780 was out, men in the ranks found a month's pay too little with which to buy even a single bushel of wheat. Washington was obliged to levy supplies from the country round him to feed his army; and in spite of their stanch loyalty to him, his men grew mutinous, in sheer disgust with the weak and faithless government they were expected to serve. Wholesale desertion began, as many as one hundred men a month going over to the enemy, to get at least pay and food and clothing. The country seemed not so much dismayed as worn out and indifferent; weary of waiting and hoping; looking stolidly to see the end come. Washington was helpless. Without the co-operation of a naval force, it was impossible to do more than hold the British in New York. France, it was true, was bestirring herself again. On the 10th of July a French fleet put in at Newport and landed a force of six thousand men, under Count Bochambeau, a most sensible and capable officer, who was directed to join Washington and put himself entirely under his command. But a powerful British fleet presently made its appearance in the Sound; the French admiral dared not stir; Bochambeau dared not leave him without succor; and the reinforcements that were to have followed out of France were blockaded in the harbor of Brest.

Then, while things stood so, treason was added. Benedict Arnold, the man whom Washington trusted with a deep affection, and whom the army loved for his gallantry, entered into correspondence with the enemy; arranged to give West Point and the posts dependent upon it into their hands; and, his treason suddenly detected, escaped without punishment to the British sloop of war that waited in the river for the British agent in the plot. Washington was at hand when the discovery was made. His aides were breakfasting with Arnold when the traitor was handed the note which told him he was found out; and Arnold had scarcely excused himself and made good his flight when the commander-in-chief reached the house. When Washington learned what had happened, it smote him so that mighty sobs burst from him, as if his great heart would break; and all the night through the guard could hear him pacing his room endlessly, in a lonely vigil with his bitter thoughts. He did not in his own grief forget the stricken wife upstairs. "Go to Mrs. Arnold," he said to one of his officers, " and tell her that, though my duty required that no means should be neglected to arrest General Arnold, I have great pleasure in acquainting her that he is now safe on board a British vessel." Arnold had deemed himself wronged and insulted by congress-but what officer that Washington trusted might not? Who could be confided in if such men turned traitors?

Bat a sudden turning of affairs marked the close of the year. Cornwallis had penetrated too far into the Carolinas; had advanced into North Carolina, and was beset, as Burgoyne had been, by a rising of the country. He lost twelve hundred men at King's Mountain (October 7th, 1780), as Burgoyne had lost a thousand at Bennington; and everywhere, as he moved, he found himself checked by the best officers the long war had bred —Nathanael Greene, who had been Washington's right hand the war through; Henry Lee, the daring master of cavalry, whom Washington loved; the veteran Steuben; Morgan, who had won Saratoga with Arnold; and partisan leaders a score, whom he had learned to dread in that wide forested country. He was outgener-ailed; his forces were taken in detail and beaten, and he himself was forced at last into Virginia. By midsummer, 1781, all his interior posts were lost, and he was cut off from Charleston and Savannah by a country he dared not cross again. In Virginia, though at first he raided as he pleased, he was checked more and more as the season advanced by a growing force under Lafayette; and by the first week in August he had taken counsel of prudence, and established himself, seven thousand strong, at Yorktown, near the sea, his base of supplies. Then it was that Washington struck the blow which ended the war. At last Rochambeau was free to move; at last a French fleet was at hand to block the free passage of the sea. The Count de Grasse, with twenty-eight ships of the line, six frigates, and twenty thousand men, was in the West Indies, and in August sent word to Washington that he was about to bring his whole fleet to the Chesapeake, as Washington had urged. Either the Chesapeake or New York, had been Washington's prayer to him. Making as if he were bat moving about New York from north to south for some advantage of position, Washington suddenly took two thousand Continentats and four thousand Frenchmen, under Rochambeuu, all the long four hundred miles to York River in Virginia, to find Cornwallis already entrapped there, as he had planned, between Grasse's fleet in the bay and Lafayette intrenched across the peninsula with eight thousand men, now the French had loaned him three thousand. A few weeks' siege and the decisive work was done, to the admiration of Cornwallis himself. The British army was taken. The generous Englishman could not withhold an expression of his admiration for the extraordinary skill with which Washington had struck all the way from New York with six thousand men as easily as if with six hundred. "But, after all," he added, "your Excellency's achievements in New Jersey were such that nothing could surpass them."

THE ESCAPE OF ARNOLD

Chapter VIII
The Stress of Victory

The victory at Yorktown brought neither peace nor ease in affairs. The revolution was indeed accomplished —that every man could see who had the candor to look facts in the face; but its accomplishment brought tasks harder even than the tasks of war. Hostilities slackened-were almost wholly done with before another spring had come. No more troops came over sea. The ministry in England were discredited and ousted. Every one knew that the proud mother country must yield, for all her stout defiance of the world. But a long year dragged by, nevertheless, before even preliminary articles of accommodation were signed; and still another before definitive peace came, with independence and the full fruits of victory. Meanwhile there was an army to be maintained, despite desperate incompetence on the part of the congress and a hopeless indifference among the people; and a government to be kept presentably afoot, despite lack of money and lack of men. The Articles of Confederation proposed at the heart of the war-time (November 15th, 1777) had at last been adopted (March 1st, 1781), in season to create at least a government which could sign treaties and conclude wars, but neither soon enough nor wisely enough to bring order out of chaos. The states, glad to think the war over, would do nothing for the army, nothing for the public credit, nothing even for the maintenance of order; and the Articles of Confederation only gave the congress written warranty for offering advice: they did not make its shadowy powers real.

It was beyond measure fortunate that at such a critical time as this Washington still kept his command, still held affairs under the steady pressure of his will His successes had at last given him a place of authority in the thoughts and affections of his countrymen in some sort commensurate with his capacity and his vision in affairs. He had risen to a very safe footing of power among all the people as the war drew towards its close, filling their imaginations, and reigning among them as securely as among his troops, who for so long had felt his will wrought upon them day-by day. His very reserve, and the large dignity and pride of his stately bearing, made him seem the more like a hero in the people's eyes. They could understand a man made in this ample and simple kind, give them but time enough to see him in his full proportions. It answered to their thought of him to find him too proud to dissemble, too masterful to brook unreasonable faults, and yet slow to grow impatient, though he must wait a whole twelvemonth to see a plan mature, or coax a half-score states to get a purpose made good. And they could not deem him cold, though they found him self-possessed, keeping his own counsel; for was not the country full of talk how passionately he was like to act at a moment of crisis and in the field? They only feared to lose a leader so reckless of himself when danger was sharpest. "Our army love their general very much," one of his officers had said, "but they have one thing against him, which is the little care he takes of himself in any action"; for he had seen how Washington pressed at Trenton and at Princeton to the points that were most exposed, thinking of his troops, not of himself. The spirit of fight had ran high in him the whole war through. Even during those dismal weeks of 1776, when affairs looked darkest, and he had but a handful of men about him as he all but fled before Howe through New Jersey, he had spoken, as if in the very pleasantry of daring, of what he would do should things come to the worst with him. His thought turned to those western fastnesses he knew so well, where the highlands of his own state lay, and he spoke calmly of a desperate venture thither. " Reed," he exclaimed, to one of his aides, "my neck does not feel as though it was made for a halter. We must retire to Augusta County, in Virginia, and if overpowered, must pass the Alleghany Mountains." And when the last movement of the war came, it was still with the same feeling that he drew his lines about Cornwallis. "We may be beaten by the English," he said; " it is the chance of war; but there is the army they will never conquer."

"The privates are all generals, but not soldiers," the gallant Montgomery had cried, in his hot impatience with the heady militia-men he was bidden command; but it was not so in the presence of Washington, when once these men had taken his measure. They were then "rivals in praising him," the Abbe Robin declared, "fearing him even when he was silent, and retaining their full confidence in him after defeats and disgrace." The singular majesty and poise of this revolutionary hero struck the French officers as infinitely more remarkable than his mastery in the field and his ascendency in council. They had looked to find him great in action, but they had not thought to see in him a great gentleman, a man after their own kind in grace and courtesy and tact, and yet so lifted above the manner of courts and drawing-rooms by an incommunicable quality of grave sincerity which they were at a loss how to describe. No one could tell whether it were a gift of the mind or of the heart. It was certain only that it constituted the atmosphere and apotheosis of the man. The Marquis de Chastellux noted, with a sort of reverent awe for this hero not yet turned of fifty, how perfect a union reigned between his physical and moral qualities. "One alone," he declared, "will enable you to judge of all the rest." "It is not my intention to exaggerate," he said; "I wish only to express my impression of a perfect whole, which cannot be the product of enthusiasm, since the effect of proportion is rather to diminish the idea of greatness."

Strangers who had noted his appearance in the earlier years of the war had remarked the spirit and life that sat in Washington's eyes: but when the war was over, and its strain relaxed, they found those eyes grown pensive, " more attentive than sparkling"; steady still, and noble in their frankness and good feeling, but touched a little with care, dimmed with watching. The Prince de Broglie found him " still as fresh and active as a young man " in 1782, but thought "he must have been much handsomer three years ago," for " the gentlemen who had remained with him during all that time said that he seemed to have grown much older." 'Twould have been no marvel had he broken under the burden he had carried, athletic soldier and hardened campaigner though he was. " This is the seventh year that he has commanded the army and that he has obeyed the congress: more need not be said," the Marquis de Chastellux declared, unconsciously uttering a very bitter gibe against the government, when he meant only to praise its general.

Such service told the more heavily upon Washington because he had rendered it in silence. No man among all the Revolutionary leaders, it is true, had been more at the desk than he. Letters of command and persuasion, reports that carried every detail of the army's life and hopes in their careful phrases, orders of urgency and of provident arrangement, writings of any and every sort that might keep the hard war afoot, he had poured forth incessantly, and as if incapable of fatigue or discouragement. No one who was under orders, no man who could lend the service a hand or take a turn at counsel, was likely to escape seeing the commander-in-chiefs handwriting often enough to keep him in mind of his tireless power to foresee and to direct. Washington seemed present in every transaction of the war. And yet always and to every one he seemed a silent man. What he said and what he wrote never touched himself. He spoke seldom of motives, always of what was to be done and considered; and even his secretaries, though they handled the multitude of his papers, were left oftentimes to wonder and speculate about the man himself-so frank and yet so reserved, so straightforward and simple and yet so proud and self-contained, revealing powers, but somehow not revealing himself. It must have seemed at times to those who followed him and pondered what they saw that he had caught from Nature her own manner while he took his breeding as a boy and his preparation as a man amidst the forests of a wild frontier; that his character spoke in what he did and without self-consciousness that he had no moods but those of action.

Nor did men know him for what he really was until the war was over. His own officers then found they had something more to learn of the man they had fought under for six years-and those six, all of them, years such as lay bare the characters of men. What remained to be done during the two trying, anxious years 1782 and 1783 seemed as if in tended for a supreme and final test of the qualities of the man whose genius and character had made the Revolution possible. "At the end of a long civil war," said the Marquis de Chas-tellux, with a noble pride for his friend, "he had nothing with which he could reproach himself"; but it was these last years which were to crown this perfect praise with its full meaning. In the absence of any real government, Washington proved almost the only prop of authority and law. What the crisis was no one knew quite so thoroughly or so particularly as he. It consisted in the ominous fact that the army was the only organized and central power in the country, and that it had deep reason for discontent and insubordination. When once it had served its purpose greatly at York-town, and the war seemed ended at a stroke, the country turned from it in indifference-left it without money; talked of disbanding it without further ceremony, and with no provision made for arrears of pay; seemed almost to challenge it to indignation and mutiny. It was necessary, for every reason of prudence and good statesmanship, to keep the army still upon a war footing. There were sure signs of peace, no doubt, but no man could foretell what might be the course of politics ere England should have compounded her quarrel with France and Spain, and ended the wars with which the Revolution had become inextricably involved. 'Twere folly to leave the English army at New York unchecked. Premature confidence that peace had come might bring some sudden disaster of arms, should the enemy take the field again. The army must be ready to fight, if only to make fighting unnecessary. Washington would have assumed the offensive again, would have crushed Clinton where he lay in New York; and the congress was not slack-as slackness was counted there-in sustaining his counsels. But the congress had no power to raise money; had no power to command. The states alone could make it possible to tax the country to pay the army: their thirteen governments were the only civil authority, and they took the needs and the discontents of the army very lightly, deemed peace secure and war expenses unnecessary, and let matters drift as they would.

THE BUST BY ECKSTEIN

They came very near drifting to another revolution —a revolution such as politicians had left out of their reckoning, and only Washington could avert. After Yorktown, Washington spent four months in Philadelphia, helping the congress forward with the business of the winter; but as March of the new year (1782) drew towards its close, he rejoined the army at Newburgh, to resume his watch upon New York. He had been scarcely two months at his post when a letter was placed in his hands which revealed, more fully than any observations of his own could have revealed it, the pass to which affairs had come. The letter was from Colonel Lewis Nicola, an old and respected officer, who stood nearer than did most of his fellow-officers to the commander-in-chief in intimacy and affection, and who felt it his privilege to speak plainly. The letter was calm in temper, grave and moderate in tone, with something of the gravity and method of a disquisition written upon abstract questions of government; did not broach its meaning like a revolutionary document. But what it proposed was nothing less, when read between the lines, than that Washington should suffer himself to be made king, and that so an end should be put to the incompetency and ingratitude of a band of weak and futile republics. Washington met the suggestion with a rebuke so direct and overwhelming that Colonel Nicola must himself have wondered how he had ever dared make such a venture. "Be assured, sir," said the indignant commander, "no occurrence in the course of the war has given me more painful sensations than your information of there being such ideas existing in the army.... I am much at a loss to conceive what part of my conduct could have given encouragement to an address which to me seems big with the greatest mischiefs that can befall my country. If I am not deceived in the knowledge of myself, you could not have found a person to whom your schemes are more disagreeable....Let me conjure you, if you have any regard for your country, concern for yourself or posterity, or respect for me, to banish these thoughts from your mind, and never communicate, as from yourself or any one else, a sentiment of the like nature." He was cut to the quick that his own officers should deem him an adventurer, willing to advance his own power at the expense of the very principles he had fought for. His thought must have gone back at a bound to his old comradeship with his brother Lawrence, with the Fairfaxes, George Mason, and the Lees, and all that free company of gentlemen in the Northern Neck who revered law, loved liberty, and hated a usurper.

But he could not blink the just complaints and real grievances of the array; nor did he wish to. Though others were angry after a manner he scorned, no man's grief or indignation was deeper than his that the army should be left penniless after all it had suffered and done, and be threatened, besides, with being turned adrift without reward or hope of provision for the future. "No man possesses a more sincere wish to see ample justice done to the army than I do," he had declared to Colonel Nicola; "and as far as my power and influence, in a constitutional way, extend, they shall be employed to the utmost of my abilities to effect it." The pledge was fulfilled in almost every letter he wrote, private or public. He urged the states, as he urged the congress, in season and out of season, to see justice done the men who had won the Revolution, and whom he loved as if they had been of his own blood. But even his great voice went too long unheeded. "The spirit of party, private interest, slowness, and national indolence slacken, suspend, and overthrow the best concerted measures," the Abbe Robin had observed, upon his first coming with Rochambeau; and now measures were not so much as concerted until a final menace from the army brought the country to its senses. A troubled summer came and went, and another winter of anxious doubt and ineffectual counsel. The very approach of peace, as it grew more certain, quickened the angry fears of the army, lest peace should be made a pretext, when it came, to disperse them before their demands could be driven home upon the demoralized and reluctant government they were learning to despise.

Another spring and the mischief so long maturing was ripe; it looked as if even Washington could not prevent it. It had been rumored in Philadelphia, while the winter held, "that the army had secretly determined not to lay down their arms until due provision and a satisfactory prospect should be afforded on the subject of their pay," and that Washington had grown unpopular among almost all ranks because of his harshness against every unlawful means of securing justice. "His extreme reserve, mixed sometimes with a degree of asperity of temper, both of which were said to have increased of late, had contributed to the decline of his popularity " —so ran the report-and it grew every week the more unlikely he could check the treasonable purposes of his men.

In March, 1783, the mine was sprung; and then men learned, by a new sign, what power there was in the silent man: how he could handle disaffection and disarm reproach. An open address was spread broadcast through the camp, calling upon the army to use its power to obtain its rights, and inviting a meeting of the officers to devise a way. " Can you consent to be the only sufferers by this Revolution? ...If you can...go,.. carry with you the ridicule, and, what is worse, the pity of the world. Go, starve, and be forgotten. ... . But if you have sense enough to discover, and spirit enough to oppose, tyranny...awake; attend to your situation, and redress yourselves." Such were its kindling phrases; and no man need deceive himself with thinking they would go unheeded. Washington showed his tact and mastery by assuming immediate control of the movement, with a sharp rebuke for such a breach of manly propriety and soldierly discipline, but with no thought to stay a righteous protest. He himself summoned the officers; and when they had come together stepped to the desk before them, with no show of anger or offended dignity, but very gravely, with a sort of majesty it moved one strangely to see, and taking a written paper from his pocket, adjusted his spectacles to read it. "Gentlemen," he said, very simply, "you will permit me to put on my spectacles, for I have not only grown gray, but almost blind, in the service of my country." There were wet eyes upon the instant in the room; no man stirred while he read — read words of admonition, of counsel, and of hope which burned at the ear; and when he was done, and had withdrawn, leaving them to do what they would, they did nothing of which he could be ashamed. They spoke manfully, as was right, of what they deemed it just and imperative the congress should do for them; but they "Resolved unanimously, that at the commencement of the present war the officers of the American army engaged in the service of their country from the purest love and attachment to the rights and liberties of human nature, which motives still exist in the highest degree; and that no circumstances of distress or danger shall induce a conduct that may tend to sully the reputation and glory which they have acquired at the price of their blood and eight years' faithful services."

Washington knew, nevertheless, how black a danger lurked among these distressed men; did not fail to speak plainly of it to the congress; and breathed freely again only when the soldiers' just demands had at last in some measure been met, by at any rate the proper legislation. He grew weary with longing for peace, when the work seemed done and his thoughts had leisure to turn towards his home again. But once in all the lengthened days of fighting had he seen Mount Vernon. He had turned aside to spend a night or two there on his way to Yorktown, and he had seen the loved place again for a little after the victory was won. Now, amidst profitless days at Newburgh, or in counsel with the committees of the congress upon business that was never finished, while affairs stood as it were in a sort of paralysis, waiting upon the interminable conferences of the three powers who haggled over definitive terms of peace at Paris, home seemed to him, in his weariness, more to be desired than ever before. Private griefs had stricken him at the very moment of his triumph. Scarcely had the victory at Yorktown been celebrated when he was called (November, 1781) to the death-bed of Jack Custis, his wayward but dearly loved step-son, and had there to endure the sight of his wife's grief and the young widow's hopeless sorrow added to his own. The two youngest children he claimed for himself, with that wistful fatherly longing that had always marked him; and Mount Vernon seemed to him more like a haven than ever, where to seek rest and solace. The two years he had yet to wait may well have seemed to him the longest of his life, and may have added a touch of their own to what strangers deemed his sternness.

He had seldom seemed so stern, indeed, as in one incident of those trying months. An officer of the American army had been taken in a skirmish, and the English had permitted a brutal company of loyalists, under one Captain Lippincott, to take him from his prison in New York and wantonly hang him in broad daylight on the heights near Middletown. Washington at once notified the British commander that unless the murderers were delivered up to be punished, a British officer would be chosen by lot from among his prisoners to suffer in their stead; and, when reparation was withheld, proceeded without hesitation to carry his threat into execution. The lot fell upon Captain Charles Asgill, an engaging youth of only nineteen, the heir of a great English family. Lady Asgill, the lad's mother, did not stop short of moving the very French court itself to intervene to save her son, and at last the congress counselled his release, the English commander having disavowed the act of the murderers in whose place he was to suffer, and Washington himself having asked to be directed what he should do. "Captain Asgill has been released," Washington wrote to Vergennes, in answer to the great minister's intercession. "I have no right to assume any particular merit from the lenient manner in which this disagreeable affair has terminated. But I beg you to believe, sir, that I most sincerely rejoice, not only because your humane intentions are gratified, but because the event accords with the wishes of his Most Christian Majesty." It lifted a great weight from his heart to have the innocent boy go unhurt from his hands, and he wrote almost tenderly to him in acquainting him with his release; but it was of his simple nature to have sent the lad to the gallows, nevertheless, had things continued to stand as they were at the first. He was inexorable to check perfidy and vindicate the just rules of war. Men were reminded, while the affair pended, of the hanging of Andre, Arnold's British confederate in treason, and how pitiless the commander-in-chief had seemed in sending the frank, accomplished, lovable gentleman to his disgraceful death, like any common spy, granting him not even the favor to be shot, like a soldier. It seemed hard to learn the inflexible lines upon which that consistent mind worked, as if it had gone to school to Fate.

But no one deemed him hard or stern, or so much as a thought more or less than human, when at last the British had withdrawn from New York, and he stood amidst his officers in Fraunce's Tavern to say good-bye. He could hardly speak for emotion: he could only lift his glass and say: "With a heart full of love and gratitude, I now take my leave of you, most devoutly wishing that your latter days may be as prosperous and happy as your former ones have been glorious and honorable....I cannot come to each of you and take my leave," he said, "but shall be obliged if you will come and take me by the hand." When General Knox, who stood nearest, approached him, he drew him to him with a sudden impulse and kissed him, and not a soldier among them all went away without an embrace from this man who was deemed cold and distant. After the parting they followed him in silence to Whitehall Ferry, and saw him take boat for his journey.

And then, standing before the congress at Annapolis to resign his commission, he added the crowning touch of simplicity to his just repute as a man beyond others noble and sincere. " I have now the honor of offering my sincere congratulations to congress," he said, as he stood amidst the august scene they had prepared for him, " and of presenting myself before them to surrender into their hands the trust committed to me, and to claim the indulgence of retiring from the service of my country. Happy in the confirmation of our independence and sovereignty, and pleased with the opportunity afforded the United States of becoming a respectable nation, I resign with satisfaction the appointment I accepted with diffidence — a diffidence in my abilities to accomplish so arduous a task, which, however, was superseded by a confidence in the rectitude of our cause, the support of the supreme power of the Union, and the patronage of Heaven. The successful termination of the war has verified the most sanguine expectations; and my gratitude for the interposition of Providence and the assistance I have received from my countrymen increases with every review of the momentous contest....I consider it my indispensable duty to close this last solemn act of my official life by commending the interests of our dearest country to the protection of Almighty God, and those who have the superintendence of them to His holy keeping." It was as if spoken on the morrow of the day upon which he accepted his commission: the same diffidence, the same trust in a power greater and higher than his own. The plaudits that had but just now filled his ears at every stage of his long journey from New York seemed utterly forgotten; he seemed not to know how his fellow countrymen had made of him an idol and a hero; his simplicity was once again his authentic badge of genuineness. He knew, it would seem, no other way in which to act. A little child remembered afterwards how he had prayed at her father's house upon the eve of battle; how he had taken scripture out of Joshua, and had cried," The Lord God of gods, the Lord God of gods, He knoweth, and Israel he shall know; if it be in rebellion, or if in transgression against the Lord (save us not this day)." There was here the same note of solemnity and of self-forgetful devotion, as if duty and honor were alike inevitable.

FRAUNCE'S TAVERN, NEW YORK

On Christmas Eve, 1783, he was once more at Mount Vernon, to resume the life he loved more than victory and power. He had a zest for the means and the labor of succeeding, but not for the mere content of success. He put the Revolution behind him as he would have laid aside a book that was read; turned from it as quietly as he had turned from receiving the surrender of Cornwallis at Yorktown-interested in victory not as a pageant and field of glory, but only as a means to an end. He looked to find very sweet satisfaction in the peace which war had earned, as sufficient a scope for his powers at home as in the field. Once more he would be a

Virginian, and join his strength to his neighbors' in all the tasks of good citizenship. He had seen nothing of the old familiar places since that far-away spring of the year 1775, when he had left his farming and his foxhunting, amidst rumors of war, to attend the congress which was to send him to Cambridge. He had halted at Fredericksburg, indeed, with the Count de Rochambeau, two years ago, ere he followed his army from York to its posts upon the Hudson. Mrs. Lewis, his sister, had returned one day from visiting a neighbor in the quiet town to look in astonishment upon an officer's horses and attendants at her door, and had entered to find her beloved brother stretched upon her own bed within, sound asleep in his clothes, like a boy returned from hunting. There had been a formal ball given, too, in celebration of the victory, before the French officers and the commander-in-chief left Fredericksburg to go northward again, and Washington had had the joy of entering the room in the face of the gay company with his aged mother on his arm, not a whit bent for all her seventy-four years, and as quiet as a queen at receiving the homage of her son's comrades in arms. He had got his imperious spirit of command from her. A servant bad told her that "Mars George" had pot up at the tavern. "Go and tell George to come here instantly," she bad commanded; and he had come, masterful man though he was. He had felt every old affection and every old allegiance renew itself as he saw former neighbors crowd around him; and that little glimpse of Virginia had refreshed him like a tonic-deeply, and as if it renewed his very nature, as only a silent man can be refreshed. But a few days in Fredericksburg and at Mount Vernon then had been only an incident of campaigning, only a grateful pause on a march. Now at last he had come back to keep his home and be a neighbor again, as he had not been these nine years.

Chapter IX
First in Peace

It was not the same Virginia, nor even the same home and neighborhood he had gone from, that Washington came back to when the war was done. He had left Mount Vernon in the care of Lund Washington, his nephew, while the war lasted, and had not forgotten amidst all his letter writing to send seasonable directions and maintain a constant oversight upon the management of his estate. It was part of his genius to find time for everything; and Mount Vernon had suffered something less than the ordinary hazards and neglects of war. It had suffered less upon one occasion, indeed, than its proud owner could have found it in his heart to wish. In the spring of 1781 several British vessels had come pillaging within the Potomac, and the anxious Lund had regaled their officers with refreshments from Mount Vernon to buy them off from mischief. "It would have been a less painful circumstance to me," his uncompromising uncle had written him, "to have heard that, in consequence of your non-compliance with their request, they had burnt my house and laid the plantation in ruin. You ought to have considered yourself as my representative." Kept though it was from harm, however, the place had suffered many things for lack of his personal care. There was some part of the task to be done over again that had confronted him when he came to take possession of the old plantation with his bride after the neglects of the French war.

But Virginia was more changed than Mount Vernon. He had left it a colony, at odds with a royal Governor; he returned to find it a State, with Benjamin Harrison, that stout gentleman and good planter, for Governor, by the free suffrages of his fellow Virginians. There had been no radical break with the aristocratic traditions of the past. Mr. Harrison's handsome seat at Lower Brandon lay where the long reaches of the James marked the oldest regions of Virginia's life upon broad, half-feudal estates; where there were good wine and plate upon the table, and gentlemen kept old customs bright and honored in the observance. But the face of affairs had greatly changed, nevertheless. The old generation of statesmen had passed away, almost with the colony, and a younger generation was in the saddle, notwithstanding a gray-haired figure here and there. Richard Bland had died in the year of the Declaration; Peyton Randolph had not lived to see it. Edmund Pendleton, after presiding over Virginia's making as a State, as chairman of her revolutionary Committee of Safety, was now withdrawn from active affairs to the bench, his fine figure marred by a fall from his horse, his old power as an advocate transmuted into the cooler talents of the judge. Patrick Henry, the ardent leader of the Revolution, had been chosen the State's first Governor, in the year of the Declaration of Independence; three years later Thomas Jefferson had succeeded him in the office, the philosophical radical of times of change; the choice of Mr. Harrison had but completed the round of the new variety in affairs. Men who, like Richard Henry Lee, had counselled revolution and the breaking of old bonds, were now in all things at the front of the State's business; and younger men, of a force and power of origination equal to their own, were pressing forward, as if to hurry a new generation to the stage which had known nothing but independence and a free field for statesmanship. Among the rest, James Madison, only a little more than ten years out of college, but already done with serving his novitiate in the Congress of the Confederation, a publicist and leader in the Old Dominion at thirty-two. Edmund Randolph, of the new generation of the commonwealth's great family of lawyers, like his forebears in gifts and spirit, was already received, at thirty, into a place of influence among public men. John Marshall, just turned of twenty-eight, but a veteran of the long war none the less, having been at the thick of the fighting, a lieutenant and a captain among the Virginian forces, from the time Dunmore was driven from Norfolk till the eve of Yorktown, was, now that that duty was done, a lawyer in quiet Fauquier, drawing to himself the eyes of every man who had the perception to note qualities of force and leadership. James Monroe had come out of the war at twenty-five to go at once into the public councils of his

State, an equal among his elders. Young men came forward upon every side to take their part in the novel rush of affairs that followed upon the heels of revolution.

Washington found himself no stranger in the new State, for all it had grown of a sudden so unlike that old community in which his own life had been formed. He found a very royal welcome awaiting him at his home-coming. The old commonwealth loved a hero still as much as ever; was as loyal to him now as it had been in the far-away days of the French war, when Dinwiddle alone fretted against him; received him with every tribute of affection; offered him gifts, and loved him all the better for refusing them. Bat he must have felt that a deep change had come upon his life, none the less, and even upon his relations with his old familiars and neighbors. He had gone away honored indeed, and marked for responsible services among his people —a Burgess as a matter of course, a notable citizen, whose force no man who knew him could fail to remark; but by no means accounted greatest, even among the men who gathered for the colony's business at Williamsburg; chosen only upon occasion for special services of action; no debater or statesman, so far as ordinary men could see; too reserved to be popular with the crowd, though it should like his frankness and taking address, and go out of its way to see him on horseback; a man for his neighbors, who could know him, not for the world, which he refused to court. But the war had suddenly lifted him to the view of all mankind ; had set him among the great captains of the world; had marked him a statesman in the midst of affairs-more a statesman than a soldier even, men must have thought who had read his letters or heard them read in Congress, on the floor or in the committee rooms; had drawn to himself the admiration of the very men he had been fighting, the very nation whose dominion he had helped to cast off. He had come home perhaps the most famous man of his day, and could not take up the old life where he had left it off, much as he wished to; was obliged, in spite of himself, to play a new part in affairs.

For a few weeks, indeed, after he had reached Mount Vernon, Nature herself assisted him to a little privacy and real retirement. The winter (1783-4) was an uncommonly severe one. Snow lay piled, all but impassable, upon the roads; frosts hardened all the country against travel; he could not get even to Fredericksburg to see his aged mother; and not many visitors, though they were his near neighbors, could reach him at Mount Vernon. " At length, my dear Marquis," he could write to Lafayette in his security, "I am become a private citizen on the banks of the Potomac; and under the shadow of my own vine and my own fig-tree, free from the bustle of a camp and the busy scenes of public life, I am solacing myself with those tranquil enjoyments of which the soldier, who is ever in pursuit of fame, the statesman, whose watchful days and sleepless nights are spent in devising schemes to promote the welfare of his own, perhaps the ruin of other countries, as if this globe was insufficient for us all, and the courtier, who is always watching the countenance of his prince, can have very little conception. I have not only retired from all public employments, but I am retiring within myself. . . . Envious of none, I am determined to be pleased with all; and this, my dear friend, being the order of my march, I will move gently down the stream of time until I sleep with my fathers." The simple gentleman did not yet realize what the breaking up of the frosts would bring.

With the spring the whole life of the world seemed to come pouring in upon him. Men of note everywhere pressed their correspondence upon him; no stranger visited America but thought first of Mount Vernon in planning where he should go and what he should see; new friends and old sat every day at his table; a year and a half had gone by since his home-coming before he could note in his diary (June 30th, 1785): "Dined with only Mrs. Washington, which, I believe, is the first instance of it since my retirement from public life" —for some visitors had broken their way even through the winter roads. Authors sent him what they wrote; inventors submitted their ideas and models to him; everything that was being said, everything that was being done, seemed to find its way, if nowhere else, to Mount Yemen-till those who knew his occupations could speak of Washington, very justly, as "the focus of political intelligence for the New World." He would not alter his way of living even in the face of such overwhelming interruptions. His guests saw him for a little after dinner, and once and again, it might be, in the evening also; but he kept to his business throughout all the working hours of the day; was at his desk even before breakfast, and after breakfast was always early in the saddle and off to his farms.

Only at table did he play the host, lingering over the wine to give and call for toasts and relax in genial conversation, losing, as the months passed by, some of the deep gravity that had settled upon him in the camp, and showing once more an enjoying relish for "a pleasant story, an unaffected sally of wit, or a burlesque description," as in the old days after hunting. Strangers were often in awe of him. It did not encourage talk in those who had little to say to sit in the presence of a man who so looked his greatness in the very proportions of his strong figure even, and whose grave and steady eyes so challenged the significance of what was said. Young people would leave off dancing and romping when he came into the room, and force him to withdraw, and peep at the fan from without the door, unobserved. It was only among his intimates that he was suffered and taken to be the simple, straightforward, sympathizing man he was, exciting, not awe, but only a warm and affectionate allegiance. "The General, with a few glasses of champagne, got quite merry," a young Englishman could report who had had the good luck to be introduced by Richard Henry Lee, " and, being with his intimate friends, laughed and talked a good deal."

As much as he could, he resumed the old life, and the thoughts and pastimes that had gone with it. Once more he became the familiar of his hounds at the kennels, and followed them as often as might be in the hunt at sunrise. He asked but one thing of a horse, as of old, " and that was to go along. He ridiculed the idea that he could be unhorsed, provided the animal kept on his legs." The two little children, a tiny boy and a romping, mischievous lassie, not much bigger, whom he had adopted at Jack Custis's death-bed, took strong hold upon his heart, and grew slowly to an intimacy with him such as few ventured to claim any longer amidst those busy days in the guest-crowded house. It seemed to Lafayette a very engaging picture when he saw Washington and the little toddling boy together — "a very little gentleman with a feather in his hat, holding fast to one finger of the good General's remarkable hand, which (so large that hand!)" was all the tiny fellow could manage. These children took Washington back more completely than anything else to the old days when he had brought his bride home with her own little ones. He felt those days come back, too, when he was on his horse in the open, going the round of good twelve miles and more that carried him to all the quarters of his plantation.

Once more he was the thorough farmer, ransacking books, when men and his own observation failed him, to come at the best methods of cultivation. Once more he took daily account of the character of his slaves and servants, and of the progress of their work, talking with them when he could, and gaining a personal mastery over them. Contracts for work he drew up with his own hand, with a minuteness and particularity which were sometimes whimsical and shot through with a gleam of grim humor. He agreed with Philip Barter that if he would serve him faithfully as gardener and keep sober at all other times, he would allow him "four dollars at Christmas, with which to be drunk four days and four nights; two dollars at Easter, to effect the same purpose; two dollars at Whitsuntide, to be drunk for two days; a dram in the morning, and a drink of grog at dinner, at noon"; and the contract was drawn, signed, and witnessed with all formality. Philip no doubt found short shrift of consideration from his thorough-going master if there was any drunkenness in the garden beyond the limit of the eight days nominated in the bond, and found the contract no jest in the end, for Washington had small patience and no soft words for a breach of agreement, whatever its kind. He would help men in distress with a generosity and wise choice of means which few took the pains to exercise, but he had only sharp rebuke for carelessness or neglect or any slackness in the performance of a duty. Men who had cheated or sought to impose upon him deemed him harsh and called him a hard master, so sharply did they smart after he had reckoned with them. He exacted the uttermost farthing. But he spent it, with the other hand, to relieve genuine suffering and real want, though it were deserved and the fruit of a crying fault. In his home dealings, as in everything else, his mind kept that trait by which men had been awed in the camp — that trick, as if of Fate, of letting every act come at its consequences and its full punishment or reward, as if he but presided at a process which was just Nature's own. When he succored distress, he did it in pity, not in justice-not excusing fault, but giving leave to mercy. If he urged the government to pension and reward the soldiers of the war, who had only done their duty, he himself set an example. There were black pensioners not a few about his own homestead. Bishop, his old body-servant, lived like a retired gentleman in his cottage there; even Nelson, the good sorrel who had borne him so bravely in the field till Yorktown, now went forever unsaddled, free in his own pasture.

WASHINGTON BRINGING HIS MOTHER INTO THE BALL-ROOM, FREDERICKSBURG

But, much as he loved his home and courted retirement amidst the duties of a planter, the old life would not come back, was gone forever. He was too famous, and there was an end on 't. He could not go abroad without drawing crowds about him. If he attended service on a Sunday away from home, though it were in never so quiet a parish, the very walls of the church groaned threateningly under the unaccustomed weight of people gathered in the galleries and packed upon the floor to see the hero of the Revolution. Not even a ride into the far west, to view his lands and pull together bis neglected business on the Ohio, was long enough to take him beyond the reach of public affairs. On the 1st of September, 1784, with Dr. Craik for company, he set out on horseback to go by Braddock's road again into the west. For nearly five weeks he was deep in the wilderness, riding close upon seven hundred miles through the forested mountains, and along the remote courses of the long rivers that ran into the Mississippi; camping out as in the old days when he was a surveyor and a soldier in his 'prenticeship in these very wilds; renewing his zest for the rough life and the sudden adventures of the frontiersman. But, though he had come upon his own business, it was the seat of a future empire he saw rather than his own acres scattered here and there.

When last he had ridden the long stages from settlement to settlement and cabin to cabin in this far country of the Ohio, he had been a Virginian and nothing more, a colonial colonel merely, come to pick out lands for his comrades and himself, their reward for serving the crown against the French. A transformation had been worked upon him since then. He had led the armies of the whole country; had been the chief instrument of a new nation in winning independence; had carried its affairs by his own counsels as no other man had done; had seen through all the watches of those long campaigns the destinies and the hopes that were at stake. Now he saw the crowding immigrants come into the west with a new solicitude he had not felt before. A new vision was in his thought. This western country was now a "rising world," to be kept or lost, husbanded or squandered, by the raw nation he had helped put upon its feet. His thought was stretched at last to a continental measure; problems of statesmanship that were national, questions of policy that had a scope great as schemes of empire, stood foremost in his view. He returned home more engrossed than ever by interests not his own, but central to public affairs, and of the very stuff of politics.

And so not the letters merely which poured in with every mail, not only his host of visitors, great and small —the Governor of the State, the President of Congress, foreign noblemen, soldiers, diplomatists, travellers, neighbors, friends, acquaintances, intruders — but his own unbidden thoughts as well, and the very suggestions of his own interest as a citizen and landowner, drew him from his dreams of retirement and forced him upon the open stage again. Even hunting ceased before many seasons were out. The savage boar-hounds which Lafayette bad sent, in his kindness, from the Old World, proved too fierce and great a breed for even the sharp sport with the gray fox; the old hunting companions were gone-the Fairfaxes over sea; Belvoir deserted and burned ; George Mason too much engaged — none but boys and strangers left to ride with. 'Twas poor sport, after all, without the right sportsmen. It must needs give way before a statesman's cares.

Upon his first home-coming, Washington had found it hard to break himself of his habit of waking very early in the morning with a sense of care concerning the affairs of the day, as if he were still in camp and in the midst of public duties. Now a new sense of responsibility possessed him, and more and more gained ascendency over him. He began to feel a deep anxiety lest a weak government should make independence little better than a reproach, and the country should fall into a hopeless impotency. At first he had been very sanguine. "Notwithstanding the jealous and contracted temper which seems to prevail in some of the States," he wrote to Jonathan Trumbull in January, 1784, "yet I cannot but hope and believe that the good sense of the people will ultimately get the better of their prejudices, and that order and sound policy, though they do not come so soon as one could wish, will be produced from the present unsettled and deranged state of public affairs....Everything, my dear Trumbull, will come right at last, as we have often prophesied. My only fear is that we shall lose a little reputation first." But the more he observed the temper of the time, the more uneasy he grew. " Like a young heir," he cried," come a little prematurely to a large inheritance, we shall wanton and run riot until we have brought our reputation to the brink of ruin, and then, like him, shall have to labor with the current of opinion, when compelled, perhaps, to do what prudence and common policy pointed out, as plain as any problem in Euclid, in the first instance....I think we have opposed

Great Britain, and have arrived at the present state of peace and independency, to very little purpose, if we cannot conquer our own prejudices."

For the present he saw little that could be done beyond holding up the hands of the Congress, and increaseing, as it might prove possible to do so, the meagre powers of the Confederation. "My political creed," he said, "is to be wise in the choice of delegates, support them like gentlemen while they are our representatives, give them competent powers for all federal purposes, support them in the due exercise thereof, and, lastly, to compel them to close attendance in Congress during their delegation." But his thoughts took wider scope as the months passed; and nothing quickened them more than his western trip. He saw how much of the future travelled with those slow wagon trains of immigrants into the west; realized how they were leaving behind them the rivers that ran to the old ports at the sea, and going down into the valleys whose outlet was the great highway of the Mississippi and the ports of the Gulf; how the great ridge of the Alleghanies lay piled between them and the older seats of settlement, with only here and there a gap to let a road through, only here and there two rivers lying close enough at their sources to link the east with the west; and the likelihood of a separation between the two populations seemed to him as obvious as the tilt of the mountains upon either slope. " There is nothing which binds one country or one State to another but interest," he said. "Without this cement the western inhabitants, who more than probably will be composed in a great degree of foreigners, can have no predilection for us, and a commercial connection is the only tie we can have upon them." "The western settlers," he declared, while still fresh from the Ohio, "stand as it were upon a pivot. The touch of a feather would turn them any way " —down the Mississippi to join their interests with those of the Spaniard, or back to the mountain roads and the headwaters of the eastern streams, to make for themselves a new allegiance in the east. He was glad to see the Spaniard so impolitic as to close the Mississippi against the commerce offered him, and hoped that things might stand so until there should have been "a little time allowed to open and make easy the ways between the Atlantic States and the western territory."

The opening of the upper reaches of the Potomac to navigation had long been a favorite object with Washington; now it seemed nothing less than a necessity. It had been part of the original scheme of the old Ohio Company to use this means of winning a way for commerce through the mountains. Steps had been taken more than twenty years ago to act in the matter through private subscription; and active measures for securing the necessary legislation from the Assemblies of Virginia and Maryland were still in course when Washington was called to Cambridge and revolution drew men's minds imperatively off from the business. In 1770 Washington had written to Jefferson of the project as a means of opening a channel for "the extensive trade of a rising empire"; now the empire of which he had had a vision was no longer Britain's, but America's own, and it was become a matter of exigent political necessity to keep that western country against estrangement, winning it by commerce and close sympathy to join itself with the old colonies in building up a free company of united States upon the great continent.

Already the west was astir for the formation of new States. Virginia had taken the broad and national view of her duty that Washington himself held, and had ceded to the Confederation all her ancient claims to the lands that lay northwest of the Ohio River, reserving for herself only the fair region that stretch south of that great stream, from her own mountains to the Mississippi. North Carolina would have ceded her western lands beyond the mountains also, had they been empty and unclaimed, like the vast territory that lay beyond the Ohio. But for many a year settlers had been crossing the mountains into those fertile valleys, and both this region and that which Virginia still kept showed many a clearing now and many a rude hamlet where hardy frontiersmen were making a new home for civilization. Bather than be handed over to Congress, to be disposed of by an authority which no one else was bound to obey, North Carolina's western settlers declared they would form a State of their own, and North Carolina had to recall her gift of their lands to the Confederation before their plans of defiance could be checked and defeated. Virginia found her own frontiersmen no less ready to take the initiative in whatever affair touched their interest. Spain offered the United States trade at her ports, but refused to grant them the use of the lower courses of the Mississippi, lest territorial aggression should be pushed too shrewdly in that quarter; and news reached the settlers beyond the mountains, in the far counties of North Carolina and Virginia, that Mr. Jay, the Confederation's Secretary for Foreign Affairs, had proposed to the Congress to yield the navigation of the Mississippi for a generation in exchange for trade on the seas. They flatly declared they would give themselves, and their lands too, into the hands of England again rather than submit to be so robbed, cramped, and deserted. The New England States, on their part, threatened to withdraw from the Confederation if treaties were to be made to wait upon the assent of frontiersmen on the far Mississippi.

The situation was full of menace of no ordinary sort. It could profit the Confederation little that great States like Virginia and New York had grown magnanimous, and were endowing the Confederation with vast gifts of territory in the west, if such gifts were but to loosen still further the already slackened bonds of the common government, leaving settlers in the unclaimed lands no allegiance they could respect. Without a national government spirited and strong enough to frame policies and command obedience, " we shall never establish a national character or be considered as on a respectable footing by the powers of Europe," Washington had said from the first. He had made a most solemn appeal to the States in his last circular to them, ere he resigned his commission, urging them to strengthen the powers of Congress, put faction and jealousy away, and make sure of "an indissoluble union under one federal head." "An option is still left to the United States of America," he had told them, with all his plain and stately eloquence; "it is in their choice, and depends upon their conduct, whether they will be respectable and prosperous, or contemptible and miserable, as a nation. This is the time of their political probation." The hazards of that probation had been a burden upon his heart through all the toil of the Revolution, and now it seemed as if the States must needs make every evil choice in meeting them. Congress could not so much as carry out the provisions of the treaty of peace, for its commissioners had made promises in the name of the States which the States would not redeem. England consequently refused to keep her part of the agreement and relinquish the western posts. She levied commercial war against the country, besides, without fear of reprisal; for Congress had no power to regulate trade, and the States were too jealous of each other to co-operate in this or any other matter. English statesmen had consented to give up the colonies, and recognize their independence as a nation, rather than face any longer the world in arms; but they now looked to see them presently drop back into their hands again, out of sheer helplessness and hopeless division in counsel; and there were observant men in America who deemed the thing possible, though it brought an intolerable fire into their blood to think of it.

Other nations, too, were fast conceiving a like contempt for the Confederation. It was making no provision for the payment of the vast sums of money it had borrowed abroad, in France and Poland and Spain; and it could not make any. It could only ask the States for money, and must count itself fortunate to get enough to pay even the interest on its debts. It was this that foreign courts were finding out, that the Confederation was a mere "government of supplication," as Randolph had dubbed it; and its credit broke utterly down. Frenchman and Spaniard alike would only have laughed in contemptuous derision to see the whole fabric go to pieces, and were beginning to interest themselves with surmises as to what plunder it would afford. The States which lay neighbors to each other were embroiled in boundary disputes, and were fallen to levying duties on each other's commerce. They were individually in debt, besides, and were many of them resorting to issues of irredeemable paper money to relieve themselves of the inevitable taxation that must sooner or later pay their reckonings. "We are either a united people, or we are not so," cried Washington. "If the former, let us in all matters of general concern act as a nation which has a national character to support; if we are not, let us no longer act a farce by pretending to it." As the months passed it began to look as if the farce might be turned into a tragedy.

The troubles of the country, though he filled his letters with them and wrung his heart for phrases of protest and persuasion that would tell effectually in the deep labor of working out the sufficient remedy of a roused and united opinion, though he deemed them personal to himself, and knew his own fame in danger to be undone by them, did not break the steady self-possession of Washington's life at Mount Vernon. " It's astonishing the packets of letters that daily come for him, from all parts of the world," exclaimed an English visitor; but it was not till he had struggled to keep pace with his correspondence unassisted for a year and a half that he employed a secretary to help him. "Letters of friendship require no study," he wrote to General Knox; " the communications are easy, and allowances are expected and made. This is not the case with those that require researches, consideration, recollection, and the de —I knows what to prevent error, and to answer the ends for which they are written." He grew almost docile, nevertheless, under the gratuitous tasks of courtesy thrust upon him. His gallantry, bred in him since a boy, the sense of duty to which he was born, his feeling that what he had done had in some sort committed him to serve his countrymen and his friends everywhere, though it were only in answering questions, disposed him to sacrifice his comfort and his privacy to every one who had the slightest claim upon his attention. He even found sitting for his portrait grow easy at last. " In for a penny, in for a pounds is an old adage," he laughed, writing to Francis Hopkinson. " I am so hackneyed to the touches of the painter's pencil that I am now altogether at their beck; and sit like Patience on a monument' whilst they are delineating the lines of my face. ...At first I was as impatient at the request, and as restive under the operation, as a colt is of the saddle. The next time I submitted very reluctantly, but with less flouncing. Now no dray-horse moves more readily to his thill than I do to the painter's chair." Besides the failure of the public credit, it concerned him to note the fact that, though he kept a hundred cows, he was obliged to buy butter for his innumerable guests. He saw to it that there should be at least a very definite and efficient government upon his own estate, and, when there was need, put his own hand to the work. He "often works with his men himself— strips off his coat and labors like a common man," measures with his own hands every bit of building or construction that is going forward, and " shows a great turn for mechanics," one of his guests noted, amidst comments on his greatness and his gracious dignity. It was such constancy and candor and spirit in living that took the admiration of all men alike upon the instant; and his neighbors every day saw here the same strenuous and simple gentleman they had known before ever the war began.

It was through the opening of the Potomac, after all —the thing nearest his hand-that a way was found to cure the country of its malady of weakness and disorder. Washington had been chosen president of the Potomac Company, that it might have the advantage both of his name and of his capacity in affairs; and he had gone upon a tour of inspection, with the directors of the company, to the falls of the river in the summer of 1785, keeping steadily to the business he had come upon, and insisting upon being in fact a private gentleman busy with his own affairs, despite the efforts made everywhere he went to see and to entertain him; and it presently became evident even to the least sanguine that the long-talked-of work was really to be carried through. A visitor at Mount Vernon in the autumn of 1785 found Washington "quite pleased at the idea of the Baltimore merchants laughing at him, and saying it was a ridiculous plan, and would never succeed. They begin now, says the General, to look a little serious about the matter, as they know it must hurt their commerce amazingly."

The scheme had shown its real consequence in the spring of that very year, when it brought commissioners from the two States that lay upon the river together in conference to devise plans of co-operation. Both Virginia and Maryland had appointed commissioners, and a meeting had been set for March, 1785, at Alexandria. For some reason the Virginian commissioners were not properly notified of the place and time of conference. The meeting was held, nevertheless, a minority of the Virginian commissioners being present; and, as if to give it more the air of a cordial conference of neighbors, Washington invited the representatives of both States to adjourn from Alexandria to Mount Vernon. There they sat, his guests, from Friday to Monday. He was not formally of the commission; but conference was not confined to their formal sessions, and his counsel entered into their determinations. It was evident that two States were not enough to decide the questions submitted to them. Pennsylvania, at least, must be consulted before the full line of trade they sought could be drawn from the head-waters of the Ohio to the head-waters of the Potomac; and if three States were to consult upon questions of trade which concerned the whole continent, why should not more be invited, and the conference be made general? Such was the train of suggestion, certainly, that ran in Washington's mind, and which the commissioners carried home with them. Every sign of the time served to deepen its significance for Washington. Just before quitting the army he had ridden upon a tour of inspection into the valley of the Mohawk, where a natural way, like this of the Potomac, ran from the northern settlements into the west. He knew that the question of joining the Potomac with the Ohio was but one item of a policy which all the States must consider and settle-nothing less than the policy which must make them an empire or doom them to remain a weak and petty confederacy.

The commissioners did not put all that they had heard at Mount Vernon into their reports to their respective Assemblies. They recommended only that, besides co-operating with each other and with Pennsylvania in opening a way to the western waters, Virginia and Maryland should adopt a uniform system of duties and of commercial regulations, and should establish uniform rules regarding their currency. But the Maryland Assembly itself went further. It presently informed the Virginian Legislature that it had not only adopted the measures recommended by the commissioners, but thought it wise to do something more. Delaware ought to be consulted, with a view to carrying a straight watercourse, by canal, from Chesapeake Bay to the Delaware River; and, since conference could do no harm and bind nobody, it would be as well to invite all the States to confer with them, for the questions involved seemed far-reaching enough to justify it, if not to make it necessary. Governor Bowdoin, of Massachusetts, had that very year urged his Legislature to invite a general convention of the States in the interest of trade. The whole country was in a tangle of disagreement about granting to Congress the power to lay imposts; Gardoqui, it was rumored, was insisting, for Spain, upon closing the Mississippi: 'twas evident enough conference was needed. Every thoughtful man might well pray that it would bring peace and accommodation. When Maryland's suggestion was read in the Virginian Assembly, there was prompt acquiescence. Virginia asked all the States of the Union (January, 1786) to send delegates to a general conference to be held at Annapolis on the first Monday in September, to consider and recommend such additions to the powers of Congress as might conduce to a better regulation of trade. "There is more wickedness than ignorance in the conduct of the States, or, in other words, in the conduct of those who have too much influence in the government of them," Washington wrote hotly to Henry Lee, upon hearing to what lengths contempt of the authority of Congress had been carried; "and until the curtain is withdrawn, and the private views and selfish principles upon which these men act are exposed to public notice, I have little hope of amendment without another convulsion." Perhaps the conference at Annapolis would withdraw the curtain and give the light leave to work a purification; and he waited anxiously for the issue.

But when the commissioners assembled they found only five States represented-Virginia, Pennsylvania, Delaware, New Jersey, and New York. Maryland had suddenly fallen indifferent, and had not appointed delegates. New Hampshire, Massachusetts, Rhode Island, and North Carolina had appointed delegates, but they had not taken the trouble to come. Connecticut, South Carolina, and Georgia had ignored the call altogether. The delegates who were in attendance, besides, had come with only the most jealously restricted powers; only New Jersey, in her great uneasiness at being neighbor to the powerful States of New York and Pennsylvania, had authorized her representatives to "consider how far a uniform system in their commercial regulations and other important matters might be necessary to the common interest and permanent harmony of the several States." The other delegates had no such scope; all deemed it futile to attempt their business in so small a convention; and it was resolved to make another opportunity. Alexander Hamilton, of New York, drew up their address to the States, and in it made bold to adopt New Jersey's hint, and ask for a conference which should not merely consider questions of trade, but also "devise such further provisions as should appear to them necessary to render the constitution of the federal government adequate to the exigencies of the Union." Hamilton held with Washington for a national government. He had been born, and bred as a lad, in the West Indies, and had never received the local pride of any colony-state into his blood. He had served with the army, too, in close intimacy with Washington, and, though twenty-five years his captain's junior, had seen as clearly as he saw the deep hazards of a nation's birth.

The Congress was indifferent, if not hostile, to the measures which the address proposed; and the States would have acted on the call as slackly as before, had not the winter brought with it something like a threat of social revolution, and fairly startled them out of their negligent humor. The central counties of Massachusetts broke into violent rebellion, under one Shays, a veteran of the Revolution-not to reform the government, but to rid themselves of it altogether; to shut the courts and escape the payment of debts and taxes. The insurgents worked their will for weeks together; drove out the officers of the law, burned and plundered at pleasure through whole districts, living upon the land like a hostile army, and were brought to a reckoning at last only when a force thousands strong had been levied against them. The contagion spread to Vermont and New Hampshire; and, even when the outbreak had been crushed, the States concerned were irresolute in the punishment of the leaders. Rhode Island declared her sympathy with the insurgents; Vermont offered them asylum; Massachusetts brought the leaders to trial and conviction only to pardon and set them free again. Congress dared do no more than make covert preparation to check a general rising. "You talk, my good sir," wrote Washington to Henry Lee, in Congress, "of employing influence to appease the present tumults in Massachusetts. I know not where that influence is to be found, or, if attainable, that it would be a proper remedy for the disorders. Influence is no government Let us have one by which our lives, liberties, and properties will be secured, or let us know the worst at once." It was an object-lesson for the whole country; the dullest and the most lethargic knew now what slack government and financial disorder would produce. The States one and all-save Rhode Island-bethought them of the convention called to meet in Philadelphia on the second Monday in May, 1787, and delegates were appointed. Even Congress took the lesson to heart, and gave its sanction to the conference.

The Legislature of Virginia put Washington's name at the head of its own list of delegates, and after his name the names of Patrick Henry, Edmund Randolph, John Blair, James Madison, George Mason, and George Wythe-the leading names of the State, no man could doubt. But Washington hesitated. He had already declined to meet the Society of the Cincinnati in Philadelphia about the same time, he said, and thought it would be disrespectful to that body, to whom he owed much, "to be there on any other occasion." He even hinted a doubt whether the convention was constitutionaly its avowed purposes being what they were, until Congress tardily sanctioned it. His real reason his intimate friends must have divined from the first. They knew him better in such matters than he knew himself. He not only loved his retirement; he deemed himself a soldier and man of action, and no statesman. The floor of assemblies had never seemed to him his principal sphere of duty. He had thought of staying away from the House of Burgesses on private business twenty years ago, when he knew that the Stamp Act was to be debated. But it was not for the floor of the approaching convention that his friends wanted him; they told him from the first he must preside. He was known to be in favor of giving the Confederation powers that would make it a real government, and he thought that enough; but they wanted the whole country to see him pledged to the actual work, and, when they had persuaded him to attend, knew that they had at any rate won the confidence of the people in their patriotic purpose. His mere presence would give them power.

Washington and the other Virginians were prompt to be in Philadelphia on the day appointed, but only the Pennsylvanian delegates were there to meet them. They had to wait an anxious week before so many as seven States were represented. Meanwhile, those who gathered from day to day were nervous and apprehensive, and there was talk of compromise and halfway measures, should the convention prove weak or threaten to miscarry. They remembered for many a long year afterwards how nobly Washington, "standing self-collected in the midst of them," had uttered brave counsels of wisdom in their rebuke. "It is too probable," he said, "that no plan we propose will be adopted. Perhaps another dreadful conflict is to be sustained. If, to please the people, we offer what we ourselves disapprove, how can we afterwards defend our work? Let us raise a standard to which the wise and honest can repair. The event is in the hand of God." It was an utterance, they knew, not of statesmanship merely, but of character; and it was that character, if anything could, that would win the people to their support. When at last seven States were represented—a quorum of the thirteen-an organization was effected, and Washington unanimously chosen president of the convention. He spoke, when led to the chair, "of the novelty of the scene of business in which he was to act, lamented his want of better qualifications, and claimed the indulgence of the house towards the involuntary errors which his inexperience might occasion"; but no mere parliamentarian could have given that anxious body such steadiness in business or such grave earnestness in counsel as it got from his presence and influence in the chair. Five more States were in attendance before deliberation was very far advanced; but he had the satisfaction to see his own friends lead upon the floor.

It was the plan which Edmund Randolph proposed, for his fellow Virginians, which the convention accepted as a model to work from; it was James Madison, that young master of counsel, who guided the deliberations from day to day, little as he showed his hand in the work or seemed to put himself forward in debate. No speeches came from the president; only once or twice did he break the decorum of his office to temper some difference of opinion or facilitate some measure of accommodation. It was the 17th of September when the convention at last broke up; the 19th when the Constitution it had wrought out was published to the country. All the slow summer through, Washington had kept counsel with the rest as to the anxious work that was going forward behind the closed doors of the long conference; it was a grateful relief to be rid of the painful strain, and he returned to Mount Vernon like one whose part in the work was done.

"I never saw him so keen for anything in my life as he is for the adoption of the new scheme of government," wrote a visitor at Mount Vernon to Jefferson; but he took no other part than his correspondence afforded him in the agitation for its acceptance. Throughout all those long four months in Philadelphia he had given his whole mind and energy to every process of difficult counsel by which it had been wrought to completion ; but he was no politician. Earnestly as he commended the plan to his friends, he took no public part either in defence or in advocacy of it. He read not only the Federalist papers, in which Hamilton and Madison and Jay made their masterly plea for the adoption of the Constitution, but also "every performance which has been printed on the one side and the other on the great question," he said, so far as he was able to obtain them; and he felt as poignantly as any man the deep excitement of the momentous contest. It disturbed him keenly to find George Mason opposing the Constitution —the dear friend from whom he had always accepted counsel hitherto in public affairs-and Richard Henry Lee and Patrick Henry, too, in their passionate attachment to what they deemed the just sovereignty of Virginia. He could turn away with all his old self-possession, nevertheless, to discuss questions of culture and tillage, in the midst of the struggle, with Arthur Young over sea, and to write very gallant compliments to the Marquis de Chastellux on his marriage. "So your day has at length come," he laughed. "I am glad of it with all my heart and soul. It is quite good enough for you. Now you are well served for coming to fight in favor of the American rebels all the way across the Atlantic Ocean, by catching that terrible contagion-domestic felicity-which, like the small-pox or the plague, a man can have only once in his life, because it commonly lasts him (at least with us in America — I don't know how you manage such matters in France) for his whole lifetime."

Ten months of deep but quiet agitation — the forces of opinion in close grapple-and the future seemed to clear. The Constitution was adopted, only two States dissenting. It had been a tense and stubborn fight: in such States as Massachusetts and New York, the concerted action of men at the centres of trade against the instinctive dread of centralization or change in the regions that lay back from the rivers and the sea; in States like Virginia, where the mass of men waited to be led, the leaders who had vision against those who bad only the slow wisdom of caution and presentiment. But, though she acted late in the business, and some home-keeping spirits among even her greater men held back, Virginia did not lose the place of initiative she had had in all this weighty business of reform. Something in her air or her life had given her in these latter years an extraordinary breed of public men-men liberated from local prejudice, possessed of a vision and an efficacy in affairs worthy of the best traditions of statesmanship among the English race from which they were sprung, capable of taking the long view, of seeing the permanent lines of leadership upon great questions, and shaping ordinary views to meet extraordinary ends. Even Henry and Mason could take their discomfiture gracefully, loyally, like men bred to free institutions; and Washington had the deep satisfaction to see his State come without hesitation to his view and hope.

The new Constitution made sure of, and a time set by Congress for the elections and the organization of a new government under it, the country turned as one man to Washington to be the first President of the United States. " We cannot, sir, do without you," cried Governor Johnson, of Maryland," and I and thousands more can explain to anybody but yourself why we cannot do without you." To make any one else President, it seemed to men everywhere, would be like crowning a subject while the king was by. But Washington held back, as he had held back from attending the Constitutional Convention. He doubted his civil capacity, called himself an old man, said "it would be to forego repose and domestic enjoyment for trouble, perhaps for public obloquy." " The acceptance," he declared, "would be attended with more diffidence and reluctance than I ever experienced before in my life." But he was not permitted to decline. Hamilton told him that his attendance upon the Constitutional Convention must be taken to have pledged him in the view of the country to take part also in the formation of the government. " In a matter so essential to the well-being of society as the prosperity of a newly instituted government," said the great advocate," a citizen of so much consequence as yourself to its success has no option bat to lend his services, if called for. Permit me to say it would be inglorious, in such a situation, not to hazard the glory, however great, which he might have previously acquired."

Washington of course yielded, like the simple-minded gentleman and soldier he was, when it was made thus a matter of duty. When the votes of the electors were opened in the new Congress, and it was found that they were one and all for him, he no longer doubted. He did not know how to decline such a call, and turned with all bis old courage to the new task.

Chapter X
The First President of the United States

The members of the new Congress were so laggard in coming together that it was the 6th of April, 1789, before both Houses could count a quorum, though the 4th of March had been appointed the day for their convening. Their first business was the opening and counting of the electoral votes; and on the 7th Charles Thomson, the faithful and sedulous gentleman who had been clerk of every congress since that first one in the old colonial days fifteen years ago, got away on his long ride to Mount Vernon to notify Washington of his election. Affairs waited upon the issue of his errand. Washington had for long known what was coming, and was ready and resolute, as of old. There had been no formal nominations for the presidency, and the votes of the electors had lain under seal till the new Congress met and found a quorum; but it was an open secret who had been chosen President, and Washington had made up his mind what to do. Mr. Thomson reached Mount Vernon on the 14th, and found Washington ready to obey his summons at once. He waited only for a hasty ride to Fredericksburg to bid his aged mother farewell. She was not tender in the parting. Her last days had come, and she had set herself to bear with grim resolution the fatal disease that had long been upon her. She had never been tender, and these latter days had added their touch of hardness. But it was a tonic to her son to take her farewell, none the less; to hear her once more bid him God-speed, and once more command him, as she did, to his duty. On the morning of the 16th he took the northern road again, as so often before, and pressed forward on the way for New York.

The setting out was made with a very heavy heart; for duty had never seemed to him so unattractive as it seemed now, and his diffidence had never been so distressing. "For myself the delay may be compared to a reprieve," he had written to Knox, when he learned how slow Congress was in coming together, "for in confidence I tell you that my movements to the chair of government will be accompanied by feelings not unlike those of a culprit who is going to the place of execution." When the day for his departure came, his diary spoke the same heaviness of heart. "About ten o'clock," he wrote, "I bade adieu to Mount Vernon, to private life, and to domestic felicity; and, with a mind oppressed with more anxious and painful sensations than I have words to express, set out for New York." He did not doubt that he was doing right; he doubted his capacity in civil affairs, and loved the sweet retirement and the free life he was leaving behind him. Grief and foreboding did not in the least relax his proud energy and promptness in action. He was not a whit the less resolute to attempt this new role, and stretch his powers to the uttermost to play it in masterful fashion. He was only wistful and full of a sort of manly sadness; lacking not resolution, but only alacrity.

Be had hoped to the last that he would be suffered to spend the rest of his days at Mount Vernon; he knew the place must lack efficient keeping, and fall once more out of repair under hired overseers; he feared his strength would be spent and his last years come ere he could return to look to it and enjoy it himself again. He had but just now been obliged to borrow a round sum of money to meet pressing obligations; and the expenses of this very journey had made it necessary to add a full hundred pounds to the new debt. If the estate brought money so slowly in while he farmed it, he must count upon its doing even less while he was away; and yet he had determined to accept no salary as President, but only his necessary expenses while in the discharge of his official duties, as in the old days of the war. It had brought distressing perplexities upon him to be thus drawn from his private business to serve the nation. Private cares passed off, no doubt, and were forgotten as the journey lengthened. But the other anxiety, how he should succeed in this large business of statesmanship to which he had been called, did not pass off; the incidents of that memorable ride only served to heighten it. When he had ridden to Cambridge that anxious summer of 1775, he had been hailed by cheering crowds upon the way, who admired the fine figure he made, and shouted for the cause he was destined to lead; but he knew himself a soldier then, was but forty-three, and did not fear to find his duty uncongenial. The people had loved him and had thronged about him with looks and words it had quickened his heart to see and hear as he made his way from New York to Annapolis to resign his commission but six years ago; but that was upon the morrow of a task accomplished, and the plaudits he heard upon the way were but greetings to speed him the more happily homeward. Things stood very differently now. Though he felt himself grown old, he had come out to meet a hope he could not share, and it struck a subtle pain to his heart that the people should so trust him—should give him so royal a progress as he fared on his way to attempt an untried task.

THOMSON, THE CLERK OF CONGRESS, ANNOUNCING TO WASHINGTON, AT MOUNT VERNON, HIS ELECTION TO THE PRESIDENCY

No king in days of kings' divinity could have looked for so heartfelt a welcome to his throne as this modest gentleman got to the office he feared to take. Not only were there civil fete and military parade at every stage of the journey; there was everywhere, besides, a running together from all the country roundabout of people who bore themselves not as mere sightseers, but as if they had come out of love for the man they were to see pass by. It was not their numbers but their manner that struck their hero with a new sense of responsibility: their earnest gaze, their unpremeditated cries of welcome, their simple joy to see the new government put into the hands of a man they perfectly trusted. He was to be their guarantee of its good faith, of its respect for law and its devotion to liberty; and they made him know their hope and their confidence in the very tone of their greeting. There was the manifest touch of love in the reception everywhere prepared for him. Refined women broke their reserve to greet him in the open road; put their young daughters forward, in their enthusiasm, to strew roses before him in the way; brought tears to his eyes by the very artlessness of their affection. When at last the triumphal journey was ended, the display of every previous stage capped and outdone by the fine pageant of his escort of boats from Newark and of his reception at the ferry stairs in New York, the demonstration seemed almost more than he could bear. "The display of boats which attended and joined us," he confessed to his diary, "the decorations of the ships, the roar of the cannon, and the loud acclamation of the people which rent the skies as I walked along the streets, filled my mind with sensations as painful as they are pleasant"; for his fears foreboded scenes the opposite of these, when he should have shown himself unable to fulfill the hopes which were the burden of all the present joy.

It was the 27th of April when he reached New York. Notwithstanding his executive fashion of making haste, the rising of the country to bid him Godspeed had kept him four days longer on the way than Mr. Thomson had taken to carry the summons to Mount Vernon. Three days more elapsed before Congress had completed its preparations for his inauguration. On the 80th of April, in the presence of a great concourse of people, who first broke into wild cheers at sight of him, and then fell silent again upon the instant to see him so moved, Washington stood face to face with the Chancellor of the State upon the open balcony of the Federal Hall in Wall Street, and took the oath of office. "Do you solemnly swear," asked Livingston, "that you will faithfully execute the office of President of the United States, and will, to the best of your ability, preserve, protect, and defend the Constitution of the United States?" "I do solemnly swear," replied Washington, "that I will faithfully execute the office of President of the United States, and will, to the best of my ability, preserve, protect, and defend the Constitution of the United States," and then, bending to kiss the Bible held before him, bowed his head and said " So help me God!" in tones no man could mistake, so deep was their thrill of feeling. "Long live George Washington, President of the United States!" cried Livingston to the people; and a great shout went up with the booming of the cannon in the narrow streets.

Washington was profoundly moved, and, with all his extraordinary mastery of himself, could not hide his agitation. It was a company of friends, the Senators and Representatives who stood about him within the Senate chamber as he read his address, after the taking of the oath. Some very old friends were there-men who had been with him in the first continental congress, men who had been his intimate correspondents the long years through, men who were now his close confidants and sworn supporters. Not many strangers could crowd into the narrow hall; and it was not mere love of ceremony, but genuine and heartfelt respect, that made the whole company stand while he read. He visibly trembled, nevertheless, as he stood in their presence, strong and steadfast man though he was, "and several times could scarce make out to read"; shifted his manuscript uneasily from hand to hand; gestured with awkward effort; let his voice fall almost inaudible; was every way unlike himself, except for the simple majesty and sincerity that shone in him through it all. His manner but gave emphasis, after all, to the words he was reading. " The magnitude and difficulty of the trust," he declared," could not but overwhelm with despondence one who, inheriting inferior endowments from nature, and unpractised in the duties of civil administration, ought to be peculiarly conscious of his own deficiencies"; and no one there could look at him and deem him insincere when he added," All I dare aver is that it has been my faithful study to collect my duty from a just appreciation of every circumstance by which it might be affected. All I dare hope is that, if in executing this task I have been too much swayed by a grateful remembrance of former instances, or by an affectionate sensibility to this transcendent proof of the confidence of my fellow-citizens, and have thence too little consulted my incapacity as well as disinclination for the weighty and untried cares before me, my error will be palliated by the motives which misled me, and its consequences be judged by my country with some share of the partiality with which they originated." His hearers knew how near the truth he struck when he said, "The smiles of Heaven can never be expected on a nation that disregards the eternal rules of order and right which Heaven itself has ordained; and the preservation of the sacred fire of liberty, and the destiny of the republican model of government, are justly considered as deeply, perhaps as finally, staked on the experiment intrusted to the hands of the American people." It was, no doubt," a novelty in the history of society to see a great people turn a calm and scrutinizing eye upon itself," as the people of America had done; "to see it carefully examine the extent of the evil" into which disunion and disorder had brought it; " patiently wait for two years until a remedy was discovered"; and at last voluntarily adopt a new order and government " without having wrung a tear or a drop of blood from mankind." But Washington knew that the praise deserved for such mastery and self-possession would be shortlived enough if the new government should fail or be discredited. It was the overpowering thought that he himself would be chiefly responsible for its success or failure that shook his nerves as he stood there at the beginning of his task; and no man of right sensibility in that audience failed to like him the better and trust him the more implicitly for bis emotion. "It was a very touching scene," wrote Fisher Ames, of Massachusetts. "It seemed to me an allegory in which virtue was personified as addressing those whom she would make her votaries. Her power over the heart was never greater, and the illustration of her doctrine by her own example was never more perfect." "I feel how much I shall stand in need of the countenance and aid of every friend to myself, of every friend to the Revolution, and of every lover of good government," were Washington's words of appeal to Edward Rutledge, of South Carolina; and he never seemed to his friends more attractive or more noble than now.

The inauguration over, the streets fallen quiet again, the legislative business of the Houses resumed, Washington regained his old self-possession, and turned to master his new duties with a calm thoroughness of purpose which seemed at once to pass into the action of the government itself. Perhaps it was true, as he thought, that he had been no statesman hitherto; though those who had known him would have declared themselves of another mind. He had carried the affairs of the Confederation upon his own shoulders, while the war lasted, after a fashion the men of that time were not likely to forget, so full of energy had he been, so provident and capable upon every point of policy. His letters, too, since the war ended, had shown his correspondents the country over such an appreciation of the present, so sure a forecast of the future, so masculine an under-Standing of what waited to be done and of the means at hand to do it, that they, at least, accounted him their leader in peace no less than in war. But statesmanship hitherto had been only incidental to his duties as a soldier and a citizen. It had been only an accident of the Revolution that he had had himself, oftentimes, to supply the foresight and the capacity in action which the halting congress lacked. He had had no experience at all in actual civil administration. He did not know bis own abilities, or realize how rich his experience in affairs had, in fact, been. He went about his new tasks with diffidence, therefore, but with the full-pulsed heartiness, too, of the man who thoroughly trusts himself, for the capacity at any rate of taking pains. Statesmanship was now his duty-his whole duty-and it was his purpose to understand and execute the office of President as he had understood and administered the office of General.

THE FIRST PRESIDENTIAL MANSION, AT PEARL AND CHERRY STREETS, NEW YORK

WASHINGTON MANSION, 190 MARKET STREET, PHILADELPHIA

He knew what need there was for caution. This was to be, " in the first instance, in a considerable degree, a government of accommodation as well as a government of laws. Much was to be done by prudence, much by conciliation, much by firmness." "I walk," he said, " on untrodden ground. There is scarcely an action the motive of which may not be subjected to a double interpretation. There is scarcely any part of my conduct which may not hereafter be drawn into precedent." But, though he sought a prudent course, he had no mind to be timid; though he asked advice, he meant to be his own master.

Washington had, no doubt, a more precise understanding of what the new government must be made to mean than any other man living, except, perhaps. Hamilton and Madison, the men whom he most consulted. The Confederation had died in contempt, despised for its want of dignity and power. The new government must deserve and get preeminent standing from the first. Its policy must make the States a nation, must stir the people out of their pettiness as colonists and provincials, and give them a national character and spirit. It was not a government only that was to be created, but the definite body of opinion also which should sustain and perfect it. It must be made worth believing in, and the best spirits of the country must be rallied to its support. It was not the question simply of how strong the government should be. Its action must, as Washington said, be mixed of firmness, prudence, and conciliation, if it would win liking and loyalty as well as respect. It must cultivate tact as well as eschew weakness; must win as well as compel obedience. It was of the first consequence to the country, therefore, that the man it had chosen to preside in this delicate business of establishing a government which should be vigorous without being overbearing was a thoroughbred gentleman, whose instincts would carry him a great way towards the solution of many a nice question of conduct. While he waited to be made President he called upon every Senator and Representative then in attendance upon Congress, with the purpose to show them upon how cordial and natural a basis of personal acquaintance he wished, for his part, to see the government conducted; but, the oath of office once taken, he was no longer a simple citizen, as he had been during those two days of waiting; the dignity of the government had come into his keeping with the office. Henceforth he would pay no more calls, accept no invitations. On a day fixed he would receive calls; and he would show himself once a week at Mrs. Washington's general receptions. He would invite persons of official rank or marked distinction to his table at suitable intervals. There should be no pretence of seclusion, no parade of inaccessibility. The President should be a republican officer, the servant of the people. But he would not be common. It should be known that his office and authority were the first in the land. Every proper outward form of dignity, ceremony, and self-respect should be observed that might tell wholesomely upon the imagination of the people; that might be made to serve as a visible sign, which no man could miss, that there was here no vestige of the old federal authority, at which it had been the fashion to laugh, but a real government, and that the greatest in the land. It was not that the President was not to be seen by anybody who had the curiosity to wish to see him. Many a fine afternoon he was to be seen walking, an unmistakable figure, upon the Battery, whither all persons of fashion in the town resorted for their daily promenade, his secretaries walking behind him, but otherwise unattended. Better still, he could be seen almost any day on horseback, riding in his noble way through the streets. People drew always aside to give him passage wherever he went, whether he walked or rode; no doubt there was something in his air and bearing which seemed to expect them to do so; but their respect had the alacrity of affection, and he would have borne himself with a like proud figure in his own Virginia. Some thought him stiff, but only the churlish could deem him unrepublican, so evident was it to every candid man that it was not himself but his office he was exalting. His old passion for success was upon him, and he meant that this government of which he had been made the head should have prestige from the first. Count de Moustier, the French Minister to the United States, deeming America, no doubt, a protege of France, claimed the right to deal directly with the President in person, as if upon terms of familiar privilege, when conducting his diplomatic business; but was checked very promptly. It was not likely a man bred in the proud school of Virginian country gentlemen would miss so obvious a point of etiquette as this. To demand intimacy was to intimate superiority, and Washington's reply drew from the Count an instant apology. That the United States had every reason to hold France in loyal affection Washington gladly admitted with all stately courtesy; but affection became servility when it lost self-respect, and France must approach the President of the United States as every other country did, through the properly constituted department. "If there are rules of proceeding," he said, quietly, "which have originated from the wisdom of statesmen, and are sanctioned by the common assent of nations, it would not be prudent for a young state to dispense with them altogether," — particularly a young state (his thought added) which foreign states had despised and might now try to patronize. These small matters would carry an infinite weight of suggestion with them, as he knew, and every suggestion that proceeded from the President should speak of dignity and independence.

For the first few months of the new government's life these small matters that marked its temper and its self-respect were of as much consequence as its laws or its efficient organization for the tasks of actual administration. The country evidently looked to Washington to set the tone and show what manner of government it was to have. Congress, though diligent and purposeful enough, could linger, meanwhile, the whole summer through upon its task of framing the laws necessary for the erection and organization of Departments of State, for Foreign Affairs, of the Treasury, and of War, and the creation of the office of Attorney-General — a simple administrative structure to suffice for the present. In the interval the treasury board of the Confederation and its secretaries of war and foreign affairs were continued in service, and the President found time to digest the business of the several departments preparatory to their reorganization. He sent for all the papers concerning their transactions since the treaty of peace of 1783, and mastered their contents after his own thorough fashion, making copious notes and abstracts as he read.

WASHINGTON

He had been scarcely six weeks in office when he was stricken with a sharp illness. A malignant tumor in bis thigh seemed to his physicians for a time to threaten mortification. It was three weeks before he could take the air again, stretched painfully at length in his coach; even his stalwart strength was slow to rally from the draught made upon it by the disease, and its cure with the knife. There was deep anxiety for a little among those who knew, so likely did it seem that the life of the government was staked upon his life. He himself had looked very calmly into the doctor's troubled face, and had bidden him tell him the worst with that placid firmness that always came to him in moments of danger. "I am not afraid to die," he said. " Whether tonight or twenty years hence makes no difference. I know that I am in the hands of a good Providence." A chain had been stretched across the street in front of the house where he lay, to check the noisy traffic that might have disturbed him more deeply in his fever. But the government had not stood still the while. He had steadily attended to important matters as he could. 'Twas scarcely necessary he should be out of bed and abroad again to make all who handled affairs feel his mastery; and by the time the summer was ended that mastery was founded upon knowledge. He understood the affairs of the new government, as of the old, better than any other man; knew the tasks that waited to be attempted, the questions that waited to be answered, the difficulties that awaited solution, and the means at hand for solving them, with a grasp and thoroughness such as made it impossible henceforth that any man who might be called to serve with him in executive business, of whatever capacity in affairs, should be more than his counsellor. He had made himself once for all head and master of the government.

By the end of September (1789) Congress had completed its work of organization and Washington had drawn his permanent advisers about him. The federal courts, too, had been erected and given definitive jurisdiction. The new government had taken distinct shape, and was ready to digest its business in detail. Washington chose Alexander Hamilton to be Secretary of the Treasury, Henry Knox to be Secretary of War, Thomas Jefferson Secretary of State, and Edmund Randolph Attorney - General — young men all, except Jefferson, and he was but forty-six.

The fate of the government was certain to turn, first of all, upon questions of finance. It was hopeless poverty that had brought the Confederation into deep disgrace; the new government had inherited from it nothing bat a great debt; and the first test of character to which the new plan in affairs would be put, whether at home or abroad, was the test of its ability to sustain its financial credit with businesslike thoroughness and statesmanlike wisdom. Alexander Hamilton was only thirty-two years old. He had been a spirited and capable soldier and an astute and eloquent advocate; but he had not had a day's experience in the administration of a great governmental department, and had never handled-so far as men knew, had never studied-questions of public finance. "Washington chose him, nevertheless, without hesitation, for what must certainly turn out to be the most critical post in his administration. No man saw more clearly than Washington did how large a capacity for statesmanship Hamilton had shown in his masterly papers in advocacy of the Constitution. He had known Hamilton, moreover, through all the quick years that had brought him from precocious youth to wise maturity; had read his letters and felt the singular power that moved in them; and was ready to trust him with whatever task he would consent to assume.

Henry Knox, that gallant officer of the Revolution, had been already four years Secretary of "War for the Confederation. In appointing him to the same office under the new Constitution, "Washington was but retaining a man whom he loved and to whom he had for long been accustomed to look for friendship and counsel. He chose Thomas Jefferson to handle the delicate questions of foreign affairs which must press upon the young state because, John Adams being Vice-President, there was no other man of equal gifts available who had had so large an experience in the field of diplomacy. Again and again Jefferson had been chosen for foreign missions under the Confederation; he was American Minister to France when Washington's summons called him to the Secretaryship of State; and he came of that race of Virginian statesmen from whom Washington might reasonably count upon receiving a support touched with personal loyalty. Richard Henry Lee, Patrick Henry, and George Mason were home-keeping spirits, and doubted of the success of the new government; but Jefferson, though he bad looked upon its making from across the sea, approved, and was ready to lend his aid to its successful establishment. In appointing Edmund Randolph to be Attorney - General, Washington was but choosing a brilliant young man whom he loved out of a great family of lawyers who had held a sort of primacy at the bar in Virginia ever since he could remember-almost ever since she had been called the Old Dominion. Knox was thirty-nine, Edmund Randolph thirty-six; but if Washington chose young men to be his comrades and guides in counsel, it was but another capital proof of his own mastery in affairs. Himself a natural leader, he recognized the like gift and capacity in others, even when fortune had not yet disclosed or brought them to the test.

It was hard, in filling even the greater offices, to find men of eminence who were willing to leave the service of their States or the security and ease of private life to try the untrodden paths of federal government The States were old and secure-so men thought-the federal government was new and an experiment. The stronger sort of men, particularly amongst those bred to the law, showed, many of them, a great reluctance to identify themselves with new institutions set up but five or six months ago; and Washington, though he meant to make every liberal allowance for differences of opinion, would invite no man to stand with him in the new service who did not thoroughly believe in it. He was careful to seek out six of the best lawyers to be had in the country when he made up the Supreme Court, and to choose them from as many States-John Jay, of New York, to be chief justice; John Rutledge, of South Carolina; William Cushing, of Massachusetts; John Blair, of Virginia; James Wilson, of Pennsylvania, and R. H. Harrison, of Maryland — for he knew that the government must draw its strength from the men who administered it, and that the common run of people must learn to respect it in the persons of its officers. But he was equally careful to find out in advance of every appointment what the man whom he wished to ask thought of the new government and wished its future to be. Many to whom he offered appointment declined; minor offices seemed almost to go a-begging amongst men of assured position such as it was his object to secure. It needed all the tact and patience he could command to draw about him a body of men such as the country must look up to and revere. His letters again went abroad by the hundred, as so often before, to persuade men to their duty, build a bulwark of right opinion round about the government, make his purposes clear and his plans effective. He would spare no pains to make the government both great and permanent.

In October, 1789, his principal appointments all made, the government in full operation, and affairs standing still till Congress should meet again, he went upon a four weeks' tour through the eastern States, to put the people in mind there, by his own presence, of the existence and dignity of the federal government, and to make trial of their feeling towards it. They received him with cordial enthusiasm, for he was secure of their love and admiration; and he had once more a royal progress from place to place all the way to far New Hampshire and back again. He studiously contrived to make it everywhere felt, nevertheless, by every turn of ceremonial and behavior, that he had come, not as the hero of the Revolution, but as the President of the United States. At Boston Governor Hancock sought by cordial notes and pleas of illness to force Washington to waive the courtesy of a first call from him, and so give the executive of Massachusetts precedence, if only for old friendship's sake. But Washington would not be so defeated of his errand; forced the perturbed old patriot to come to him, swathed as he was in flannels and borne upon men's shoulders up the stairs, received him with grim courtesy, and satisfied the gossips of the town once and for all that precedence belonged to the federal government-at any rate, so long as George Washington was President. Having seen him and feted him, the eastern towns had seen and done homage to the new authority set over them. Washington was satisfied, and returned with a noticeable accession of spirits to the serious work of federal administration.

No man stood closer to him in his purpose to strengthen and give prestige to the government than Hamilton; and no man was able to discover the means with a surer genius. Hamilton knew who the well-wishers of the new government were, whence its strength was to be drawn, what it must do to approve itself great and permanent, with an insight and thoroughness Washington himself could not match: for Hamilton knew Washington and the seats of his strength in the country as that self-forgetful man himself could not. He knew that it was the commercial classes of the country — such men as he had himself dwelt amongst at the great port at New York-who were bound by self-interest to the new government, which promised them a single policy in trade, in the stead of policies a half-score; and that the men who were standing to its support out of a reasoned prudence, out of a high-minded desire to secure good government and a place of consideration for their country amongst the nations of the world, were individuals merely, to be found only in small groups here and there, where a special light shone in some minds. He knew that Washington was loved most for his national character and purpose amongst the observant middle classes of substantial people in the richer counties of Pennsylvania, New Jersey, New York, and New England, while his neighbors in the South loved him with an individual affection only, and rather as their hero than as their leader in affairs. He saw that the surest way to get both popular support and international respect was to give to the government at once and in the outset a place of command in the business and material interests of the country. Such a policy every man could comprehend, and a great body of energetic and influential men would certainly support; that alone could make the government seem real from the first—a veritable power, not an influence and a shadow merely.

CONGRESS HALL 1790-1800

Here was a man, unquestionably, who had a quick genius in affairs; and Washington gave him leave and initiative with such sympathy and comprehension and support as only a nature equally bold and equally originative could have given. Hamilton's measures jumped with Washington's purpose, ran with Washington's perception of national interests; and they were with Washington's aid put into execution with a promptness and decision which must have surprised the friends of the new government no less than it chagrined and alarmed its enemies.

Having done its work of organization during its first summer session, the Congress came together again, January 4th, 1790, to attempt the formulation of a policy of government, and Hamilton at once laid before it a "plan for the settlement of the public debt" which he had drawn and Washington had sanctioned. He proposed that provision should be made for the payment of the foreign debt in full-that of course; that the domestic debt, the despised promises and paper of the Confederation, should be funded and paid; and that the debts contracted by the several States in the prosecution of the war for independence should be assumed by the general government as the debt of the nation. No one could doubt that the foreign debt must be paid in full: to that Congress agreed heartily and without hesitation. But there was much in the rest of the plan to give prudent men pause. To pay off the paper of the Confederation would be to give to the speculators, who had bought it up in the hope of just such a measure, a gratuity of many times what they had paid for it. To assume the State debts would be taken to mean that the States were bankrupt or delinquent, that the federal government was to be their guardian and financial providence, and that the capital of the country must look only to the government of the nation, not to the government of the States, for security and profitable employment. This was nationalizing the government with a vengeance, and was a plain bid, besides, to win the moneyed class to its support. Members whose constituencies lay away from the centres of trade looked askance at such measures, and deemed them no better than handing the government over to the money lenders of the towns. But boldness and energy prevailed, as they had prevailed in the adoption of the Constitution itself, and both measures were carried through the Houses-the first at once, the second after a close and doubtful struggle-by stratagem and barter.

Jefferson had been in France when Washington called him to assume the headship of foreign affairs at home; had not reached New York on his return voyage until December 23d, 1789; and did not take his place in Washington's council till March 21st, 1790. All of Hamilton's great plan had by that time passed Congress, except the assumption of the State debts. Upon that question a crisis had been reached. It had wrought Congress to a dangerous heat of feeling. Members from the South, where trade was not much astir and financial interests told for less than local pride and sharp jealousy of a too great central power, were set hotly against the measure; most of the Northern members were as hotly resolved upon its adoption. Mr. Jefferson must have caught echoes and rumors of the great debate as he lingered at Monticello in order to adjust his private affairs before entering upon his duties in the cabinet. The measure had been lost at last in the House by the narrow margin of two votes. But the minority were in no humor to submit. They declined to transact any business at all till they should be yielded to in this matter. There were even ugly threats to be heard that some would withdraw from Congress and force a dissolution of the Union rather than make concessions upon the one side or the other.

It was to this pass that things had come when Mr. Jefferson reached the seat of government; and his arrival gave Hamilton an opportunity to show how consummate a politician he could be in support of his statesmanship. The Southern members wanted the seat of the federal government established within their reach, upon the Potomac, where Congress might at least be rid of importunate merchants and money lenders clamoring at its doors, and of impracticable Quakers with their petitions for the abolition of slavery; and were almost as hot at their failure to get their will in that matter as the Northern men were to find themselves defeated upon the question of the State debts. Mr. Jefferson was fresh upon the field, was strong among the Southern members, was not embroiled or committed in the quarrel. Hamilton besought him to intervene. The success of the government was at stake, he said, and Mr. Jefferson could pluck it out of peril. Might it not be that the Southern men would consent to vote for the assumption of the State debts if the Northern members would vote for a capital on the Potomac? The suggestion came as if upon the thought of the moment, at a chance meeting on the street, as the two men walked and talked of matters of the day; but it was very eloquently urged. Mr. Jefferson declared he was " really a stranger to the whole subject," but would be glad to lend what aid he could. Would not Mr. Hamilton dine with him the next day, to meet and confer with a few of the Southern members? In the genial air of the dinner-table the whole difficulty was talked away. Two of the diners agreed to vote for the assumption of the State debts if Mr. Hamilton could secure a majority for a capital on the Potomac; and Congress presently ratified the bargain. There was not a little astonishment at the sudden clearing of the skies. The waters did not go down at once; hints of a scandal and of the shipwreck of a fair name or two went about the town and spread to the country. But Congress had come out of its angry tangle of factions, calm had returned to the government, and Hamilton's plan stood finished and complete. He had nationalized the government as he wished.

ELEANOR PARKE CUSTIS

It was this fact that most struck the eye of Jefferson when he had settled to his work and had come to see affairs steadily and as a whole at the seat of government. He saw Hamilton supreme in the cabinet and in legislation — not because either the President or Congress was weak, but because Hamilton was a master in his new field, and both Congress and the President had accepted his leadership. It chagrined Jefferson deeply to see that he had himself assisted at Hamilton's triumph, had himself made it complete, indeed. He could not easily brook successful rivalry in leadership; must have expected to find himself, not Hamilton, preferred in the counsels of a Virginian President; was beyond measure dismayed to see the administration already in the hands, as it seemed, of a man just two months turned of thirty-three. He began ere long to declare that he had been "most ignorantly and innocently made to hold the candle" to the sharp work of the Secretary of the Treasury, having been "a stranger to the circumstances."

But it was not the circumstances of which he had been ignorant; it was the effect of what he had done upon his own wish to play the chief role in the new government. When he came to a calm scrutiny of the matter, he did not like the assumption of the State debts, and, what was more serious for a man of political ambition, it was bitterly distasteful to the very men from whom he must look to draw a following when parties should form. He felt that he had been tricked; he knew that he had been outrun in the race for leadership. What he did not understand or know how to reckon with was the place and purpose of Washington in the government. Hamilton had been Washington's aide and confidant when a lad of twenty, and knew in what way those must rule who served under such a chief. He knew that Washington must first be convinced and won; did not for a moment doubt that the President held the reins and was master; was aware that his own plans had prospered both in the making and in the adoption because the purpose they spoke was the purpose Washington most cherished. Washington had adopted the fiscal measures as his own; Hamilton's strength consisted in having his confidence and support. Jefferson had slowly to discover that leadership in the cabinet was to be had, not by winning a majority of the counsellors who sat in it, but by winning Washington. That masterful man asked counsel upon every question of consequence, but took none his own judgment did not approve. He had chosen Hamilton because he knew his views, Jefferson only because he knew his influence, ability, and experience in affairs. When he did test Jefferson's views he found them less to his liking than he had expected.

He had taken Jefferson direct from France, where for five years he had been watching a revolution come on apace, hurried from stage to stage, not by statesmen who were masters in the art and practice of freedom, like those who had presided in the counsels of America, but by demagogues and philosophers rather; and the subtle air of that age of change had crept into the man's thought He had come back a philosophical radical rather than a statesman. He had yet to learn, in the practical air of America, what plain and steady policy must serve him to win hard-headed men to his following; and Washington found him a guide who needed watching. Foreign affairs, over which it was Jefferson's duty to preside, began of a sudden to turn upon the politics of France, where Jefferson's thought was so much engaged. The year 1789, in which America gained self-possession and set up a government soberly planned to last, was the year in which France lost self-possession and set out upon a wild quest for liberty which was to cost her both her traditional polity and all the hopes she had of a new one. In that year broke the storm of the French revolution.

It was a dangerous infection that went abroad from France in those first days of her ardor, and nowhere was it more likely to spread than in America.

"Bliss was it io that dawn to be alive.

> But to be young was very heaven! O times
> In which the meagre, stale, forbidding ways
> Of custom, law, and statute took at once
> The attraction of a country in romance!
> When Reason seemed the most to assert her rights
> When most intent on making of herself
> A prime Enchantress, to assist the work
> Which then was going forward in her name!
> Not favored spots alone, but the whole earth.
> The beauty wore of promise, that which sets
> (As at some moments might not be unfelt
> Among the bowers of paradise itself)
> The budding rose above the rose full blown."

Was not this spirit that had sprang to such sudden might in France the very spirit that had made America free, her people sovereign, her government liberal as men could dream of? Was not France now more than ever America's friend and close ally against the world I 'Twould be niggardly to grudge her aid and love to the full in this day of her emulation of America's great example. The Bastile was down, tyranny at an end, Lafayette the people's leader. The gallant Frenchman himself could think of nothing more appropriate than to send the great key of the fallen fortress to Washington. But Washington's vision in affairs was not obscured. He had not led revolutionary armies without learning what revolution meant. "The revolution which has been effected in France," he said, "is of so wonderful a nature that the mind can hardly realize the fact" —his calm tones ringing strangely amidst the enthusiastic cries of the time. " I fear, though it has gone triumphantly through the first paroxysm, it is not the last it has to encounter before matters are finally settled. The revolution is of too great a magnitude to be effected in so short a space and with the loss of so little blood." He hoped, but did not believe, that it would run its course without fatal disorders; and he meant, in any case, to keep America from the infection. She was herself but "in a convalescent state," as he said, after her own great struggle. She was too observant still, moreover, of European politics and opinion, like a province rather than like a nation-inclined to take sides as if she were still a child of the European family, who had flung away from her mother England to cling in pique to an ancient foe. Washington's first and almost single object, at every point of policy, was to make of the provincial States of the Union a veritable nation, independent, at any rate, and ready to be great when its growth should come, and its self-knowledge. "Every true friend to this country," he said, at last, "must see feel that the policy of it is not to embroil ourselves with any nation whatever, but to avoid their disputes and their politics, and, if they will harass one another, to avail ourselves of the neutral conduct we have adopted. Twenty years' peace, with such an increase of population and resources as we have a right to expect, added to our remote situation from the jarring powers, will in all probability enable us, in a just cause, to bid defiance to any power on earth"; and such were his thought and purpose from the first. "I want an American, character," he cried, that the powers of Europe may be convinced we act for ourselves, and not for others." He had been given charge of a nation in the making, and he meant it should form, under his care, an independent character.

It was thus he proved himself no sentimentalist, but a statesman. It was stuff of his character, this purpose of independence. He would have played a like part of self-respect for himself among his neighbors on the Virginian plantations; and he could neither understand nor tolerate the sentiment which made men like Jefferson eager to fling themselves into European broils. Truly this man was the first American, the men about him provincials merely, dependent still for their life and thought upon the breath of the Old World, unless, like Hamilton, they had been born and had stood aloof, or, like Governor Morris, had divined Europe in her own capitals with clear, unenamoured eyes. Fortunately affairs could be held steadily enough to a course of wise neutrality and moderation at first, while France's revolution wrought only its work of internal overthrow and destruction; and while things went thus opinion began slowly to cool. 'Twas plain to be seen, as the months went by, that the work being done in France bore no real likeness at all to the revolution in America; and wise men began to see it for what it was, a social distemper, not a reformation of government-effective enough as a purge, no doubt; inevitable, perhaps; a cure of nature's own devising; but by no means to be taken part in by a people not likewise stricken, still free to choose. At first Washington and a few men of like insight stood almost alone in their cool self-possession. Every man of generous spirit deemed it his mere duty to extol the French, to join clubs after their manner, in the name of the rights of man, to speak everywhere in praise of the revolution. But by the time it became necessary to act-to declare the position and policy of the nation's government towards France —a sober second thought had come, and Washington's task was a little simplified.

The crisis came with the year 1793. In 1792 France took arms against her European neighbors, let her mobs sack the King's palace, declared herself a republic, and put her monarch on trial for his life. The opening days of 1793 saw Louis dead upon the scaffold; England, Holland,

Spain, and the Empire joined with the alliance against the fevered nation; and war as it were spread suddenly to all the world. Would not America succor her old ally? Was there no compulsion in the name of liberty? Would she stand selfishly off to save herself from danger? There was much in such a posture of affairs to give pause even to imperative men like Washington. Those who favored France seemed the spokesmen of the country. The thoughtful men, to whom the real character of the great revolution over sea was beginning to be made plain, were silent. It would have required a veritable art of divination to distinguish the real sentiment of the country, upon which, after all, the general government must depend. "It is on great occasions only, and after time has been given for cool and deliberate reflection." Washington held, "that the real voice of the people can be known"; but a great risk must be run in waiting to know it.

The measures already adopted by the government, though well enough calculated to render it strong, had not been equally well planned to make it popular. The power to tax, so jealously withheld but the other day from the Confederation, the new Congress had begun promptly and confidently to exercise upon a great scale, not only laying duties upon imports, the natural resource of the general government, but also imposing taxes upon distilled spirits, and so entering the fiscal field of the States. Not only had the war debts of the States been assumed, but a national bank had been set up (1791), as if still further to make the general government sure of a complete mastery in the field of finance. Jefferson and Randolph had fought the measure in the cabinet, as many a moderate man had fought it in Congress, and Washington had withheld his signature from it till he should hear what they had to urge. But he had sent their arguments to Hamilton for criticism, and had accepted his answer in favor of the bank. Jefferson and Randolph had challenged the measure on the ground that it was without warrant in the Constitution, which nowhere gave Congress the right to create corporations, fiscal or other. Hamilton replied that, besides the powers explicitly enumerated, the Constitution gave to Congress the power to pass any measure "necessary and proper" for executing those set forth; that Congress was itself left to determine what might thus seem necessary; and that if it deemed the erection of a bank a proper means of executing the undoubted financial powers of the government, the constitutional question was answered. By accepting such a view Washington sanctioned the whole doctrine of "implied powers," which Jefferson deemed the very annulment of a written and explicit constitution. No bounds, Jefferson believed, could be set to the aggressive sweep of congressional pretension if the two Houses were to be given leave to do whatever they thought expedient in exercising their in any case great and commanding powers. No man could doubt, in the face of such measures, what the spirit and purpose of Hamilton were, or of the President whom Hamilton so strangely dominated.

Strong measures bred strong opposition. When the first Congress came together there seemed to be no parties in the country. All men seemed agreed upon a fair and spirited trial of the new Constitution. But an opposition had begun to gather form before its two years' term was out; and in the second. Congress party lines began to grow definite-not for and against the Constitution, but for and against an extravagant use of constitutional powers. There was still a majority for the principal measures of the administration; but the minority had clearly begun to gather force both in the votes and in the debates. The reaction was unmistakable. Even Madison, Washington's stanch friend and intimate counsellor, who had at first been his spokesman in the House, began to draw back-first doubted and then opposed the policy of the Treasury. He had led the opposition to the bank, and grew more and more uneasy to note the course affairs were taking. It looked as if the administration were determined of set purpose to increase the expenses of the government, in order that they might add to the loans,which were so acceptable to influential men of wealth, and double the taxes which made the power of the government so real in the eyes of the people. Steps were urged to create a navy; to develop an army with permanent organization and equipment; and the President insisted upon vigorous action at the frontiers against the western Indians. This was part of his cherished policy. It was his way of fulfilling the vision that had long ago come to him, of a nation spreading itself down the western slopes of the mountains and over all the broad reaches of fertile land that looked towards the Mississippi; but to many a member of Congress from the quiet settlements in the east it looked like nothing better than a waste of men and of treasure. The President seemed even a little too imperious in the business: would sometimes come into the Senate in no temper to brook delay in the consideration and adoption of what he proposed in such matters. When things went wrong through the fault of the commanders he had sent to the frontier, he stormed in a sudden fury, as sometimes in the old days of the war, scorning soldiers who must needs blunder and fail. The compulsion of his will grew often a little irksome to the minority in Congress; and the opposition slowly pulled itself together as the months went by to concert a definite policy of action.

Washington saw as plainly as any man what was taking place. He was sensitive to the movements of opinion; wished above all things to have the government supported by the people's approval; was never weary of writing to those who were in a position to know, to ask them what they and their neighbors soberly thought about the questions and policies under debate; was never so impatient as to run recklessly ahead of manifest public opinion. He knew how many men had been repelled by the measures he had supported Hamilton in proposing; knew that a reaction had set in; that even to seem to repulse France and to refuse her aid or sympathy would surely strengthen it. The men who were opposed to his financial policy were also the men who most loved France, now she was mad with revolution. They were the men who dreaded a strong government as a direct menace to the rights alike of individuals and of the separate States; the men who held a very imperative philosophy of separation and of revolt against any too great authority. If he showed himself cold towards France, he would certainly strengthen them in their charge that the new government craved power and was indifferent to the guarantees of freedom.

But Washington's spirit was of the majestic sort that keeps a great and hopeful confidence that the right view will prevail; that the "standard to which the wise and honest will repair" is also the standard to which the whole people will rally at last, if it be but held long and steadily enough on high to be seen of all. When the moment for action came he acted promptly, unhesitatingly, as if in indifference to opinion. The outbreak of war between France and England made it necessary he should let the country know what he meant to do. " War having actually commenced between France and Great Britain," he wrote to Jefferson in April, 1793," it behooves the government of this country to use every means in its power to prevent the citizens thereof from embroiling us with either of those powers, by endeavoring to maintain a strict neutrality. I therefore require that you will give the subject mature consideration, that such measures as shall be deemed most likely to effect this desirable purpose may be adopted without delay. . . . Such other measures as may be necessary for us to pursue against events which it may not be in our power to avoid or control, you will also think of, and lay them before me at my arrival in Philadelphia; for which place I shall set out to-morrow." He was at Mount Vernon when he despatched these instructions; but it did not take him long to reach the seat of government, to consult his cabinet, and to issue a proclamation of neutrality whose terms no man could mistake. It contained explicit threat of exemplary action against any who should presume to disregard it.

That very month (April, 1793) Edmond Charles Genet, a youth still in his twenties whom the new republic over sea had commissioned Minister to the United States, landed at Charleston. It pleased him to take possession of the country, as if it were of course an appanage of France. He was hardly ashore before he had begun to arrange for the fitting out of privateers, to issue letters of marque to American citizens, and to authorize French consuls at American ports to act as judges of admiralty in the condemnation of prizes. As he journeyed northward to Philadelphia he was joyfully confirmed in his views and purposes by his reception at the hands of the people. He was everywhere dined and toasted and feted, as if he had been a favorite prince returned to his subjects. His speeches by the way rang in a tone of authority and patronage. He reached Philadelphia fairly mad with the sense of power, and had no conception of his real situation till he stood face to face with the President. Of that grim countenance and cold greeting there could be but one interpretation; and the fellow winced to feel that at last he had come to a grapple with the country's government. It was, no doubt, in the eyes of the sobering man, a strange and startling thing that then took place. The country itself had not fully known Washington till then-or its own dignity either. It had deemed the proclamation of neutrality a party measure, into which the President had been led by the enemies of France, the partisans of England. But the summer undeceived everybody, even Genet. Not content with the lawless mischief he had set afoot on the coasts by the commissioning of privateersmen, that mad youth had hastened to send agents into the south and west to enlist men for armed expeditions against the Floridas and against New Orleans, on the coveted Mississippi; bat his work was everywhere steadily undone. Washington acted slowly, deliberately even, with that majesty of self-control, that awful courtesy and stillness in wrath, that had ever made him a master to be feared in moments of sharp trial. One by one the unlawful prizes were seized; justice was done upon their captors; the false admiralty courts were shut up. The array of the United States was made ready to check the risings in the south and west, should there be need; the complaints of the British Minister were silenced by deeds as well as by words; the clamor of those who had welcomed the Frenchman so like provincials was ignored, though for a season it seemed the voice of the country itself; and the humiliating work, which ought never to have been necessary, was at last made effective and complete.

Towards the close of June, Washington ventured to go for a little while to Mount Vernon for rest. At once there was trouble. A privateer was found taking arms and stores aboard in the very river at Philadelphia; Jefferson allowed her to drop down to Chester, believing Genet instead of the agents of the government; and she was upon the point of getting to sea before Washington could reach the seat of government. Jefferson was not in town when the President arrived. "What is to be done in the case of the Little Sarah now at Chester?" came Washington's, hot questions after him. "Is the Minister of the French Republic to set the acts of this government at defiance with impunity? And then threaten the executive with an appeal to the people ? What must the world think of such conduct, and of the United States in submitting to it? Circumstances press for decision; and as you have had time to consider them, I wish to know your opinion upon them, even before to-morrow, for the vessel may then be gone." It was indeed too late to stop her: a gross violation of neutrality had been permitted under the very eyes of the Secretary of State. Washington stayed henceforth in Philadelphia, in personal control of affairs.

It was an appeal to the people that finally delivered Genet into his hands. Washington revoked the exequatur of one Duplaine, French consul at Boston, for continuing to ignore the laws of neutrality; Genet declared he would appeal from the President to the sovereign State of Massachusetts; rumors of the silly threat got abroad, and Genet demanded of the President that he deny them. Washington answered with a chilling rebuke; the correspondence was given to the public prints; and at last the country saw the French Minister for what he was. A demand for his recall had been resolved upon in the cabinet in August; by February, 1794, the slow processes of diplomatic action were complete, and a successor had arrived. Genet did not venture to return to his distracted country; but he was as promptly and as readily forgotten in America. Some might find it possible to love France still; but no one could any longer stomach Genet.

Washington had divined French affairs much too clearly to be for a moment tempted to think with anything but contempt of the French party who had truckled to Genet. "The affairs of France," he said to Lee, in the midst of Genet's heyday, "seem to me to be in the highest paroxysm of disorder; not so much from the presence of foreign enemies, but because those in whose hands the government is intrusted are ready to tear each other to pieces, and will more than probably prove the worst foes the country has." It was his clear perception what the danger would be should America be drawn into the gathering European wars that had led him to accept a second term as President. It had been his wish to remain only four years in the arduous office: but he had no thought to leave a task unfinished; knew that he was in the very midst of the critical business of holding the country to the course which should make it a self-respecting nation; and consented to submit himself once more to the vote of the electors. Parties were organizing, but there was no opposition to Washington. He received again a unanimous vote; and John Adams was again chosen Vice-President. The second inauguration (March, 1793) seemed but a routine confirmation of the first. But the elections to Congress showed a change setting in. In the Senate the avowed supporters of the administration had still a narrow majority; but in the House they fell ten votes short of control; and Washington had to put his policy of neutrality into execution against the mad Genet with nothing but doubts how he should be supported. The insane folly of Genet saved the President serious embarrassment, after all; made the evidence that Washington was right too plain to be missed by anybody; and gave the country at last vision enough to see what was in fact the course of affairs abroad, within and without unhappy France. Before that trying year 1793 was out, an attack upon Hamilton in the House, though led by Madison, had failed; Jefferson had left the cabinet; and the hands of those who definitely and heartily supported the President were not a little strengthened. There was sharp bitterness between parties—a bitterness sharper as yet, indeed, than their differences of view; but the "federalists," who stood to the support of Washington and Hamilton, were able, none the less, to carry their more indispensable measures — even an act of neutrality which made the President's policy the explicit law of the land. The sober second thought of the country was slowly coming about to their aid.

WASHINGTON AND NELLY CUSTIS

The air might have cleared altogether had the right method of dealing with France been the only question that pressed; but the ill fortune of the time forced the President to seem not only the recreant friend of France, but also the too complacent partisan of England. Great Britain seemed as mischievously bent upon forcing the United States to war as Genet himself had been. She would not withdraw her garrisons from the border posts; it was believed that she was inciting the Indians to their savage inroads upon the border, as the French had done in the old days; she set herself to destroy neutral trade by seizing all vessels that carried the products of the French islands or were laden with provisions for their ports; she would admit American vessels to her own West Indian harbors only upon sufferance, and within the limits of a most jealous restriction. It gave a touch of added bitterness to the country's feeling against her that she should thus levy as it were covert war upon the Union while affecting to be at peace with it, as if she counted on its weakness, especially on the seas; and Congress would have taken measures of retaliation, which must certainly have led to open hostilities, had not Washington intervened, despatching John Jay, the trusted Chief Justice, across sea as minister extraordinary, to negotiate terms of accommodation; and so giving pause to the trouble.

While the country waited upon the negotiation, it witnessed a wholesome object-lesson in the power of its new government. In March, 1791, Congress had passed an act laying taxes on distilled spirits: 'twas part of Hamilton's plan to show that the federal government could and would use its great authority. The act bore nowhere so hard upon the people as in the vast far counties of Pennsylvania and Virginia, beyond the mountains-and there the very allegiance of the people had been but the other day doubtful, as Washington very well knew. How were they to get their corn to market over the long roads if they were not to be permitted to reduce its bulk and increase its value by turning it into whiskey? The tax seemed to them intolerable, and the remedy plain. They would not pay it. They had not been punctilious to obey the laws of the States; they would not begin obedience now by submitting to the worst laws of the United States. At first they only amused themselves by tarring and feathering an exciseman here and there; but resistance could not stop with that in the face of a government bent upon having its own way. Opposition organized itself and spread, till the writs of federal courts had been defied by violent mobs and the western counties of Pennsylvania were fairly quick with incipient insurrection.

For two years Washington watched the slow gathering of the storm, warning those who resisted, keeping Congress abreast of him in preparation for action when the right time should come, letting all the country know what was afoot and prepare its mind for what was to come. It must have won him to a stern humor to learn that seven thousand armed men had gathered in mass-meeting on Braddock's field to defy him. At last he summoned an army of militia out of the States, sent it straight to the lawless counties, going with it himself till he learned there would be no serious resistance — and taught the country what was back of federal law. Hamilton had had his way, the country its lesson. "The servile copyist of Mr. Pitt thought he must have his alarms, his insurrections and plots against the Constitution," sneered Jefferson. "It aroused the favorite purposes- of strengthening government and increasing the public debt; and therefore an insurrection was announced and proclaimed and armed against and marched against, but could never be found. And all this under the sanction of a name which has done too much good not to be sufficient to cover harm also." " The powers of the executive of this country are more definite and better understood, perhaps, than those of any other country," Washington had said, "and my aim has been, and will continue to be, neither to stretch nor to relax from them in any instance whatever, unless compelled to it by imperious circumstances," and that was what he meant the country to know, whether the law's purpose was good or bad.

The next year the people knew what Mr. Jay had done. He reached New York May 28th, 1796; and the treaty he brought with him was laid before the Senate on the 8th of June. On the 2d of July the country knew what he had agreed to and the Senate had ratified. There was an instant outburst of wrath. It swept from one end of the country to the other. The treaty yielded so much, gained so little, that to accept it seemed a veritable humiliation. The northwestern posts were, indeed, to be given up at last; the boundaries between English and American territory were to be determined by commissioners; unrestricted commerce with England herself, and a free direct trade with her East Indian possessions, were conceded; but not a word was said about the impressment of American seamen; American claims for damages for unjust seizures in the West Indies were referred to a commission, along with American debts to Englishmen; the coveted trade with the West Indian islands was secured only to vessels of seventy tons and under, and at the cost of renouncing the right to export sugar, molasses, coffee, cocoa, or cotton to Europe. Washington agreed with the Senate that ratifications of the treaty ought not to be exchanged without a modification of the clauses respecting the West Indian trade, and October had come before new and better terms could be agreed upon; but he had no doubt that the treaty as a whole ought to be accepted. The opposition party in Congress had refused to vote money for an efficient navy, and so had made it impossible to check British aggressions: they must now accept this unpalatable treaty as better at any rate than war.

It was hard to stand steady in the storm. The country took fire as it had done at the passage of the Stamp Act. Harder things had never been said of king and parliament than were now said of Washington and his advisers. Many stout champions stood to his defence — none stouter or more formidable than Hamilton, no longer a member of the cabinet, for imperative private interests had withdrawn him these six months and more, but none the less redoubtable in the field of controversy. For long, nevertheless, the battle went heavily against the treaty. Even Washington, for once, stood a little while perplexed, not doubting his own purpose, indeed, but very anxious what the outcome should be. Protests against his signing the treaty poured in upon him from every quarter of the country: many of them earnest almost to the point of entreaty, some hot with angry comment. His reply, when he vouchsafed any, was always that his very gratitude for the approbation of the country in the past fixed him but the more firmly in his resolution to deserve it now by obeying his own conscience. "It is very desirable," he wrote to Hamilton, "to ascertain, if possible, after the paroxysm of the fever is a little abated, what the real temper of the people is concerning it; for at present the cry against the Treaty is like that against a mad dog;" but he showed himself very calm to the general eye, making his uneasiness known only to his intimates. The cruel abuse heaped upon him cut him to the quick. "Such exaggerated and indecent terms," he cried, "could scarcely be applied to a Nero, a notorious defaulter, or even to a common pickpocket." But the men who sneered and stormed, talked of usurpation and impeachment, called him base, incompetent, traitorous even, were permitted to see not so much as the quiver of an eyelid as they watched him go steadily from step to step in the course he had chosen.

At last the storm cleared; the bitter months were over; men at the ports saw at length how much more freely trade ran under the terms of the treaty, and remembered that, while they had been abusing Jay and maligning the President, Thomas Pinckney had obtained a treaty from Spain which settled the Florida boundary, opened the Mississippi without restriction, secured a place of deposit at New Orleans and made commerce with the Spaniards as free as commerce with the French. The whole country felt a new impulse of prosperity. The "paroxysm of the fever" was over, and shame came upon the men who had so vilely abused the great President and had made him wish, in his bitterness, that he were in his grave rather than in the Presidency; who had even said that he had played false in the Revolution, and had squandered public moneys; who had gone beyond threats of impeachment and dared to hint at assassination! They saw the end of his term approach, and would have recalled their insults. But they had alienated his great spirit forever.

When he had seen parties forming in his cabinet in the quiet days of his first term as President, he had sought to placate differences; had tried to bring Hamilton and Jefferson to a cordial understanding which should be purged of partisan bias, as he meant his own judgments to be; had deemed parties unnecessary and loyalty to the new Constitution the only standard of preferment to office. But he had come to another mind in the hard years that followed. "I shall not, whilst I have the honor to administer the government, bring a man into any office of consequence knowingly," he declared in the closing days of 1795, "whose political tenets are adverse to the tenets which the general government are pursuing; for this, in my opinion, would be a sort of political suicide;" and he left the Presidency ready to call himself very flatly a "Federalist " —of the party that stood for the Constitution and abated nothing of its powers. "You could as soon scrub a blackamore white," he cried, "as to change the principle of a profest Democrat"—"he will leave nothing unattempted to overturn the Government of this Country."

Affairs fell very quiet again as the last year of his Presidency drew towards its close. Brisk trade under the new treaties heartened the country more and more; the turbulent democratic clubs that had so noisily affected French principles and French modes of agitation were sobered and discredited, now the Reign of Terror had come and wrought its bloody work in France; the country turned once more to Washington with its old confidence and affection, and would have had him take the Presidency a third time, to keep the government steady in its new ways.

But he would not have the hard office again. On the 19th of September, 1796, he published to the people a farewell address, quick with the solemn eloquence men had come to expect from him. He wrote to Hamilton and to Madison for advice as to what he should say, as in the old

243

days of his diffident beginnings in the great office-though Hamilton was the arch-Federalist and Madison was turning Democrat-took their phrases for his thought where they seemed better than his own; put the address forth as his mature and last counsel to the little nation he loved. "It was designed," he said, "in a more especial manner for the yeomanry of the country," and spoke the advice he hoped they might take to heart. The circumstances which had given his services a temporary value, he told them, were passed; they had now a unified and national government, which might serve them for great ends. He exhorted them to preserve it intact, and not to degrade it in the using; to put down party spirit, make religion, education, and good faith the guides and safeguards of their government, and keep it national and their own by excluding foreign influences and entanglements. 'Twas a noble document. No thoughtful man could read it without emotion, knowing how it spoke in all its solemn sentences the great character of the man whose career was ended.

When the day came on which he should resign his office to John Adams, the great civilian who was to succeed him, there was a scene which left no one in doubt-not even Washington himself-what the people thought of the leader they had trusted these twenty years. A great crowd was assembled to see the simple ceremonies of the inauguration, as on that April day in New York eight years ago; but very few in the throng watched Adams. All eyes were bent upon that great figure in black velvet, with a light sword slung at his side. No one stirred till he had left the room, to follow and pay his respects to the new President. Then they and all the crowd in the streets moved after him, an immense company, going as one man, "in total silence," his escort all the way. He turned upon the threshold of the President's lodgings and looked, as if for the last time, upon this multitude of nameless friends. " No man ever saw him so moved." The tears rolled unchecked down his cheeks; and when at last he went within, a great smothered common voice went through the stirred throng, as if they sobbed to see their hero go from their sight forever.

It had been noted how cheerful he looked, at thought of his release, as he entered the hall of the Representatives, where Mr. Adams was to take the oath. As soon as possible he was at his beloved Mount Vernon once more, to pick up such threads as he might of the old life again. "I begin my diurnal course with the sun," he wrote, in grave playfulness, to a friend; "if my hirelings are not in their places by that time, I send them messages of sorrow for their indisposition; having put these wheels in motion, I examine the state of things further; the more they are probed the deeper I find the wounds which my buildings have sustained by an absence and neglect of eight years; by the time I have accomplished these matters breakfast (a little after seven o'clock, about the time, I presume, that you are taking leave of Mrs. McHenry) is ready; this being over, I mount my horse and ride round my farms, which employs me until it is time to dress for dinner.... The usual time of sitting at the table, a walk, and tea bring me within the dawn of candlelight; previous to which, if not prevented by company, I resolve that as soon as the glimmering taper supplies the place of the great luminary I will retire to my writing-table and acknowledge the letters I have received; when the lights are brought I feel tired and disinclined to engage in this work, conceiving that the next night will do as well. The next night comes, and with it the same causes for postponement, and so on. Having given you the history of a day, it will serve for a year, and I am persuaded that you will not require a second edition of it." He had kept his overseers under his hand all the time he was President; had not forgotten to write to Dr. Young upon methods of cultivation; had shown the same passion as ever for speeding and regulating at its best every detail of his private business; but matters had gone ill for lack of his personal supervision. He was obliged to sell no less than fifty thousand dollars worth of his lands in the course of four or five years to defray the great expenses he was put to in the Presidency and the cost of bringing his estate into solvent shape again. He did not try to begin anew; he only set things in order, and kept his days serene.

A spark of war was kindled by the new administration's dealings with France, and Washington was called once more to prepare for command, should the fighting leave the sea and come ashore. But formal war did not come. The flurry only kept him a little nearer the movements of politics than he cared to be. He was the more uneasy to see how the Democrats bore themselves in the presence of the moment's peril; doubted the expediency of assigning men of that party to places of command in the army; approved the laws passed against aliens and against those who should utter seditious libel against the government; showed again, and without reserve, how deeply his affections were engaged on the side of the institutions he had so labored to set up and protect; was intolerant towards any who sought to touch or question at any point their new authority — imperious as of old in question of action.

HANOVER COURT-HOUSE

THE OLD TOMB, MOUNT VERNON

But it was his home that chiefly held his thought now. He had not changed towards his friends through all the long years of public care and engrossing business. An old comrade, who had come in his rough frontier dress all the way from far Kentucky to Philadelphia to see the President, had been told "that Washington had become puffed up with the importance of his station, and was too much of an aristocrat to welcome him in that garb." But the old soldier was not daunted, pressed on to make his call, and came back to tell his friends how the President and his lady had both seen him and recognized him from the window, and had hurried to the door to draw him cordially in. "I never was better treated," he said. "I had not believed a word against him; and I found that he was 'Old Hoss' still." 'Twas the same with his neighbors, and with strangers too. He was the simple gentleman of the old days. A strolling actor, riding Mount Vernon way on a day in July, stopped to help a man and woman who had been thrown from their chaise, and did not recognize the stalwart horseman who galloped up to his assistance till the overturned vehicle had been set up again, they had dusted each the other's coat, and the stately stranger, saying he had had the pleasure of seeing him play in Philadelphia, had bidden him come to the house yonder and be refreshed. "Have I the honor of addressing General Washington?" exclaimed the astonished player. "An odd sort of introduction, Mr. Bernard," smiled the heated soldier; "but I am pleased to find you can play so active a part in private, and without a prompter."

Those who saw him now at Mount Vernon thought him gentler with little children than Mrs. Washington even, and remembered how he had always shown a like love and tenderness for them, going oftentimes out of his way to warn them of danger, with a kindly pat on the head, when he saw them watching the soldiers in the war days. Now all at Mount Vernon looked forward to the evening. That "was the children's hour." He had written sweet Nelly Custis a careful letter of advice upon love matters, half grave, half playful, in the midst of his Presidency, when the troubles with England were beginning to darken; she had always found him a comrade, and had loved him with an intimacy very few could know. Now she was to be married, to his own sister's son, and upon his birthday, February 22d, 1799. She begged him to wear the "grand embroidered uniform," just made for the French war, at her wedding; but he shook his head and donned instead the worn buff and blue that had seen real campaigns. Then the delighted girl told him, with her arm about his neck, that she loved him better in that.

The quiet days went by without incident. He served upon a petty jury of the county when summoned; and was more than content to be the simple citizen again, great duties put by, small ones diligently resumed.

Once and again his anger flamed at perverse neglects and tasks ill done. Even while he was President, he had stormed to find his horses put to the chariot with unpolished hoofs upon a day of ceremony. But old age, and the consciousness of a lifework done, had added serenity now to his self-control; and at last the end came, when he was ready. On the 12th of December, 1799, he was chilled through by the keen winds and cold rain and sleet that beat upon him as he went his round about the farms. He spent the evening cheerfully, listening to his secretary read; but went to bed with a gathering hoarseness and cold, and woke in the night sharply stricken in his throat. Physicians came almost at dawn, but the disease was already beyond their control. Nothing that they' tried could stay it; and by evening the end had come. He was calm the day through, as in a time of battle; knowing what be-tided, but not fearing it; steady, noble, a warrior figure to the last; and he died as those who loved him might have wished to see him die.

The country knew him when he was dead: knew the majesty, the nobility, the unsulh'ed greatness of the man who was gone, and knew not whether to mourn or give praise. He could not serve them any more; but they saw his light shine already upon the future as upon the past, and were glad. They knew him now the Happy Warrior,

> "Whose powers shed round him, in the common strife
>   Or mild concerns of ordinary life,
>   A constant influence, a peculiar grace;
>   But who, if he be called upon to face

Some awful moment to which Heaven has joined
Great issues, good or bad, for humankind,
Is happy as a Lover; and attired
With sudden brightness, like a man inspired;
And, through the heat of conflict, keeps the law
In calmness made, and sees what he foresaw.

* *

A soul whose master-bias leans
To homefelt pleasures and to gentle scenes;

* *

More brave for this, that he hath much to love:-

* * * the man, who, lifted high,
Conspicuous object in a nation's eye,
Or left unthought of in obscurity.-
Who, with a toward or untoward lot,
Prosperous or adverse, to his wish or not,
Plays, in the many games of life, that one
Where what he most doth value must be won."

On Being Human

I

"The rarest sort of a book," says Mr. Bagehot, slyly, is "a book to read"; and "the knack in style is to write like a human being." It is painfully evident, upon experiment, that not many of the books which come teeming from our presses every year are meant to be read. They are meant, it may be, to be pondered; it is hoped, no doubt, they may instruct, or inform, or startle, or arouse, or reform, or provoke, or amuse us; but we read, if we have the true reader's zest and plate, not to grow more knowing, but to be less pent up and bound within a little circle, —as those who take their pleasure, and not as those who laboriously seek instruction, —as a means of seeing and enjoying the world of men and affairs. We wish companionship and renewal of spirit, enrichment of thought and the full adventure of the mind; and we desire fair company, and a larger world in which to find them.

No one who loves the masters who may be communed with and read but must see, therefore, and resent the error of making the text of any one of them a source to draw grammar from, forcing the parts of speech to stand out stark and cold from the warm text; or a store of samples whence to draw rhetorical instances, setting up figures of speech singly and without support of any neighbor phrase, to be stared at curiously and with intent to copy or dissect! Here is grammar done without deliberation: the phrases carry their meaning simply and by a sort of limpid reflection; the thought is a living thing, not an image ingeniously contrived and wrought. Pray leave the text whole: it has no meaning piecemeal; at any rate, not that best, wholesome meaning, as of a frank and genial friend who talks, not for himself or for his phrase, but for you. It is questionable morals to dismember a living frame to seek for its obscure fountains of life!

When you say that a book was meant to be read, you mean, for one thing, of course, that it was not meant to be studied. You do not study a good story, or a haunting poem, or a battle song, or a love ballad, or any moving narrative, whether it be out of history or out of fiction-nor any argument, even, that moves vital in the field of action. You do not have to study these things; they reveal themselves, you do not stay to see how. They remain with you, and will not be forgotten or laid by. They cling like a personal experience, and become the mind's intimates. You devour a book meant to be read, not because you would fill yourself or have an anxious care to be nourished, but because it contains such stuff as it makes the mind hungry to look upon. Neither do you read it to kill time, but to lengthen time, rather, adding to its natural usury by living the more abundantly while it lasts, joining another's life and thought to your own.

There are a few children in every generation, as Mr. Bagehot reminds us, who think the natural thing to do with any book is to read it. "There is an argument from design in the subject," as he says; "if the book was not meant to be read for that purpose, for what purpose was it meant?" These are the young eyes to which books yield up great treasure, almost in spite of themselves, as if they had been penetrated by some swift, enlarging power of vision which only the young know. It is these youngsters to whom books give up the long ages of history, "the wonderful series going back to the times of old patriarchs with their flocks and herds"—I am quoting Mr. Bagehot again—"the keen-eyed Greek, the stately Roman, the watching Jew, the uncouth Goth, the horrid Hun, the settled picture of the unchanging East, the restless shifting of the rapid West, the rise of the cold and classical civilization, its fall, the rough impetuous Middle Ages, the vague warm picture of ourselves and home. When did we learn these? Not yesterday nor today, but long ago, in the first dawn of reason, in the original flow of fancy." Books will not yield to us so richly when we are older. The argument from design fails. We return to the staid authors we read long ago, and do not find in them the vital, speaking images that used to lie there upon the page. Our own fancy is gone, and the author never had any. We are driven in upon the books meant to be read.

These are books written by human beings, indeed, but with no general quality belonging to the kind-with a special tone and temper, rather, a spirit out of the common, touched with a light that shines clear out of some great source of light which not every man can uncover. We call this spirit human because it moves us, quickens a like life in ourselves, makes us glow with a sort of ardor of self-discovery. It touches the springs of fancy or of action within us, and makes our own life seem more quick and vital. We do not call every book that moves us human. Some seem written with knowledge of the black art, set our base passions aflame, disclose motives at which we shudder-the more because we feel their reality and power; and we know that this is of the devil, and not the fruitage of any quality that distinguishes us as men. We are distinguished as men by the qualities that mark us different from the beasts. When we call a thing human we have a spiritual ideal in mind. It may not be an ideal of that which is perfect, but it moves at least upon an upland level where the air is sweet; it holds an image of man erect and constant, going abroad with undaunted steps, looking with frank and open gaze upon all the fortunes of his day, feeling even and again —

> ". . . the joy
> Of elevated thoughts; a sense sublime
> Of something far more deeply interfused.
> Whose dwelling is the light of setting suns.
> And the round ocean and the living air,
> And the blue sky, and in the mind of man:
> A motion and a spirit, that impels
> All thinking things."

Say what we may of the errors and the degrading sins of our kind, we do not willingly make what is worst in us the distinguishing trait of what is human. When we declare, with Bagehot, that the author whom we love writes like a human being, we are not sneering at him; we do not say it with a leer. It is in token of admiration, rather. He makes us like our humankind. There is a noble passion in what he says, a wholesome humor that echoes genial comradeships; a certain reasonableness and moderation in what is thought and said; an air of the open day, in which things are seen whole and in their right colors, rather than of the close study or the academic class-room. We do not want our poetry from grammarians, nor our tales from philologists, nor our history from theorists. Their human nature is subtly transmuted into something less broad and catholic and of the general world. Neither do we want our political economy from tradesmen nor our statesmanship from mere politicians, but from those who see more and care for more than these men see or care for.

II

Once-it is a thought which troubles us-once it was a simple enough matter to be a human being, but now it is deeply difficult; because life was once simple, but is now complex, confused, multifarious. Haste, anxiety, preoccupation, the need to specialize and make machines of ourselves, have transformed the once simple world, and we are apprised that it will not be without effort that we shall keep the broad human traits which have so far made the earth habitable. We have seen our modern life accumulate, hot and restless, in great cities-and we cannot say that the change is not natural: we see in it, on the contrary, the fulfillment of an inevitable law of change, which is no doubt a law of growth, and not of decay. And yet we look upon the portentous thing with a great distaste, and doubt with what altered passions we shall come out of it. The huge, rushing, aggregate life of a great city-the crushing crowds in the streets, where friends seldom meet and there are few greetings; the thunderous noise of trade and industry that speaks of nothing but gain and competition, and a consuming fever that checks the natural courses of the kindly blood; no leisure anywhere, no quiet, no restful ease, no wise repose-all this shocks us. It is inhumane. It does not seem human. How much more likely does it appear that we shall find men sane and human about a country fireside, upon the streets of quiet villages, where all are neighbors, where groups of friends gather easily, and a constant sympathy makes the very air seem native! Why should not the city seem infinitely more human than the hamlet? Why should not human traits the more abound where human beings teem millions strong?

Because the city curtails man of his wholeness, specializes him, quickens some powers, stunts others, gives him a sharp edge, and a temper like that of steel, makes him unfit for nothing so much as to sit still. Men have indeed written like human beings in the midst of great cities, but not often when they have shared the city's characteristic life, its struggle for place and for gain. There are not many places that belong to a city's life to which you can "invite your soul." Its haste, its preoccupations, its anxieties, its rushing noise as of men driven, its ringing cries, distract you. It offers no quiet for reflection; it permits no retirement to any who share its life. It is a place of little tasks, of narrowed functions, of aggregate and not of individual strength. The great machine dominates its little parts, and its Society is as much of a machine as its business.

"This tract which the river of Time
  Now flows through with us, is the plain.
  Gone is the calm of its earlier shore.
  Border'd by cities, and hoarse
  With a thousand cries is its stream.
  And we on its breast, our minds
  Are confused as the cries which we hear,
  Changing and shot as the sights which we see.

"And we say that repose has fled
  Forever the course of the river of Time
  That cities will crowd to its edge
  In a blacker, incessanter line;
  That the din will be more on its banks,
  Denser the trade on its stream,
  Flatter the plain where it flows,
  Fiercer the sun overhead,
  That never will those on its breast
  See an enobling sight,
  Drink of the feeling of quiet again.

"But what was before us we know not,
    And we know not what shall succeed.

"Haply, the river of Time —
    As it grows, as the towns on its marge
    Fling their wavering lights
    On a wider, statelier stream —
    May acquire, if not the calm
    Of its early mountainous shore,
    Yet a solemn peace of its own.

"And the width of the waters, the hush
    Of the gray expanse where he floats,
    Freshening its current and spotted with foam
    As it draws to the Ocean, may strike
    Peace to the soul of the man on its breast —
    As the pale waste widens around him,
    As the banks fade dimmer away,
    As the stars come out, and the night-wind
    Brings up the stream
    Murmurs and scents of the infinite sea."

We cannot easily see the large measure and abiding purpose of the novel age in which we stand young and confused. The view that shall clear our minds and quicken us to act as those who know their task and its distant consummation will come with better knowledge and completer self-possession. It shall not be a night-wind, but an air that shall blow out of the widening east and with the coming of the light, and shall bring us, with the morning, "murmurs and scents of the infinite sea." Who can doubt that man has grown more and more human with each step of that slow process which has brought him knowledge, self-restraint, the arts of intercourse, and the revelations of real joy? Man has more and more lived with his fellow-men, and it is society that has humanized him-the development of society into an infinitely various school of discipline and ordered skill. He has been made more human by schooling, by growing more self-possessed —less violent, less tumultuous; holding himself in hand, and moving always with a certain poise of spirit; not forever clapping his hand to the hilt of his sword, but preferring, rather, to play with a subtler skill upon the springs of action. This is our conception of the truly human man: a man in whom there is a just balance of faculties, a catholic sympathy-no brawler, no fanatic, no pharisee; not too credulous in hope, not too desperate in purpose; warm, but not hasty; ardent, and full of definite power, but not running about to be pleased and deceived by every new thing.

    It is a genial image of men we love-an image of men warm and true of heart, direct and unhesitating in courage, generous, magnanimous, faithful, steadfast, capable of a deep devotion and self-forgetfulness. But the age changes, and with it must change our ideals of human quality. Not that we would give up what we have loved: we would add what a new life demands. In a new age men must acquire a new capacity, must be men upon a new scale, and with added qualities. We shall need a new Renaissance, ushered in by a new "humanistic" movement, in which we shall add our present minute, introspective study of ourselves, our jails, our slums, our nerve centers, our shifts to live, almost as morbid as medieval religion, a rediscovery of the round world, and of man's place in it, now that its face has changed. We study the world, but not yet with intent to school our hearts and tastes, broaden our natures, and know our fellow-men as comrades rather than as phenomena; with purpose, rather, to build up bodies of critical doctrine and provide ourselves with theses. That, surely, is not the truly humanizing way in which to take the air of the world. Man is much more than a "rational being," and lives more by sympathies and impressions than by conclusions. It darkens his eyes and dries up the wells of his humanity to be forever in search of doctrine. We need wholesome, experiencing natures, I dare affirm, much more than we need sound reasoning.

III

Take life in the large view, and we are most reasonable when we seek that which is most wholesome and tonic for our natures as a whole; and we know, when we put aside pedantry, that the great middle object in life-the object that lies between religion on one hand, and food and clothing on the other, establishing our average levels of achievement-the excellent golden mean, is, not to be learned, but to be human beings in all the wide and genial meaning of the term. Does the age hinder? Do its many interests distract us when we would plan our discipline, determine our duty, clarify our ideals? It is the more necessary that we should ask ourselves what it is that is demanded of us, if we would fit our qualities to meet the new tests. Let us remind ourselves that to be human is, for one thing, to speak and act with a certain note of genuineness, a quality mixed of spontaneity and intelligence. This is necessary for wholesome life in any age, but particularly amidst confused affairs and shifting standards. Genuineness is not mere simplicity, for that may lack vitality, and genuineness does not. We expect what we call genuine to have pith and strength of fiber. Genuineness is a quality which we sometimes mean to include when we speak of individuality. Individuality is lost the moment you submit to passing modes or fashions, the creations of an artificial society; and so is genuineness. No man is genuine who is forever trying to pattern his life after the lives of other people-unless, indeed, he be a genuine dolt. But individuality is by no means the same as genuineness; for individuality may be associated with the most extreme and even ridiculous eccentricity, while genuineness we conceive to be always wholesome, balanced, and touched with dignity. It is a quality that goes with good sense and self-respect. It is a sort of robust moral sanity, mixed of elements both moral and intellectual. It is found in natures too strong to be mere trimmers and conformers, too well poised and thoughtful to fling off into intemperate protest and revolt. Laughter is genuine which has in it neither the shrill, hysterical note of mere excitement nor the hard, metallic twang of the cynic's sneer-which rings in the honest voice of gracious good humor, which is innocent and unsatirical. Speech is genuine which is without silliness, affectation, or pretense. That character is genuine which seems built by nature rather than by convention, which is stuff of independence and of good courage. Nothing spurious, bastard, begotten out of true wedlock of the mind; nothing adulterated and seeming to be what it is not; nothing unreal, can ever get place among the nobility of things genuine, natural, of pure stock and unmistakable lineage. It is a prerogative of every truly human being to come out from the low estate of those who are merely gregarious and of the herd, and show his innate powers cultivated and yet unspoiled-sound, unmixed, free from imitation; showing that individualization without extravagance which is genuineness.

But how? By what means is this self-liberation to be effected-this emancipation from affectation and the bondage of being like other people? Is it open to us to choose to be genuine? I see nothing insuperable in the way, except for those who are hopelessly lacking in a sense of humor. It depends upon the range and scale of your observation whether you can strike the balance of genuineness or not. If you live in a small and petty world, you will be subject to its standards; but if you live in a large world, you will see that standards are innumerable-some old, some new, some made by the noble-minded and made to last, some made by the weak-minded and destined to perish, some lasting from age to age, some only from day to day-and that a choice must be made among them. It is then that your sense of humor will assist you. You are, you will perceive, upon a long journey, and it will seem to you ridiculous to change your life and discipline your instincts to conform with the usages of a single inn by the way. You will distinguish the essentials from the accidents, and deem the accidents something meant for your amusement. The strongest natures do not need to wait for these slow lessons of observation, to be got by conning life: their sheer vigor makes it impossible for them to conform to fashion or care for times and seasons. But the rest of us must cultivate knowledge of the world in the large, get our offing, reaching a comparative point of view, before we can become with steady confidence our own masters and pilots. The art of being human begins with the practice of being genuine, and following standards of conduct which the world has tested. If your life is not various and you cannot know the best people, who set the standards of sincerity, your reading at least can be various, and you may look at your little circle through the best books, under the guidance of writers who have known life and loved the truth.

IV

And then genuineness will bring serenity-which I take to be another mark of the right development of the true human being, certainly in an age passionate and confused as this in which we live. Of course serenity does not always go with genuineness. We must say of Dr. Johnson that he was genuine, and yet we know that the stormy tyrant of the Turk's Head Tavern was not serene. Carlyle was genuine (though that is not quite the first adjective we should choose to describe him), but of serenity he allowed cooks and cocks and every modern and every ancient sham to deprive him. Serenity is a product, no doubt, of two very different things, namely, vision and digestion. Not the eye only, but the courses of the blood must be clear, if we would find serenity. Our word "serene" contains a picture. Its image is of the calm evening when the stars are out and the still night comes on; when the dew is on the grass and the wind does not stir; when the day's work is over, and the evening meal, and thought falls clear in the quiet hour. It is the hour of reflection-and it is human to reflect. Who shall contrive to be human without this evening hour, which drives turmoil out, and gives the soul its seasons of self-recollection? Serenity is not a thing to beget inaction. It only checks excitement and uncalculating haste. It does not exclude ardor or the heat of battle: it keeps ardor from extravagance, prevents the battle from becoming a mere aimless melee. The great captains of the world have been men who were calm in the moment of crisis; who were calm, too, in the long planning which preceded crisis; who went into battle with a serenity infinitely ominous for those whom they attack. We instinctively associate serenity with the highest types of power among men, seeing in it the poise of knowledge and calm vision, the supreme heat and mastery which is without splutter or noise of any kind. The art of power in this sort is no doubt learned in hours of reflection, by those who are not born with it. What rebuke of aimless excitement there is to be got out of a little reflection, when we have been inveighing against the corruption and decadence of our own days, if only we have provided ourselves with a little knowledge of the past wherewith to balance our thought! As bad times as these, or any we shall see, have been reformed, but not by protests. They have been made glorious instead of shameful by the men who kept their heads and struck with sure self-possession in the fight. The world is very human, not a bit given to adopting virtues for the sakes of those who merely bemoan its vices, and we are most effective when we are most calmly in possession of our senses.

So far is serenity from being a thing of slackness or inaction that it seems bred, rather, by an equable energy, a satisfying activity. It may be found in the midst of that alert interest in affairs which is, it may be, the distinguishing trait of developed manhood. You distinguish man from the brute by his intelligent curiosity, his play of mind beyond the narrow field of instinct, his perception of cause and effect in matters to him indifferent, his appreciation of motive and calculation of results. He is interested in the world about him, and even in the great universe of which it forms a part, not merely as a thing he would use, satisfy his wants and grow great by, but as a field to stretch his mind in, for love of journeyings and excursions in the large realm of thought. Your full-bred human being loves a run afield with his understanding. With what images does he not surround himself and store his mind! With what fondness does he con travelers' tales and credit poets' fancies! With what patience does he follow science and pore upon old records, and with what eagerness does he ask the news of the day! No great part of what he learns immediately touches his own life or the course of his own affairs: he is not pursuing a business, but satisfying as he can an insatiable mind. No doubt the highest form of this noble curiosity is that which leads us, without self-interest, to look abroad upon all the field of man's life at home and in society, seeking more excellent forms of government, more righteous ways of labor, more elevating forms of art, and which makes the greater among us statesmen, reformers, philanthropists, artists, critics, men of letters. It is certainly human to mind your neighbor's business as well as your own. Gossips are only sociologists upon a mean and petty scale. The art of being human lifts to be a better level than that of gossip; it leaves mere chatter behind, as too reminiscent of a lower stage of existence, and is compassed by those whose outlook is wide enough to serve for guidance and a choosing of ways.

V

Luckily we are not the first human beings. We have come into a great heritage of interesting things, collected and piled all about us by the curiosity of past generations. And so our interest is selective. Our education consists in learning intelligent choice. Our energies do not clash or compete: each is free to take his own path to knowledge. Each has that choice, which is man's alone, of the life he shall live, and finds out first or last that the art in living is not only to be genuine and one's own master, but also to learn mastery in perception and preference. Your true woodsman needs not to follow the dusty highway through the forest nor search for any path, but goes straight from glade to glade as if upon an open way, having some privy understanding with the taller trees, some compass in his senses. So there is the subtle craft in finding ways for the mind, too. Keep but your eyes alert and your ears quick, as you move among men and among books, and you shall find yourself possessed at last of a new sense, the sense of the pathfinder. Have you never marked the eyes of a man who has seen the world he has lived in: the eyes of the sea-captain, who has watched his life through the changes of the heavens; the eyes of the huntsman, nature's gossip and familiar; the eyes of the man of affairs, accustomed to command in moments of exigency? You are at once aware that they are eyes which can see. There is something in them that you do not find in other eyes, and you have read the life of the man when you have divined what it is. Let the thing serve as a figure. So ought alert interest in the world of men and thought to serve each one of us that we shall have the quick perceiving vision, taking meanings at a glance, reading suggestions as if they were expositions. You shall not otherwise get full value of your humanity. What good shall it do you else that the long generations of men which have gone before have filled the world with great store of everything that may make you wise and your life various? Will you not take the usury of the past, if it may be had for the taking? Here is the world humanity has made: will you take full citizenship in it, or will you live in it as dull, as slow to receive, as unenfranchised, as the idlers for whom civilization has no uses, or the deadened toilers, men or beasts, whose labor shuts the door on choice?

That man seems to me a little less than human who lives as if our life in the world were but just begun, thinking only of the things of sense, reckoning nothing of the infinite thronging and assemblage of affairs the great stage over, or of the old wisdom that has ruled the world. That is, if he have the choice. Great masses of our fellow-men are shut out from choosing, by reason of absorbing toil, and it is part of the enlightenment of our age that our understandings are being opened to the workingman's need of a little leisure wherein to look about him and clear his vision of the dust of the workshop. We know that there is a drudgery which is inhuman, let it but encompass the whole life, with only heavy sleep between task and task. We know that those who are so bound can have no freedom to be men, that their very spirits are in bondage. It is part of our philanthropy-it should be part of our statesmanship-to ease the burden as we can, and enfranchise those who spend and are spent for the sustenance of the race. But what shall we say of those who are free and yet choose littleness and bondage, or of those who, though they might see the whole face of society, nevertheless choose to spend all a life's space poring upon some single vice or blemish? I would not for the world discredit any sort of philanthropy except the small and churlish sort which seeks to reform by nagging-the sort which exaggerates petty vices into great ones, and runs atilt against windmills, while everywhere colossal shams and abuses go unexposed, unrebuked. Is it because we are better at being common scolds than at being wise advisers that we prefer little reforms to big ones? Are we to allow the poor personal habits of other people to absorb and quite use up all our fine indignation? It will be a bad day for society when sentimentalists are encouraged to suggest all the measures that shall be taken for the betterment of the race. I, for one, sometimes sigh for the generation of "leading people" and of good people who shall see things steadily and see them whole; who shall show a handsome justness and a large sanity of view, an opportune tolerance for details, that happen to be awry, in order that they may spend their energy, not without self-possession, in some generous mission which shall make right principles shine upon the people's life. They would bring with them an age of large moralities, a spacious time, a day of vision.

Knowledge has come into the world in vain if it is not to emancipate those who may have it from narrowness, censoriousness, fussiness, an intemperate zeal for petty things. It would be a most pleasant, a truly humane world, would we but open our ears with a more generous welcome to the clear voices that ring in those writings upon life and affairs which mankind has chosen to keep. Not many splenetic books, not many intemperate, not many bigoted, have kept men's confidence; and the mind that is impatient, or intolerant, or hoodwinked, or shut in to a petty view shall have no part in carrying men forward to a true humanity, shall never stand as examples of the true humankind. What is truly human has always upon it the broad light of what is genial, fit to support life, cordial, and of a catholic spirit of helpfulness. Your true human being has eyes and keeps his balance in the world; deems nothing uninteresting that comes from life; clarifies his vision and gives health to his eyes by using them upon things near and things far. The brute beast has but a single neighborhood, a single, narrow round of existence; the gain of being human accrues in the choice of change and variety and of experience far and wide, with all the world for stage —a stage set and appointed by this very art of choice-all future generations for witnesses and audience. When you talk with a man who has in his nature and acquirements that freedom from constraint which goes with the full franchise of humanity, he turns easily with topic to topic; does not fall silent or dull when you leave some single field of thought such as unwise men make a prison of. The men who will not be broken from a little set of subjects, who talk earnestly, hotly, with a sort of fierceness, of certain special schemes of conduct, and look coldly upon everything else, render you infinitely uneasy, as if there were in them a force abnormal and which rocked toward an upset of the mind; but from the man whose interest swings from thought to thought with the zest and poise and pleasure of the old traveler, eager for what is new, glad to look again upon what is old, you come away with faculties warmed and heartened-with the feeling of having been comrade for a little with a genuine human being. It is a large world and a round world, and men grow human by seeing all its play of force and folly.

VI

Let no one suppose that efficiency is lost by such breadth and catholicity of view. We deceive ourselves with instances, look at sharp crises in the world's affairs, and imagine that intense and narrow men have made history for us. Poise, balance, a nice and equable exercise of force, are not, it is true, the things the world ordinarily seeks for or most applauds in its heroes. It is apt to esteem that man most human who has his qualities in a certain exaggeration, whose courage is passionate, whose generosity is without deliberation, whose just action is without premeditation, whose spirit runs toward its favorite objects with an infectious and reckless ardor, whose wisdom is no child of slow prudence. We love Achilles more than Diomedes, and Ulysses not at all. But these are standards left over from a ruder state of society: we should have passed by this time the Homeric stage of mind-should have heroes suited to our age. Nay, we have erected different standards, and do make a different choice, when we see in any man fulfillment of our real ideals. Let a modern instance serve as test. Could any man hesitate to say that Abraham Lincoln was more human than William Lloyd Garrison? Does not every one know that it was the practical Free-Soilers who made emancipation possible, and not the hot, impracticable Abolitionists; that the country was infinitely more moved by Lincoln's temperate sagacity than by any man's enthusiasm, instinctively trusted the man who saw the whole situation and kept his balance, instinctively held off from those who refused to see more than one thing? We know how serviceable the intense and headlong agitator was in bringing to their feet men fit for action; but we feel uneasy while he lives, and vouchsafe him our full sympathy only when he is dead. We know that the genial forces of nature which work daily, equably, and without violence are infinitely more serviceable, infinitely more admirable, than the rude violence of the storm, however necessary or excellent the purification it may have wrought. Should we seek to name the most human man among those who led the nation to its struggle with slavery, and yet was no statesmen, we should, of course, name Lowell. We know that his humor went further than any man's passion toward setting tolerant men atingle with the new impulses of the day. We naturally hold back from those who are intemperate and can never stop to smile, and are deeply reassured to see a twinkle in a reformer's eye. We are glad to see earnest men laugh. It breaks the strain. If it be wholesome laughter, it dispels all suspicion of spite, and is like the gleam of light upon running water, lifting sullen shadows, suggesting clear depths.

Surely it is this soundness of nature, this broad and genial quality, this full-blooded, full-orbed sanity of spirit, which gives the men we love that wide-eyed sympathy which gives hope and power to humanity, which gives range to every good quality and is so excellent a credential of genuine manhood. Let your life and your thought be narrow, and your sympathy will shrink to a like scale. It is a quality which follows the seeing mind afield, which waits on experience. It is not a mere sentiment. It goes not with pity so much as with a penetrative understanding of other men's lives and hopes and temptations. Ignorance of these things makes it worthless. Its best tutors are observations and experience, and these serve only those who keep clear eyes and a wide field of vision. It is exercise and discipline upon such a scale, too, which strengthen, which for ordinary men come near to creating, that capacity to reason upon affairs and to plan for action which we always reckon upon finding in every man who has studied to perfect his native force. This new day in which we live cries a challenge to us. Steam and electricity have reduced nations to neighborhoods; have made travel pastime, and news a thing for everybody. Cheap printing has made knowledge a vulgar commodity. Our eyes look, almost without choice, upon the very world itself, and the word "human" is filled with new meaning. Our ideals broaden to suit the wide day in which we live. We crave, not cloistered virtue-it is impossible any longer to keep the cloister-but a robust spirit that shall take the air in the great world, know men in all their kinds, choose its way amid the bustle with all self-possession, with wise genuineness, in calmness, and yet with the quick eye of interest and the quick pulse of power. It is again a day for Shakespeare's spirit —a day more various, more ardent, more provoking to valor and every large design, even than "the spacious times of great Elizabeth," when all the world seemed new; and if we cannot find another bard, come out of a new Warwickshire, to hold once more the mirror up to nature, it will not be because the stage is not set for him. The time is such an one as he might rejoice to look upon; and if we would serve it as it should be served, we should seek to be human after his wide-eyed sort. The serenity of power; the naturalness that is nature's poise and mark of genuineness; the unsleeping interest in all affairs, all fancies, all things believed or done; the catholic understanding, tolerance, enjoyment, of all classes and conditions of men; the conceiving imagination, the planning purpose, the creating thought, the wholesome, laughing humor, the quiet insight, the universal coinage of the brain-are not these the marvelous gifts and qualities we mark in Shakespeare when we call him the greatest among men? And shall not these rounded and perfect powers serve us as our ideal of what it is to be a finished human being?

We live for our own age-an age like Shakespeare's, when an old world is passing away, a new world coming in-an age of new speculation and every new adventure of the mind; a full stage, an intricate plot, a universal play of passion, an outcome no man can foresee. It is to this world, this sweep of action, that our understandings must be stretched and fitted; it is in this age we must show our human quality. We must measure ourselves by the task, accept the pace set for us, make shift to know what we are about. How free and liberal should be the scale of our sympathy, how catholic our understanding of the world in which we live, how poised and masterful our action in the midst of so great affairs! We should school our ears to know the voices that are genuine, our thought to take the truth when it is spoken, our spirits to feel the zest of the day. It is within our choice to be with mean company or with great, to consort with the wise or with the foolish, now that the great world has spoken to us in the literature of all tongues and voices. The best selected human nature will tell in the making of the future, and the art of being human is the art of freedom and of force.

Essays

The New Freedom

Preface

I have not written a book since the campaign. I did not write this book at all. It is the result of the editorial literary skill of Mr. William Bayard Hale, who has put together here in their right sequences the more suggestive portions of my campaign speeches.

And yet it is not a book of campaign speeches. It is a discussion of a number of very vital subjects in the free form of extemporaneously spoken words. I have left the sentences in the form in which they were stenographically reported. I have not tried to alter the easy-going and often colloquial phraseology in which they were uttered from the platform, in the hope that they would seem the more fresh and spontaneous because of their very lack of pruning and recasting. They have been suffered to run their unpremeditated course even at the cost of such repetition and redundancy as the extemporaneous speaker apparently inevitably falls into.

The book is not a discussion of measures or of programs. It is an attempt to express the new spirit of our politics and to set forth, in large terms which may stick in the imagination, what it is that must be done if we are to restore our politics to their full spiritual vigor again, and our national life, whether in trade, in industry, or in what concerns us only as families and individuals, to its purity, its self-respect, and its pristine strength and freedom. The New Freedom is only the old revived and clothed in the unconquerable strength of modern America.

WOODROW WILSON.

I
The Old Order Changeth

There is one great basic fact which underlies all the questions that are discussed on the political platform at the present moment. That singular fact is that nothing is done in this country as it was done twenty years ago.

We are in the presence of a new organization of society. Our life has broken away from the past. The life of America is not the life that it was twenty years ago; it is not the life that it was ten years ago. We have changed our economic conditions, absolutely, from top to bottom; and, with our economic society, the organization of our life. The old political formulas do not fit the present problems; they read now like documents taken out of a forgotten age. The older cries sound as if they belonged to a past age which men have almost forgotten. Things which used to be put into the party platforms of ten years ago would sound antiquated if put into a platform now. We are facing the necessity of fitting a new social organization, as we did once fit the old organization, to the happiness and prosperity of the great body of citizens; for we are conscious that the new order of society has not been made to fit and provide the convenience or prosperity of the average man. The life of the nation has grown infinitely varied. It does not centre now upon questions of governmental structure or of the distribution of governmental powers. It centres upon questions of the very structure and operation of society itself, of which government is only the instrument. Our development has run so fast and so far along the lines sketched in the earlier day of constitutional definition, has so crossed and interlaced those lines, has piled upon them such novel structures of trust and combination, has elaborated within them a life so manifold, so full of forces which transcend the boundaries of the country itself and fill the eyes of the world, that a new nation seems to have been created which the old formulas do not fit or afford a vital interpretation of.

We have come upon a very different age from any that preceded us. We have come upon an age when we do not do business in the way in which we used to do business,—when we do not carry on any of the operations of manufacture, sale, transportation, or communication as men used to carry them on. There is a sense in which in our day the individual has been submerged. In most parts of our country men work, not for themselves, not as partners in the old way in which they used to work, but generally as employees,—in a higher or lower grade,—of great corporations. There was a time when corporations played a very minor part in our business affairs, but now they play the chief part, and most men are the servants of corporations.

You know what happens when you are the servant of a corporation. You have in no instance access to the men who are really determining the policy of the corporation. If the corporation is doing the things that it ought not to do, you really have no voice in the matter and must obey the orders, and you have oftentimes with deep mortification to co-operate in the doing of things which you know are against the public interest. Your individuality is swallowed up in the individuality and purpose of a great organization.

It is true that, while most men are thus submerged in the corporation, a few, a very few, are exalted to a power which as individuals they could never have wielded. Through the great organizations of which they are the heads, a few are enabled to play a part unprecedented by anything in history in the control of the business operations of the country and in the determination of the happiness of great numbers of people.

Yesterday, and ever since history began, men were related to one another as individuals. To be sure there were the family, the Church, and the State, institutions which associated men in certain wide circles of relationship. But in the ordinary concerns of life, in the ordinary work, in the daily round, men dealt freely and directly with one another. To-day, the everyday relationships of men are largely with great impersonal concerns, with organizations, not with other individual men.

Now this is nothing short of a new social age, a new era of human relationships, a new stage-setting for the drama of life.

In this new age we find, for instance, that our laws with regard to the relations of employer and employee are in many respects wholly antiquated and impossible. They were framed for another age, which nobody now living remembers, which is, indeed, so remote from our life that it would be difficult for many of us to understand it if it were described to us. The employer is now generally a corporation or a huge company of some kind; the employee is one of hundreds or of thousands brought together, not by individual masters whom they know and with whom they have personal relations, but by agents of one sort or another. Workingmen are marshaled in great numbers for the performance of a multitude of particular tasks under a common discipline. They generally use dangerous and powerful machinery, over whose repair and renewal they have no control. New rules must be devised with regard to their obligations and their rights, their obligations to their employers and their responsibilities to one another. Rules must be devised for their protection, for their compensation when injured, for their support when disabled.

There is something very new and very big and very complex about these new relations of capital and labor. A new economic society has sprung up, and we must effect a new set of adjustments. We must not pit power against weakness. The employer is generally, in our day, as I have said, not an individual, but a powerful group; and yet the workingman when dealing with his employer is still, under our existing law, an individual.

Why is it that we have a labor question at all? It is for the simple and very sufficient reason that the laboring man and the employer are not intimate associates now as they used to be in time past. Most of our laws were formed in the age when employer and employees knew each other, knew each other's characters, were associates with each other, dealt with each other as man with man. That is no longer the case. You not only do not come into personal contact with the men who have the supreme command in those corporations, but it would be out of the question for you to do it. Our modern corporations employ thousands, and in some instances hundreds of thousands, of men. The only persons whom you see or deal with are local superintendents or local representatives of a vast organization, which is not like anything that the workingmen of the time in which our laws were framed knew anything about. A little group of workingmen, seeing their employer every day, dealing with him in a personal way, is one thing, and the modern body of labor engaged as employees of the huge enterprises that spread all over the country, dealing with men of whom they can form no personal conception, is another thing. A very different thing. You never saw a corporation, any more than you ever saw a government. Many a workingman to-day never saw the body of men who are conducting the industry in which he is employed. And they never saw him. What they know about him is written in ledgers and books and letters, in the correspondence of the office, in the reports of the superintendents. He is a long way off from them.

So what we have to discuss is, not wrongs which individuals intentionally do, —I do not believe there are a great many of those, —but the wrongs of a system. I want to record my protest against any discussion of this matter which would seem to indicate that there are bodies of our fellow-citizens who are trying to grind us down and do us injustice. There are some men of that sort. I don't know how they sleep o' nights, but there are men of that kind. Thank God, they are not numerous. The truth is, we are all caught in a great economic system which is heartless. The modern corporation is not engaged in business as an individual. When we deal with it, we deal with an impersonal element, an immaterial piece of society. A modern corporation is a means of co-operation in the conduct of an enterprise which is so big that no one man can conduct it, and which the resources of no one man are sufficient to finance. A company is formed; that company puts out a prospectus; the promoters expect to raise a certain fund as capital stock. Well, how are they going to raise it? They are going to raise it from the public in general, some of whom will buy their stock. The moment that begins, there is formed-what? A joint stock corporation. Men begin to pool their earnings, little piles, big piles. A certain number of men are elected by the stockholders to be directors, and these directors elect a president. This president is the head of the undertaking, and the directors are its managers.

Now, do the workingmen employed by that stock corporation deal with that president and those directors? Not at all. Does the public deal with that president and that board of directors? It does not. Can anybody bring them to account? It is next to impossible to do so. If you undertake it you will find it a game of hide and seek, with the objects of your search taking refuge now behind the tree of their individual personality, now behind that of their corporate irresponsibility.

And do our laws take note of this curious state of things? Do they even attempt to distinguish between a man's act as a corporation director and as an individual? They do not. Our laws still deal with us on the basis of the old system. The law is still living in the dead past which we have left behind. This is evident, for instance, with regard to the matter of employers' liability for workingmen's injuries. Suppose that a superintendent wants a workman to use a certain piece of machinery which it is not safe for him to use, and that the workman is injured by that piece of machinery. Some of our courts have held that the superintendent is a fellow-servant, or, as the law states it, a fellow-employee, and that, therefore, the man cannot recover damages for his injury. The superintendent who probably engaged the man is not his employer. Who is his employer? And whose negligence could conceivably come in there? The board of directors did not tell the employee to use that piece of machinery; and the president of the corporation did not tell him to use that piece of machinery. And so forth. Don't you see by that theory that a man never can get redress for negligence on the part of the employer? When I hear judges reason upon the analogy of the relationships that used to exist between workmen and their employers a generation ago, I wonder if they have not opened their eyes to the modern world. You know, we have a right to expect that judges will have their eyes open, even though the law which they administer hasn't awakened.

Yet that is but a single small detail illustrative of the difficulties we are in because we have not adjusted the law to the facts of the new order.

Since I entered politics, I have chiefly had men's views confided to me privately. Some of the biggest men in the United States, in the field of commerce and manufacture, are afraid of somebody, are afraid of something. They know that there is a power somewhere so organized, so subtle, so watchful, so interlocked, so complete, so pervasive, that they had better not speak above their breath when they speak in condemnation of it.

They know that America is not a place of which it can be said, as it used to be, that a man may choose his own calling and pursue it just as far as his abilities enable him to pursue it; because to-day, if he enters certain fields, there are organizations which will use means against him that will prevent his building up a business which they do not want to have built up; organizations that will see to it that the ground is cut from under him and the markets shut against him. For if he begins to sell to certain retail dealers, to any retail dealers, the monopoly will refuse to sell to those dealers, and those dealers, afraid, will not buy the new man's wares.

And this is the country which has lifted to the admiration of the world its ideals of absolutely free opportunity, where no man is supposed to be under any limitation except the limitations of his character and of his mind; where there is supposed to be no distinction of class, no distinction of blood, no distinction of social status, but where men win or lose on their merits.

I lay it very close to my own conscience as a public man whether we can any longer stand at our doors and welcome all newcomers upon those terms. American industry is not free, as once it was free; American enterprise is not free; the man with only a little capital is finding it harder to get into the field, more and more impossible to compete with the big fellow. Why? Because the laws of this country do not prevent the strong from crushing the weak. That is the reason, and because the strong have crushed the weak the strong dominate the industry and the economic life of this country. No man can deny that the lines of endeavor have more and more narrowed and stiffened; no man who knows anything about the development of industry in this country can have failed to observe that the larger kinds of credit are more and more difficult to obtain, unless you obtain them upon the terms of uniting your efforts with those who already control the industries of the country; and nobody can fail to observe that any man who tries to set himself up in competition with any process of manufacture which has been taken under the control of large combinations of capital will presently find himself either squeezed out or obliged to sell and allow himself to be absorbed.

There is a great deal that needs reconstruction in the United States. I should like to take a census of the business men, —I mean the rank and file of the business men, —as to whether they think that business conditions in this country, or rather whether the organization of business in this country, is satisfactory or not. I know what they would say if they dared. If they could vote secretly they would vote overwhelmingly that the present organization of business was meant for the big fellows and was not meant for the little fellows; that it was meant for those who are at the top and was meant to exclude those who are at the bottom; that it was meant to shut out beginners, to prevent new entries in the race, to prevent the building up of competitive enterprises that would interfere with the monopolies which the great trusts have built up.

What this country needs above everything else is a body of laws which will look after the men who are on the make rather than the men who are already made. Because the men who are already made are not going to live indefinitely, and they are not always kind enough to leave sons as able and as honest as they are.

The originative part of America, the part of America that makes new enterprises, the part into which the ambitious and gifted workingman makes his way up, the class that saves, that plans, that organizes, that presently spreads its enterprises until they have a national scope and character, —that middle class is being more and more squeezed out by the processes which we have been taught to call processes of prosperity. Its members are sharing prosperity, no doubt; but what alarms me is that they are not *originating* prosperity. No country can afford to have its prosperity originated by a small controlling class. The treasury of America does not lie in the brains of the small body of men now in control of the great enterprises that have been concentrated under the direction of a very small number of persons. The treasury of America lies in those ambitions, those energies, that cannot be restricted to a special favored class. It depends upon the inventions of unknown men, upon the originations of unknown men, upon the ambitions of unknown men. Every country is renewed out of the ranks of the unknown, not out of the ranks of those already famous and powerful and in control.

There has come over the land that un-American set of conditions which enables a small number of men who control the government to get favors from the government; by those favors to exclude their fellows from equal business opportunity; by those favors to extend a network of control that will presently dominate every industry in the country, and so make men forget the ancient time when America lay in every hamlet, when America was to be seen in every fair valley, when America displayed her great forces on the broad prairies, ran her fine fires of enterprise up over the mountain-sides and down into the bowels of the earth, and eager men were everywhere captains of industry, not employees; not looking to a distant city to find out what they might do, but looking about among their neighbors, finding credit according to their character, not according to their connections, finding credit in proportion to what was known to be in them and behind them, not in proportion to the securities they held that were approved where they were not known. In order to start an enterprise now, you have to be authenticated, in a perfectly impersonal way, not according to yourself, but according to what you own that somebody else approves of your owning. You cannot begin such an enterprise as those that have made America until you are so authenticated, until you have succeeded in obtaining the good-will of large allied capitalists. Is that freedom? That is dependence, not freedom.

We used to think in the old-fashioned days when life was very simple that all that government had to do was to put on a policeman's uniform, and say, "Now don't anybody hurt anybody else." We used to say that the ideal of government was for every man to be left alone and not interfered with, except when he interfered with somebody else; and that the best government was the government that did as little governing as possible. That was the idea that obtained in Jefferson's time. But we are coming now to realize that life is so complicated that we are not dealing with the old conditions, and that the law has to step in and create new conditions under which we may live, the conditions which will make it tolerable for us to live.

Let me illustrate what I mean: It used to be true in our cities that every family occupied a separate house of its own, that every family had its own little premises, that every family was separated in its life from every other family. That is no longer the case in our great cities. Families live in tenements, they live in flats, they live on floors; they are piled layer upon layer in the great tenement houses of our crowded districts, and not only are they piled layer upon layer, but they are associated room by room, so that there is in every room, sometimes, in our congested districts, a separate family. In some foreign countries they have made much more progress than we in handling these things. In the city of Glasgow, for example (Glasgow is one of the model cities of the world), they have made up their minds that the entries and the hallways of great tenements are public streets. Therefore, the policeman goes up the stairway, and patrols the corridors; the lighting department of the city sees to it that the halls are abundantly lighted. The city does not deceive itself into supposing that that great building is a unit from which the police are to keep out and the civic authority to be excluded, but it says: "These are public highways, and light is needed in them, and control by the authority of the city."

I liken that to our great modern industrial enterprises. A corporation is very like a large tenement house; it isn't the premises of a single commercial family; it is just as much a public affair as a tenement house is a network of public highways.

When you offer the securities of a great corporation to anybody who wishes to purchase them, you must open that corporation to the inspection of everybody who wants to purchase. There must, to follow out the figure of the tenement house, be lights along the corridors, there must be police patrolling the openings, there must be inspection wherever it is known that men may be deceived with regard to the contents of the premises. If we believe that fraud lies in wait for us, we must have the means of determining whether our suspicions are well founded or not. Similarly, the treatment of labor by the great corporations is not what it was in Jefferson's time. Whenever bodies of men employ bodies of men, it ceases to be a private relationship. So that when courts hold that workingmen cannot peaceably dissuade other workingmen from taking employment, as was held in a notable case in New Jersey, they simply show that their minds and understandings are lingering in an age which has passed away. This dealing of great bodies of men with other bodies of men is a matter of public scrutiny, and should be a matter of public regulation.

Similarly, it was no business of the law in the time of Jefferson to come into my house and see how I kept house. But when my house, when my so-called private property, became a great mine, and men went along dark corridors amidst every kind of danger in order to dig out of the bowels of the earth things necessary for the industries of a whole nation, and when it came about that no individual owned these mines, that they were owned by great stock companies, then all the old analogies absolutely collapsed and it became the right of the government to go down into these mines to see whether human beings were properly treated in them or not; to see whether accidents were properly safeguarded against; to see whether modern economical methods of using these inestimable riches of the earth were followed or were not followed. If somebody puts a derrick improperly secured on top of a building or overtopping the street, then the government of the city has the right to see that that derrick is so secured that you and I can walk under it and not be afraid that the heavens are going to fall on us. Likewise, in these great beehives where in every corridor swarm men of flesh and blood, it is the privilege of the government, whether of the State or of the United States, as the case may be, to see that human life is protected, that human lungs have something to breathe.

These, again, are merely illustrations of conditions. We are in a new world, struggling under old laws. As we go inspecting our lives to-day, surveying this new scene of centralized and complex society, we shall find many more things out of joint.

One of the most alarming phenomena of the time, —or rather it would be alarming if the nation had not awakened to it and shown its determination to control it, —one of the most significant signs of the new social era is the degree to which government has become associated with business. I speak, for the moment, of the control over the government exercised by Big Business. Behind the whole subject, of course, is the truth that, in the new order, government and business must be associated closely. But that association is at present of a nature absolutely intolerable; the precedence is wrong, the association is upside down. Our government has been for the past few years under the control of heads of great allied corporations with special interests. It has not controlled these interests and assigned them a proper place in the whole system of business; it has submitted itself to their control. As a result, there have grown up vicious systems and schemes of governmental favoritism (the most obvious being the extravagant tariff), far-reaching in effect upon the whole fabric of life, touching to his injury every inhabitant of the land, laying unfair and impossible handicaps upon competitors, imposing taxes in every direction, stifling everywhere the free spirit of American enterprise.

Now this has come about naturally; as we go on we shall see how very naturally. It is no use denouncing anybody, or anything, except human nature. Nevertheless, it is an intolerable thing that the government of the republic should have got so far out of the hands of the people; should have been captured by interests which are special and not general. In the train of this capture follow the troops of scandals, wrongs, indecencies, with which our politics swarm.

There are cities in America of whose government we are ashamed. There are cities everywhere, in every part of the land, in which we feel that, not the interests of the public, but the interests of special privileges, of selfish men, are served; where contracts take precedence over public interest. Not only in big cities is this the case. Have you not noticed the growth of socialistic sentiment in the smaller towns? Not many months ago I stopped at a little town in Nebraska, and while my train lingered I met on the platform a very engaging young fellow dressed in overalls who introduced himself to me as the mayor of the town, and added that he was a Socialist. I said, "What does that mean? Does that mean that this town is socialistic?" "No, sir," he said; "I have not deceived myself; the vote by which I was elected was about 20 per cent. socialistic and 80 per cent. protest." It was protest against the treachery to the people of those who led both the other parties of that town.

All over the Union people are coming to feel that they have no control over the course of affairs. I live in one of the greatest States in the union, which was at one time in slavery. Until two years ago we had witnessed with increasing concern the growth in New Jersey of a spirit of almost cynical despair. Men said: "We vote; we are offered the platform we want; we elect the men who stand on that platform, and we get absolutely nothing." So they began to ask: "What is the use of voting? We know that the machines of both parties are subsidized by the same persons, and therefore it is useless to turn in either direction."

This is not confined to some of the state governments and those of some of the towns and cities. We know that something intervenes between the people of the United States and the control of their own affairs at Washington. It is not the people who have been ruling there of late.

Why are we in the presence, why are we at the threshold, of a revolution? Because we are profoundly disturbed by the influences which we see reigning in the determination of our public life and our public policy. There was a time when America was blithe with self-confidence. She boasted that she, and she alone, knew the processes of popular government; but now she sees her sky overcast; she sees that there are at work forces which she did not dream of in her hopeful youth.

Don't you know that some man with eloquent tongue, without conscience, who did not care for the nation, could put this whole country into a flame? Don't you know that this country from one end to the other believes that something is wrong? What an opportunity it would be for some man without conscience to spring up and say: "This is the way. Follow me!" —and lead in paths of destruction!

The old order changeth-changeth under our very eyes, not quietly and equably, but swiftly and with the noise and heat and tumult of reconstruction.

I suppose that all struggle for law has been conscious, that very little of it has been blind or merely instinctive. It is the fashion to say, as if with superior knowledge of affairs and of human weakness, that every age has been an age of transition, and that no age is more full of change than another; yet in very few ages of the world can the struggle for change have been so widespread, so deliberate, or upon so great a scale as in this in which we are taking part.

The transition we are witnessing is no equable transition of growth and normal alteration; no silent, unconscious unfolding of one age into another, its natural heir and successor. Society is looking itself over, in our day, from top to bottom; is making fresh and critical analysis of its very elements; is questioning its oldest practices as freely as its newest, scrutinizing every arrangement and motive of its life; and it stands ready to attempt nothing less than a radical reconstruction, which only frank and honest counsels and the forces of generous co-operation can hold back from becoming a revolution. We are in a temper to reconstruct economic society, as we were once in a temper to reconstruct political society, and political society may itself undergo a radical modification in the process. I doubt if any age was ever more conscious of its task or more unanimously desirous of radical and extended changes in its economic and political practice.

We stand in the presence of a revolution, —not a bloody revolution; America is not given to the spilling of blood, —but a silent revolution, whereby America will insist upon recovering in practice those ideals which she has always professed, upon securing a government devoted to the general interest and not to special interests.

We are upon the eve of a great reconstruction. It calls for creative statesmanship as no age has done since that great age in which we set up the government under which we live, that government which was the admiration of the world until it suffered wrongs to grow up under it which have made many of our own compatriots question the freedom of our institutions and preach revolution against them. I do not fear revolution. I have unshaken faith in the power of America to keep its self-possession. Revolution will come in peaceful guise, as it came when we put aside the crude government of the Confederation and created the great Federal Union which governs individuals, not States, and which has been these hundred and thirty years our vehicle of progress. Some radical changes we must make in our law and practice. Some reconstructions we must push forward, which a new age and new circumstances impose upon us. But we can do it all in calm and sober fashion, like statesmen and patriots.

I do not speak of these things in apprehension, because all is open and above-board. This is not a day in which great forces rally in secret. The whole stupendous program must be publicly planned and canvassed. Good temper, the wisdom that comes of sober counsel, the energy of thoughtful and unselfish men, the habit of co-operation and of compromise which has been bred in us by long years of free government, in which reason rather than passion has been made to prevail by the sheer virtue of candid and universal debate, will enable us to win through to still another great age without violence.

II
What is Progress?

In that sage and veracious chronicle, "Alice Through the Looking-Glass," it is recounted how, on a noteworthy occasion, the little heroine is seized by the Red Chess Queen, who races her off at a terrific pace. They run until both of them are out of breath; then they stop, and Alice looks around her and says, "Why, we are just where we were when we started!" "Oh, yes," says the Red Queen; "you have to run twice as fast as that to get anywhere else."

That is a parable of progress. The laws of this country have not kept up with the change of economic circumstances in this country; they have not kept up with the change of political circumstances; and therefore we are not even where we were when we started. We shall have to run, not until we are out of breath, but until we have caught up with our own conditions, before we shall be where we were when we started; when we started this great experiment which has been the hope and the beacon of the world. And we should have to run twice as fast as any rational program I have seen in order to get anywhere else.

I am, therefore, forced to be a progressive, if for no other reason, because we have not kept up with our changes of conditions, either in the economic field or in the political field. We have not kept up as well as other nations have. We have not kept our practices adjusted to the facts of the case, and until we do, and unless we do, the facts of the case will always have the better of the argument; because if you do not adjust your laws to the facts, so much the worse for the laws, not for the facts, because law trails along after the facts. Only that law is unsafe which runs ahead of the facts and beckons to it and makes it follow the will-o'-the-wisps of imaginative projects.

Business is in a situation in America which it was never in before; it is in a situation to which we have not adjusted our laws. Our laws are still meant for business done by individuals; they have not been satisfactorily adjusted to business done by great combinations, and we have got to adjust them. I do not say we may or may not; I say we must; there is no choice. If your laws do not fit your facts, the facts are not injured, the law is damaged; because the law, unless I have studied it amiss, is the expression of the facts in legal relationships. Laws have never altered the facts; laws have always necessarily expressed the facts; adjusted interests as they have arisen and have changed toward one another.

Politics in America is in a case which sadly requires attention. The system set up by our law and our usage doesn't work,—or at least it can't be depended on; it is made to work only by a most unreasonable expenditure of labor and pains. The government, which was designed for the people, has got into the hands of bosses and their employers, the special interests. An invisible empire has been set up above the forms of democracy.

There are serious things to do. Does any man doubt the great discontent in this country? Does any man doubt that there are grounds and justifications for discontent? Do we dare stand still? Within the past few months we have witnessed (along with other strange political phenomena, eloquently significant of popular uneasiness) on one side a doubling of the Socialist vote and on the other the posting on dead walls and hoardings all over the country of certain very attractive and diverting bills warning citizens that it was "better to be safe than sorry" and advising them to "let well enough alone." Apparently a good many citizens doubted whether the situation they were advised to let alone was really well enough, and concluded that they would take a chance of being sorry. To me, these counsels of do-nothingism, these counsels of sitting still for fear something would happen, these counsels addressed to the hopeful, energetic people of the United States, telling them that they are not wise enough to touch their own affairs without marring them, constitute the most extraordinary argument of fatuous ignorance I ever heard. Americans are not yet cowards. True, their self-reliance has been sapped by years of submission to the doctrine that prosperity is something that benevolent magnates provide for them with the aid of the government; their self-reliance has been weakened, but not so utterly destroyed that you can twit them about it. The American people are not naturally stand-patters. Progress is the word that charms their ears and stirs their hearts.

There are, of course, Americans who have not yet heard that anything is going on. The circus might come to town, have the big parade and go, without their catching a sight of the camels or a note of the calliope. There are people, even Americans, who never move themselves or know that anything else is moving.

A friend of mine who had heard of the Florida "cracker," as they call a certain ne'er-do-weel portion of the population down there, when passing through the State in a train, asked some one to point out a "cracker" to him. The man asked replied, "Well, if you see something off in the woods that looks brown, like a stump, you will know it is either a stump or a cracker; if it moves, it is a stump."

Now, movement has no virtue in itself. Change is not worth while for its own sake. I am not one of those who love variety for its own sake. If a thing is good to-day, I should like to have it stay that way to-morrow. Most of our calculations in life are dependent upon things staying the way they are. For example, if, when you got up this morning, you had forgotten how to dress, if you had forgotten all about those ordinary things which you do almost automatically, which you can almost do half awake, you would have to find out what you did yesterday. I am told by the psychologists that if I did not remember who I was yesterday, I should not know who I am to-day, and that, therefore, my very identity depends upon my being able to tally to-day with yesterday. If they do not tally, then I am confused; I do not know who I am, and I have to go around and ask somebody to tell me my name and where I came from.

I am not one of those who wish to break connection with the past; I am not one of those who wish to change for the mere sake of variety. The only men who do that are the men who want to forget something, the men who filled yesterday with something they would rather not recollect to-day, and so go about seeking diversion, seeking abstraction in something that will blot out recollection, or seeking to put something into them which will blot out all recollection. Change is not worth while unless it is improvement. If I move out of my present house because I do not like it, then I have got to choose a better house, or build a better house, to justify the change.

It would seem a waste of time to point out that ancient distinction,—between mere change and improvement. Yet there is a class of mind that is prone to confuse them. We have had political leaders whose conception of greatness was to be forever frantically doing something,—it mattered little what; restless, vociferous men, without sense of the energy of concentration, knowing only the energy of succession. Now, life does not consist of eternally running to a fire. There is no virtue in going anywhere unless you will gain something by being there. The direction is just as important as the impetus of motion.

All progress depends on how fast you are going, and where you are going, and I fear there has been too much of this thing of knowing neither how fast we were going or where we were going. I have my private belief that we have been doing most of our progressiveness after the fashion of those things that in my boyhood days we called "treadmills,"—a treadmill being a moving platform, with cleats on it, on which some poor devil of a mule was forced to walk forever without getting anywhere. Elephants and even other animals have been known to turn treadmills, making a good deal of noise, and causing certain wheels to go round, and I daresay grinding out some sort of product for somebody, but without achieving much progress. Lately, in an effort to persuade the elephant to move, really, his friends tried dynamite. It moved,—in separate and scattered parts, but it moved.

A cynical but witty Englishman said, in a book, not long ago, that it was a mistake to say of a conspicuously successful man, eminent in his line of business, that you could not bribe a man like that, because, he said, the point about such men is that they have been bribed-not in the ordinary meaning of that word, not in any gross, corrupt sense, but they have achieved their great success by means of the existing order of things and therefore they have been put under bonds to see that that existing order of things is not changed; they are bribed to maintain the *status quo.*

It was for that reason that I used to say, when I had to do with the administration of an educational institution, that I should like to make the young gentlemen of the rising generation as unlike their fathers as possible. Not because their fathers lacked character or intelligence or knowledge or patriotism, but because their fathers, by reason of their advancing years and their established position in society, had lost touch with the processes of life; they had forgotten what it was to begin; they had forgotten what it was to rise; they had forgotten what it was to be dominated by the circumstances of their life on their way up from the bottom to the top, and, therefore, they were out of sympathy with the creative, formative and progressive forces of society.

Progress! Did you ever reflect that that word is almost a new one? No word comes more often or more naturally to the lips of modern man, as if the thing it stands for were almost synonymous with life itself, and yet men through many thousand years never talked or thought of progress. They thought in the other direction. Their stories of heroisms and glory were tales of the past. The ancestor wore the heavier armor and carried the larger spear. "There were giants in those days." Now all that has altered. We think of the future, not the past, as the more glorious time in comparison with which the present is nothing. Progress, development, —those are modern words. The modern idea is to leave the past and press onward to something new.

But what is progress going to do with the past, and with the present? How is it going to treat them? With ignominy, or respect? Should it break with them altogether, or rise out of them, with its roots still deep in the older time? What attitude shall progressives take toward the existing order, toward those institutions of conservatism, the Constitution, the laws, and the courts?

Are those thoughtful men who fear that we are now about to disturb the ancient foundations of our institutions justified in their fear? If they are, we ought to go very slowly about the processes of change. If it is indeed true that we have grown tired of the institutions which we have so carefully and sedulously built up, then we ought to go very slowly and very carefully about the very dangerous task of altering them. We ought, therefore, to ask ourselves, first of all, whether thought in this country is tending to do anything by which we shall retrace our steps, or by which we shall change the whole direction of our development?

I believe, for one, that you cannot tear up ancient rootages and safely plant the tree of liberty in soil which is not native to it. I believe that the ancient traditions of a people are its ballast; you cannot make a *tabula rasa* upon which to write a political program. You cannot take a new sheet of paper and determine what your life shall be to-morrow. You must knit the new into the old. You cannot put a new patch on an old garment without ruining it; it must be not a patch, but something woven into the old fabric, of practically the same pattern, of the same texture and intention. If I did not believe that to be progressive was to preserve the essentials of our institutions, I for one could not be a progressive.

One of the chief benefits I used to derive from being president of a university was that I had the pleasure of entertaining thoughtful men from all over the world. I cannot tell you how much has dropped into my granary by their presence. I had been casting around in my mind for something by which to draw several parts of my political thought together when it was my good fortune to entertain a very interesting Scotsman who had been devoting himself to the philosophical thought of the seventeenth century. His talk was so engaging that it was delightful to hear him speak of anything, and presently there came out of the unexpected region of his thought the thing I had been waiting for. He called my attention to the fact that in every generation all sorts of speculation and thinking tend to fall under the formula of the dominant thought of the age. For example, after the Newtonian Theory of the universe had been developed, almost all thinking tended to express itself in the analogies of the Newtonian Theory, and since the Darwinian Theory has reigned amongst us, everybody is likely to express whatever he wishes to expound in terms of development and accommodation to environment.

Now, it came to me, as this interesting man talked, that the Constitution of the United States had been made under the dominion of the Newtonian Theory. You have only to read the papers of *The Federalist* to see that fact written on every page. They speak of the "checks and balances" of the Constitution, and use to express their idea the simile of the organization of the universe, and particularly of the solar system,—how by the attraction of gravitation the various parts are held in their orbits; and then they proceed to represent Congress, the Judiciary, and the President as a sort of imitation of the solar system.

They were only following the English Whigs, who gave Great Britain its modern constitution. Not that those Englishmen analyzed the matter, or had any theory about it; Englishmen care little for theories. It was a Frenchman, Montesquieu, who pointed out to them how faithfully they had copied Newton's description of the mechanism of the heavens.

The makers of our Federal Constitution read Montesquieu with true scientific enthusiasm. They were scientists in their way,—the best way of their age,—those fathers of the nation. Jefferson wrote of "the laws of Nature,"—and then by way of afterthought,—"and of Nature's God." And they constructed a government as they would have constructed an orrery,—to display the laws of nature. Politics in their thought was a variety of mechanics. The Constitution was founded on the law of gravitation. The government was to exist and move by virtue of the efficacy of "checks and balances."

The trouble with the theory is that government is not a machine, but a living thing. It falls, not under the theory of the universe, but under the theory of organic life. It is accountable to Darwin, not to Newton. It is modified by its environment, necessitated by its tasks, shaped to its functions by the sheer pressure of life. No living thing can have its organs offset against each other, as checks, and live. On the contrary, its life is dependent upon their quick co-operation, their ready response to the commands of instinct or intelligence, their amicable community of purpose. Government is not a body of blind forces; it is a body of men, with highly differentiated functions, no doubt, in our modern day, of specialization, with a common task and purpose. Their co-operation is indispensable, their warfare fatal. There can be no successful government without the intimate, instinctive co-ordination of the organs of life and action. This is not theory, but fact, and displays its force as fact, whatever theories may be thrown across its track. Living political constitutions must be Darwinian in structure and in practice. Society is a living organism and must obey the laws of life, not of mechanics; it must develop.

All that progressives ask or desire is permission-in an era when "development," "evolution," is the scientific word-to interpret the Constitution according to the Darwinian principle; all they ask is recognition of the fact that a nation is a living thing and not a machine.

Some citizens of this country have never got beyond the Declaration of Independence, signed in Philadelphia, July 4th, 1776. Their bosoms swell against George III, but they have no consciousness of the war for freedom that is going on to-day.

The Declaration of Independence did not mention the questions of our day. It is of no consequence to us unless we can translate its general terms into examples of the present day and substitute them in some vital way for the examples it itself gives, so concrete, so intimately involved in the circumstances of the day in which it was conceived and written. It is an eminently practical document, meant for the use of practical men; not a thesis for philosophers, but a whip for tyrants; not a theory of government, but a program of action. Unless we can translate it into the questions of our own day, we are not worthy of it, we are not the sons of the sires who acted in response to its challenge.

What form does the contest between tyranny and freedom take to-day? What is the special form of tyranny we now fight? How does it endanger the rights of the people, and what do we mean to do in order to make our contest against it effectual? What are to be the items of our new declaration of independence?

By tyranny, as we now fight it, we mean control of the law, of legislation and adjudication, by organizations which do not represent the people, by means which are private and selfish. We mean, specifically, the conduct of our affairs and the shaping of our legislation in the interest of special bodies of capital and those who organize their use. We mean the alliance, for this purpose, of political machines with selfish business. We mean the exploitation of the people by legal and political means. We have seen many of our governments under these influences cease to be representative governments, cease to be governments representative of the people, and become governments representative of special interests, controlled by machines, which in their turn are not controlled by the people.

Sometimes, when I think of the growth of our economic system, it seems to me as if, leaving our law just about where it was before any of the modern inventions or developments took place, we had simply at haphazard extended the family residence, added an office here and a workroom there, and a new set of sleeping rooms there, built up higher on our foundations, and put out little lean-tos on the side, until we have a structure that has no character whatever. Now, the problem is to continue to live in the house and yet change it.

Well, we are architects in our time, and our architects are also engineers. We don't have to stop using a railroad terminal because a new station is being built. We don't have to stop any of the processes of our lives because we are rearranging the structures in which we conduct those processes. What we have to undertake is to systematize the foundations of the house, then to thread all the old parts of the structure with the steel which will be laced together in modern fashion, accommodated to all the modern knowledge of structural strength and elasticity, and then slowly change the partitions, relay the walls, let in the light through new apertures, improve the ventilation; until finally, a generation or two from now, the scaffolding will be taken away, and there will be the family in a great building whose noble architecture will at last be disclosed, where men can live as a single community, co-operative as in a perfected, co-ordinated beehive, not afraid of any storm of nature, not afraid of any artificial storm, any imitation of thunder and lightning, knowing that the foundations go down to the bedrock of principle, and knowing that whenever they please they can change that plan again and accommodate it as they please to the altering necessities of their lives.

But there are a great many men who don't like the idea. Some wit recently said, in view of the fact that most of our American architects are trained in a certain *École* in Paris, that all American architecture in recent years was either bizarre or "Beaux Arts." I think that our economic architecture is decidedly bizarre; and I am afraid that there is a good deal to learn about matters other than architecture from the same source from which our architects have learned a great many things. I don't mean the School of Fine Arts at Paris, but the experience of France; for from the other side of the water men can now hold up against us the reproach that we have not adjusted our lives to modern conditions to the same extent that they have adjusted theirs. I was very much interested in some of the reasons given by our friends across the Canadian border for being very shy about the reciprocity arrangements. They said: "We are not sure whither these arrangements will lead, and we don't care to associate too closely with the economic conditions of the United States until those conditions are as modern as ours." And when I resented it, and asked for particulars, I had, in regard to many matters, to retire from the debate. Because I found that they had adjusted their regulations of economic development to conditions we had not yet found a way to meet in the United States.

Well, we have started now at all events. The procession is under way. The stand-patter doesn't know there is a procession. He is asleep in the back part of his house. He doesn't know that the road is resounding with the tramp of men going to the front. And when he wakes up, the country will be empty. He will be deserted, and he will wonder what has happened. Nothing has happened. The world has been going on. The world has a habit of going on. The world has a habit of leaving those behind who won't go with it. The world has always neglected stand-patters. And, therefore, the stand-patter does not excite my indignation; he excites my sympathy. He is going to be so lonely before it is all over. And we are good fellows, we are good company; why doesn't he come along? We are not going to do him any harm. We are going to show him a good time. We are going to climb the slow road until it reaches some upland where the air is fresher, where the whole talk of mere politicians is stilled, where men can look in each other's faces and see that there is nothing to conceal, that all they have to talk about they are willing to talk about in the open and talk about with each other; and whence, looking back over the road, we shall see at last that we have fulfilled our promise to mankind. We had said to all the world, "America was created to break every kind of monopoly, and to set men free, upon a footing of equality, upon a footing of opportunity, to match their brains and their energies." and now we have proved that we meant it.

III
Freemen Need No Guardians

There are two theories of government that have been contending with each other ever since government began. One of them is the theory which in America is associated with the name of a very great man, Alexander Hamilton. A great man, but, in my judgment, not a great American. He did not think in terms of American life. Hamilton believed that the only people who could understand government, and therefore the only people who were qualified to conduct it, were the men who had the biggest financial stake in the commercial and industrial enterprises of the country.

That theory, though few have now the hardihood to profess it openly, has been the working theory upon which our government has lately been conducted. It is astonishing how persistent it is. It is amazing how quickly the political party which had Lincoln for its first leader, —Lincoln, who not only denied, but in his own person so completely disproved the aristocratic theory, —it is amazing how quickly that party, founded on faith in the people, forgot the precepts of Lincoln and fell under the delusion that the "masses" needed the guardianship of "men of affairs."

For indeed, if you stop to think about it, nothing could be a greater departure from original Americanism, from faith in the ability of a confident, resourceful, and independent people, than the discouraging doctrine that somebody has got to provide prosperity for the rest of us. And yet that is exactly the doctrine on which the government of the United States has been conducted lately. Who have been consulted when important measures of government, like tariff acts, and currency acts, and railroad acts, were under consideration? The people whom the tariff chiefly affects, the people for whom the currency is supposed to exist, the people who pay the duties and ride on the railroads? Oh, no! What do they know about such matters! The gentlemen whose ideas have been sought are the big manufacturers, the bankers, and the heads of the great railroad combinations. The masters of the government of the United States are the combined capitalists and manufacturers of the United States. It is written over every intimate page of the records of Congress, it is written all through the history of conferences at the White House, that the suggestions of economic policy in this country have come from one source, not from many sources. The benevolent guardians, the kind-hearted trustees who have taken the troubles of government off our hands, have become so conspicuous that almost anybody can write out a list of them. They have become so conspicuous that their names are mentioned upon almost every political platform. The men who have undertaken the interesting job of taking care of us do not force us to requite them with anonymously directed gratitude. We know them by name.

Suppose you go to Washington and try to get at your government. You will always find that while you are politely listened to, the men really consulted are the men who have the biggest stake, —the big bankers, the big manufacturers, the big masters of commerce, the heads of railroad corporations and of steamship corporations. I have no objection to these men being consulted, because they also, though they do not themselves seem to admit it, are part of the people of the United States. But I do very seriously object to these gentlemen being *chiefly* consulted, and particularly to their being exclusively consulted, for, if the government of the United States is to do the right thing by the people of the United States, it has got to do it directly and not through the intermediation of these gentlemen. Every time it has come to a critical question these gentlemen have been yielded to, and their demands have been treated as the demands that should be followed as a matter of course.

The government of the United States at present is a foster-child of the special interests. It is not allowed to have a will of its own. It is told at every move: "Don't do that; you will interfere with our prosperity." And when we ask, "Where is our prosperity lodged?" a certain group of gentlemen say, "With us." The government of the United States in recent years has not been administered by the common people of the United States. You know just as well as

I do, —it is not an indictment against anybody, it is a mere statement of the facts, —that the people have stood outside and looked on at their own government and that all they have had to determine in past years has been which crowd they would look on at; whether they would look on at this little group or that little group who had managed to get the control of affairs in its hands. Have you ever heard, for example, of any hearing before any great committee of the Congress in which the people of the country as a whole were represented, except it may be by the Congressmen themselves? The men who appear at those meetings in order to argue for or against a schedule in the tariff, for this measure or against that measure, are men who represent special interests. They may represent them very honestly, they may intend no wrong to their fellow-citizens, but they are speaking from the point of view always of a small portion of the population. I have sometimes wondered why men, particularly men of means, men who didn't have to work for their living, shouldn't constitute themselves attorneys for the people, and every time a hearing is held before a committee of Congress should not go and ask: "Gentlemen, in considering these things suppose you consider the whole country? Suppose you consider the citizens of the United States?"

I don't want a smug lot of experts to sit down behind closed doors in Washington and play Providence to me. There is a Providence to which I am perfectly willing to submit. But as for other men setting up as Providence over myself, I seriously object. I have never met a political savior in the flesh, and I never expect to meet one. I am reminded of Gillet Burgess' verses:

> I never saw a purple cow,
>   I never hope to see one,
> But this I'll tell you anyhow,
>   I'd rather see than be one.

That is the way I feel about this saving of my fellow-countrymen. I'd rather see a savior of the United States than set up to be one; because I have found out, I have actually found out, that men I consult with know more than I do, —especially if I consult with enough of them. I never came out of a committee meeting or a conference without seeing more of the question that was under discussion than I had seen when I went in. And that to my mind is an image of government. I am not willing to be under the patronage of the trusts, no matter how providential a government presides over the process of their control of my life.

I am one of those who absolutely reject the trustee theory, the guardianship theory. I have never found a man who knew how to take care of me, and, reasoning from that point out, I conjecture that there isn't any man who knows how to take care of all the people of the United States. I suspect that the people of the United States understand their own interests better than any group of men in the confines of the country understand them. The men who are sweating blood to get their foothold in the world of endeavor understand the conditions of business in the United States very much better than the men who have arrived and are at the top. They know what the thing is that they are struggling against. They know how difficult it is to start a new enterprise. They know how far they have to search for credit that will put them upon an even footing with the men who have already built up industry in this country. They know that somewhere, by somebody, the development of industry is being controlled.

I do not say this with the slightest desire to create any prejudice against wealth; on the contrary, I should be ashamed of myself if I excited class feeling of any kind. But I do mean to suggest this: That the wealth of the country has, in recent years, come from particular sources; it has come from those sources which have built up monopoly. Its point of view is a special point of view. It is the point of view of those men who do not wish that the people should determine their own affairs, because they do not believe that the people's judgment is sound. They want to be commissioned to take care of the United States and of the people of the United States, because they believe that they, better than anybody else, understand the interests of the United States. I do not challenge their character; I challenge their point of view. We cannot afford to be governed as we have been governed in the last generation, by men who occupy so narrow, so prejudiced, so limited a point of view.

The government of our country cannot be lodged in any special class. The policy of a great nation cannot be tied up with any particular set of interests. I want to say, again and again, that my arguments do not touch the character of the men to whom I am opposed. I believe that the very wealthy men who have got their money by certain kinds of corporate enterprise have closed in their horizon, and that they do not see and do not understand the rank and file of the people. It is for that reason that I want to break up the little coterie that has determined what the government of the nation should do. The list of the men who used to determine what New Jersey should and should not do did not exceed half a dozen, and they were always the same men. These very men now are, some of them, frank enough to admit that New Jersey has finer energy in her because more men are consulted and the whole field of action is widened and liberalized. We have got to relieve our government from the domination of special classes, not because these special classes are bad, necessarily, but because no special class can understand the interests of a great community.

I believe, as I believe in nothing else, in the average integrity and the average intelligence of the American people, and I do not believe that the intelligence of America can be put into commission anywhere. I do not believe that there is any group of men of any kind to whom we can afford to give that kind of trusteeship.

I will not live under trustees if I can help it. No group of men less than the majority has a right to tell me how I have got to live in America. I will submit to the majority, because I have been trained to do it,—though I may sometimes have my private opinion even of the majority. I do not care how wise, how patriotic, the trustees may be, I have never heard of any group of men in whose hands I am willing to lodge the liberties of America in trust.

If any part of our people want to be wards, if they want to have guardians put over them, if they want to be taken care of, if they want to be children, patronized by the government, why, I am sorry, because it will sap the manhood of America. But I don't believe they do. I believe they want to stand on the firm foundation of law and right and take care of themselves. I, for my part, don't want to belong to a nation, I believe that I do not belong to a nation, that needs to be taken care of by guardians. I want to belong to a nation, and I am proud that I do belong to a nation, that knows how to take care of itself. If I thought that the American people were reckless, were ignorant, were vindictive, I might shrink from putting the government into their hands. But the beauty of democracy is that when you are reckless you destroy your own established conditions of life; when you are vindictive, you wreak vengeance upon yourself; the whole stability of a democratic polity rests upon the fact that every interest is every man's interest.

The theory that the men of biggest affairs, whose field of operation is the widest, are the proper men to advise the government is, I am willing to admit, rather a plausible theory. If my business covers the United States not only, but covers the world, it is to be presumed that I have a pretty wide scope in my vision of business. But the flaw is that it is my own business that I have a vision of, and not the business of the men who lie outside of the scope of the plans I have made for a profit out of the particular transactions I am connected with. And you can't, by putting together a large number of men who understand their own business, no matter how large it is, make up a body of men who will understand the business of the nation as contrasted with their own interest.

In a former generation, half a century ago, there were a great many men associated with the government whose patriotism we are not privileged to deny nor to question, who intended to serve the people, but had become so saturated with the point of view of a governing class that it was impossible for them to see America as the people of America themselves saw it. Then there arose that interesting figure, the immortal figure of the great Lincoln, who stood up declaring that the politicians, the men who had governed this country, did not see from the point of view of the people. When I think of that tall, gaunt figure rising in Illinois, I have a picture of a man free, unentangled, unassociated with the governing influences of the country, ready to see things with an open eye, to see them steadily, to see them whole, to see them as the men he rubbed shoulders with and associated with saw them. What the country needed in 1860 was a leader who understood and represented the thought of the whole people, as contrasted with that of a class which imagined itself the guardian of the country's welfare.

Now, likewise, the trouble with our present political condition is that we need some man who has not been associated with the governing classes and the governing influences of this country to stand up and speak for us; we need to hear a voice from the outside calling upon the American people to assert again their rights and prerogatives in the possession of their own government.

My thought about both Mr. Taft and Mr. Roosevelt is that of entire respect, but these gentlemen have been so intimately associated with the powers that have been determining the policy of this government for almost a generation, that they cannot look at the affairs of the country with the view of a new age and of a changed set of circumstances. They sympathize with the people; their hearts no doubt go out to the great masses of unknown men in this country; but their thought is in close, habitual association with those who have framed the policies of the country during all our lifetime. Those men have framed the protective tariff, have developed the trusts, have co-ordinated and ordered all the great economic forces of this country in such fashion that nothing but an outside force breaking in can disturb their domination and control. It is with this in mind, I believe, that the country can say to these gentlemen: "We do not deny your integrity; we do not deny your purity of purpose; but the thought of the people of the United States has not yet penetrated to your consciousness. You are willing to act for the people, but you are not willing to act *through* the people. Now we propose to act for ourselves."

I sometimes think that the men who are now governing us are unconscious of the chains in which they are held. I do not believe that men such as we know, among our public men at least-most of them-have deliberately put us into leading strings to the special interests. The special interests have grown up. They have grown up by processes which at last, happily, we are beginning to understand. And, having grown up, having occupied the seats of greatest advantage nearest the ear of those who are conducting government, having contributed the money which was necessary to the elections, and therefore having been kindly thought of after elections, there has closed around the government of the United States a very interesting, a very able, a very aggressive coterie of gentlemen who are most definite and explicit in their ideas as to what they want.

They don't have to consult us as to what they want. They don't have to resort to anybody. They know their plans, and therefore they know what will be convenient for them. It may be that they have really thought what they have said they thought; it may be that they know so little of the history of economic development and of the interests of the United States as to believe that their leadership is indispensable for our prosperity and development. I don't have to prove that they believe that, because they themselves admit it. I have heard them admit it on many occasions.

I want to say to you very frankly that I do not feel vindictive about it. Some of the men who have exercised this control are excellent fellows; they really believe that the prosperity of the country depends upon them. They really believe that if the leadership of economic development in this country dropped from their hands, the rest of us are too muddle-headed to undertake the task. They not only comprehend the power of the United States within their grasp, but they comprehend it within their imagination. They are honest men, they have just as much right to express their views as I have to express mine or you to express yours, but it is just about time that we examined their views for ourselves and determined their validity.

As a matter of fact, their thought does not cover the processes of their own undertakings. As a university president, I learned that the men who dominate our manufacturing processes could not conduct their business for twenty-four hours without the assistance of the experts with whom the universities were supplying them. Modern industry depends upon technical knowledge; and all that these gentlemen did was to manage the external features of great combinations and their financial operation, which had very little to do with the intimate skill with which the enterprises were conducted. I know men not catalogued in the public prints, men not spoken of in public discussion, who are the very bone and sinew of the industry of the United States.

Do our masters of industry speak in the spirit and interest even of those whom they employ? When men ask me what I think about the labor question and laboring men, I feel that I am being asked what I know about the vast majority of the people, and I feel as if I were being asked to separate myself, as belonging to a particular class, from that great body of my fellow-citizens who sustain and conduct the enterprises of the country. Until we get away from that point of view it will be impossible to have a free government.

I have listened to some very honest and eloquent orators whose sentiments were noteworthy for this: that when they spoke of the people, they were not thinking of themselves; they were thinking of somebody whom they were commissioned to take care of. They were always planning to do things *for* the American people, and I have seen them visibly shiver when it was suggested that they arrange to have something done by the people for themselves. They said, "What do they know about it?" I always feel like replying, "What do *you* know about it? You know your own interest, but who has told you our interests, and what do you know about them?" For the business of every leader of government is to hear what the nation is saying and to know what the nation is enduring. It is not his business to judge *for* the nation, but to judge *through* the nation as its spokesman and voice. I do not believe that this country could have safely allowed a continuation of the policy of the men who have viewed affairs in any other light.

The hypothesis under which we have been ruled is that of government through a board of trustees, through a selected number of the big business men of the country who know a lot that the rest of us do not know, and who take it for granted that our ignorance would wreck the prosperity of the country. The idea of the Presidents we have recently had has been that they were Presidents of a National Board of Trustees. That is not my idea. I have been president of one board of trustees, and I do not care to have another on my hands. I want to be President of the people of the United States. There was many a time when I was president of the board of trustees of a university when the undergraduates knew more than the trustees did; and it has been in my thought ever since that if I could have dealt directly with the people who constituted Princeton University I could have carried it forward much faster than I could dealing with a board of trustees.

Mark you, I am not saying that these leaders knew that they were doing us an evil, or that they intended to do us an evil. For my part, I am very much more afraid of the man who does a bad thing and does not know it is bad than of the man who does a bad thing and knows it is bad; because I think that in public affairs stupidity is more dangerous than knavery, because harder to fight and dislodge. If a man does not know enough to know what the consequences are going to be to the country, then he cannot govern the country in a way that is for its benefit. These gentlemen, whatever may have been their intentions, linked the government up with the men who control the finances. They may have done it innocently, or they may have done it corruptly, without affecting my argument at all. And they themselves cannot escape from that alliance.

Here, for example, is the old question of campaign funds: If I take a hundred thousand dollars from a group of men representing a particular interest that has a big stake in a certain schedule of the tariff, I take it with the knowledge that those gentlemen will expect me not to forget their interest in that schedule, and that they will take it as a point of implicit honor that I should see to it that they are not damaged by too great a change in that schedule. Therefore, if I take their money, I am bound to them by a tacit implication of honor. Perhaps there is no ground for objection to this situation so long as the function of government is conceived to be to look after the trustees of prosperity, who in turn will look after the people; but on any other theory than that of trusteeship no interested campaign contributions can be tolerated for a moment,—save those of the millions of citizens who thus support the doctrines they believe and the men whom they recognized as their spokesmen.

I tell you the men I am interested in are the men who, under the conditions we have had, never had their voices heard, who never got a line in the newspapers, who never got a moment on the platform, who never had access to the ears of Governors or Presidents or of anybody who was responsible for the conduct of public affairs, but who went silently and patiently to their work every day carrying the burden of the world. How are they to be understood by the masters of finance, if only the masters of finance are consulted?

That is what I mean when I say, "Bring the government back to the people." I do not mean anything demagogic; I do not mean to talk as if we wanted a great mass of men to rush in and destroy something. That is not the idea. I want the people to come in and take possession of their own premises; for I hold that the government belongs to the people, and that they have a right to that intimate access to it which will determine every turn of its policy.

America is never going to submit to guardianship. America is never going to choose thralldom instead of freedom. Look what there is to decide! There is the tariff question. Can the tariff question be decided in favor of the people, so long as the monopolies are the chief counselors at Washington? There is the currency question. Are we going to settle the currency question so long as the government listens only to the counsel of those who command the banking situation?

Then there is the question of conservation. What is our fear about conservation? The hands that are being stretched out to monopolize our forests, to prevent or pre-empt the use of our great power-producing streams, the hands that are being stretched into the bowels of the earth to take possession of the great riches that lie hidden in Alaska and elsewhere in the incomparable domain of the United States, are the hands of monopoly. Are these men to continue to stand at the elbow of government and tell us how we are to save ourselves, —from themselves? You can not settle the question of conservation while monopoly is close to the ears of those who govern. And the question of conservation is a great deal bigger than the question of saving our forests and our mineral resources and our waters; it is as big as the life and happiness and strength and elasticity and hope of our people.

There are tasks awaiting the government of the United States which it cannot perform until every pulse of that government beats in unison with the needs and the desires of the whole body of the American people. Shall we not give the people access of sympathy, access of authority, to the instrumentalities which are to be indispensable to their lives?

IV
Life Comes from the Soil

When I look back on the processes of history, when I survey the genesis of America, I see this written over every page: that the nations are renewed from the bottom, not from the top; that the genius which springs up from the ranks of unknown men is the genius which renews the youth and energy of the people. Everything I know about history, every bit of experience and observation that has contributed to my thought, has confirmed me in the conviction that the real wisdom of human life is compounded out of the experiences of ordinary men. The utility, the vitality, the fruitage of life does not come from the top to the bottom; it comes, like the natural growth of a great tree, from the soil, up through the trunk into the branches to the foliage and the fruit. The great struggling unknown masses of the men who are at the base of everything are the dynamic force that is lifting the levels of society. A nation is as great, and only as great, as her rank and file.

So the first and chief need of this nation of ours to-day is to include in the partnership of government all those great bodies of unnamed men who are going to produce our future leaders and renew the future energies of America. And as I confess that, as I confess my belief in the common man, I know what I am saying. The man who is swimming against the stream knows the strength of it. The man who is in the mêlée knows what blows are being struck and what blood is being drawn. The man who is on the make is the judge of what is happening in America, not the man who has made good; not the man who has emerged from the flood; not the man who is standing on the bank looking on, but the man who is struggling for his life and for the lives of those who are dearer to him than himself. That is the man whose judgment will tell you what is going on in America; that is the man by whose judgment I, for one, wish to be guided.

We have had the wrong jury; we have had the wrong group, —no, I will not say the wrong group, but too small a group, —in control of the policies of the United States. The average man has not been consulted, and his heart had begun to sink for fear he never would be consulted again. Therefore, we have got to organize a government whose sympathies will be open to the whole body of the people of the United States, a government which will consult as large a proportion of the people of the United States as possible before it acts. Because the great problem of government is to know what the average man is experiencing and is thinking about. Most of us are average men; very few of us rise, except by fortunate accident, above the general level of the community about us; and therefore the man who thinks common thoughts, the man who has had common experiences, is almost always the man who interprets America aright. Isn't that the reason that we are proud of such stories as the story of Abraham Lincoln, —a man who rose out of the ranks and interpreted America better than any man had interpreted it who had risen out of the privileged classes or the educated classes of America?

The hope of the United States in the present and in the future is the same that it has always been: it is the hope and confidence that out of unknown homes will come men who will constitute themselves the masters of industry and of politics. The average hopefulness, the average welfare, the average enterprise, the average initiative, of the United States are the only things that make it rich. We are not rich because a few gentlemen direct our industry; we are rich because of our own intelligence and our own industry. America does not consist of men who get their names into the newspapers; America does not consist politically of the men who set themselves up to be political leaders; she does not consist of the men who do most of her talking, —they are important only so far as they speak for that great voiceless multitude of men who constitute the great body and the saving force of the nation. Nobody who cannot speak the common thought, who does not move by the common impulse, is the man to speak for America, or for any of her future purposes. Only he is fit to speak who knows the thoughts of the great body of citizens, the men who go about their business every day, the men who toil from morning till night, the men who go home tired in the evenings, the men who are carrying on the things we are so proud of.

You know how it thrills our blood sometimes to think how all the nations of the earth wait to see what America is going to do with her power, her physical power, her enormous resources, her enormous wealth. The nations hold their breath to see what this young country will do with her young unspoiled strength; we cannot help but be proud that we are strong. But what has made us strong? The toil of millions of men, the toil of men who do not boast, who are inconspicuous, but who live their lives humbly from day to day; it is the great body of toilers that constitutes the might of America. It is one of the glories of our land that nobody is able to predict from what family, from what region, from what race, even, the leaders of the country are going to come. The great leaders of this country have not come very often from the established, "successful" families.

I remember speaking at a school not long ago where I understood that almost all the young men were the sons of very rich people, and I told them I looked upon them with a great deal of pity, because, I said: "Most of you fellows are doomed to obscurity. You will not do anything. You will never try to do anything, and with all the great tasks of the country waiting to be done, probably you are the very men who will decline to do them. Some man who has been 'up against it,' some man who has come out of the crowd, somebody who has had the whip of necessity laid on his back, will emerge out of the crowd, will show that he understands the crowd, understands the interests of the nation, united and not separated, and will stand up and lead us."

If I may speak of my own experience, I have found audiences made up of the "common people" quicker to take a point, quicker to understand an argument, quicker to discern a tendency and to comprehend a principle, than many a college class that I have lectured to, —not because the college class lacked the intelligence, but because college boys are not in contact with the realities of life, while "common" citizens are in contact with the actual life of day by day; you do not have to explain to them what touches them to the quick.

There is one illustration of the value of the constant renewal of society from the bottom that has always interested me profoundly. The only reason why government did not suffer dry rot in the Middle Ages under the aristocratic system which then prevailed was that so many of the men who were efficient instruments of government were drawn from the church, —from that great religious body which was then the only church, that body which we now distinguish from other religious bodies as the Roman Catholic Church. The Roman Catholic Church was then, as it is now, a great democracy. There was no peasant so humble that he might not become a priest, and no priest so obscure that he might not become Pope of Christendom; and every chancellery in Europe, every court in Europe, was ruled by these learned, trained and accomplished men, —the priesthood of that great and dominant body. What kept government alive in the Middle Ages was this constant rise of the sap from the bottom, from the rank and file of the great body of the people through the open channels of the priesthood. That, it seems to me, is one of the most interesting and convincing illustrations that could possibly be adduced of the thing that I am talking about.

The only way that government is kept pure is by keeping these channels open, so that nobody may deem himself so humble as not to constitute a part of the body politic, so that there will constantly be coming new blood into the veins of the body politic; so that no man is so obscure that he may not break the crust of any class he may belong to, may not spring up to higher levels and be counted among the leaders of the state. Anything that depresses, anything that makes the organization greater than the man, anything that blocks, discourages, dismays the humble man, is against all the principles of progress. When I see alliances formed, as they are now being formed, by successful men of business with successful organizers of politics, I know that something has been done that checks the vitality and progress of society. Such an alliance, made at the top, is an alliance made to depress the levels, to hold them where they are, if not to sink them; and, therefore, it is the constant business of good politics to break up such partnerships, to re-establish and reopen the connections between the great body of the people and the offices of government.

To-day, when our government has so far passed into the hands of special interests; to-day, when the doctrine is implicitly avowed that only select classes have the equipment necessary for carrying on government; to-day, when so many conscientious citizens, smitten with the scene of social wrong and suffering, have fallen victims to the fallacy that benevolent government can be meted out to the people by kind-hearted trustees of prosperity and guardians of the welfare of dutiful employees,—to-day, supremely, does it behoove this nation to remember that a people shall be saved by the power that sleeps in its own deep bosom, or by none; shall be renewed in hope, in conscience, in strength, by waters welling up from its own sweet, perennial springs. Not from above; not by patronage of its aristocrats. The flower does not bear the root, but the root the flower. Everything that blooms in beauty in the air of heaven draws its fairness, its vigor, from its roots. Nothing living can blossom into fruitage unless through nourishing stalks deep-planted in the common soil. The rose is merely the evidence of the vitality of the root; and the real source of its beauty, the very blush that it wears upon its tender cheek, comes from those silent sources of life that lie hidden in the chemistry of the soil. Up from that soil, up from the silent bosom of the earth, rise the currents of life and energy. Up from the common soil, up from the quiet heart of the people, rise joyously to-day streams of hope and determination bound to renew the face of the earth in glory.

I tell you, the so-called radicalism of our times is simply the effort of nature to release the generous energies of our people. This great American people is at bottom just, virtuous, and hopeful; the roots of its being are in the soil of what is lovely, pure, and of good report, and the need of the hour is just that radicalism that will clear a way for the realization of the aspirations of a sturdy race.

V
The Parliament of the People

For a long time this country of ours has lacked one of the institutions which freemen have always and everywhere held fundamental. For a long time there has been no sufficient opportunity of counsel among the people; no place and method of talk, of exchange of opinion, of parley. Communities have outgrown the folk-moot and the town-meeting. Congress, in accordance with the genius of the land, which asks for action and is impatient of words,—Congress has become an institution which does its work in the privacy of committee rooms and not on the floor of the Chamber; a body that makes laws,—a legislature; not a body that debates,—not a parliament. Party conventions afford little or no opportunity for discussion; platforms are privately manufactured and adopted with a whoop. It is partly because citizens have foregone the taking of counsel together that the unholy alliances of bosses and Big Business have been able to assume to govern for us.

I conceive it to be one of the needs of the hour to restore the processes of common counsel, and to substitute them for the processes of private arrangement which now determine the policies of cities, states, and nation. We must learn, we freemen, to meet, as our fathers did, somehow, somewhere, for consultation. There must be discussion and debate, in which all freely participate.

It must be candid debate, and it must have for its honest purpose the clearing up of questions and the establishing of the truth. Too much political discussion is not to honest purpose, but only for the confounding of an opponent. I am often reminded, when political debate gets warm and we begin to hope that the truth is making inroads on the reason of those who have denied it, of the way a debate in Virginia once seemed likely to end:

When I was a young man studying at Charlottesville, there were two factions in the Democratic party in the State of Virginia which were having a pretty hot contest with each other. In one of the counties one of these factions had practically no following at all. A man named Massey, one of its redoubtable debaters, though a little, slim, insignificant-looking person, sent a messenger up into this county and challenged the opposition to debate with him. They didn't quite like the idea, but they were too proud to decline, so they put up their best debater, a big, good-natured man whom everybody was familiar with as "Tom," and it was arranged that Massey should have the first hour and that Tom Whatever-his-name-was should succeed him the next hour. When the occasion came, Massey, with his characteristic shrewdness, began to get underneath the skins of the audience, and he hadn't made more than half his speech before it was evident that he was getting that hostile crowd with him; whereupon one of Tom's partisans in the back of the room, seeing how things were going, cried out: "Tom, call him a liar and make it a fight!"

Now, that kind of debate, that spirit in discussion, gets us nowhere. Our national affairs are too serious, they lie too close to the well-being of each one of us, to excuse our talking about them except in earnestness and candor and a willingness to speak and listen with open minds. It is a misfortune that attends the party system that in the heat of a campaign partisan passions are so aroused that we cannot have frank discussion. Yet I am sure that I observe, and that all citizens must observe, an almost startling change in the temper of the people in this respect. The campaign just closed was markedly different from others that had preceded it in the degree to which party considerations were forgotten in the seriousness of the things we had to discuss as common citizens of an endangered country.

There is astir in the air of America something that I for one never saw before, never felt before. I have been going to political meetings all my life, though not all my life playing an immodestly conspicuous part in them; and there is a spirit in our political meetings now that I never saw before. It hasn't been very many years, let me say for example, that women attended political meetings. And women are attending political meetings now not simply because there is a woman question in politics; they are attending them because the modern political meeting is not like the political meeting of five or ten years ago. That was a mere ratification rally. That was a mere occasion for "whooping it up" for somebody. That was merely an occasion upon which one party was denounced unreasonably and the other was lauded unreasonably. No party has ever deserved quite the abuse that each party has got in turn, and nobody has ever deserved the praise that both parties have got in turn. The old political meeting was a wholly irrational performance; it was got together for the purpose of saying things that were chiefly not so and that were known by those who heard them not to be so, and were simply to be taken as a tonic in order to produce cheers.

But I am very much mistaken in the temper of my fellow-countrymen if the meetings I have seen in the last two years bear any resemblance to those older meetings. Men now get together in a political meeting in order to hear things of the deepest consequence discussed. And you will find almost as many Republicans in a Democratic meeting as you will find Democrats in a Republican meeting; the spirit of frank discussion, of common counsel, is abroad.

Good will it be for the country if the interest in public concerns manifested so widely and so sincerely be not suffered to expire with the election! Why should political debate go on only when somebody is to be elected? Why should it be confined to campaign time?

There is a movement on foot in which, in common with many men and women who love their country, I am greatly interested,—the movement to open the schoolhouse to the grown-up people in order that they may gather and talk over the affairs of the neighborhood and the state. There are schoolhouses all over the land which are not used by the teachers and children in the summer months, which are not used in the winter time in the evening for school purposes. These buildings belong to the public. Why not insist everywhere that they be used as places of discussion, such as of old took place in the town-meetings to which everybody went and where every public officer was freely called to account? The schoolhouse, which belongs to all of us, is a natural place in which to gather to consult over our common affairs.

I was very much interested in the remark of a fellow-citizen of ours who had been born on the other side of the water. He said that not long ago he wandered into one of those neighborhood schoolhouse meetings, and there found himself among people who were discussing matters in which they were all interested; and when he came out he said to me: "I have been living in America now ten years, and to-night for the first time I saw America as I had imagined it to be. This gathering together of men of all sorts upon a perfect footing of equality to discuss frankly with one another what concerned them all,—that is what I dreamed America was."

That set me to thinking. He hadn't seen the America he had come to find until that night. Had he not felt like a neighbor? Had men not consulted him? He had felt like an outsider. Had there been no little circles in which public affairs were discussed?

You know that the great melting-pot of America, the place where we are all made Americans of, is the public school, where men of every race and of every origin and of every station in life send their children, or ought to send their children, and where, being mixed together, the youngsters are all infused with the American spirit and developed into American men and American women. When, in addition to sending our children to school to paid teachers, we go to school to one another in those same schoolhouses, then we shall begin more fully to realize than we ever have realized before what American life is. And let me tell you this, confidentially, that wherever you find school boards that object to opening the schoolhouses in the evening for public meetings of every proper sort, you had better look around for some politician who is objecting to it; because the thing that cures bad politics is talk by the neighbors. The thing that brings to light the concealed circumstances of our political life is the talk of the neighborhood; and if you can get the neighbors together, get them frankly to tell everything they know, then your politics, your ward politics, and your city politics, and your state politics, too, will be turned inside out,—in the way they ought to be. Because the chief difficulty our politics has suffered is that the inside didn't look like the outside. Nothing clears the air like frank discussion.

One of the valuable lessons of my life was due to the fact that at a comparatively early age in my experience as a public speaker I had the privilege of speaking in Cooper Union in New York. The audience in Cooper Union is made up of every kind of man and woman, from the poor devil who simply comes in to keep warm up to the man who has come in to take a serious part in the discussion of the evening. I want to tell you this, that in the questions that are asked there after the speech is over, the most penetrating questions that I have ever had addressed to me came from some of the men who were the least well-dressed in the audience, came from the plain fellows, came from the fellows whose muscle was daily up against the whole struggle of life. They asked questions which went to the heart of the business and put me to my mettle to answer them. I felt as if those questions came as a voice out of life itself, not a voice out of any school less severe than the severe school of experience. And what I like about this social centre idea of the schoolhouse is that there is the place where the ordinary fellow is going to get his innings, going to ask his questions, going to express his opinions, going to convince those who do not realize the vigor of America that the vigor of America pulses in the blood of every true American, and that the only place he can find the true American is in this clearing-house of absolutely democratic opinion.

No one man understands the United States. I have met some gentlemen who professed they did. I have even met some business men who professed they held in their own single comprehension the business of the United States; but I am educated enough to know that they do not. Education has this useful effect, that it narrows of necessity the circles of one's egotism. No student knows his subject. The most he knows is where and how to find out the things he does not know with regard to it. That is also the position of a statesman. No statesman understands the whole country. He should make it his business to find out where he will get the information necessary to understand at least a part of it at a time when dealing with complex affairs. What we need is a universal revival of common counsel.

I have sometimes reflected on the lack of a body of public opinion in our cities, and once I contrasted the habits of the city man with those of the countryman in a way which got me into trouble. I described what a man in a city generally did when he got into a public vehicle or sat in a public place. He doesn't talk to anybody, but he plunges his head into a newspaper and presently experiences a reaction which he calls his opinion, but which is not an opinion at all, being merely the impression that a piece of news or an editorial has made upon him. He cannot be said to be participating in public opinion at all until he has laid his mind alongside the minds of his neighbors and discussed with them the incidents of the day and the tendencies of the time.

Where I got into trouble was, that I ventured on a comparison. I said that public opinion was not typified on the streets of a busy city, but was typified around the stove in a country store where men sat and probably chewed tobacco and spat into a sawdust box, and made up, before they got through, what was the neighborhood opinion both about persons and events; and then, inadvertently, I added this philosophical reflection, that, whatever might be said against the chewing of tobacco, this at least could be said for it: that it gave a man time to think between sentences. Ever since then I have been represented, particularly in the advertisements of tobacco firms, as in favor of the use of chewing tobacco!

The reason that some city men are not more catholic in their ideas is that they do not share the opinion of the country, and the reason that some countrymen are rustic is that they do not know the opinion of the city; they are both hampered by their limitations. I heard the other day of a woman who had lived all her life in a city and in an hotel. She made a first visit to the country last summer, and spent a week in a farmhouse. Asked afterward what had interested her most about her experience, she replied that it was hearing the farmer "page his cows!"

A very urban point of view with regard to a common rustic occurrence, and yet that language showed the sharp, the inelastic limits of her thought. She was provincial in the extreme; she thought even more narrowly than in the terms of a city; she thought in the terms of an hotel. In proportion as we are confined within the walls of one hostelry or one city or one state, we are provincial. We can do nothing more to advance our country's welfare than to bring the various communities within the counsels of the nation. The real difficulty of our nation has been that not enough of us realized that the matters we discussed were matters of common concern. We have talked as if we had to serve now this part of the country and again that part, now this interest and again that interest; as if all interests were not linked together, provided we understood them and knew how they were related to one another.

If you would know what makes the great river as it nears the sea, you must travel up the stream. You must go up into the hills and back into the forests and see the little rivulets, the little streams, all gathering in hidden places to swell the great body of water in the channel. And so with the making of public opinion: Back in the country, on the farms, in the shops, in the hamlets, in the homes of cities, in the schoolhouses, where men get together and are frank and true with one another, there come trickling down the streams which are to make the mighty force of the river, the river which is to drive all the enterprises of human life as it sweeps on into the great common sea of humanity.

I feel nothing so much as the intensity of the common man. I can pick out in any audience the men who are at ease in their fortunes: they are seeing a public man go through his stunts. But there are in every crowd other men who are not doing that,—men who are listening as if they were waiting to hear if there were somebody who could speak the thing that is stirring in their own hearts and minds. It makes a man's heart ache to think that he cannot be sure that he is doing it for them; to wonder whether they are longing for something that he does not understand. He prays God that something will bring into his consciousness what is in theirs, so that the whole nation may feel at last released from its dumbness, feel at last that there is no invisible force holding it back from its goal, feel at last that there is hope and confidence and that the road may be trodden as if we were brothers, shoulder to shoulder, not asking each other anything about differences of class, not contesting for any selfish advance, but united in the common enterprise.

The burden that is upon the heart of every conscientious public man is the burden of the thought that perhaps he does not sufficiently comprehend the national life. For, as a matter of fact, no single man does comprehend it. The whole purpose of democracy is that we may hold counsel with one another, so as not to depend upon the understanding of one man, but to depend upon the counsel of all. For only as men are brought into counsel, and state their own needs and interests, can the general interests of a great people be compounded into a policy that will be suitable to all.

I have realized all my life, as a man connected with the tasks of education, that the chief use of education is to open the understanding to comprehend as many things as possible. That it is not what a man knows,—for no man knows a great deal,—but what a man has upon his mind to find out; it is his ability to understand things, it is his connection with the great masses of men that makes him fit to speak for others,—and only that. I have associated with some of the gentlemen who are connected with the special interests of this country (and many of them are pretty fine men, I can tell you), but, fortunately for me, I have associated with a good many other persons besides; I have not confined my acquaintance to these interesting groups, and I can actually tell those gentlemen some things that they have not had time to find out. It has been my great good fortune not to have had my head buried in special undertakings, and, therefore, I have had an occasional look at the horizon. Moreover, I found out, a long time ago, fortunately for me, when I was a boy, that the United States did not consist of that part of it in which I lived. There was a time when I was a very narrow provincial, but happily the circumstances of my life made it necessary that I should go to a very distant part of the country, and I early found out what a very limited acquaintance I had with the United States, found out that the only thing that would give me any sense at all in discussing the affairs of the United States was to know as many parts of the United States as possible.

The men who have been ruling America must consent to let the majority into the game. We will no longer permit any system to go uncorrected which is based upon private understandings and expert testimony; we will not allow the few to continue to determine what the policy of the country is to be. It is a question of access to our own government. There are very few of us who have had any real access to the government. It ought to be a matter of common counsel; a matter of united counsel; a matter of mutual comprehension.

So, keep the air clear with constant discussion. Make every public servant feel that he is acting in the open and under scrutiny; and, above all things else, take these great fundamental questions of your lives with which political platforms concern themselves and search them through and through by every process of debate. Then we shall have a clear air in which we shall see our way to each kind of social betterment. When we have freed our government, when we have restored freedom of enterprise, when we have broken up the partnerships between money and power which now block us at every turn, then we shall see our way to accomplish all the handsome things which platforms promise in vain if they do not start at the point where stand the gates of liberty.

I am not afraid of the American people getting up and doing something. I am only afraid they will not; and when I hear a popular vote spoken of as mob government, I feel like telling the man who dares so to speak that he has no right to call himself an American. You cannot make a reckless, passionate force out of a body of sober people earning their living in a free country. Just picture to yourselves the voting population of this great land, from the sea to the far borders in the mountains, going calmly, man by man, to the polls, expressing its judgment about public affairs: is that your image of "a mob?"

What is a mob? A mob is a body of men in hot contact with one another, moved by ungovernable passion to do a hasty thing that they will regret the next day. Do you see anything resembling a mob in that voting population of the countryside, men tramping over the mountains, men going to the general store up in the village, men moving in little talking groups to the corner grocery to cast their ballots, —is that your notion of a mob? Or is that your picture of a free, self-governing people? I am not afraid of the judgments so expressed, if you give men time to think, if you give them a clear conception of the things they are to vote for; because the deepest conviction and passion of my heart is that the common people, by which I mean all of us, are to be absolutely trusted.

So, at this opening of a new age, in this its day of unrest and discontent, it is our part to clear the air, to bring about common counsel; to set up the parliament of the people; to demonstrate that we are fighting no man, that we are trying to bring all men to understand one another; that we are not the friends of any class against any other class, but that our duty is to make classes understand one another. Our part is to lift so high the incomparable standards of the common interest and the common justice that all men with vision, all men with hope, all men with the convictions of America in their hearts, will crowd to that standard and a new day of achievement may come for the liberty which we love.

VI
Let There Be Light

The concern of patriotic men is to put our government again on its right basis, by substituting the popular will for the rule of guardians, the processes of common counsel for those of private arrangement. In order to do this, a first necessity is to open the doors and let in the light on all affairs which the people have a right to know about.

In the first place, it is necessary to open up all the processes of our politics. They have been too secret, too complicated, too roundabout; they have consisted too much of private conferences and secret understandings, of the control of legislation by men who were not legislators, but who stood outside and dictated, controlling oftentimes by very questionable means, which they would not have dreamed of allowing to become public. The whole process must be altered. We must take the selection of candidates for office, for example, out of the hands of small groups of men, of little coteries, out of the hands of machines working behind closed doors, and put it into the hands of the people themselves again by means of direct primaries and elections to which candidates of every sort and degree may have free access. We must substitute public for private machinery.

It is necessary, in the second place, to give society command of its own economic life again by denying to those who conduct the great modern operations of business the privacy that used to belong properly enough to men who used only their own capital and their individual energy in business. The processes of capital must be as open as the processes of politics. Those who make use of the great modern accumulations of wealth, gathered together by the dragnet process of the sale of stocks and bonds, and piling up of reserves, must be treated as under a public obligation; they must be made responsible for their business methods to the great communities which are in fact their working partners, so that the hand which makes correction shall easily reach them and a new principle of responsibility be felt throughout their structure and operation.

What are the right methods of politics? Why, the right methods are those of public discussion: the methods of leadership open and above board, not closeted with "boards of guardians" or anybody else, but brought out under the sky, where honest eyes can look upon them and honest eyes can judge of them.

If there is nothing to conceal, then why conceal it? If it is a public game, why play it in private? If it is a public game, then why not come out into the open and play it in public? You have got to cure diseased politics as we nowadays cure tuberculosis, by making all the people who suffer from it live out of doors; not only spend their days out of doors and walk around, but sleep out of doors; always remain in the open, where they will be accessible to fresh, nourishing, and revivifying influences.

I, for one, have the conviction that government ought to be all outside and no inside. I, for my part, believe that there ought to be no place where anything can be done that everybody does not know about. It would be very inconvenient for some gentlemen, probably, if government were all outside, but we have consulted their susceptibilities too long already. It is barely possible that some of these gentlemen are unjustly suspected; in that case they owe it to themselves to come out and operate in the light. The very fact that so much in politics is done in the dark, behind closed doors, promotes suspicion. Everybody knows that corruption thrives in secret places, and avoids public places, and we believe it a fair presumption that secrecy means impropriety. So, our honest politicians and our honorable corporation heads owe it to their reputations to bring their activities out into the open.

At any rate, whether they like it or not, these affairs are going to be dragged into the open. We are more anxious about their reputations than they are themselves. We are too solicitous for their morals, —if they are not, —to permit them longer to continue subject to the temptations of secrecy. You know there is temptation in loneliness and secrecy. Haven't you experienced it? I have. We are never so proper in our conduct as when everybody can look and see exactly what we are doing. If you are off in some distant part of the world and suppose that nobody who lives within a mile of your home is anywhere around, there are times when you adjourn your ordinary standards. You say to yourself: "Well, I'll have a fling this time; nobody will know anything about it." If you were on the desert of Sahara, you would feel that you might permit yourself,—well, say, some slight latitude in conduct; but if you saw one of your immediate neighbors coming the other way on a camel,—you would behave yourself until he got out of sight. The most dangerous thing in the world is to get off where nobody knows you. I advise you to stay around among the neighbors, and then you may keep out of jail. That is the only way some of us can keep out of jail.

Publicity is one of the purifying elements of politics. The best thing that you can do with anything that is crooked is to lift it up where people can see that it is crooked, and then it will either straighten itself out or disappear. Nothing checks all the bad practices of politics like public exposure. You can't be crooked in the light. I don't know whether it has ever been tried or not; but I venture to say, purely from observation, that it can't be done.

And so the people of the United States have made up their minds to do a healthy thing for both politics and big business. Permit me to mix a few metaphors: They are going to open doors; they are going to let up blinds; they are going to drag sick things into the open air and into the light of the sun. They are going to organize a great hunt, and smoke certain animals out of their burrows. They are going to unearth the beast in the jungle in which when they hunted they were caught by the beast instead of catching him. They have determined, therefore, to take an axe and raze the jungle, and then see where the beast will find cover. And I, for my part, bid them God-speed. The jungle breeds nothing but infection and shelters nothing but the enemies of mankind.

And nobody is going to get caught in our hunt except the beasts that prey. Nothing is going to be cut down or injured that anybody ought to wish preserved.

You know the story of the Irishman who, while digging a hole, was asked, "Pat, what are you doing,—digging a hole?" And he replied, "No, sir; I am digging the dirt, and laying the hole." It was probably the same Irishman who, seen digging around the wall of a house, was asked, "Pat, what are you doing?" And he answered, "Faith, I am letting the dark out of the cellar." Now, that's exactly what we want to do,—let the dark out of the cellar.

Take, first, the relations existing between politics and business.

It is perfectly legitimate, of course, that the business interests of the country should not only enjoy the protection of the law, but that they should be in every way furthered and strengthened and facilitated by legislation. The country has no jealousy of any connection between business and politics which is a legitimate connection. It is not in the least averse from open efforts to accommodate law to the material development which has so strengthened the country in all that it has undertaken by supplying its extraordinary life with its necessary physical foundations.

But the illegitimate connections between business and legislation are another matter. I would wish to speak on this subject with soberness and circumspection. I have no desire to excite anger against anybody. That would be easy, but it would do no particular good. I wish, rather, to consider an unhappy situation in a spirit that may enable us to account for it, to some extent, and so perhaps get at the causes and the remedy. Mere denunciation doesn't help much to clear up a matter so involved as is the complicity of business with evil politics in America.

Every community is vaguely aware that the political machine upon which it looks askance has certain very definite connections with men who are engaged in business on a large scale, and the suspicion which attaches to the machine itself has begun to attach also to business enterprises, just because these connections are known to exist. If these connections were open and avowed, if everybody knew just what they involved and just what use was being made of them, there would be no difficulty in keeping an eye upon affairs and in controlling them by public opinion. But, unfortunately, the whole process of law-making in America is a very obscure one. There is no highway of legislation, but there are many by-ways. Parties are not organized in such a way in our legislatures as to make any one group of men avowedly responsible for the course of legislation. The whole process of discussion, if any discussion at all takes place, is private and shut away from public scrutiny and knowledge. There are so many circles within circles, there are so many indirect and private ways of getting at legislative action, that our communities are constantly uneasy during legislative sessions. It is this confusion and obscurity and privacy of our legislative method that gives the political machine its opportunity. There is no publicly responsible man or group of men who are known to formulate legislation and to take charge of it from the time of its introduction until the time of its enactment. It has, therefore, been possible for an outside force,—the political machine, the body of men who nominated the legislators and who conducted the contest for their election,—to assume the rôle of control. Business men who desired something done in the way of changing the law under which they were acting, or who wished to prevent legislation which seemed to them to threaten their own interests, have known that there was this definite body of persons to resort to, and they have made terms with them. They have agreed to supply them with money for campaign expenses and to stand by them in all other cases where money was necessary if in return they might resort to them for protection or for assistance in matters of legislation. Legislators looked to a certain man who was not even a member of their body for instructions as to what they were to do with particular bills. The machine, which was the centre of party organization, was the natural instrument of control, and men who had business interests to promote naturally resorted to the body which exercised the control.

There need have been nothing sinister about this. If the whole matter had been open and candid and honest, public criticism would not have centred upon it. But the use of money always results in demoralization, and goes beyond demoralization to actual corruption. There are two kinds of corruption,—the crude and obvious sort, which consists in direct bribery, and the much subtler, more dangerous, sort, which consists in a corruption of the will. Business men who have tried to set up a control in politics through the machine have more and more deceived themselves, have allowed themselves to think that the whole matter was a necessary means of self-defence, have said that it was a necessary outcome of our political system. Having reassured themselves in this way, they have drifted from one thing to another until the questions of morals involved have become hopelessly obscured and submerged. How far away from the ideals of their youth have many of our men of business drifted, enmeshed in the vicious system,—how far away from the days when their fine young manhood was wrapped in "that chastity of honor which felt a stain like a wound!"

It is one of the happy circumstances of our time that the most intelligent of our business men have seen the mistake as well as the immorality of the whole bad business. The alliance between business and politics has been a burden to them,—an advantage, no doubt, upon occasion, but a very questionable and burdensome advantage. It has given them great power, but it has also subjected them to a sort of slavery and a bitter sort of subserviency to politicians. They are as anxious to be freed from bondage as the country is to be rid of the influences and methods which it represents. Leading business men are now becoming great factors in the emancipation of the country from a system which was leading from bad to worse. There are those, of course, who are wedded to the old ways and who will stand out for them to the last, but they will sink into a minority and be overcome. The rest have found that their old excuse (namely, that it was necessary to defend themselves against unfair legislation) is no longer a good excuse; that there is a better way of defending themselves than through the private use of money. That better way is to take the public into their confidence, to make absolutely open all their dealings with legislative bodies and legislative officers, and let the public judge as between them and those with whom they are dealing.

This discovery on their part of what ought to have been obvious all along points out the way of reform; for undoubtedly publicity comes very near being the cure-all for political and economic maladies of this sort. But publicity will continue to be very difficult so long as our methods of legislation are so obscure and devious and private. I think it will become more and more obvious that the way to purify our politics is to simplify them, and that the way to simplify them is to establish responsible leadership. We now have no leadership at all inside our legislative bodies,—at any rate, no leadership which is definite enough to attract the attention and watchfulness of the country. Our only leadership being that of irresponsible persons outside the legislatures who constitute the political machines, it is extremely difficult for even the most watchful public opinion to keep track of the circuitous methods pursued. This undoubtedly lies at the root of the growing demand on the part of American communities everywhere for responsible leadership, for putting in authority and keeping in authority those whom they know and whom they can watch and whom they can constantly hold to account. The business of the country ought to be served by thoughtful and progressive legislation, but it ought to be served openly, candidly, advantageously, with a careful regard to letting everybody be heard and every interest be considered, the interest which is not backed by money as well as the interest which is; and this can be accomplished only by some simplification of our methods which will centre the public trust in small groups of men who will lead, not by reason of legal authority, but by reason of their contact with and amenability to public opinion.

I am striving to indicate my belief that our legislative methods may well be reformed in the direction of giving more open publicity to every act, in the direction of setting up some form of responsible leadership on the floor of our legislative halls so that the people may know who is back of every bill and back of the opposition to it, and so that it may be dealt with in the open chamber rather than in the committee room. The light must be let in on all processes of law-making.

Legislation, as we nowadays conduct it, is not conducted in the open. It is not threshed out in open debate upon the floors of our assemblies. It is, on the contrary, framed, digested, and concluded in committee rooms. It is in committee rooms that legislation not desired by the interests dies. It is in committee rooms that legislation desired by the interests is framed and brought forth. There is not enough debate of it in open house, in most cases, to disclose the real meaning of the proposals made. Clauses lie quietly unexplained and unchallenged in our statutes which contain the whole gist and purpose of the act; qualifying phrases which escape the public attention, casual definitions which do not attract attention, classifications so technical as not to be generally understood, and which every one most intimately concerned is careful not to explain or expound, contain the whole purpose of the law. Only after it has been enacted and has come to adjudication in the courts is its scheme as a whole divulged. The beneficiaries are then safe behind their bulwarks.

Of course, the chief triumphs of committee work, of covert phrase and unexplained classification, are accomplished in the framing of tariffs. Ever since the passage of the outrageous Payne-Aldrich Tariff Act our people have been discovering the concealed meanings and purposes which lay hidden in it. They are discovering item by item how deeply and deliberately they were deceived and cheated. This did not happen by accident; it came about by design, by elaborated, secret design. Questions put upon the floor in the House and Senate were not frankly or truly answered, and an elaborate piece of legislation was foisted on the country which could not possibly have passed if it had been generally comprehended.

And we know, those of us who handle the machinery of politics, that the great difficulty in breaking up the control of the political boss is that he is backed by the money and the influence of these very people who are intrenched in these very schedules. The tariff could never have been built up item by item by public discussion, and it never could have passed, if item by item it had been explained to the people of this country. It was built up by arrangement and by the subtle management of a political organization represented in the Senate of the United States by the senior Senator from Rhode Island, and in the House of Representatives by one of the Representatives from Illinois. These gentlemen did not build that tariff upon the evidence that was given before the Committee on Ways and Means as to what the manufacturer and the workingmen, the consumers and the producers, of this country want. It was not built upon what the interests of the country called for. It was built upon understandings arrived at outside of the rooms where testimony was given and debate was held.

I am not even now suggesting corrupt influence. That is not my point. Corruption is a very difficult thing to manage in its literal sense. The payment of money is very easily detected, and men of this kind who control these interests by secret arrangement would not consent to receive a dollar in money. They are following their own principles, —that is to say, the principles which they think and act upon, —and they think that they are perfectly honorable and incorruptible men; but they believe one thing that I do not believe and that it is evident the people of the country do not believe: they believe that the prosperity of the country depends upon the arrangements which certain party leaders make with certain business leaders. They believe that, but the proposition has merely to be stated to the jury to be rejected. The prosperity of this country depends upon the interests of all of us and cannot be brought about by arrangement between any groups of persons. Take any question you like out to the country, —let it be threshed out in public debate, —and you will have made these methods impossible.

This is what sometimes happens: They promise you a particular piece of legislation. As soon as the legislature meets, a bill embodying that legislation is introduced. It is referred to a committee. You never hear of it again. What happened? Nobody knows what happened.

I am not intimating that corruption creeps in; I do not know what creeps in. The point is that we not only do not know, but it is intimated, if we get inquisitive, that it is none of our business. My reply is that it is our business, and it is the business of every man in the state; we have a right to know all the particulars of that bill's history. There is not any legitimate privacy about matters of government. Government must, if it is to be pure and correct in its processes, be absolutely public in everything that affects it. I cannot imagine a public man with a conscience having a secret that he would keep from the people about their own affairs.

I know how some of these gentlemen reason. They say that the influences to which they are yielding are perfectly legitimate influences, but that if they were disclosed they would not be understood. Well, I am very sorry, but nothing is legitimate that cannot be understood. If you cannot explain it properly, then there is something about it that cannot *be* explained at all. I know from the circumstances of the case, not what is happening, but that something private is happening, and that every time one of these bills gets into committee, something private stops it, and it never comes out again unless forced out by the agitation of the press or the courage and revolt of brave men in the legislature. I have known brave men of that sort. I could name some splendid examples of men who, as representatives of the people, demanded to be told by the chairman of the committee why the bill was not reported, and who, when they could not find out from him, investigated and found out for themselves and brought the bill out by threatening to tell the reason on the floor of the House.

Those are private processes. Those are processes which stand between the people and the things that are promised them, and I say that until you drive all of those things into the open, you are not connected with your government; you are not represented; you are not participants in your government. Such a scheme of government by private understanding deprives you of representation, deprives the people of representative institutions. It has got to be put into the heads of legislators that public business is public business. I hold the opinion that there can be no confidences as against the people with respect to their government, and that it is the duty of every public officer to explain to his fellow-citizens whenever he gets a chance, —explain exactly what is going on inside of his own office.

There is no air so wholesome as the air of utter publicity.

There are other tracts of modern life where jungles have grown up that must be cut down. Take, for example, the entirely illegitimate extensions made of the idea of private property for the benefit of modern corporations and trusts. A modern joint stock corporation cannot in any proper sense be said to base its rights and powers upon the principles of private property. Its powers are wholly derived from legislation. It possesses them for the convenience of business at the sufferance of the public. Its stock is widely owned, passes from hand to hand, brings multitudes of men into its shifting partnerships and connects it with the interests and the investments of whole communities. It is a segment of the public; bears no analogy to a partnership or to the processes by which private property is safeguarded and managed, and should not be suffered to afford any covert whatever to those who are managing it. Its management is of public and general concern, is in a very proper sense everybody's business. The business of many of those corporations which we call public-service corporations, and which are indispensable to our daily lives and serve us with transportation and light and water and power, —their business, for instance, is clearly public business; and, therefore, we can and must penetrate their affairs by the light of examination and discussion.

In New Jersey the people have realized this for a long time, and a year or two ago we got our ideas on the subject enacted into legislation. The corporations involved opposed the legislation with all their might. They talked about ruin, —and I really believe they did think they would be somewhat injured. But they have not been. And I hear I cannot tell you how many men in New Jersey say: "Governor, we were opposed to you; we did not believe in the things you wanted to do, but now that you have done them, we take off our hats. That was the thing to do, it did not hurt us a bit; it just put us on a normal footing; it took away suspicion from our business." New Jersey, having taken the cold plunge, cries out to the rest of the states, "Come on in! The water's fine!" I wonder whether these men who are controlling the government of the United States realize how they are creating every year a thickening atmosphere of suspicion, in which presently they will find that business cannot breathe?

So I take it to be a necessity of the hour to open up all the processes of politics and of public business, —open them wide to public view; to make them accessible to every force that moves, every opinion that prevails in the thought of the people; to give society command of its own economic life again, not by revolutionary measures, but by a steady application of the principle that the people have a right to look into such matters and to control them; to cut all privileges and patronage and private advantage and secret enjoyment out of legislation.

Wherever any public business is transacted, wherever plans affecting the public are laid, or enterprises touching the public welfare, comfort, or convenience go forward, wherever political programs are formulated, or candidates agreed on, —over that place a voice must speak, with the divine prerogative of a people's will, the words: "Let there be light!"

VII
The Tariff—"Protection," or Special Privilege?

Every business question, in this country, comes back, sooner or later, to the question of the tariff. You cannot escape from it, no matter in which direction you go. The tariff is situated in relation to other questions like Boston Common in the old arrangement of that interesting city. I remember seeing once, in *Life*, a picture of a man standing at the door of one of the railway stations in Boston and inquiring of a Bostonian the way to the Common. "Take any of these streets," was the reply, "in either direction." Now, as the Common was related to the winding streets of Boston, so the tariff question is related to the economic questions of our day. Take any direction and you will sooner or later get to the Common. And, in discussing the tariff you may start at the centre and go in any direction you please.

Let us illustrate by standing at the centre, the Common itself. As far back as 1828, when they knew nothing about "practical politics" as compared with what we know now, a tariff bill was passed which was called the "Tariff of Abominations," because it had no beginning nor end nor plan. It had no traceable pattern in it. It was as if the demands of everybody in the United States had all been thrown indiscriminately into one basket and that basket presented as a piece of legislation. It had been a general scramble and everybody who scrambled hard enough had been taken care of in the schedules resulting. It was an abominable thing to the thoughtful men of that day, because no man guided it, shaped it, or tried to make an equitable system out of it. That was bad enough, but at least everybody had an open door through which to scramble for his advantage. It was a go-as-you-please, free-for-all struggle, and anybody who could get to Washington and say he represented an important business interest could be heard by the Committee on Ways and Means.

We have a very different state of affairs now. The Committee on Ways and Means and the Finance Committee of the Senate in these sophisticated days have come to discriminate by long experience among the persons whose counsel they are to take in respect of tariff legislation. There has been substituted for the unschooled body of citizens that used to clamor at the doors of the Finance Committee and the Committee on Ways and Means, one of the most interesting and able bodies of expert lobbyists that has ever been developed in the experience of any country,—men who know so much about the matters they are talking of that you cannot put your knowledge into competition with theirs. They so overwhelm you with their familiarity with detail that you cannot discover wherein their scheme lies. They suggest the change of an innocent fraction in a particular schedule and explain it to you so plausibly that you cannot see that it means millions of dollars additional from the consumers of this country. They propose, for example, to put the carbon for electric lights in two-foot pieces instead of one-foot pieces,—and you do not see where you are getting sold, because you are not an expert. If you will get some expert to go through the schedules of the present Payne-Aldrich tariff, you will find a "nigger" concealed in almost every woodpile,—some little word, some little clause, some unsuspected item, that draws thousands of dollars out of the pockets of the consumer and yet does not seem to mean anything in particular. They have calculated the whole thing beforehand; they have analyzed the whole detail and consequence, each one in his specialty. With the tariff specialist the average business man has no possibility of competition. Instead of the old scramble, which was bad enough, we get the present expert control of the tariff schedules. Thus the relation between business and government becomes, not a matter of the exposure of all the sensitive parts of the government to all the active parts of the people, but the special impression upon them of a particular organized force in the business world.

Furthermore, every expedient and device of secrecy is brought into use to keep the public unaware of the arguments of the high protectionists, and ignorant of the facts which refute them; and uninformed of the intentions of the framers of the proposed legislation. It is notorious, even, that many members of the Finance Committee of the Senate did not know the significance of the tariff schedules which were reported in the present tariff bill to the Senate, and that members of the Senate who asked Mr. Aldrich direct questions were refused the information they sought; sometimes, I dare say, because he could not give it, and sometimes, I venture to say, because disclosure of the information would have embarrassed the passage of the measure. There were essential papers, moreover, which could not be got at.

Take that very interesting matter, that will-o'-the-wisp, known as "the cost of production." It is hard for any man who has ever studied economics at all to restrain a cynical smile when he is told that an intelligent group of his fellow-citizens are looking for "the cost of production" as a basis for tariff legislation. It is not the same in any one factory for two years together. It is not the same in one industry from one season to another. It is not the same in one country at two different epochs. It is constantly eluding your grasp. It nowhere exists, as a scientific, demonstrable fact. But, in order to carry out the pretences of the "protective" program, it was necessary to go through the motions of finding out what it was. I am credibly informed that the government of the United States requested several foreign governments, among others the government of Germany, to supply it with as reliable figures as possible concerning the cost of producing certain articles corresponding with those produced in the United States. The German government put the matter into the hands of certain of her manufacturers, who sent in just as complete answers as they could procure from their books. The information reached our government during the course of the debate on the Payne-Aldrich Bill and was transmitted, — for the bill by that time had reached the Senate, —to the Finance Committee of the Senate. But I am told, —and I have no reason to doubt it, —that it never came out of the pigeonholes of the committee. I don't know, and that committee doesn't know, what the information it contained was. When Mr. Aldrich was asked about it, he first said it was not an official report from the German government. Afterward he intimated that it was an impudent attempt on the part of the German government to interfere with tariff legislation in the United States. But he never said what the cost of production disclosed by it was. If he had, it is more than likely that some of the schedules would have been shown to be entirely unjustifiable.

Such instances show you just where the centre of gravity is, —and it is a matter of gravity indeed, for it is a very grave matter! It lay during the last Congress in the one person who was the accomplished intermediary between the expert lobbyists and the legislation of Congress. I am not saying this in derogation of the character of Mr. Aldrich. It is no concern of mine what kind of man Mr. Aldrich is; now, particularly, when he has retired from public life, is it a matter of indifference. The point is that he, because of his long experience, his long handling of these delicate and private matters, was the usual and natural instrument by which the Congress of the United States informed itself, not as to the wishes of the people of the United States or of the rank and file of business men of the country, but as to the needs and arguments of the experts who came to arrange matters with the committees.

The moral of the whole matter is this: The business of the United States is not as a whole in contact with the government of the United States. So soon as it is, the matters which now give you, and justly give you, cause for uneasiness will disappear. Just so soon as the business of this country has general, free, welcome access to the councils of Congress, all the friction between business and politics will disappear.

The tariff question is not the question that it was fifteen or twenty or thirty years ago. It used to be said by the advocates of the tariff that it made no difference even if there were a great wall separating us from the commerce of the world, because inside the United States there was so enormous an area of absolute free trade that competition within the country kept prices down to a normal level; that so long as one state could compete with all the others in the United States, and all the others compete with it, there would be only that kind of advantage gained which is gained by superior brain, superior economy, the better plant, the better administration; all of the things that have made America supreme, and kept prices in America down, because

American genius was competing with American genius. I must add that so long as that was true, there was much to be said in defence of the protective tariff.

But the point now is that the protective tariff has been taken advantage of by some men to destroy domestic competition, to combine all existing rivals within our free-trade area, and to make it impossible for new men to come into the field. Under the high tariff there has been formed a network of factories which in their connection dominate the market of the United States and establish their own prices. Whereas, therefore, it was once arguable that the high tariff did not create the high cost of living, it is now no longer arguable that these combinations do not, —not by reason of the tariff, but by reason of their combination under the tariff, —settle what prices shall be paid; settle how much the product shall be; and settle, moreover, what shall be the market for labor.

The "protective" policy, as we hear it proclaimed to-day, bears no relation to the original doctrine enunciated by Webster and Clay. The "infant industries," which those statesmen desired to encourage, have grown up and grown gray, but they have always had new arguments for special favors. Their demands have gone far beyond what they dared ask for in the days of Mr. Blaine and Mr. McKinley, though both those apostles of "protection" were, before they died, ready to confess that the time had even then come to call a halt on the claims of the subsidized industries. William McKinley, before he died, showed symptoms of adjustment to the new age such as his successors have not exhibited. You remember what the utterances of Mr. McKinley's last month were with regard to the policy with which his name is particularly identified; I mean the policy of "protection." You remember how he joined in opinion with what Mr. Blaine before him had said-namely, that we had devoted the country to a policy which, too rigidly persisted in, was proving a policy of restriction; and that we must look forward to a time that ought to come very soon when we should enter into reciprocal relations of trade with all the countries of the world. This was another way of saying that we must substitute elasticity for rigidity; that we must substitute trade for closed ports. McKinley saw what his successors did not see. He saw that we had made for ourselves a strait-jacket.

When I reflect upon the "protective" policy of this country, and observe that it is the later aspects and the later uses of that policy which have built up trusts and monopoly in the United States, I make this contrast in my thought: Mr. McKinley had already uttered his protest against what he foresaw; his successor saw what McKinley had only foreseen, but he took no action. His successor saw those very special privileges, which Mr. McKinley himself began to suspect, used by the men who had obtained them to build up a monopoly for themselves, making freedom of enterprise in this country more and more difficult. I am one of those who have the utmost confidence that Mr. McKinley would not have sanctioned the later developments of the policy with which his name stands identified.

What is the present tariff policy of the protectionists? It is not the ancient protective policy to which I would give all due credit, but an entirely new doctrine. I ask anybody who is interested in the history of high "protective" tariffs to compare the latest platforms of the two "protective" tariff parties with the old doctrine. Men have been struck, students of this matter, by an entirely new departure. The new doctrine of the protectionist is that the tariff should represent the difference between the cost of production in America and the cost of production in other countries, *plus* a reasonable profit to those who are engaged in industry. This is the new part of the protective doctrine: "*plus* a reasonable profit." It openly guarantees profit to the men who come and ask favors of Congress. The old idea of a protective tariff was designed to keep American industries alive and, therefore, keep American labor employed. But the favors of protection have become so permanent that this is what has happened: Men, seeing that they need not fear foreign competition, have drawn together in great combinations. These combinations include factories (if it is a combination of factories) of all grades: old factories and new factories, factories with antiquated machinery and factories with brand-new machinery; factories that are economically and factories that are not economically administered; factories that have been long in the family, which have been allowed to run down, and factories with all the new modern inventions. As soon as the combination is effected the less efficient factories are generally put out of operation. But the stock issued in payment for them has to pay dividends. And the United States government guarantees profit on investment in factories that have gone out of business. As soon as these combinations see prices falling they reduce the hours of labor, they reduce production, they reduce wages, they throw men out of employment, —in order to do what? In order to keep the prices up in spite of their lack of efficiency.

There may have been a time when the tariff did not raise prices, but that time is past; the tariff is now taken advantage of by the great combinations in such a way as to give them control of prices. These things do not happen by chance. It does not happen by chance that prices are and have been rising faster here than in any other country. That river that divides us from Canada divides us from much cheaper living, notwithstanding that the Canadian Parliament levies duties on importations.

But "Ah!" exclaim those who do not understand what is going on; "you will ruin the country with your free trade!" Who said free trade? Who proposed free trade? You can't have free trade in the United States, because the government of the United States is of necessity, with our present division of the field of taxation between the federal and state governments, supported in large part by the duties collected at the ports. I should like to ask some gentlemen if very much is collected in the way of duties at the ports under the particular tariff schedules under which they operate. Some of the duties are practically prohibitive, and there is no tariff to be got from them.

When you buy an imported article, you pay a part of the price to the Federal government in the form of customs duty. But, as a rule, what you buy is, not the imported article, but a domestic article, the price of which the manufacturer has been able to raise to a point equal to, or higher than, the price of the foreign article *plus the duty*. But who gets the tariff tax in this case? The government? Oh, no; not at all. The manufacturer. The American manufacturer, who says that while he can't sell goods as low as the foreign manufacturer, all good Americans ought to buy of him and pay him a tax on every article for the privilege. Perhaps we ought. The original idea was that, when he was just starting and needed support, we ought to buy of him, even if we had to pay a higher price, till he could get on his feet. Now it is said that we ought to buy of him and pay him a price 15 to 120 per cent. higher than we need pay the foreign manufacturer, even if he is a six-foot, bearded "infant," because the cost of production is necessarily higher here than anywhere else. I don't know why it should be. The American workingman used to be able to do so much more and better work than the foreigner that that more than compensated for his higher wages and made him a good bargain at any wage.

Of course, if we are going to agree to give any fellow-citizen who takes a notion to go into some business or other for which the country is not especially adapted, —if we are going to give him a bonus on every article he produces big enough to make up for the handicap he labors under because of some natural reason or other, —why, we may indeed gloriously diversify our industries, but we shall beggar ourselves. On this principle, we shall have in Connecticut, or Michigan, or somewhere else, miles of hothouses in which thousands of happy American workingmen, with full dinner-pails, will be raising bananas, —to be sold at a quarter apiece. Some foolish person, a benighted Democrat like as not, might timidly suggest that bananas were a greater public blessing when they came from Jamaica and were three for a nickel, but what patriotic citizen would listen for a moment to the criticisms of a person without any conception of the beauty and glory of the great American banana industry, without realization of the proud significance of the fact that Old Glory floats over the biggest banana hothouses in the world!

But that is a matter on one side. What I am trying to point out to you now is that this "protective" tariff, so-called, has become a means of fostering the growth of particular groups of industry at the expense of the economic vitality of the rest of the country. What the people now propose is a very practical thing indeed: They propose to unearth these special privileges and to cut them out of the tariff. They propose not to leave a single concealed private advantage in the statutes concerning the duties that can possibly be eradicated without affecting the part of the business that is sound and legitimate and which we all wish to see promoted.

Some men talk as if the tariff-reformers, as if the Democrats, weren't part of the United States. I met a lady the other day, not an elderly lady, who said to me with pride: "Why, I have been a Democrat ever since they hunted them with dogs." And you would really suppose, to hear some men talk, that Democrats were outlaws and did not share the life of the United States. Why, Democrats constitute nearly one half the voters of this country. They are engaged in all sorts of enterprises, big and little. There isn't a walk of life or a kind of occupation in which you won't find them; and, as a Philadelphia paper very wittily said the other day, they can't commit economic murder without committing economic suicide. Do you suppose, therefore, that half of the population of the United States is going about to destroy the very foundations of our economic life by simply running amuck amidst the schedules of the tariff? Some of the schedules are so tough that they wouldn't be hurt, if it did. But that isn't the program, and anybody who says that it is simply doesn't understand the situation at all. All that the tariff-reformers claim is this: that the partnership ought to be bigger than it is. Just because there are so many of them, they know how many are outside. And let me tell you, just as many Republicans are outside. The only thing I have against my protectionist fellow-citizens is that they have allowed themselves to be imposed upon so many years. Think of saying that the "protective" tariff is for the benefit of the workingman, in the presence of all those facts that have just been disclosed in Lawrence, Mass., where the worst schedule of all —"Schedule K" — operates to keep men on wages on which they cannot live. Why, the audacity, the impudence, of the claim is what strikes one; and in face of the fact that the workingmen of this country who are in unprotected industries are better paid than those who are in "protected" industries; at any rate, in the conspicuous industries! The Steel schedule, I dare say, is rather satisfactory to those who manufacture steel, but is it satisfactory to those who make the steel with their own tired hands? Don't you know that there are mills in which men are made to work seven days in the week for twelve hours a day, and in the three hundred and sixty-five weary days of the year can't make enough to pay their bills? And this in one of the giants among our industries, one of the undertakings which have thriven to gigantic size upon this very system.

Ah, the whole mass of the fraud is falling away, and men are beginning to see disclosed little groups of persons maintaining a control over the dominant party and through the dominant party over the government, in their own interest, and not in the interest of the people of the United States!

Let me repeat: There cannot be free trade in the United States so long as the established fiscal policy of the federal government is maintained. The federal government has chosen throughout all the generations that have preceded us to maintain itself chiefly on indirect instead of direct taxation. I dare say we shall never see a time when it can alter that policy in any substantial degree; and there is no Democrat of thoughtfulness that I have met who contemplates a program of free trade.

But what we intend to do, what the House of Representatives has been attempting to do and will attempt to do again, and succeed in doing, is to weed this garden that we have been cultivating. Because, if we have been laying at the roots of our industrial enterprises this fertilization of protection, if we have been stimulating it by this policy, we have found that the stimulation was not equal in respect of all the growths in the garden, and that there are some growths, which every man can distinguish with the naked eye, which have so overtopped the rest, which have so thrown the rest into destroying shadow, that it is impossible for the industries of the United States as a whole to prosper under their blighting shade. In other words, we have found out that this that professes to be a process of protection has become a process of favoritism, and that the favorites of this policy have flourished at the expense of all the rest. And now we are going into this garden and weed it. We are going into this garden and give the little plants air and light in which to grow. We are going to pull up every root that has so spread itself as to draw the nutriment of the soil from the other roots. We are going in there to see to it that the fertilization of intelligence, of invention, of origination, is once more applied to a set of industries now threatening to be stagnant, because threatening to be too much concentrated. The policy of freeing the country from the restrictive tariff will so variegate and multiply the undertakings in the country that there will be a wider market and a greater competition for labor; it will let the sun shine through the clouds again as once it shone on the free, independent, unpatronized intelligence and energy of a great people.

One of the counts of the indictment against the so-called "protective" tariff is that it has robbed Americans of their independence, resourcefulness, and self-reliance. Our industry has grown invertebrate, cowardly, dependent on government aid. When I hear the argument of some of the biggest business men in this country, that if you took the "protection" of the tariff off they would be overcome by the competition of the world, I ask where and when it happened that the boasted genius of America became afraid to go out into the open and compete with the world? Are we children, are we wards, are we still such puerile infants that we have to be fed out of a bottle? Isn't it true that we know how to make steel in America better than anybody else in the world? Yet they say, "For Heaven's sake don't expose us to the chill of prices coming from any other quarter of the globe." Mind you, we can compete with those prices. Steel is sold abroad, steel made in America is sold abroad in many of its forms, much cheaper than it is sold in America. It is so hard for people to get that into their heads!

We set up a kindergarten in New York. We called it the Chamber of Horrors. We exhibited there a great many things manufactured in the United States, with the prices at which they were sold in the United States, and the prices at which they were sold outside of the United States, marked on them. If you tell a woman that she can buy a sewing machine for eighteen dollars in Mexico that she has to pay thirty dollars for in the United States, she will not heed it or she will forget it unless you take her and show her the machine with the price marked on it. My very distinguished friend, Senator Gore, of Oklahoma, made this interesting proposal: that we should pass a law that every piece of goods sold in the United States should have on it a label bearing the price at which it sells under the tariff and the price at which it would sell if there were no tariff, and then the Senator suggests that we have a very easy solution for the tariff question. He does not want to oblige that great body of our fellow-citizens who have a conscientious belief in "protection" to turn away from it. He proposes that everybody who believes in the "protective" tariff should pay it and the rest of us should not; if they want to subscribe, it is open to them to subscribe.

As for the rest of us, the time is coming when we shall not have to subscribe. The people of this land have made up their minds to cut all privilege and patronage out of our fiscal legislation, particularly out of that part of it which affects the tariff. We have come to recognize in the tariff as it is now constructed, not a system of protection, but a system of favoritism, of privilege, too often granted secretly and by subterfuge, instead of openly and frankly and legitimately, and we have determined to put an end to the whole bad business, not by hasty and drastic changes, but by the adoption of an entirely new principle, —by the reformation of the whole purpose of legislation of that kind. We mean that our tariff legislation henceforth shall have as its object, not private profit, but the general public development and benefit. We shall make our fiscal laws, not like those who dole out favors, but like those who serve a nation. We are going to begin with those particular items where we find special privilege intrenched. We know what those items are; these gentlemen have been kind enough to point them out themselves. What we are interested in first of all with regard to the tariff is getting the grip of special interests off the throat of Congress. We do not propose that special interests shall any longer camp in the rooms of the Committee on Ways and Means of the House and the Finance Committee of the Senate. We mean that those shall be places where the people of the United States shall come and be represented, in order that everything may be done in the general interest, and not in the interest of particular groups of persons who already dominate the industries and the industrial development of this country. Because no matter how wise these gentlemen may be, no matter how patriotic, no matter how singularly they may be gifted with the power to divine the right courses of business, there isn't any group of men in the United States or in any other country who are wise enough to have the destinies of a great people put into their hands as trustees. We mean that business in this land shall be released, emancipated.

VIII
Monopoly, or Opportunity?

Gentlemen say, they have been saying for a long time, and, therefore, I assume that they believe, that trusts are inevitable. They don't say that big business is inevitable. They don't say merely that the elaboration of business upon a great co-operative scale is characteristic of our time and has come about by the natural operation of modern civilization. We would admit that. But they say that the particular kind of combinations that are now controlling our economic development came into existence naturally and were inevitable; and that, therefore, we have to accept them as unavoidable and administer our development through them. They take the analogy of the railways. The railways were clearly inevitable if we were to have transportation, but railways after they are once built stay put. You can't transfer a railroad at convenience; and you can't shut up one part of it and work another part. It is in the nature of what economists, those tedious persons, call natural monopolies; simply because the whole circumstances of their use are so stiff that you can't alter them. Such are the analogies which these gentlemen choose when they discuss the modern trust.

I admit the popularity of the theory that the trusts have come about through the natural development of business conditions in the United States, and that it is a mistake to try to oppose the processes by which they have been built up, because those processes belong to the very nature of business in our time, and that therefore the only thing we can do, and the only thing we ought to attempt to do, is to accept them as inevitable arrangements and make the best out of it that we can by regulation.

I answer, nevertheless, that this attitude rests upon a confusion of thought. Big business is no doubt to a large extent necessary and natural. The development of business upon a great scale, upon a great scale of co-operation, is inevitable, and, let me add, is probably desirable. But that is a very different matter from the development of trusts, because the trusts have not grown. They have been artificially created; they have been put together, not by natural processes, but by the will, the deliberate planning will, of men who were more powerful than their neighbors in the business world, and who wished to make their power secure against competition.

The trusts do not belong to the period of infant industries. They are not the products of the time, that old laborious time, when the great continent we live on was undeveloped, the young nation struggling to find itself and get upon its feet amidst older and more experienced competitors. They belong to a very recent and very sophisticated age, when men knew what they wanted and knew how to get it by the favor of the government.

Did you ever look into the way a trust was made? It is very natural, in one sense, in the same sense in which human greed is natural. If I haven't efficiency enough to beat my rivals, then the thing I am inclined to do is to get together with my rivals and say: "Don't let's cut each other's throats; let's combine and determine prices for ourselves; determine the output, and thereby determine the prices: and dominate and control the market." That is very natural. That has been done ever since freebooting was established. That has been done ever since power was used to establish control. The reason that the masters of combination have sought to shut out competition is that the basis of control under competition is brains and efficiency. I admit that any large corporation built up by the legitimate processes of business, by economy, by efficiency, is natural; and I am not afraid of it, no matter how big it grows. It can stay big only by doing its work more thoroughly than anybody else. And there is a point of bigness,—as every business man in this country knows, though some of them will not admit it,—where you pass the limit of efficiency and get into the region of clumsiness and unwieldiness. You can make your combine so extensive that you can't digest it into a single system; you can get so many parts that you can't assemble them as you would an effective piece of machinery. The point of efficiency is overstepped in the natural process of development oftentimes, and it has been overstepped many times in the artificial and deliberate formation of trusts.

A trust is formed in this way: a few gentlemen "promote" it-that is to say, they get it up, being given enormous fees for their kindness, which fees are loaded on to the undertaking in the form of securities of one kind or another. The argument of the promoters is, not that every one who comes into the combination can carry on his business more efficiently than he did before; the argument is: we will assign to you as your share in the pool twice, three times, four times, or five times what you could have sold your business for to an individual competitor who would have to run it on an economic and competitive basis. We can afford to buy it at such a figure because we are shutting out competition. We can afford to make the stock of the combination half a dozen times what it naturally would be and pay dividends on it, because there will be nobody to dispute the prices we shall fix.

Talk of that as sound business? Talk of that as inevitable? It is based upon nothing except power. It is not based upon efficiency. It is no wonder that the big trusts are not prospering in proportion to such competitors as they still have in such parts of their business as competitors have access to; they are prospering freely only in those fields to which competition has no access. Read the statistics of the Steel Trust, if you don't believe it. Read the statistics of any trust. They are constantly nervous about competition, and they are constantly buying up new competitors in order to narrow the field. The United States Steel Corporation is gaining in its supremacy in the American market only with regard to the cruder manufactures of iron and steel, but wherever, as in the field of more advanced manufactures of iron and steel, it has important competitors, its portion of the product is not increasing, but is decreasing, and its competitors, where they have a foothold, are often more efficient than it is.

Why? Why, with unlimited capital and innumerable mines and plants everywhere in the United States, can't they beat the other fellows in the market? Partly because they are carrying too much. Partly because they are unwieldy. Their organization is imperfect. They bought up inefficient plants along with efficient, and they have got to carry what they have paid for, even if they have to shut some of the plants up in order to make any interest on their investments; or, rather, not interest on their investments, because that is an incorrect word, —on their alleged capitalization. Here we have a lot of giants staggering along under an almost intolerable weight of artificial burdens, which they have put on their own backs, and constantly looking about lest some little pigmy with a round stone in a sling may come out and slay them.

For my part, I want the pigmy to have a chance to come out. And I foresee a time when the pigmies will be so much more athletic, so much more astute, so much more active, than the giants, that it will be a case of Jack the giant-killer. Just let some of the youngsters I know have a chance and they'll give these gentlemen points. Lend them a little money. They can't get any now. See to it that when they have got a local market they can't be squeezed out of it. Give them a chance to capture that market and then see them capture another one and another one, until these men who are carrying an intolerable load of artificial securities find that they have got to get down to hard pan to keep their foothold at all. I am willing to let Jack come into the field with the giant, and if Jack has the brains that some Jacks that I know in America have, then I should like to see the giant get the better of him, with the load that he, the giant, has to carry, —the load of water. For I'll undertake to put a water-logged giant out of business any time, if you will give me a fair field and as much credit as I am entitled to, and let the law do what from time immemorial law has been expected to do, —see fair play.

As for watered stock, I know all the sophistical arguments, and they are many, for capitalizing earning capacity. It is a very attractive and interesting argument, and in some instances it is legitimately used. But there is a line you cross, above which you are not capitalizing your earning capacity, but capitalizing your control of the market, capitalizing the profits which you got by your control of the market, and didn't get by efficiency and economy. These things are not hidden even from the layman. These are not half-hidden from college men. The college men's days of innocence have passed, and their days of sophistication have come. They know what is going on, because we live in a talkative world, full of statistics, full of congressional inquiries, full of trials of persons who have attempted to live independently of the statutes of the United States; and so a great many things have come to light under oath, which we must believe upon the credibility of the witnesses who are, indeed, in many instances very eminent and respectable witnesses.

I take my stand absolutely, where every progressive ought to take his stand, on the proposition that private monopoly is indefensible and intolerable. And there I will fight my battle. And I know how to fight it. Everybody who has even read the newspapers knows the means by which these men built up their power and created these monopolies. Any decently equipped lawyer can suggest to you statutes by which the whole business can be stopped. What these gentlemen do not want is this: they do not want to be compelled to meet all comers on equal terms. I am perfectly willing that they should beat any competitor by fair means; but I know the foul means they have adopted, and I know that they can be stopped by law. If they think that coming into the market upon the basis of mere efficiency, upon the mere basis of knowing how to manufacture goods better than anybody else and to sell them cheaper than anybody else, they can carry the immense amount of water that they have put into their enterprises in order to buy up rivals, then they are perfectly welcome to try it. But there must be no squeezing out of the beginner, no crippling his credit; no discrimination against retailers who buy from a rival; no threats against concerns who sell supplies to a rival; no holding back of raw material from him; no secret arrangements against him. All the fair competition you choose, but no unfair competition of any kind. And then when unfair competition is eliminated, let us see these gentlemen carry their tanks of water on their backs. All that I ask and all I shall fight for is that they shall come into the field against merit and brains everywhere. If they can beat other American brains, then they have got the best brains.

But if you want to know how far brains go, as things now are, suppose you try to match your better wares against these gentlemen, and see them undersell you before your market is any bigger than the locality and make it absolutely impossible for you to get a fast foothold. If you want to know how brains count, originate some invention which will improve the kind of machinery they are using, and then see if you can borrow enough money to manufacture it. You may be offered something for your patent by the corporation,—which will perhaps lock it up in a safe and go on using the old machinery; but you will not be allowed to manufacture. I know men who have tried it, and they could not get the money, because the great money lenders of this country are in the arrangement with the great manufacturers of this country, and they do not propose to see their control of the market interfered with by outsiders. And who are outsiders? Why, all the rest of the people of the United States are outsiders.

They are rapidly making us outsiders with respect even of the things that come from the bosom of the earth, and which belong to us in a peculiar sense. Certain monopolies in this country have gained almost complete control of the raw material, chiefly in the mines, out of which the great body of manufactures are carried on, and they now discriminate, when they will, in the sale of that raw material between those who are rivals of the monopoly and those who submit to the monopoly. We must soon come to the point where we shall say to the men who own these essentials of industry that they have got to part with these essentials by sale to all citizens of the United States with the same readiness and upon the same terms. Or else we shall tie up the resources of this country under private control in such fashion as will make our independent development absolutely impossible.

There is another injustice that monopoly engages in. The trust that deals in the cruder products which are to be transformed into the more elaborate manufactures often will not sell these crude products except upon the terms of monopoly,—that is to say, the people that deal with them must buy exclusively from them. And so again you have the lines of development tied up and the connections of development knotted and fastened so that you cannot wrench them apart.

Again, the manufacturing monopolies are so interlaced in their personal relationships with the great shipping interests of this country, and with the great railroads, that they can often largely determine the rates of shipment.

The people of this country are being very subtly dealt with. You know, of course, that, unless our Commerce Commissions are absolutely sleepless, you can get rebates without calling them such at all. The most complicated study I know of is the classification of freight by the railway company. If I wanted to make a special rate on a special thing, all I should have to do is to put it in a special class in the freight classification, and the trick is done. And when you reflect that the twenty-four men who control the United States Steel Corporation, for example, are either presidents or vice-presidents or directors in 55 per cent. of the railways of the United States, reckoning by the valuation of those railroads and the amount of their stock and bonds, you know just how close the whole thing is knitted together in our industrial system, and how great the temptation is. These twenty-four gentlemen administer that corporation as if it belonged to them. The amazing thing to me is that the people of the United States have not seen that the administration of a great business like that is not a private affair; it is a public affair.

I have been told by a great many men that the idea I have, that by restoring competition you can restore industrial freedom, is based upon a failure to observe the actual happenings of the last decades in this country; because, they say, it is just free competition that has made it possible for the big to crush the little.

I reply, it is not free competition that has done that; it is illicit competition. It is competition of the kind that the law ought to stop, and can stop, —this crushing of the little man.

You know, of course, how the little man is crushed by the trusts. He gets a local market. The big concerns come in and undersell him in his local market, and that is the only market he has; if he cannot make a profit there, he is killed. They can make a profit all through the rest of the Union, while they are underselling him in his locality, and recouping themselves by what they can earn elsewhere. Thus their competitors can be put out of business, one by one, wherever they dare to show a head. Inasmuch as they rise up only one by one, these big concerns can see to it that new competitors never come into the larger field. You have to begin somewhere. You can't begin in space. You can't begin in an airship. You have got to begin in some community. Your market has got to be your neighbors first and those who know you there. But unless you have unlimited capital (which of course you wouldn't have when you were beginning) or unlimited credit (which these gentlemen can see to it that you shan't get), they can kill you out in your local market any time they try, on the same basis exactly as that on which they beat organized labor; for they can sell at a loss in your market because they are selling at a profit everywhere else, and they can recoup the losses by which they beat you by the profits which they make in fields where they have beaten other fellows and put them out. If ever a competitor who by good luck has plenty of money does break into the wider market, then the trust has to buy him out, paying three or four times what the business is worth. Following such a purchase it has got to pay the interest on the price it has paid for the business, and it has got to tax the whole people of the United States, in order to pay the interest on what it borrowed to do that, or on the stocks and bonds it issued to do it with. Therefore the big trusts, the big combinations, are the most wasteful, the most uneconomical, and, after they pass a certain size, the most inefficient, way of conducting the industries of this country.

A notable example is the way in which Mr. Carnegie was bought out of the steel business. Mr. Carnegie could build better mills and make better steel rails and make them cheaper than anybody else connected with what afterward became the United States Steel Corporation. They didn't dare leave him outside. He had so much more brains in finding out the best processes; he had so much more shrewdness in surrounding himself with the most successful assistants; he knew so well when a young man who came into his employ was fit for promotion and was ripe to put at the head of some branch of his business and was sure to make good, that he could undersell every mother's son of them in the market for steel rails. And they bought him out at a price that amounted to three or four times, —I believe actually five times, —the estimated value of his properties and of his business, because they couldn't beat him in competition. And then in what they charged afterward for their product, —the product of his mills included, —they made us pay the interest on the four or five times the difference.

That is the difference between a big business and a trust. A trust is an arrangement to get rid of competition, and a big business is a business that has survived competition by conquering in the field of intelligence and economy. A trust does not bring efficiency to the aid of business; it *buys efficiency out of business*. I am for big business, and I am against the trusts. Any man who can survive by his brains, any man who can put the others out of the business by making the thing cheaper to the consumer at the same time that he is increasing its intrinsic value and quality, I take off my hat to, and I say: "You are the man who can build up the United States, and I wish there were more of you."

There will not be more, unless we find a way to prevent monopoly. You know perfectly well that a trust business staggering under a capitalization many times too big is not a business that can afford to admit competitors into the field; because the minute an economical business, a business with its capital down to hard pan, with every ounce of its capital working, comes into the field against such an overloaded corporation, it will inevitably beat it and undersell it; therefore it is to the interest of these gentlemen that monopoly be maintained. They cannot rule the markets of the world in any way but by monopoly. It is not surprising to find them helping to found a new party with a fine program of benevolence, but also with a tolerant acceptance of monopoly.

There is another matter to which we must direct our attention, whether we like or not. I do not take these things into my mouth because they please my palate; I do not talk about them because I want to attack anybody or upset anything; I talk about them because only by open speech about them among ourselves shall we learn what the facts are.

You will notice from a recent investigation that things like this take place: A certain bank invests in certain securities. It appears from evidence that the handling of these securities was very intimately connected with the maintenance of the price of a particular commodity. Nobody ought, and in normal circumstances nobody would, for a moment think of suspecting the managers of a great bank of making such an investment in order to help those who were conducting a particular business in the United States maintain the price of their commodity; but the circumstances are not normal. It is beginning to be believed that in the big business of this country nothing is disconnected from anything else. I do not mean in this particular instance to which I have referred, and I do not have in mind to draw any inference at all, for that would be unjust; but take any investment of an industrial character by a great bank. It is known that the directorate of that bank interlaces in personnel with ten, twenty, thirty, forty, fifty, sixty boards of directors of all sorts, of railroads which handle commodities, of great groups of manufacturers which manufacture commodities, and of great merchants who distribute commodities; and the result is that every great bank is under suspicion with regard to the motive of its investments. It is at least considered possible that it is playing the game of somebody who has nothing to do with banking, but with whom some of its directors are connected and joined in interest. The ground of unrest and uneasiness, in short, on the part of the public at large, is the growing knowledge that many large undertakings are interlaced with one another, are indistinguishable from one another in personnel.

Therefore, when a small group of men approach Congress in order to induce the committee concerned to concur in certain legislation, nobody knows the ramifications of the interests which those men represent; there seems no frank and open action of public opinion in public counsel, but every man is suspected of representing some other man and it is not known where his connections begin or end.

I am one of those who have been so fortunately circumstanced that I have had the opportunity to study the way in which these things come about in complete disconnection from them, and I do not suspect that any man has deliberately planned the system. I am not so uninstructed and misinformed as to suppose that there is a deliberate and malevolent combination somewhere to dominate the government of the United States. I merely say that, by certain processes, now well known, and perhaps natural in themselves, there has come about an extraordinary and very sinister concentration in the control of business in the country.

However it has come about, it is more important still that the control of credit also has become dangerously centralized. It is the mere truth to say that the financial resources of the country are not at the command of those who do not submit to the direction and domination of small groups of capitalists who wish to keep the economic development of the country under their own eye and guidance. The great monopoly in this country is the monopoly of big credits. So long as that exists, our old variety and freedom and individual energy of development are out of the question. A great industrial nation is controlled by its system of credit. Our system of credit is privately concentrated. The growth of the nation, therefore, and all our activities are in the hands of a few men who, even if their action be honest and intended for the public interest, are necessarily concentrated upon the great undertakings in which their own money is involved and who necessarily, by very reason of their own limitations, chill and check and destroy genuine economic freedom. This is the greatest question of all, and to this statesmen must address themselves with an earnest determination to serve the long future and the true liberties of men.

This money trust, or, as it should be more properly called, this credit trust, of which Congress has begun an investigation, is no myth; it is no imaginary thing. It is not an ordinary trust like another. It doesn't do business every day. It does business only when there is occasion to do business. You can sometimes do something large when it isn't watching, but when it is watching, you can't do much. And I have seen men squeezed by it; I have seen men who, as they themselves expressed it, were put "out of business by Wall Street," because Wall Street found them inconvenient and didn't want their competition.

Let me say again that I am not impugning the motives of the men in Wall Street. They may think that that is the best way to create prosperity for the country. When you have got the market in your hand, does honesty oblige you to turn the palm upside down and empty it? If you have got the market in your hand and believe that you understand the interest of the country better than anybody else, is it patriotic to let it go? I can imagine them using this argument to themselves.

The dominating danger in this land is not the existence of great individual combinations, — that is dangerous enough in all conscience, — but the combination of the combinations, — of the railways, the manufacturing enterprises, the great mining projects, the great enterprises for the development of the natural water-powers of the country, threaded together in the personnel of a series of boards of directors into a "community of interest" more formidable than any conceivable single combination that dare appear in the open.

The organization of business has become more centralized, vastly more centralized, than the political organization of the country itself. Corporations have come to cover greater areas than states; have come to live under a greater variety of laws than the citizen himself, have excelled states in their budgets and loomed bigger than whole commonwealths in their influence over the lives and fortunes of entire communities of men. Centralized business has built up vast structures of organization and equipment which overtop all states and seem to have no match or competitor except the federal government itself.

What we have got to do, — and it is a colossal task not to be undertaken with a light head or without judgment, — what we have got to do is to disentangle this colossal "community of interest." No matter how we may purpose dealing with a single combination in restraint of trade, you will agree with me in this, that no single, avowed, combination is big enough for the United States to be afraid of; but when all the combinations are combined and this final combination is not disclosed by any process of incorporation or law, but is merely an identity of personnel, or of interest, then there is something that even the government of the nation itself might come to fear, — something for the law to pull apart, and gently, but firmly and persistently, dissect.

You know that the chemist distinguishes between a chemical combination and an amalgam. A chemical combination has done something which I cannot scientifically describe, but its molecules have become intimate with one another and have practically united, whereas an amalgam has a mere physical union created by pressure from without. Now, you can destroy that mere physical contact without hurting the individual elements, and this community of interest is an amalgam; you can break it up without hurting any one of the single interests combined. Not that I am particularly delicate of some of the interests combined,—I am not under bonds to be unduly polite to them,—but I am interested in the business of the country, and believe its integrity depends upon this dissection. I do not believe any one group of men has vision enough or genius enough to determine what the development of opportunity and the accomplishment by achievement shall be in this country.

The facts of the situation amount to this: that a comparatively small number of men control the raw material of this country; that a comparatively small number of men control the water-powers that can be made useful for the economical production of the energy to drive our machinery; that that same number of men largely control the railroads; that by agreements handed around among themselves they control prices, and that that same group of men control the larger credits of the country.

When we undertake the strategy which is going to be necessary to overcome and destroy this far-reaching system of monopoly, we are rescuing the business of this country, we are not injuring it; and when we separate the interests from each other and dismember these communities of connection, we have in mind a greater community of interest, a vaster community of interest, the community of interest that binds the virtues of all men together, that community of mankind which is broad and catholic enough to take under the sweep of its comprehension all sorts and conditions of men; that vision which sees that no society is renewed from the top but that every society is renewed from the bottom. Limit opportunity, restrict the field of originative achievement, and you have cut out the heart and root of all prosperity.

The only thing that can ever make a free country is to keep a free and hopeful heart under every jacket in it. Honest American industry has always thriven, when it has thriven at all, on freedom; it has never thriven on monopoly. It is a great deal better to shift for yourselves than to be taken care of by a great combination of capital. I, for my part, do not want to be taken care of. I would rather starve a free man than be fed a mere thing at the caprice of those who are organizing American industry as they please to organize it. I know, and every man in his heart knows, that the only way to enrich America is to make it possible for any man who has the brains to get into the game. I am not jealous of the size of any business that has *grown* to that size. I am not jealous of any process of growth, no matter how huge the result, provided the result was indeed obtained by the processes of wholesome development, which are the processes of efficiency, of economy, of intelligence, and of invention.

IX
Benevolence, or Justice?

The doctrine that monopoly is inevitable and that the only course open to the people of the United States is to submit to and regulate it found a champion during the campaign of 1912 in the new party, or branch of the Republican party, founded under the leadership of Mr. Roosevelt, with the conspicuous aid, —I mention him with no satirical intention, but merely to set the facts down accurately, —of Mr. George W. Perkins, organizer of the Steel Trust and the Harvester Trust, and with the support of more than three millions of citizens, many of them among the most patriotic, conscientious and high-minded men and women of the land. The fact that its acceptance of monopoly was a feature of the new party platform from which the attention of the generous and just was diverted by the charm of a social program of great attractiveness to all concerned for the amelioration of the lot of those who suffer wrong and privation, and the further fact that, even so, the platform was repudiated by the majority of the nation, render it no less necessary to reflect on the significance of the confession made for the first time by any party in the country's history. It may be useful, in order to the relief of the minds of many from an error of no small magnitude, to consider now, the heat of a presidential contest being past, exactly what it was that Mr. Roosevelt proposed.

Mr. Roosevelt attached to his platform some very splendid suggestions as to noble enterprises which we ought to undertake for the uplift of the human race; but when I hear an ambitious platform put forth, I am very much more interested in the dynamics of it than in the rhetoric of it. I have a very practical mind, and I want to know who are going to do those things and how they are going to be done. If you have read the trust plank in that platform as often as I have read it, you have found it very long, but very tolerant. It did not anywhere condemn monopoly, except in words; its essential meaning was that the trusts have been bad and must be made to be good. You know that Mr. Roosevelt long ago classified trusts for us as good and bad, and he said that he was afraid only of the bad ones. Now he does not desire that there should be any more bad ones, but proposes that they should all be made good by discipline, directly applied by a commission of executive appointment. All he explicitly complains of is lack of publicity and lack of fairness; not the exercise of power, for throughout that plank the power of the great corporations is accepted as the inevitable consequence of the modern organization of industry. All that it is proposed to do is to take them under control and regulation. The national administration having for sixteen years been virtually under the regulation of the trusts, it would be merely a family matter were the parts reversed and were the other members of the family to exercise the regulation. And the trusts, apparently, which might, in such circumstances, comfortably continue to administer our affairs under the mollifying influences of the federal government, would then, if you please, be the instrumentalities by which all the humanistic, benevolent program of the rest of that interesting platform would be carried out!

I have read and reread that plank, so as to be sure that I get it right. All that it complains of is, —and the complaint is a just one, surely, —that these gentlemen exercise their power in a way that is secret. Therefore, we must have publicity. Sometimes they are arbitrary; therefore they need regulation. Sometimes they do not consult the general interests of the community; therefore they need to be reminded of those general interests by an industrial commission. But at every turn it is the trusts who are to do us good, and not we ourselves.

Again, I absolutely protest against being put into the hands of trustees. Mr. Roosevelt's conception of government is Mr. Taft's conception, that the Presidency of the United States is the presidency of a board of directors. I am willing to admit that if the people of the United States cannot get justice for themselves, then it is high time that they should join the third party and get it from somebody else. The justice proposed is very beautiful; it is very attractive; there were planks in that platform which stir all the sympathies of the heart; they proposed things that we all want to do; but the question is, Who is going to do them? Through whose instrumentality? Are Americans ready to ask the trusts to give us in pity what we ought, in justice, to take?

The third party says that the present system of our industry and trade has come to stay. Mind you, these artificially built up things, these things that can't maintain themselves in the market without monopoly, have come to stay, and the only thing that the government can do, the only thing that the third party proposes should be done, is to set up a commission to regulate them. It accepts them. It says: "We will not undertake, it were futile to undertake, to prevent monopoly, but we will go into an arrangement by which we will make these monopolies kind to you. We will guarantee that they shall be pitiful. We will guarantee that they shall pay the right wages. We will guarantee that they shall do everything kind and public-spirited, which they have never heretofore shown the least inclination to do."

Don't you realize that that is a blind alley? You can't find your way to liberty that way. You can't find your way to social reform through the forces that have made social reform necessary.

The fundamental part of such a program is that the trusts shall be recognized as a permanent part of our economic order, and that the government shall try to make trusts the ministers, the instruments, through which the life of this country shall be justly and happily developed on its industrial side. Now, everything that touches our lives sooner or later goes back to the industries which sustain our lives. I have often reflected that there is a very human order in the petitions in our Lord's prayer. For we pray first of all, "Give us this day our daily bread," knowing that it is useless to pray for spiritual graces on an empty stomach, and that the amount of wages we get, the kind of clothes we wear, the kind of food we can afford to buy, is fundamental to everything else.

Those who administer our physical life, therefore, administer our spiritual life; and if we are going to carry out the fine purpose of that great chorus which supporters of the third party sang almost with religious fervor, then we have got to find out through whom these purposes of humanity are going to be realized. It is a mere enterprise, so far as that part of it is concerned, of making the monopolies philanthropic.

I do not want to live under a philanthropy. I do not want to be taken care of by the government, either directly, or by any instruments through which the government is acting. I want only to have right and justice prevail, so far as I am concerned. Give me right and justice and I will undertake to take care of myself. If you enthrone the trusts as the means of the development of this country under the supervision of the government, then I shall pray the old Spanish proverb, "God save me from my friends, and I'll take care of my enemies." Because I want to be saved from these friends. Observe that I say these friends, for I am ready to admit that a great many men who believe that the development of industry in this country through monopolies is inevitable intend to be the friends of the people. Though they profess to be my friends, they are undertaking a way of friendship which renders it impossible that they should do me the fundamental service that I demand-namely, that I should be free and should have the same opportunities that everybody else has.

For I understand it to be the fundamental proposition of American liberty that we do not desire special privilege, because we know special privilege will never comprehend the general welfare. This is the fundamental, spiritual difference between adherents of the party now about to take charge of the government and those who have been in charge of it in recent years. They are so indoctrinated with the idea that only the big business interests of this country understand the United States and can make it prosperous that they cannot divorce their thoughts from that obsession. They have put the government into the hands of trustees, and Mr. Taft and Mr. Roosevelt were the rival candidates to preside over the board of trustees. They were candidates to serve the people, no doubt, to the best of their ability, but it was not their idea to serve them directly; they proposed to serve them indirectly through the enormous forces already set up, which are so great that there is almost an open question whether the government of the United States with the people back of it is strong enough to overcome and rule them.

Shall we try to get the grip of monopoly away from our lives, or shall we not? Shall we withhold our hand and say monopoly is inevitable, that all that we can do is to regulate it? Shall we say that all that we can do is to put government in competition with monopoly and try its strength against it? Shall we admit that the creature of our own hands is stronger than we are? We have been dreading all along the time when the combined power of high finance would be greater than the power of the government. Have we come to a time when the President of the United States or any man who wishes to be the President must doff his cap in the presence of this high finance, and say, "You are our inevitable master, but we will see how we can make the best of it?"

We are at the parting of the ways. We have, not one or two or three, but many, established and formidable monopolies in the United States. We have, not one or two, but many, fields of endeavor into which it is difficult, if not impossible, for the independent man to enter. We have restricted credit, we have restricted opportunity, we have controlled development, and we have come to be one of the worst ruled, one of the most completely controlled and dominated, governments in the civilized world-no longer a government by free opinion, no longer a government by conviction and the vote of the majority, but a government by the opinion and the duress of small groups of dominant men.

If the government is to tell big business men how to run their business, then don't you see that big business men have to get closer to the government even than they are now? Don't you see that they must capture the government, in order not to be restrained too much by it? Must capture the government? They have already captured it. Are you going to invite those inside to stay inside? They don't have to get there. They are there. Are you going to own your own premises, or are you not? That is your choice. Are you going to say: "You didn't get into the house the right way, but you are in there, God bless you; we will stand out here in the cold and you can hand us out something once in a while?"

At the least, under the plan I am opposing, there will be an avowed partnership between the government and the trusts. I take it that the firm will be ostensibly controlled by the senior member. For I take it that the government of the United States is at least the senior member, though the younger member has all along been running the business. But when all the momentum, when all the energy, when a great deal of the genius, as so often happens in partnerships the world over, is with the junior partner, I don't think that the superintendence of the senior partner is going to amount to very much. And I don't believe that benevolence can be read into the hearts of the trusts by the superintendence and suggestions of the federal government; because the government has never within my recollection had its suggestions accepted by the trusts. On the contrary, the suggestions of the trusts have been accepted by the government.

There is no hope to be seen for the people of the United States until the partnership is dissolved. And the business of the party now entrusted with power is going to be to dissolve it.

Those who supported the third party supported, I believe, a program perfectly agreeable to the monopolies. How those who have been fighting monopoly through all their career can reconcile the continuation of the battle under the banner of the very men they have been fighting, I cannot imagine. I challenge the program in its fundamentals as not a progressive program at all. Why did Mr. Gary suggest this very method when he was at the head of the Steel Trust? Why is this very method commended here, there, and everywhere by the men who are interested in the maintenance of the present economic system of the United States? Why do the men who do not wish to be disturbed urge the adoption of this program? The rest of the program is very handsome; there is beating in it a great pulse of sympathy for the human race. But I do not want the sympathy of the trusts for the human race. I do not want their condescending assistance.

And I warn every progressive Republican that by lending his assistance to this program he is playing false to the very cause in which he had enlisted. That cause was a battle against monopoly, against control, against the concentration of power in our economic development, against all those things that interfere with absolutely free enterprise. I believe that some day these gentlemen will wake up and realize that they have misplaced their trust, not in an individual, it may be, but in a program which is fatal to the things we hold dearest.

If there is any meaning in the things I have been urging, it is this: that the incubus that lies upon this country is the present monopolistic organization of our industrial life. That is the thing which certain Republicans became "insurgents" in order to throw off. And yet some of them allowed themselves to be so misled as to go into the camp of the third party in order to remove what the third party proposed to legalize. My point is that this is a method conceived from the point of view of the very men who are to be controlled, and that this is just the wrong point of view from which to conceive it.

I said not long ago that Mr. Roosevelt was promoting a plan for the control of monopoly which was supported by the United States Steel Corporation. Mr. Roosevelt denied that he was being supported by more than one member of that corporation. He was thinking of money. I was thinking of ideas. I did not say that he was getting money from these gentlemen; it was a matter of indifference to me where he got his money; but it was a matter of a great deal of difference to me where he got his ideas. He got his idea with regard to the regulation of monopoly from the gentlemen who form the United States Steel Corporation. I am perfectly ready to admit that the gentlemen who control the United States Steel Corporation have a perfect right to entertain their own ideas about this and to urge them upon the people of the United States; but I want to say that their ideas are not my ideas; and I am perfectly certain that they would not promote any idea which interfered with their monopoly. Inasmuch, therefore, as I hope and intend to interfere with monopoly just as much as possible, I cannot subscribe to arrangements by which they know that it will not be disturbed.

The Roosevelt plan is that there shall be an industrial commission charged with the supervision of the great monopolistic combinations which have been formed under the protection of the tariff, and that the government of the United States shall see to it that these gentlemen who have conquered labor shall be kind to labor. I find, then, the proposition to be this: That there shall be two masters, the great corporation, and over it the government of the United States; and I ask who is going to be master of the government of the United States? It has a master now, —those who in combination control these monopolies. And if the government controlled by the monopolies in its turn controls the monopolies, the partnership is finally consummated.

I don't care how benevolent the master is going to be, I will not live under a master. That is not what America was created for. America was created in order that every man should have the same chance as every other man to exercise mastery over his own fortunes. What I want to do is analogous to what the authorities of the city of Glasgow did with tenement houses. I want to light and patrol the corridors of these great organizations in order to see that nobody who tries to traverse them is waylaid and maltreated. If you will but hold off the adversaries, if you will but see to it that the weak are protected, I will venture a wager with you that there are some men in the United States, now weak, economically weak, who have brains enough to compete with these gentlemen and who will presently come into the market and put these gentlemen on their mettle. And the minute they come into the market there will be a bigger market for labor and a different wage scale for labor.

Because it is susceptible of convincing proof that the high-paid labor of America, —where it is high paid, —is cheaper than the low-paid labor of the continent of Europe. Do you know that about ninety per cent. of those who are employed in labor in this country are not employed in the "protected" industries, and that their wages are almost without exception higher than the wages of those who are employed in the "protected" industries? There is no corner on carpenters, there is no corner on bricklayers, there is no corner on scores of individual classes of skilled laborers; but there is a corner on the poolers in the furnaces, there is a corner on the men who dive down into the mines; they are in the grip of a controlling power which determines the market rates of wages in the United States. Only where labor is free is labor highly paid in America.

When I am fighting monopolistic control, therefore, I am fighting for the liberty of every man in America, and I am fighting for the liberty of American industry.

It is significant that the spokesman for the plan of adopting monopoly declares his devoted adherence to the principle of "protection." Only those duties which are manifestly too high even to serve the interests of those who are directly "protected" ought in his view to be lowered. He declares that he is not troubled by the fact that a very large amount of money is taken out of the pocket of the general taxpayer and put into the pocket of particular classes of "protected" manufacturers, but that his concern is that so little of this money gets into the pocket of the laboring man and so large a proportion of it into the pockets of the employers. I have searched his program very thoroughly for an indication of what he expects to do in order to see to it that a larger proportion of this "prize" money gets into the pay envelope, and have found none. Mr. Roosevelt, in one of his speeches, proposed that manufacturers who did not share their profits liberally enough with their workmen should be penalized by a sharp cut in the "protection" afforded them; but the platform, so far as I could see, proposed nothing.

Moreover, under the system proposed, most employers,—at any rate, practically all of the most powerful of them,—would be, to all intents and purposes, wards and protégés of the government which is the master of us all; for no part of this program can be discussed intelligently without remembering that monopoly, as handled by it, is not to be prevented, but accepted. It is to be accepted and regulated. All attempt to resist it is to be given up. It is to be accepted as inevitable. The government is to set up a commission whose duty it will be, not to check or defeat it, but merely to regulate it under rules which it is itself to frame and develop. So that the chief employers will have this tremendous authority behind them: what they do, they will have the license of the federal government to do.

And it is worth the while of the workingmen of the country to recall what the attitude toward organized labor has been of these masters of consolidated industries whom it is proposed that the federal government should take under its patronage as well as under its control. They have been the stoutest and most successful opponents of organized labor, and they have tried to undermine it in a great many ways. Some of the ways they have adopted have worn the guise of philanthropy and good-will, and have no doubt been used, for all I know, in perfect good faith. Here and there they have set up systems of profit sharing, of compensation for injuries, and of bonuses, and even pensions; but every one of these plans has merely bound their workingmen more tightly to themselves. Rights under these various arrangements are not legal rights. They are merely privileges which employees enjoy only so long as they remain in the employment and observe the rules of the great industries for which they work. If they refuse to be weaned away from their independence they cannot continue to enjoy the benefits extended to them.

When you have thought the whole thing out, therefore, you will find that the program of the new party legalizes monopolies and systematically subordinates workingmen to them and to plans made by the government both with regard to employment and with regard to wages. Take the thing as a whole, and it looks strangely like economic mastery over the very lives and fortunes of those who do the daily work of the nation; and all this under the overwhelming power and sovereignty of the national government. What most of us are fighting for is to break up this very partnership between big business and the government. We call upon all intelligent men to bear witness that if this plan were consummated, the great employers and capitalists of the country would be under a more overpowering temptation than ever to take control of the government and keep it subservient to their purpose.

What a prize it would be to capture! How unassailable would be the majesty and the tyranny of monopoly if it could thus get sanction of law and the authority of government! By what means, except open revolt, could we ever break the crust of our life again and become free men, breathing an air of our own, living lives that we wrought out for ourselves?

You cannot use monopoly in order to serve a free people. You cannot use great combinations of capital to be pitiful and righteous when the consciences of great bodies of men are enlisted, not in the promotion of special privilege, but in the realization of human rights. When I read those beautiful portions of the program of the third party devoted to the uplift of mankind and see noble men and women attaching themselves to that party in the hope that regulated monopoly may realize these dreams of humanity, I wonder whether they have really studied the instruments through which they are going to do these things. The man who is leading the third party has not changed his point of view since he was President of the United States. I am not asking him to change it. I am not saying that he has not a perfect right to retain it. But I do say that it is not surprising that a man who had the point of view with regard to the government of this country which he had when he was President was not chosen as President again, and allowed to patent the present processes of industry and personally direct them how to treat the people of the United States.

There has been a history of the human race, you know, and a history of government; it is recorded; and the kind of thing proposed has been tried again and again and has always led to the same result. History is strewn all along its course with the wrecks of governments that tried to be humane, tried to carry out humane programs through the instrumentality of those who controlled the material fortunes of the rest of their fellow-citizens.

I do not trust any promises of a change of temper on the part of monopoly. Monopoly never was conceived in the temper of tolerance. Monopoly never was conceived with the purpose of general development. It was conceived with the purpose of special advantage. Has monopoly been very benevolent to its employees? Have the trusts had a soft heart for the working people of America? Have you found trusts that cared whether women were sapped of their vitality or not? Have you found trusts who are very scrupulous about using children in their tender years? Have you found trusts that were keen to protect the lungs and the health and the freedom of their employees? Have you found trusts that thought as much of their men as they did of their machinery? Then who is going to convert these men into the chief instruments of justice and benevolence?

If you will point me to the least promise of disinterestedness on the part of the masters of our lives, then I will conceive you some ray of hope; but only upon this hypothesis, only upon this conjecture: that the history of the world is going to be reversed, and that the men who have the power to oppress us will be kind to us, and will promote our interests, whether our interests jump with theirs or not.

After you have made the partnership between monopoly and your government permanent, then I invite all the philanthropists in the United States to come and sit on the stage and go through the motions of finding out how they are going to get philanthropy out of their masters.

I do not want to see the special interests of the United States take care of the workingmen, women, and children. I want to see justice, righteousness, fairness and humanity displayed in all the laws of the United States, and I do not want any power to intervene between the people and their government. Justice is what we want, not patronage and condescension and pitiful helpfulness. The trusts are our masters now, but I for one do not care to live in a country called free even under kind masters. I prefer to live under no masters at all.

I agree that as a nation we are now about to undertake what may be regarded as the most difficult part of our governmental enterprises. We have gone along so far without very much assistance from our government. We have felt, and felt more and more in recent months, that the American people were at a certain disadvantage as compared with the people of other countries, because of what the governments of other countries were doing for them and our government omitting to do for us.

It is perfectly clear to every man who has any vision of the immediate future, who can forecast any part of it from the indications of the present, that we are just upon the threshold of a time when the systematic life of this country will be sustained, or at least supplemented, at every point by governmental activity. And we have now to determine what kind of governmental activity it shall be; whether, in the first place, it shall be direct from the government itself, or whether it shall be indirect, through instrumentalities which have already constituted themselves and which stand ready to supersede the government.

I believe that the time has come when the governments of this country, both state and national, have to set the stage, and set it very minutely and carefully, for the doing of justice to men in every relationship of life. It has been free and easy with us so far; it has been go as you please; it has been every man look out for himself; and we have continued to assume, up to this year when every man is dealing, not with another man, in most cases, but with a body of men whom he has not seen, that the relationships of property are the same that they always were. We have great tasks before us, and we must enter on them as befits men charged with the responsibility of shaping a new era.

We have a great program of governmental assistance ahead of us in the co-operative life of the nation; but we dare not enter upon that program until we have freed the government. That is the point. Benevolence never developed a man or a nation. We do not want a benevolent government. We want a free and a just government. Every one of the great schemes of social uplift which are now so much debated by noble people amongst us is based, when rightly conceived, upon justice, not upon benevolence. It is based upon the right of men to breathe pure air, to live; upon the right of women to bear children, and not to be overburdened so that disease and breakdown will come upon them; upon the right of children to thrive and grow up and be strong; upon all these fundamental things which appeal, indeed, to our hearts, but which our minds perceive to be part of the fundamental justice of life.

Politics differs from philanthropy in this: that in philanthropy we sometimes do things through pity merely, while in politics we act always, if we are righteous men, on grounds of justice and large expediency for men in the mass. Sometimes in our pitiful sympathy with our fellow-men we must do things that are more than just. We must forgive men. We must help men who have gone wrong. We must sometimes help men who have gone criminally wrong. But the law does not forgive. It is its duty to equalize conditions, to make the path of right the path of safety and advantage, to see that every man has a fair chance to live and to serve himself, to see that injustice and wrong are not wrought upon any.

We ought not to permit passion to enter into our thoughts or our hearts in this great matter; we ought not to allow ourselves to be governed by resentment or any kind of evil feeling, but we ought, nevertheless, to realize the seriousness of our situation. That seriousness consists, singularly enough, not in the malevolence of the men who preside over our industrial life, but in their genius and in their honest thinking. These men believe that the prosperity of the United States is not safe unless it is in their keeping. If they were dishonest, we might put them out of business by law; since most of them are honest, we can put them out of business only by making it impossible for them to realize their genuine convictions. I am not afraid of a knave. I am not afraid of a rascal. I am afraid of a strong man who is wrong, and whose wrong thinking can be impressed upon other persons by his own force of character and force of speech. If God had only arranged it that all the men who are wrong were rascals, we could put them out of business very easily, because they would give themselves away sooner or later; but God has made our task heavier than that,—he has made some good men who think wrong. We cannot fight them because they are bad, but because they are wrong. We must overcome them by a better force, the genial, the splendid, the permanent force of a better reason.

The reason that America was set up was that she might be different from all the nations of the world in this: that the strong could not put the weak to the wall, that the strong could not prevent the weak from entering the race. America stands for opportunity. America stands for a free field and no favor. America stands for a government responsive to the interests of all. And until America recovers those ideals in practice, she will not have the right to hold her head high again amidst the nations as she used to hold it.

It is like coming out of a stifling cellar into the open where we can breathe again and see the free spaces of the heavens to turn away from such a doleful program of submission and dependence toward the other plan, the confident purpose for which the people have given their mandate. Our purpose is the restoration of freedom. We purpose to prevent private monopoly by law, to see to it that the methods by which monopolies have been built up are legally made impossible. We design that the limitations on private enterprise shall be removed, so that the next generation of youngsters, as they come along, will not have to become protégés of benevolent trusts, but will be free to go about making their own lives what they will; so that we shall taste again the full cup, not of charity, but of liberty,—the only wine that ever refreshed and renewed the spirit of a people.

X
The Way to Resume is to Resume

One of the wonderful things about America, to my mind, is this: that for more than a generation it has allowed itself to be governed by persons who were not invited to govern it. A singular thing about the people of the United States is their almost infinite patience, their willingness to stand quietly by and see things done which they have voted against and do not want done, and yet never lay the hand of disorder upon any arrangement of government.

There is hardly a part of the United States where men are not aware that secret private purposes and interests have been running the government. They have been running it through the agency of those interesting persons whom we call political "bosses." A boss is not so much a politician as the business agent in politics of the special interests. The boss is not a partisan; he is quite above politics! He has an understanding with the boss of the other party, so that, whether it is heads or tails, we lose. The two receive contributions from the same sources, and they spend those contributions for the same purposes.

Bosses are men who have worked their way by secret methods to the place of power they occupy; men who were never elected to anything; men who were not asked by the people to conduct their government, and who are very much more powerful than if you had asked them, so long as you leave them where they are, behind closed doors, in secret conference. They are not politicians; they have no policies, —except concealed policies of private aggrandizement. A boss isn't a leader of a party. Parties do not meet in back rooms; parties do not make arrangements which do not get into the newspapers. Parties, if you reckon them by voting strength, are great masses of men who, because they can't vote any other ticket, vote the ticket that was prepared for them by the aforesaid arrangement in the aforesaid back room in accordance with the aforesaid understanding. A boss is the manipulator of a "machine." A "machine" is that part of a political organization which has been taken out of the hands of the rank and file of the party, captured by half a dozen men. It is the part that has ceased to be political and has become an agency for the purposes of unscrupulous business.

Do not lay up the sins of this kind of business to political organizations. Organization is legitimate, is necessary, is even distinguished, when it lends itself to the carrying out of great causes. Only the man who uses organization to promote private purposes is a boss. Always distinguish between a political leader and a boss. I honor the man who makes the organization of a great party strong and thorough, in order to use it for public service. But he is not a boss. A boss is a man who uses this splendid, open force for secret purposes.

One of the worst features of the boss system is this fact, that it works secretly. I would a great deal rather live under a king whom I should at least know, than under a boss whom I don't know. A boss is a much more formidable master than a king, because a king is an obvious master, whereas the hands of the boss are always where you least expect them to be.

When I was in Oregon, not many months ago, I had some very interesting conversations with Mr. U'Ren, who is the father of what is called the Oregon System, a system by which he has put bosses out of business. He is a member of a group of public-spirited men who, whenever they cannot get what they want through the legislature, draw up a bill and submit it to the people, by means of the initiative, and generally get what they want. The day I arrived in Portland, a morning paper happened to say, very ironically, that there were two legislatures in Oregon, one at Salem, the state capital, and the other going around under the hat of Mr. U'Ren. I could not resist the temptation of saying, when I spoke that evening, that, while I was the last man to suggest that power should be concentrated in any single individual or group of individuals, I would, nevertheless, after my experience in New Jersey, rather have a legislature that went around under the hat of somebody in particular whom I knew I could find than a legislature that went around under God knows who's hat; because then you could at least put your finger on your governing force; you would know where to find it.

Why do we continue to permit these things? Isn't it about time that we grew up and took charge of our own affairs? I am tired of being under age in politics. I don't want to be associated with anybody except those who are politically over twenty-one. I don't wish to sit down and let any man take care of me without my having at least a voice in it; and if he doesn't listen to my advice, I am going to make it as unpleasant for him as I can. Not because my advice is necessarily good, but because no government is good in which every man doesn't insist upon his advice being heard, at least, whether it is heeded or not.

Some persons have said that representative government has proved too indirect and clumsy an instrument, and has broken down as a means of popular control. Others, looking a little deeper, have said that it was not representative government that had broken down, but the effort to get it. They have pointed out that, with our present methods of machine nomination and our present methods of election, which give us nothing more than a choice between one set of machine nominees and another, we do not get representative government at all,—at least not government representative of the people, but merely government representative of political managers who serve their own interests and the interests of those with whom they find it profitable to establish partnerships.

Obviously, this is something that goes to the root of the whole matter. Back of all reform lies the method of getting it. Back of the question, What do you want, lies the question,—the fundamental question of all government,—How are you going to get it? How are you going to get public servants who will obtain it for you? How are you going to get genuine representatives who will serve your interests, and not their own or the interests of some special group or body of your fellow-citizens whose power is of the few and not of the many? These are the queries which have drawn the attention of the whole country to the subject of the direct primary, the direct choice of their officials by the people, without the intervention of the nominating machine; to the subject of the direct election of United States Senators; and to the question of the initiative, referendum, and recall.

The critical moment in the choosing of officials is that of their nomination more often than that of their election. When two party organizations, nominally opposing each other but actually working in perfect understanding and co-operation, see to it that both tickets have the same kind of men on them, it is Tweedledum or Tweedledee, so far as the people are concerned; the political managers have us coming and going. We may delude ourselves with the pleasing belief that we are electing our own officials, but of course the fact is we are merely making an indifferent and ineffectual choice between two sets of men named by interests which are not ours.

So that what we establish the direct primary for is this: to break up the inside and selfish determination of the question who shall be elected to conduct the government and make the laws of our commonwealths and our nation. Everywhere the impression is growing stronger that there can be no means of dominating those who have dominated us except by taking this process of the original selection of nominees into our own hands. Does that upset any ancient foundations? Is it not the most natural and simple thing in the world? You say that it does not always work; that the people are too busy or too lazy to bother about voting at primary elections? True, sometimes the people of a state or a community do let a direct primary go by without asserting their authority as against the bosses. The electorate of the United States is occasionally like the god Baal: it is sometimes on a journey or it is sometimes asleep; but when it does awake, it does not resemble the god Baal in the slightest degree. It is a great self-possessed power which effectually takes control of its own affairs. I am willing to wait. I am among those who believe so firmly in the essential doctrines of democracy that I am willing to wait on the convenience of this great sovereign, provided I know that he has got the instrument to dominate whenever he chooses to grasp it.

Then there is another thing that the conservative people are concerned about: the direct election of United States Senators. I have seen some thoughtful men discuss that with a sort of shiver, as if to disturb the original constitution of the United States Senate was to do something touched with impiety, touched with irreverence for the Constitution itself. But the first thing necessary to reverence for the United States Senate is respect for United States Senators. I am not one of those who condemn the United States Senate as a body; for, no matter what has happened there, no matter how questionable the practices or how corrupt the influences which have filled some of the seats in that high body, it must in fairness be said that the majority in it has all the years through been untouched by stain, and that there has always been there a sufficient number of men of integrity to vindicate the self-respect and the hopefulness of America with regard to her institutions.

But you need not be told, and it would be painful to repeat to you, how seats have been bought in the Senate; and you know that a little group of Senators holding the balance of power has again and again been able to defeat programs of reform upon which the whole country had set its heart; and that whenever you analyzed the power that was behind those little groups you have found that it was not the power of public opinion, but some private influence, hardly to be discerned by superficial scrutiny, that had put those men there to do that thing.

Now, returning to the original principles upon which we profess to stand, have the people of the United States not the right to see to it that every seat in the Senate represents the unbought United States of America? Does the direct election of Senators touch anything except the private control of seats in the Senate? We remember another thing: that we have not been without our suspicions concerning some of the legislatures which elect Senators. Some of the suspicions which we entertained in New Jersey about them turned out to be founded upon very solid facts indeed. Until two years ago New Jersey had not in half a generation been represented in the United States Senate by the men who would have been chosen if the process of selecting them had been free and based upon the popular will.

We are not to deceive ourselves by putting our heads into the sand and saying, "Everything is all right." Mr. Gladstone declared that the American Constitution was the most perfect instrument ever devised by the brain of man. We have been praised all over the world for our singular genius for setting up successful institutions, but a very thoughtful Englishman, and a very witty one, said a very instructive thing about that: he said that to show that the American Constitution had worked well was no proof that it is an excellent constitution, because Americans could run any constitution, —a compliment which we laid like sweet unction to our soul; and yet a criticism which ought to set us thinking.

While it is true that when American forces are awake they can conduct American processes without serious departure from the ideals of the Constitution, it is nevertheless true that we have had many shameful instances of practices which we can absolutely remove by the direct election of Senators by the people themselves. And therefore I, for one, will not allow any man who knows his history to say to me that I am acting inconsistently with either the spirit or the essential form of the American government in advocating the direct election of United States Senators.

Take another matter. Take the matter of the initiative and referendum, and the recall. There are communities, there are states in the Union, in which I am quite ready to admit that it is perhaps premature, that perhaps it will never be necessary, to discuss these measures. But I want to call your attention to the fact that they have been adopted to the general satisfaction in a number of states where the electorate had become convinced that they did not have representative government.

Why do you suppose that in the United States, the place in all the world where the people were invited to control their own government, we should set up such an agitation as that for the initiative and referendum and the recall. When did this thing begin? I have been receiving circulars and documents from little societies of men all over the United States with regard to these matters, for the last twenty-five years. But the circulars for a long time kindled no fire.

Men felt that they had representative government and they were content. But about ten or fifteen years ago the fire began to burn,—and it has been sweeping over wider and wider areas of the country, because of the growing consciousness that something intervenes between the people and the government, and that there must be some arm direct enough and strong enough to thrust aside the something that comes in the way.

I believe that we are upon the eve of recovering some of the most important prerogatives of a free people, and that the initiative and referendum are playing a great part in that recovery. I met a man the other day who thought that the referendum was some kind of an animal, because it had a Latin name; and there are still people in this country who have to have it explained to them. But most of us know and are deeply interested. Why? Because we have felt that in too many instances our government did not represent us, and we have said: "We have got to have a key to the door of our own house. The initiative and referendum and the recall afford such a key to our own premises. If the people inside the house will run the place as we want it run, they may stay inside and we will keep the latchkeys in our pockets. If they do not, we shall have to re-enter upon possession."

Let no man be deceived by the cry that somebody is proposing to substitute direct legislation by the people, or the direct reference of laws passed in the legislature, to the vote of the people, for representative government. The advocates of these reforms have always declared, and declared in unmistakable terms, that they were intending to recover representative government, not supersede it; that the initiative and referendum would find no use in places where legislatures were really representative of the people whom they were elected to serve. The initiative is a means of seeing to it that measures which the people want shall be passed,—when legislatures defy or ignore public opinion. The referendum is a means of seeing to it that the unrepresentative measures which they do not want shall not be placed upon the statute book.

When you come to the recall, the principle is that if an administrative officer,—for we will begin with the administrative officer,—is corrupt or so unwise as to be doing things that are likely to lead to all sorts of mischief, it will be possible by a deliberate process prescribed by the law to get rid of that officer before the end of his term. You must admit that it is a little inconvenient sometimes to have what has been called an astronomical system of government, in which you can't change anything until there has been a certain number of revolutions of the seasons. In many of our oldest states the ordinary administrative term is a single year. The people of those states have not been willing to trust an official out of their sight more than twelve months. Elections there are a sort of continuous performance, based on the idea of the constant touch of the hand of the people on their own affairs. That is exactly the principle of the recall. I don't see how any man grounded in the traditions of American affairs can find any valid objection to the recall of administrative officers. The meaning of the recall is merely this,—not that we should have unstable government, not that officials should not know how long their power might last,—but that we might have government exercised by officials who know whence their power came and that if they yield to private influences they will presently be displaced by public influences.

You will of course understand that, both in the case of the initiative and referendum and in that of the recall, the very existence of these powers, the very possibilities which they imply, are half,—indeed, much more than half,—the battle. They rarely need to be actually exercised. The fact that the people may initiate keeps the members of the legislature awake to the necessity of initiating themselves; the fact that the people have the right to demand the submission of a legislative measure to popular vote renders the members of the legislature wary of bills that would not pass the people; the very possibility of being recalled puts the official on his best behavior.

It is another matter when we come to the judiciary. I myself have never been in favor of the recall of judges. Not because some judges have not deserved to be recalled. That isn't the point. The point is that the recall of judges is treating the symptom instead of the disease. The disease lies deeper, and sometimes it is very virulent and very dangerous. There have been courts in the United States which were controlled by private interests. There have been supreme courts in our states before which plain men could not get justice. There have been corrupt judges; there have been controlled judges; there have been judges who acted as other men's servants and not as the servants of the public. Ah, there are some shameful chapters in the story! The judicial process is the ultimate safeguard of the things that we must hold stable in this country. But suppose that that safeguard is corrupted; suppose that it does not guard my interests and yours, but guards merely the interests of a very small group of individuals; and, whenever your interest clashes with theirs, yours will have to give way, though you represent ninety per cent. of the citizens, and they only ten per cent. Then where is your safeguard?

The just thought of the people must control the judiciary, as it controls every other instrument of government. But there are ways and ways of controlling it. If, —mark you, I say *if*, —at one time the Southern Pacific Railroad owned the supreme court of the State of California, would you remedy that situation by recalling the judges of the court? What good would that do, so long as the Southern Pacific Railroad could substitute others for them? You would not be cutting deep enough. Where you want to go is to the process by which those judges were selected. And when you get there, you will reach the moral of the whole of this discussion, because the moral of it all is that the people of the United States have suspected, until their suspicions have been justified by all sorts of substantial and unanswerable evidence, that, in place after place, at turning-points in the history of this country, we have been controlled by private understandings and not by the public interest; and that influences which were improper, if not corrupt, have determined everything from the making of laws to the administration of justice. The disease lies in the region where these men get their nominations; and if you can recover for the people the *selecting* of judges, you will not have to trouble about their recall. Selection is of more radical consequence than election.

I am aware that those who advocate these measures which we have been discussing are denounced as dangerous radicals. I am particularly interested to observe that the men who cry out most loudly against what they call radicalism are the men who find that their private game in politics is being spoiled. Who are the arch-conservatives nowadays? Who are the men who utter the most fervid praise of the Constitution of the United States and the constitutions of the states? They are the gentlemen who used to get behind those documents to play hide-and-seek with the people whom they pretended to serve. They are the men who entrenched themselves in the laws which they misinterpreted and misused. If now they are afraid that "radicalism" will sweep them away, —and I believe it will, —they have only themselves to thank.

Yet how absurd is the charge that we who are demanding that our government be made representative of the people and responsive to their demands, —how fictitious and hypocritical is the charge that we are attacking the fundamental principles of republican institutions! These very men who hysterically profess their alarm would declaim loudly enough on the Fourth of July of the Declaration of Independence; they would go on and talk of those splendid utterances in our earliest state constitutions, which have been copied in all our later ones, taken from the Petition of Rights, or the Declaration of Rights, those great fundamental documents of the struggle for liberty in England; and yet in these very documents we read such uncompromising statements as this: that, when at any time the people of a commonwealth find that their government is not suitable to the circumstances of their lives or the promotion of their liberties, it is their privilege to alter it at their pleasure, and alter it in any degree. That is the foundation, that is the very central doctrine, that is the ground principle, of American institutions.

I want you to read a passage from the Virginia Bill of Rights, that immortal document which has been a model for declarations of liberty throughout the rest of the continent:

> That all power is vested in, and consequently derived from, the people; that magistrates are their trustees and servants, and at all times amenable to them.
>
> That government is, or ought to be, instituted for the common benefit, protection, and security of the people, nation, or community; of all the various modes and

forms of government, that is the best which is capable of producing the greatest degree of happiness and safety, and is most effectually secured against the danger of mal-administration; and that, when any government shall be found inadequate or contrary to these purposes, a majority of the community bath an indubitable, inalienable, and indefeasible right to reform, alter, or abolish it, in such manner as shall be judged most conducive to the public weal.

I have heard that read a score of times on the Fourth of July, but I never heard it read where actual measures were being debated. No man who understands the principles upon which this Republic was founded has the slightest dread of the gentle, —though very effective, —measures by which the people are again resuming control of their own affairs.

Nor need any lover of liberty be anxious concerning the outcome of the struggle upon which we are now embarked. The victory is certain, and the battle is not going to be an especially sanguinary one. It is hardly going to be worth the name of a battle. Let me tell the story of the emancipation of one State, —New Jersey:

It has surprised the people of the United States to find New Jersey at the front in enterprises of reform. I, who have lived in New Jersey the greater part of my mature life, know that there is no state in the Union which, so far as the hearts and intelligence of its people are concerned, has more earnestly desired reform than has New Jersey. There are men who have been prominent in the affairs of the State who again and again advocated with all the earnestness that was in them the things that we have at last been able to do. There are men in New Jersey who have spent some of the best energies of their lives in trying to win elections in order to get the support of the citizens of New Jersey for programs of reform.

The people had voted for such things very often before the autumn of 1910, but the interesting thing is that nothing had happened. They were demanding the benefit of remedial measures such as had been passed in every progressive state of the Union, measures which had proved not only that they did not upset the life of the communities to which they were applied but that they quickened every force and bettered every condition in those communities. But the people of New Jersey could not get them, and there had come upon them a certain pessimistic despair. I used to meet men who shrugged their shoulders and said: "What difference does it make how we vote? Nothing ever results from our votes." The force that is behind the new party that has recently been formed, the so-called "Progressive Party," is a force of discontent with the old parties of the United States. It is the feeling that men have gone into blind alleys often enough, and that somehow there must be found an open road through which men may pass to some purpose.

In the year 1910 there came a day when the people of New Jersey took heart to believe that something could be accomplished. I had no merit as a candidate for Governor, except that I said what I really thought, and the compliment that the people paid me was in believing that I meant what I said. Unless they had believed in the Governor whom they then elected, unless they had trusted him deeply and altogether, he could have done absolutely nothing. The force of the public men of a nation lies in the faith and the backing of the people of the country, rather than in any gifts of their own. In proportion as you trust them, in proportion as you back them up, in proportion as you lend them your strength, are they strong. The things that have happened in New Jersey since 1910 have happened because the seed was planted in this fine fertile soil of confidence, of trust, of renewed hope.

The moment the forces in New Jersey that had resisted reform realized that the people were backing new men who meant what they had said, they realized that they dare not resist them. It was not the personal force of the new officials; it was the moral strength of their backing that accomplished the extraordinary result.

And what was accomplished? Mere justice to classes that had not been treated justly before.

Every schoolboy in the State of New Jersey, if he cared to look into the matter, could comprehend the fact that the laws applying to laboring-men with respect of compensation when they were hurt in their various employments had originated at a time when society was organized very differently from the way in which it is organized now, and that because the law had not been changed, the courts were obliged to go blindly on administering laws which were cruelly unsuitable to existing conditions, so that it was practically impossible for the workingmen of New Jersey to get justice from the courts; the legislature of the commonwealth had not come to their assistance with the necessary legislation. Nobody seriously debated the circumstances; everybody knew that the law was antiquated and impossible; everybody knew that justice waited to be done. Very well, then, why wasn't it done?

There was another thing that we wanted to do: We wanted to regulate our public service corporations so that we could get the proper service from them, and on reasonable terms. That had been done elsewhere, and where it had been done it had proved just as much for the benefit of the corporations themselves as for the benefit of the people. Of course it was somewhat difficult to convince the corporations. It happened that one of the men who knew the least about the subject was the president of the Public Service Corporation of New Jersey. I have heard speeches from that gentleman that exhibited a total lack of acquaintance with the circumstances of our times. I have never known ignorance so complete in its detail; and, being a man of force and ignorance, he naturally set all his energy to resist the things that he did not comprehend.

I am not interested in questioning the motives of men in such positions. I am only sorry that they don't know more. If they would only join the procession they would find themselves benefited by the healthful exercise, which, for one thing, would renew within them the capacity to learn which I hope they possessed when they were younger. We were not trying to do anything novel in New Jersey in regulating the Public Service Corporation; we were simply trying to adopt there a tested measure of public justice. We adopted it. Has anybody gone bankrupt since? Does anybody now doubt that it was just as much for the benefit of the Public Service Corporation as for the people of the State?

Then there was another thing that we modestly desired: We wanted fair elections; we did not want candidates to buy themselves into office. That seemed reasonable. So we adopted a law, unique in one particular, namely: that if you bought an office, you didn't get it. I admit that that is contrary to all commercial principles, but I think it is pretty good political doctrine. It is all very well to put a man in jail for buying an office, but it is very much better, besides putting him in jail, to show him that if he has paid out a single dollar for that office, he does not get it, though a huge majority voted for him. We reversed the laws of trade; when you buy something in politics in New Jersey, you do not get it. It seemed to us that that was the best way to discourage improper political argument. If your money does not produce the goods, then you are not tempted to spend your money.

We adopted a Corrupt Practices Act, the reasonable foundation of which no man could question, and an Election Act, which every man predicted was not going to work, but which did work,—to the emancipation of the voters of New Jersey.

All these things are now commonplaces with us. We like the laws that we have passed, and no man ventures to suggest any material change in them. Why didn't we get them long ago? What hindered us? Why, because we had a closed government; not an open government. It did not belong to us. It was managed by little groups of men whose names we knew, but whom somehow we didn't seem able to dislodge. When we elected men pledged to dislodge them, they only went into partnership with them. Apparently what was necessary was to call in an amateur who knew so little about the game that he supposed that he was expected to do what he had promised to do.

There are gentlemen who have criticised the Governor of New Jersey because he did not do certain things,—for instance, bring a lot of indictments. The Governor of New Jersey does not think it necessary to defend himself; but he would like to call attention to a very interesting thing that happened in his State: When the people had taken over control of the government, a curious change was wrought in the souls of a great many men; a sudden moral awakening took place, and we simply could not find culprits against whom to bring indictments; it was like a Sunday school, the way they obeyed the laws.

So I say, there is nothing very difficult about resuming our own government. There is nothing to appall us when we make up our minds to set about the task. "The way to resume is to resume," said Horace Greeley, once, when the country was frightened at a prospect which turned out to be not in the least frightful; it was at the moment of the resumption of specie payments for Treasury notes. The Treasury simply resumed, —there was not a ripple of danger or excitement when the day of resumption came around.

It will be precisely so when the people resume control of their own government. The men who conduct the political machines are a small fraction of the party they pretend to represent, and the men who exercise corrupt influences upon them are only a small fraction of the business men of the country. What we are banded together to fight is not a party, is not a great body of citizens; we have to fight only little coteries, groups of men here and there, a few men, who subsist by deceiving us and cannot subsist a moment after they cease to deceive us.

I had occasion to test the power of such a group in the State of New Jersey, and I had the satisfaction of discovering that I had been right in supposing that they did not possess any power at all. It looked as if they were entrenched in a fortress; it looked as if the embrasures of the fortress showed the muzzles of guns; but, as I told my good fellow-citizens, all they had to do was to press a little upon it and they would find that the fortress was a mere cardboard fabric; that it was a piece of stage property; that just so soon as the audience got ready to look behind the scenes they would learn that the army which had been marching and counter-marching in such terrifying array consisted of a single company that had gone in one wing and around and out at the other wing, and could have thus marched in procession for twenty-four hours. You only need about twenty-four men to do the trick. These men are impostors. They are powerful only in proportion as we are susceptible to absurd fear of them. Their capital is our ignorance and our credulity.

To-day we are seeing something that some of us have waited all of our lives to see. We are witnessing a rising of the country. We are seeing a whole people stand up and decline any longer to be imposed upon. The day has come when men are saying to each other: "It doesn't make a peppercorn's difference to me what party I have voted with. I am going to pick out the men I want and the policies I want, and let the label take care of itself. I do not find any great difference between my table of contents and the table of contents of those who have voted with the other party, and who, like me, are very much dissatisfied with the way in which their party has rewarded their faithfulness. They want the same things that I want, and I don't know of anything under God's heaven to prevent our getting together. We want the same things, we have the same faith in the old traditions of the American people, and we have made up our minds that we are going to have now at last the reality instead of the shadow."

We Americans have been too long satisfied with merely going through the motions of government. We have been having a mock game. We have been going to the polls and saying: "This is the act of a sovereign people, but we won't be the sovereign yet; we will postpone that; we will wait until another time. The managers are still shifting the scenes; we are not ready for the real thing yet."

My proposal is that we stop going through the mimic play; that we get out and translate the ideals of American politics into action; so that every man, when he goes to the polls on election day, will feel the thrill of executing an actual judgment, as he takes again into his own hands the great matters which have been too long left to men deputized by their own choice, and seriously sets about carrying into accomplishment his own purposes.

XI
The Emancipation of Business

In the readjustments that are about to be undertaken in this country not one single legitimate or honest arrangement is going to be disturbed; but every impediment to business is going to be removed, every illegitimate kind of control is going to be destroyed. Every man who wants an opportunity and has the energy to seize it, is going to be given a chance. All that we are going to ask the gentlemen who now enjoy monopolistic advantages to do is to match their brains against the brains of those who will then compete with them. The brains, the energy, of the rest of us are to be set free to go into the game,—that is all. There is to be a general release of the capital, the enterprise, of millions of people, a general opening of the doors of opportunity. With what a spring of determination, with what a shout of jubilance, will the people rise to their emancipation!

I am one of those who believe that we have had such restrictions upon the prosperity of this country that we have not yet come into our own, and that by removing those restrictions we shall set free an energy which in our generation has not been known. It is for that reason that I feel free to criticise with the utmost frankness these restrictions, and the means by which they have been brought about. I do not criticise as one without hope; in describing conditions which so hamper, impede, and imprison, I am only describing conditions from which we are going to escape into a contrasting age. I believe that this is a time when there should be unqualified frankness. One of the distressing circumstances of our day is this: I cannot tell you how many men of business, how many important men of business, have communicated their real opinions about the situation in the United States to me privately and confidentially. They are afraid of somebody. They are afraid to make their real opinions known publicly; they tell them to me behind their hand. That is very distressing. That means that we are not masters of our own opinions, except when we vote, and even then we are careful to vote very privately indeed.

It is alarming that this should be the case. Why should any man in free America be afraid of any other man? Or why should any man fear competition,—competition either with his fellow-countrymen or with anybody else on earth?

It is part of the indictment against the protective policy of the United States that it has weakened and not enhanced the vigor of our people. American manufacturers who know that they can make better things than are made elsewhere in the world, that they can sell them cheaper in foreign markets than they are sold in these very markets of domestic manufacture, are afraid,—afraid to venture out into the great world on their own merits and their own skill. Think of it, a nation full of genius and yet paralyzed by timidity! The timidity of the business men of America is to me nothing less than amazing. They are tied to the apron strings of the government at Washington. They go about to seek favors. They say: "For pity's sake, don't expose us to the weather of the world; put some homelike cover over us. Protect us. See to it that foreign men don't come in and match their brains with ours." And, as if to enhance this peculiarity of ours, the strongest men amongst us get the biggest favors; the men of peculiar genius for organizing industries, the men who could run the industries of any country, are the men who are most strongly intrenched behind the highest rates in the schedules of the tariff. They are so timid morally, furthermore, that they dare not stand up before the American people, but conceal these favors in the verbiage of the tariff schedule itself,—in "jokers." Ah! but it is a bitter joke when men who seek favors are so afraid of the best judgment of their fellow-citizens that they dare not avow what they take.

Happily, the general revival of conscience in this country has not been confined to those who were consciously fighting special privilege. The awakening of conscience has extended to those who were *enjoying* special privileges, and I thank God that the business men of this country are beginning to see our economic organization in its true light, as a deadening aristocracy of privilege from which they themselves must escape. The small men of this country are not deluded, and not all of the big business men of this country are deluded. Some men who have been led into wrong practices, who have been led into the practices of monopoly, because that seemed to be the drift and inevitable method of supremacy, are just as ready as we are to turn about and adopt the process of freedom. For American hearts beat in a lot of these men, just as they beat under our jackets. They will be as glad to be free as we shall be to set them free. And then the splendid force which has lent itself to things that hurt us will lend itself to things that benefit us.

And we,—we who are not great captains of industry or business,—shall do them more good than we do now, even in a material way. If you have to be subservient, you are not even making the rich fellows as rich as they might be, because you are not adding your originative force to the extraordinary production of wealth in America. America is as rich, not as Wall Street, not as the financial centres in Chicago and St. Louis and San Francisco; it is as rich as the people that make those centres rich. And if those people hesitate in their enterprise, cower in the face of power, hesitate to originate designs of their own, then the very fountains which make these places abound in wealth are dried up at the source. By setting the little men of America free, you are not damaging the giants.

It may be that certain things will happen, for monopoly in this country is carrying a body of water such as men ought not to be asked to carry. When by regulated competition,—that is to say, fair competition, competition that fights fair,—they are put upon their mettle, they will have to economize, and they cannot economize unless they get rid of that water. I do not know how to squeeze the water out, but they will get rid of it, if you will put them to the necessity. They will have to get rid of it, or those of us who don't carry tanks will outrun them in the race. Put all the business of America upon the footing of economy and efficiency, and then let the race be to the strongest and the swiftest.

Our program is a program of prosperity; a program of prosperity that is to be a little more pervasive than the present prosperity,—and pervasive prosperity is more fruitful than that which is narrow and restrictive. I congratulate the monopolies of the United States that they are not going to have their way, because, quite contrary to their own theory, the fact is that the people are wiser than they are. The people of the United States understand the United States as these gentlemen do not, and if they will only give us leave, we will not only make them rich, but we will make them happy. Because, then, their conscience will have less to carry. I have lived in a state that was owned by a series of corporations. They handed it about. It was at one time owned by the Pennsylvania Railroad; then it was owned by the Public Service Corporation. It was owned by the Public Service Corporation when I was admitted, and that corporation has been resentful ever since that I interfered with its tenancy. But I really did not see any reason why the people should give up their own residence to so small a body of men to monopolize; and, therefore, when I asked them for their title deeds and they couldn't produce them, and there was no court except the court of public opinion to resort to, they moved out. Now they eat out of our hands; and they are not losing flesh either. They are making just as much money as they made before, only they are making it in a more respectable way. They are making it without the constant assistance of the legislature of the State of New Jersey. They are making it in the normal way, by supplying the people of New Jersey with the service in the way of transportation and gas and water that they really need. I do not believe that there are any thoughtful officials of the Public Service Corporation of New Jersey that now seriously regret the change that has come about. We liberated government in my state, and it is an interesting fact that we have not suffered one moment in prosperity.

What we propose, therefore, in this program of freedom, is a program of general advantage. Almost every monopoly that has resisted dissolution has resisted the real interests of its own stockholders. Monopoly always checks development, weighs down natural prosperity, pulls against natural advance.

Take but such an everyday thing as a useful invention and the putting of it at the service of men. You know how prolific the American mind has been in invention; how much civilization has been advanced by the steamboat, the cotton-gin, the sewing-machine, the reaping-machine, the typewriter, the electric light, the telephone, the phonograph. Do you know, have you had occasion to learn, that there is no hospitality for invention nowadays? There is no encouragement for you to set your wits at work to improve the telephone, or the camera, or some piece of machinery, or some mechanical process; you are not invited to find a shorter and cheaper way to make things or to perfect them, or to invent better things to take their place. There is too much money invested in old machinery; too much money has been spent advertising the old camera; the telephone plants, as they are, cost too much to permit their being superseded by something better. Wherever there is monopoly, not only is there no incentive to improve, but, improvement being costly in that it "scraps" old machinery and destroys the value of old products, there is a positive motive against improvement. The instinct of monopoly is against novelty, the tendency of monopoly is to keep in use the old thing, made in the old way; its disposition is to "standardize" everything. Standardization may be all very well, —but suppose everything had been standardized thirty years ago, —we should still be writing by hand, by gas-light, we should be without the inestimable aid of the telephone (sometimes, I admit, it is a nuisance), without the automobile, without wireless telegraphy. Personally, I could have managed to plod along without the aeroplane, and I could have been happy even without moving-pictures.

Of course, I am not saying that all invention has been stopped by the growth of trusts, but I think it is perfectly clear that invention in many fields has been discouraged, that inventors have been prevented from reaping the full fruits of their ingenuity and industry, and that mankind has been deprived of many comforts and conveniences, as well as of the opportunity of buying at lower prices.

The damper put on the inventive genius of America by the trusts operates in half a dozen ways: The first thing discovered by the genius whose device extends into a field controlled by a trust is that he can't get capital to make and market his invention. If you want money to build your plant and advertise your product and employ your agents and make a market for it, where are you going to get it? The minute you apply for money or credit, this proposition is put to you by the banks: "This invention will interfere with the established processes and the market control of certain great industries. We are already financing those industries, their securities are in our hands; we will consult them."

It may be, as a result of that consultation, you will be informed that it is too bad, but it will be impossible to "accommodate" you. It may be you will receive a suggestion that if you care to make certain arrangements with the trust, you will be permitted to manufacture. It may be you will receive an offer to buy your patent, the offer being a poor consolation dole. It may be that your invention, even if purchased, will never be heard of again.

That last method of dealing with an invention, by the way, is a particularly vicious misuse of the patent laws, which ought not to allow property in an idea which is never intended to be realized. One of the reforms waiting to be undertaken is a revision of our patent laws.

In any event, if the trust doesn't want you to manufacture your invention, you will not be allowed to, unless you have money of your own and are willing to risk it fighting the monopolistic trust with its vast resources. I am generalizing the statement, but I could particularize it. I could tell you instances where exactly that thing happened. By the combination of great industries, manufactured products are not only being standardized, but they are too often being kept at a single point of development and efficiency. The increase of the power to produce in proportion to the cost of production is not studied in America as it used to be studied, because if you don't have to improve your processes in order to excel a competitor, if you are human you aren't going to improve your processes; and if you can prevent the competitor from coming into the field, then you can sit at your leisure, and, behind this wall of protection which prevents the brains of any foreigner competing with you, you can rest at your ease for a whole generation.

Can any one who reflects on merely this attitude of the trusts toward invention fail to understand how substantial, how actual, how great will be the effect of the release of the genius of our people to originate, improve, and perfect the instruments and circumstances of our lives? Who can say what patents now lying, unrealized, in secret drawers and pigeonholes, will come to light, or what new inventions will astonish and bless us, when freedom is restored?

Are you not eager for the time when the genius and initiative of all the people shall be called into the service of business? when newcomers with new ideas, new entries with new enthusiasms, independent men, shall be welcomed? when your sons shall be able to look forward to becoming, not employees, but heads of some small, it may be, but hopeful, business, where their best energies shall be inspired by the knowledge that they are their own masters, with the paths of the world open before them? Have you no desire to see the markets opened to all? to see credit available in due proportion to every man of character and serious purpose who can use it safely and to advantage? to see business disentangled from its unholy alliance with politics? to see raw material released from the control of monopolists, and transportation facilities equalized for all? and every avenue of commercial and industrial activity levelled for the feet of all who would tread it? Surely, you must feel the inspiration of such a new dawn of liberty!

There is the great policy of conservation, for example; and I do not conceive of conservation in any narrow sense. There are forests to conserve, there are great water powers to conserve, there are mines whose wealth should be deemed exhaustible, not inexhaustible, and whose resources should be safeguarded and preserved for future generations. But there is much more. There are the lives and energies of the people to be physically safeguarded.

You know what has been the embarrassment about conservation. The federal government has not dared relax its hold, because, not *bona fide* settlers, not men bent upon the legitimate development of great states, but men bent upon getting into their own exclusive control great mineral, forest, and water resources, have stood at the ear of the government and attempted to dictate its policy. And the government of the United States has not dared relax its somewhat rigid policy because of the fear that these forces would be stronger than the forces of individual communities and of the public interest. What we are now in dread of is that this situation will be made permanent. Why is it that Alaska has lagged in her development? Why is it that there are great mountains of coal piled up in the shipping places on the coast of Alaska which the government at Washington will not permit to be sold? It is because the government is not sure that it has followed all the intricate threads of intrigue by which small bodies of men have tried to get exclusive control of the coal fields of Alaska. The government stands itself suspicious of the forces by which it is surrounded.

The trouble about conservation is that the government of the United States hasn't any policy at present. It is simply marking time. It is simply standing still. Reservation is not conservation. Simply to say, "We are not going to do anything about the forests," when the country needs to use the forests, is not a practicable program at all. To say that the people of the great State of Washington can't buy coal out of the Alaskan coal fields doesn't settle the question. You have got to have that coal sooner or later. And if you are so afraid of the Guggenheims and all the rest of them that you can't make up your mind what your policies are going to be about those coal fields, how long are we going to wait for the government to throw off its fear? There can't be a working program until there is a free government. The day when the government is free to set about a policy of positive conservation, as distinguished from mere negative reservation, will be an emancipation day of no small importance for the development of the country.

But the question of conservation is a very much bigger question than the conservation of our natural resources; because in summing up our natural resources there is one great natural resource which underlies them all, and seems to underlie them so deeply that we sometimes overlook it. I mean the people themselves.

What would our forests be worth without vigorous and intelligent men to make use of them? Why should we conserve our natural resources, unless we can by the magic of industry transmute them into the wealth of the world? What transmutes them into that wealth, if not the skill and the touch of the men who go daily to their toil and who constitute the great body of the American people? What I am interested in is having the government of the United States more concerned about human rights than about property rights. Property is an instrument of humanity; humanity isn't an instrument of property. And yet when you see some men riding their great industries as if they were driving a car of juggernaut, not looking to see what multitudes prostrate themselves before the car and lose their lives in the crushing effect of their industry, you wonder how long men are going to be permitted to think more of their machinery than they think of their men. Did you never think of it,—men are cheap, and machinery is dear; many a superintendent is dismissed for overdriving a delicate machine, who wouldn't be dismissed for overdriving an overtaxed man. You can discard your man and replace him; there are others ready to come into his place; but you can't without great cost discard your machine and put a new one in its place. You are less apt, therefore, to look upon your men as the essential vital foundation part of your whole business. It is time that property, as compared with humanity, should take second place, not first place. We must see to it that there is no over-crowding, that there is no bad sanitation, that there is no unnecessary spread of avoidable diseases, that the purity of food is safeguarded, that there is every precaution against accident, that women are not driven to impossible tasks, nor children permitted to spend their energy before it is fit to be spent. The hope and elasticity of the race must be preserved; men must be preserved according to their individual needs, and not according to the programs of industry merely. What is the use of having industry, if we perish in producing it? If we die in trying to feed ourselves, why should we eat? If we die trying to get a foothold in the crowd, why not let the crowd trample us sooner and be done with it? I tell you that there is beginning to beat in this nation a great pulse of irresistible sympathy which is going to transform the processes of government amongst us. The strength of America is proportioned only to the health, the energy, the hope, the elasticity, the buoyancy of the American people.

Is not that the greatest thought that you can have of freedom,—the thought of it as a gift that shall release men and women from all that pulls them back from being their best and from doing their best, that shall liberate their energy to its fullest limit, free their aspirations till no bounds confine them, and fill their spirits with the jubilance of realizable hope?

XII
The Liberation of a People's Vital Energies

No matter how often we think of it, the discovery of America must each time make a fresh appeal to our imaginations. For centuries, indeed from the beginning, the face of Europe had been turned toward the east. All the routes of trade, every impulse and energy, ran from west to east. The Atlantic lay at the world's back-door. Then, suddenly, the conquest of Constantinople by the Turk closed the route to the Orient. Europe had either to face about or lack any outlet for her energies; the unknown sea at the west at last was ventured upon, and the earth learned that it was twice as big as it had thought. Columbus did not find, as he had expected, the civilization of Cathay; he found an empty continent. In that part of the world, upon that new-found half of the globe, mankind, late in its history, was thus afforded an opportunity to set up a new civilization; here it was strangely privileged to make a new human experiment.

Never can that moment of unique opportunity fail to excite the emotion of all who consider its strangeness and richness; a thousand fanciful histories of the earth might be contrived without the imagination daring to conceive such a romance as the hiding away of half the globe until the fulness of time had come for a new start in civilization. A mere sea captain's ambition to trace a new trade route gave way to a moral adventure for humanity. The race was to found a new order here on this delectable land, which no man approached without receiving, as the old voyagers relate, you remember, sweet airs out of woods aflame with flowers and murmurous with the sound of pellucid waters. The hemisphere lay waiting to be touched with life,—life from the old centres of living, surely, but cleansed of defilement, and cured of weariness, so as to be fit for the virgin purity of a new bride. The whole thing springs into the imagination like a wonderful vision, an exquisite marvel which once only in all history could be vouchsafed.

One other thing only compares with it; only one other thing touches the springs of emotion as does the picture of the ships of Columbus drawing near the bright shores,—and that is the thought of the choke in the throat of the immigrant of to-day as he gazes from the steerage deck at the land where he has been taught to believe he in his turn shall find an earthly paradise, where, a free man, he shall forget the heartaches of the old life, and enter into the fulfilment of the hope of the world. For has not every ship that has pointed her prow westward borne hither the hopes of generation after generation of the oppressed of other lands? How always have men's hearts beat as they saw the coast of America rise to their view! How it has always seemed to them that the dweller there would at last be rid of kings, of privileged classes, and of all those bonds which had kept men depressed and helpless, and would there realize the full fruition of his sense of honest manhood, would there be one of a great body of brothers, not seeking to defraud and deceive one another, but seeking to accomplish the general good!

What was in the writings of the men who founded America,—to serve the selfish interests of America? Do you find that in their writings? No; to serve the cause of humanity, to bring liberty to mankind. They set up their standards here in America in the tenet of hope, as a beacon of encouragement to all the nations of the world; and men came thronging to these shores with an expectancy that never existed before, with a confidence they never dared feel before, and found here for generations together a haven of peace, of opportunity, of equality.

God send that in the complicated state of modern affairs we may recover the standards and repeat the achievements of that heroic age!

For life is no longer the comparatively simple thing it was. Our relations one with another have been profoundly modified by the new agencies of rapid communication and transportation, tending swiftly to concentrate life, widen communities, fuse interests, and complicate all the processes of living. The individual is dizzily swept about in a thousand new whirlpools of activities. Tyranny has become more subtle, and has learned to wear the guise of mere industry, and even of benevolence. Freedom has become a somewhat different matter. It cannot,—eternal principle that it is,—it cannot have altered, yet it shows itself in new aspects. Perhaps it is only revealing its deeper meaning.

What is liberty?

I have long had an image in my mind of what constitutes liberty. Suppose that I were building a great piece of powerful machinery, and suppose that I should so awkwardly and unskilfully assemble the parts of it that every time one part tried to move it would be interfered with by the others, and the whole thing would buckle up and be checked. Liberty for the several parts would consist in the best possible assembling and adjustment of them all, would it not? If you want the great piston of the engine to run with absolute freedom, give it absolutely perfect alignment and adjustment with the other parts of the machine, so that it is free, not because it is let alone or isolated, but because it has been associated most skilfully and carefully with the other parts of the great structure.

What it liberty? You say of the locomotive that it runs free. What do you mean? You mean that its parts are so assembled and adjusted that friction is reduced to a minimum, and that it has perfect adjustment. We say of a boat skimming the water with light foot, "How free she runs," when we mean, how perfectly she is adjusted to the force of the wind, how perfectly she obeys the great breath out of the heavens that fills her sails. Throw her head up into the wind and see how she will halt and stagger, how every sheet will shiver and her whole frame be shaken, how instantly she is "in irons," in the expressive phrase of the sea. She is free only when you have let her fall off again and have recovered once more her nice adjustment to the forces she must obey and cannot defy.

Human freedom consists in perfect adjustments of human interests and human activities and human energies.

Now, the adjustments necessary between individuals, between individuals and the complex institutions amidst which they live, and between those institutions and the government, are infinitely more intricate to-day than ever before. No doubt this is a tiresome and roundabout way of saying the thing, yet perhaps it is worth while to get somewhat clearly in our mind what makes all the trouble to-day. Life has become complex; there are many more elements, more parts, to it than ever before. And, therefore, it is harder to keep everything adjusted,—and harder to find out where the trouble lies when the machine gets out of order.

You know that one of the interesting things that Mr. Jefferson said in those early days of simplicity which marked the beginnings of our government was that the best government consisted in as little governing as possible. And there is still a sense in which that is true. It is still intolerable for the government to interfere with our individual activities except where it is necessary to interfere with them in order to free them. But I feel confident that if Jefferson were living in our day he would see what we see: that the individual is caught in a great confused nexus of all sorts of complicated circumstances, and that to let him alone is to leave him helpless as against the obstacles with which he has to contend; and that, therefore, law in our day must come to the assistance of the individual. It must come to his assistance to see that he gets fair play; that is all, but that is much. Without the watchful interference, the resolute interference, of the government, there can be no fair play between individuals and such powerful institutions as the trusts. Freedom to-day is something more than being let alone. The program of a government of freedom must in these days be positive, not negative merely.

Well, then, in this new sense and meaning of it, are we preserving freedom in this land of ours, the hope of all the earth?

Have we, inheritors of this continent and of the ideals to which the fathers consecrated it,—have we maintained them, realizing them, as each generation must, anew? Are we, in the consciousness that the life of man is pledged to higher levels here than elsewhere, striving still to bear aloft the standards of liberty and hope, or, disillusioned and defeated, are we feeling the disgrace of having had a free field in which to do new things and of not having done them?

The answer must be, I am sure, that we have been in a fair way of failure,—tragic failure. And we stand in danger of utter failure yet except we fulfil speedily the determination we have reached, to deal with the new and subtle tyrannies according to their deserts. Don't deceive yourselves for a moment as to the power of the great interests which now dominate our development. They are so great that it is almost an open question whether the government of the United States can dominate them or not. Go one step further, make their organized power permanent, and it may be too late to turn back. The roads diverge at the point where we stand. They stretch their vistas out to regions where they are very far separated from one another; at the end of one is the old tiresome scene of government tied up with special interests; and at the other shines the liberating light of individual initiative, of individual liberty, of individual freedom, the light of untrammeled enterprise. I believe that that light shines out of the heavens itself that God has created. I believe in human liberty as I believe in the wine of life. There is no salvation for men in the pitiful condescensions of industrial masters. Guardians have no place in a land of freemen. Prosperity guaranteed by trustees has no prospect of endurance. Monopoly means the atrophy of enterprise. If monopoly persists, monopoly will always sit at the helm of the government. I do not expect to see monopoly restrain itself. If there are men in this country big enough to own the government of the United States, they are going to own it; what we have to determine now is whether we are big enough, whether we are men enough, whether we are free enough, to take possession again of the government which is our own. We haven't had free access to it, our minds have not touched it by way of guidance, in half a generation, and now we are engaged in nothing less than the recovery of what was made with our own hands, and acts only by our delegated authority.

I tell you, when you discuss the question of the tariffs and of the trusts, you are discussing the very lives of yourselves and your children. I believe that I am preaching the very cause of some of the gentlemen whom I am opposing when I preach the cause of free industry in the United States, for I think they are slowly girding the tree that bears the inestimable fruits of our life, and that if they are permitted to gird it entirely nature will take her revenge and the tree will die.

I do not believe that America is securely great because she has great men in her now. America is great in proportion as she can make sure of having great men in the next generation. She is rich in her unborn children; rich, that is to say, if those unborn children see the sun in a day of opportunity, see the sun when they are free to exercise their energies as they will. If they open their eyes in a land where there is no special privilege, then we shall come into a new era of American greatness and American liberty; but if they open their eyes in a country where they must be employees or nothing, if they open their eyes in a land of merely regulated monopoly, where all the conditions of industry are determined by small groups of men, then they will see an America such as the founders of this Republic would have wept to think of. The only hope is in the release of the forces which philanthropic trust presidents want to monopolize. Only the emancipation, the freeing and heartening of the vital energies of all the people will redeem us. In all that I may have to do in public affairs in the United States I am going to think of towns such as I have seen in Indiana, towns of the old American pattern, that own and operate their own industries, hopefully and happily. My thought is going to be bent upon the multiplication of towns of that kind and the prevention of the concentration of industry in this country in such a fashion and upon such a scale that towns that own themselves will be impossible. You know what the vitality of America consists of. Its vitality does not lie in New York, nor in Chicago; it will not be sapped by anything that happens in St. Louis. The vitality of America lies in the brains, the energies, the enterprise of the people throughout the land; in the efficiency of their factories and in the richness of the fields that stretch beyond the borders of the town; in the wealth which they extract from nature and originate for themselves through the inventive genius characteristic of all free American communities.

That is the wealth of America, and if America discourages the locality, the community, the self-contained town, she will kill the nation. A nation is as rich as her free communities; she is not as rich as her capital city or her metropolis. The amount of money in Wall Street is no indication of the wealth of the American people. That indication can be found only in the fertility of the American mind and the productivity of American industry everywhere throughout the

United States. If America were not rich and fertile, there would be no money in Wall Street. If Americans were not vital and able to take care of themselves, the great money exchanges would break down. The welfare, the very existence of the nation, rests at last upon the great mass of the people; its prosperity depends at last upon the spirit in which they go about their work in their several communities throughout the broad land. In proportion as her towns and her country-sides are happy and hopeful will America realize the high ambitions which have marked her in the eyes of all the world.

The welfare, the happiness, the energy and spirit of the men and women who do the daily work in our mines and factories, on our railroads, in our offices and ports of trade, on our farms and on the sea, is the underlying necessity of all prosperity. There can be nothing wholesome unless their life is wholesome; there can be no contentment unless they are contented. Their physical welfare affects the soundness of the whole nation. How would it suit the prosperity of the United States, how would it suit business, to have a people that went every day sadly or sullenly to their work? How would the future look to you if you felt that the aspiration had gone out of most men, the confidence of success, the hope that they might improve their condition? Do you not see that just so soon as the old self-confidence of America, just so soon as her old boasted advantage of individual liberty and opportunity, is taken away, all the energy of her people begins to subside, to slacken, to grow loose and pulpy, without fibre, and men simply cast about to see that the day does not end disastrously with them?

So we must put heart into the people by taking the heartlessness out of politics, business, and industry. We have got to make politics a thing in which an honest man can take his part with satisfaction because he knows that his opinion will count as much as the next man's, and that the boss and the interests have been dethroned. Business we have got to untrammel, abolishing tariff favors, and railroad discrimination, and credit denials, and all forms of unjust handicaps against the little man. Industry we have got to humanize,—not through the trusts,—but through the direct action of law guaranteeing protection against dangers and compensation for injuries, guaranteeing sanitary conditions, proper hours, the right to organize, and all the other things which the conscience of the country demands as the workingman's right. We have got to cheer and inspirit our people with the sure prospects of social justice and due reward, with the vision of the open gates of opportunity for all. We have got to set the energy and the initiative of this great people absolutely free, so that the future of America will be greater than the past, so that the pride of America will grow with achievement, so that America will know as she advances from generation to generation that each brood of her sons is greater and more enlightened than that which preceded it, know that she is fulfilling the promise that she has made to mankind.

Such is the vision of some of us who now come to assist in its realization. For we Democrats would not have endured this long burden of exile if we had not seen a vision. We could have traded; we could have got into the game; we could have surrendered and made terms; we could have played the rôle of patrons to the men who wanted to dominate the interests of the country,—and here and there gentlemen who pretended to be of us did make those arrangements. They couldn't stand privation. You never can stand it unless you have within you some imperishable food upon which to sustain life and courage, the food of those visions of the spirit where a table is set before us laden with palatable fruits, the fruits of hope, the fruits of imagination, those invisible things of the spirit which are the only things upon which we can sustain ourselves through this weary world without fainting. We have carried in our minds, after you had thought you had obscured and blurred them, the ideals of those men who first set their foot upon America, those little bands who came to make a foothold in the wilderness, because the great teeming nations that they had left behind them had forgotten what human liberty was, liberty of thought, liberty of religion, liberty of residence, liberty of action.

Since their day the meaning of liberty has deepened. But it has not ceased to be a fundamental demand of the human spirit, a fundamental necessity for the life of the soul. And the day is at hand when it shall be realized on this consecrated soil,—a New Freedom,—a Liberty widened and deepened to match the broadened life of man in modern America, restoring to him in very truth the control of his government, throwing wide all gates of lawful enterprise, unfettering his energies, and warming the generous impulses of his heart, —a process of release, emancipation, and inspiration, full of a breath of life as sweet and wholesome as the airs that filled the sails of the caravels of Columbus and gave the promise and boast of magnificent Opportunity in which America *dare not fail.*

When A Man Comes To Himself

I

It is a very wholesome and regenerating change which a man undergoes when he "comes to himself." It is not only after periods of recklessness or infatuation, when he has played the spendthrift or the fool, that a man comes to himself. He comes to himself after experiences of which he alone may be aware: when he has left off being wholly preoccupied with his own powers and interests and with every petty plan that centers in himself; when he has cleared his eyes to see the world as it is, and his own true place and function in it.

It is a process of disillusionment. The scales have fallen away. He sees himself soberly, and knows under what conditions his powers must act, as well as what his powers are. He has got rid of earlier prepossessions about the world of men and affairs, both those which were too favorable and those which were too unfavorable-both those of the nursery and those of a young man's reading. He has learned his own paces, or, at any rate, is in a fair way to learn them; has found his footing and the true nature of the "going" he must look for in the world; over what sorts of roads he must expect to make his running, and at what expenditure of effort; whither his goal lies, and what cheer he may expect by the way. It is a process of disillusionment, but it disheartens no soundly made man. It brings him into a light which guides instead of deceiving him; a light which does not make the way look cold to any man whose eyes are fit for use in the open, but which shines wholesomely, rather upon the obvious path, like the honest rays of the frank sun, and makes traveling both safe and cheerful.

II

There is no fixed time in a man's life at which he comes to himself, and some men never come to themselves at all. It is a change reserved for the thoroughly sane and healthy, and for those who can detach themselves from tasks and drudgery long and often enough to get, at any rate once and again, a view of the proportions of life and of the stage and plot of its action. We speak often with amusement, sometimes with distaste and uneasiness, of men who "have no sense of humor," who take themselves too seriously, who are intense, self-absorbed, over-confident in matters of opinion, or else go plumed with conceit, proud of we cannot tell what, enjoying, appreciating, thinking of nothing so much as themselves. These are men who have not suffered that wholesome change. They have not come to themselves. If they be serious men, and real forces in the world, we may conclude that they have been too much and too long absorbed; that their tasks and responsibilities long ago rose about them like a flood, and have kept them swimming with sturdy stroke the years through, their eyes level with the troubled surface-no horizon in sight, no passing fleets, no comrades but those who struggled in the flood like themselves. If they be frivolous, light-headed men without purpose or achievement, we may conjecture, if we do not know, that they were born so, or spoiled by fortune, or befuddled by self-indulgence. It is no great matter what we think of them.

It is enough to know that there are some laws which govern a man's awakening to know himself and the right part to play. A man is the part he plays among his fellows. He is not isolated; he cannot be. His life is made up of the relations he bears to others-is made or marred by those relations, guided by them, judged by them, expressed in them. There is nothing else upon which he can spend his spirit-nothing else that we can see. It is by these he gets his spiritual growth; it is by these we see his character revealed, his purpose and his gifts. Some play with a certain natural passion, an unstudied directness, without grace, without modulation, with no study of the masters or consciousness of the pervading spirit of the plot; others give all their thought to their costume and think only of the audience; a few act as those who have mastered the secrets of a serious art, with deliberate subordination of themselves to the great end and motive of the play, spending themselves like good servants, indulging no wilfulness, obtruding no eccentricity, lending heart and tone and gesture to the perfect progress of the action. These have "found themselves," and have all the ease of a perfect adjustment.

Adjustment is exactly what a man gains when he comes to himself. Some men gain it late, some early; some get it all at once, as if by one distinct act of deliberate accommodation; others get it by degrees and quite imperceptibly. No doubt to most men it comes by slow processes of experience-at each stage of life a little. A college man feels the first shock of it at graduation, when the boy's life has been lived out and the man's life suddenly begins. He has measured himself with boys; he knows their code and feels the spur of their ideals of achievement. But what the world expects of him he has yet to find out, and it works, when he has discovered, a veritable revolution in his ways both of thought and of action. He finds a new sort of fitness demanded of him, executive, thorough-going, careful of details, full of drudgery and obedience to orders. Everybody is ahead of him. Just now he was a senior, at the top of the world he knows and reigned in, a finished product and pattern of good form. Of a sudden he is a novice again, as green as in his first school year, studying a thing that seems to have no rules-at sea amid crosswinds, and a bit seasick withal. Presently, if he be made of stuff that will shake into shape and fitness, he settles to his tasks and is comfortable. He has come to himself: understands what capacity is, and what it is meant for; sees that his training was not for ornament or personal gratification, but to teach him how to use himself and develop faculties worth using. Henceforth there is a zest in action, and he loves to see his strokes tell.

The same thing happens to the lad come from the farm into the city, a big and novel field, where crowds rush and jostle, and a rustic boy must stand puzzled for a little how to use his placid and unjaded strength. It happens, too, though in a deeper and more subtle way, to the man who marries for love, if the love be true and fit for foul weather. Mr. Bagehot used to say that a bachelor was "an amateur at life," and wit and wisdom are married in the jest. A man who lives only for himself has not begun to live-has yet to learn his use, and his real pleasure, too, in the world. It is not necessary he should marry to find himself out, but it is necessary he should love. Men have come to themselves serving their mothers with an unselfish devotion, or their sisters, or a cause for whose sake they forsook ease and left off thinking of themselves. It is unselfish action, growing slowly into the high habit of devotion, and at last, it may be, into a sort of consecration, that teaches a man the wide meaning of his life, and makes of him a steady professional in living, if the motive be not necessity, but love. Necessity may make a mere drudge of a man, and no mere drudge ever made a professional of himself; that demands a higher spirit and a finer incentive than his.

III

Surely a man has come to himself only when he has found the best that is in him, and has satisfied his heart with the highest achievement he is fit for. It is only then that he knows of what he is capable and what his heart demands. And, assuredly, no thoughtful man ever came to the end of his life, and had time and a little space of calm from which to look back upon it, who did not know and acknowledge that it was what he had done unselfishly and for others, and nothing else, that satisfied him in the retrospect, and made him feel that he had played the man. That alone seems to him the real measure of himself, the real standard of his manhood. And so men grow by having responsibility laid upon them, the burden of other people's business. Their powers are put out at interest, and they get usury in kind. They are like men multiplied. Each counts manifold. Men who live with an eye only upon what is their own are dwarfed beside them-seem fractions while they are integers. The trustworthiness of men trusted seems often to grow with the trust.

It is for this reason that men are in love with power and greatness: it affords them so pleasurable an expansion of faculty, so large a run for their minds, an exercise of spirit so various and refreshing; they have the freedom of so wide a tract of the world of affairs. But if they use power only for their own ends, if there be no unselfish service in it, if its object be only their personal aggrandizement, their love to see other men tools in their hands, they go out of the world small, disquieted, beggared, no enlargement of soul vouchsafed them, no usury of satisfaction. They have added nothing to themselves. Mental and physical powers alike grow by use, as every one knows; but labor for oneself is like exercise in a gymnasium. No healthy man can remain satisfied with it, or regard it as anything but a preparation for tasks in the open, amid the affairs of the world-not sport, but business-where there is no orderly apparatus, and every man must devise the means by which he is to make the most of himself. To make the most of himself means the multiplication of his activities, and he must turn away from himself for that. He looks about him, studies the facts of business or of affairs, catches some intimation of their larger objects, is guided by the intimation, and presently finds himself part of the motive force of communities or of nations. It makes no difference how small a part, how insignificant, how unnoticed. When his powers begin to play outward, and he loves the task at hand, not because it gains him a livelihood, but because it makes him a life, he has come to himself.

Necessity is no mother to enthusiasm. Necessity carries a whip. Its method is compulsion, not love. It has no thought to make itself attractive; it is content to drive. Enthusiasm comes with the revelation of true and satisfying objects of devotion; and it is enthusiasm that sets the powers free. It is a sort of enlightenment. It shines straight upon ideals, and for those who see it the race and struggle are henceforth toward these. An instance will point the meaning. One of the most distinguished and most justly honored of our great philanthropists spent the major part of his life absolutely absorbed in the making of money-so it seemed to those who did not know him. In fact, he had very early passed the stage at which he looked upon his business as a means of support or of material comfort. Business had become for him an intellectual pursuit, a study in enterprise and increment. The field of commerce lay before him like a chess-board; the moves interested him like the manoeuvers of a game. More money was more power, a great advantage in the game, the means of shaping men and events and markets to his own ends and uses. It was his will that set fleets afloat and determined the havens they were bound for; it was his foresight that brought goods to market at the right time; it was his suggestion that made the industry of unthinking men efficacious; his sagacity saw itself justified at home not only, but at the ends of the earth. And as the money poured in, his government and mastery increased, and his mind was the more satisfied. It is so that men make little kingdoms for themselves, and an international power undarkened by diplomacy, undirected by parliaments.

IV

It is a mistake to suppose that the great captains of industry, the great organizers and directors of manufacture and commerce and monetary exchange, are engrossed in a vulgar pursuit of wealth. Too often they suffer the vulgarity of wealth to display itself in the idleness and ostentation of their wives and children, who "devote themselves," it may be, "to expense regardless of pleasure"; but we ought not to misunderstand even that, or condemn it unjustly. The masters of industry are often too busy with their own sober and momentous calling to have time or spare thought enough to govern their own households. A king may be too faithful a statesman to be a watchful father. These men are not fascinated by the glitter of gold: the appetite for power has got hold upon them. They are in love with the exercise of their faculties upon a great scale; they are organizing and overseeing a great part of the life of the world. No wonder they are captivated. Business is more interesting than pleasure, as Mr. Bagehot said, and when once the mind has caught its zest, there's no disengaging it. The world has reason to be grateful for the fact.

It was this fascination that had got hold upon the faculties of the man whom the world was afterward to know, not as a prince among merchants-for the world forgets merchant princes-but as a prince among benefactors; for beneficence breeds gratitude, gratitude admiration, admiration fame, and the world remembers its benefactors. Business, and business alone, interested him, or seemed to him worthwhile. The first time he was asked to subscribe money for a benevolent object he declined. Why should he subscribe? What affair would be set forward, what increase of efficiency would the money buy, what return would it bring in? Was good money to be simply given away, like water poured on a barren soil, to be sucked up and yield nothing? It was not until men who understood benevolence on its sensible, systematic, practical, and really helpful side explained it to him as an investment that his mind took hold of it and turned to it for satisfaction. He began to see that education was a thing of infinite usury; that money devoted to it would yield a singular increase to which there was no calculable end, an increase in perpetuity-increase of knowledge, and therefore of intelligence and efficiency, touching generation after generation with new impulses, adding to the sum total of the world's fitness for affairs-an invisible but intensely real spiritual usury beyond reckoning, because compounded in an unknown ratio from age to age. Henceforward beneficence was as interesting to him as business-was, indeed, a sort of sublimated business in which money moved new forces in a commerce which no man could bind or limit.

He had come to himself-to the full realization of his powers, the true and clear perception of what it was his mind demanded for its satisfaction. His faculties were consciously stretched to their right measure, were at last exercised at their best. He felt the keen zest, not of success merely, but also of honor, and was raised to a sort of majesty among his fellow-men, who attended him in death like a dead sovereign. He had died dwarfed had he not broken the bonds of mere money-getting; would never have known himself had he not learned how to spend it; and ambition itself could not have shown him a straighter road to fame.

This is the positive side of a man's discovery of the way in which his faculties are to be made to fit into the world's affairs, and released for effort in a way that will bring real satisfaction. There is a negative side also. Men come to themselves by discovering their limitations no less than by discovering their deeper endowments and the mastery that will make them happy. It is the discovery of what they can not do, and ought not to attempt, that transforms reformers into statesmen; and great should be the joy of the world over every reformer who comes to himself. The spectacle is not rare; the method is not hidden. The practicability of every reform is determined absolutely and always by "the circumstances of the case," and only those who put themselves into the midst of affairs, either by action or by observation, can know what those circumstances are or perceive what they signify. No statesman dreams of doing whatever he pleases; he knows that it does not follow that because a point of morals or of policy is obvious to him it will be obvious to the nation, or even to his own friends; and it is the strength of a democratic polity that there are so many minds to be consulted and brought to agreement, and that nothing can be wisely done for which the thought, and a good deal more than the thought, of the country, its sentiment and its purpose, have not been prepared. Social reform is a matter of cooperation, and if it be of a novel kind, requires an infinite deal of converting to bring the efficient majority to believe in it and support it. Without their agreement and support it is impossible.

V

It is this that the more imaginative and impatient reformers find out when they come to themselves, if that calming change ever comes to them. Oftentimes the most immediate and drastic means of bringing them to themselves is to elect them to legislative or executive office. That will reduce over-sanguine persons to their simplest terms. Not because they find their fellow-legislators or officials incapable of high purpose or indifferent to the betterment of the communities which they represent. Only cynics hold that to be the chief reason why we approach the millennium so slowly, and cynics are usually very ill-informed persons. Nor is it because under our modern democratic arrangements we so subdivide power and balance parts in government that no one man can tell for much or turn affairs to his will. One of the most instructive studies a politician could undertake would be a study of the infinite limitations laid upon the power of the Russian Czar, notwithstanding the despotic theory of the Russian constitution-limitations of social habit, of official prejudice, of race jealousies, of religious predilections, of administrative machinery even, and the inconvenience of being himself only one man, caught amidst a rush of duties and responsibilities which never halt or pause. He can do only what can be done with the Russian people. He cannot change them at will. He is himself of their own stuff, and immersed in the life which forms them, as it forms him. He is simply the leader of the Russians.

An English or American statesman is better off. He leads a thinking nation, not a race of peasants topped by a class of revolutionists and a caste of nobles and officials. He can explain new things to men able to understand, persuade men willing and accustomed to make independent and intelligent choices of their own. An English statesman has an even better opportunity to lead than an American statesman, because in England executive power and legislative initiative are both intrusted to the same grand committee, the ministry of the day. The ministers both propose what shall be law and determine how it shall be enforced when enacted. And yet English reformers, like American, have found office a veritable cold-water bath for their ardor for change. Many a man who has made his place in affairs as the spokesman of those who see abuses and demand their reformation has passed from denunciation to calm and moderate advice when he got into Parliament, and has turned veritable conservative when made a minister of the crown. Mr. Bright was a notable example. Slow and careful men had looked upon him as little better than a revolutionist so long as his voice rang free and imperious from the platforms of public meetings. They greatly feared the influence he should exercise in Parliament, and would have deemed the constitution itself unsafe could they have foreseen that he would some day be invited to take office and a hand of direction in affairs. But it turned out that there was nothing to fear. Mr. Bright lived to see almost every reform he had urged accepted and embodied in legislation; but he assisted at the process of their realization with greater and greater temperateness and wise deliberation as his part in affairs became more and more prominent and responsible, and was at the last as little like an agitator as any man that served the queen.

It is not that such men lose courage when they find themselves charged with the actual direction of the affairs concerning which they have held and uttered such strong, unhesitating, drastic opinions. They have only learned discretion. For the first time they see in its entirety what it was that they were attempting. They are at last at close quarters with the world. Men of every interest and variety crowd about them; new impressions throng them; in the midst of affairs the former special objects of their zeal fall into new environments, a better and truer perspective; seem no longer so susceptible to separate and radical change. The real nature of the complex stuff of life they were seeking to work in is revealed to them-its intricate and delicate fiber, and the subtle, secret interrelationship of its parts-and they work circumspectly, lest they should mar more than they mend. Moral enthusiasm is not, uninstructed and of itself, a suitable guide to practicable and lasting reformation; and if the reform sought be the reformation of others as well as of himself, the reformer should look to it that he knows the true relation of his will to the wills of those he would change and guide. When he has discovered that relation, he has come to himself: has discovered his real use and planning part in the general world of men; has come to the full command and satisfying employment of his faculties. Otherwise he is doomed to live for ever in a fool's paradise, and can be said to have come to himself only on the supposition that he is a fool.

VI

Every man-if I may adopt and paraphrase a passage from Dr. South-every man hath both an absolute and a relative capacity: an absolute in that he hath been endued with such a nature and such parts and faculties; and a relative in that he is part of the universal community of men, and so stands in such a relation to the whole. When we say that a man has come to himself, it is not of his absolute capacity that we are thinking, but of his relative. He has begun to realize that he is part of a whole, and to know what part, suitable for what service and achievement.

It was once fashionable-and that not a very long time ago-to speak of political society with a certain distaste, as a necessary evil, an irritating but inevitable restriction upon the "natural" sovereignty and entire self-government of the individual. That was the dream of the egotist. It was a theory in which men were seen to strut in the proud consciousness of their several and "absolute" capacities. It would be as instructive as it would be difficult to count the errors it has bred in political thinking. As a matter of fact, men have never dreamed of wishing to do without the "trammels" of organized society, for the very good reason that those trammels are in reality but no trammels at all, but indispensable aids and spurs to the attainment of the highest and most enjoyable things man is capable of. Political society, the life of men in states, is an abiding natural relationship. It is neither a mere convenience nor a mere necessity. It is not a mere voluntary association, not a mere corporation. It is nothing deliberate or artificial, devised for a special purpose. It is in real truth the eternal and natural expression and embodiment of a form of life higher than that of the individual-that common life of mutual helpfulness, stimulation, and contest which gives leave and opportunity to the individual life, makes it possible, makes it full and complete.

It is in such a scene that man looks about to discover his own place and force. In the midst of men organized, infinitely cross-related, bound by ties of interest, hope, affection, subject to authorities, to opinion, to passion, to visions and desires which no man can reckon, he casts eagerly about to find where he may enter in with the rest and be a man among his fellows. In making his place he finds, if he seek intelligently and with eyes that see, more than ease of spirit and scope for his mind. He finds himself-as if mists had cleared away about him and he knew at last his neighborhood among men and tasks.

What every man seeks is satisfaction. He deceives himself so long as he imagines it to lie in self-indulgence, so long as he deems himself the center and object of effort. His mind is spent in vain upon itself. Not in action itself, not in "pleasure," shall it find its desires satisfied, but in consciousness of right, of powers greatly and nobly spent. It comes to know itself in the motives which satisfy it, in the zest and power of rectitude. Christianity has liberated the world, not as a system of ethics, not as a philosophy of altruism, but by its revelation of the power of pure and unselfish love. Its vital principle is not its code, but its motive. Love, clear-sighted, loyal, personal, is its breath and immortality. Christ came, not to save Himself, assuredly, but to save the world. His motive, His example, are every man's key to his own gifts and happiness. The ethical code he taught may no doubt be matched, here a piece and there a piece, out of other religions, other teachings and philosophies. Every thoughtful man born with a conscience must know a code of right and of pity to which he ought to conform; but without the motive of Christianity, without love, he may be the purest altruist and yet be as sad and as unsatisfied as Marcus Aurelius.

Christianity gave us, in the fullness of time, the perfect image of right living, the secret of social and of individual well-being; for the two are not separable, and the man who receives and verifies that secret in his own living has discovered not only the best and only way to serve the world, but also the one happy way to satisfy himself. Then, indeed, has he come to himself. Henceforth he knows what his powers mean, what spiritual air they breathe, what ardors of service clear them of lethargy, relieve them of all sense of effort, put them at their best. After this fretfulness passes away, experience mellows and strengthens and makes more fit, and old age brings, not senility, not satiety, not regret, but higher hope and serene maturity.

The Study of Administration

The Study of Administration

Wilson, Woodrow

I suppose that no practical science is ever studied where there is no need to know it. The very fact, therefore, that the eminently practical science of administration is finding its way into college courses in this country would prove that this country needs to know more about administration, were such proof of the fact required to make out a case. It need not be said, however, that we do not look into college programmes for proof of this fact. It is a thing almost taken for granted among us, that the present movement called civil service reform must, after the accomplishment of its first purpose, expand into efforts to improve, not the personnel only, but also the organization and methods of our government offices: because it is plain that their organization and methods need improvement only less than their personnel. It is the object of administrative study to discover, first, what government can properly and success-fully do, and, secondly, how it can do these proper things with the utmost possible efficiency and at the least possible cost either of money or of energy. On both these points there is obviously much need of light among us; and only careful study can supply that light.

Before entering on that study, however, it is needful:

I. To take some account of what others have done in the same line; that is to say, of the history of the study.

II. To ascertain just what is its subject-matter.

III. To determine just what are the best methods by which to develop it, and the most clarifying political conceptions to carry with us into it.

Unless we know and settle these things, we shall set out with-out chart or compass.

I.

The science of administration is the latest fruit of that study of the science of politics which was begun some twenty-two hundred years ago. It is a birth of our own century, almost of our own generation.

Why was it so late in coming? Why did it wait till this too busy century of ours to demand attention for itself? Administration is the most obvious part of government; it is government in action; it is the executive, the operative, the most visible side of government, and is of course as old as government itself. It is government in action, and one might very naturally expect to find that government in action had arrested the attention and provoked the scrutiny of writers of politics very early in the history of systematic thought.

But such was not the case. No one wrote systematically of administration as a branch of the science of government until the present century had passed its first youth and had begun to put forth its characteristic flower of systematic knowledge. Up to our own day all the political writers whom we now read had thought, argued, dogmatized only about the constitution of government; about the nature of the state, the essence and seat of sovereignty, popular power and kingly prerogative; about the greatest meanings lying at the heart of government, and the high ends set before the purpose of government by man's nature and man's aims. The central field of controversy was that great field of theory in which monarchy rode tilt against democracy,in which oligarchy would have built for itself strongholds of privilege, and in which tyranny sought opportunity to make good its claim to receive submission from all competitors. Amidst this high warfare of principles, administration could command no pause for its own consideration. The question was always: Who shall make law, and what shall that law be ?The other question, how law should be administered with enlightenment, with equity, with speed, and without friction, was put aside as " practical detail " which clerks could arrange after doctors had agreed upon principles.

That political philosophy took this direction was of course no accident, no chance preference or perverse whim of political philosophers. The philosophy of any time is, as Hegel says,"nothing but the spirit of that time expressed in abstract thought"; and political philosophy, like philosophy of every other kind, has only held up the mirror to contemporary affairs. The trouble in early times was almost altogether about the constitution of government; and consequently that was what engrossed men's thoughts. There was little or no trouble about administration, — at least little that was heeded by administrators. The functions of government were simple, because life itself was simple. Government went about imperatively and compelled men, without thought of consulting their wishes.There was no complex system of public revenues and public debts to puzzle financiers; there were, consequently, no financiers to be puzzled. No one who possessed power was long at a loss how to use it. The great and only question was: Whos hall possess it? Populations were of manageable numbers; property was of simple sorts. There were plenty of farms, but no stocks and bonds: more cattle than vested interests.

I have said that all this was true of "early times"; but it was substantially true also of comparatively late times. One does not have to look back of the last century for the beginnings of the present complexities of trade and perplexities of commercial speculation, nor for the portentous birth of national debts. Good Queen Bess, doubtless, thought that the monopolies of the sixteenth century were hard enough to handle without burning her hands; but they are not remembered in the presence of the giant monopolies of the nineteenth century. When Black stone lamented that corporations had no bodies to be kicked and no souls to be damned, he was anticipating the proper time for such regrets by full a century. The perennial discords between master and workmen which now so often disturb industrial society began before the Black Death and the Statute of Laborers; but never before our own day did they assume such ominous proportions as they wear now. In brief, if difficulties of governmental action are to be seen gathering in other centuries,they are to be seen culminating in our own.

This is the reason why administrative tasks have now a days to be so studiously and systematically adjusted to carefully tested standards of policy, the reason why we are having now what we never had before, a science of administration. The weightier debates of constitutional principle are even yet by no means concluded; but they are no longer of more immediate practical moment than questions of administration. It is getting to be harder to run a constitution than to frame one.

Here is Mr. Bagehot's graphic, whimsical way of depicting the difference between the old and the new in administration:

In early times, when a despot wishes to govern a distant province,he sends down a satrap on a grand horse, and other people on little horses; and very little is heard of the satrap again unless he send back some of the little people to tell what he has been doing. No great labour of superintendence is possible. Common rumour and casual report are the sources of intelligence. If it seems certain that the provinceis in a bad state, satrap No. 1 is recalled, and satrap No. 2 sent out in his stead. In civilized countries the process is different. You erect a bureau in the province you want to govern; you make it write letters and copy letters; it sends home eight reports per diem to the head bureau in St. Petersburg. Nobody does a sum in the province without some one doing the same sum in the capital, to "check" him, and see that he does it correctly. The consequence of this is, to throw on the heads of departments an amount of reading and labour which can only be accomplished by the greatest natural aptitude, the most efficient training, the most firm and regular industry.

There is scarcely a single duty of government which was once simple which is not now complex; government once had but a few masters; it now has scores of masters. Majorities formerly only underwent government; they now conduct government. Where government once might follow the whims of a court, it must now follow the views of a nation.

And those views are steadily widening to new conceptions of state duty; so that, at the same time that the functions of government are every day becoming more complex and difficult, they are also vastly multiplying in number. Administration is everywhere putting its hands to new undertakings. The utility, cheapness, and success of the government's postal service, for instance, point towards the early establishment of governmental control of the telegraph system. Or, even if our government is not to follow the lead of the governments of Europe in buying or building both telegraph and railroad lines, no one can doubt that in some way it must make itself master of masterful corporations. The creation of national commissioners of railroads, in addition to the older state commissions, involves a very important and delicate extension of administrative functions. Whatever hold of authority state or federal governments are to take upon corporations, there must follow cares and responsibilities which will require not a little wisdom, knowledge, and experience. Such things must be studied in order to be well done. And these, as I have said,are only a few of the doors which are being opened to offices of government. The idea of the state and the consequent ideal of its duty are undergoing noteworthy change; and "the idea of the state is the conscience of administration." Seeing every day new things which the state ought to do, the next thing is to see clearly how it ought to do them.

This is why there should be a science of administration which shall seek to straighten the paths of government, to make its business less unbusiness like, to strengthen and purify its organization, and to crown its duties with dutifulness. This is one reason why there is such a science.

But where has this science grown up? Surely not on this side the sea. Not much impartial scientific method is to be discerned in our administrative practices. The poisonous atmosphere of city government, the crooked secrets of state administration, the confusion, sinecurism, and corruption ever and again discovered in the bureaus at Washington forbid us to believe that any clear conceptions of what constitutes good administration are as yet very widely current in the United States. No; American writers have hitherto taken no very important part in the advancement of this science. It has found its doctors in Europe. It is not of our making; it is a foreign science, speaking very little of the language of English or American principle. It employs only foreign tongues; it utters none but what are to our minds alien ideas. Its aims, its examples, its conditions, are almost exclusively grounded in the histories of foreign races, in the precedents of foreign systems, in the lessons of foreign revolutions. It has been developed by French and German professors, and is consequently in all parts adapted to the needs of a compact state, and made to fit highly centralized forms of government; whereas, to answer our purposes, it must be adapted, not to a simple and compact, but to a complex and multiform state, and made to fit highly decentralized forms of government. If we would employ it, we must Americanize it, and that not formally, in language merely, but radically, in thought, principle, and aim as well. It must learn our constitutions by heart; must get the bureaucratic fever out of its veins; must inhale much free American air.

If an explanation be sought why a science manifestly so susceptible of being made useful to all governments alike should have received attention first in Europe, where government has long been a monopoly, rather than in England or the United States, where government has long been a common franchise, the reason will doubtless be found to be twofold: first, that in Europe, just because government was independent of popular assent, there was more governing to be done; and, second, that the desire to keep government a monopoly made the monopolists interested in discovering the least irritating means of governing. They were, besides, few enough to adopt means promptly.

It will be instructive to look into this matter a little more closely. In speaking of European governments I do not, of course, include England. She has not refused to change with the times. She has simply tempered the severity of the transition from a polity of aristocratic privilege to a system of democratic power by slow measures of constitutional reform which, without preventing revolution, has confined it to paths of peace.

But the countries of the continent for a long time desperately struggled against all change, and would have diverted revolution by softening the asperities of absolute government. They sought so to perfect their machinery as to destroy all wearing friction, so to sweeten their methods with consideration for the interests of the governed as to placate all hindering hatred, and so assiduously and opportunely to offer their aid to all classes of undertakings as to render themselves indispensable to the industrious. They did at last give the people constitutions and the franchise; but even after that they obtained leave to continue despotic by becoming paternal. They made themselves too efficient to be dispensed with, too smoothly operative to be noticed, too enlightened to be inconsiderately questioned, too benevolent to be suspected, too powerful to be coped with. All this has required study; and they have closely studied it.

On this side the sea we, the while, had known no great difficulties of government. With a new country, in which there was room and remunerative employment for everybody, with liberal principles of government and unlimited skill in practical politics, we were long exempted from the need of being anxiously careful about plans and methods of administration. We have naturally been slow to see the use or significance of those many volumes of learned research and painstaking examination into the ways and means of conducting government which the presses of Europe have been sending to our libraries. Like a lusty child, government with us has expanded in nature and grown great in stature, but has also become awkward in movement. The vigor and increase of its life has been altogether out of proportion to its skill in living. It has gained strength, but it has not acquired deportment. Great, therefore, as has been our advantage over the countries of Europe in point of ease and health of constitutional development, now that the time for more careful administrative adjustments and larger administrative knowledge has come to us, we are at a signal disadvantage as compared with the transatlantic nations; and this for reasons which I shall try to make clear.

Judging by the constitutional histories of the chief nations of the modern world, there may be said to be three periods of growth through which government has passed in all the most highly developed of existing systems, and through which it promises to pass in all the rest. The first of these periods is that of absolute rulers, and of an administrative system adapted to absolute rule; the second is that in which constitutions are framed to do away with absolute rulers and substitute popular control, and in which administration is neglected for these higher concerns; and the third is that in which the sovereign people undertake to develop administration under this new constitution which has brought them into power.

Those governments are now in the lead in administrative practice which had rulers still absolute but also enlightened when those modern days of political illumination came in which it was made evident to all but the blind that governors are properly only the servants of the governed. In such governments administration has been organized to subserve the general weal with the simplicity and effectiveness vouchsafed only to the undertakings of a single will.

Such was the case in Prussia, for instance, where administration has been most studied and most nearly perfected. Fredericthe Great, stern and masterful as was his rule, still sincerely professed to regard himself as only the chief servant of the state, to consider his great office a public trust; and it was he who, building upon the foundations laid by his father, began to organize the public service of Prussia as in very earnest a service of the public. His no less absolute successor, Frederic William III, under the inspiration of Stein, again, in his turn, advanced the work still further, planning many of the broader structural features which give firmness and form to Prussian administration to-day. Almost the whole of the admirable system has been developed by kingly initiative.

Of similar origin was the practice, if not the plan, of modern French administration, with its symmetrical divisions of territory and its orderly gradations of office. The days of the Revolution — of the Constituent Assembly — were days of constitution-writing, but they can hardly be called days of constitution-making. The Revolution heralded a period of constitutional development, — the entrance of France upon the second of those periods which I have enumerated, — but it did not itself inaugurate such a period. It interrupted and unsettled absolutism, but did not destroy it. Napoleon succeeded the monarchs of France, to exercise a power as unrestricted as they had ever possessed.

The recasting of French administration by Napoleon is, therefore, my second example of the perfecting of civil machinery by the single will of an absolute ruler before the dawn of a constitutional era. No corporate, popular will could ever have effected arrangements such as those which Napoleon commanded. Arrangements so simple at the expense of local prejudice, so logical in their indifference to popular choice, might be decreed by a Constituent Assembly, but could be established only by the unlimited authority of a despot. The system of the year VIII was ruthlessly thorough and heartlessly perfect. It was, besides, in large part, a return to the despotism that had been overthrown.

Among those nations, on the other hand, which entered upon a season of constitution-making and popular reform before administration had received the impress of liberal principle, administrative improvement has been tardy and half-done. Once a nation has embarked in the business of manufacturing constitutions, it finds it exceedingly difficult to close out that business and open for the public a bureau of skilled, economical administration. There seems to be no end to the tinkering of constitutions. Your ordinary constitution will last you hardly ten years without repairs or additions; and the time for administrative detail comes late.

Here, of course, our examples are England and our own country. In the days of the Angevin kings, before constitutional life had taken root in the Great Charter, legal and administrative reforms began to proceed with sense and vigor under the impulse of Henry II's shrewd, busy, pushing, indomitable spirit and purpose; and kingly initiative seemed destined in England, as elsewhere, to shape governmental growth at its will. But impulsive, errant Richard and weak, despicable John were not the men to carry out such schemes as their father's. Administrative development gave place in their reigns to constitutional struggles; and Parliament became king before any English monarch had had the practical genius or the enlightened conscience to devise just and lasting forms for the civil service of the state.

The English race, consequently, has long and successfully studied the art of curbing executive power to the constant neglect of the art of perfecting executive methods. It has exercised itself much more in controlling than in energizing government. It has been more concerned to render government just and moderate than to make it facile, well-ordered,and effective. English and American political history has been a history, not of administrative development, but of legislative oversight, — not of progress in governmental organization, but of advance in law-making and political criticism. Consequently,we have reached a time when administrative study and creation are imperatively necessary to the well-being of our governments saddled with the habits of a long period of constitution-making. That period has practically closed, so far as the establishment of essential principles is concerned, but we cannot shake off its atmosphere. We go on criticizing when we ought to be creating. We have reached the third of the periods I have mentioned, — the period, namely, when the people have to develop administration in accordance with the constitutions they won for themselves in a previous period of struggle with absolute power; but we are not prepared for the tasks of the new period.

Such an explanation seems to afford the only escape from blank astonishment at the fact that, in spite of our vast advantages in point of political liberty, and above all in point of practical political skill and sagacity, so many nations are ahead of us in administrative organization and administrative skill. Why,for instance, have we but just begun purifying a civil service which was rotten full fifty years ago? To say that slavery diverted us is but to repeat what I have said — that flaws in our constitution delayed us.

Of course all reasonable preference would declare for this English and American course of politics rather than for that of any European country. We should not like to have had Prussia's history for the sake of having Prussia's administrative skill; and Prussia's particular system of administration would quite suffocate us. It is better to be untrained and free than to be servile and systematic. Still there is' no denying that it would be better yet to be both free in spirit and proficient in practice. It is this even more reasonable preference which impels us to discover what there may be to hinder or delay us in naturalizing this much-to-be-desired science of administration.

What, then, is there to prevent?

Well, principally, popular sovereignty. It is harder for democracy to organize administration than for monarchy. The very completeness of our most cherished political successes in the past embarrasses us. We have enthroned public opinion; and it is forbidden us to hope during its reign for any quick schooling of the sovereign in executive expertness or in the conditions of perfect functional balance in government. The very fact that we have realized popular rule in its fulness has made the task of organizing that rule just so much the more difficult.In order to make any advance at all we must instruct and persuade a multitudinous monarch called public opinion, — a much less feasible undertaking than to influence a single monarch called a king. An individual sovereign will adopt a simple plan and carry it out directly: he will have but one opinion, and he will embody that one opinion in one command. But this other sovereign, the people, will have a score of differing opinions.They can agree upon nothing simple: advance must be made through compromise, by a compounding of differences, by at rimming of plans and a suppression of too straightforward principles. There will be a succession of resolves running through a course of years, a dropping fire of commands running through a whole gamut of modifications.

In government, as in virtue, the hardest of hard things is to make progress. Formerly the reason for this was that the single person who was sovereign was generally either selfish,ignorant, timid, or a fool, — albeit there was now and again one who was wise. Nowadays the reason is that the many, the people, who are sovereign have no single ear which one can approach, and are selfish, ignorant, timid, stubborn, or foolish with the selfishnesses, the ignorances, the stubbornnesses, the timidities, or the follies of several thousand persons, — albeit there are hundreds who are wise. Once the advantage of the reformer was that the sovereign's mind had a definite locality,that it was contained in one man's head, and that consequently it could be gotten at; though it was his disadvantage that that mind learned only reluctantly or only in small quantities, or was under the influence of some one who let it learn only the wrong things. Now, on the contrary, the reformer is bewildered by the fact that the sovereign's mind has no definite locality, but is contained in a voting majority of several million heads; and embarrassed by the fact that the mind of this sovereign also is under the influence of favorites, who are none the less favorites in a good old-fashioned sense of the word because they are not persons but preconceived opinions; i.e., prejudices which are not to be reasoned with because they are not the children of reason.

Wherever regard for public opinion is a first principle of government, practical reform must be slow and all reform must be full of compromises. For wherever public opinion exists it must rule. This is now an axiom half the world over, and will presently come to be believed even in Russia. Whoever would effect a change in a modern constitutional government must first educate his fellow-citizens to want some change. That done, he must persuade them to want the particular change he wants. He must first make public opinion willing to listen and then see to it that it listen to the right things. He must stir it up to search for an opinion, and then manage to put the right opinion in its way.

The first step is not less difficult than the second. With opinions, possession is more than nine points of the law. It is next to impossible to dislodge them. Institutions which one generation regards as only a makeshift approximation to the realization of a principle, the next generation honors as the nearest possible approximation to that principle, and the next worships as the principle itself. It takes scarcely three generations for the apotheosis. The grandson accepts his grand-father's hesitating experiment as an integral part of the fixed constitution of nature.

Even if we had clear insight into all the political past, and could form out of perfectly instructed heads a few steady, infallible, placidly wise maxims of government into which all sound political doctrine would be ultimately resolvable, would the country act on them f That is the question. The bulk of mankind is rigidly unphilosophical, and nowadays the bulk of mankind votes. A truth must become not only plain but also commonplace before it will be seen by the people who go to their work very early in the morning; and not to act upon it must involve great and pinching inconveniences before the sesame people will make up their minds to act upon it.

And where is this unphilosophical bulk of mankind more multifarious in its composition than in the United States? To know the public mind of this country, one must know the mind, not of Americans of the older stocks only, but also of Irishmen, of Germans, of negroes. In order to get a footing for new doctrine, one must influence minds cast in every mould of race, minds inheriting every bias of environment, warped by the histories of a score of different nations, warmed or chilled, closed or expanded by almost every climate of the globe.

So much, then, for the history of the study of administration, and the peculiarly difficult conditions under which, entering upon it when we do, we must undertake it. What, now, is the subject-matter of this study, and what are its characteristic objects?

II.

The field of administration is a field of business. It is removed from the hurry and strife of politics; it at most points stands apart even from the debatable ground of constitutional study. It is a part of political life only as the methods of the counting-house are a part of the life of society; only as machinery is part of the manufactured product. But it is, at the same time, raised very far above the dull level of mere technical detail by the fact that through its greater principles it is directly connected with the lasting maxims of political wisdom,the permanent truths of political progress.

The object of administrative study is to rescue executive methods from the confusion and costliness of empirical experiment and set them upon foundations laid deep in stable principle.

It is for this reason that we must regard civil-service reform in its present stages as but a prelude to a fuller administrative reform. We are now rectifying methods of appointment; we must go on to adjust executive functions more fitly and to prescribe better methods of executive organization and action. Civil-service reform is thus but a moral preparation for what is to follow. It is clearing the moral atmosphere of official life by establishing the sanctity of public office as a public trust, and,by making the service unpartisan, it is opening the way for making it businesslike. By sweetening its motives it is renering it capable of improving its methods of work.

Let me expand a little what I have said of the province of administration. Most important to be observed is the truth already so much and so fortunately insisted upon by our civil-service reformers; namely, that administration lies outside the proper sphere of politics. Administrative questions are not political questions. Although politics sets the tasks for administration, it should not be suffered to manipulate its offices.

This is distinction of high authority; eminent German writers insist upon it as of course. Bluntschli, for instance, bids us separate administration alike from politics and from law. Politics, he says, is state activity "in things great and universal,"while "administration, on the other hand," is "the activity of the state in individual and small things. Politics is thus the special province of the statesman, administration of the technical official." "Policy does nothing without the aid of administration"; but administration is not therefore politics. But we do not require German authority for this position; this discrimination between administration and politics is now, happily, too obvious to need further discussion.

There is another distinction which must be worked into all our conclusions, which, though but another side of that between administration and politics, is not quite so easy to keep sight of: I mean the distinction between constitutional and administrative questions, between those governmental adjustments which are essential to constitutional principle and those which are merely instrumental to the possibly changing purposes of a wisely adapting convenience-One cannot easily make clear to every one just where administration resides in the various departments of any practicable government without entering upon particulars so numerous as to confuse and distinctions so minute as to distract. No lines of demarcation, setting apart administrative from non-administrative functions, can be run between this and that department of government without being run up hill and down dale, over dizzy heights of distinction and through dense jungles of statutory enactment, hither and thither around " ifs" and " buts,"" whens " and " howevers," until they become altogether lost to the common eye not accustomed to this sort of surveying, and consequently not acquainted with the use of the theodolite of logical discernment. A great deal of administration goes about incognito to most of the world, being confounded now with political "management," and again with constitutional principle.

Perhaps this ease of confusion may explain such utterancesas that of Niebuhr's: " Liberty," he says, " depends in comparably more upon administration than upon constitution." At first sight this appears to be largely true. Apparently facility in the actual exercise of liberty does depend more upon administrative arrangements than upon constitutional guarantees;although constitutional guarantees alone secure the existence of liberty. But — upon second thought

— is even so much as this true? Liberty no more consists in easy functional movement than intelligence consists in the ease and vigor with which the limbs of a strong man move. The principles that rule within the man, or the constitution, are the vital springs of liberty or servitude. Because dependence and subjection are without chains, are lightened by every easy-working device of considerate, paternal government, they are not thereby transformed into liberty. Liberty cannot live apart from constitutional principle; and no administration, however perfect and liberal its methods, can give men more than a poor counterfeit of liberty if it rest upon illiberal principles of government.

A clear view of the difference between the province of constitutional law and the province of administrative function ought to leave no room for misconception; and it is possible to name some roughly definite criteria upon which such a view can be built. Public administration is detailed and systematic execution of public law. Every particular application of general law is an act of administration. The assessment and raising of taxes, for instance, the hanging of a criminal, the transportation and delivery of the mails, the equipment and recruiting of the army and navy, etc., are all obviously acts of administration; but the general laws which direct these things to be done areas obviously outside of and above administration. The broad plans of governmental action are not administrative; the detailed execution of such plans is administrative. Constitutions,therefore, properly concern themselves only with those instrumentalities of government which are to control general law. Our federal constitution observes this principle in saying nothing of even the greatest of the purely executive offices, and speaking only of that President of the Union who was to share the legislative and policy-making functions of government, only of those judges of highest jurisdiction who were to interpret and guard its principles, and not of those who were merely to give utterance to them.

This is not quite the distinction between Will and answering Deed, because the administrator should have and does have a will of his own in the choice of means for accomplishing his work. He is not and ought not to be a mere passive instrument. The distinction is between general plans and special means.

There is, indeed, one point at which administrative studie strench on constitutional ground — or at least upon what seems constitutional ground. The study of administration, philosophically viewed, is closely connected with the study of the proper distribution of constitutional authority. To be efficient it must discover the simplest arrangements by which responsibility can be unmistakably fixed upon officials; the best way of dividing authority without hampering it, and responsibility without obscuring it. And this question of the distribution of authority,when taken into the sphere of the higher, the originating functions of government, is obviously a central constitutional question. If administrative study can discover the best principles upon which to base such distribution, it will have done constitutional study an invaluable service. Montesquieu did not, I am convinced, say the last word on this head.

To discover the best principle for the distribution of authority is of greater importance, possibly, under a democratic system, where officials serve many masters, than under others where they serve but a few. All sovereigns are suspicious of their servants, and the sovereign people is no exception to the rule; but how is its suspicion to be allayed by knowledge? If that suspicion could but be clarified into wise vigilance, it would be altogether salutary; if that vigilance could be aided by the unmistakable placing of responsibility, it would be altogether beneficent. Suspicion in itself is never healthful either in the private or in the public mind. Trust is strength in all relations of life; and, as it is the office of the constitutional reformer to create conditions of trustfulness, so it is the office of the administrative organizer to fit administration with conditions of clearcut responsibility which shall insure trustworthiness.

And let me say that large powers and unhampered discretion seem to me the indispensable conditions of responsibility. Public attention must be easily directed, in each case of good or bad administration, to just the man deserving of praise or blame. There is no danger in power, if only it be not irresponsible. If it be divided, dealt out in shares to many, it is obscured; and if it be obscured, it is made irresponsible. But if it be centred in heads of the service and in heads of branches of the service, it is easily watched and brought to book. If to keep his office a man must achieve open and honest success, and if at the same time he feels himself in trusted with large freedom of discretion, the greater his power the less likely is he to abuse it, the more is he nerved and sobered and elevated by it. The less his power, the more safely obscure and unnoticed does he feel his position to be, and the more readily does he relapse into remissness.

Just here we manifestly emerge upon the field of that still larger question, — the proper relations between public opinion and administration.

To whom is official trustworthiness to be disclosed, and by whom is it to be rewarded? Is the official to look to the public for his meed of praise and his push of promotion, or only to his superior in office? Are the people to be called in to settle administrative discipline as they are called in to settle constitutional principles? These questions evidently find their root in what is undoubtedly the fundamental problem of this whole study. That problem is: What part shall public opinion take in the conduct of administration?

The right answer seems to be, that public opinion shall play the part of authoritative critic.

But the method by which its authority shall be made to tell? Our peculiar American difficulty in organizing administration is not the danger of losing liberty, but the danger of not being able or willing to separate its essentials from its accidents.Our success is made doubtful by that besetting error of ours,the error of trying to do too much by vote. Self-government does not consist in having a hand in everything, any more than housekeeping consists necessarily in cooking dinner with one'sown hands. The cook must be trusted with a large discretion as to the management of the fires and the ovens.

In those countries in which public opinion has yet to be instructed in its privileges, yet to be accustomed to having its own way, this question as to the province of public opinion is much more readily soluble than in this country, where public opinion is wide awake and quite intent upon having its own way anyhow. It is pathetic to see a whole book written by a German professor of political science for the purpose of saying to his countrymen, " Please try to have an opinion about national affairs "; but a public which is so modest may at least be expected to be very docile and acquiescent in learning what things it has not a right to think and speak about imperatively. It may be sluggish, but it will not be meddlesome. It will submit to be instructed before it tries to instruct. Its political education will come before its political activity. In trying to instruct our own public opinion, we are dealing with a pupil apt to think itself quite sufficiently instructed beforehand.

The problem is to make public opinion efficient without suffering it to be meddlesome. Directly exercised, in the oversight of the daily details and in the choice of the daily means of government, public criticism is of course a clumsy nuisance, a rustic handling delicate machinery. But as superintending the greater forces of formative policy alike in politics and administration, public criticism is altogether safe and beneficent, altogether indispensable. Let administrative study find the best means for giving public criticism this control and for shutting it out from all other interference.

But is the whole duty of administrative study done when it has taught the people what sort of administration to desire and demand, and how to get what they demand? Ought it not to go on to drill candidates for the public service?

There is an admirable movement towards universal political education now afoot in this country. The time will soon come when no college of respectability can afford to do without a well filled chair of political science. But the education thus imparted will go but a certain length. It will multiply the number of intelligent critics of government, but it will create no competent body of administrators. It will prepare the way for the development of a surefooted understanding of the general principles of government, but it will not necessarily foster skill in conducting government. It is an education which will equip legislators, perhaps, but not executive officials. If we are to improve public opinion, which is the motive power of government, we must prepare better officials as the apparatus of government. If we are to put in new boilers and to mend the fires which drive our governmental machinery, we must not leave the old wheels and joints and valves and bands to creak and buzz and clatter on as best they may at bidding of the new force. We must put in new running parts wherever there is the least lack of strength or adjustment. It will be necessary to organize democracy by sending up to the competitive examinations for the civil service men definitely prepared for standing liberal tests as to technical knowledge. A technically schooled civil service will presently have become indispensable.

I know that a corps of civil servants prepared by a special schooling and drilled, after appointment, into a perfected organization, with appropriate hierarchy and characteristic discipline, seems to a great many very thoughtful persons to contain elements which might combine to make an offensive official class, — a distinct, semi-corporate body with sympathies divorced from those of a progressive, free-spirited people, and with hearts narrowed to the meanness of a bigoted officialism. Certainly such a class would be altogether hateful and harmful in the United States. Any measures calculated to produce it would for us be measures of reaction and of folly.

But to fear the creation of a domineering, illiberal officialism as a result of the studies I am here proposing is to miss altogether the principle upon which I wish most to insist. That principle is, that administration in the United States must beat all points sensitive to public opinion. A body of thoroughly trained officials serving during good behavior we must have in any case: that is a plain business necessity. But the apprehension that such a body will be anything un-American clears away the moment it is asked, What is to constitute good behavior? For that question obviously carries its own answer on its face. Steady, hearty allegiance to the policy of the government they serve will constitute good behavior. That policy will have no taint of officialism about it. It will not be the creation of permanent officials, but of statesmen whose responsibility to public opinion will be direct and inevitable. Bureaucracy can exist only where the whole service of the state is removed from the common political life of the people, its chiefs as well as its rank and file. Its motives, its objects, its policy, its standards, must be bureaucratic. It would be difficult to point out any examples of impudent exclusiveness and arbitrariness on the part of officials doing service under a chief of department who really served the people, as all our chiefs of departments must be made to do. It would be easy, on the other hand, to adduce other instances like that of the influence of Stein in Prussia, where the leadership of one statesman imbued with true public spirit transformed arrogant and perfunctory bureaux into public-spirited instruments of just government.

The ideal for us is a civil service cultured and self-sufficient enough to act with sense and vigor, and yet so intimately connected with the popular thought, by means of elections and constant public counsel, as to find arbitrariness or class spirit quite out of the question.

III.

Having thus viewed in some sort the subject-matter and the objects of this study of administration, what are we to conclude as to the methods best suited to it — the points of view most advantageous for it?

Government is so near us, so much a thing of our daily familiar handling, that we can with difficulty see the need of any philosophical study of it, or the exact point of such study, should it be undertaken. We have been on our feet too long to study now the art of walking. We are a practical people, made so apt, so adept in self-government by centuries of experimental drill that we are scarcely any longer capable of perceiving the awkwardness of the particular system we may be using, just because it is so easy for us to use any system. We do not study the art of governing: we govern. But mere unschooled genius for affairs will not save us from sad blunders in administration. Though democrats by long inheritance and repeated choice, we are still rather crude democrats. Old as democracy is, its organization on a basis of modern ideas and conditions is still an unaccomplished work. The democratic state has yet to be equipped for carrying those enormous burdens of administration which the needs of this industrial and trading age are so fast accumulating. Without comparative studies in government we cannot rid ourselves of the misconception that administration stands upon an essentially different basis in a democratic state from that on which it stands in a non-democratic state.

After such study we could grant democracy the sufficient honor of ultimately determining by debate all essential questions affecting the public weal, of basing all structures of policy upon the major will; but we would have found but one rule of good administration for all governments alike. So far as administrative functions are concerned, all governments have a strong structural likeness; more than that, if they are to be uniformly useful and efficient, they must have a strong structural likeness. A free man has the same bodily organs, the same executive parts, as the slave, however different may be his motives, his services, his energies. Monarchies and democracies, radically different as they are in other respects, have in reality much the same business to look to.

It is abundantly safe nowadays to insist upon this actual likeness of all governments, because these are days when abuses of power are easily exposed and arrested, in countries like our own, by a bold, alert, inquisitive, detective public thought and a sturdy popular self-dependence such as never existed before. We are slow to appreciate this; but it is easy to appreciate it. Try to imagine personal government in the United States. It is like trying to imagine a national worship of Zeus. Our imaginations are too modern for the feat.

But, besides being safe, it is necessary to see that for all governments alike the legitimate ends of administration are the same, in order not to be frightened at the idea of looking into foreign systems of administration for instruction and suggestion; in order to get rid of the apprehension that we might perchance blindly borrow something incompatible with our principles. That man is blindly astray who denounces attempts to transplant foreign systems into this country. It is impossible: they simply would not grow here. But why should we not use such parts of foreign contrivances as we want, if they be in any way serviceable? We are in no danger of using them in a foreign way. We borrowed rice, but we do not eat it with chopsticks. We borrowed our whole political language from England, but we leave the words "king" and "lords" out of it. What did we ever originate, except the action of the federal government upon individuals and some of the functions of the federal supreme court?

We can borrow the science of administration with safety and profit if only we read all fundamental differences of condition into its essential tenets. We have only to filter it through our constitutions, only to put it over a slow fire of criticism and distil away its foreign gases.

I know that there is a sneaking fear in some conscientiously patriotic minds that studies of European systems might signalize some foreign methods as better than some American methods; and the fear is easily to be understood. But it would scarcely be avowed in just any company.

It is the more necessary to insist upon thus putting away all prejudices against looking anywhere in the world but at home for suggestions in this study, because nowhere else in the whole field of politics, it would seem, can we make use of the historical, comparative method more safely than in this province of administration. Perhaps the more novel the forms we study the better. We shall the sooner learn the peculiarities of our own methods. We can never learn either our own weaknesses or our own virtues by comparing ourselves with ourselves. We are too used to the appearance and procedure of our own system to see its true significance. Perhaps even the English system is too much like our own to be used to the most profit in illustration. It is best on the whole to get entirely away from our own atmosphere and to be most careful in examining such systems as those of France and Germany. Seeing our own institutions through such media, we see ourselves as foreigners might see us were they to look at us without preconceptions. Of ourselves, so long as we know only ourselves, we know nothing.

Let it be noted that it is the distinction, already drawn, between administration and politics which makes the comparative method so safe in the field of administration. When we study the administrative systems of France and Germany, knowing that we are not in search of political principles, we need not care a peppercorn for the constitutional or political reasons which Frenchmen or Germans give for their practices when explaining them to us. If I see a murderous fellow sharpening a knife cleverly, I can borrow his way of sharpening the knife without borrowing his probable intention to commit murder with it; and so, if I see a monarchist dyed in the wool managing a public bureau well, I can learn his business methods without changing one of my republican spots. He may serve his king; I will continue to serve the people; but I should like to serve my sovereign as well as he serves his. By keeping this distinction in view, — that is, by studying administration as a means of putting our own politics into convenient practice, as a means of making what is democratically politic towards all administratively possible towards each, — we are on perfectly safe ground, and can learn without error what foreign systems have to teach us. We thus devise an adjusting weight for our comparative method of study. We can thus scrutinize the anatomy of foreign governments without fear of getting any of their diseases into our veins; dissect alien systems without apprehension of blood-poisoning.

Our own politics must be the touchstone for all theories. The principles on which to base a science of administration for America must be principles which have democratic policy very much at heart. And, to suit American habit, all general theories must, as theories, keep modestly in the background, not in open argument only, but even in our own minds, — lest opinions satisfactory only to the standards of the library should be dogmatically used, as if they must be quite as satisfactory to the standards of practical politics as well. Doctrinaire devices must be postponed to tested practices. Arrangements not only santioned by conclusive experience elsewhere but also congenial to American habit must be preferred without hesitation to theoretical perfection. In a word, steady, practical statesmanship must come first, closet doctrine second. The cosmopolitan what-to-do must always be commanded by the American how-to-do-it.

Our duty is, to supply the best possible life to a federal organization, to systems within systems; to make town, city, county, state, and federal governments live with a like strength and an equally assured healthfulness, keeping each unquestionably its own master and yet making all interdependent and cooperative, combining independence with mutual helpfulness. The task is great and important enough to attract the best minds.

This interlacing of local self-government with federal self-government is quite a modern conception. It is not like the arrangements of imperial federation in Germany. There local government is not yet, fully, local-government. The bureaucrat is everywhere busy. His efficiency springs out of espritde corps, out of care to make ingratiating obeisance to the authority of a superior, or, at best, out of the soil of a sensitive conscience. He serves, not the public, but an irresponsible minister. The question for us is, how shall our series of governments within governments be so administered that it shall always be to the interest of the public officer to serve, no this superior alone but the community also, with the best efforts of his talents and the soberest service of his conscience ? How shall such service be made to his commonest interest by contributing abundantly to his sustenance, to his dearest interest by furthering his ambition, and to his highest interest by advancing his honor and establishing his character? And how shall this be done alike for the local part and for the national whole?

If we solve this problem we shall again pilot the world. There is a tendency — is there not? — a tendency as yet dim, but already steadily impulsive and clearly destined to prevail, towards, first the confederation of parts of empires like the British, and finally of great states themselves. Instead of centralization of power, there is to be wide union with tolerated divisions of prerogative. This is a tendency towards the American type — of governments joined with governments for the pursuit of common purposes, in honorary equality and honorable subordination. Like principles of civil liberty are every where fostering like methods of government; and if comparative studies of the ways and means of government should enable us to offer suggestions which will practicably combine openness and vigor in the administration of such governments with ready docility to all serious, well-sustained public criticism, they will have approved themselves worthy to be ranked among the highest and most fruitful of the great departments of political study. That they will issue in such suggestions I confidently hope.

Woodrow Wilson.

Leaders of Men

Woodrow Wilson

June 17, 1890

Only those are 'leaders of men,' in the general eye, who lead in action. The title belongs, if the whole field of the world be justly viewed, no more rightfully to the men who lead in action than to those who lead in silent thought. A book is often quite as quickening a trumpet as any made of brass and sounded in the field. But it is the estimate of the world that bestows their meaning upon words: and that estimate is not often very far from the fact. The men who act stand nearer to the mass of men than do the men who write; and it is at their hands that new thought gets its translation into the crude language of deeds. The very crudity of that language of deeds exasperates the sensibilities of the author; and his exasperation proves the world's point. He may be back of the leaders, but he is not the leader. In his thought there is due and studied proportion; all limiting considerations are set in their right places, as guards to ward off misapprehension. Every cadence of right utterance is made to sound in the careful phrases, in the perfect adjustments of sense. Translate the thought into action and all its shadings disappear. It stands out a naked, lusty thing, sure to rasp the sensibilities of every man of fastidious taste. Stripped for action, a thought must always shock those who cultivate the nice fashions of literary dress, as authors do. But it is only when thought does thus stand forth in unabashed force that it can perform deeds of strength in the arena round about which the great public sit as spectators, awarding the prizes by the suffrage of their applause.

Here, unquestionably, we come upon the heart of the perennial misunderstanding between the men who write and the men who act. The men who write love proportion; the men who act must strike out practicable lines of action, and neglect proportion. This would seem to explain the well-nigh universal repugnance felt by literary men towards Democracy. The arguments which induce popular action must always be broad and obvious arguments. Only a very gross substance of concrete conception can make any impression on the minds of the masses; they must get their ideas very absolutely put, and are much readier to receive a half-truth which they can promptly understand than a whole truth which has too many sides to be seen all at once. How can any man whose method is the method of artistic completeness of thought and expression, whose mood is the mood of contemplation, for a moment understand or tolerate the majority whose purpose and practice it is to strike out broad, rough-hewn policies, whose mood is the mood of action? The great stream of freedom which "broadens down from precedent to precedent," is not a clear mountain current such as the fastidious man of chastened taste likes to drink from: it is polluted with not a few of the coarse elements of the gross world on its banks; it is heavy with the drainage of a very material universe.

One of the nicest tests of the repugnance felt by the literary nature for the sort of leadership and action which commends itself to the world of common men you may yourself supply. Asking some author of careful, discriminative thought to utter his ideas to a mass-meeting, from a platform occupied by 'representative citizens.' He will shrink from it as he would shrink from being publicly dissected! Even to hear some one else, who's given to apt public speech, re-render his thoughts in oratorical phrase and make them acceptable to a miscellaneous audience, is often a mild, sometimes an acute, form of torture for him. If the world would really know his thoughts for what they are, let them go to his written words, con his phrases, join paragraph with paragraph, chapter with chapter: then, the whole form and fashion of his conceptions impressed upon their minds, they will know him as no platform speaker can ever him known. Of course such preferences greatly limit his audience. Not many out of the multitudes who crowd about him buy his books. But, if the few who can understand read and are convinced, will not his thoughts finally leaven the mass?

The true leader of men, it is plain, is equipped by lacking such sensibilities, which the literary man, when analyzed, is found to possess as a chief part of his make-up. He lacks that subtle power of sympathy which enables the men who write the great works of the imagination to put their minds under the spell of a thousand individual motives not their own but the living force in several characters they interpret. No popular leader could write fiction. He could not write fiction. He could not conceive the Ring and the Book the impersonation of a half-score points of view. An imaginative realization of other natures and minds than his own is as impossible for him, as his own commanding, dominating frame of mind and character is impossible for the sensitive seer whose imagination can give life to a thousand separate characters. Mr. Browning could no more have been a statesman-if statesmen are to be popular leaders also-than Mr. Disraeli could write a novel. Mr. Browning could see from individual's point of view intellectual sympathy came amiss to him. Mr. Disraeli could see from no point of view but his own,-and the characters which he put into those works of his which were meant to be novels move as mere puppets to his will, -as the men he governed did. They are his mouthpieces simply and are as little like themselves as were the Tory squires in the Commons like themselves after they became his chessmen.

One of the most interesting and suggestive criticisms made upon Mr. Gladstone's leadership during the life of his ministries was that he was not decisive in the House of Commons as Palmerston and Peel had been before him. He could not help seeing two sides of a question: the force of objections evidently told upon him. His conclusions seemed the nice result of a balancing of considerations, not the commands of an unhesitating conviction. A party likes to be led by very absolute opinions: it chills it to hear it admitted that there is some reason on the other side. Mr. Peel saw both sides of many questions; but he never saw both sides at once. He saw now one, and afterwards, by slow and honest conversion, the other. While he is in opposition Mr. Gladstone's transparent honesty adds to his moral weight with the people: for in opposition only the whole attitude is significant. But it was different when he was in power. For a governing party particulars of posture and policy tell. For them the consistency of unhesitating opinion counts heavily as an element of success and prestige.

That the leader of men must have such sympathetic and penetrative insight as shall enable him to discern quite unerringly the motives which move other men in the mass is of course self-evident; but the insight which he must have is not the Shakespearian insight. It need not pierce the particular secrets of individual men: it need only know what it is that lies waiting to be stirred in the minds and purposes of groups and masses of men. Besides, it is not a sympathy that serves, but a sympathy whose power is to command, to command by knowing its instrument. The seer, whose function is imaginative interpretation, is the man of science; the leader is the mechanic. The chemist knows his materials interpretatively: he can make subtlest analysis of all their affinities, of all their antipathies; can give you the point of view of every gas or metal or liquid with regard to every other liquid or gas or metal; he can marry, he can divorce, he can destroy them. He could suppose fictitious cases with regard to the conduct of the 'elements' which would appear most clever and probable to other chemists: which would appear witty and credible, doubtless, to the 'elements' themselves, could they know. But the mining-engineer's point of view is very different. He, too, must know chemical properties, but only in order that he may use them-only in order to have the right sort of explosion at the right place. So, too, the mechanic's point of view must be quite different from that of the physicist. He must know what his tools can do and what they will stand; but he must be something more than interpreter of their qualities-and something quite different. "It is the general opinion of locomotive superintendents that it is not essential that the men who run locomotives should be good mechanics. Brunel, the distinguished civil engineer, said that he never would trust himself to run a locomotive because he was sure to think of some problem relating to his profession which would distract his attention from the engine. It is probably a similar reason which unfits good mechanics for being good locomotive runners."

Imagine Thackeray leading the House of Commons, or Mr. Lowell on the stump. How comically would their very genius defeat them. The special gift of these two men is a critical understanding of other men, their fallible fellow-creatures. How could their keen humorous sense of what was transpiring in the breasts of their followers and fellow-partisans be held back from banter? How could they take the mass seriously-themselves refrain from laughter and also from the temptation of provoking it? Thackeray argue patiently and respectfully with a dense country member, equipped with nothing but diverting scruples and laughable prejudices? Impossible. As well ask a biologist to treat a cat or a rabbit as if it were a pet with no admirable machinery inside to tempt the dissecting knife.

The competent leader of men cares little for the interior niceties of other people's characters: he cares much-everything for the external uses to which they may be put. His will seeks the lines of least resistance; but the whole question with him is a question of the application of force. There are men to be moved: how shall he move them? He supplies the power; others supply only the materials upon which that power operates. The power will fail if it be misapplied; it will be misapplied if it be not suitable both in kind and method to the nature of the materials upon which it is spent; but that nature is, after all, only its means. It is the power which dictates, dominates: the materials yield. Men are as clay in the hands of the consummate leader.

It often happens that the leader displays a sagacity and an insight in the handling of men in the mass which quite baffle the wits of the shrewdest analyst of individual character. Men in the mass differ from men as individuals. A man who knows, and keenly knows, every man in town may yet fail to understand a mob or a mass-meeting of his fellow-townsmen. Just as the whole tone and method suitable for a public speech are foreign to the tone and method proper in individual, face to face dealings with separate men, so is the art of leading different from the art of writing novels.

Some of the gifts and qualities which most commend the literary man to success would inevitably doom the would-be leader to failure. One could wish for no better proof and example of this than is furnished by the career of that most table of great Irishmen, Edmund Burke. Everyone knows that Burke's life was spent in Parliament, and everyone knows that the eloquence he poured forth there is as deathless as our literature; and yet everyone is left to wonder in presence of the indubitable fact that he was of so little consequence in the actual direction of affairs. How noble a figure in the history of English politics: how large a man; how commanding a mind; and yet how ineffectual in the work of bringing men to turn their faces as he would have them, toward the high purposes he had ever in view! We hear with astonishment that after the delivery of that consummate speech on the Nabob of Arcot's debts, which everybody has read, Pitt and Grenville easily agree that they need not trouble themselves to make any reply. His speech on conciliation with America is not only wise beyond precedent in the annals of debate, but marches also with a force of phrase which, it would seen, must have been irresistible; and yet we know that it emptied the House of all audience! You remember what Goldsmith playfully suggested for Burke's epitaph:

> "Here lies our good Edmund, whose genius was such,
> We scarcely can praise it, or blame it, too much;
> Who, too deep for his hearers, still went on refining,
> And thought of convincing while they thought of dining:
> Though equal to all things, for all things unfit,
> Too nice for a statesman, too proud for a wit;
> For a patriot too cool; for a drudge disobedient,
> And too fond of the right to pursue the expedient.
> In short, 'twas his fate, unemploy'd, or in place, sir,
> To eat mutton cold, and cut blocks with a razor."

Certainly this is too small a measure for so big a man, as Goldsmith himself would probably have been the first to admit; but the description is almost as true as it is clever. It is better to read Burke than to have heard him. The thoughts which miscarried in parliaments of George III have had their triumphs in parliaments of a later day, -have established themselves at the heart of such policies as are to-day liberalizing the world. His power is literary, not forensic. He was no leader of men. He was an organizer of thought, but not of party victories. "Burke is a wise man," said Fox, "but he is wise too soon." He was wise also too much. He went on from the wisdom of to-day to the wisdom of to-morrow, to the wisdom which is for all time. It was impossible he should be followed so far. Men want the wisdom which they are expected to apply to be obvious, and to be conveniently limited in amount. They want a thoroughly trustworthy article, with very simple adjustments and manifest present uses. Elaborate it, increase the expenditure of thought necessary to obtain it, and they will decline to listen, you must keep it in stock for the use of the next generation.

Men are not led by being told what they do not know. Persuasion is a force, but not information; and persuasion is accomplished by creeping into the confidence of those you would lead. Their confidence is not gained by preaching new thoughts to them. It is gained by qualities which they can recognize at first sight by arguments which they can assimilate at once: by the things which find easy and intermediate entrance into their minds, and which are easily transmitted to the palms of their hands or to the ends of their walking-sticks in the shape of applause. Burke's thoughts penetrate the mind and possess the heart of the quiet student. His style of saying things fills the attention as if it were finest music. But his are not thoughts to be shouted over; his is not a style to ravish the ear of the voter at the hustings. If you would be a leader of men, you must lead your own generation, not the next. Your playing must be good now, while the play is on the boards and the audience in the seats: it will not get you the repute of a great actor to have excellencies discovered in you afterwards. Burke's genius, besides, made conservative men uneasy. How could a man be safe who had so many ideas?

Englishmen of the present generation wonder that England should ever have been ruled by John Addington, a man about whom nothing was accentuated but his dullness; by Mr. Perceval, a sort of Tory squire without the usual rich and diverting blood or any irregularity of his kind; by Lord Castlereagh, whose speaking was so bad as to drive his hearers to assume that there must be some great purpose lurking behind its amorphous masses somewhere, simply because it was inconceivable that there should be in it so little purpose as it revealed. Accustomed to the aggressive and persistent power of Gladstone, the epigrammatic variety of Disraeli, the piquant indiscretions of Salisbury, they naturally marvel that they could have been interested enough in such men to follow or in any wise heed them. But, after all, the Englishman has not changed. He still has a sneaking distrust of successful men of thought like Mr. John Morley. An Englishmen is made as uncomfortable and as indignant now by the vagaries of a man like Lord Randolph Churchill as he formally was, in times he has forgotten, by the equally bumptious young Disraeli. The story is told of a thorough-going old country Tory of the time when Pitt was displaced by Addington that, going to tell a friend of the formation of a new ministry by that excellent mediocrity, he repeated with unction the whole list of common-place men who were to constitute the new Government, and then, rubbing his hands in demonstrative satisfaction, exclaimed, "Well, thank God, we have at last got a ministry without one of those confounded men of genius in it!" Cobden was doubtless right when he said that "the only way in which the soul of a great nation can be stirred, is by appealing to its sympathies with a true principle in its unalloyed simplicity," and that it was "necessary for the concentration of a people's mind that an individual should become the incarnation of a principle"; but the emphasis should be laid on the "unalloyed simplicity" of the principle. It will not do to incarnate too many ideas at a time if you are to be universally understood and numerously followed.

Cobden himself is an excellent case in point. Embodying a true principle of unhampered commerce in its "unalloyed simplicity," he became a power in England second to none. Never did England so steadily yield to argument, so steadily thaw under persuasion, as while Cobden occupied the platform. Cobden was singularly equipped for leadership, -especially for leadership of this practical, business like kind. He had in him nothing of the literary mind, which combines images and is dominated by associations: he conceived only facts, and was dominated by programs of reform. Going to Greece, he found Issus and Cephisus, the famed streams of Attica, ridiculous rivulets and wondered that the world should pause so often to study such Lilliputian states as classical Hellas contained when there were the politics of the United States and the vast rivers and mountains of the new continents to think about. "What famous puffers those old Greeks were!" he exclaims. He journeyed to Egypt and sat beside Mehemet Ali, one of the fiercest warriors and most accomplished tyrants of our century, with a practical eye open to the fact that the royal viceroy was a somewhat fat personage who fell into blunders when he boasted of the cotton crops of the land he had under his heel, and a shrewd perception that his conductor and introducer, Col. C., had hit upon the wrong resource in beginning the conversation by a reference to the excellent weather in a latitude "where unlimited sunshine prevails for seven years together. He keeps the world of practical details under constant cross-examination. And when, in later days, the great anti-corn-law League is in the heat of its task of reforming the English tariff, how seriously this earnest man takes the vast fairs, the colossal bazaars, and all the other homely, bourgeois machinery by means of which the League keeps itself supplied at once with funds for its work and with that large measure of popular attention necessary to its success. This is the organizer, who is incapable of being fatigued by the commonplace-or amused by it-and who is thoroughly in love with working at a single idea.

Mark the simplicity and directness of the arguments and ideas of such men. The motives which they urge are elemental; the morality which they seek to enforce is large and obvious; the policy they emphasize purged of all subtlety. They give you the fine gold of truth in the nugget, not cunningly beaten into elaborate shapes and chased with intricate patterns. "If oratory were a business and not an art," says Mr. Justin McCarthy, "then it might be contended reasonably enough that Mr. Cobden was one of the greatest orators England has ever known. Nothing could exceed the persuasiveness of his style. His manner was simple, sweet, and earnest. It persuaded by convincing. It was transparently sincere.

But we see the same things in the oratory of Bright, with whom oratory was not a business but an art. Hear him appeal to his constituents in Birmingham, that capital of the spirit of gain, touching what he deemed an iniquitous foreign policy;

"I believe," he exclaims, "there is no permanent greatness in a nation except it be based upon morality. I do not care for military greatness or military renown. I care for the condition of the people among whom I live. There is no man in England who is less likely to speak irreverently of the Crown and Monarchy of England than I am; but crowns, coronets, mitres, military display, the pomp of war, wide colonies, and a huge empire, are, in my view, all trifles light as air, and not worth considering, unless with them you can have a fair share of comfort, contentment, and happiness among the great body of the people. Palaces, baronial castles, great halls, stately mansions, do not make a nation. The nation in every country dwells in the cottage; and unless the light of your constitution can shine there, unless the beauty of your legislation and the excellence of your statesmanship are impressed there on the feelings and conditions of the people, rely upon it you have yet to learn the duties of government.

"May I ask you, then, to believe, as I do most devoutly believe, that the moral law was not written for men alone in their individual character, but that it was written as well for nations, and for nations great as this of which we are citizens. If nations reject and deride that moral law, there is a penalty which will inevitably follow. It may not come at once, it may not come in our lifetime; but, rely upon it, the great Italian poet is not a poet only, but a prophet, when he says,-

> 'The sword of heaven is not in haste to smite,
> Nor yet doth linger.'

We have experience, we have beacons, we have landmarks enough. We know what the past has cost us, we know how much and how far we have wandered, but we are not left without a guide. It is true we have not, as an ancient people had, Urim and Thummim-those oraculous gems on Aaron's breast-from which to take counsel, but we have the unchangeable and eternal principles of the moral law to guide us, and only so far as we walk by that guidance can we be permanently a great nation, or our people a happy people."

How simple, how evident it all is, -how commonplace the motives appealed to, -how old the moral maxim-how obvious every consideration urged. And yet how effective such a passage is, -how it carries, -what a thrill of life and of power there is in it. As simple as the quiet argument of Cobden, it is yet alight with passionate feeling. As direct and unpretentious as a bit of conversation, though elevated above the level of conversation by a sweep of accumulating phrase such as may be made effectual for the throwing down of strongholds.

Style has of course a great deal to do with such effects in popular oratory. Armies have not won battles by sword-fencing, but by the fierce cut of the sabre, the direct volley of musketry, the straightforward argument of artillery, the impetuous dash of cavalry. And it is in the same way that oratorical battles are won: not by the nice refinements of statement, the deft sword-play of dialectic fence, but by the straight and speedy thrusts of speech sent through and through the gross and obvious frame of a subject. It must be clear and always clear what the sentences would be about. They must be advanced with the firm tread of disciplined march. Their meaning must ring clear and loud.

There is also much in physical gifts, as everybody knows. The popular leader should be satisfying to the eye and to the ear: broad, sturdy, clear-eyed, musically voiced, like John Bright; built with the stature and mien of a Norse god, like Webster; towering, imperious, persuading by voice and carriage, like Clay; or vast, rugged, fulminating, like Daniel O'Connell, fit for a Celtic Olympus. It is easy to call a man like Daniel O'Connell a demagogue, but it is juster to see in him a born leader of men. We remember him as the agitator, simply, loud, incessant, a bit turbulent, not a little coarse also, full of flouts and jibes, bitter and abusive, in headlong pursuit of the aims of Irish liberty. We ought to remember him as the ardent supporter of every policy that made for English and for human liberty also, a friend of reform when reform was unpopular, a champion of oppressed classes who had almost no one else to speak for them, a battler for what was liberal and enlightened and against what was unfair and prejudiced, all along the line. He was no courter of popularity: but his heart was the heart of his people: their cause and their hopes were his. He was not their slave, nor were they his dupes. He was their mouth-piece. And what a mouth-piece! Nature seems to have planned him for utterance. His figure and influence loom truly grand as we look back to him standing, as he so often did, before concourses mustered, scores of thousands strong, upon the open heath to hear and to protest of Ireland's wrongs.

> "His Titan strength must touch what gave it birth;
> Hear him to mobs and on his mother earth."

Here is the testimony of one who saw one of those immeasurable assemblies stand round about the giant Celt and saw the Master wield his spell:

> "Methought no clarion could have sent its sound
>   Even to the centre of the hosts around;
> And, as I thought, rose the sonorous swell,
> As from some church-tower swings the silvery bell.
> Aloft and clear, from airy tide to tide,
> It glided, easy as a bird may glide;
> To the last verge of that vast audience sent,
> It play'd with each wild passion as it went;
> Now stirred the uproar, now the murmur still'd,
> And sobs or laughter answer'd as it will'd.
> Then did I know what spells of infinite choice,

To rouse or lull, has the sweet human voice;
Then did I seem to seize the sudden clue
To the grand troublous Life Antique-to view
Under the rock-stand of Demosthenes,
Mutable Athens heave her noisy seas."

This huge organization, this thrilling voice, ringing out clear and effectual over vast multitudes were, it would seem, too big, too voluminous for Parliament. There were no channels offered there which were broad and free enough to give effective course to the crude force of the man. The gross and obvious vigour of him shocked sensitive, slow, and decorous men, not accustomed to have sense served up to them with a shout. The open heath was needed to contain O'Connell. But even in Parliament where the decorum and reserve of debate offered him no effective play, his honesty, his ardour for liberty, his good humour, his transparent genuineness won for him at last almost his due meed of respect.

The whole question of leadership receives sharp practical test in a popular legislative assembly. The revolutions which have changed the whole principle and method of government within the last hundred years have created a new kind of leadership in legislation: a leadership which is not yet, perhaps, fully understood. It used to be thought that legislation was an affair proper to be conducted only by the few who were instructed, for the benefit of the many who were uninstructed: that statesmanship was a function of origination for which only trained and instructed men were fit. Those who actually conducted legislation and undertook affairs were rather whimsically chosen by Fortune to illustrate this theory, but such was the ruling thought in politics. The Sovereignty of the People, however, that great modern dogma of politics, has erected a different conception-or, if so be that, in the slowness of our thought, we adhere to the old conception, has at least created a very different practice. When we are angry with public men nowadays we charge them with subserving instead of forming and directing public opinion. It is to be suspected that when we make such charges we are suffering our standards of judgment to lag behind our politics. When an Englishman declares that Mr. Gladstone is truckling to public opinion in his Irish policy, he surely cannot expect us to despise Mr. Gladstone on that account, even if the declaration be true, inasmuch as it is now quite indisputably the last part of the Nineteenth Century, and the nineteenth is a century, we know, which has established the principle that public opinion must be truckled to (if you will use a disagreeable word) in the conduct of government. A man, surely, would not fish for votes, (if that be what Mr. Gladstone is doing) among the minority-particularly if he be in his eightieth year and in need of getting the votes at once if he is to get them at all. He must believe, at any rate, that he is throwing his bait among the majority. And it is a dignified proposition with us-is it not?-that as is the majority, so ought the government to be.

Pray do not misunderstand me. I am not radical. I would not for the world be instrumental in discrediting the ancient and honorable pastime of abusing demagogues. Demagogues were quite evidently, it seems to me, meant for abuse, if we are to argue by exclusion: for assuredly they were never known to serve any other useful purpose. I will follow the hounds any day in pursuit of one of the wily, doubling rascals, however rough the country to be ridden over. But you must allow me to make my condemnations tally with my theory of government. Is Irish opinion ripe for Home Rule, as the Liberals claim? Very well then: let it have Home Rule. Every community, says my political philosophy, should be governed for its own interests, as it understands them, and not for the satisfaction of any other community.

Still I seem radical, without in reality being so. I advance my explanation, therefore, another step. Society is not a crowd, but an organism; and, like every organism, it must grow as a whole or else be deformed. The world is agreed, too, that it is an organism also in this, that it will die unless it be vital in every part. That is the only line of reasoning by which we can really establish the majority in legitimate authority. This organic whole, Society, is made up, obviously, for the most part, of the majority. It grows by the development of its aptitudes and desires, and under their guidance. The evolution of its institutions must take place by slow modification and nice all-round adjustment. And all this is but a careful and abstract way of saying that no reform may succeed for which the major thought of the nation is not prepared: that the instructed few may not be safe leaders except in so far as they have communicated their instruction to the many -except in so far as they have transmuted their thought into a common, a popular thought.

Let us fairly distinguish, therefore, the peculiar and delicate duties of the popular leader from the not very peculiar or delicate misdemeanors of the demagogue. Leadership, for the statesman, is interpretation. He must read the common thought: he must test and calculate very circumspectly the preparation of the nation for the next move in the progress of politics. If he fairly hit the popular thought, when we have missed it, are we to say that he is a demagogue? The nice point is to distinguish the firm and progressive popular thought from the momentary and whimsical popular mood, the transitory or mistaken popular passion. But it is fatally easy to blame or misunderstand the statesman.

Our temperament is one of logic, let us say. We hold that one and one make two and we see no salvation for the people except they receive the truth. The statesman is of another opinion. 'One and one doubtless make two', he is ready to admit, 'but the people think that one and one make more than two and until they see otherwise we shall have to legislate on that supposition'. This is not to talk nonsense. The Roman augurs very soon discovered that sacred fowls drank water and pecked grain with no sage intent of prophecy, but from motives quite mundane and simple. But it would have been a revolution to say so in the face of a people who believed otherwise, and executive policy had to proceed on the theory of a divine method of fowl appetite and digestion. The divinity that once did hedge a king, grows not now very high about the latest Hohenzollern; but who that prefers growth to revolution would propose that legislation in Germany proceed independently of this accident of hereditary succession?

In no case may we safely hurry the organism away from its habit: for it is held together by that habit, and by it is enabled to perform its functions completely. The constituent habit of a people inheres in its thought, and to that thought legislation, -even the legislation that advances and modifies habit, -just keep very near. The ear of the leader must ring with the voices of the people. He cannot be of the school of the prophets; he must be of the number of those who studiously serve the slow-paced daily demand.

In what, then, does political leadership consist? It is leadership in conduct, and leadership in conduct must discern and strengthen the tendencies that make for development. The legislative leader must perceive the direction of the nation's permanent forces, and must feel the speed of their operation. There is initiative here, but not novelty. There are old thoughts, but a progressive application of them.

There is such initiative as we may conceive the man part of the mythical centaur to have exercised. Doubtless the centaur acted, not as a man, but as a horse, would act, the head conceiving only such things as were possible for the performance of its lower and nether equine parts. He never dared to climb where hoofs could gain no sure foothold: and he knew that there were four feet, not two, to be provided with standing-room. There must have been the caper of the beast in all his schemes. He would have had as much respect we may suppose, for a blacksmith as for a haberdasher. He must have had the standards of the stable rather than the standards of the drawing-room. The headship of the mind over the body is a like headship for all of us: it is observant of possibility and of physical environment.

The inventing mind is impatient of such restraints: the aspiring soul has at all times longed to be loosed from the body. But such are the conditions of organic life that if the body is to be put off dissolution must be endured. As the conceiving mind is tenant of the body, so is the conceiving legislator tenant of that greater body, Society. Practical leadership may not beckon to the slow masses of men from beyond some dim unexplored space or some intervening chasm: it must daily feel under its own feet the road that leads to the goal proposed, knowing that it is a slow, a very slow, evolution to wings, and that for the present, and for a very long future also, Society must walk, dependent upon practicable paths, incapable of scaling sudden, precipitous heights, a road-breaker, not a fowl of the air. In the words of the master, Burke, "to follow, not to force, the public inclination, -to give a direction, a form, a technical dress, and a specific sanction, to the general sense of the community, is the true end of legislation." That general sense of the community may wait to be aroused, and the statesman must arouse it; may be inchoate and vague, and the statesman must formulate and make it explicit. But he cannot and he should not do more. The forces of the public thought may be blind: he must lend them sight; they may blunder: he must set them right. He can do something, indeed, to create such forces of opinion; but it is a creation of forms, not of substance:- and without such forces at his back he can do nothing effective.

This function of interpretation, this careful exclusion of individual origination it is that makes it difficult for the impatient original mind to distinguish the popular statesman from the demagogue. The demagogue sees and seeks self-interest in an acquiescent reading of that part of the public thought upon which he depends for votes; the statesman, also reading the common inclination, also, when he reads aright, obtains the votes that keep him in power. But if you will justly observe the two, you will find the one trimming to the inclinations of the moment, the other obedient only to the permanent purposes of the public mind. The one adjusts his sails to the breeze of the day; the other makes his plans to ripen with the slow progress of the years. While the one solicitously watches the capricious changes of the weather, the other diligently sows the grains in their seasons. The one ministers to himself, the other to the race.

To the literary temperament leadership in both kinds is impossible. The literary mind conceives images, images rounded, perfect, ideal; unlimited and unvaried by accident. It craves outlooks. It handles such stuff as dreams are made of. It is not guided by principles, as statesmen conceive principles, but by conceptions. Principles, as statesmen conceive them, are threads to the labyrinth of circumstances; principles, as the literary mind holds them, are unities, instrumental to nothing, sufficient unto themselves. Throw the conceiving mind, habituated to contemplating wholes, into the arena of politics, and it seems to itself to be standing upon shifting sands, where no sure foothold and no upright posture are possible. Its ideals are to it more real and more solid than any actuality of the world in which men are managed.

The late Mr. Matthew Arnold was wont now and again to furnish excellent illustration of these points. In the presence of the acute political crisis in Ireland, he urged that no radical remedy be undertaken, -except the very radical remedy of changing the character of the English people. What was needed was not home rule for Ireland but a sounder home conscience and less Philistinism in England. 'Wait', he said, in effect, 'don't legislate. Let me talk to these middle classes a little more, and then, without radical measures of relief, they will treat Ireland in the true human spirit.' Doubtless he was right. When America was discontented, and, because England resisted of home rule, began to clamour for home sovereignty, peradventure the truest remedy would have been, not revolution, but the enlightenment of the English people. But the process of enlightenment was slow; while the injustice was pressing: and revolution came on apace. Unquestionably culture is the best cure for anarchy; but anarchy is swifter than her adversary. Culture lags behind the practicable remedy.

There is a familiar anecdote that belongs just here. The captain of a Mississippi steamboat had made fast to the shore because of a thick fog lying upon the river. The fog lay low and dense upon the surface of the water, but overhead all was clear. A cloudless sky showed a thousand points of starry light. An impatient passenger inquired the cause of the delay. "We can't see to steer," said the captain. "But all's clear overhead," suggested the passenger, "you can see the North Star." "Yes," replied the officer, "but we are not going that way." Politics must follow the actual windings of the channel: if it steer by the stars it will run aground.

You may say that if all this be truth: if practical political thought may not run in straight lines, but must twist and turn through all the sinuous paths of various circumstance, then compromise is the true gospel of politics. I cannot wholly gainsay the proposition. But it depends almost altogether upon how you conceive and define compromise whether it seem hateful or not, -whether it be hateful or not. I understand the biologists to say that all growth is a process of compromise: a compromise of the vital forces within the organism with the physical forces without, which constitute the environment. Yet growth is not dishonest. Neither need compromise in politics be dishonest, -if only it be progressive. Is not compromise the law of society in all things? Do we not in all dealings adjust views, compound differences, placate antagonisms? Uncompromising thought is the luxury of the closeted recluse. Untrammelled reasoning is the indulgence of the philosopher, of the dreamer of sweet dreams. We make always a sharp distinction between the literature of conduct and the literature of the imagination. 'Poetic justice' we recognize as being quite out of the common run of experience.

Nevertheless, leadership does not always wear the harness of compromise. Once and again one of those great Influences which we call a Cause arises in the midst of a nation. Men of strenuous minds and high ideals come forward, with a sort of gentle majesty, as champions of a political or moral principle. They wear no armour; they bestride no chargers; they only speak their thought, in season and out of season. But the attacks they sustain are more cruel than the collisions of arms. Their souls are pierced with a thousand keen arrows of obloquy. Friends desert and despise them. They stand alone: and oftentimes are made bitter by their isolation. They are doing nothing less than defy public opinion, and shall they convert it by blows? Yes. Presently the forces of the popular thought hesitate, waver, seem to doubt their power to subdue a half score stubborn minds. Again a little while and those forces have actually yielded. Masses come over to the side of the reform. Resistance is left to the minority, and such as will not be convinced are crushed.

What has happened? Has it been given to a handful of men to revolutionize by the foolishness of preaching the whole thought of a nation and of an epoch? By no means. None but Christian doctrine was ever permitted to dig entirely new channels for human thought, and turn that thought rapidly about from its old courses: and even Christianity came only in the "fullness of time" and has had a triumph as slow-paced as history itself. No cause is born out of time. Every successful reform movement has had as its efficient cry some principle of equity or morality already accepted well-nigh universally, but not yet universally applied in the affairs of life. Every such movement has been the awakening of a people to see a new field for old principles. These men who stood alone at the inception of the movement and whose voices then seemed as it were the voices of men crying in the wilderness, have in reality been simply the more sensitive organs of Society-the parts first awakened to consciousness of a situation. With the start and irritation of a rude and sudden summons from sleep, Society at first resents the disturbance of its restful unconsciousness, and for a moment racks itself with hasty passion. But, once completely aroused, it will sanely meet the necessities of conduct revealed by the hour of its awakening.

Great reformers do not indeed observe times and circumstances. Theirs is not a service of opportunity. They have no thought for occasion, no capacity for compromise. But they are none the less produced by occasions. They are early vehicles of the Spirit of the Age. They are born of the very times that oppose them: their success is the acknowledgment of their legitimacy. For how many centuries had the world heard single, isolated voices summoning it to religious toleration before that toleration became inevitable, because not to have had it would have been an anomaly, an anachronism. It was postponed until it should fit into the world's whole system, -and only in this latter time did its advocates become leaders. Did not Protestantism come first to Germany, which had already unconsciously drifted very far away from Rome? Did not parliamentary reform come in England only as the tardy completion of tendencies long established and long drilled for success? Were not the Corn Laws repealed because they were a belated remnant of an effete system of economy and politics? Did not the abolition of slavery come just in the nick of time to restore to a system already sorely deranged the symmetry and wholeness of its original plan? Take what example you please and in every case what took place was the destruction of an anomaly, the wiping out of an anachronism. Does not every historian of insight perceive the timeliness of these reforms? Is it not the judgment of history that they were the products of a period, that there was laid upon their originators, not the gift of creation, but in a superior degree the gift of insight, the spirit of the age? It was theirs to hear the inarticulate voices that stir in the night-watches, apprising the lonely sentinel of what the day will bring forth.

Turn to religious leaders, and similar principles will be found to govern their rise and influence. Of course among religious leaders there is one type which stands out above all the rest, catching the eye of the world. This is the type to which Bernard of Clairvaux, Calvin, and Savonarola belong. Of course Bernard was no Protestant reformer, as Calvin was, and Savonarola played the part towards the Church neither of Calvin nor of Bernard. But I do not now speak of ecclesiastical reform; I speak simply of leadership. There is one transcendent feature in which these three men are alike. Each spoke to his generation of righteousness and judgment to come. Each withstood men because of their sins, and each himself dominated because of eloquence and purity and personal force.

Perhaps there is no beauty in any career that may justly be preferred to the beauty which was wrought into the life of the saintly abbot of Clairvaux, the man who, without self-assertion, was yet raised to rule, first over his fellows in the church, afterwards once and again over kings and in the affairs of nations, because he feared God but not man, because he loved righteousness and hated the wrong. When caught in the entanglements of fierce international disputes, men called to quiet Clairvaux for help, and there came out of the cloister a man simple in mien and habit, simple also in life and purpose, but bearing upon his sweet, grave face a stamp of godly courage that sent to the heart of the haughtiest men a thrill of awe; a man regarding his fellowmen with a calm gaze that nevertheless glowed with such a clear perception of the truth as held the proudest men in check. Pride and Self-Will broke against the spirit of this quiet man as if they were the mist and he the rock. He stood in the midst of his generation a master, a living rebuke to sin, a lively inspiration to good.

There is much less of grace, but there is no less of power in the figure of Savonarola, the pale, burning man who substituted a pulpit for the throne of the Medici, who made the dimly lighted, church where were to be heard the oracles of God, the only centre of power. How excellent, and how terrible, is the force of the man, lashing Florence into obedience with the quick whips of his almost inspired utterances. And then there is Calvin, ruler and priest of Geneva:- how singular and how elevated is the place such men hold among the greater figures and forces of history. Theirs, it would seem, was a leadership of rebuke. With how stern a menace did they apprise men of their sins and constrain them to their duty. Their sceptre was a scourge of small whips; their words purified as with flame; they were supreme by reason of the spirit that was in them.

And yet it does not seem to me that even these men escape from the analysis which must be made of all leadership. I have said that no man thinking thoughts born out of time can succeed in leading his generation, and that successful leadership is a product of sympathy, not of antagonism. I do not believe that any man can lead who does not act, whether it be consciously or unconsciously, under the impulse of a profound sympathy with those whom he leads,-a sympathy which is insight,-an insight which is of the heart rather than of the intellect. The law unto every such leader as these whom we now have in mind is the law of love. In the face of Savonarola, marked and hollowed as it is by the fierce flames of his nature, solemn, sombre, cast in the mould of anxious fear rather than in the mould of hope, is nevertheless to be seen but a close mask for an inward beauty of tenderness. The sensitiveness of a woman lurks in the stern features, not to be identified with any one of them, and yet not to be overlooked. In Calvin, too, love is the sanction of justice. And in Bernard it is love that reigns, not enmity towards his fellowmen. Such men incarnate the consciences of the men whom they rule. They compel obedience, not so much by reason of fear as by reason of their infallible analysis of character. Men know that they speak justice, and obey by instinct. By methods which would infallibly alienate individuals they master multitudes, and that is their indisputable title to be named leaders of men.

It is a long cry from Savonarola and Calvin to Voltaire, but it is to Voltaire that I at this point find it convenient to resort for illustration and comment. The transition is the more abrupt because I cannot claim leadership for Voltaire in any of the senses to which I have limited the word. But there are literary men, nevertheless, who fail of being leaders only for lack of initiative in action; who have the thought, but not the executive parts of leaders; whose minds, if we may put it so, contain all the materials for leadership, but whose wills spend their force, not upon men, but upon paper. Standing as they do, half way between the men who act and the men who merely think and imagine, they may very neatly serve our present purpose, of differentiating leaders from the quieter race of those who content themselves with thought. And of this class Voltaire was a perfect type.

Our slow world spends its time catching up with the ideas of its best minds. It would seem that in almost every generation men are born who embody the projected consciousness of their time and people. Their thought runs forward apace into the regions whither the race is advancing, but where it will not for many a weary day arrive. A few generations, and that point, thus early descried, is passed; the new thoughts of one age are the commonplaces of the next. Such is the literary function: it reads the present fragments of thought as completed wholes, and thus enables the fragments, no doubt, in due time to achieve their completion. There are, on the other hand, again, other periods which we call periods of critical thought, and these do not project their ideas as wholes, but speak them incomplete, as parts. Whoever can hit the latent conceptions of such a period will receive immediate recognition: he is simply the articulate utterance of itself.

Such a man, of such fortune, was Voltaire. No important distinction can be drawn between his mind and the mind of France in the period in which he lived, – except, no doubt, that the mind of France was diffused, Voltaire's concentrated. It was an Englishman, doubtless who said he would like to slap Voltaire's face, for then he could feel that he had given France the affront direct. I suppose we cannot imagine how happy it must have made a Frenchman of the last century to laugh with Voltaire. His hits are indeed palpable: no literary swordsman but must applaud them. The speed of his style, too, and the swift critical destructiveness of it are in the highest degree exhilarating and admirable. It is capital sport to ride atilt with him against some belated superstition, to see him unseat priest and courtier alike in his dashing overthrow of shams. But for us it is not vital sport. The things that he killed are now long dead; the things he found it impossible to slay, still triumph over all opponents-are grown old in conquest. But for a Frenchman of the last century the thing was being done. To read Voltaire must have made him feel that he was reading his own thoughts; laughing his own laugh; speaking his own scorn; speeding his own present impulses. Voltaire shocked political and ecclesiastical magnates, but he rejoiced the general mind of France. The men whom he attacked felt at once and instinctively that this was not the mere premonitory flash from a distant storm, but a bolt from short range; that the danger was immediate, the need for some shelter of authority an instantaneous need. No wonder the people of Paris took the horses from Voltaire's coach and themselves dragged him through the streets. The load ought to have been light, as light as the carriage, for they were pulling themselves. The old man inside the coach was presently to die and carry away with him the spirit of the eighteenth century. If Voltaire seriously doubted the existence of a future life, we have no grounds for wonder. It is hard to think of him in any world but this. It is awkward to conceive the Eighteenth Century given a place in either of the realms of eternity. It would chill the one; it would surely liberalize the other. That singular century does not seem to belong in the line of succession to any immortality.

Men who hit the critical, floating thought of their age, seem to me leaders in all but initiative. They are not ahead of their age. They do not conceive its thoughts in future wholes. They gather to a head each characteristic sentiment of their day. They are at once listened to; they would be followed, if they would but lead.

There are some qualities of the mind of Thomas Carlyle which seem to place him in this class. To speak of him is to go a good part of our way back to the great preachers of whom I have spoken. Carlyle was the apostle of a vague sort of lay religion, as imperative as Calvinism, though less provocative of organization-a religion with a sanction but without a hierarchy. He was not all preacher, however; and while he was something less than a prophet, he was also something more than a Jeremiah. He throbbed, as much as a Scotch peasant could, with the pulses of the nineteenth century. He was hotly moved by its forces; he felt with a keenness which reached the pitch of suffering the puissant influences abroad in his day. He withstood them, it is true; he would have beaten many of them back with denunciations; but there is a deep significance in his fierce longing for action, in his keen desire to be a leader. It is noteworthy that there is no wholeness in his thought, either, as in most products of the purely literary mind there would be. Its parts are disjecta membra. His ideas are flashes stuck out by hot contact with the forces of thought active about him. With almost inarticulate fervour, he seems once and again to break forth with the very spirit of our century on his lips. It would of course be absurd to compare Carlyle with Voltaire, the spiritual man with the intellectual; and yet it seems to me that Carlyle is as representative of the spiritual aspects of our own century as Voltaire was of all the mental aspects of his own very different age. Incoherent and impossible in his proposition of measures, sadly in need of interpretation to the common mind even in his utterance of the thoughts brought to him out of his century, eager often to revert to old standards of action, a figure rugged, amorphous, needing to be explained, Carlyle was yet the very voice of his own age, not a prophet of the next. In his writings are thrown up, as if by a convulsion of nature, the hidden things of the modem mind. Those who lead may well look and learn. His mind is a sub-soil plow and in its furrows may crops be sown.

If there were no other quality which marked the absence of any practical gift of leadership in Carlyle, his fierce impatience would be sufficient evidence. The dynamics of leadership lie in persuasion, and persuasion is never impatient. "You are poor fishers of men," it has been said of a certain class of preachers; "you do not go fishing with a rod and a line, and with the patient sagacity of the true sportsman. You use a telegraph pole and a cable: with these you savagely beat the water, and bid men bite or be damned. And you expect they will be caught!"

A wide sympathy and tolerance is needed in dealing with men, and uncompromising men cannot lead. We are sometimes struck in a rather unpleasant way by the apparent pliancy of public men, their apparent laxness as towards the principles they profess. We are inclined to exact of a public character, not only that he incarnate a principle "in its unalloyed simplicity," to use Cobden's phrase again, but also that he incarnate it in active and continuous antagonism to all other principles and their incarnations. It is a bit disconcerting to learn that men who sit and debate on opposite sides of the Senate or the House afterwards go off to lunch together between sessions and are always great cronies in private. It throws us out of all our political reckonings to hear that the Irish members of the House of Commons are received into hale fellowship in the smoking-room of the House by the very men who habitually vote for coercion measures when the House is sitting. How can the Irishmen themselves consent thus to smoke and joke with those who are abusing and injuring Ireland every day; and how can obstructionists be acceptable company for Tory ministerialists? We have an uncomfortable impression that these men must surely hold their political principles only in a Pickwickian sense; that their public motives and their private characters are somehow separable; that it is quite unbearable from a moral point of view that the incarnation of one principle should smoke and chat and hobnob with the incarnation of an opposite principle. And in conversation with public men we have received the same disquieting impressions. They are so unstrenuous in it all! They have such an easy, unimpressed way of talking about influences which they are supposed to be combating with might and main. Surely they are like lawyers, engaging their minds in certain causes, but not themselves, as easily to be obtained by one side as by the other.

And yet it seems to me that these phenomena of conduct which so disturb us are but further illustrations of the principles of leadership upon which I have most insisted. There is and must be in politics a sort of pervasive sense of compromise, an abiding consciousness of the fact that there is in the general growth and progress of affairs no absolute initiative for any one man, but that each must both give and take. If I am so strenuous in every point of belief and conduct that I cannot meet those of opposite opinions in good fellowship wherever and whenever conduct does not tell immediately upon the action of the state, you may be sure that when you examine my schemes you will find them impracticable,-impracticable, that is, to be voted upon. You may be sure that I am a man who must have his own way wholly or not at all. Of course there is much in mere everyday association. Men of opposite parties, seeing each other every day, are enabled to discover that there are no more tails and cloven hoofs on one side in politics than on the other. But it is not all the effect of use and companionship. More than that, it is the effect of openness of mind to impressions of the general opinion, to the influences of the whole situation as to character and strategy. Now and again their arises the figure of a leader silent, reserved, intense, uncompanionable, shut in upon his own thoughts and plans; and such a man will oftentimes prove a great force; but you will find him generally useful for the advancement of but a single cause. He holds a narrow commission, and his work is soon finished. He may count himself happy if he escape the misfortune of being esteemed a fanatic.

What a lesson it is in the organic wholeness of Society, this study of leadership! How subtle and delicate is the growth of the organism, and how difficult initiative in it! Where is rashness? It is excluded. And raw invention? It is discredited. How, as we look about us into the great maze of Society, see its solidarity, its complexity, its restless forces surging amidst its delicate tissues, its hazards and its exalted hopes, -how can we but be filled with awe! Many are the functions that enter into, quick unresting life. There is the lonely seer, seeking the truths that shall stand permanent and endure; the poet, tracing all perfected lines of beauty, sounding full-voiced all notes of love or hope, of duty or gladness; the toilers in the world's massy stuffs, moulders of metals, forgers of steel, refiners of gold; there are the winds of commerce; the errors and despairs of war; the old things and the new; the vast things that dominate and the small things that constitute the world; passions of men, loves of women; the things that are visible and which pass away and the things that are invisible and eternal. And in the midst of all stands the leader, gathering, as best he can, the thoughts that are completed, that are perceived, that have told upon the common mind; judging also of the work that is now at length ready to be completed; reckoning the gathered gain; perceiving the fruits of toil and of war, -and combining all these into words of progress, into acts of recognition and completion. Who shall say that this is not an exalted function? Who shall doubt or dispraise the titles of leadership?

Shall we wonder, either, if the leader be a man open at all points to all men, ready to break into coarse laughter with the Rabelaisian vulgar; ready also to prose with the moralist and the reformer; with an eye of tolerance and shrewd appreciation for life of every mode and degree; a sort of sensitive dial registering all forces that move upon the face of Society? I do not conceive the leader a trimmer, weak to yield what clamour claims, but the deeply human man, quick to know and to do the things that the hour and his people need.

"How beautiful to see
Once more a shepherd of mankind indeed,
Who loves his charge, and ever loves to lead;
One whose meek flock the people joy to be,
Not lured by any cheat of birth,
But by his clear-grained human worth,
And brave old wisdom of sincerity!
They know that outward grace is dust;
They cannot choose but trust
In that sure-footed mind's unfaltering skill,
And supple-tempered will
That bends like perfect steel to spring again and thrust.
His is no [lonely] mountain-peak of mind,
Thrusting to thin air o'er our cloudy bars,
A sea-mark now, now lost in vapours blind;
Broad prairie rather, genial, level-lined,

Fruitful and friendly for all human kind,
Yet also nigh to heaven and loved of loftiest stars."

The New Democracy

THE FORCES OF CHANGE DOMINATE AMERICA A.D. 1913

WOODROW WILSON

On March 4, 1913, Woodrow Wilson was inaugurated as President of the United States, and thus became the central figure of a new and tremendously important movement. He was, it is true, elected as the candidate of what is known as the Democratic party, which has existed since the days of Thomas Jefferson. But the ideas advanced by President Wilson as being democratic were so different from the original theories and policies of Jefferson that President Wilson himself felt called on to formulate his principles in a now celebrated work entitled "The New Freedom." From the opening pages of this, as originally published in *The World's Work*, we here, by permission of both the President and the magazine, give his own statement of the ideas of the new era.

The voting body of Americans who stand behind President Wilson are obviously of the type now generally called progressive. In the convention which nominated him, the conservative element of the old Democracy struggled long and bitterly against the naming of any "progressive" candidate. In the Republican party, the strife between conservatism and progress was so bitter as to produce a complete split; and the progressives nominated a candidate of their own, preferring, if they could not control the government themselves, to hand it over to the progressive element among the Democrats. The former political parties in the United States seem to have been so completely disrupted by recent events that even though they continue to hold some power under the old names, they now stand for wholly different things. The two parties which in the triangular presidential contest polled the largest numbers of votes were both "progressive."

So it seems settled that we are to "progress." But whither — and into what? Is there any clear purpose before our new leaders, and how does it differ from mankind's former purposes? That is what President Wilson tries to tell us.

There is one great basic fact which underlies all the questions that are discussed on the political platform at the present moment. That singular fact is that nothing is done in this country as it was done twenty years ago.

We are in the presence of a new organization of society. Our life has broken away from the past. The life of America is not the life that it was twenty years ago; it is not the life that it was ten years ago. We have changed our economic conditions, absolutely, from top to bottom; and, with our economic society, the organization of our life. The old political formulae do not fit the present problems; they read now like documents taken out of a forgotten age. The older cries sound as if they belonged to a past age which men have almost forgotten. Things which used to be put into the party platforms of ten years ago would sound antiquated if put into a platform now. We are facing the necessity of fitting a new social organization, as we did once fit the old organization, to the happiness and prosperity of the great body of citizens; for we are conscious that the new order of society has not been made to fit and provide the convenience or prosperity of the average man. The life of the nation has grown infinitely varied. It does not center now upon questions of governmental structure or of the distribution of governmental powers. It centers upon questions of the very structure and operation of society itself, of which government is only the instrument. Our development has run so fast and so far along the line sketched in the earlier days of constitutional definition, has so crossed and interlaced those lines, has piled upon them such novel structures of trust and combination, has elaborated within them a life so manifold, so full of forces which transcend the boundaries of the country itself and fill the eyes of the world, that a new nation seems to have been created which the old formulae do not fit or afford a vital interpretation of.

We have come upon a very different age from any that preceded us. We have come upon an age when we do not do business in the way in which we used to do business — when we do not carry on any of the operations of manufacture, sale, transportation, or communication as men used to carry them on. There is a sense in which in our day the individual has been submerged. In most parts of our country men work for themselves, not as partners in the old way in which they used to work, but as employees — in a higher or lower grade — of great corporations. There was a time when corporations played a very minor part in our business affairs, but now they play the chief part, and most men are the servants of corporations.

You know what happens when you are the servant of a corporation. You have in no instance access to the men who are really determining the policy of the corporation. If the corporation is doing the things that it ought not to do, you really have no voice in the matter and must obey the orders, and you have, with deep mortification, to cooperate in the doing of things which you know are against the public interest. Your individuality is swallowed up in the individuality and purpose of a great organization.

It is true that, while most men are thus submerged in the corporation, a few, a very few, are exalted to power which as individuals they could never have wielded. Through the great organizations of which they are the heads, a few are enabled to play a part unprecedented by anything in history in the control of the business operations of the country and in the determination of the happiness of great numbers of people.

Yesterday, and ever since history began, men were related to one another as individuals. To be sure there were the family, the Church, and the State, institutions which associated men in certain limited circles of relationships. But in the ordinary concerns of life, in the ordinary work, in the daily round, men dealt freely and directly with one another. To-day, the everyday relationships of men are largely with great impersonal concerns, with organizations, not with other individual men.

Now this is nothing short of a new social age, a new era of human relationships, a new stage-setting for the drama of life.

In this new age we find, for instance, that our laws with regard to the relations of employer and employee are in many respects wholly antiquated and impossible. They were framed for another age, which nobody now living remembers, which is, indeed, so remote from our life that it would be difficult for many of us to understand it if it were described to us. The employer is now generally a corporation or a huge company of some kind; the employee is one of hundreds or of thousands brought together, not by individual masters whom they know and with whom they have personal relations, but by agents of one sort or another. Working men are marshaled in great numbers for the performance of a multitude of particular tasks under a common discipline. They generally use dangerous and powerful machinery, over whose repair and renewal they have no control. New rules must be devised with regard to their obligations and their rights, their obligations to their employers and their responsibilities to one another. New rules must be devised for their protection, for their compensation when injured, for their support when disabled.

There is something very new and very big and very complex about these new relations of capital and labor. A new economic society has sprung up, and we must effect a new set of adjustments. We must not pit power against weakness. The employer is generally, in our day, as I have said, not an individual, but a powerful group; and yet the working man when dealing with his employer is still, under our existing law, an individual.

Why is it that we have a labor question at all? It is for the simple and very sufficient reason that the laboring man and the employer are not intimate associates now, as they used to be in time past. Most of our laws were formed in the age when employer and employees knew each other, knew each other's characters, were associates with each other, dealt with each other as man with man. That is no longer the case. You not only do not come into personal contact with the men who have the supreme command in those corporations, but it would be out of the question for you to do it. Our modern corporations employ thousands, and in some instances hundreds of thousands, of men. The only persons whom you see or deal with are local superintendents or local representatives of a vast organization, which is not like anything that the working men of the time in which our laws were framed knew anything about. A little group of working men, seeing their employer every day, dealing with him in a personal way, is one thing, and the modern body of labor engaged as employees of the huge enterprises that spread all over the country, dealing with men of whom they can form no personal conception, is another thing. A very different thing. You never saw a corporation, any more than you ever saw a government. Many a working man to-day never saw the body of men who are conducting the industry in which he is employed. And they never saw him. What they know about him is written in ledgers and books and letters, in the correspondence of the office, in the reports of the superintendents. He is a long way off from them.

So what we have to discuss is, not wrongs which individuals intentionally do — I do not believe there are a great many of those — but the wrongs of the system. I want to record my protest against any discussion of this matter which would seem to indicate that there are bodies of our fellow citizens who are trying to grind us down and do us injustice. There are some men of that sort. I don't know how they sleep o' nights, but there are men of that kind. Thank God they are not numerous. The truth is, we are all caught in a great economic system which is heartless. The modern corporation is not engaged in business as an individual. When we deal with it we deal with an impersonal element, a material piece of society. A modern corporation is a means of cooperation in the conduct of an enterprise which is so big that no one can conduct it, and which the resources of no one man are sufficient to finance. A company is formed; that company puts out a prospectus; the promoters expect to raise a certain fund as capital stock. Well, how are they going to raise it? They are going to raise it from the public in general, some of whom will buy their stock. The moment that begins, there is formed — what? A joint-stock corporation. Men begin to pool their earnings, little piles, big piles. A certain number of men are elected by the stockholders to be directors, and these directors elect a president. This president is the head of the undertaking, and the directors are its managers.

Now, do the working men employed by that stock corporation deal with that president and those directors? Not at all. Does the public deal with that president and that board of directors? It does not. Can anybody bring them to account? It is next to impossible to do so. If you undertake it you will find it a game of hide and seek, with the objects of your search taking refuge now behind the tree of their individual personality, now behind that of their corporate irresponsibility.

And do our laws take note of this curious state of things? Do they even attempt to distinguish between a man's act as a corporation director and as an individual? They do not. Our laws still deal with us on the basis of the old system. The law is still living in the dead past which we have left behind. This is evident, for instance, with regard to the matter of employers' liability for working men's injuries. Suppose that a superintendent wants a workman to use a certain piece of machinery which it is not safe for him to use, and that the workman is injured by that piece of machinery. Our courts have held that the superintendent is a fellow servant, or, as the law states it, a fellow employee, and that, therefore, the man can not recover damages for his injury. The superintendent who probably engaged the man is not his employer. Who is his employer? And whose negligence could conceivably come in there? The board of directors did not tell the employee to use that piece of machinery; and the president of the corporation did not tell him to use that piece of machinery. And so forth. Don't you see by that theory that a man never can get redress for negligence on the part of the employer? When I hear judges reason upon the analogy of the relationships that used to exist between workmen and their employers a generation ago, I wonder if they have not opened their eyes to the modern world.

You know, we have a right to expect that judges will have their eyes open, even though the law which they administer hasn't awakened.

Yet that is but a single small detail illustrative of the difficulties we are in because we have not adjusted the law to the facts of the new order.

Since I entered politics, I have chiefly had men's views confided to me privately. Some of the biggest men in the United States, in the field of commerce and manufacture, are afraid of somebody, are afraid of something. They know that there is a power somewhere so organized, so subtle, so watchful, so interlocked, so complete, so pervasive, that they had better not speak above their breath when they speak in condemnation of it.

They know that America is not a place of which it can be said, as it used to be, that a man may choose his own calling and pursue it just so far as his abilities enable him to pursue it; because to-day, if he enters certain fields, there are organizations which will use means against him that will prevent his building up a business which they do not want to have built up; organizations that will see to it that the ground is cut from under him and the markets shut against him. For if he begins to sell to certain retail dealers, to any retail dealers, the monopoly will refuse to sell to those dealers, and those dealers will be afraid and will not buy the new man's wares.

And this is the country which has lifted to the admiration of the world its ideals of absolutely free opportunity, where no man is supposed to be under any limitation except the limitations of his character and of his mind; where there is supposed to be no distinction of class, no distinction of blood, no distinction of social status, but where men win or lose on their merits.

I lay it very close to my own conscience as a public man whether we can any longer stand at our doors and welcome all newcomers upon those terms. American industry is not free, as once it was free; American enterprise is not free; the man with only a little capital is finding it harder to get into the field, more and more impossible to compete with the big fellow. Why? Because the laws of this country do not prevent the strong from crushing the weak. That is the reason, and because the strong have crushed the weak, the strong dominate the industry and the economic life of this country. No man can deny that the lines of endeavor have more and more narrowed and stiffened; no man who knows anything about the development of industry in this country can have failed to observe that the larger kinds of credit are more and more difficult to obtain, unless you obtain them upon the terms of uniting your efforts with those who already control the industries of the country; and nobody can fail to observe that any man who tries to set himself up in competition with any process of manufacture which has been taken under the control of large combinations of capital will presently find himself either squeezed out or obliged to sell and allow himself to be absorbed.

There is a great deal that needs reconstruction in the United States. I should like to take a census of the business men — I mean the rank and file of the business men — as to whether they think that business conditions in this country, or rather whether the organization of business in this country, is satisfactory or not. I know what they would say if they dared. If they could vote secretly they would vote overwhelmingly that the present organization of business was meant for the big fellows and was not meant for the little fellows; that it was meant for those who are at the top and was meant to exclude those who are at the bottom; that it was meant to shut out beginners, to prevent new entries in the race, to prevent the building up of competitive enterprise that would interfere with the monopolies which the great trusts have built up.

What this country needs, above everything else, is a body of laws which will look after the men who are on the make rather than the men who are already made. Because the men who are already made are not going to live indefinitely, and they are not always kind enough to leave sons as able and as honest as they are.

The originative part of America, the part of America that makes new enterprises, the part into which the ambitious and gifted working man makes his way up, the class that saves, that plans, that organizes, that presently spreads its enterprises until they have a national scope and character — that middle class is being more and more squeezed out by the processes which we have been taught to call processes of prosperity. Its members are sharing prosperity, no doubt;

but what alarms me is that they are not _originating_ prosperity. No country can afford to have its prosperity originated by a small controlling class. The treasury of America does not lie in the brains of the small body of men now in control of the great enterprises that have been concentrated under the direction of a very small number of persons. The treasury of America lies in those ambitions, those energies, that can not be restricted to a special, favored class. It depends upon the inventions of unknown men, upon the originations of unknown men, upon the ambitions of unknown men. Every country is renewed out of the ranks of the unknown, not out of the ranks of those already famous and powerful and in control.

There has come over the land that un-American set of conditions which enables a small number of men who control the Government to get favors from the Government; by those favors to exclude their fellows from equal business opportunity; by those favors to extend a network of control that will presently drive every industry in the country, and so make men forget the ancient time when America lay in every hamlet, when America was to be seen on every fair valley, when America displayed her great forces on the broad prairies, ran her fine fires of enterprise up over the mountain sides and down into the bowels of the earth, and eager men were everywhere captains of industry, not employees; not looking to a distant city to find out what they might do, but looking about among their neighbors, finding credit according to their character, not according to their connections, finding credit in proportion to what was known to be in them and behind them, not in proportion to the securities they held that were approved where they were not known. In order to start an enterprise now, you have to be authenticated, in a perfectly impersonal way, not according to yourself, but according to what you own that somebody else approves of your owning. You can not begin such an enterprise as those that have made America until you are so authenticated, until you have succeeded in obtaining the good-will of large allied capitalists. Is that freedom? That is dependence, not freedom.

We used to think, in the old-fashioned days when life was very simple, that all that government had to do was to put on a policeman's uniform and say, "Now don't anybody hurt anybody else." We used to say that the ideal of government was for every man to be left alone and not interfered with, except when he interfered with somebody else; and that the best government was the government that did as little governing as possible. That was the idea that obtained in Jefferson's time. But we are coming now to realize that life is so complicated that we are not dealing with the old conditions, and that the law has to step in and create the conditions under which we live, the conditions which will make it tolerable for us to live.

Let me illustrate what I mean: It used to be true in our cities that every family occupied a separate house of its own, that every family had its own little premises, that every family was separated in its life from every other family. That is no longer the case in our great cities. Families live in tenements, they live in flats, they live on floors; they are piled layer upon layer in the great tenement houses of our crowded districts, and not only are they piled layer upon layer, but they are associated room by room, so that there is in every room, sometimes, in our congested districts, a separate family. In some foreign countries they have made much more progress than we in handling these things. In the city of Glasgow, for example (Glasgow is one of the model cities of the world), they have made up their minds that the entries and the hall-ways of great tenements are public streets. Therefore, the policeman goes up the stairway and patrols the corridors; the lighting department of the city sees to it that the halls are abundantly lighted. The city does not deceive itself into supposing that that great building is a unit from which the police are to keep out and the civic authority to be excluded, but it says: "These are public highways, and light is needed in them, and control by the authority of the city."

I liken that to our great modern industrial enterprises. A corporation is very like a large tenement house; it isn't the premises of a single commercial family; it is just as much a public affair as a tenement house is a network of public highways.

When you offer the securities, of a great corporation to anybody who wishes to purchase them, you must open that corporation to the inspection of everybody who wants to purchase. There must, to follow out the figure of the tenement house, be lights along the corridors, there must be police patrolling the openings, there must be inspection wherever it is known that men may be deceived with regard to the contents of the premises. If we believe that fraud lies in wait for us, we must have the means of determining whether our suspicions are well founded or not. Similarly, the treatment of labor by the great corporations is not what it was in Jefferson's time. Whenever bodies of men employ bodies of men, it ceases to be a private relationship. So that when courts hold that working men can not peaceably dissuade other working men from taking employment, and base the decision upon the analogy of domestic servants, they simply show that their minds and understandings are lingering in an age which has passed away. This dealing of great bodies of men with other bodies of men is a matter of public scrutiny, and should be a matter of public regulation.

Similarly, it was no business of the law in the time of Jefferson to come into my house and see how I kept house. But when my house, when my so-called private property, became a great mine, and men went along dark corridors amidst every kind of danger in order to dig out of the bowels of the earth things necessary for the industries of a whole nation, and when it came about that no individual owned these mines, that they were owned by great stock companies, then all the old analogies absolutely collapsed, and it became the right of the government to go down into these mines to see whether human beings were properly treated in them or not; to see whether accidents were properly safeguarded against; to see whether modern economical methods of using these inestimable riches of the earth were followed or were not followed. If somebody puts a derrick improperly secured on top of a building or overtopping the street, then the government of the city has the right to see that that derrick is so secured that you and I can walk under it and not be afraid that the heavens are going to fall on us. Likewise in these great beehives where in every corridor swarm men of flesh and blood, it is the privilege of the government, whether of the State or of the United States, as the case may be, to see that human life is properly cared for, and that human lungs have something to breathe.

These, again, are merely illustrations of conditions. We are in a new world, struggling under old laws. As we go inspecting our lives to-day, surveying this new scene of centralized and complex society, we shall find many more things out of joint.

One of the most alarming phenomena of the time — or rather it would be alarming if the Nation had not awakened to it and shown its determination to control it — one of the most significant signs of the new social era is the degree to which government has become associated with business. I speak, for the moment, of the control over the Government exercised by Big Business. Behind the whole subject, of course, is the truth that, in the new order, government and business must be associated, closely. But that association is, at present, of a nature absolutely intolerable; the precedence is wrong, the association is upside down. Our Government has been for the past few years under the control of heads of great allied corporations with special interests. It has not controlled these interests and assigned them a proper place in the whole system of business; it has submitted itself to their control. As a result, there have grown up vicious systems and schemes of governmental favoritism (the most obvious being the extravagant tariff), far-reaching in effect upon the whole fabric of life, touching to his injury every inhabitant of the land, laying unfair and impossible handicaps upon competitors, imposing taxes in every direction, stifling everywhere the free spirit of American enterprise.

Now this has come about naturally; as we go on, we shall see how very naturally. It is no use denouncing anybody or anything, except human nature. Nevertheless, it is an intolerable thing that the government of the Republic should have got so far out of the hands of the people; should have been captured by interests which are special and not general. In the train of this capture follow the troops of scandals, wrongs, indecencies, with which our politics swarm.

There are cities in America of whose government we are ashamed. There are cities everywhere, in every part of the land, in which we feel that, not the interests of the public, but the interests of special privileges of selfish men, are served; where contracts take precedence over public interest. Not only in big cities is this the case. Have you not noticed the growth of socialistic sentiment in the smaller towns? Not many months ago I stopped at a little town in

Nebraska while my train lingered, and I met on the platform, a very engaging young fellow, dressed in overalls, who introduced himself to me as the mayor of the town, and added that he was a Socialist. I said, "What does that mean? Does that mean that this town is socialistic?" "No, sir," he said; "I have not deceived myself; the vote by which I was elected was about 20 per cent. socialistic and 80 per cent, protest." It was protest against the treachery to the people and those who led both the other parties of that town.

All over the Union people are coming to feel that they have no control over the course of affairs. I live in one of the greatest States in the Union, which was at one time in slavery. Until two years ago we had witnessed with increasing concern the growth in New Jersey of a spirit of almost cynical despair. Men said, "We vote; we are offered the platform we want; we elect the men who stand on that platform, and we get absolutely nothing." So they began to ask, "What is the use of voting? We know that the machines of both parties are subsidized by the same persons, and therefore it is useless to turn in either direction."

It is not confined to some of the State governments and those of some of the towns and cities. We know that something intervenes between the people of the United States and the control of their own affairs at Washington. It is not the people who have been ruling there of late.

Why are we in the presence, why are we at the threshold, of a revolution? Because we are profoundly disturbed by the influences which we see reigning in the determination of our public life and our public policy. There was a time when America was blithe with self-confidence. She boasted that she, and she alone, knew the processes of popular government; but now she sees her sky overcast; she sees that there are at work forces which she did not dream of in her hopeful youth.

Don't you know that some man with eloquent tongue, without conscience, who did not care for the Nation, could put this whole country into a flame? Don't you know that this country from one end to another believes that something is wrong? What an opportunity it would be for some man without conscience to spring up and say: "This is the way. Follow me!" — and lead in paths of destruction.

The old order changeth — changeth under our very eyes, not quietly and equably, but swiftly and with the noise and heat and tumult of reconstruction.

I suppose that all struggle for law has been conscious, that very little of it has been blind or merely instinctive. It is the fashion to say, as if with superior knowledge of affairs and of human weakness, that every age has been an age of transition, and that no age is more full of change than another; yet in very few ages of the world can the struggle for change have been so widespread, so deliberate, or upon so great a scale as in this in which we are taking part.

The transition we are witnessing is no equable transition of growth and normal alteration; no silent, unconscious unfolding of one age into another, its natural heir and successor. Society is looking itself over, in our day, from top to bottom; is making fresh and critical analysis of its very elements; is questioning its oldest practises as freely as its newest, scrutinizing every arrangement and motive of its life; and it stands ready to attempt nothing less than a radical reconstruction, which only frank and honest counsels and the forces of generous cooperation can hold back from becoming a revolution. We are in a temper to reconstruct economic society, as we were once in a temper to reconstruct political society, and political society may itself undergo a radical modification in the process. I doubt if any age was ever more conscious of its task or more unanimously desirous of radical and extended changes in its economic and political practise.

We stand in the presence of a revolution — not a bloody revolution, America is not given to the spilling of blood — but a silent revolution whereby America will insist upon recovering in practise those ideals which she has always professed, upon securing a government devoted to the general interest and not to special interests.

We are upon the eve of a great reconstruction. It calls for creative statesmanship as no age has done since that great age in which we set up the government under which we live, that government which was the admiration of the world until it suffered wrongs to grow up under it which have made many of our own compatriots question the freedom of our institutions and preach revolution against them. I do not fear revolution. I have unshaken faith in the power of America to keep its self-possession. Revolution will come in peaceful guise, as it came when we put aside the crude government of the Confederation, and created the great Federal Union which governed individuals, not States, and which has been these one hundred and thirty years our vehicle of progress. Some radical changes we must make in our law and practise. Some reconstructions we must push forward, which a new age and new circumstances impose upon us. But we can do it all in calm and sober fashion, like statesmen and patriots.

I do not speak of these things in apprehension, because all is open and above-board. This is not a day in which great forces rally in secret. The whole stupendous program must be publicly planned and canvassed. Good temper, the wisdom that comes of sober counsel, the energy of thoughtful and unselfish men, the habit of cooperation and of compromise which has been bred in us by long years of free government in which reason rather than passion has been made to prevail by the sheer virtue of candid and universal debate, will enable us to win through to still another great age without violence.

Inaugural Addresses

First Inaugural Address

There has been a change of government. It began two years ago, when the House of Representatives became Democratic by a decisive majority. It has now been completed. The Senate about to assemble will also be Democratic. The offices of President and Vice-President have been put into the hands of Democrats. What does the change mean? That is the question that is uppermost in our minds to-day. That is the question I am going to try to answer, in order, if I may, to interpret the occasion.

It means much more than the mere success of a party. The success of a party means little except when the Nation is using that party for a large and definite purpose. No one can mistake the purpose for which the Nation now seeks to use the Democratic Party. It seeks to use it to interpret a change in its own plans and point of view. Some old things with which we had grown familiar, and which had begun to creep into the very habit of our thought and of our lives, have altered their aspect as we have latterly looked critically upon them, with fresh, awakened eyes; have dropped their disguises and shown themselves alien and sinister. Some new things, as we look frankly upon them, willing to comprehend their real character, have come to assume the aspect of things long believed in and familiar, stuff of our own convictions. We have been refreshed by a new insight into our own life.

We see that in many things that life is very great. It is incomparably great in its material aspects, in its body of wealth, in the diversity and sweep of its energy, in the industries which have been conceived and built up by the genius of individual men and the limitless enterprise of groups of men. It is great, also, very great, in its moral force. Nowhere else in the world have noble men and women exhibited in more striking forms the beauty and the energy of sympathy and helpfulness and counsel in their efforts to rectify wrong, alleviate suffering, and set the weak in the way of strength and hope. We have built up, moreover, a great system of government, which has stood through a long age as in many respects a model for those who seek to set liberty upon foundations that will endure against fortuitous change, against storm and accident. Our life contains every great thing, and contains it in rich abundance.

But the evil has come with the good, and much fine gold has been corroded. With riches has come inexcusable waste. We have squandered a great part of what we might have used, and have not stopped to conserve the exceeding bounty of nature, without which our genius for enterprise would have been worthless and impotent, scorning to be careful, shamefully prodigal as well as admirably efficient. We have been proud of our industrial achievements, but we have not hitherto stopped thoughtfully enough to count the human cost, the cost of lives snuffed out, of energies overtaxed and broken, the fearful physical and spiritual cost to the men and women and children upon whom the dead weight and burden of it all has fallen pitilessly the years through. The groans and agony of it all had not yet reached our ears, the solemn, moving undertone of our life, coming up out of the mines and factories, and out of every home where the struggle had its intimate and familiar seat. With the great Government went many deep secret things which we too long delayed to look into and scrutinize with candid, fearless eyes. The great Government we loved has too often been made use of for private and selfish purposes, and those who used it had forgotten the people.

At last a vision has been vouchsafed us of our life as a whole. We see the bad with the good, the debased and decadent with the sound and vital. With this vision we approach new affairs. Our duty is to cleanse, to reconsider, to restore, to correct the evil without impairing the good, to purify and humanize every process of our common life without weakening or sentimentalizing it. There has been something crude and heartless and unfeeling in our haste to succeed and be great. Our thought has been "Let every man look out for himself, let every generation look out for itself," while we reared giant machinery which made it impossible that any but those who stood at the levers of control should have a chance to look out for themselves. We had not forgotten our morals. We remembered well enough that we had set up a policy which was meant to serve the humblest as well as the most powerful, with an eye single to the standards of justice and fair play, and remembered it with pride. But we were very heedless and in a hurry to be great.

We have come now to the sober second thought. The scales of heedlessness have fallen from our eyes. We have made up our minds to square every process of our national life again with the standards we so proudly set up at the beginning and have always carried at our hearts. Our work is a work of restoration.

We have itemized with some degree of particularity the things that ought to be altered and here are some of the chief items: A tariff which cuts us off from our proper part in the commerce of the world, violates the just principles of taxation, and makes the Government a facile instrument in the hand of private interests; a banking and currency system based upon the necessity of the Government to sell its bonds fifty years ago and perfectly adapted to concentrating cash and restricting credits; an industrial system which, take it on all its sides, financial as well as administrative, holds capital in leading strings, restricts the liberties and limits the opportunities of labor, and exploits without renewing or conserving the natural resources of the country; a body of agricultural activities never yet given the efficiency of great business undertakings or served as it should be through the instrumentality of science taken directly to the farm, or afforded the facilities of credit best suited to its practical needs; watercourses undeveloped, waste places unreclaimed, forests untended, fast disappearing without plan or prospect of renewal, unregarded waste heaps at every mine. We have studied as perhaps no other nation has the most effective means of production, but we have not studied cost or economy as we should either as organizers of industry, as statesmen, or as individuals.

Nor have we studied and perfected the means by which government may be put at the service of humanity, in safeguarding the health of the Nation, the health of its men and its women and its children, as well as their rights in the struggle for existence. This is no sentimental duty. The firm basis of government is justice, not pity. These are matters of justice. There can be no equality or opportunity, the first essential of justice in the body politic, if men and women and children be not shielded in their lives, their very vitality, from the consequences of great industrial and social processes which they can not alter, control, or singly cope with. Society must see to it that it does not itself crush or weaken or damage its own constituent parts. The first duty of law is to keep sound the society it serves. Sanitary laws, pure food laws, and laws determining conditions of labor which individuals are powerless to determine for themselves are intimate parts of the very business of justice and legal efficiency.

These are some of the things we ought to do, and not leave the others undone, the old-fashioned, never-to-be-neglected, fundamental safeguarding of property and of individual right. This is the high enterprise of the new day: To lift everything that concerns our life as a Nation to the light that shines from the hearthfire of every man's conscience and vision of the right. It is inconceivable that we should do this as partisans; it is inconceivable we should do it in ignorance of the facts as they are or in blind haste. We shall restore, not destroy. We shall deal with our economic system as it is and as it may be modified, not as it might be if we had a clean sheet of paper to write upon; and step by step we shall make it what it should be, in the spirit of those who question their own wisdom and seek counsel and knowledge, not shallow self-satisfaction or the excitement of excursions whither they can not tell. Justice, and only justice, shall always be our motto.

And yet it will be no cool process of mere science. The Nation has been deeply stirred, stirred by a solemn passion, stirred by the knowledge of wrong, of ideals lost, of government too often debauched and made an instrument of evil. The feelings with which we face this new age of right and opportunity sweep across our heartstrings like some air out of God's own presence, where justice and mercy are reconciled and the judge and the brother are one. We know our task to be no mere task of politics but a task which shall search us through and through, whether we be able to understand our time and the need of our people, whether we be indeed their spokesmen and interpreters, whether we have the pure heart to comprehend and the rectified will to choose our high course of action.

This is not a day of triumph; it is a day of dedication. Here muster, not the forces of party, but the forces of humanity. Men's hearts wait upon us; men's lives hang in the balance; men's hopes call upon us to say what we will do. Who shall live up to the great trust? Who dares fail to try? I summon all honest men, all patriotic, all forward-looking men, to my side. God helping me, I will not fail them, if they will but counsel and sustain me!

Second Inaugural Address

My Fellow Citizens:

The four years which have elapsed since last I stood in this place have been crowded with counsel and action of the most vital interest and consequence. Perhaps no equal period in our history has been so fruitful of important reforms in our economic and industrial life or so full of significant changes in the spirit and purpose of our political action. We have sought very thoughtfully to set our house in order, correct the grosser errors and abuses of our industrial life, liberate and quicken the processes of our national genius and energy, and lift our politics to a broader view of the people's essential interests.

It is a record of singular variety and singular distinction. But I shall not attempt to review it. It speaks for itself and will be of increasing influence as the years go by. This is not the time for retrospect. It is time rather to speak our thoughts and purposes concerning the present and the immediate future.

Although we have centered counsel and action with such unusual concentration and success upon the great problems of domestic legislation to which we addressed ourselves four years ago, other matters have more and more forced themselves upon our attention — matters lying outside our own life as a nation and over which we had no control, but which, despite our wish to keep free of them, have drawn us more and more irresistibly into their own current and influence.

It has been impossible to avoid them. They have affected the life of the whole world. They have shaken men everywhere with a passion and an apprehension they never knew before. It has been hard to preserve calm counsel while the thought of our own people swayed this way and that under their influence. We are a composite and cosmopolitan people. We are of the blood of all the nations that are at war. The currents of our thoughts as well as the currents of our trade run quick at all seasons back and forth between us and them. The war inevitably set its mark from the first alike upon our minds, our industries, our commerce, our politics and our social action. To be indifferent to it, or independent of it, was out of the question.

And yet all the while we have been conscious that we were not part of it. In that consciousness, despite many divisions, we have drawn closer together. We have been deeply wronged upon the seas, but we have not wished to wrong or injure in return; have retained throughout the consciousness of standing in some sort apart, intent upon an interest that transcended the immediate issues of the war itself.

As some of the injuries done us have become intolerable we have still been clear that we wished nothing for ourselves that we were not ready to demand for all mankind-fair dealing, justice, the freedom to live and to be at ease against organized wrong.

It is in this spirit and with this thought that we have grown more and more aware, more and more certain that the part we wished to play was the part of those who mean to vindicate and fortify peace. We have been obliged to arm ourselves to make good our claim to a certain minimum of right and of freedom of action. We stand firm in armed neutrality since it seems that in no other way we can demonstrate what it is we insist upon and cannot forget. We may even be drawn on, by circumstances, not by our own purpose or desire, to a more active assertion of our rights as we see them and a more immediate association with the great struggle itself. But nothing will alter our thought or our purpose. They are too clear to be obscured. They are too deeply rooted in the principles of our national life to be altered. We desire neither conquest nor advantage. We wish nothing that can be had only at the cost of another people. We always professed unselfish purpose and we covet the opportunity to prove our professions are sincere.

There are many things still to be done at home, to clarify our own politics and add new vitality to the industrial processes of our own life, and we shall do them as time and opportunity serve, but we realize that the greatest things that remain to be done must be done with the whole world for stage and in cooperation with the wide and universal forces of mankind, and we are making our spirits ready for those things.

We are provincials no longer. The tragic events of the thirty months of vital turmoil through which we have just passed have made us citizens of the world. There can be no turning back. Our own fortunes as a nation are involved whether we would have it so or not.

And yet we are not the less Americans on that account. We shall be the more American if we but remain true to the principles in which we have been bred. They are not the principles of a province or of a single continent. We have known and boasted all along that they were the principles of a liberated mankind. These, therefore, are the things we shall stand for, whether in war or in peace:

That all nations are equally interested in the peace of the world and in the political stability of free peoples, and equally responsible for their maintenance; that the essential principle of peace is the actual equality of nations in all matters of right or privilege; that peace cannot securely or justly rest upon an armed balance of power; that governments derive all their just powers from the consent of the governed and that no other powers should be supported by the common thought, purpose or power of the family of nations; that the seas should be equally free and safe for the use of all peoples, under rules set up by common agreement and consent, and that, so far as practicable, they should be accessible to all upon equal terms; that national armaments shall be limited to the necessities of national order and domestic safety; that the community of interest and of power upon which peace must henceforth depend imposes upon each nation the duty of seeing to it that all influences proceeding from its own citizens meant to encourage or assist revolution in other states should be sternly and effectually suppressed and prevented.

I need not argue these principles to you, my fellow countrymen; they are your own part and parcel of your own thinking and your own motives in affairs. They spring up native amongst us. Upon this as a platform of purpose and of action we can stand together. And it is imperative that we should stand together. We are being forged into a new unity amidst the fires that now blaze throughout the world. In their ardent heat we shall, in God's Providence, let us hope, be purged of faction and division, purified of the errant humors of party and of private interest, and shall stand forth in the days to come with a new dignity of national pride and spirit. Let each man see to it that the dedication is in his own heart, the high purpose of the nation in his own mind, ruler of his own will and desire.

I stand here and have taken the high and solemn oath to which you have been audience because the people of the United States have chosen me for this august delegation of power and have by their gracious judgment named me their leader in affairs.

I know now what the task means. I realize to the full the responsibility which it involves. I pray God I may be given the wisdom and the prudence to do my duty in the true spirit of this great people. I am their servant and can succeed only as they sustain and guide me by their confidence and their counsel. The thing I shall count upon, the thing without which neither counsel nor action will avail, is the unity of America-an America united in feeling, in purpose and in its vision of duty, of opportunity and of service.

We are to beware of all men who would turn the tasks and the necessities of the nation to their own private profit or use them for the building up of private power.

United alike in the conception of our duty and in the high resolve to perform it in the face of all men, let us dedicate ourselves to the great task to which we must now set our hand. For myself I beg your tolerance, your countenance and your united aid.

The shadows that now lie dark upon our path will soon be dispelled, and we shall walk with the light all about us if we be but true to ourselves-to ourselves as we have wished to be known in the counsels of the world and in the thought of all those who love liberty and justice and the right exalted.

State of the Union Addresses

First State of the Union address

December 2, 1913

Gentlemen of the Congress:

In pursuance of my constitutional duty to "give to the Congress information of the state of the Union," I take the liberty of addressing you on several matters which ought, as it seems to me, particularly to engage the attention of your honorable bodies, as of all who study the welfare and progress of the Nation.

I shall ask your indulgence if I venture to depart in some degree from the usual custom of setting before you in formal review the many matters which have engaged the attention and called for the action of the several departments of the Government or which look to them for early treatment in the future, because the list is long, very long, and would suffer in the abbreviation to which I should have to subject it. I shall submit to you the reports of the heads of the several departments, in which these subjects are set forth in careful detail, and beg that they may receive the thoughtful attention of your committees and of all Members of the Congress who may have the leisure to study them. Their obvious importance, as constituting the very substance of the business of the Government, makes comment and emphasis on my part unnecessary.

The country, I am thankful to say, is at peace with all the world, and many happy manifestations multiply about us of a growing cordiality and sense of community of interest among the nations, foreshadowing an age of settled peace and good will. More and more readily each decade do the nations manifest their willingness to bind themselves by solemn treaty to the processes of peace, the processes of frankness and fair concession. So far the United States has stood at the front of such negotiations. She will, I earnestly hope and confidently believe, give fresh proof of her sincere adherence to the cause of international friendship by ratifying the several treaties of arbitration awaiting renewal by the Senate. In addition to these, it has been the privilege of the Department of State to gain the assent, in principle, of no less than 31 nations, representing four-fifths of the population of the world, to the negotiation of treaties by which it shall be agreed that whenever differences of interest or of policy arise which can not be resolved by the ordinary processes of diplomacy they shall be publicly analyzed, discussed, and reported upon by a tribunal chosen by the parties before either nation determines its course of action.

There is only one possible standard by which to determine controversies between the United States and other nations, and that is compounded of these two elements: Our own honor and our obligations to the peace of the world. A test so compounded ought easily to be made to govern both the establishment of new treaty obligations and the interpretation of those already assumed.

There is but one cloud upon our horizon. That has shown itself to the south of us, and hangs over Mexico. There can be no certain prospect of peace in America until Gen. Huerta has surrendered his usurped authority in Mexico; until it is understood on all hands, indeed, that such pretended governments will not be countenanced or dealt with by the Government of the United States. We are the friends of constitutional government in America; we are more than its friends, we are its champions; because in no other way can our neighbors, to whom we would wish in every way to make proof of our friendship, work out their own development in peace and liberty. Mexico has no Government. The attempt to maintain one at the City of Mexico has broken down, and a mere military despotism has been set up which has hardly more than the semblance of national authority. It originated in the usurpation of Victoriano Huerta, who, after a brief attempt to play the part of constitutional President, has at last cast aside even the pretense of legal right and declared himself dictator. As a consequence, a condition of affairs now exists in Mexico which has made it doubtful whether even the most elementary and fundamental rights either of her own people or of the citizens of other countries resident within her territory can long be successfully safeguarded, and which threatens, if long continued, to imperil the interests of peace, order, and tolerable life in the lands immediately to the south of us. Even if the usurper had succeeded in his purposes, in despite of the constitution of the Republic and the rights of its people, he would have set up nothing but a precarious and hateful power, which could have lasted but a little while, and whose eventual downfall would have left the country in a more deplorable condition than ever. But he has not succeeded. He has forfeited the respect and the moral support even of those who were at one time willing to see him succeed. Little by little he has been completely isolated. By a little every day his power and prestige are crumbling and the collapse is not far away. We shall not, I believe, be obliged to alter our policy of watchful waiting. And then, when the end comes, we shall hope to see constitutional order restored in distressed Mexico by the concert and energy of such of her leaders as prefer the liberty of their people to their own ambitions.

I turn to matters of domestic concern. You already have under consideration a bill for the reform of our system of banking and currency, for which the country waits with impatience, as for something fundamental to its whole business life and necessary to set credit free from arbitrary and artificial restraints. I need not say how earnestly I hope for its early enactment into law. I take leave to beg that the whole energy and attention of the Senate be concentrated upon it till the matter is successfully disposed of. And yet I feel that the request is not needed-that the Members of that great House need no urging in this service to the country.

I present to you, in addition, the urgent necessity that special provision be made also for facilitating the credits needed by the farmers of the country. The pending currency bill does the farmers a great service. It puts them upon an equal footing with other business men and masters of enterprise, as it should; and upon its passage they will find themselves quit of many of the difficulties which now hamper them in the field of credit. The farmers, of course, ask and should be given no special privilege, such as extending to them the credit of the Government itself. What they need and should obtain is legislation which will make their own abundant and substantial credit resources available as a foundation for joint, concerted local action in their own behalf in getting the capital they must use. It is to this we should now address ourselves.

It has, singularly enough, come to pass that we have allowed the industry of our farms to lag behind the other activities of the country in its development. I need not stop to tell you how fundamental to the life of the Nation is the production of its food. Our thoughts may ordinarily be concentrated upon the cities and the hives of industry, upon the cries of the crowded market place and the clangor of the factory, but it is from the quiet interspaces of the open valleys and the free hillsides that we draw the sources of life and of prosperity, from the farm and the ranch, from the forest and the mine. Without these every street would be silent, every office deserted, every factory fallen into disrepair. And yet the farmer does not stand upon the same footing with the forester and the miner in the market of credit. He is the servant of the seasons. Nature determines how long he must wait for his crops, and will not be hurried in her processes. He may give his note, but the season of its maturity depends upon the season when his crop matures, lies at the gates of the market where his products are sold. And the security he gives is of a character not known in the broker's office or as familiarly as it might be on the counter of the banker.

The Agricultural Department of the Government is seeking to assist as never before to make farming an efficient business, of wide co-operative effort, in quick touch with the markets for foodstuffs. The farmers and the Government will henceforth work together as real partners in this field, where we now begin to see our way very clearly and where many intelligent plans are already being put into execution. The Treasury of the United States has, by a timely and well-considered distribution of its deposits, facilitated the moving of the crops in the present season and prevented the scarcity of available funds too often experienced at such times. But we must not allow ourselves to depend upon extraordinary expedients. We must add the means by which the, farmer may make his credit constantly and easily available and command when he will the capital by which to support and expand his business. We lag behind many other great countries of the modern world in attempting to do this. Systems of rural credit have been studied and developed on the other side of the water while we left our farmers to shift for themselves in the ordinary money market. You have but to look about you in any rural district to see the result, the handicap and embarrassment which have been put upon those who produce our food.

Conscious of this backwardness and neglect on our part, the Congress recently authorized the creation of a special commission to study the various systems of rural credit which have been put into operation in Europe, and this commission is already prepared to report. Its report ought to make it easier for us to determine what methods will be best suited to our own farmers. I hope and believe that the committees of the Senate and House will address themselves to this matter with the most fruitful results, and I believe that the studies and recently formed plans of the Department of Agriculture may be made to serve them very greatly in their work of framing appropriate and adequate legislation. It would be indiscreet and presumptuous in anyone to dogmatize upon so great and many-sided a question, but I feel confident that common counsel will produce the results we must all desire.

Turn from the farm to the world of business which centers in the city and in the factory, and I think that all thoughtful observers will agree that the immediate service we owe the business communities of the country is to prevent private monopoly more effectually than it has yet been prevented. I think it will be easily agreed that we should let the Sherman anti-trust law stand, unaltered, as it is, with its debatable ground about it, but that we should as much as possible reduce the area of that debatable ground by further and more explicit legislation; and should also supplement that great act by legislation which will not only clarify it but also facilitate its administration and make it fairer to all concerned. No doubt we shall all wish, and the country will expect, this to be the central subject of our deliberations during the present session; but it is a subject so many-sided and so deserving of careful and discriminating discussion that I shall take the liberty of addressing you upon it in a special message at a later date than this. It is of capital importance that the business men of this country should be relieved of all uncertainties of law with regard to their enterprises and investments and a clear path indicated which they can travel without anxiety. It is as important that they should be relieved of embarrassment and set free to prosper as that private monopoly should be destroyed. The ways of action should be thrown wide open.

I turn to a subject which I hope can be handled promptly and without serious controversy of any kind. I mean the method of selecting nominees for the Presidency of the United States. I feel confident that I do not misinterpret the wishes or the expectations of the country when I urge the prompt enactment of legislation which will provide for primary elections throughout the country at which the voters of the several parties may choose their nominees for the Presidency without the intervention of nominating conventions. I venture the suggestion that this legislation should provide for the retention of party conventions, but only for the purpose of declaring and accepting the verdict of the primaries and formulating the platforms of the parties; and I suggest that these conventions should consist not of delegates chosen for this single purpose, but of the nominees for Congress, the nominees for vacant seats in the Senate of the United States, the Senators whose terms have not yet closed, the national committees, and the candidates for the Presidency themselves, in order that platforms may be framed by those responsible to the people for carrying them into effect.

These are all matters of vital domestic concern, and besides them, outside the charmed circle of our own national life in which our affections command us, as well as our consciences, there stand out our obligations toward our territories over sea. Here we are trustees. Porto Rico, Hawaii, the Philippines, are ours, indeed, but not ours to do what we please with. Such territories, once regarded as mere possessions, are no longer to be selfishly exploited; they are part of the domain of public conscience and of serviceable and enlightened statesmanship. We must administer them for the people who live in them and with the same sense of responsibility to them as toward our own people in our domestic affairs. No doubt we shall successfully enough bind Porto Rico and the Hawaiian Islands to ourselves by ties of justice and interest and affection, but the performance of our duty toward the Philippines is a more difficult and debatable matter. We can satisfy the obligations of generous justice toward the people of Porto Rico by giving them the ample and familiar rights and privileges accorded our own citizens in our own territories and our obligations toward the people of Hawaii by perfecting the provisions for self-government already granted them, but in the Philippines we must go further. We must hold steadily in view their ultimate independence, and we must move toward the time of that independence as steadily as the way can be cleared and the foundations thoughtfully and permanently laid.

Acting under the authority conferred upon the President by Congress, I have already accorded the people of the islands a majority in both houses of their legislative body by appointing five instead of four native citizens to the membership of the commission. I believe that in this way we shall make proof of their capacity in counsel and their sense of responsibility in the exercise of political power, and that the success of this step will be sure to clear our view for the steps which are to follow. Step by step we should extend and perfect the system of self-government in the islands, making test of them and modifying them as experience discloses their successes and their failures; that we should more and more put under the control of the native citizens of the archipelago the essential instruments of their life, their local instrumentalities of government, their schools, all the common interests of their communities, and so by counsel and experience set up a government which all the world will see to be suitable to a people whose affairs are under their own control. At last, I hope and believe, we are beginning to gain the confidence of the Filipino peoples. By their counsel and experience, rather than by our own, we shall learn how best to serve them and how soon it will be possible and wise to withdraw our supervision. Let us once find the path and set out with firm and confident tread upon it and we shall not wander from it or linger upon it.

A duty faces us with regard to Alaska which seems to me very pressing and very imperative; perhaps I should say a double duty, for it concerns both the political and the material development of the Territory. The people of Alaska should be given the full Territorial form of government, and Alaska, as a storehouse, should be unlocked. One key to it is a system of railways. These the Government should itself build and administer, and the ports and terminals it should itself control in the interest of all who wish to use them for the service and development of the country and its people.

But the construction of railways is only the first step; is only thrusting in the key to the storehouse and throwing back the lock and opening the door. How the tempting resources of the country are to be exploited is another matter, to which I shall take the liberty of from time to time calling your attention, for it is a policy which must be worked out by well-considered stages, not upon theory, but upon lines of practical expediency. It is part of our general problem of conservation. We have a freer hand in working out the problem in Alaska than in the States of the Union; and yet the principle and object are the same, wherever we touch it. We must use the resources of the country, not lock them up. There need be no conflict or jealousy as between State and Federal authorities, for there can be no essential difference of purpose between them. The resources in question must be used, but not destroyed or wasted; used, but not monopolized upon any narrow idea of individual rights as against the abiding interests of communities. That a policy can be worked out by conference and concession which will release these resources and yet not jeopard or dissipate them, I for one have no doubt; and it can be done on lines of regulation which need be no less acceptable to the people and governments of the States concerned than to the people and Government of the Nation at large, whose heritage these resources are. We must bend our counsels to this end. A common purpose ought to make agreement easy.

Three or four matters of special importance and significance I beg, that you will permit me to mention in closing.

Our Bureau of Mines ought to be equipped and empowered to render even more effectual service than it renders now in improving the conditions of mine labor and making the mines more economically productive as well as more safe. This is an all-important part of the work of conservation; and the conservation of human life and energy lies even nearer to our interests than the preservation from waste of our material resources.

We owe it, in mere justice to the railway employees of the country, to provide for them a fair and effective employers' liability act; and a law that we can stand by in this matter will be no less to the advantage of those who administer the railroads of the country than to the advantage of those whom they employ. The experience of a large number of the States abundantly proves that.

We ought to devote ourselves to meeting pressing demands of plain justice like this as earnestly as to the accomplishment of political and economic reforms. Social justice comes first. Law is the machinery for its realization and is vital only as it expresses and embodies it.

An international congress for the discussion of all questions that affect safety at sea is now sitting in London at the suggestion of our own Government. So soon as the conclusions of that congress can be learned and considered we ought to address ourselves, among other things, to the prompt alleviation of the very unsafe, unjust, and burdensome conditions which now surround the employment of sailors and render it extremely difficult to obtain the services of spirited and competent men such as every ship needs if it is to be safely handled and brought to port.

May I not express the very real pleas-are I have experienced in co-operating with this Congress and sharing with it the labors of common service to which it has devoted itself so unreservedly during the past seven months of uncomplaining concentration upon the business of legislation? Surely it is a proper and pertinent part of my report on "the state of the Union" to express my admiration for the diligence, the good temper, and the full comprehension of public duty which has already been manifested by both the Houses; and I hope that it may not be deemed an impertinent intrusion of myself into the picture if I say with how much and how constant satisfaction I have availed myself of the privilege of putting my time and energy at their disposal alike in counsel and in action.

Second State of the Union address

Woodrow Wilson
December 8, 1914
GENTLEMEN OF THE CONGRESS:
The session upon which you are now entering will be the closing session of the Sixty-third Congress, a Congress, I venture to say, which will long be remembered for the great body of thoughtful and constructive work which it has done, in loyal response to the thought and needs of the country. I should like in this address to review the notable record and try to make adequate assessment of it; but no doubt we stand too near the work that has been done and are ourselves too much part of it to play the part of historians toward it.

Our program of legislation with regard to the regulation of business is now virtually complete. It has been put forth, as we intended, as a whole, and leaves no conjecture as to what is to follow. The road at last lies clear and firm before business. It is a road which it can travel without fear or embarrassment. It is the road to ungrudged, unclouded success. In it every honest man, every man who believes that the public interest is part of his own interest, may walk with perfect confidence.

Moreover, our thoughts are now more of the future than of the past. While we have worked at our tasks of peace the circumstances of the whole age have been altered by war. What we have done for our own land and our own people we did with the best that was in us, whether of character or of intelligence, with sober enthusiasm and a confidence in the principles upon which we were acting which sustained us at every step of the difficult undertaking; but it is done. It has passed from our hands. It is now an established part of the legislation of the country. Its usefulness, its effects will disclose themselves in experience. What chiefly strikes us now, as we look about us during these closing days of a year which will be forever memorable in the history of the world, is that we face new tasks, have been facing them these six months, must face them in the months to come,-face them without partisan feeling, like men who have forgotten everything but a common duty and the fact that we are representatives of a great people whose thought is not of us but of what America owes to herself and to all mankind in such circumstances as these upon which we look amazed and anxious.

War has interrupted the means of trade not only but also the processes of production. In Europe it is destroying men and resources wholesale and upon a scale unprecedented and appalling, There is reason to fear that the time is near, if it be not already at hand, when several of the countries of Europe will find it difficult to do for their people what they have hitherto been always easily able to do,—many essential and fundamental things. At any rate, they will need our help and our manifold services as they have never needed them before; and we should be ready, more fit and ready than we have ever been.

It is of equal consequence that the nations whom Europe has usually supplied with innumerable articles of manufacture and commerce of which they are in constant need and without which their economic development halts and stands still can now get only a small part of what they formerly imported and eagerly look to us to supply their all but empty markets. This is particularly true of our own neighbors, the States, great and small, of Central and South America. Their lines of trade have hitherto run chiefly athwart the seas, not to our ports but to the ports of Great Britain and of the older continent of Europe. I do not stop to inquire why, or to make any comment on probable causes. What interests us just now is not the explanation but the fact, and our duty and opportunity in the presence of it. Here are markets which we must supply, and we must find the means of action. The United States, this great people for whom we speak and act, should be ready, as never before, to serve itself and to serve mankind; ready with its resources, its energies, its forces of production, and its means of distribution.

It is a very practical matter, a matter of ways and means. We have the resources, but are we fully ready to use them? And, if we can make ready what we have, have we the means at hand to distribute it? We are not fully ready; neither have we the means of distribution. We are willing, but we are not fully able. We have the wish to serve and to serve greatly, generously; but we are not prepared as we should be. We are not ready to mobilize our resources at once. We are not prepared to use them immediately and at their best, without delay and without waste.

To speak plainly, we have grossly erred in the way in which we have stunted and hindered the development of our merchant marine. And now, when we need ships, we have not got them. We have year after year debated, without end or conclusion, the best policy to pursue with regard to the use of the ores and forests and water powers of our national domain in the rich States of the West, when we should have acted; and they are still locked up. The key is still turned upon them, the door shut fast at which thousands of vigorous men, full of initiative, knock clamorously for admittance. The water power of our navigable streams outside the national domain also, even in the eastern States, where we have worked and planned for generations, is still not used as it might be, because we will and we won't; because the laws we have made do not intelligently balance encouragement against restraint. We withhold by regulation.

I have come to ask you to remedy and correct these mistakes and omissions, even at this short session of a Congress which would certainly seem to have done all the work that could reasonably be expected of it. The time and the circumstances are extraordinary, and so must our efforts be also.

Fortunately, two great measures, finely conceived, the one to unlock, with proper safeguards, the resources of the national domain, the other to encourage the use of the navigable waters outside that domain for the generation of power, have already passed the House of Representatives and are ready for immediate consideration and action by the Senate. With the deepest earnestness I urge their prompt passage. In them both we turn our backs upon hesitation and makeshift and formulate a genuine policy of use and conservation, in the best sense of those words. We owe the one measure not only to the people of that great western country for whose free and systematic development, as it seems to me, our legislation has done so little, but also to the people of the Nation as a whole; and we as clearly owe the other fulfillment of our repeated promises that the water power of the country should in fact as well as in name be put at the disposal of great industries which can make economical and profitable use of it, the rights of the public being adequately guarded the while, and monopoly in the use prevented. To have begun such measures and not completed them would indeed mar the record of this great Congress very seriously. I hope and confidently believe that they will be completed.

And there is another great piece of legislation which awaits and should receive the sanction of the Senate: I mean the bill which gives a larger measure of self-government to the people of the Philippines. How better, in this time of anxious questioning and perplexed policy, could we show our confidence in the principles of liberty, as the source as well as the expression of life, how better could we demonstrate our own self-possession and steadfastness in the courses of justice and disinterestedness than by thus going calmly forward to fulfill our promises to a dependent people, who will now look more anxiously than ever to see whether we have indeed the liberality, the unselfishness, the courage, the faith we have boasted and professed. I can not believe that the Senate will let this great measure of constructive justice await the action of another Congress. Its passage would nobly crown the record of these two years of memorable labor.

But I think that you will agree with me that this does not complete the toll of our duty. How are we to carry our goods to the empty markets of which I have spoken if we have not the ships? How are we to build up a great trade if we have not the certain and constant means of transportation upon which all profitable and useful commerce depends? And how are we to get the ships if we wait for the trade to develop without them? To correct the many mistakes by which we have discouraged and all but destroyed the merchant marine of the country, to retrace the steps by which we have.. it seems almost deliberately, withdrawn our flag from the seas.. except where, here and there, a ship of war is bidden carry it or some wandering yacht displays it, would take a long time and involve many detailed items of legislation, and the trade which we ought immediately to handle would disappear or find other channels while we debated the items.

The case is not unlike that which confronted us when our own continent was to be opened up to settlement and industry, and we needed long lines of railway, extended means of transportation prepared beforehand, if development was not to lag intolerably and wait interminably. We lavishly subsidized the building of transcontinental railroads. We look back upon that with regret now, because the subsidies led to many scandals of which we are ashamed; but we know that the railroads had to be built, and if we had it to do over again we should of course build them, but in another way. Therefore I propose another way of providing the means of transportation, which must precede, not tardily follow, the development of our trade with our neighbor states of America. It may seem a reversal of the natural order of things, but it is true, that the routes of trade must be actually opened-by many ships and regular sailings and moderate charges-before streams of merchandise will flow freely and profitably through them.

Hence the pending shipping bill, discussed at the last session but as yet passed by neither House. In my judgment such legislation is imperatively needed and can not wisely be postponed. The Government must open these gates of trade, and open them wide; open them before it is altogether profitable to open them, or altogether reasonable to ask private capital to open them at a venture. It is not a question of the Government monopolizing the field. It should take action to make it certain that transportation at reasonable rates will be promptly provided, even where the carriage is not at first profitable; and then, when the carriage has become sufficiently profitable to attract and engage private capital, and engage it in abundance, the Government ought to withdraw. I very earnestly hope that the Congress will be of this opinion, and that both Houses will adopt this exceedingly important bill.

The great subject of rural credits still remains to be dealt with, and it is a matter of deep regret that the difficulties of the subject have seemed to render it impossible to complete a bill for passage at this session. But it can not be perfected yet, and therefore there are no other constructive measures the necessity for which I will at this time call your attention to; but I would be negligent of a very manifest duty were I not to call the attention of the Senate to the fact that the proposed convention for safety at sea awaits its confirmation and that the limit fixed in the convention itself for its acceptance is the last day of the present month. The conference in which this convention originated was called by the United States; the representatives of the United States played a very influential part indeed in framing the provisions of the proposed convention; and those provisions are in themselves for the most part admirable. It would hardly be consistent with the part we have played in the whole matter to let it drop and go by the board as if forgotten and neglected. It was ratified in May by the German Government and in August by the Parliament of Great Britain. It marks a most hopeful and decided advance in international civilization. We should show our earnest good faith in a great matter by adding our own acceptance of it.

There is another matter of which I must make special mention, if I am to discharge my conscience, lest it should escape your attention. It may seem a very small thing. It affects only a single item of appropriation. But many human lives and many great enterprises hang upon it. It is the matter of making adequate provision for the survey and charting of our coasts. It is immediately pressing and exigent in connection with the immense coast line of Alaska, a coast line greater than that of the United States themselves, though it is also very important indeed with regard to the older coasts of the continent. We can not use our great Alaskan domain, ships will not ply thither, if those coasts and their many hidden dangers are not thoroughly surveyed and charted. The work is incomplete at almost every point. Ships and lives have been lost in threading what were supposed to be well-known main channels. We have not provided adequate vessels or adequate machinery for the survey and charting. We have used old vessels that were not big enough or strong enough and which were so nearly unseaworthy that our inspectors would not have allowed private owners to send them to sea. This is a matter which, as I have said, seems small, but is in reality very great. Its importance has only to be looked into to be appreciated.

Before I close may I say a few words upon two topics, much discussed out of doors, upon which it is highly important that our judgment should be clear, definite, and steadfast?

One of these is economy in government expenditures. The duty of economy is not debatable. It is manifest and imperative. In the appropriations we pass we are spending the money of the great people whose servants we are,-not our own. We are trustees and responsible stewards in the spending. The only thing debatable and upon which we should be careful to make our thought and purpose clear is the kind of economy demanded of us. I assert with the greatest confidence that the people of the United States are not jealous of the amount their Government costs if they are sure that they get what they need and desire for the outlay, that the money is being spent for objects of which they approve, and that it is being applied with good business sense and management.

Governments grow, piecemeal, both in their tasks and in the means by which those tasks are to be performed, and very few Governments are organized, I venture to say, as wise and experienced business men would organize them if they had a clean sheet of paper to write upon. Certainly the Government of the United States is not. I think that it is generally agreed that there should be a systematic reorganization and reassembling of its parts so as to secure greater efficiency and effect considerable savings in expense. But the amount of money saved in that way would, I believe, though no doubt considerable in itself, running, it may be, into the millions, be relatively small,-small, I mean, in proportion to the total necessary outlays of the Government. It would be thoroughly worth effecting, as every saving would, great or small. Our duty is not altered by the scale of the saving. But my point is that the people of the United States do not wish to curtail the activities of this Government; they wish, rather, to enlarge them; and with every enlargement, with the mere growth, indeed, of the country itself, there must come, of course, the inevitable increase of expense. The sort of economy we ought to practice may be effected, and ought to be effected, by a careful study and assessment of the tasks to be performed; and the money spent ought to be made to yield the best possible returns in efficiency and achievement. And, like good stewards, we should so account for every dollar of our appropriations as to make it perfectly evident what it was spent for and in what way it was spent.

It is not expenditure but extravagance that we should fear being criticized for; not paying for the legitimate enterprise and undertakings of a great Government whose people command what it should do, but adding what will benefit only a few or pouring money out for what need not have been undertaken at all or might have been postponed or better and more economically conceived and carried out. The Nation is not niggardly; it is very generous. It will chide us only if we forget for whom we pay money out and whose money it is we pay. These are large and general standards, but they are not very difficult of application to particular cases.

The other topic I shall take leave to mention goes deeper into the principles of our national life and policy. It is the subject of national defense.

It can not be discussed without first answering some very searching questions. It is said in some quarters that we are not prepared for war. What is meant by being prepared? Is it meant that we are not ready upon brief notice to put a nation in the field, a nation of men trained to arms? Of course we are not ready to do that; and we shall never be in time of peace so long as we retain our present political principles and institutions. And what is it that it is suggested we should be prepared to do? To defend ourselves against attack? We have always found means to do that, and shall find them whenever it is necessary without calling our people away from their necessary tasks to render compulsory military service in times of peace.

Allow me to speak with great plainness and directness upon this great matter and to avow my convictions with deep earnestness. I have tried to know what America is, what her people think, what they are, what they most cherish and hold dear. I hope that some of their finer passions are in my own heart,—some of the great conceptions and desires which gave birth to this Government and which have made the voice of this people a voice of peace and hope and liberty among the peoples of the world, and that, speaking my own thoughts, I shall, at least in part, speak theirs also, however faintly and inadequately, upon this vital matter.

We are at peace with all the world. No one who speaks counsel based on fact or drawn from a just and candid interpretation of realities can say that there is reason to fear that from any quarter our independence or the integrity of our territory is threatened. Dread of the power of any other nation we are incapable of. We are not jealous of rivalry in the fields of commerce or of any other peaceful achievement. We mean to live our own lives as we will; but we mean also to let live. We are, indeed, a true friend to all the nations of the world, because we threaten none, covet the possessions of none, desire the overthrow of none. Our friendship can be accepted and is accepted without reservation, because it is offered in a spirit and for a purpose which no one need ever question or suspect. Therein lies our greatness. We are the champions of peace and of concord. And we should be very jealous of this distinction which we have sought to earn. Just now we should be particularly jealous of it because it is our dearest present hope that this character and reputation may presently, in God's providence, bring us an opportunity such as has seldom been vouchsafed any nation, the opportunity to counsel and obtain peace in the world and reconciliation and a healing settlement of many a matter that has cooled and interrupted the friendship of nations. This is the time above all others when we should wish and resolve to keep our strength by self-possession, our influence by preserving our ancient principles of action.

From the first we have had a clear and settled policy with regard to military establishments. We never have had, and while we retain our present principles and ideals we never shall have, a large standing army. If asked, Are you ready to defend yourselves? we reply, Most assuredly, to the utmost; and yet we shall not turn America into a military camp. We will not ask our young men to spend the best years of their lives making soldiers of themselves. There is another sort of energy in us. It will know how to declare itself and make itself effective should occasion arise. And especially when half the world is on fire we shall be careful to make our moral insurance against the spread of the conflagration very definite and certain and adequate indeed.

Let us remind ourselves, therefore, of the only thing we can do or will do. We must depend in every time of national peril, in the future as in the past, not upon a standing army, nor yet upon a reserve army, but upon a citizenry trained and accustomed to arms. It will be right enough, right American policy, based upon our accustomed principles and practices, to provide a system by which every citizen who will volunteer for the training may be made familiar with the use of modern arms, the rudiments of drill and maneuver, and the maintenance and sanitation of camps. We should encourage such training and make it a means of discipline which our young men will learn to value. It is right that we should provide it not only, but that we should make it as attractive as possible, and so induce our young men to undergo it at such times as they can command a little freedom and can seek the physical development they need, for mere health's sake, if for nothing more. Every means by which such things can be stimulated is legitimate, and such a method smacks of true American ideas. It is right, too, that the National Guard of the States should be developed and strengthened by every means which is not inconsistent with our obligations to our own people or with the established policy of our Government. And this, also, not because the time or occasion specially calls for such measures, but because it should be our constant policy to make these provisions for our national peace and safety.

More than this carries with it a reversal of the whole history and character of our polity. More than this, proposed at this time, permit me to say, would mean merely that we had lost our self-possession, that we had been thrown off our balance by a war with which we have nothing to do, whose causes can not touch us, whose very existence affords us opportunities of friendship and disinterested service which should make us ashamed of any thought of hostility or fearful preparation for trouble. This is assuredly the opportunity for which a people and a government like ours were raised up, the opportunity not only to speak but actually to embody and exemplify the counsels of peace and amity and the lasting concord which is based on justice and fair and generous dealing.

A powerful navy we have always regarded as our proper and natural means of defense, and it has always been of defense that we have thought, never of aggression or of conquest. But who shall tell us now what sort of navy to build? We shall take leave to be strong upon the seas, in the future as in the past; and there will be no thought of offense or of provocation in that. Our ships are our natural bulwarks. When will the experts tell us just what kind we should construct-and when will they be right for ten years together, if the relative efficiency of craft of different kinds and uses continues to change as we have seen it change under our very eyes in these last few months?

But I turn away from the subject. It is not new. There is no new need to discuss it. We shall not alter our attitude toward it because some amongst us are nervous and excited. We shall easily and sensibly agree upon a policy of defense. The question has not changed its aspects because the times are not normal. Our policy will not be for an occasion. It will be conceived as a permanent and settled thing, which we will pursue at all seasons, without haste and after a fashion perfectly consistent with the peace of the world, the abiding friendship of states, and the unhampered freedom of all with whom we deal. Let there be no misconception. The country has been misinformed. We have not been negligent of national defense. We are not unmindful of the great responsibility resting upon us. We shall learn and profit by the lesson of every experience and every new circumstance; and what is needed will be adequately done.

I close, as I began, by reminding you of the great tasks and duties of peace which challenge our best powers and invite us to build what will last, the tasks to which we can address ourselves now and at all times with free-hearted zest and with all the finest gifts of constructive wisdom we possess. To develop our life and our resources; to supply our own people, and the people of the world as their need arises, from the abundant plenty of our fields and our marts of trade to enrich the commerce of our own States and of the world with the products of our mines, our farms, and our factories, with the creations of our thought and the fruits of our character,-this is what will hold our attention and our enthusiasm steadily, now and in the years to come, as we strive to show in our life as a nation what liberty and the inspirations of an emancipated spirit may do for men and for societies, for individuals, for states, and for mankind.

Third State of the Union address

Woodrow Wilson
December 7, 1915
GENTLEMEN OF THE CONGRESS:

Since I last had the privilege of addressing you on the state of the Union the war of nations on the other side of the sea, which had then only begun to disclose its portentous proportions, has extended its threatening and sinister scope until it has swept within its flame some portion of every quarter of the globe, not excepting our own hemisphere, has altered the whole face of international affairs, and now presents a prospect of reorganization and reconstruction such as statesmen and peoples have never been called upon to attempt before.

We have stood apart, studiously neutral. It was our manifest duty to do so. Not only did we have no part or interest in the policies which seem to have brought the conflict on; it was necessary, if a universal catastrophe was to be avoided, that a limit should be set to the sweep of destructive war and that some part of the great family of nations should keep the processes of peace alive, if only to prevent collective economic ruin and the breakdown throughout the world of the industries by which its populations are fed and sustained. It was manifestly the duty of the self-governed nations of this hemisphere to redress, if possible, the balance of economic loss and confusion in the other, if they could do nothing more. In the day of readjustment and recuperation we earnestly hope and believe that they can be of infinite service.

In this neutrality, to which they were bidden not only by their separate life and their habitual detachment from the politics of Europe but also by a clear perception of international duty, the states of America have become conscious of a new and more vital community of interest and moral partnership in affairs, more clearly conscious of the many common sympathies and interests and duties which bid them stand together.

There was a time in the early days of our own great nation and of the republics fighting their way to independence in Central and South America when the government of the United States looked upon itself as in some sort the guardian of the republics to the South of her as against any encroachments or efforts at political control from the other side of the water; felt it its duty to play the part even without invitation from them; and I think that we can claim that the task was undertaken with a true and disinterested enthusiasm for the freedom of the Americas and the unmolested Self-government of her independent peoples. But it was always difficult to maintain such a role without offense to the pride of the peoples whose freedom of action we sought to protect, and without provoking serious misconceptions of our motives, and every thoughtful man of affairs must welcome the altered circumstances of the new day in whose light we now stand, when there is no claim of guardianship or thought of wards but, instead, a full and honorable association as of partners between ourselves and our neighbors, in the interest of all America, north and south. Our concern for the independence and prosperity of the states of Central and South America is not altered. We retain unabated the spirit that has inspired us throughout the whole life of our government and which was so frankly put into words by President Monroe. We still mean always to make a common cause of national independence and of political liberty in America. But that purpose is now better understood so far as it concerns ourselves. It is known not to be a selfish purpose. It is known to have in it no thought of taking advantage of any government in this hemisphere or playing its political fortunes for our own benefit. All the governments of America stand, so far as we are concerned, upon a footing of genuine equality and unquestioned independence.

We have been put to the test in the case of Mexico, and we have stood the test. Whether we have benefited Mexico by the course we have pursued remains to be seen. Her fortunes are in her own hands. But we have at least proved that we will not take advantage of her in her distress and undertake to impose upon her an order and government of our own choosing. Liberty is often a fierce and intractable thing, to which no bounds can be set, and to which no bounds of a few men's choosing ought ever to be set. Every American who has drunk at the true fountains of principle and tradition must subscribe without reservation to the high doctrine of the Virginia Bill of Rights, which in the great days in which our government was set up was everywhere amongst us accepted as the creed of free men. That doctrine is, "That government is, or ought to be, instituted for the common benefit, protection, and security of the people, nation, or community"; that "of all the various modes and forms of government, that is the best which is capable of producing the greatest degree of happiness and safety, and is most effectually secured against the danger of maladministration; and that, when any government shall be found inadequate or contrary to these purposes, a majority of the community hath an indubitable, inalienable, and indefeasible right to reform, alter, or abolish it, in such manner as shall be judged most conducive to the public weal." We have unhesitatingly applied that heroic principle to the case of Mexico, and now hopefully await the rebirth of the troubled Republic, which had so much of which to purge itself and so little sympathy from any outside quarter in the radical but necessary process. We will aid and befriend Mexico, but we will not coerce her; and our course with regard to her ought to be sufficient proof to all America that we seek no political suzerainty or selfish control.

The moral is, that the states of America are not hostile rivals but cooperating friends, and that their growing sense of community or interest, alike in matters political and in matters economic, is likely to give them a new significance as factors in international affairs and in the political history of the world. It presents them as in a very deep and true sense a unit in world affairs, spiritual partners, standing together because thinking together, quick with common sympathies and common ideals. Separated they are subject to all the cross currents of the confused politics of a world of hostile rivalries; united in spirit and purpose they cannot be disappointed of their peaceful destiny.

This is Pan-Americanism. It has none of the spirit of empire in it. It is the embodiment, the effectual embodiment, of the spirit of law and independence and liberty and mutual service.

A very notable body of men recently met in the City of Washington, at the invitation and as the guests of this Government, whose deliberations are likely to be looked back to as marking a memorable turning point in the history of America. They were representative spokesmen of the several independent states of this hemisphere and were assembled to discuss the financial and commercial relations of the republics of the two continents which nature and political fortune have so intimately linked together. I earnestly recommend to your perusal the reports of their proceedings and of the actions of their committees. You will get from them, I think, a fresh conception of the ease and intelligence and advantage with which Americans of both continents may draw together in practical cooperation and of what the material foundations of this hopeful partnership of interest must consist,-of how we should build them and of how necessary it is that we should hasten their building.

There is, I venture to point out, an especial significance just now attaching to this whole matter of drawing the Americans together in bonds of honorable partnership and mutual advantage because of the economic readjustments which the world must inevitably witness within the next generation, when peace shall have at last resumed its healthful tasks. In the performance of these tasks I believe the Americas to be destined to play their parts together. I am interested to fix your attention on this prospect now because unless you take it within your view and permit the full significance of it to command your thought I cannot find the right light in which to set forth the particular matter that lies at the very font of my whole thought as I address you to-day. I mean national defense.

No one who really comprehends the spirit of the great people for whom we are appointed to speak can fail to perceive that their passion is for peace, their genius best displayed in the practice of the arts of peace. Great democracies are not belligerent. They do not seek or desire war. Their thought is of individual liberty and of the free labor that supports life and the uncensored thought that quickens it. Conquest and dominion are not in our reckoning, or agreeable to our principles. But just because we demand unmolested development and the undisturbed government of our own lives upon our own principles of right and liberty, we resent, from whatever quarter it may come, the aggression we ourselves will not practice. We insist upon security in prosecuting our self-chosen lines of national development. We do more than that. We demand it also for others. We do not confine our enthusiasm for individual liberty and free national development to the incidents and movements of affairs which affect only ourselves. We feel it wherever there is a people that tries to walk in these difficult paths of independence and right. From the first we have made common cause with all partisans of liberty on this side the sea, and have deemed it as important that our neighbors should be free from all outside domination as that we ourselves should be. We have set America aside as a whole for the uses of independent nations and political freemen.

Out of such thoughts grow all our policies. We regard war merely as a means of asserting the rights of a people against aggression. And we are as fiercely jealous of coercive or dictatorial power within our own nation as of aggression from without. We will not maintain a standing army except for uses which are as necessary in times of peace as in times of war; and we shall always see to it that our military peace establishment is no larger than is actually and continuously needed for the uses of days in which no enemies move against us. But we do believe in a body of free citizens ready and sufficient to take care of themselves and of the governments which they have set up to serve them. In our constitutions themselves we have commanded that "the right of the people to keep and bear arms shall not be infringed," and our confidence has been that our safety in times of danger would lie in the rising of the nation to take care of itself, as the farmers rose at Lexington.

But war has never been a mere matter of men and guns. It is a thing of disciplined might. If our citizens are ever to fight effectively upon a sudden summons, they must know how modern fighting is done, and what to do when the summons comes to render themselves immediately available and immediately effective. And the government must be their servant in this matter, must supply them with the training they need to take care of themselves and of it. The military arm of their government, which they will not allow to direct them, they may properly use to serve them and make their independence secure,-and not their own independence merely but the rights also of those with whom they have made common cause, should they also be put in jeopardy. They must be fitted to play the great role in the world, and particularly in this hemisphere, for which they are qualified by principle and by chastened ambition to play.

It is with these ideals in mind that the plans of the Department of War for more adequate national defense were conceived which will be laid before you, and which I urge you to sanction and put into effect as soon as they can be properly scrutinized and discussed. They seem to me the essential first steps, and they seem to me for the present sufficient.

They contemplate an increase of the standing force of the regular army from its present strength of five thousand and twenty-three officers and one hundred and two thousand nine hundred and eighty-five enlisted men of all services to a strength of seven thousand one hundred and thirty-six officers and one hundred and thirty-four thousand seven hundred and seven enlisted men, or 141,843, all told, all services, rank and file, by the addition of fifty-two companies of coast artillery, fifteen companies of engineers, ten regiments of infantry, four regiments of field artillery, and four aero squadrons, besides seven hundred and fifty officers required for a great variety of extra service, especially the all important duty of training the citizen force of which I shall presently speak, seven hundred and ninety-two noncommissioned officers for service in drill, recruiting and the like, and the necessary quota of enlisted men for the Quartermaster Corps, the Hospital Corps, the Ordnance Department, and other similar auxiliary services. These are the additions necessary to render the army adequate for its present duties, duties which it has to perform not only upon our own continental coasts and borders and at our interior army posts, but also in the Philippines, in the Hawaiian Islands, at the Isthmus, and in Porto Rico.

By way of making the country ready to assert some part of its real power promptly and upon a larger scale, should occasion arise, the plan also contemplates supplementing the army by a force of four hundred thousand disciplined citizens, raised in increments of one hundred and thirty-three thousand a year throughout a period of three years. This it is proposed to do by a process of enlistment under which the serviceable men of the country would be asked to bind themselves to serve with the colors for purposes of training for short periods throughout three years, and to come to the colors at call at any time throughout an additional "furlough" period of three years. This force of four hundred thousand men would be provided with personal accoutrements as fast as enlisted and their equipment for the field made ready to be supplied at any time. They would be assembled for training at stated intervals at convenient places in association with suitable units of the regular army. Their period of annual training would not necessarily exceed two months in the year.

It would depend upon the patriotic feeling of the younger men of the country whether they responded to such a call to service or not. It would depend upon the patriotic spirit of the employers of the country whether they made it possible for the younger men in their employ to respond under favorable conditions or not. I, for one, do not doubt the patriotic devotion either of our young men or of those who give them employment,–those for whose benefit and protection they would in fact enlist. I would look forward to the success of such an experiment with entire confidence.

At least so much by way of preparation for defense seems to me to be absolutely imperative now. We cannot do less.

The programme which will be laid before you by the Secretary of the Navy is similarly conceived. It involves only a shortening of the time within which plans long matured shall be carried out; but it does make definite and explicit a programme which has heretofore been only implicit, held in the minds of the Committees on Naval Affairs and disclosed in the debates of the two Houses but nowhere formulated or formally adopted. It seems to me very clear that it will be to the advantage of the country for the Congress to adopt a comprehensive plan for putting the navy upon a final footing of strength and efficiency and to press that plan to completion within the next five years. We have always looked to the navy of the country as our first and chief line of defense; we have always seen it to be our manifest course of prudence to be strong on the seas. Year by year we have been creating a navy which now ranks very high indeed among the navies of the maritime nations. We should now definitely determine how we shall complete what we have begun, and how soon.

The programme to be laid before you contemplates the construction within five years of ten battleships, six battle cruisers, ten scout cruisers, fifty destroyers, fifteen fleet submarines, eighty-five coast submarines, four gunboats, one hospital ship, two ammunition ships, two fuel oil ships, and one repair ship. It is proposed that of this number we shall the first year provide for the construction of two battleships, two battle cruisers, three scout cruisers, fifteen destroyers, five fleet submarines, twenty-five coast submarines, two gunboats, and one hospital ship; the second year, two battleships, one scout cruiser, ten destroyers, four fleet submarines, fifteen coast submarines, one gunboat, and one fuel oil ship; the third year, two battleships, one battle cruiser, two scout cruisers, five destroyers, two fleet sub marines, and fifteen coast submarines; the fourth year, two battleships, two battle cruisers, two scout cruisers, ten destroyers, two fleet submarines, fifteen coast submarines, one ammunition ship, and one fuel oil ship; and the fifth year, two battleships, one battle cruiser, two scout cruisers, ten destroyers, two fleet submarines, fifteen coast submarines, one gunboat, one ammunition ship, and one repair ship.

The Secretary of the Navy is asking also for the immediate addition to the personnel of the navy of seven thousand five hundred sailors, twenty-five hundred apprentice seamen, and fifteen hundred marines. This increase would be sufficient to care for the ships which are to be completed within the fiscal year 1917 and also for the number of men which must be put in training to man the ships which will be completed early in 1918. It is also necessary that the number of midshipmen at the Naval academy at Annapolis should be increased by at least three hundred in order that the force of officers should be more rapidly added to; and authority is asked to appoint, for engineering duties only, approved graduates of engineering colleges, and for service in the aviation corps a certain number of men taken from civil life.

If this full programme should be carried out we should have built or building in 1921, according to the estimates of survival and standards of classification followed by the General Board of the Department, an effective navy consisting of twenty-seven battleships of the first line, six battle cruisers, twenty-five battleships of the second line, ten armored cruisers, thirteen scout cruisers, five first class cruisers, three second class cruisers, ten third class cruisers, one hundred and eight destroyers, eighteen fleet submarines, one hundred and fifty-seven coast submarines, six monitors, twenty gunboats, four supply ships, fifteen fuel ships, four transports, three tenders to torpedo vessels, eight vessels of special types, and two ammunition ships. This would be a navy fitted to our needs and worthy of our traditions.

But armies and instruments of war are only part of what has to be considered if we are to provide for the supreme matter of national self-sufficiency and security in all its aspects. There are other great matters which will be thrust upon our attention whether we will or not. There is, for example, a very pressing question of trade and shipping involved in this great problem of national adequacy. It is necessary for many weighty reasons of national efficiency and development that we should have a great merchant marine. The great merchant fleet we once used to make us rich, that great body of sturdy sailors who used to carry our flag into every sea, and who were the pride and often the bulwark of the nation, we have almost driven out of existence by inexcusable neglect and indifference and by a hopelessly blind and provincial policy of so-called economic protection. It is high time we repaired our mistake and resumed our commercial independence on the seas.

For it is a question of independence. If other nations go to war or seek to hamper each other's commerce, our merchants, it seems, are at their mercy, to do with as they please. We must use their ships, and use them as they determine. We have not ships enough of our own. We cannot handle our own commerce on the seas. Our independence is provincial, and is only on land and within our own borders. We are not likely to be permitted to use even the ships of other nations in rivalry of their own trade, and are without means to extend our commerce even where the doors are wide open and our goods desired. Such a situation is not to be endured. It is of capital importance not only that the United States should be its own carrier on the seas and enjoy the economic independence which only an adequate merchant marine would give it, but also that the American hemisphere as a whole should enjoy a like independence and self-sufficiency, if it is not to be drawn into the tangle of European affairs. Without such independence the whole question of our political unity and self-determination is very seriously clouded and complicated indeed.

Moreover, we can develop no true or effective American policy without ships of our own,—not ships of war, but ships of peace, carrying goods and carrying much more: creating friendships and rendering indispensable services to all interests on this side the water. They must move constantly back and forth between the Americas. They are the only shuttles that can weave the delicate fabric of sympathy, comprehension, confidence, and mutual dependence in which we wish to clothe our policy of America for Americans.

The task of building up an adequate merchant marine for America private capital must ultimately undertake and achieve, as it has undertaken and achieved every other like task amongst us in the past, with admirable enterprise, intelligence, and vigor; and it seems to me a manifest dictate of wisdom that we should promptly remove every legal obstacle that may stand in the way of this much to be desired revival of our old independence and should facilitate in every possible way the building, purchase, and American registration of ships. But capital cannot accomplish this great task of a sudden. It must embark upon it by degrees, as the opportunities of trade develop. Something must be done at once; done to open routes and develop opportunities where they are as yet undeveloped; done to open the arteries of trade where the currents have not yet learned to run,—especially between the two American continents, where they are, singularly enough, yet to be created and quickened; and it is evident that only the government can undertake such beginnings and assume the initial financial risks. When the risk has passed and private capital begins to find its way in sufficient abundance into these new channels, the government may withdraw. But it cannot omit to begin. It should take the first steps, and should take them at once. Our goods must not lie piled up at our ports and stored upon side tracks in freight cars which are daily needed on the roads; must not be left without means of transport to any foreign quarter. We must not await the permission of foreign ship-owners and foreign governments to send them where we will.

With a view to meeting these pressing necessities of our commerce and availing ourselves at the earliest possible moment of the present unparalleled opportunity of linking the two Americas together in bonds of mutual interest and service, an opportunity which may never return again if we miss it now, proposals will be made to the present Congress for the purchase or construction of ships to be owned and directed by the government similar to those made to the last Congress, but modified in some essential particulars. I recommend these proposals to you for your prompt acceptance with the more confidence because every month that has elapsed since the former proposals were made has made the necessity for such action more and more manifestly imperative. That need was then foreseen; it is now acutely felt and everywhere realized by those for whom trade is waiting but who can find no conveyance for their goods. I am not so much interested in the particulars of the programme as I am in taking immediate advantage of the great opportunity which awaits us if we will but act in this emergency. In this matter, as in all others, a spirit of common counsel should prevail, and out of it should come an early solution of this pressing problem.

There is another matter which seems to me to be very intimately associated with the question of national safety and preparation for defense. That is our policy towards the Philippines and the people of Porto Rico. Our treatment of them and their attitude towards us are manifestly of the first consequence in the development of our duties in the world and in getting a free hand to perform those duties. We must be free from every unnecessary burden or embarrassment; and there is no better way to be clear of embarrassment than to fulfil our promises and promote the interests of those dependent on us to the utmost. Bills for the alteration and reform of the government of the Philippines and for rendering fuller political justice to the people of Porto Rico were submitted to the sixty-third Congress. They will be submitted also to you. I need not particularize their details. You are most of you already familiar with them. But I do recommend them to your early adoption with the sincere conviction that there are few measures you could adopt which would more serviceably clear the way for the great policies by which we wish to make good, now and always, our right to lead in enterprises of peace and good will and economic and political freedom.

The plans for the armed forces of the nation which I have outlined, and for the general policy of adequate preparation for mobilization and defense, involve of course very large additional expenditures of money,-expenditures which will considerably exceed the estimated revenues of the government. It is made my duty by law, whenever the estimates of expenditure exceed the estimates of revenue, to call the attention of the Congress to the fact and suggest any means of meeting the deficiency that it may be wise or possible for me to suggest. I am ready to believe that it would be my duty to do so in any case; and I feel particularly bound to speak of the matter when it appears that the deficiency will arise directly out of the adoption by the Congress of measures which I myself urge it to adopt. Allow me, therefore, to speak briefly of the present state of the Treasury and of the fiscal problems which the next year will probably disclose.

On the thirtieth of June last there was an available balance in the general fund of the Treasury Of $104,170,105.78. The total estimated receipts for the year 1916, on the assumption that the emergency revenue measure passed by the last Congress will not be extended beyond its present limit, the thirty-first of December, 1915, and that the present duty of one cent per pound on sugar will be discontinued after the first of May, 1916, will be $670,365,500. The balance of June last and these estimated revenues come, therefore, to a grand total of $774,535,605-78. The total estimated disbursements for the present fiscal year, including twenty-five millions for the Panama Canal, twelve millions for probable deficiency appropriations, and fifty thousand dollars for miscellaneous debt redemptions, will be $753,891,000; and the balance in the general fund of the Treasury will be reduced to $20,644,605.78. The emergency revenue act, if continued beyond its present time limitation, would produce, during the half year then remaining, about forty-one millions. The duty of one cent per pound on sugar, if continued, would produce during the two months of the fiscal year remaining after the first of May, about fifteen millions. These two sums, amounting together to fifty-six millions, if added to the revenues of the second half of the fiscal year, would yield the Treasury at the end of the year an available balance Of $76,644,605-78.

The additional revenues required to carry out the programme of military and naval preparation of which I have spoken, would, as at present estimated, be for the fiscal year, 1917, $93,800,000. Those figures, taken with the figures for the present fiscal year which I have already given, disclose our financial problem for the year 1917. Assuming that the taxes imposed by the emergency revenue act and the present duty on sugar are to be discontinued, and that the balance at the close of the present fiscal year will be only $20,644,605.78, that the disbursements for the Panama Canal will again be about twenty-five millions, and that the additional expenditures for the army and navy are authorized by the Congress, the deficit in the general fund of the Treasury on the thirtieth of June, 1917, will be nearly two hundred and thirty-five millions. To this sum at least fifty millions should be added to represent a safe working balance for the Treasury, and twelve millions to include the usual deficiency estimates in 1917; and these additions would make a total deficit of some two hundred and ninety-seven millions. If the present taxes should be continued throughout this year and the next, however, there would be a balance in the Treasury of some seventy-six and a half millions at the end of the present fiscal year, and a deficit at the end of the next year of only some fifty millions, or, reckoning in sixty-two millions for deficiency appropriations and a safe Treasury balance at the end of the year, a total deficit of some one hundred and twelve millions. The obvious moral of the figures is that it is a plain counsel of prudence to continue all of the present taxes or their equivalents, and confine ourselves to the problem of providing one hundred and twelve millions of new revenue rather than two hundred and ninety-seven millions.

How shall we obtain the new revenue? We are frequently reminded that there are many millions of bonds which the Treasury is authorized under existing law to sell to reimburse the sums paid out of current revenues for the construction of the Panama Canal; and it is true that bonds to the amount of approximately $222,000,000 are now available for that purpose. Prior to 1913, $134,631,980 of these bonds had actually been sold to recoup the expenditures at the Isthmus; and now constitute a considerable item of the public debt. But I, for one, do not believe that the people of this country approve of postponing the payment of their bills. Borrowing money is short-sighted finance. It can be justified only when permanent things are to be accomplished which many generations will certainly benefit by and which it seems hardly fair that a single generation should pay for. The objects we are now proposing to spend money for cannot be so classified, except in the sense that everything wisely done may be said to be done in the interest of posterity as well as in our own. It seems to me a clear dictate of prudent statesmanship and frank finance that in what we are now, I hope, about to undertake we should pay as we go. The people of the country are entitled to know just what burdens of taxation they are to carry, and to know from the outset, now. The new bills should be paid by internal taxation.

To what sources, then, shall we turn? This is so peculiarly a question which the gentlemen of the House of Representatives are expected under the Constitution to propose an answer to that you will hardly expect me to do more than discuss it in very general terms. We should be following an almost universal example of modern governments if we were to draw the greater part or even the whole of the revenues we need from the income taxes. By somewhat lowering the present limits of exemption and the figure at which the surtax shall begin to be imposed, and by increasing, step by step throughout the present graduation, the surtax itself, the income taxes as at present apportioned would yield sums sufficient to balance the books of the Treasury at the end of the fiscal year 1917 without anywhere making the burden unreasonably or oppressively heavy. The precise reckonings are fully and accurately set out in the report of the Secretary of the Treasury which will be immediately laid before you.

And there are many additional sources of revenue which can justly be resorted to without hampering the industries of the country or putting any too great charge upon individual expenditure. A tax of one cent per gallon on gasoline and naphtha would yield, at the present estimated production, $10,000,000; a tax of fifty cents per horse power on automobiles and internal explosion engines, $15,000,000; a stamp tax on bank cheques, probably $18,000,000; a tax of twenty-five cents per ton on pig iron, $10,000,000; a tax of twenty-five cents per ton on fabricated iron and steel, probably $10,000,000. In a country of great industries like this it ought to be easy to distribute the burdens of taxation without making them anywhere bear too heavily or too exclusively upon any one set of persons or undertakings. What is clear is, that the industry of this generation should pay the bills of this generation.

I have spoken to you to-day, Gentlemen, upon a single theme, the thorough preparation of the nation to care for its own security and to make sure of entire freedom to play the impartial role in this hemisphere and in the world which we all believe to have been providentially assigned to it. I have had in my mind no thought of any immediate or particular danger arising out of our relations with other nations. We are at peace with all the nations of the world, and there is reason to hope that no question in controversy between this and other Governments will lead to any serious breach of amicable relations, grave as some differences of attitude and policy have been land may yet turn out to be. I am sorry to say that the gravest threats against our national peace and safety have been uttered within our own borders. There are citizens of the United States, I blush to admit, born under other flags but welcomed under our generous naturalization laws to the full freedom and opportunity of America, who have poured the poison of disloyalty into the very arteries of our national life; who have sought to bring the authority and good name of our Government into contempt, to destroy our industries wherever they thought it effective for their vindictive purposes to strike at them, and to debase our politics to the uses of foreign intrigue. Their number is not great as compared with the whole number of those sturdy hosts by which our nation has been enriched in recent generations out of virile foreign stock; but it is great enough to have brought deep disgrace upon us and to have made it necessary that we should promptly make use of processes of law by which we may be purged of their corrupt distempers. America never witnessed anything like this before. It never dreamed it possible that men sworn into its own citizenship, men drawn out of great free stocks such as supplied some of the best and strongest elements of that little, but how heroic, nation that in a high day of old staked its very life to free itself from every entanglement that had darkened the fortunes of the older nations and set up a new standard here, that men of such origins and such free choices of allegiance would ever turn in malign reaction against the Government and people who had welcomed and nurtured them and seek to make this proud country once more a hotbed of European passion. A little while ago such a thing would have seemed incredible. Because it was incredible we made no preparation for it. We would have been almost ashamed to prepare for it, as if we were suspicious of ourselves, our own comrades and neighbors! But the ugly and incredible thing has actually come about and we are without adequate federal laws to deal with it. I urge you to enact such laws at the earliest possible moment and feel that in doing so I am urging you to do nothing less than save the honor and self-respect of the nation. Such creatures of passion, disloyalty, and anarchy must be crushed out. They are not many, but they are infinitely malignant, and the hand of our power should close over them at once. They have formed plots to destroy property, they have entered into conspiracies against the neutrality of the Government, they have sought to pry into every confidential transaction of the Government in order to serve interests alien to our own. It is possible to deal with these things very effectually. I need not suggest the terms in which they may be dealt with.

I wish that it could be said that only a few men, misled by mistaken sentiments of allegiance to the governments under which they were born, had been guilty of disturbing the self-possession and misrepresenting the temper and principles of the country during these days of terrible war, when it would seem that every man who was truly an American would instinctively make it his duty and his pride to keep the scales of judgment even and prove himself a partisan of no nation but his own. But it cannot. There are some men among us, and many resident abroad who, though born and bred in the United States and calling themselves Americans, have so forgotten themselves and their honor as citizens as to put their passionate sympathy with one or the other side in the great European conflict above their regard for the peace and dignity of the United States. They also preach and practice disloyalty. No laws, I suppose, can reach corruptions of the mind and heart; but I should not speak of others without also speaking of these and expressing the even deeper humiliation and scorn which every self-possessed and thoughtfully patriotic American must feel when he thinks of them and of the discredit they are daily bringing upon us.

While we speak of the preparation of the nation to make sure of her security and her effective power we must not fall into the patent error of supposing that her real strength comes from armaments and mere safeguards of written law. It comes, of course, from her people, their energy, their success in their undertakings, their free opportunity to use the natural resources of our great home land and of the lands outside our continental borders which look to us for protection, for encouragement, and for assistance in their development; from the organization and freedom and vitality of our economic life. The domestic questions which engaged the attention of the last Congress are more vital to the nation in this its time of test than at any other time. We cannot adequately make ready for any trial of our strength unless we wisely and promptly direct the force of our laws into these all-important fields of domestic action. A matter which it seems to me we should have very much at heart is the creation of the right instrumentalities by which to mobilize our economic resources in any time of national necessity. I take it for granted that I do not need your authority to call into systematic consultation with the directing officers of the army and navy men of recognized leadership and ability from among our citizens who are thoroughly familiar, for example, with the transportation facilities of the country and therefore competent to advise how they may be coordinated when the need arises, those who can suggest the best way in which to bring about prompt cooperation among the manufacturers of the country, should it be necessary, and those who could assist to bring the technical skill of the country to the aid of the Government in the solution of particular problems of defense. I only hope that if I should find it feasible to constitute such an advisory body the Congress would be willing to vote the small sum of money that would be needed to defray the expenses that would probably be necessary to give it the clerical and administrative Machinery with which to do serviceable work.

What is more important is, that the industries and resources of the country should be available and ready for mobilization. It is the more imperatively necessary, therefore, that we should promptly devise means for doing what we have not yet done: that we should give intelligent federal aid and stimulation to industrial and vocational education, as we have long done in the large field of our agricultural industry; that, at the same time that we safeguard and conserve the natural resources of the country we should put them at the disposal of those who will use them promptly and intelligently, as was sought to be done in the admirable bills submitted to the last Congress from its committees on the public lands, bills which I earnestly recommend in principle to your consideration; that we should put into early operation some provision for rural credits which will add to the extensive borrowing facilities already afforded the farmer by the Reserve Bank Act, adequate instrumentalities by which long credits may be obtained on land mortgages; and that we should study more carefully than they have hitherto been studied the right adaptation of our economic arrangements to changing conditions.

Many conditions about which we I-lave repeatedly legislated are being altered from decade to decade, it is evident, under our very eyes, and are likely to change even more rapidly and more radically in the days immediately ahead of us, when peace has returned to the world and the nations of Europe once more take up their tasks of commerce and industry with the energy of those who must bestir themselves to build anew. Just what these changes will be no one can certainly foresee or confidently predict. There are no calculable, because no stable, elements in the problem. The most we can do is to make certain that we have the necessary instrumentalities of information constantly at our service so that we may be sure that we know exactly what we are dealing with when we come to act, if it should be necessary to act at all. We must first certainly know what it is that we are seeking to adapt ourselves to. I may ask the privilege of addressing you more at length on this important matter a little later in your session.

In the meantime may I make this suggestion? The transportation problem is an exceedingly serious and pressing one in this country. There has from time to time of late been reason to fear that our railroads would not much longer be able to cope with it successfully, as at present equipped and coordinated I suggest that it would be wise to provide for a commission of inquiry to ascertain by a thorough canvass of the whole question whether our laws as at present framed and administered are as serviceable as they might be in the solution of the problem. It is obviously a problem that lies at the very foundation of our efficiency as a people. Such an inquiry ought to draw out every circumstance and opinion worth considering and we need to know all sides of the matter if we mean to do anything in the field of federal legislation.

No one, I am sure, would wish to take any backward step. The regulation of the railways of the country by federal commission has had admirable results and has fully justified the hopes and expectations of those by whom the policy of regulation was originally proposed. The question is not what should we undo? It is, whether there is anything else we can do that would supply us with effective means, in the very process of regulation, for bettering the conditions under which the railroads are operated and for making them more useful servants of the country as a whole. It seems to me that it might be the part of wisdom, therefore, before further legislation in this field is attempted, to look at the whole problem of coordination and efficiency in the full light of a fresh assessment of circumstance and opinion, as a guide to dealing with the several parts of it.

For what we are seeking now, what in my mind is the single thought of this message, is national efficiency and security. We serve a great nation. We should serve it in the spirit of its peculiar genius. It is the genius of common men for self-government, industry, justice, liberty and peace. We should see to it that it lacks no instrument, no facility or vigor of law, to make it sufficient to play its part with energy, safety, and assured success. In this we are no partisans but heralds and prophets of a new age.

Fourth State of the Union address

Woodrow Wilson

December 5, 1916

GENTLEMEN OF THE CONGRESS:

In fulfilling at this time the duty laid upon me by the Constitution of communicating to you from time to time information of the state of the Union and recommending to your consideration such legislative measures as may be judged necessary and expedient, I shall continue the practice, which I hope has been acceptable to you, of leaving to the reports of the several heads of the executive departments the elaboration of the detailed needs of the public service and confine myself to those matters of more general public policy with which it seems necessary and feasible to deal at the present session of the Congress.

I realize the limitations of time under which you will necessarily act at this session and shall make my suggestions as few as possible; but there were some things left undone at the last session which there will now be time to complete and which it seems necessary in the interest of the public to do at once.

In the first place, it seems to me imperatively necessary that the earliest possible consideration and action should be accorded the remaining measures of the program of settlement and regulation which I had occasion to recommend to you at the close of your last session in view of the public dangers disclosed by the unaccommodated difficulties which then existed, and which still unhappily continue to exist, between the railroads of the country and their locomotive engineers, conductors and trainmen.

I then recommended:

First, immediate provision for the enlargement and administrative reorganization of the Interstate Commerce Commission along the lines embodied in the bill recently passed by the House of Representatives and now awaiting action by the Senate; in order that the Commission may be enabled to deal with the many great and various duties now devolving upon it with a promptness and thoroughness which are, with its present constitution and means of action, practically impossible.

Second, the establishment of an eight-hour day as the legal basis alike of work and wages in the employment of all railway employes who are actually engaged in the work of operating trains in interstate transportation.

Third, the authorization of the appointment by the President of a small body of men to observe actual results in experience of the adoption of the eight-hour day in railway transportation alike for the men and for the railroads.

Fourth, explicit approval by the Congress of the consideration by the Interstate Commerce Commission of an increase of freight rates to meet such additional expenditures by the railroads as may have been rendered necessary by the adoption of the eight-hour day and which have not been offset by administrative readjustments and economies, should the facts disclosed justify the increase.

Fifth, an amendment of the existing Federal statute which provides for the mediation, conciliation and arbitration of such controversies as the present by adding to it a provision that, in case the methods of accommodation now provided for should fail, a full public investigation of the merits of every such dispute shall be instituted and completed before a strike or lockout may lawfully be attempted.

And, sixth, the lodgment in the hands of the Executive of the power, in case of military necessity, to take control of such portions and such rolling stock of the railways of the country as may be required for military use and to operate them for military purposes, with authority to draft into the military service of the United States such train crews and administrative officials as the circumstances require for their safe and efficient use.

The second and third of these recommendations the Congress immediately acted on: it established the eight-hour day as the legal basis of work and wages in train service and it authorized the appointment of a commission to observe and report upon the practical results, deeming these the measures most immediately needed; but it postponed action upon the other suggestions until an opportunity should be offered for a more deliberate consideration of them.

The fourth recommendation I do not deem it necessary to renew. The power of the Interstate Commerce Commission to grant an increase of rates on the ground referred to is indisputably clear and a recommendation by the Congress with regard to such a matter might seem to draw in question the scope of the commission's authority or its inclination to do justice when there is no reason to doubt either.

The other suggestions-the increase in the Interstate Commerce Commission's membership and in its facilities for performing its manifold duties; the provision for full public investigation and assessment of industrial disputes, and the grant to the Executive of the power to control and operate the railways when necessary in time of war or other like public necessity-I now very earnestly renew.

The necessity for such legislation is manifest and pressing. Those who have entrusted us with the responsibility and duty of serving and safeguarding them in such matters would find it hard, I believe, to excuse a failure to act upon these grave matters or any unnecessary postponement of action upon them.

Not only does the Interstate Commerce Commission now find it practically impossible, with its present membership and organization, to perform its great functions promptly and thoroughly, but it is not unlikely that it may presently be found advisable to add to its duties still others equally heavy and exacting. It must first be perfected as an administrative instrument.

The country cannot and should not consent to remain any longer exposed to profound industrial disturbances for lack of additional means of arbitration and conciliation which the Congress can easily and promptly supply.

And all will agree that there must be no doubt as to the power of the Executive to make immediate and uninterrupted use of the railroads for the concentration of the military forces of the nation wherever they are needed and whenever they are needed.

This is a program of regulation, prevention and administrative efficiency which argues its own case in the mere statement of it. With regard to one of its items, the increase in the efficiency of the Interstate Commerce Commission, the House of Representatives has already acted; its action needs only the concurrence of the Senate.

I would hesitate to recommend, and I dare say the Congress would hesitate to act upon the suggestion should I make it, that any man in any I occupation should be obliged by law to continue in an employment which he desired to leave.

To pass a law which forbade or prevented the individual workman to leave his work before receiving the approval of society in doing so would be to adopt a new principle into our jurisprudence, which I take it for granted we are not prepared to introduce.

But the proposal that the operation of the railways of the country shall not be stopped or interrupted by the concerted action of organized bodies of men until a public investigation shall have been instituted, which shall make the whole question at issue plain for the judgment of the opinion of the nation, is not to propose any such principle.

It is based upon the very different principle that the concerted action of powerful bodies of men shall not be permitted to stop the industrial processes of the nation, at any rate before the nation shall have had an opportunity to acquaint itself with the merits of the case as between employe and employer, time to form its opinion upon an impartial statement of the merits, and opportunity to consider all practicable means of conciliation or arbitration.

I can see nothing in that proposition but the justifiable safeguarding by society of the necessary processes of its very life. There is nothing arbitrary or unjust in it unless it be arbitrarily and unjustly done. It can and should be done with a full and scrupulous regard for the interests and liberties of all concerned as well as for the permanent interests of society itself.

Three matters of capital importance await the action of the Senate which have already been acted upon by the House of Representatives; the bill which seeks to extend greater freedom of combination to those engaged in promoting the foreign commerce of the country than is now thought by some to be legal under the terms of the laws against monopoly; the bill amending the present organic law of Porto Rico; and the bill proposing a more thorough and systematic regulation of the expenditure of money in elections, commonly called the Corrupt Practices Act.

I need not labor my advice that these measures be enacted into law. Their urgency lies in the manifest circumstances which render their adoption at this time not only opportune but necessary. Even delay would seriously jeopard the interests of the country and of the Government.

Immediate passage of the bill to regulate the expenditure of money in elections may seem to be less necessary than the immediate enactment of the other measures to which I refer, because at least two years will elapse before another election in which Federal offices are to be filled; but it would greatly relieve the public mind if this important matter were dealt with while the circumstances and the dangers to the public morals of the present method of obtaining and spending campaign funds stand clear under recent observation, and the methods of expenditure can be frankly studied in the light of present experience; and a delay would have the further very serious disadvantage of postponing action until another election was at hand and some special object connected with it might be thought to be in the mind of those who urged it. Action can be taken now with facts for guidance and without suspicion of partisan purpose.

I shall not argue at length the desirability of giving a freer hand in the matter of combined and concerted effort to those who shall undertake the essential enterprise of building up our export trade. That enterprise will presently, will immediately assume, has indeed already assumed a magnitude unprecedented in our experience. We have not the necessary instrumentalities for its prosecution; it is deemed to be doubtful whether they could be created upon an adequate scale under our present laws.

We should clear away all legal obstacles and create a basis of undoubted law for it which will give freedom without permitting unregulated license. The thing must be done now, because the opportunity is here and may escape us if we hesitate or delay.

The argument for the proposed amendments of the organic law of Porto Rico is brief and conclusive. The present laws governing the island and regulating the rights and privileges of its people are not just. We have created expectations of extended privilege which we have not satisfied. There is uneasiness among the people of the island and even a suspicious doubt with regard to our intentions concerning them which the adoption of the pending measure would happily remove. We do not doubt what we wish to do in any essential particular. We ought to do it at once.

At the last session of the Congress a bill was passed by the Senate which provides for the promotion of vocational and industrial education, which is of vital importance to the whole country because it concerns a matter, too long neglected, upon which the thorough industrial preparation of the country for the critical years of economic development immediately ahead of us in very large measure depends.

May I not urge its early and favorable consideration by the House of Representatives and its early enactment into law? It contains plans which affect all interests and all parts of the country, and I am sure that there is no legislation now pending before the Congress whose passage the country awaits with more thoughtful approval or greater impatience to see a great and admirable thing set in the way of being done.

There are other matters already advanced to the stage of conference between the two houses of which it is not necessary that I should speak. Some practicable basis of agreement concerning them will no doubt be found an action taken upon them.

Inasmuch as this is, gentlemen, probably the last occasion I shall have to address the Sixty-fourth Congress, I hope that you will permit me to say with what genuine pleasure and satisfaction I have co-operated with you in the many measures of constructive policy with which you have enriched the legislative annals of the country. It has been a privilege to labor in such company. I take the liberty of congratulating you upon the completion of a record of rare serviceableness and distinction.

Fifth State of the Union address

Woodrow Wilson

December 4, 1917

GENTLEMEN OF THE CONGRESS:

Eight months have elapsed since I last had the honor of addressing you. They have been months crowded with events of immense and grave significance for us. I shall not undertake to detail or even to summarize those events. The practical particulars of the part we have played in them will be laid before you in the reports of the executive departments. I shall discuss only our present outlook upon these vast affairs, our present duties, and the immediate means of accomplishing the objects we shall hold always in view.

I shall not go back to debate the causes of the war. The intolerable wrongs done and planned against us by the sinister masters of Germany have long since become too grossly obvious and odious to every true American to need to be rehearsed. But I shall ask you to consider again and with a very grave scrutiny our objectives and the measures by which we mean to attain them; for the purpose of discussion here in this place is action, and our action must move straight toward definite ends. Our object is, of course, to win the war; and we shall not slacken or suffer ourselves to be diverted until it is won. But it is worth while asking and answering the question, When shall we consider the war won?

From one point of view it is not necessary to broach this fundamental matter. I do not doubt that the American people know what the war is about and what sort of an outcome they will regard as a realization of their purpose in it.

As a nation we are united in spirit and intention. I pay little heed to those who tell me otherwise. I hear the voices of dissent-who does not? I bear the criticism and the clamor of the noisily thoughtless and troublesome. I also see men here and there fling themselves in impotent disloyalty against the calm, indomitable power of the Nation. I hear men debate peace who understand neither its nature nor the way in which we may attain it with uplifted eyes and unbroken spirits. But I know that none of these speaks for the Nation. They do not touch the heart of anything. They may safely be left to strut their uneasy hour and be forgotten.

But from another point of view I believe that it is necessary to say plainly what we here at the seat of action consider the war to be for and what part we mean to play in the settlement of its searching issues. We are the spokesmen of the American people, and they have a right to know whether their purpose is ours. They desire peace by the overcoming of evil, by the defeat once for all of the sinister forces that interrupt peace and render it impossible, and they wish to know how closely our thought runs with theirs and what action we propose. They are impatient with those who desire peace by any sort of compromise deeply and indignantly impatient--but they will be equally impatient with us if we do not make it plain to them what our objectives are and what we are planning for in seeking to make conquest of peace by arms.

I believe that I speak for them when I say two things: First, that this intolerable thing of which the masters of Germany have shown us the ugly face, this menace of combined intrigue and force which we now see so clearly as the German power, a thing without conscience or honor of capacity for covenanted peace, must be crushed and, if it be not utterly brought to an end, at least shut out from the friendly intercourse of the nations; and second, that when this thing and its power are indeed defeated and the time comes that we can discuss peace when the German people have spokesmen whose word we can believe and when those spokesmen are ready in the name of their people to accept the common judgment of the nations as to what shall henceforth be the bases of law and of covenant for the life of the world-we shall be willing and glad to pay the full price for peace, and pay it ungrudgingly.

We know what that price will be. It will be full, impartial justice-justice done at every point and to every nation that the final settlement must affect, our enemies as well as our friends.

You catch, with me, the voices of humanity that are in the air. They grow daily more audible, more articulate, more persuasive, and they come from the hearts of men everywhere. They insist that the war shall not end in vindictive action of any kind; that no nation or people shall be robbed or punished because the irresponsible rulers of a single country have themselves done deep and abominable wrong. It is this thought that has been expressed in the formula, "No annexations, no contributions, no punitive indemnities."

Just because this crude formula expresses the instinctive judgment as to right of plain men everywhere, it has been made diligent use of by the masters of German intrigue to lead the people of Russia astray and the people of every other country their agents could reach-in order that a premature peace might be brought about before autocracy has been taught its final and convincing lesson and the people of the world put in control of their own destinies.

But the fact that a wrong use has been made of a just idea is no reason why a right use should not be made of it. It ought to be brought under the patronage of its real friends. Let it be said again that autocracy must first be shown the utter futility of its claim to power or leadership in the modern world. It is impossible to apply any standard of justice so long as such forces are unchecked and undefeated as the present masters of Germany command. Not until that has been done can right be set up as arbiter and peacemaker among the nations. But when that has been done-as, God willing, it assuredly will be-we shall at last be free to do an unprecedented thing, and this is the time to avow our purpose to do it. We shall be free to base peace on generosity and justice, to the exclusions of all selfish claims to advantage even on the part of the victors.

Let there be no misunderstanding. Our present and immediate task is to win the war and nothing shall turn us aside from it until it is accomplished. Every power and resource we possess, whether of men, of money, or of materials, is being devoted and will continue to be devoted to that purpose until it is achieved. Those who desire to bring peace about before that purpose is achieved I counsel to carry their advice elsewhere. We will not entertain it. We shall regard the war as won only when the German people say to us, through properly accredited representatives, that they are ready to agree to a settlement based upon justice and reparation of the wrongs their rulers have done. They have done a wrong to Belgium which must be repaired. They have established a power over other lands and peoples than their own--over the great empire of Austria-Hungary, over hitherto free Balkan states, over Turkey and within Asia-which must be relinquished.

Germany's success by skill, by industry, by knowledge, by enterprise we did not grudge or oppose, but admired, rather. She had built up for herself a real empire of trade and influence, secured by the peace of the world. We were content to abide by the rivalries of manufacture, science and commerce that were involved for us in her success, and stand or fall as we had or did not have the brains and the initiative to surpass her. But at the moment when she had conspicuously won her triumphs of peace she threw them away, to establish in their stead what the world will no longer permit to be established, military and political domination by arms, by which to oust where she could not excel the rivals she most feared and hated. The peace we make must remedy that wrong. It must deliver the once fair lands and happy peoples of Belgium and Northern France from the Prussian conquest and the Prussian menace, but it must deliver also the peoples of Austria-Hungary, the peoples of the Balkans and the peoples of Turkey, alike in Europe and Asia, from the impudent and alien dominion of the Prussian military and commercial autocracy.

We owe it, however, to ourselves, to say that we do not wish in any way to impair or to rearrange the Austro-Hungarian Empire. It is no affair of ours what they do with their own life, either industrially or politically. We do not purpose or desire to dictate to them in any way. We only desire to see that their affairs are left in their own hands, in all matters, great or small. We shall hope to secure for the peoples of the Balkan peninsula and for the people of the Turkish Empire the right and opportunity to make their own lives safe, their own fortunes secure against oppression or injustice and from the dictation of foreign courts or parties.

And our attitude and purpose with regard to Germany herself are of a like kind. We intend no wrong against the German Empire, no interference with her internal affairs. We should deem either the one or the other absolutely unjustifiable, absolutely contrary to the principles we have professed to live by and to hold most sacred throughout our life as a nation.

The people of Germany are being told by the men whom they now permit to deceive them and to act as their masters that they are fighting for the very life and existence of their empire, a war of desperate self-defense against deliberate aggression. Nothing could be more grossly or wantonly false, and we must seek by the utmost openness and candor as to our real aims to convince them of its falseness. We are in fact fighting for their emancipation from the fear, along with our own-from the fear as well as from the fact of unjust attack by neighbors or rivals or schemers after world empire. No one is threatening the existence or the independence of the peaceful enterprise of the German Empire.

The worst that can happen to the detriment the German people is this, that if they should still, after the war is over, continue to be obliged to live under ambitious and intriguing masters interested to disturb the peace of the world, men or classes of men whom the other peoples of the world could not trust, it might be impossible to admit them to the partnership of nations which must henceforth guarantee the world's peace. That partnership must be a partnership of peoples, not a mere partnership of governments. It might be impossible, also, in such untoward circumstances, to admit Germany to the free economic intercourse which must inevitably spring out of the other partnerships of a real peace. But there would be no aggression in that; and such a situation, inevitable, because of distrust, would in the very nature of things sooner or later cure itself, by processes which would assuredly set in.

The wrongs, the very deep wrongs, committed in this war will have to be righted. That, of course. But they cannot and must not be righted by the commission of similar wrongs against Germany and her allies. The world will not permit the commission of similar wrongs as a means of reparation and settlement. Statesmen must by this time have learned that the opinion of the world is everywhere wide awake and fully comprehends the issues involved. No representative of any self-governed nation will dare disregard it by attempting any such covenants of selfishness and compromise as were entered into at the Congress of Vienna. The thought of the plain people here and everywhere throughout the world, the people who enjoy no privilege and have very simple and unsophisticated standards of right and wrong, is the air all governments must henceforth breathe if they would live.

It is in the full disclosing light of that thought that all policies must be received and executed in this midday hour of the world's life. Ger. man rulers have been able to upset the peace of the world only because the German people were not suffered under their tutelage to share the comradeship of the other peoples of the world either in thought or in purpose. They were allowed to have no opinion of their own which might be set up as a rule of conduct for those who exercised authority over them. But the Congress that concludes this war will feel the full strength of the tides that run now in the hearts and consciences of free men everywhere. Its conclusions will run with those tides.

All those things have been true from the very beginning of this stupendous war; and I cannot help thinking that if they had been made plain at the very outset the sympathy and enthusiasm of the Russian people might have been once for all enlisted on the side of the Allies, suspicion and distrust swept away, and a real and lasting union of purpose effected. Had they believed these things at the very moment of their revolution, and had they been confirmed in that belief since, the sad reverses which have recently marked the progress of their affairs towards an ordered and stable government of free men might have been avoided. The Russian people have been poisoned by the very same falsehoods that have kept the German people in the dark, and the poison has been administered by the very same hand. The only possible antidote is the truth. It cannot be uttered too plainly or too often.

From every point of view, therefore, it has seemed to be my duty to speak these declarations of purpose, to add these specific interpretations to what I took the liberty of saying to the Senate in January. Our entrance into the war has not altered out attitude towards the settlement that must come when it is over.

When I said in January that the nations of the world were entitled not only to free pathways upon the sea, but also to assured and unmolested access to those-pathways, I was thinking, and I am thinking now, not of the smaller and weaker nations alone which need our countenance and support, but also of the great and powerful nations and of our present enemies as well as our present associates in the war. I was thinking, and am thinking now, of Austria herself, among the rest, as well as of Serbia and of Poland.

Justice and equality of rights can be had only at a great price. We are seeking permanent, not temporary, foundations for the peace of the world, and must seek them candidly and fearlessly. As always, the right will prove to be the expedient.

What shall we do, then, to push this great war of freedom and justice to its righteous conclusion? We must clear away with a thorough hand all impediments to success, and we must make every adjustment of law that will facilitate the full and free use of our whole capacity and force as a fighting unit.

One very embarrassing obstacle that stands hi our way is that we are at war with Germany but not with her allies. I, therefore, very earnestly recommend that the Congress immediately declare the United States in a state of war with Austria-Hungary. Does it seem strange to you that this should be the conclusion of the argument I have just addressed to you? It is not. It is in fact the inevitable logic of what I have said. Austria-Hungary is for the time being not her own mistress but simply the vassal of the German Government.

We must face the facts as they are and act upon them without sentiment in this stern business. The Government of Austria and Hungary is not acting upon its own initiative or in response to the wishes and feelings of its own peoples, but as the instrument of another nation. We must meet its force with our own and regard the Central Powers as but one. The war can be successfully conducted in no other way.

The same logic would lead also to a declaration of war against Turkey and Bulgaria. They also are the tools of Germany, but they are mere tools and do not yet stand in the direct path of our necessary action. We shall go wherever the necessities of this war carry us, but it seems to me that we should go only where immediate and practical considerations lead us, and not heed any others.

The financial and military measures which must be adopted will suggest themselves as the war and its undertakings develop, but I will take the liberty of proposing to you certain other acts of legislation which seem to me to be needed for the support of the war and for the release of our whole force and energy.

It will be necessary to extend in certain particulars the legislation of the last session with regard to alien enemies, and also necessary, I believe, to create a very definite and particular control over the entrance and departure of all persons into and from the United States.

Legislation should be enacted defining as a criminal offense every wilful violation of the presidential proclamation relating to alien enemies promulgated under section 4067 of the revised statutes and providing appropriate punishments; and women, as well as men, should be included under the terms of the acts placing restraints upon alien enemies.

It is likely that as time goes on many alien enemies will be willing to be fed and housed at the expense of the Government in the detention camps, and it would be the purpose of the legislation I have suggested to confine offenders among them in the penitentiaries and other similar institutions where they could be made to work as other criminals do.

Recent experience has convinced me that the Congress must go further in authorizing the Government to set limits to prices. The law of supply and demand, I am sorry to say, has been replaced by the law of unrestrained selfishness. While we have eliminated profiteering in several branches of industry, it still runs impudently rampant in others. The farmers for example, complain with a great deal of justice that, while the regulation of food prices restricts their incomes, no restraints are placed upon the prices of most of the things they must themselves purchase; and similar inequities obtain on all sides.

It is imperatively necessary that the consideration of the full use of the water power of the country, and also of the consideration of the systematic and yet economical development of such of the natural resources of the country as are still under the control of the Federal Government should be immediately resumed and affirmatively and constructively dealt with at the earliest possible moment. The pressing need of such legislation is daily becoming more obvious.

The legislation proposed at the last session with regard to regulated combinations among our exporters in order to provide for our foreign trade a more effective organization and method of co-operation ought by all means to be completed at this session.

And I beg that the members of the House of Representatives will permit me to express the opinion that it will be impossible to deal in any but a very wasteful and extravagant fashion with the enormous appropriations of the public moneys which must continue to be made if the war is to be properly sustained, unless the House will consent to return to its former practice of initiating and preparing all appropriation bills through a single committee, in order that responsibility may be centered, expenditures standardized and made uniform, and waste and duplication as much as possible avoided.

Additional legislation may also become necessary before the present Congress again adjourns in order to effect the most efficient co-ordination and operation of the railways and other transportation systems of the country; but to that I shall, if circumstances should demand, call the attention of Congress upon another occasion.

If I have overlooked anything that ought to be done for the more effective conduct of the war, your own counsels will supply the omission. What I am perfectly clear about is that in the present session of the Congress our whole attention and energy should be concentrated on the vigorous, rapid and successful prosecution of the great task of winning the war.

We can do this with all the greater zeal and enthusiasm because we know that for us this is a war of high principle, debased by no selfish ambition of conquest or spoliation; because we know, and all the world knows, that we have been forced into it to save the very institutions we live under from corruption and destruction. The purpose of the Central Powers strikes straight at the very heart of everything we believe in; their methods of warfare outrage every principle of humanity and of knightly honor; their intrigue has corrupted the very thought and spirit of many of our people; their sinister and secret diplomacy has sought to take our very territory away from us and disrupt the union of the states. Our safety would be at an end, our honor forever sullied and brought into contempt, were we to permit their triumph. They are striking at the very existence of democracy and liberty.

It is because it is for us a war of high, disinterested purpose, in which all the free peoples of the world are banded together for the vindication of right, a war for the preservation of our nation, of all that it has held dear, of principle and of purpose, that we feel ourselves doubly constrained to propose for its outcome only that which is righteous and of irreproachable intention, for our foes as well as for our friends. The cause being just and holy, the settlement must be of like motive and equality. For this we can fight, but for nothing less noble or less worthy of our traditions. For this cause we entered the war and for this cause will we battle until the last gun is fired.

I have spoken plainly because this seems to me the time when it is most necessary to speak plainly, in order that all the world may know that, even in the heat and ardor of the struggle and when our whole thought is of carrying the war through to its end, we have not forgotten any ideal or principle for which the name of America has been held in honor among the nations and for which it has been our glory to contend in the great generations that went before us. A supreme moment of history has come. The eyes of the people have been opened and they see. The hand of God is laid upon the nations. He will show them favor, I devoutly believe, only if they rise to the clear heights of His own justice and mercy.

Sixth State of the Union address

Woodrow Wilson
December 2, 1918
GENTLEMEN OF THE CONGRESS:

The year that has elapsed since I last stood before you to fulfil my constitutional duty to give to the Congress from time to time information on the state of the Union has been so crowded with great events, great processes, and great results that I cannot hope to give you an adequate picture of its transactions or of the far-reaching changes which have been wrought of our nation and of the world. You have yourselves witnessed these things, as I have. It is too soon to assess them; and we who stand in the midst of them and are part of them are less qualified than men of another generation will be to say what they mean, or even what they have been. But some great outstanding facts are unmistakable and constitute, in a sense, part of the public business with which it is our duty to deal. To state them is to set the stage for the legislative and executive action which must grow out of them and which we have yet to shape and determine.

A year ago we had sent 145,918 men overseas. Since then we have sent 1,950,513, an average of 162,542 each month, the number in fact rising, in May last, to 245,951, in June to 278,760, in July to 307,182, and continuing to reach similar figures in August and September, in August 289,570 and in September 257,438. No such movement of troops ever took place before, across three thousand miles of sea, followed by adequate equipment and supplies, and carried safely through extraordinary dangers of attack,-dangers which were alike strange and infinitely difficult to guard against. In all this movement only seven hundred and fifty-eight men were lost by enemy attack, six hundred and thirty of whom were upon a single English transport which was sunk near the Orkney Islands.

I need not tell you what lay back of this great movement of men and material. It is not invidious to say that back of it lay a supporting organization of the industries of the country and of all its productive activities more complete, more thorough in method and effective in result, more spirited and unanimous in purpose and effort than any other great belligerent had been able to effect. We profited greatly by the experience of the nations which had already been engaged for nearly three years in the exigent and exacting business, their every resource and every executive proficiency taxed to the utmost. We were their pupils. But we learned quickly and acted with a promptness and a readiness of cooperation that justify our great pride that we were able to serve the world with unparalleled energy and quick accomplishment.

But it is not the physical scale and executive efficiency of preparation, supply, equipment and despatch that I would dwell upon, but the mettle and quality of the officers and men we sent over and of the sailors who kept the seas, and the spirit of the nation that stood behind them. No soldiers or sailors ever proved themselves more quickly ready for the test of battle or acquitted themselves with more splendid courage and achievement when put to the test. Those of us who played some part in directing the great processes by which the war was pushed irresistibly forward to the final triumph may now forget all that and delight our thoughts with the story of what our men did. Their officers understood the grim and exacting task they had undertaken and performed it with an audacity, efficiency, and unhesitating courage that touch the story of convoy and battle with imperishable distinction at every turn, whether the enterprise were great or small, from their great chiefs, Pershing and Sims, down to the youngest lieutenant; and their men were worthy of them,-such men as hardly need to be commanded, and go to their terrible adventure blithely and with the quick intelligence of those who know just what it is they would accomplish. I am proud to be the fellow-countryman of men of such stuff and valor. Those of us who stayed at home did our duty; the war could not have been won or the gallant men who fought it given their opportunity to win it otherwise; but for many a long day we shall think ourselves "accurs'd we were not there, and hold our manhoods cheap while any speaks that fought" with these at St. Mihiel or Thierry. The memory of those days of triumphant battle will go with these fortunate men to their graves; and each will have his favorite memory. "Old men forget; yet all shall be forgot, but he'll remember with advantages what feats he did that day!"

What we all thank God for with deepest gratitude is that our men went in force into the line of battle just at the critical moment when the whole fate of the world seemed to hang in the balance and threw their fresh strength into the ranks of freedom in time to turn the whole tide and sweep of the fateful struggle,-turn it once for all, so that thenceforth it was back, back, back for their enemies, always back, never again forward! After that it was only a scant four months before the commanders of the Central Empires knew themselves beaten; and now their very empires are in liquidation!

And throughout it all how fine the spirit of the nation was: what unity of purpose, what untiring zeal! What elevation of purpose ran through all its splendid display of strength, its untiring accomplishment! I have said that those of us who stayed at home to do the work of organization and supply will always wish that we had been with the men whom we sustained by our labor; but we can never be ashamed. It has been an inspiring thing to be here in the midst of fine men who had turned aside from every private interest of their own and devoted the whole of their trained capacity to the tasks that supplied the sinews of the whole great undertaking! The patriotism, the unselfishness, the thoroughgoing devotion and distinguished capacity that marked their toilsome labors, day after day, month after month, have made them fit mates and comrades of the men in the trenches and on the sea. And not the men here in Washington only. They have but directed the vast achievement. Throughout innumerable factories, upon innumerable farms, in the depths of coal mines and iron mines and copper mines, wherever the stuffs of industry were to be obtained and prepared, in the shipyards, on the railways, at the docks, on the sea, in every labor that was needed to sustain the battle lines, men have vied with each other to do their part and do it well. They can look any man-at-arms in the face, and say, We also strove to win and gave the best that was in us to make our fleets and armies sure of their triumph!

And what shall we say of the women,-of their instant intelligence, quickening every task that they touched; their capacity for organization and cooperation, which gave their action discipline and enhanced the effectiveness of everything they attempted; their aptitude at tasks to which they had never before set their hands; their utter self-sacrifice alike in what they did and in what they gave? Their contribution to the great result is beyond appraisal. They have added a new lustre to the annals of American womanhood.

The least tribute we can pay them is to make them the equals of men in political rights as they have proved themselves their equals in every field of practical work they have entered, whether for themselves or for their country. These great days of completed achievement would be sadly marred were we to omit that act of justice. Besides the immense practical services they have rendered the women of the country have been the moving spirits in the systematic economies by which our people have voluntarily assisted to supply the suffering peoples of the world and the armies upon every front with food and everything else that we had that might serve the common cause. The details of such a story can never be fully written, but we carry them at our hearts and thank God that we can say that we are the kinsmen of such.

And now we are sure of the great triumph for which every sacrifice was made. It has come, come in its completeness, and with the pride and inspiration of these days of achievement quick within us, we turn to the tasks of peace again,-a peace secure against the violence of irresponsible monarchs and ambitious military coteries and made ready for a new order, for new foundations of justice and fair dealing.

We are about to give order and organization to this peace not only for ourselves but for the other peoples of the world as well, so far as they will suffer us to serve them. It is international justice that we seek, not domestic safety merely. Our thoughts have dwelt of late upon Europe, upon Asia, upon the near and the far East, very little upon the acts of peace and accommodation that wait to be performed at our own doors. While we are adjusting our relations with the rest of the world is it not of capital importance that we should clear away all grounds of misunderstanding with our immediate neighbors and give proof of the friendship we really feel? I hope that the members of the Senate will permit me to speak once more of the unratified treaty of friendship and adjustment with the Republic of Colombia. I very earnestly urge upon them an early and favorable action upon that vital matter. I believe that they will feel, with me, that the stage of affairs is now set for such action as will be not only just but generous and in the spirit of the new age upon which we have so happily entered.

So far as our domestic affairs are concerned the problem of our return to peace is a problem of economic and industrial readjustment. That problem is less serious for us than it may turn out too he for the nations which have suffered the disarrangements and the losses of war longer than we. Our people, moreover, do not wait to be coached and led. They know their own business, are quick and resourceful at every readjustment, definite in purpose, and self-reliant in action. Any leading strings we might seek to put them in would speedily become hopelessly tangled because they would pay no attention to them and go their own way. All that we can do as their legislative and executive servants is to mediate the process of change here, there, and elsewhere as we may. I have heard much counsel as to the plans that should be formed and personally conducted to a happy consummation, but from no quarter have I seen any general scheme of "reconstruction" emerge which I thought it likely we could force our spirited business men and self-reliant laborers to accept with due pliancy and obedience.

While the war lasted we set up many agencies by which to direct the industries of the country in the services it was necessary for them to render, by which to make sure of an abundant supply of the materials needed, by which to check undertakings that could for the time be dispensed with and stimulate those that were most serviceable in war, by which to gain for the purchasing departments of the Government a certain control over the prices of essential articles and materials, by which to restrain trade with alien enemies, make the most of the available shipping, and systematize financial transactions, both public and private, so that there would be no unnecessary conflict or confusion,-by which, in short, to put every material energy of the country in harness to draw the common load and make of us one team in the accomplishment of a great task. But the moment we knew the armistice to have been signed we took the harness off. Raw materials upon which the Government had kept its hand for fear there should not be enough for the industries that supplied the armies have been released and put into the general market again. Great industrial plants whose whole output and machinery had been taken over for the uses of the Government have been set free to return to the uses to which they were put before the war. It has not been possible to remove so readily or so quickly the control of foodstuffs and of shipping, because the world has still to be fed from our granaries and the ships are still needed to send supplies to our men overseas and to bring the men back as fast as the disturbed conditions on the other side of the water permit; but even there restraints are being relaxed as much as possible and more and more as the weeks go by.

Never before have there been agencies in existence in this country which knew so much of the field of supply, of labor, and of industry as the War Industries Board, the War Trade Board, the Labor Department, the Food Administration, and the Fuel Administration have known since their labors became thoroughly systematized; and they have not been isolated agencies; they have been directed by men who represented the permanent Departments of the Government and so have been the centres of unified and cooperative action. It has been the policy of the Executive, therefore, since the armistice was assured (which is in effect a complete submission of the enemy) to put the knowledge of these bodies at the disposal of the business men of the country and to offer their intelligent mediation at every point and in every matter where it was desired. It is surprising how fast the process of return to a peace footing has moved in the three weeks since the fighting stopped. It promises to outrun any inquiry that may be instituted and any aid that may be offered. It will not be easy to direct it any better than it will direct itself. The American business man is of quick initiative.

The ordinary and normal processes of private initiative will not, however, provide immediate employment for all of the men of our returning armies. Those who are of trained capacity, those who are skilled workmen, those who have acquired familiarity with established businesses, those who are ready and willing to go to the farms, all those whose aptitudes are known or will be sought out by employers will find no difficulty, it is safe to say, in finding place and employment. But there will be others who will be at a loss where to gain a livelihood unless pains are taken to guide them and put them in the way of work. There will be a large floating residuum of labor which should not be left wholly to shift for itself. It seems to me important, therefore, that the development of public works of every sort should be promptly resumed, in order that opportunities should be created for unskilled labor in particular, and that plans should be made for such developments of our unused lands and our natural resources as we have hitherto lacked stimulation to undertake.

I particularly direct your attention to the very practical plans which the Secretary of the Interior has developed in his annual report and before your Committees for the reclamation of arid, swamp, and cutover lands which might, if the States were willing and able to cooperate, redeem some three hundred million acres of land for cultivation. There are said to be fifteen or twenty million acres of land in the West, at present arid, for whose reclamation water is available, if properly conserved. There are about two hundred and thirty million acres from which the forests have been cut but which have never yet been cleared for the plow and which lie waste and desolate. These lie scattered all over the Union. And there are nearly eighty million acres of land that lie under swamps or subject to periodical overflow or too wet for anything but grazing, which it is perfectly feasible to drain and protect and redeem. The Congress can at once direct thousands of the returning soldiers to the reclamation of the arid lands which it has already undertaken, if it will but enlarge the plans and appropriations which it has entrusted to the Department of the Interior. It is possible in dealing with our unused land to effect a great rural and agricultural development which will afford the best sort of opportunity to men who want to help themselves and the Secretary of the Interior has thought the possible methods out in a way which is worthy of your most friendly attention.

I have spoken of the control which must yet for a while, perhaps for a long long while, be exercised over shipping because of the priority of service to which our forces overseas are entitled and which should also be accorded the shipments which are to save recently liberated peoples from starvation and many devastated regions from permanent ruin. May I not say a special word about the needs of Belgium and northern France? No sums of money paid by way of indemnity will serve of themselves to save them from hopeless disadvantage for years to come. Something more must be done than merely find the money. If they had money and raw materials in abundance to-morrow they could not resume their place in the industry of the world to-morrow,-the very important place they held before the flame of war swept across them. Many of their factories are razed to the ground. Much of their machinery is destroyed or has been taken away. Their people are scattered and many of their best workmen are dead. Their markets will be taken by others, if they are not in some special way assisted to rebuild their factories and replace their lost instruments of manufacture. They should not be left to the vicissitudes of the sharp competition for materials and for industrial facilities which is now to set in. I hope, therefore, that the Congress will not be unwilling, if it should become necessary, to grant to some such agency as the War Trade Board the right to establish priorities of export and supply for the benefit of these people whom we have been so happy to assist in saving from the German terror and whom we must not now thoughtlessly leave to shift for themselves in a pitiless competitive market.

For the steadying, and facilitation of our own domestic business readjustments nothing is more important than the immediate determination of the taxes that are to be levied for 1918, 1919, and 1920. As much of the burden of taxation must be lifted from business as sound methods of financing the Government will permit, and those who conduct the great essential industries of the country must be told as exactly as possible what obligations to the Government they will be expected to meet in the years immediately ahead of them. It will be of serious consequence to the country to delay removing all uncertainties in this matter a single day longer than the right processes of debate justify. It is idle to talk of successful and confident business reconstruction before those uncertainties are resolved.

If the war had continued it would have been necessary to raise at least eight billion dollars by taxation payable in the year 1919; but the war has ended and I agree with the Secretary of the Treasury that it will be safe to reduce the amount to six billions. An immediate rapid decline in the expenses of the Government is not to be looked for. Contracts made for war supplies will, indeed, be rapidly cancelled and liquidated, but their immediate liquidation will make heavy drains on the Treasury for the months just ahead of us. The maintenance of our forces on the other side of the sea is still necessary. A considerable proportion of those forces must remain in Europe during the period of occupation, and those which are brought home will be transported and demobilized at heavy expense for months to come. The interest on our war debt must of course be paid and provision made for the retirement of the obligations of the Government which represent it. But these demands will of course fall much below what a continuation of military operations would have entailed and six billions should suffice to supply a sound foundation for the financial operations of the year.

I entirely concur with the Secretary of the Treasury in recommending that the two billions needed in addition to the four billions provided by existing law be obtained from the profits which have accrued and shall accrue from war contracts and distinctively war business, but that these taxes be confined to the war profits accruing in 1918, or in 1919 from business originating in war contracts. I urge your acceptance of his recommendation that provision be made now, not subsequently, that the taxes to be paid in 1920 should be reduced from six to four billions. Any arrangements less definite than these would add elements of doubt and confusion to the critical period of industrial readjustment through which the country must now immediately pass, and which no true friend of the nation's essential business interests can afford to be responsible for creating or prolonging. Clearly determined conditions, clearly and simply charted, are indispensable to the economic revival and rapid industrial development which may confidently be expected if we act now and sweep all interrogation points away.

I take it for granted that the Congress will carry out the naval programme which was undertaken before we entered the war. The Secretary of the Navy has submitted to your Committees for authorization that part of the programme which covers the building plans of the next three years. These plans have been prepared along the lines and in accordance with the policy which the Congress established, not under the exceptional conditions of the war, but with the intention of adhering to a definite method of development for the navy. I earnestly recommend the uninterrupted pursuit of that policy. It would clearly be unwise for us to attempt to adjust our programmes to a future world policy as yet undetermined.

The question which causes me the greatest concern is the question of the policy to be adopted towards the railroads. I frankly turn to you for counsel upon it. I have no confident judgment of my own. I do not see how any thoughtful man can have who knows anything of the complexity of the problem. It is a problem which must be studied, studied immediately, and studied without bias or prejudice. Nothing can be gained by becoming partisans of any particular plan of settlement.

It was necessary that the administration of the railways should be taken over by the Government so long as the war lasted. It would have been impossible otherwise to establish and carry through under a single direction the necessary priorities of shipment. It would have been impossible otherwise to combine maximum production at the factories and mines and farms with the maximum possible car supply to take the products to the ports and markets; impossible to route troop shipments and freight shipments without regard to the advantage or-disadvantage of the roads employed; impossible to subordinate, when necessary, all questions of convenience to the public necessity; impossible to give the necessary financial support to the roads from the public treasury. But all these necessities have now been served, and the question is, What is best for the railroads and for the public in the future?

Exceptional circumstances and exceptional methods of administration were not needed to convince us that the railroads were not equal to the immense tasks of transportation imposed upon them by the rapid and continuous development of the industries of the country. We knew that already. And we knew that they were unequal to it partly because their full cooperation was rendered impossible by law and their competition made obligatory, so that it has been impossible to assign to them severally the traffic which could best be carried by their respective lines in the interest of expedition and national economy.

We may hope, I believe, for the formal conclusion of the war by treaty by the time Spring has come. The twenty-one months to which the present control of the railways is limited after formal proclamation of peace shall have been made will run at the farthest, I take it for granted, only to the January of 1921. The full equipment of the railways which the federal administration had planned could not be completed within any such period. The present law does not permit the use of the revenues of the several roads for the execution of such plans except by formal contract with their directors, some of whom will consent while some will not, and therefore does not afford sufficient authority to undertake improvements upon the scale upon which it would be necessary to undertake them. Every approach to this difficult subject-matter of decision brings us face to face, therefore, with this unanswered question: What is it right that we should do with the railroads, in the interest of the public and in fairness to their owners?

Let me say at once that I have no answer ready. The only thing that is perfectly clear to me is that it is not fair either to the public or to the owners of the railroads to leave the question unanswered and that it will presently become my duty to relinquish control of the roads, even before the expiration of the statutory period, unless there should appear some clear prospect in the meantime of a legislative solution. Their release would at least produce one element of a solution, namely certainty and a quick stimulation of private initiative.

I believe that it will be serviceable for me to set forth as explicitly as possible the alternative courses that lie open to our choice. We can simply release the roads and go back to the old conditions of private management, unrestricted competition, and multiform regulation by both state and federal authorities; or we can go to the opposite extreme and establish complete government control, accompanied, if necessary, by actual government ownership; or we can adopt an intermediate course of modified private control, under a more unified and affirmative public regulation and under such alterations of the law as will permit wasteful competition to be avoided and a considerable degree of unification of administration to be effected, as, for example, by regional corporations under which the railways of definable areas would be in effect combined in single systems.

The one conclusion that I am ready to state with confidence is that it would be a disservice alike to the country and to the owners of the railroads to return to the old conditions unmodified. Those are conditions of restraint without development. There is nothing affirmative or helpful about them. What the country chiefly needs is that all its means of transportation should be developed, its railways, its waterways, its highways, and its countryside roads. Some new element of policy, therefore, is absolutely necessary--necessary for the service of the public, necessary for the release of credit to those who are administering the railways, necessary for the protection of their security holders. The old policy may be changed much or little, but surely it cannot wisely be left as it was. I hope that the Con will have a complete and impartial study of the whole problem instituted at once and prosecuted as rapidly as possible. I stand ready and anxious to release the roads from the present control and I must do so at a very early date if by waiting until the statutory limit of time is reached I shall be merely prolonging the period of doubt and uncertainty which is hurtful to every interest concerned.

I welcome this occasion to announce to the Congress my purpose to join in Paris the representatives of the governments with which we have been associated in the war against the Central Empires for the purpose of discussing with them the main features of the treaty of peace. I realize the great inconveniences that will attend my leaving the country, particularly at this time, but the conclusion that it was my paramount duty to go has been forced upon me by considerations which I hope will seem as conclusive to you as they have seemed to me.

The Allied governments have accepted the bases of peace which I outlined to the Congress on the eighth of January last, as the Central Empires also have, and very reasonably desire my personal counsel in their interpretation and application, and it is highly desirable that I should give it in order that the sincere desire of our Government to contribute without selfish purpose of any kind to settlements that will be of common benefit to all the nations concerned may be made fully manifest. The peace settlements which are now to be agreed upon are of transcendent importance both to us and to the rest of the world, and I know of no business or interest which should take precedence of them. The gallant men of our armed forces on land and sea have consciously fought for the ideals which they knew to be the ideals of their country; I have sought to express those ideals; they have accepted my statements of them as the substance of their own thought and purpose, as the associated governments have accepted them; I owe it to them to see to it, so far as in me lies, that no false or mistaken interpretation is put upon them, and no possible effort omitted to realize them. It is now my duty to play my full part in making good what they offered their life's blood to obtain. I can think of no call to service which could transcend this.

I shall be in close touch with you and with affairs on this side the water, and you will know all that I do. At my request, the French and English governments have absolutely removed the censorship of cable news which until within a fortnight they had maintained and there is now no censorship whatever exercised at this end except upon attempted trade communications with enemy countries. It has been necessary to keep an open wire constantly available between Paris and the Department of State and another between France and the Department of War. In order that this might be done with the least possible interference with the other uses of the cables, I have temporarily taken over the control of both cables in order that they may be used as a single system. I did so at the advice of the most experienced cable officials, and I hope that the results will justify my hope that the news of the next few months may pass with the utmost freedom and with the least possible delay from each side of the sea to the other.

May I not hope, Gentlemen of the Congress, that in the delicate tasks I shall have to perform on the other side of the sea, in my efforts truly and faithfully to interpret the principles and purposes of the country we love, I may have the encouragement and the added strength of your united support? I realize the magnitude and difficulty of the duty I am undertaking; I am poignantly aware of its grave responsibilities. I am the servant of the nation. I can have no private thought or purpose of my own in performing such an errand. I go to give the best that is in me to the common settlements which I must now assist in arriving at in conference with the other working heads of the associated governments. I shall count upon your friendly countenance and encouragement. I shall not be inaccessible. The cables and the wireless will render me available for any counsel or service you may desire of me, and I shall be happy in the thought that I am constantly in touch with the weighty matters of domestic policy with which we shall have to deal. I shall make my absence as brief as possible and shall hope to return with the happy assurance that it has been possible to translate into action the great ideals for which America has striven.

Seventh State of the Union address

Woodrow Wilson
December 2, 1919
TO THE SENATE AND HOUSE OF REPRESENTATIVES:
I sincerely regret that I cannot be present at the opening of this session of the Congress. I am thus prevented from presenting in as direct a way as I could wish the many questions that are pressing for solution at this time. Happily, I have had the advantage of the advice of the heads of the several executive departments who have kept in close touch with affairs in their detail and whose thoughtful recommendations I earnestly second.

In the matter of the railroads and the readjustment of their affairs growing out of Federal control, I shall take the liberty at a later date of addressing you.

I hope that Congress will bring to a conclusion at this session legislation looking to the establishment of a budget system. That there should be one single authority responsible for the making of all appropriations and that appropriations should be made not independently of each other, but with reference to one single comprehensive plan of expenditure properly related to the nation's income, there can be no doubt I believe the burden of preparing the budget must, in the nature of the case, if the work is to be properly done and responsibility concentrated instead of divided, rest upon the executive. The budget so prepared should be submitted to and approved or amended by a single committee of each House of Congress and no single appropriation should be made by the Congress, except such as may have been included in the budget prepared by the executive or added by the particular committee of Congress charged with the budget legislation.

Another and not less important aspect of the problem is the ascertainment of the economy and efficiency with which the moneys appropriated are expended. Under existing law the only audit is for the purpose of ascertaining whether expenditures have been lawfully made within the appropriations. No one is authorized or equipped to ascertain whether the money has been spent wisely, economically and effectively. The auditors should be highly trained officials with permanent tenure in the Treasury Department, free of obligations to or motives of consideration for this or any subsequent administration, and authorized and empowered to examine into and make report upon the methods employed and the results obtained by the executive departments of the Government. Their reports should be made to the Congress and to the Secretary of the Treasury.

I trust that the Congress will give its immediate consideration to the problem of future taxation. Simplification of the income and profits taxes has become an immediate necessity. These taxes performed indispensable service during the war. They must, however, be simplified, not only to save the taxpayer inconvenience and expense, but in order that his liability may be made certain and definite.

With reference to the details of the Revenue Law, the Secretary of the Treasury and the Commissioner of Internal Revenue will lay before you for your consideration certain amendments necessary or desirable in connection with the administration of the law-recommendations which have my approval and support. It is of the utmost importance that in dealing with this matter the present law should not be disturbed so far as regards taxes for the calendar year 1920 payable in the calendar year 1921. The Congress might well consider whether the higher rates of income and profits taxes can in peace times be effectively productive of revenue, and whether they may not, on the contrary, be destructive of business activity and productive of waste and inefficiency. There is a point at which in peace times high rates of income and profits taxes discourage energy, remove the incentive to new enterprises, encourage extravagant expenditures and produce industrial stagnation with consequent unemployment and other attendant evils.

The problem is not an easy one. A fundamental change has taken place with reference to the position of America in the world's affairs. The prejudice and passions engendered by decades of controversy between two schools of political and economic thought,-the one believers in protection of American industries, the other believers in tariff for revenue only,-must be subordinated to the single consideration of the public interest in the light of utterly changed conditions. Before the war America was heavily the debtor of the rest of the world and the interest payments she had to make to foreign countries on American securities held abroad, the expenditures of American travelers abroad and the ocean freight charges she had to pay to others, about balanced the value of her pre-war favorable balance of trade. During the war America's exports have been greatly stimulated, and increased prices have increased their value. On the other hand, she has purchased a large proportion of the American securities previously held abroad, has loaned some $9,000,000,000 to foreign governments, and has built her own ships. Our favorable balance of trade has thus been greatly increased and Europe has been deprived of the means of meeting it heretofore existing. Europe can have only three ways of meeting the favorable balance of trade in peace times: by imports into this country of gold or of goods, or by establishing new credits. Europe is in no position at the present time to ship gold to us nor could we contemplate large further imports of gold into this country without concern. The time has nearly passed for international governmental loans and it will take time to develop in this country a market for foreign securities. Anything, therefore, which would tend to prevent foreign countries from settling for our exports by shipments of goods into this country could only have the effect of preventing them from paying for our exports and therefore of preventing the exports from being made. The productivity of the country, greatly stimulated by the war, must find an outlet by exports to foreign countries, and any measures taken to prevent imports will inevitably curtail exports, force curtailment of production, load the banking machinery of the country with credits to carry unsold products and produce industrial stagnation and unemployment. If we want to sell, we must be prepared to buy. Whatever, therefore, may have been our views during the period of growth of American business concerning tariff legislation, we must now adjust our own economic life to a changed condition growing out of the fact that American business is full grown and that America is the greatest capitalist in the world.

No policy of isolation will satisfy the growing needs and opportunities of America. The provincial standards and policies of the past, which have held American business as if in a straitjacket, must yield and give way to the needs and exigencies of the new day in which we live, a day full of hope and promise for American business, if we will but take advantage of the opportunities that are ours for the asking. The recent war has ended our isolation and thrown upon us a great duty and responsibility. The United States must share the expanding world market. The United States desires for itself only equal opportunity with the other nations of the world, and that through the process of friendly cooperation and fair competition the legitimate interests of the nations concerned may be successfully and equitably adjusted.

There are other matters of importance upon which I urged action at the last session of Congress which are still pressing for solution. I am sure it is not necessary for me again to remind you that there is one immediate and very practicable question resulting from the war which we should meet in the most liberal spirit. It is a matter of recognition and relief to our soldiers. I can do no better than to quote from my last message urging this very action:

"We must see to it that our returning soldiers are assisted in every practicable way to find the places for which they are fitted in the daily work of the country. This can be done by developing and maintaining upon an adequate scale the admirable organization created by the Department of Labor for placing men seeking work; and it can also be done, in at least one very great field, by creating new opportunities for individual enterprise. The Secretary of the Interior has pointed out the way by which returning soldiers may be helped to find and take up land in the hitherto undeveloped regions of the country which the Federal Government has already prepared, or can readily prepare, for cultivation and also on many of the cutover or neglected areas which lie within the limits of the older states; and I once more take the liberty of recommending very urgently that his plans shall receive the immediate and substantial support of the Congress."

In the matter of tariff legislation, I beg to call your attention to the statements contained in my last message urging legislation with reference to the establishment of the chemical and dyestuffs industry in America:

"Among the industries to which special consideration should be given is that of the manufacture of dyestuffs and related chemicals. Our complete dependence upon German supplies before the war made the interruption of trade a cause of exceptional economic disturbance. The close relation between the manufacture of dyestuffs, on the one hand, and of explosive and poisonous gases, on the other, moreover, has given the industry an exceptional significance and value. Although the United States will gladly and unhesitatingly join in the programme of international disarmament, it will, nevertheless, be a policy of obvious prudence to make certain of the successful maintenance of many strong and well-equipped chemical plants. The German chemical industry, with which we will be brought into competition, was and may well be again, a thoroughly knit monopoly capable of exercising a competition of a peculiarly insidious and dangerous kind."

During the war the farmer performed a vital and willing service to the nation. By materially increasing the production of his land, he supplied America and the Allies with the increased amounts of food necessary to keep their immense armies in the field. He indispensably helped to win the war. But there is now scarcely less need of increasing the production in food -and the necessaries of life. I ask the Congress to consider means of encouraging effort along these lines. The importance of doing everything possible to promote production along economical lines, to improve marketing, and to make rural life more attractive and healthful, is obvious. I would urge approval of the plans already proposed to the Congress by the Secretary of Agriculture, to secure the essential facts required for the proper study of this question, through the proposed enlarged programmes for farm management studies and crop estimates. I would urge, also, the continuance of Federal participation in the building of good roads, under the terms of existing law and under the direction of present agencies; the need of further action on the part of the States and the Federal Government to preserve and develop our forest resources, especially through the practice of better forestry methods on private holdings and the extension of the publicly owned forests; better support for country schools and the more definite direction of their courses of study along lines related to rural problems; and fuller provision for sanitation in rural districts and the building up of needed hospital and medical facilities in these localities. Perhaps the way might be cleared for many of these desirable reforms by a fresh, comprehensive survey made of rural conditions by a conference composed of representatives of the farmers and of the agricultural agencies responsible for leadership.

I would call your attention to the widespread condition of political restlessness in our body politic. The causes of this unrest, while various and complicated, are superficial rather than deep-seated. Broadly, they arise from or are connected with the failure on the part of our Government to arrive speedily at a just and permanent peace permitting return to normal conditions, from the transfusion of radical theories from seething European centers pending such delay, from heartless profiteering resulting in the increase of the cost of living, and lastly from the machinations of passionate and malevolent agitators. With the return to normal conditions, this unrest will rapidly disappear. In the meantime, it does much evil. It seems to me that in dealing with this situation Congress should not be impatient or drastic but should seek rather to remove the causes. It should endeavor to bring our country back speedily to a peace basis, with ameliorated living conditions under the minimum of restrictions upon personal liberty that is consistent with our reconstruction problems. And it should arm the Federal Government with power to deal in its criminal courts with those persons who by violent methods would abrogate our time-tested institutions. With the free expression of opinion and with the advocacy of orderly political change, however fundamental, there must be no interference, but towards passion and malevolence tending to incite crime and insurrection under guise of political evolution there should be no leniency. Legislation to this end has been recommended by the Attorney General and should be enacted. In this direct connection, I would call your attention to my recommendations on August 8th, pointing out legislative measures which would be effective in controlling and bringing down the present cost of living, which contributes so largely to this unrest. On only one of these recommendations has the Congress acted. If the Government's campaign is to be effective, it is necessary that the other steps suggested should be acted on at once.

I renew and strongly urge the necessity of the extension of the present Food Control Act as to the period of time in which it shall remain in operation. The Attorney General has submitted a bill providing for an extension of this Act for a period of six months. As it now stands, it is limited in operation to the period of the war and becomes inoperative upon the formal proclamation of peace. It is imperative that it should be extended at once. The Department of justice has built up extensive machinery for the purpose of enforcing its provisions; all of which must be abandoned upon the conclusion of peace unless the provisions of this Act are extended.

During this period the Congress will have an opportunity to make similar permanent provisions and regulations with regard to all goods destined for interstate commerce and to exclude them from interstate shipment, if the requirements of the law are not compiled with. Some such regulation is imperatively necessary. The abuses that have grown up in the manipulation of prices by the withholding of foodstuffs and other necessaries of life cannot otherwise be effectively prevented. There can be no doubt of either the necessity of the legitimacy of such measures.

As I pointed out in my last message, publicity can accomplish a great deal in this campaign. The aims of the Government must be clearly brought to the attention of the consuming public, civic organizations and state officials, who are in a position to lend their assistance to our efforts. You have made available funds with which to carry on this campaign, but there is no provision in the law authorizing their expenditure for the purpose of making the public fully informed about the efforts of the Government. Specific recommendation has been made by the Attorney General in this regard. I would strongly urge upon you its immediate adoption, as it constitutes one of the preliminary steps to this campaign.

I also renew my recommendation that the Congress pass a law regulating cold storage as it is regulated, for example, by the laws of the State of New Jersey, which limit the time during which goods may be kept in storage, prescribe the method of disposing of them if kept beyond the permitted period, and require that goods released from storage shall in all cases bear the date of their receipt. It would materially add to the serviceability of the law, for the purpose we now have in view, if it were also prescribed that all goods released from storage for interstate shipment should have plainly marked upon each package the selling or market price at which they went into storage. By this means the purchaser would always be able to learn what profits stood between him and the producer or the wholesale dealer.

I would also renew my recommendation that all goods destined for interstate commerce should in every case, where their form or package makes it possible, be plainly marked with the price at which they left the hands of the producer.

We should formulate a law requiring a Federal license of all corporations engaged in interstate commerce and embodying in the license or in the conditions under which it is to be issued, specific regulations designed to secure competitive selling and prevent unconscionable profits in the method of marketing. Such a law would afford a welcome opportunity to effect other much needed reforms in the business of interstate shipment and in the methods of corporations which are engaged in it; but for the moment I confine my recommendations to the object immediately in hand, which is to lower the cost of living.

No one who has observed the march of events in the last year can fail to note the absolute need of a definite programme to bring about an improvement in the conditions of labor. There can be no settled conditions leading to increased production and a reduction in the cost of living if labor and capital are to be antagonists instead of partners. Sound thinking and an honest desire to serve the interests of the whole nation, as distinguished from the interests of a class, must be applied to the solution of this great and pressing problem. The failure of other nations to consider this matter in a vigorous way has produced bitterness and jealousies and antagonisms, the food of radicalism. The only way to keep men from agitating against grievances is to remove the grievances. An unwillingness even to discuss these matters produces only dissatisfaction and gives comfort to the extreme elements in our country which endeavor to stir up disturbances in order to provoke governments to embark upon a course of retaliation and repression. The seed of revolution is repression. The remedy for these things must not be negative in character. It must be constructive. It must comprehend the general interest. The real antidote for the unrest which manifests itself is not suppression, but a deep consideration of the wrongs that beset our national life and the application of a remedy.

Congress has already shown its willingness to deal with these industrial wrongs by establishing the eight-hour day as the standard in every field of labor. It has sought to find a way to prevent child labor. It has served the whole country by leading the way in developing the means of preserving and safeguarding lives and health in dangerous industries. It must now help in the difficult task of finding a method that will bring about a genuine democratization of industry, based upon the full recognition of the right of those who work, in whatever rank, to participate in some organic way in every decision which directly affects their welfare. It is with this purpose in mind that I called a conference to meet in Washington on December 1st, to consider these problems in all their broad aspects, with the idea of bringing about a better understanding between these two interests.

The great unrest throughout the world, out of which has emerged a demand for an immediate consideration of the difficulties between capital and labor, bids us put our own house in order. Frankly, there can be no permanent and lasting settlements between capital and labor which do not recognize the fundamental concepts for which labor has been struggling through the years. The whole world gave its recognition and endorsement to these fundamental purposes in the League of Notions. The statesmen gathered at Versailles recognized the fact that world stability could not be had by reverting to industrial standards and conditions against which the average workman of the world had revolted. It is, therefore, the task of the states men of this new day of change and readjustment to recognize world conditions and to seek to bring about, through legislation, conditions that will mean the ending of age-long antagonisms between capital and labor and that will hopefully lead to the building up of a comradeship which will result not only in greater contentment among the mass of workmen but also bring about a greater production and a greater prosperity to business itself.

To analyze the particulars in the demands of labor is to admit the justice of their complaint in many matters that lie at their basis. The workman demands an adequate wage, sufficient to permit him to live in comfort, unhampered by the fear of poverty and want in his old age. He demands the right to live and the right to work amidst sanitary surroundings, both in home and in workshop, surroundings that develop and do not retard his own health and wellbeing; and the right to provide for his children's wants in the matter of health and education. In other words, it is his desire to make the conditions of his life and the lives of those dear to him tolerable and easy to bear.

The establishment of the principles regarding labor laid down ill the covenant of the League of Nations offers us the way to industrial peace and conciliation. No other road lies open to us. Not to pursue this one is longer to invite enmities, bitterness, and antagonisms which in the end only lead to industrial and social disaster. The unwilling workman is not a profitable servant. An employee whose industrial life is hedged about by hard and unjust conditions, which he did not create and over which he has no control, lacks that fine spirit of enthusiasm and volunteer effort which are the necessary ingredients of a great producing entity. Let us be frank about this solemn matter. The evidences of world-wide unrest which manifest themselves in violence throughout the world bid us pause and consider the means to be found to stop the spread of this contagious thing before it saps the very vitality of the nation itself. Do we gain strength by withholding the remedy? Or is it not the business of statesmen to treat these manifestations of unrest which meet us on every hand as evidences of an economic disorder and to apply constructive remedies wherever necessary, being sure that in the application of the remedy we touch not the vital tissues of our industrial and economic life? There can be no recession of the tide of unrest until constructive instrumentalities are set up to stem that tide.

Governments must recognize the right of men collectively to bargain for humane objects that have at their base the mutual protection and welfare of those engaged in all industries. Labor must not be longer treated as a commodity. It must be regarded as the activity of human beings, possessed of deep yearnings and desires. The business man gives his best thought to the repair and replenishment of his machinery, so that its usefulness will not be impaired and its power to produce may always be at its height and kept in full vigor and motion. No less regard ought to be paid to the human machine, which after all propels the machinery of the world and is the great dynamic force that lies back of all industry and progress. Return to the old standards of wage and industry in employment are unthinkable. The terrible tragedy of war which has just ended and which has brought the world to the verge of chaos and disaster would be in vain if there should ensue a return to the conditions of the past. Europe itself, whence has come the unrest which now holds the world at bay, is an example of standpatism in these vital human matters which America might well accept as an example, not to be followed but studiously to be avoided. Europe made labor the differential, and the price of it all is enmity and antagonism and prostrated industry, The right of labor to live in peace and comfort must be recognized by governments and America should be the first to lay the foundation stones upon which industrial peace shall be built.

Labor not only is entitled to an adequate wage, but capital should receive a reasonable return upon its investment and is entitled to protection at the hands of the Government in every emergency. No Government worthy of the name can "play" these elements against each other, for there is a mutuality of interest between them which the Government must seek to express and to safeguard at all cost.

The right of individuals to strike is inviolate and ought not to be interfered with by any process of Government, but there is a predominant right and that is the right of the Government to protect all of its people and to assert its power and majesty against the challenge of any class. The Government, when it asserts that right, seeks not to antagonize a class but simply to defend the right of the whole people as against the irreparable harm and injury that might be done by the attempt by any class to usurp a power that only Government itself has a right to exercise as a protection to all.

In the matter of international disputes which have led to war, statesmen have sought to set up as a remedy arbitration for war. Does this not point the way for the settlement of industrial disputes, by the establishment of a tribunal, fair and just alike to all, which will settle industrial disputes which in the past have led to war and disaster? America, witnessing the evil consequences which have followed out of such disputes between these contending forces, must not admit itself impotent to deal with these matters by means of peaceful processes. Surely, there must be some method of bringing together in a council of peace and amity these two great interests, out of which will come a happier day of peace and cooperation, a day that will make men more hopeful and enthusiastic in their various tasks, that will make for more comfort and happiness in living and a more tolerable condition among all classes of men. Certainly human intelligence can devise some acceptable tribunal for adjusting the differences between capital and labor.

This is the hour of test and trial for America. By her prowess and strength, and the indomitable courage of her soldiers, she demonstrated her power to vindicate on foreign battlefields her conceptions of liberty and justice. Let not her influence as a mediator between capital and labor be weakened and her own failure to settle matters of purely domestic concern be proclaimed to the world. There are those in this country who threaten direct action to force their will, upon a majority. Russia today, with its blood and terror, is a painful object lesson of the power of minorities. It makes little difference what minority it is; whether capital or labor, or any other class; no sort of privilege will ever be permitted to dominate this country. We are a partnership or nothing that is worth while. We are a democracy, where the majority are the masters, or all the hopes and purposes of the men who founded this government have been defeated and forgotten. In America there is but one way by which great reforms can be accomplished and the relief sought by classes obtained, and that is through the orderly processes of representative government. Those who would propose any other method of reform are enemies of this country. America will not be daunted by threats nor lose her composure or calmness in these distressing times. We can afford, in the midst of this day of passion and unrest, to be self-contained and sure. The instrument of all reform in America is the ballot. The road to economic and social reform in America is the straight road of justice to all classes and conditions of men. Men have but to follow this road to realize the full fruition of their objects and purposes. Let those beware who would take the shorter road of disorder and revolution. The right road is the road of justice and orderly process.

Eighth State of the Union address

Woodrow Wilson
December 7, 1920
GENTLEMEN OF THE CONGRESS:
When I addressed myself to performing the duty laid upon the President by the Constitution to present to you an annual report on the state of the Union, I found my thought dominated by an immortal sentence of Abraham Lincoln's--"Let us have faith that right makes might, and in that faith let us dare to do our duty as we understand it"–a sentence immortal because it embodies in a form of utter simplicity and purity the essential faith of the nation, the faith in which it was conceived, and the faith in which it has grown to glory and power. With that faith and the birth of a nation founded upon it came the hope into the world that a new order would prevail throughout the affairs of mankind, an order in which reason and right would take precedence over covetousness and force; and I believe that I express the wish and purpose of every thoughtful American when I say that this sentence marks for us in the plainest manner the part we should play alike in the arrangement of our domestic affairs and in our exercise of influence upon the affairs of the world.

By this faith, and by this faith alone, can the world be lifted out of its present confusion and despair. It was this faith which prevailed over the wicked force of Germany. You will remember that the beginning of the end of the war came when the German people found themselves face to face with the conscience of the world and realized that right was everywhere arrayed against the wrong that their government was attempting to perpetrate. I think, therefore, that it is true to say that this was the faith which won the war. Certainly this is the faith with which our gallant men went into the field and out upon the seas to make sure of victory.

This is the mission upon which Democracy came into the world. Democracy is an assertion of the right of the individual to live and to be treated justly as against any attempt on the part of any combination of individuals to make laws which will overburden him or which will destroy his equality among his fellows in the matter of right or privilege; and I think we all realize that the day has come when Democracy is being put upon its final test. The Old World is just now suffering from a wanton rejection of the principle of democracy and a substitution of the principle of autocracy as asserted in the name, but without the authority and sanction, of the multitude. This is the time of all others when Democracy should prove its purity and its spiritual power to prevail. It is surely the manifest destiny of the United States to lead in the attempt to make this spirit prevail.

There are two ways in which the United States can assist to accomplish this great object. First, by offering the example within her own borders of the will and power of Democracy to make and enforce laws which are unquestionably just and which are equal in their administration-laws which secure its full right to Labor and yet at the same time safeguard the integrity of property, and particularly of that property which is devoted to the development of industry and the increase of the necessary wealth of the world. Second, by standing for right and justice as toward individual nations. The law of Democracy is for the protection of the weak, and the influence of every democracy in the world should be for the protection of the weak nation, the nation which is struggling toward its right and toward its proper recognition and privilege in the family of nations.

The United States cannot refuse this role of champion without putting the stigma of rejection upon the great and devoted men who brought its government into existence and established it in the face of almost universal opposition and intrigue, even in the face of wanton force, as, for example, against the Orders in Council of Great Britain and the arbitrary Napoleonic decrees which involved us in what we know as the War of 1812.

I urge you to consider that the display of an immediate disposition on the part of the Congress to remedy any injustices or evils that may have shown themselves in our own national life will afford the most effectual offset to the forces of chaos and tyranny which are playing so disastrous a part in the fortunes of the free peoples of more than one part of the world. The United States is of necessity the sample democracy of the world, and the triumph of Democracy depends upon its success.

Recovery from the disturbing and sometimes disastrous effects of the late war has been exceedingly slow on the other side of the water, and has given promise, I venture-to say, of early completion only in our own fortunate country; but even with us the recovery halts and is impeded at times, and there are immediately serviceable acts of legislation which it seems to me we ought to attempt, to assist that recovery and prove the indestructible recuperative force of a great government of the people. One of these is to prove that a great democracy can keep house as successfully and in as business-like a fashion as any other government. It seems to me that the first step toward providing this is to supply ourselves with a systematic method of handling our estimates and expenditures and bringing them to the point where they will not be an unnecessary strain upon our income or necessitate unreasonable taxation; in other words, a workable budget system. And I respectfully suggest that two elements are essential to such a system-namely, not only that the proposal of appropriations should be in the hands of a single body, such as a single appropriations committee in each house of the Congress, but also that this body should be brought into such cooperation with the Departments of the Government and with the Treasury of the United States as would enable it to act upon a complete conspectus of the needs of the Government and the resources from which it must draw its income.

I reluctantly vetoed the budget bill passed by the last session of the Congress because of a constitutional objection. The House of Representatives subsequently modified the bill in order to meet this objection. In the revised form, I believe that the bill, coupled with action already taken by the Congress to revise its rules and procedure, furnishes the foundation for an effective national budget system. I earnestly hope, therefore, that one of the first steps to be taken by the present session of the Congress will be to pass the budget bill.

The nation's finances have shown marked improvement during the last year. The total ordinary receipts of $6,694,000,000 for the fiscal year 1920 exceeded those for 1919 by $1,542,000,000, while the total net ordinary expenditures decreased from $18,514,000,000 to $6,403,000,000. The gross public debt, which reached its highest point on August 31, 1919, when it was $26,596,000,000, had dropped on November 30, 1920, to $24,175,000,000.

There has also been a marked decrease in holdings of government war securities by the banking institutions of the country, as well as in the amount of bills held by the Federal Reserve Banks secured by government war obligations. This fortunate result has relieved the banks and left them freer to finance the needs of Agriculture, Industry, and Commerce. It has been due in large part to the reduction of the public debt, especially of the floating debt, but more particularly to the improved distribution of government securities among permanent investors. The cessation of the Government's borrowings, except through short-term certificates of indebtedness, has been a matter of great consequence to the people of the country at large, as well as to the holders of Liberty Bonds and Victory Notes, and has had an important bearing on the matter of effective credit control.

The year has been characterized by the progressive withdrawal of the Treasury from the domestic credit market and from a position of dominant influence in that market. The future course will necessarily depend upon the extent to which economies are practiced and upon the burdens placed upon the Treasury, as well as upon industrial developments and the maintenance of tax receipts at a sufficiently high level. The fundamental fact which at present dominates the Government's financial situation is that seven and a half billions of its war indebtedness mature within the next two and a half years. Of this amount, two and a half billions are floating debt and five billions, Victory Notes and War. Savings Certificates. The fiscal program of the Government must be determined with reference to these maturities. Sound policy demands that Government expenditures be reduced to the lowest amount which will permit the various services to operate efficiently and that Government receipts from taxes and salvage be maintained sufficiently high to provide for current requirements, including interest and sinking fund charges on the public debt, and at the same time retire the floating debt and part of the Victory Loan before maturity.

With rigid economy, vigorous salvage operations, and adequate revenues from taxation, a surplus of current receipts over current expenditures can be realized and should be applied to the floating debt. All branches of the Government should cooperate to see that this program is realized. I cannot overemphasize the necessity of economy in Government appropriations and expenditures and the avoidance by the Congress of practices which take money from the Treasury by indefinite or revolving fund appropriations. The estimates for the present year show that over a billion dollars of expenditures were authorized by the last Congress in addition to the amounts shown in the usual compiled statements of appropriations. This strikingly illustrates the importance of making direct and specific appropriations. The relation between the current receipts and current expenditures of the Government during the present fiscal year, as well as during the last half of the last fiscal year, has been disturbed by the extraordinary burdens thrown upon the Treasury by the Transportation Act, in connection with the return of the railroads to private control. Over $600,000,000 has already been paid to the railroads under this act-$350,000,000 during the present fiscal year; and it is estimated that further payments aggregating possibly $650,000,000 must still be made to the railroads during the current year. It is obvious that these large payments have already seriously limited the Government's progress in retiring the floating debt.

Closely connected with this, it seems to me, is the necessity for an immediate consideration of the revision of our tax laws. Simplification of the income and profits taxes has become an immediate necessity. These taxes performed an indispensable service during the war. The need for their simplification, however, is very great, in order to save the taxpayer inconvenience and expense and in order to make his liability more certain and definite. Other and more detailed recommendations with regard to taxes will no doubt be laid before you by the Secretary of the Treasury and the Commissioner of Internal Revenue.

It is my privilege to draw to the attention of Congress for very sympathetic consideration the problem of providing adequate facilities for the care and treatment of former members of the military and naval forces who are sick and disabled as the result of their participation in the war. These heroic men can never be paid in money for the service they patriotically rendered the nation. Their reward will lie rather in realization of the fact that they vindicated the rights of their country and aided in safeguarding civilization. The nation's gratitude must be effectively revealed to them by the most ample provision for their medical care and treatment as well as for their vocational training and placement. The time has come when a more complete program can be formulated and more satisfactorily administered for their treatment and training, and I earnestly urge that the Congress give the matter its early consideration. The Secretary of the Treasury and the Board for Vocational Education will outline in their annual reports proposals covering medical care and rehabilitation which I am sure will engage your earnest study and commend your most generous support.

Permit me to emphasize once more the need for action upon certain matters upon which I dwelt at some length in my message to the second session of the Sixty-sixth Congress. The necessity, for example, of encouraging the manufacture of dyestuffs and related chemicals; the importance of doing everything possible to promote agricultural production along economic lines, to improve agricultural marketing, and to make rural life more attractive and healthful; the need for a law regulating cold storage in such a way as to limit the time during which goods may be kept in storage, prescribing the method of disposing of them if kept beyond the permitted period, and requiring goods released from storage in all cases to bear the date of their receipt. It would also be most serviceable if it were provided that all goods released from cold storage for interstate shipment should have plainly marked upon each package the selling or market price at which they went into storage, in order that the purchaser might be able to learn what profits stood between him and the producer or the wholesale dealer. Indeed, It would be very serviceable to the public if all goods destined for interstate commerce were made to carry upon every packing case whose form made it possible a plain statement of the price at which they left the hands of the producer. I respectfully call your attention also to the recommendations of the message referred to with regard to a federal license for all corporations engaged in interstate commerce.

In brief, the immediate legislative need of the time is the removal of all obstacles to the realization of the best ambitions of our people in their several classes of employment and the strengthening of all instrumentalities by. which difficulties are to be met and removed and justice dealt out, whether by law or by some form of mediation and conciliation. I do not feel it to be my privilege at present to, suggest the detailed and particular methods by which these objects may be attained, but I have faith that the inquiries of your several committees will discover the way and the method.

In response to what I believe to be the impulse of sympathy and opinion throughout the United States, I earnestly suggest that the Congress authorize the Treasury of the United States to make to the struggling government of Armenia such a loan as was made to several of the Allied governments during the war, and I would also suggest that it would be desirable to provide in the legislation itself that the expenditure of the money thus loaned should be under the supervision of a commission, or at least a commissioner, from the United States in order that revolutionary tendencies within Armenia itself might not be afforded by the loan a further tempting opportunity.

Allow me to call your attention to the fact that the people of the Philippine Islands have succeeded in maintaining a stable government since the last action of the Congress in their behalf, and have thus fulfilled the condition set by the Congress as precedent to a consideration of granting independence to the Islands. I respectfully submit that this condition precedent having been fulfilled, it is now our liberty and our duty to keep our promise to the people of those islands by granting them the independence which they so honorably covet.

I have not so much laid before you a series of recommendations, gentlemen, as sought to utter a confession of faith, of the faith in which I was bred and which it is my solemn purpose to stand by until my last fighting day. I believe this to be the faith of America, the faith of the future, and of all the victories which await national action in the days to come, whether in America or elsewhere.

Speeches & Addresses

First Address to Congress

[Delivered at a joint session of the two Houses of Congress, at the beginning of the first session of the Sixty-third Congress, April 8, 1913.]

Mr. Speaker, Mr. President, Gentlemen of the Congress:
I am very glad indeed to have this opportunity to address the two Houses directly and to verify for myself the impression that the President of the United States is a person, not a mere department of the Government hailing Congress from some isolated island of jealous power, sending messages, not speaking naturally and with his own voice-that he is a human being trying to coöperate with other human beings in a common service. After this pleasant experience I shall feel quite normal in all our dealings with one another.[65]

I have called the Congress together in extraordinary session because a duty was laid upon the party now in power at the recent elections which it ought to perform promptly, in order that the burden carried by the people under existing law may be lightened as soon as possible and in order, also, that the business interests of the country may not be kept too long in suspense as to what the fiscal changes are to be to which they will be required to adjust themselves. It is clear to the whole country that the tariff duties must be altered. They must be changed to meet the radical alteration in the conditions of our economic life which the country has witnessed within the last generation. While the whole face and method of our industrial and commercial life were being changed beyond recognition the tariff schedules have remained what they were before the change began, or have moved in the direction they were given when no large circumstance of our industrial development was what it is to-day. Our task is to square them with the actual facts. The sooner that is done the sooner we shall escape from suffering from the facts and the sooner our men of business will be free to thrive by the law of nature (the nature of free business) instead of by the law of legislation and artificial arrangement.

We have seen tariff legislation wander very far afield in our day-very far indeed from the field in which our prosperity might have had a normal growth and stimulation. No one who looks the facts squarely in the face or knows anything that lies beneath the surface of action can fail to perceive the principles upon which recent tariff legislation has been based. We long ago passed beyond the modest notion of "protecting" the industries of the country and moved boldly forward to the idea that they were entitled to the direct patronage of the Government. For a long time—a time so long that the men now active in public policy hardly remember the conditions that preceded it-we have sought in our tariff schedules to give each group of manufacturers or producers what they themselves thought that they needed in order to maintain a practically exclusive market as against the rest of the world. Consciously or unconsciously, we have built up a set of privileges and exemptions from competition behind which it was easy by any, even the crudest, forms of combination to organize monopoly; until at last nothing is normal, nothing is obliged to stand the tests of efficiency and economy, in our world of big business, but everything thrives by concerted arrangement. Only new principles of action will save us from a final hard crystallization of monopoly and a complete loss of the influences that quicken enterprise and keep independent energy alive.

It is plain what those principles must be. We must abolish everything that bears even the semblance of privilege or of any kind of artificial advantage, and put our business men and producers under the stimulation of a constant necessity to be efficient, economical, and enterprising, masters of competitive supremacy, better workers and merchants than any in the world. Aside from the duties laid upon articles which we do not, and probably cannot, produce, therefore, and the duties laid upon luxuries and merely for the sake of the revenues they yield, the object of the tariff duties henceforth laid must be effective competition, the whetting of American wits by contest with the wits of the rest of the world.

It would be unwise to move toward this end headlong, with reckless haste, or with strokes that cut at the very roots of what has grown up amongst us by long process and at our own invitation. It does not alter a thing to upset it and break it and deprive it of a chance to change. It destroys it. We must make changes in our fiscal laws, in our fiscal system, whose object is development, a more free and wholesome development, not revolution or upset or confusion. We must build up trade, especially foreign trade. We need the outlet and the enlarged field of energy more than we ever did before. We must build up industry as well, and must adopt freedom in the place of artificial stimulation only so far as it will build, not pull down. In dealing with the tariff the method by which this may be done will be a matter of judgment, exercised item by item. To some not accustomed to the excitements and responsibilities of greater freedom our methods may in some respects and at some points seem heroic, but remedies may be heroic and yet be remedies. It is our business to make sure that they are genuine remedies. Our object is clear. If our motive is above just challenge and only an occasional error of judgment is chargeable against us, we shall be fortunate.

We are called upon to render the country a great service in more matters than one. Our responsibility should be met and our methods should be thorough, as thorough as moderate and well considered, based upon the facts as they are, and not worked out as if we were beginners. We are to deal with the facts of our own day, with the facts of no other, and to make laws which square with those facts. It is best, indeed it is necessary, to begin with the tariff. I will urge nothing upon you now at the opening of your session which can obscure that first object or divert our energies from that clearly defined duty. At a later time I may take the liberty of calling your attention to reforms which should press close upon the heels of the tariff changes, if not accompany them, of which the chief is the reform of our banking and currency laws; but just now I refrain. For the present, I put these matters on one side and think only of this one thing-of the changes in our fiscal system which may best serve to open once more the free channels of prosperity to a great people whom we would serve to the utmost and throughout both rank and file.

I thank you for your courtesy.

Address on the Banking System

[Delivered at a joint session of the two Houses of Congress, June 23, 1913.]

Mr. Speaker, Mr. President, Gentlemen of the Congress:
It is under the compulsion of what seems to me a clear and imperative duty that I have a second time this session sought the privilege of addressing you in person. I know, of course, that the heated season of the year is upon us, that work in these chambers and in the committee rooms is likely to become a burden as the season lengthens, and that every consideration of personal convenience and personal comfort, perhaps, in the cases of some of us, considerations of personal health even, dictate an early conclusion of the deliberations of the session; but there are occasions of public duty when these things which touch us privately seem very small, when the work to be done is so pressing and so fraught with big consequence that we know that we are not at liberty to weigh against it any point of personal sacrifice. We are now in the presence of such an occasion. It is absolutely imperative that we should give the business men of this country a banking and currency system by means of which they can make use of the freedom of enterprise and of individual initiative which we are about to bestow upon them.

We are about to set them free; we must not leave them without the tools of action when they are free. We are about to set them free by removing the trammels of the protective tariff. Ever since the Civil War they have waited for this emancipation and for the free opportunities it will bring with it. It has been reserved for us to give it to them. Some fell in love, indeed, with the slothful security of their dependence upon the Government; some took advantage of the shelter of the nursery to set up a mimic mastery of their own within its walls. Now both the tonic and the discipline of liberty and maturity are to ensue. There will be some readjustments of purpose and point of view. There will follow a period of expansion and new enterprise, freshly conceived. It is for us to determine now whether it shall be rapid and facile and of easy accomplishment. This it cannot be unless the resourceful business men who are to deal with the new circumstances are to have at hand and ready for use the instrumentalities and conveniences of free enterprise which independent men need when acting on their own initiative.

It is not enough to strike the shackles from business. The duty of statesmanship is not negative merely. It is constructive also. We must show that we understand what business needs and that we know how to supply it. No man, however casual and superficial his observation of the conditions now prevailing in the country, can fail to see that one of the chief things business needs now, and will need increasingly as it gains in scope and vigor in the years immediately ahead of us, is the proper means by which readily to vitalize its credit, corporate and individual, and its originative brains. What will it profit us to be free if we are not to have the best and most accessible instrumentalities of commerce and enterprise? What will it profit us to be quit of one kind of monopoly if we are to remain in the grip of another and more effective kind? How are we to gain and keep the confidence of the business community unless we show that we know how both to aid and to protect it? What shall we say if we make fresh enterprise necessary and also make it very difficult by leaving all else except the tariff just as we found it? The tyrannies of business, big and little, lie within the field of credit. We know that. Shall we not act upon the knowledge? Do we not know how to act upon it? If a man cannot make his assets available at pleasure, his assets of capacity and character and resource, what satisfaction is it to him to see opportunity beckoning to him on every hand, when others have the keys of credit in their pockets and treat them as all but their own private possession? It is perfectly clear that it is our duty to supply the new banking and currency system the country needs, and it will need it immediately more than it has ever needed it before.

The only question is, When shall we supply it-now, or later, after the demands shall have become reproaches that we were so dull and so slow? Shall we hasten to change the tariff laws and then be laggards about making it possible and easy for the country to take advantage of the change? There can be only one answer to that question. We must act now, at whatever sacrifice to ourselves. It is a duty which the circumstances forbid us to postpone. I should be recreant to my deepest convictions of public obligation did I not press it upon you with solemn and urgent insistence.

The principles upon which we should act are also clear. The country has sought and seen its path in this matter within the last few years-sees it more clearly now than it ever saw it before-much more clearly than when the last legislative proposals on the subject were made. We must have a currency, not rigid as now, but readily, elastically responsive to sound credit, the expanding and contracting credits of everyday transactions, the normal ebb and flow of personal and corporate dealings. Our banking laws must mobilize reserves; must not permit the concentration anywhere in a few hands of the monetary resources of the country or their use for speculative purposes in such volume as to hinder or impede or stand in the way of other more legitimate, more fruitful uses. And the control of the system of banking and of issue which our new laws are to set up must be public, not private, must be vested in the Government itself, so that the banks may be the instruments, not the masters, of business and of individual enterprise and initiative.

The committees of the Congress to which legislation of this character is referred have devoted careful and dispassionate study to the means of accomplishing these objects. They have honored me by consulting me. They are ready to suggest action. I have come to you, as the head of the Government and the responsible leader of the party in power, to urge action now, while there is time to serve the country deliberately and as we should, in a clear air of common counsel. I appeal to you with a deep conviction of duty. I believe that you share this conviction. I therefore appeal to you with confidence. I am at your service without reserve to play my part in any way you may call upon me to play it in this great enterprise of exigent reform which it will dignify and distinguish us to perform and discredit us to neglect.

Address at Gettysburg

[Delivered in the presence of Union and Confederate veterans, on the occasion of the fiftieth anniversary of the battle, July 4, 1913.]

Friends and Fellow Citizens:

I need not tell you what the Battle of Gettysburg meant. These gallant men in blue and gray sit all about us here.[66] Many of them met upon this ground in grim and deadly struggle. Upon these famous fields and hillsides their comrades died about them. In their presence it were an impertinence to discourse upon how the battle went, how it ended, what it signified! But fifty years have gone by since then, and I crave the privilege of speaking to you for a few minutes of what those fifty years have meant.

What *have* they meant? They have meant peace and union and vigor, and the maturity and might of a great nation. How wholesome and healing the peace has been! We have found one another again as brothers and comrades in arms, enemies no longer, generous friends rather, our battles long past, the quarrel forgotten-except that we shall not forget the splendid valor, the manly devotion of the men then arrayed against one another, now grasping hands and smiling into each other's eyes. How complete the union has become and how dear to all of us, how unquestioned, how benign and majestic, as State after State has been added to this our great family of free men! How handsome the vigor, the maturity, the might of the great Nation we love with undivided hearts; how full of large and confident promise that a life will be wrought out that will crown its strength with gracious justice and with a happy welfare that will touch all alike with deep contentment! We are debtors to those fifty crowded years; they have made us heirs to a mighty heritage.

But do we deem the Nation complete and finished? These venerable men crowding here to this famous field have set us a great example of devotion and utter sacrifice. They were willing to die that the people might live. But their task is done. Their day is turned into evening. They look to us to perfect what they established. Their work is handed on to us, to be done in another way, but not in another spirit. Our day is not over; it is upon us in full tide.

Have affairs paused? Does the Nation stand still? Is what the fifty years have wrought since those days of battle finished, rounded out, and completed? Here is a great people, great with every force that has ever beaten in the lifeblood of mankind. And it is secure. There is no one within its borders, there is no power among the nations of the earth, to make it afraid. But has it yet squared itself with its own great standards set up at its birth, when it made that first noble, naïve appeal to the moral judgment of mankind to take notice that a government had now at last been established which was to serve men, not masters? It is secure in everything except the satisfaction that its life is right, adjusted to the uttermost to the standards of righteousness and humanity. The days of sacrifice and cleansing are not closed. We have harder things to do than were done in the heroic days of war, because harder to see clearly, requiring more vision, more calm balance of judgment, a more candid searching of the very springs of right.

Look around you upon the field of Gettysburg! Picture the array, the fierce heats and agony of battle, column hurled against column, battery bellowing to battery! Valor? Yes! Greater no man shall see in war; and self-sacrifice, and loss to the uttermost; the high recklessness of exalted devotion which does not count the cost. We are made by these tragic, epic things to know what it costs to make a nation-the blood and sacrifice of multitudes of unknown men lifted to a great stature in the view of all generations by knowing no limit to their manly willingness to serve. In armies thus marshaled from the ranks of free men you will see, as it were, a nation embattled, the leaders and the led, and may know, if you will, how little except in form its action differs in days of peace from its action in days of war.

May we break camp now and be at ease? Are the forces that fight for the Nation dispersed, disbanded, gone to their homes forgetful of the common cause? Are our forces disorganized, without constituted leaders and the might of men consciously united because we contend, not with armies, but with principalities and powers and wickedness in high places? Are we content to lie still? Does our union mean sympathy, our peace contentment, our vigor right action, our maturity self-comprehension and a clear confidence in choosing what we shall do? War fitted us for action, and action never ceases.

I have been chosen the leader of the Nation. I cannot justify the choice by any qualities of my own, but so it has come about, and here I stand. Whom do I command? The ghostly hosts who fought upon these battlefields long ago and are gone? These gallant gentlemen stricken in years whose fighting days, are over, their glory won? What are the orders for them, and who rallies them? I have in my mind another host, whom these set free of civil strife in order that they might work out in days of peace and settled order the life of a great Nation. That host is the people themselves, the great and the small, without class or difference of kind or race or origin; and undivided in interest, if we have but the vision to guide and direct them and order their lives aright in what we do. Our constitutions are their articles of enlistment. The orders of the day are the laws upon our statute books. What we strive for is their freedom, their right to lift themselves from day to day and behold the things they have hoped for, and so make way for still better days for those whom they love who are to come after them. The recruits are the little children crowding in. The quartermaster's stores are in the mines and forests and fields, in the shops and factories. Every day something must be done to push the campaign forward; and it must be done by plan and with an eye to some great destiny.

How shall we hold such thoughts in our hearts and not be moved? I would not have you live even to-day wholly in the past, but would wish to stand with you in the light that streams upon us now out of that great day gone by. Here is the nation God has builded by our hands. What shall we do with it? Who stands ready to act again and always in the spirit of this day of reunion and hope and patriotic fervor? The day of our country's life has but broadened into morning. Do not put uniforms by. Put the harness of the present on. Lift your eyes to the great tracts of life yet to be conquered in the interest of righteous peace, of that prosperity which lies in a people's hearts and outlasts all wars and errors of men. Come, let us be comrades and soldiers yet to serve our fellow-men in quiet counsel, where the blare of trumpets is neither heard nor heeded and where the things are done which make blessed the nations of the world in peace and righteousness and love.

Address on Mexican Affairs

[Delivered at a joint session of the two Houses of Congress, August 27, 1913.]

Gentlemen of the Congress:

It is clearly my duty to lay before you, very fully and without reservation, the facts concerning our present relations with the Republic of Mexico. The deplorable posture of affairs in Mexico I need not describe,[67] but I deem it my duty to speak very frankly of what this Government has done and should seek to do in fulfillment of its obligation to Mexico herself, as a friend and neighbor, and to American citizens whose lives and vital interests are daily affected by the distressing conditions which now obtain beyond our southern border.

Those conditions touch us very nearly. Not merely because they lie at our very doors. That of course makes us more vividly and more constantly conscious of them, and every instinct of neighborly interest and sympathy is aroused and quickened by them; but that is only one element in the determination of our duty. We are glad to call ourselves the friends of Mexico, and we shall, I hope, have many an occasion, in happier times as well as in these days of trouble and confusion, to show that our friendship is genuine and disinterested, capable of sacrifice and every generous manifestation. The peace, prosperity, and contentment of Mexico mean more, much more, to us than merely an enlarged field for our commerce and enterprise. They mean an enlargement of the field of self-government and the realization of the hopes and rights of a nation with whose best aspirations, so long suppressed and disappointed, we deeply sympathize. We shall yet prove to the Mexican people that we know how to serve them without first thinking how we shall serve ourselves.

But we are not the only friends of Mexico. The whole world desires her peace and progress; and the whole world is interested as never before. Mexico lies at last where all the world looks on. Central America is about to be touched by the great routes of the world's trade and intercourse running free from ocean to ocean at the Isthmus. The future has much in store for Mexico, as for all the States of Central America; but the best gifts can come to her only if she be ready and free to receive them and to enjoy them honorably. America in particular-America north and south and upon both continents-waits upon the development of Mexico; and that development can be sound and lasting only if it be the product of a genuine freedom, a just and ordered government founded upon law. Only so can it be peaceful or fruitful of the benefits of peace. Mexico has a great and enviable future before her, if only she choose and attain the paths of honest constitutional government.

The present circumstances of the Republic, I deeply regret to say, do not seem to promise even the foundations of such a peace. We have waited many months, months full of peril and anxiety, for the conditions there to improve, and they have not improved. They have grown worse, rather. The territory in some sort controlled by the provisional authorities at Mexico City has grown smaller, not larger. The prospect of the pacification of the country, even by arms, has seemed to grow more and more remote; and its pacification by the authorities at the capital is evidently impossible by any other means than force. Difficulties more and more entangle those who claim to constitute the legitimate government of the Republic. They have not made good their claim in fact. Their successes in the field have proved only temporary. War and disorder, devastation and confusion, seem to threaten to become the settled fortune of the distracted country. As friends we could wait no longer for a solution which every week seemed further away. It was our duty at least to volunteer our good offices-to offer to assist, if we might, in effecting some arrangement which would bring relief and peace and set up a universally acknowledged political authority there.

Accordingly, I took the liberty of sending the Hon. John Lind, formerly governor of Minnesota, as my personal spokesman and representative, to the City of Mexico, with *the following instructions*:

> Press very earnestly upon the attention of those who are now exercising authority or wielding influence in Mexico the following considerations and advice:
>
> The Government of the United States does not feel at liberty any longer to stand inactively by while it becomes daily more and more evident that no real progress is being made towards the establishment of a government at the City of Mexico which the country will obey and respect.
>
> The Government of the United States does not stand in the same case with the other great Governments of the world in respect of what is happening or what is likely to happen in Mexico. We offer our good offices, not only because of our genuine desire to play the part of a friend, but also because we are expected by the powers of the world to act as Mexico's nearest friend.
>
> We wish to act in these circumstances in the spirit of the most earnest and disinterested friendship. It is our purpose in whatever we do or propose in this perplexing and distressing situation not only to pay the most scrupulous regard to the sovereignty and independence of Mexico-that we take as a matter of course to which we are bound by every obligation of right and honor-but also to give every possible evidence that we act in the interest of Mexico alone, and not in the interest of any person or body of persons who may have personal or property claims in Mexico which they may feel that they have the right to press. We are seeking to counsel Mexico for her own good and in the interest of her own peace, and not for any other purpose whatever. The Government of the United States would deem itself discredited if it had any selfish or ulterior purpose in transactions where the peace, happiness, and prosperity of a whole people are involved. It is acting as its friendship for Mexico, not as any selfish interest, dictates.
>
> The present situation in Mexico is incompatible with the fulfillment of international obligations on the part of Mexico, with the civilized development of Mexico herself, and with the maintenance of tolerable political and economic conditions in Central America. It is upon no common occasion, therefore, that the United States offers her counsel and assistance. All America cries out for a settlement.
>
> A satisfactory settlement seems to us to be conditioned on —
>
> (*a*) An immediate cessation of fighting throughout Mexico, a definite armistice solemnly entered into and scrupulously observed;
>
> (*b*) Security given for an early and free election in which all will agree to take part;
>
> (*c*) The consent of Gen. Huerta to bind himself not to be a candidate for election as President of the Republic at this election; and
>
> (*d*) The agreement of all parties to abide by the results of the election and coöperate in the most loyal way in organizing and supporting the new administration.
>
> The Government of the United States will be glad to play any part in this settlement or in its carrying out which it can play honorably and consistently with international right. It pledges itself to recognize and in every way possible and proper to assist the administration chosen and set up in Mexico in the way and on the conditions suggested.
>
> Taking all the existing conditions into consideration, the Government of the United States can conceive of no reasons sufficient to justify those who are now attempting to shape the policy or exercise the authority of Mexico in declining the offices of friendship thus offered. Can Mexico give the civilized world a satisfactory reason for rejecting our good offices? If Mexico can suggest any better way in which to show our friendship, serve the people of Mexico, and meet our international obligations, we are more than willing to consider the suggestion.

Mr. Lind executed his delicate and difficult mission with singular tact, firmness, and good judgment, and made clear to the authorities at the City of Mexico not only the purpose of his visit but also the spirit in which it had been undertaken. But the proposals he submitted were rejected, in a note the full text of which I take the liberty of laying before you.

I am led to believe that they were rejected partly because the authorities at Mexico City had been grossly misinformed and misled upon two points. They did not realize the spirit of the American people in this matter, their earnest friendliness and yet sober determination that some just solution be found for the Mexican difficulties; and they did not believe that the present administration spoke, through Mr. Lind, for the people of the United States. The effect of this unfortunate misunderstanding on their part is to leave them singularly isolated and without friends who can effectually aid them. So long as the misunderstanding continues we can only await the time of their awakening to a realization of the actual facts. We cannot thrust our good offices upon them. The situation must be given a little more time to work itself out in the new circumstances; and I believe that only a little while will be necessary. For the circumstances are new. The rejection of our friendship makes them new and will inevitably bring its own alterations in the whole aspect of affairs. The actual situation of the authorities at Mexico City will presently be revealed.

Meanwhile, what is it our duty to do? Clearly, everything that we do must be rooted in patience and done with calm and disinterested deliberation. Impatience on our part would be childish, and would be fraught with every risk of wrong and folly. We can afford to exercise the self-restraint of a really great nation which realizes its own strength and scorns to misuse it. It was our duty to offer our active assistance. It is now our duty to show what true neutrality will do to enable the people of Mexico to set their affairs in order again and wait for a further opportunity to offer our friendly counsels. The door is not closed against the resumption, either upon the initiative of Mexico or upon our own, of the effort to bring order out of the confusion by friendly coöperative action, should fortunate occasion offer.

While we wait the contest of the rival forces will undoubtedly for a little while be sharper than ever, just because it will be plain that an end must be made of the existing situation, and that very promptly; and with the increased activity of the contending factions will come, it is to be feared, increased danger to the non-combatants in Mexico as well as to those actually in the field of battle. The position of outsiders is always particularly trying and full of hazard where there is civil strife and a whole country is upset. We should earnestly urge all Americans to leave Mexico at once, and should assist them to get away in every way possible-not because we would mean to slacken in the least our efforts to safeguard their lives and their interests, but because it is imperative that they should take no unnecessary risks when it is physically possible for them to leave the country. We should let every one who assumes to exercise authority in any part of Mexico know in the most unequivocal way that we shall vigilantly watch the fortunes of those Americans who cannot get away, and shall hold those responsible for their sufferings and losses to a definite reckoning. That can be and will be made plain beyond the possibility of a misunderstanding.

For the rest, I deem it my duty to exercise the authority conferred upon me by the law of March 14, 1912, to see to it that neither side to the struggle now going on in Mexico receive any assistance from this side the border. I shall follow the best practice of nations in the matter of neutrality by forbidding the exportation of arms or munitions of war of any kind from the United States to any part of the Republic of Mexico —a policy suggested by several interesting precedents and certainly dictated by many manifest considerations of practical expediency. We cannot in the circumstances be the partisans of either party to the contest that now distracts Mexico, or constitute ourselves the virtual umpire between them.

I am happy to say that several of the great Governments of the world have given this Government their generous moral support in urging upon the provisional authorities at the City of Mexico the acceptance of our proffered good offices in the spirit in which they were made. We have not acted in this matter under the ordinary principles of international obligation. All the world expects us in such circumstances to act as Mexico's nearest friend and intimate adviser. This is our immemorial relation towards her. There is nowhere any serious question that we have the moral right in the case or that we are acting in the interest of a fair settlement and of good government, not for the promotion of some selfish interest of our own. If further motive were necessary than our own good will towards a sister Republic and our own deep concern to see peace and order prevail in Central America, this consent of mankind to what we are attempting, this attitude of the great nations of the world towards what we may attempt in dealing with this distressed people at our doors, should make us feel the more solemnly bound to go to the utmost length of patience and forbearance in this painful and anxious business. The steady pressure of moral force will before many days break the barriers of pride and prejudice down, and we shall triumph as Mexico's friends sooner than we could triumph as her enemies-and how much more handsomely, with how much higher and finer satisfactions of conscience and of honor!

Understanding America

[Delivered at Philadelphia, Pa., on the occasion of the rededication of Congress Hall, Oct. 25, 1913. The United States Congress met in this hall till 1800. Here Washington was inaugurated the second time, and here he made his farewell address to the American people. Here John Adams took the oath of office when he succeeded Washington. The hall, after being long disused, was now restored and reopened. Before Mr. Wilson spoke, Mr. Frank Miles Day, representing the committee of architects, had referred to the "delightful silence, order, gravity, and personal dignity of manner" observed by the Senators of the first Congress, and had said, "They all appeared every morning full powdered, and dressed, as age or fancy might suggest, in the richest material."]

Your Honor, Mr. Chairman, Ladies, and Gentlemen:

No American could stand in this place to-day and think of the circumstances which we are come together to celebrate without being most profoundly stirred. There has come over me since I sat down here a sense of deep solemnity, because it has seemed to me that I saw ghosts crowding—a great assemblage of spirits, no longer visible, but whose influence we still feel as we feel the molding power of history itself. The men who sat in this hall, to whom we now look back with a touch of deep sentiment, were men of flesh and blood, face to face with extremely difficult problems. The population of the United States then was hardly three times the present population of the city of Philadelphia, and yet that was a Nation as this is a Nation, and the men who spoke for it were setting their hands to a work which was to last, not only that their people might be happy, but that an example might be lifted up for the instruction of the rest of the world.

I like to read the quaint old accounts such as Mr. Day has read to us this afternoon. Strangers came then to America to see what the young people that had sprung up here were like, and they found men in counsel who knew how to construct governments. They found men deliberating here who had none of the appearance of novices, none of the hesitation of men who did not know whether the work they were doing was going to last or not; men who addressed themselves to a problem of construction as familiarly as we attempt to carry out the traditions of a Government established these 137 years.

I feel to-day the compulsion of these men, the compulsion of examples which were set up in this place. And of what do their examples remind us? They remind us not merely of public service but of public service shot through with principle and honor. They were not histrionic men. They did not say—

Look upon us as upon those who shall hereafter be illustrious.

They said:

Look upon us who are doing the first free work of constitutional liberty in the world, and who must do it in soberness and truth, or it will not last.

Politics, ladies and gentlemen, is made up in just about equal parts of comprehension and sympathy. No man ought to go into politics who does not comprehend the task that he is going to attack. He may comprehend it so completely that it daunts him, that he doubts whether his own spirit is stout enough and his own mind able enough to attempt its great undertakings, but unless he comprehend it he ought not to enter it. After he has comprehended it, there should come into his mind those profound impulses of sympathy which connect him with the rest of mankind, for politics is a business of interpretation, and no men are fit for it who do not see and seek more than their own advantage and interest.

We have stumbled upon many unhappy circumstances in the hundred years that have gone by since the event that we are celebrating. Almost all of them have come from self-centered men, men who saw in their own interest the interest of the country, and who did not have vision enough to read it in wider terms, in the universal terms of equity and justice and the rights of mankind. I hear a great many people at Fourth of July celebrations laud the Declaration of Independence who in between Julys shiver at the plain language of our bills of rights. The Declaration of Independence was, indeed, the first audible breath of liberty, but the substance of liberty is written in such documents as the declaration of rights attached, for example, to the first constitution of Virginia, which was a model for the similar documents read elsewhere into our great fundamental charters. That document speaks in very plain terms. The men of that generation did not hesitate to say that every people has a right to choose its own forms of government-not once, but as often as it pleases-and to accommodate those forms of government to its existing interests and circumstances. Not only to establish but to alter is the fundamental principle of self-government.

We are just as much under compulsion to study the particular circumstances of our own day as the gentlemen were who sat in this hall and set us precedents, not of what to do but of how to do it. Liberty inheres in the circumstances of the day. Human happiness consists in the life which human beings are leading at the time that they live. I can feed my memory as happily upon the circumstances of the revolutionary and constitutional period as you can, but I cannot feed all my purposes with them in Washington now. Every day problems arise which wear some new phase and aspect, and I must fall back, if I would serve my conscience, upon those things which are fundamental rather than upon those things which are superficial, and ask myself this question, How are you going to assist in some small part to give the American people and, by example, the peoples of the world more liberty, more happiness, more substantial prosperity; and how are you going to make that prosperity a common heritage instead of a selfish possession? I came here to-day partly in order to feed my own spirit. I did not come in compliment. When I was asked to come I knew immediately upon the utterance of the invitation that I had to come, that to be absent would be as if I refused to drink once more at the original fountains of inspiration for our own Government.

The men of the day which we now celebrate had a very great advantage over us, ladies and gentlemen, in this one particular: Life was simple in America then. All men shared the same circumstances in almost equal degree. We think of Washington, for example, as an aristocrat, as a man separated by training, separated by family and neighborhood tradition, from the ordinary people of the rank and file of the country. Have you forgotten the personal history of George Washington? Do you not know that he struggled as poor boys now struggle for a meager and imperfect education; that he worked at his surveyor's tasks in the lonely forests; that he knew all the roughness, all the hardships, all the adventure, all the variety of the common life of that day; and that if he stood a little stiffly in this place, if he looked a little aloof, it was because life had dealt hardly with him? All his sinews had been stiffened by the rough work of making America. He was a man of the people, whose touch had been with them since the day he saw the light first in the old Dominion of Virginia. And the men who came after him, men, some of whom had drunk deep at the sources of philosophy and of study, were, nevertheless, also men who on this side of the water knew no complicated life but the simple life of primitive neighborhoods. Our task is very much more difficult. That sympathy which alone interprets public duty is more difficult for a public man to acquire now than it was then, because we live in the midst of circumstances and conditions infinitely complex.

No man can boast that he understands America. No man can boast that he has lived the life of America, as almost every man who sat in this hall in those days could boast. No man can pretend that except by common counsel he can gather into his consciousness what the varied life of this people is. The duty that we have to keep open eyes and open hearts and accessible understandings is a very much more difficult duty to perform than it was in their day. Yet how much more important that it should be performed, for fear we make infinite and irreparable blunders. The city of Washington is in some respects self-contained, and it is easy there to forget what the rest of the United States is thinking about. I count it a fortunate circumstance that almost all the windows of the White House and its offices open upon unoccupied spaces that stretch to the banks of the Potomac and then out into Virginia and on to the heavens themselves, and that as I sit there I can constantly forget Washington and remember the United States. Not that I would intimate that all of the United States lies south of Washington, but there is a serious thing back of my thought. If you think too much about being reëlected, it is very difficult to be worth reëlecting. You are so apt to forget that the comparatively small number of persons, numerous as they seem to be when they swarm, who come to Washington to ask for things, do not constitute an important proportion of the population of the country, that it is constantly necessary to come away from Washington and renew one's contact with the people who do not swarm there, who do not ask for anything, but who do trust you without their personal counsel to do your duty. Unless a man gets these contacts he grows weaker and weaker. He needs them as Hercules needed the touch of mother earth. If you lift him up too high or he lifts himself too high, he loses the contact and therefore loses the inspiration.

I love to think of those plain men, however far from plain their dress sometimes was, who assembled in this hall. One is startled to think of the variety of costume and color which would now occur if we were let loose upon the fashions of that age. Men's lack of taste is largely concealed now by the limitations of fashion. Yet these men, who sometimes dressed like the peacock, were, nevertheless, of the ordinary flight of their time. They were birds of a feather; they were birds come from a very simple breeding; they were much in the open heaven. They were beginning, when there was so little to distract their attention, to show that they could live upon fundamental principles of government. We talk those principles, but we have not time to absorb them. We have not time to let them into our blood, and thence have them translated into the plain mandates of action.

The very smallness of this room, the very simplicity of it all, all the suggestions which come from its restoration, are reassuring things-things which it becomes a man to realize. Therefore my theme here to-day, my only thought, is a very simple one. Do not let us go back to the annals of those sessions of Congress to find out what to do, because we live in another age and the circumstances are absolutely different; but let us be men of that kind; let us feel at every turn the compulsions of principle and of honor which thy felt; let us free our vision from temporary circumstances and look abroad at the horizon and take into our lungs the great air of freedom which has blown through this country and stolen across the seas and blessed people everywhere; and, looking east and west and north and south, let us remind ourselves that we are the custodians, in some degree, of the principles which have made men free and governments just.

Address Before the Southern Commercial Congress

[Delivered at Mobile, Alabama, October 27, 1913.]

Your Excellency, Mr. Chairman:
It is with unaffected pleasure that I find myself here to-day. I once before had the pleasure, in another southern city, of addressing the Southern Commercial Congress. I then spoke of what the future seemed to hold in store for this region, which so many of us love and toward the future of which we all look forward with so much confidence and hope. But another theme directed me here this time. I do not need to speak of the South. She has, perhaps, acquired the gift of speaking for herself. I come because I want to speak of our present and prospective relations with our neighbors to the south. I deemed it a public duty, as well as a personal pleasure, to be here to express for myself and for the Government I represent the welcome we all feel to those who represent the Latin-American States.

The future, ladies and gentlemen, is going to be very different for this hemisphere from the past. These States lying to the south of us, which have always been our neighbors, will now be drawn closer to us by innumerable ties, and, I hope, chief of all by the tie of a common understanding of each other. Interest does not tie nations together; it sometimes separates them. But sympathy and understanding does unite them, and I believe that by the new route that is just about to be opened, while we physically cut two continents asunder, we spiritually unite them. It is a spiritual union which we seek.

I wonder if you realize, I wonder if your imaginations have been filled with the significance of the tides of commerce. Your Governor alluded in very fit and striking terms to the voyage of Columbus, but Columbus took his voyage under compulsion of circumstances. Constantinople had been captured by the Turks, and all the routes of trade with the East had been suddenly closed. If there was not a way across the Atlantic to open those routes again, they were closed forever; and Columbus set out not to discover America, for he did not know that it existed, but to discover the eastern shores of Asia. He set sail for Cathay and stumbled upon America. With that change in the outlook of the world, what happened? England, that had been at the back of Europe with an unknown sea behind her, found that all things had turned as if upon a pivot and she was at the front of Europe; and since then all the tides of energy and enterprise that have issued out of Europe have seemed to be turned westward across the Atlantic. But you will notice that they have turned westward chiefly north of the Equator, and that it is the northern half of the globe that has seemed to be filled with the media of intercourse and of sympathy and of common understanding.

Do you not see now what is about to happen? These great tides which have been running along parallels of latitude will now swing southward athwart parallels of latitude, and that opening gate at the Isthmus of Panama will open the world to a commerce that she has not known before, a commerce of intelligence, of thought, and sympathy between North and South. The Latin-American States which, to their disadvantage, have been off the main lines will now be on the main lines. I feel that these gentlemen honoring us with their presence to-day will presently find that some part, at any rate, of the center of gravity of the world has shifted. Do you realize that New York, for example, will be nearer the western coast of South America than she is now to the eastern coast of South America? Do you realize that a line drawn northward parallel with the greater part of the western coast of South America will run only about one hundred and fifty miles west of New York? The great bulk of South America, if you will look at your globes (not at your Mercator's projection), lies eastward of the continent of North America. You will realize that when you realize that the canal will run southeast, not southwest, and that when you get into the Pacific you will be farther east then you were when you left the Gulf of

Mexico. These things are significant, therefore, of this, that we are closing one chapter in the history of the world and are opening another of great, unimaginable significance.

There is one peculiarity about the history of the Latin-American States which I am sure they are keenly aware of. You hear of "concessions" to foreign capitalists in Latin America. You do not hear of concessions to foreign capitalists in the United States. They are not granted concessions. They are invited to make investments. The work is ours, though they are welcome to invest in it. We do not ask them to supply the capital and do the work. It is an invitation, not a privilege; and States that are obliged, because their territory does not lie within the main field of modern enterprise and action, to grant concessions are in this condition, that foreign interests are apt to dominate their domestic affairs, a condition of affairs always dangerous and apt to become intolerable. What these States are going to see, therefore, is an emancipation from the subordination, which has been inevitable, to foreign enterprise and an assertion of the splendid character which, in spite of these difficulties, they have again and again been able to demonstrate. The dignity, the courage, the self-possession, the self-respect of the Latin-American States, their achievements in the face of all these adverse circumstances, deserve nothing but the admiration and applause of the world. They have had harder bargains driven with them in the matter of loans than any other peoples in the world. Interest has been exacted of them that was not exacted of anybody else, because the risk was said to be greater; and then securities were taken that destroyed the risk-an admirable arrangement for those who were forcing the terms! I rejoice in nothing so much as in the prospect that they will now be emancipated from these conditions; and we ought to be the first to take part in assisting in that emancipation. I think some of these gentlemen have already had occasion to bear witness that the Department of State in recent months has tried to serve them in that wise. In the future they will draw closer and closer to us because of circumstances of which I wish to speak with moderation and, I hope, without indiscretion.

We must prove ourselves their friends and champions upon terms of equality and honor. You cannot be friends upon any other terms than upon the terms of equality. You cannot be friends at all except upon the terms of honor. We must show ourselves friends by comprehending their interest whether it squares with our own interest or not. It is a very perilous thing to determine the foreign policy of a nation in the terms of material interest. It not only is unfair to those with whom you are dealing, but it is degrading as regards your own actions.

Comprehension must be the soil in which shall grow all the fruits of friendship, and there is a reason and a compulsion lying behind all this which is dearer than anything else to the thoughtful men of America. I mean the development of constitutional liberty in the world. Human rights, national integrity, and opportunity as against material interests-that, ladies and gentlemen, is the issue which we now have to face. I want to take this occasion to say that the United States will never again seek one additional foot of territory by conquest. She will devote herself to showing that she knows how to make honorable and fruitful use of the territory she has, and she must regard it as one of the duties of friendship to see that from no quarter are material interests made superior to human liberty and national opportunity. I say this, not with a single thought that anyone will gainsay it, but merely to fix in our consciousness what our real relationship with the rest of America is. It is the relationship of a family of mankind devoted to the development of true constitutional liberty. We know that that is the soil out of which the best enterprise springs. We know that this is a cause which we are making in common with our neighbors, because we have had to make it for ourselves.

Reference has been made here to-day to some of the national problems which confront us as a nation. What is at the heart of all our national problems? It is that we have seen the hand of material interest sometimes about to close upon our dearest rights and possessions. We have seen material interests threaten constitutional freedom in the United States. Therefore we will now know how to sympathize with those in the rest of America who have to contend with such powers, not only within their borders but from outside their borders also.

I know what the response of the thought and heart of America will be to the program I have outlined, because America was created to realize a program like that. This is not America because it is rich. This is not America because it has set up for a great population great opportunities of material prosperity. America is a name which sounds in the ears of men everywhere as a synonym with individual opportunity because a synonym of individual liberty. I would rather belong to a poor nation that was free than to a rich nation that had ceased to be in love with liberty. But we shall not be poor if we love liberty, because the nation that loves liberty truly sets every man free to do his best and be his best, and that means the release of all the splendid energies of a great people who think for themselves. A nation of employees cannot be free any more than a nation of employers can be.

In emphasizing the points which must unite us in sympathy and in spiritual interest with the Latin-American peoples we are only emphasizing the points of our own life, and we should prove ourselves untrue to our own traditions if we proved ourselves untrue friends to them. Do not think, therefore, gentlemen, that the questions of the day are mere questions of policy and diplomacy. They are shot through with the principles of life. We dare not turn from the principle that morality and not expediency is the thing that must guide us and that we will never condone iniquity because it is most convenient to do so. It seems to me that this is a day of infinite hope, of confidence in a future greater than the past has been, for I am fain to believe that in spite of all the things that we wish to correct the nineteenth century that now lies behind us has brought us a long stage toward the time when, slowly ascending the tedious climb that leads to the final uplands, we shall get our ultimate view of the duties of mankind. We have breasted a considerable part of that climb and shall presently-it may be in a generation or two-come out upon those great heights where there shines unobstructed the light of the justice of God.

Trusts and Monopolies

[Address delivered at a joint session of the two Houses of Congress, January 20, 1914.]

Gentlemen of the Congress:
In my report "on the state of the Union," which I had the privilege of reading to you on the 2d of December last, I ventured to reserve for discussion at a later date the subject of additional legislation regarding the very difficult and intricate matter of trusts and monopolies. The time now seems opportune to turn to that great question; not only because the currency legislation, which absorbed your attention and the attention of the country in December, is now disposed of, but also because opinion seems to be clearing about us with singular rapidity in this other great field of action. In the matter of the currency it cleared suddenly and very happily after the much-debated Act was passed; in respect of the monopolies which have multiplied about us and in regard to the various means by which they have been organized and maintained it seems to be coming to a clear and all but universal agreement in anticipation of our action, as if by way of preparation, making the way easier to see and easier to set out upon with confidence and without confusion of counsel.

Legislation has its atmosphere like everything else, and the atmosphere of accommodation and mutual understanding which we now breathe with so much refreshment is matter of sincere congratulation. It ought to make our task very much less difficult and embarrassing than it would have been had we been obliged to continue to act amidst the atmosphere of suspicion and antagonism which has so long made it impossible to approach such questions with dispassionate fairness. Constructive legislation, when successful, is always the embodiment of convincing experience, and of the mature public opinion which finally springs out of that experience. Legislation is a business of interpretation, not of origination; and it is now plain what the opinion is to which we must give effect in this matter. It is not recent or hasty opinion. It springs out of the experience of a whole generation. It has clarified itself by long contest, and those who for a long time battled with it and sought to change it are now frankly and honorably yielding to it and seeking to conform their actions to it.

The great business men who organized and financed monopoly and those who administered it in actual everyday transactions have year after year, until now, either denied its existence or justified it as necessary for the effective maintenance and development of the vast business processes of the country in the modern circumstances of trade and manufacture and finance; but all the while opinion has made head against them. The average business man is convinced that the ways of liberty are also the ways of peace and the ways of success as well; and at last the masters of business on the great scale have begun to yield their preference and purpose, perhaps their judgment also, in honorable surrender.

What we are purposing to do, therefore, is, happily, not to hamper or interfere with business as enlightened business men prefer to do it, or in any sense to put it under the ban. The antagonism between business and government is over. We are now about to give expression to the best business judgment of America, to what we know to be the business conscience and honor of the land. The Government and business men are ready to meet each other half-way in a common effort to square business methods with both public opinion and the law. The best informed men of the business world condemn the methods and processes and consequences of monopoly as we condemn them; and the instinctive judgment of the vast majority of business men everywhere goes with them. We shall now be their spokesmen. That is the strength of our position and the sure prophecy of what will ensue when our reasonable work is done.

When serious contest ends, when men unite in opinion and purpose, those who are to change their ways of business joining with those who ask for the change, it is possible to effect it in the way in which prudent and thoughtful and patriotic men would wish to see it brought about with as few, as slight, as easy and simple business readjustments as possible in the circumstances, nothing essential disturbed, nothing torn up by the roots, no parts rent asunder which can be left in wholesome combination. Fortunately, no measures of sweeping or novel change are necessary. It will be understood that our object is *not* to unsettle business or anywhere seriously to break its established courses athwart. On the contrary, we desire the laws we are now about to pass to be the bulwarks and safeguards of industry against the forces that have disturbed it. What we have to do can be done in a new spirit, in thoughtful moderation, without revolution of any untoward kind.

We are all agreed that "private monopoly is indefensible and intolerable," and our program is founded upon that conviction. It will be a comprehensive but not a radical or unacceptable program and these are its items, the changes which opinion deliberately sanctions and for which business waits:

It waits with acquiescence, in the first place, for laws which will effectually prohibit and prevent such interlockings of the *personnel* of the directorates of great corporations-banks and railroads, industrial, commercial, and public service bodies-as in effect result in making those who borrow and those who lend practically one and the same, those who sell and those who buy but the same persons trading with one another under different names and in different combinations, and those who affect to compete in fact partners and masters of some whole field of business. Sufficient time should be allowed, of course, in which to effect these changes of organization without inconvenience or confusion.

Such a prohibition will work much more than a mere negative good by correcting the serious evils which have arisen because, for example, the men who have been the directing spirits of the great investment banks have usurped the place which belongs to independent industrial management working in its own behoof. It will bring new men, new energies, a new spirit of initiative, new blood, into the management of our great business enterprises. It will open the field of industrial development and origination to scores of men who have been obliged to serve when their abilities entitled them to direct. It will immensely hearten the young men coming on and will greatly enrich the business activities of the whole country.

In the second place, business men as well as those who direct public affairs now recognize, and recognize with painful clearness, the great harm and injustice which has been done to many, if not all, of the great railroad systems of the country by the way in which they have been financed and their own distinctive interests subordinated to the interests of the men who financed them and of other business enterprises which those men wished to promote. The country is ready, therefore, to accept, and accept with relief as well as approval, a law which will confer upon the Interstate Commerce Commission the power to superintend and regulate the financial operations by which the railroads are henceforth to be supplied with the money they need for their proper development to meet the rapidly growing requirements of the country for increased and improved facilities of transportation. We cannot postpone action in this matter without leaving the railroads exposed to many serious handicaps and hazards; and the prosperity of the railroads and the prosperity of the country are inseparably connected. Upon this question those who are chiefly responsible for the actual management and operation of the railroads have spoken very plainly and very earnestly, with a purpose we ought to be quick to accept. It will be one step, and a very important one, toward the necessary separation of the business of production from the business of transportation.

The business of the country awaits also, has long awaited and has suffered because it could not obtain, further and more explicit legislative definition of the policy and meaning of the existing antitrust law. Nothing hampers business like uncertainty. Nothing daunts or discourages it like the necessity to take chances, to run the risk of falling under the condemnation of the law before it can make sure just what the law is. Surely we are sufficiently familiar with the actual processes and methods of monopoly and of the many hurtful restraints of trade to make definition possible, at any rate up to the limits of what experience has disclosed. These practices, being now abundantly disclosed, can be explicitly and item by item forbidden by statute in such terms as will practically eliminate uncertainty, the law itself and the penalty being made equally plain.

And the business men of the country desire something more than that the menace of legal process in these matters be made explicit and intelligible. They desire the advice, the definite guidance and information which can be supplied by an administrative body, an interstate trade commission.

The opinion of the country would instantly approve of such a commission. It would not wish to see it empowered to make terms with monopoly or in any sort to assume control of business, as if the Government made itself responsible. It demands such a commission only as an indispensable instrument of information and publicity, as a clearing house for the facts by which both the public mind and the managers of great business undertakings should be guided, and as an instrumentality for doing justice to business where the processes of the courts or the natural forces of correction outside the courts are inadequate to adjust the remedy to the wrong in a way that will meet all the equities and circumstances of the case.

Producing industries, for example, which have passed the point up to which combination may be consistent with the public interest and the freedom of trade, cannot always be dissected into their component units as readily as railroad companies or similar organizations can be. Their dissolution by ordinary legal process may oftentimes involve financial consequences likely to overwhelm the security market and bring upon it breakdown and confusion. There ought to be an administrative commission capable of directing and shaping such corrective processes, not only in aid of the courts but also by independent suggestion, if necessary.

Inasmuch as our object and the spirit of our action in these matters is to meet business halfway in its processes of self-correction and disturb its legitimate course as little as possible, we ought to see to it, and the judgment of practical and sagacious men of affairs everywhere would applaud us if we did see to it, that penalties and punishments should fall, not upon business itself, to its confusion and interruption, but upon the individuals who use the instrumentalities of business to do things which public policy and sound business practice condemn. Every act of business is done at the command or upon the initiative of some ascertainable person or group of persons. These should be held individually responsible and the punishment should fall upon them, not upon the business organization of which they make illegal use. It should be one of the main objects of our legislation to divest such persons of their corporate cloak and deal with them as with those who do not represent their corporations, but merely by deliberate intention break the law. Business men the country through would, I am sure, applaud us if we were to take effectual steps to see that the officers and directors of great business bodies were prevented from bringing them and the business of the country into disrepute and danger.

Other questions remain which will need very thoughtful and practical treatment. Enterprises, in these modern days of great individual fortunes, are oftentimes interlocked, not by being under the control of the same directors, but by the fact that the greater part of their corporate stock is owned by a single person or group of persons who are in some way ultimately related in interest. We are agreed, I take it, that holding *companies* should be prohibited, but what of the controlling private ownership of individuals or actually coöperative groups of individuals? Shall the private owners of capital stock be suffered to be themselves in effect holding companies? We do not wish, I suppose, to forbid the purchase of stocks by any person who pleases to buy them in such quantities as he can afford, or in any way arbitrarily to limit the sale of stocks to bona fide purchasers. Shall we require the owners of stock, when their voting power in several companies which ought to be independent of one another would constitute actual control, to make election in which of them they will exercise their right to vote? This question I venture for your consideration.

There is another matter in which imperative considerations of justice and fair play suggest thoughtful remedial action. Not only do many of the combinations effected or sought to be effected in the industrial world work an injustice upon the public in general; they also directly and seriously injure the individuals who are put out of business in one unfair way or another by the many dislodging and exterminating forces of combination. I hope that we shall agree in giving private individuals who claim to have been injured by these processes the right to found their suits for redress upon the facts and judgments proved and entered in suits by the Government where the Government has upon its own initiative sued the combinations complained of and won its suit, and that the statute of limitations shall be suffered to run against such litigants only from the date of the conclusion of the Government's action. It is not fair that the private litigant should be obliged to set up and establish again the facts which the Government has proved. He cannot afford, he has not the power, to make use of such processes of inquiry as the Government has command of. Thus shall individual justice be done while the processes of business are rectified and squared with the general conscience.

I have laid the case before you, no doubt as it lies in your own mind, as it lies in the thought of the country. What must every candid man say of the suggestions I have laid before you, of the plain obligations of which I have reminded you? That these are new things for which the country is not prepared? No; but that they are old things, now familiar, and must of course be undertaken if we are to square our laws with the thought and desire of the country. Until these things are done, conscientious business men the country over will be unsatisfied. They are in these things our mentors and colleagues. We are now about to write the additional articles of our constitution of peace, the peace that is honor and freedom and prosperity.

Panama Canal Tolls

[Address delivered at a joint session of the two Houses of Congress, March 5, 1914.]

Gentlemen of the Congress:

I have come to you upon an errand which can be very briefly performed, but I beg that you will not measure its importance by the number of sentences in which I state it. No communication I have addressed to the Congress carried with it graver or more far-reaching implications as to the interest of the country, and I come now to speak upon a matter with regard to which I am charged in a peculiar degree, by the Constitution itself, with personal responsibility.

I have come to ask you for the repeal of that provision of the Panama Canal Act of August 24, 1912, which exempts vessels engaged in the coastwise trade of the United States from payment of tolls, and to urge upon you the justice, the wisdom, and the large policy of such a repeal with the utmost earnestness of which I am capable.

In my own judgment, very fully considered and maturely formed, that exemption constitutes a mistaken economic policy from every point of view, and is, moreover, in plain contravention of the treaty with Great Britain concerning the canal concluded on November 18, 1901. But I have not come to urge upon you my personal views. I have come to state to you a fact and a situation. Whatever may be our own differences of opinion concerning this much debated measure, its meaning is not debated outside the United States. Everywhere else the language of the treaty is given but one interpretation, and that interpretation precludes the exemption I am asking you to repeal. We consented to the treaty; its language we accepted, if we did not originate it; and we are too big, too powerful, too self-respecting a nation to interpret with a too strained or refined reading the words of our own promises just because we have power enough to give us leave to read them as we please. The large thing to do is the only thing we can afford to do, a voluntary withdrawal from a position everywhere questioned and misunderstood. We ought to reverse our action without raising the question whether we were right or wrong, and so once more deserve our reputation for generosity and for the redemption of every obligation without quibble or hesitation.

I ask this of you in support of the foreign policy of the administration. I shall not know how to deal with other matters of even greater delicacy and nearer consequence if you do not grant it to me in ungrudging measure.

The Tampico Incident

[Address delivered at a joint session of the two Houses of Congress, April 20, 1914.]

Gentlemen of the Congress:

It is my duty to call your attention to a situation which has arisen in our dealings with General Victoriano Huerta at Mexico City which calls for action, and to ask your advice and coöperation in acting upon it. On the 9th of April a paymaster of the U.S.S. *Dolphin* landed at the Iturbide Bridge landing at Tampico with a whaleboat and boat's crew to take off certain supplies needed by his ship, and while engaged in loading the boat was arrested by an officer and squad of men of the army of General Huerta. Neither the paymaster nor anyone of the boat's crew was armed. Two of the men were in the boat when the arrest took place and were obliged to leave it and submit to be taken into custody, notwithstanding the fact that the boat carried, both at her bow and at her stern, the flag of the United States. The officer who made the arrest was proceeding up one of the streets of the town with his prisoners when met by an officer of higher authority, who ordered him to return to the landing and await orders; and within an hour and a half from the time of the arrest orders were received from the commander of the Huertista forces at Tampico for the release of the paymaster and his men. The release was followed by apologies from the commander and later by an expression of regret by General Huerta himself. General Huerta urged that martial law obtained at the time at Tampico; that orders had been issued that no one should be allowed to land at the Iturbide Bridge; and that our sailors had no right to land there. Our naval commanders at the port had not been notified of any such prohibition; and, even if they had been, the only justifiable course open to the local authorities would have been to request the paymaster and his crew to withdraw and to lodge a protest with the commanding officer of the fleet. Admiral Mayo regarded the arrest as so serious an affront that he was not satisfied with the apologies offered, but demanded that the flag of the United States be saluted with special ceremony by the military commander of the port.

The incident cannot be regarded as a trivial one, especially as two of the men arrested were taken from the boat itself-that is to say, from the territory of the United States-but had it stood by itself it might have been attributed to the ignorance or arrogance of a single officer. Unfortunately, it was not an isolated case. A series of incidents have recently occurred which cannot but create the impression that the representatives of General Huerta were willing to go out of their way to show disregard for the dignity and rights of this Government and felt perfectly safe in doing what they pleased, making free to show in many ways their irritation and contempt. A few days after the incident at Tampico an orderly from the U.S.S. *Minnesota* was arrested at Vera Cruz while ashore in uniform to obtain the ship's mail, and was for a time thrown into jail. An official dispatch from this Government to its embassy at Mexico City was withheld by the authorities of the telegraphic service until peremptorily demanded by our chargé d'affaires in person. So far as I can learn, such wrongs and annoyances have been suffered to occur only against representatives of the United States. I have heard of no complaints from other Governments of similar treatment. Subsequent explanations and formal apologies did not and could not alter the popular impression, which it is possible it had been the object of the Huertista authorities to create, that the Government of the United States was being singled out, and might be singled out with impunity, for slights and affronts in retaliation for its refusal to recognize the pretensions of General Huerta to be regarded as the constitutional provisional President of the Republic of Mexico.

The manifest danger of such a situation was that such offenses might grow from bad to worse until something happened of so gross and intolerable a sort as to lead directly and inevitably to armed conflict. It was necessary that the apologies of General Huerta and his representatives should go much further, that they should be such as to attract the attention of the whole population to their significance, and such as to impress upon General Huerta himself the necessity of seeing to it that no further occasion for explanations and professed regrets should arise. I, therefore, felt it my duty to sustain Admiral Mayo in the whole of his demand and to insist that the flag of the United States should be saluted in such a way as to indicate a new spirit and attitude on the part of the Huertistas.

Such a salute General Huerta has refused, and I have come to ask your approval and support in the course I now purpose to pursue.

This Government can, I earnestly hope, in no circumstances be forced into war with the people of Mexico. Mexico is torn by civil strife. If we are to accept the tests of its own constitution, it has no government. General Huerta has set his power up in the City of Mexico, such as it is, without right and by methods for which there can be no justification. Only part of the country is under his control. If armed conflict should unhappily come as a result of his attitude of personal resentment toward this Government, we should be fighting only General Huerta and those who adhere to him and give him their support, and our object would be only to restore to the people of the distracted Republic the opportunity to set up again their own laws and their own government.

But I earnestly hope that war is not now in question. I believe that I speak for the American people when I say that we do not desire to control in any degree the affairs of our sister Republic. Our feeling for the people of Mexico is one of deep and genuine friendship, and everything that we have so far done or refrained from doing has proceeded from our desire to help them, not to hinder or embarrass them. We would not wish even to exercise the good offices of friendship without their welcome and consent. The people of Mexico are entitled to settle their own domestic affairs in their own way, and we sincerely desire to respect their right. The present situation need have none of the grave implications of interference if we deal with it promptly, firmly, and wisely.

No doubt I could do what is necessary in the circumstances to enforce respect for our Government without recourse to the Congress, and yet not exceed my constitutional powers as President; but I do not wish to act in a matter possibly of so grave consequence except in close conference and coöperation with both the Senate and House. I, therefore, come to ask your approval that I should use the armed forces of the United States in such ways and to such an extent as may be necessary to obtain from General Huerta and his adherents the fullest recognition of the rights and dignity of the United States, even amidst the distressing conditions now unhappily obtaining in Mexico.

There can in what we do be no thought of aggression or of selfish aggrandizement. We seek to maintain the dignity and authority of the United States only because we wish always to keep our great influence unimpaired for the uses of liberty, both in the United States and wherever else it may be employed for the benefit of mankind.

In the Firmament of Memory

[Address at the Services in Memory of those who lost their lives at Vera Cruz, Mexico, delivered at the Brooklyn Navy Yard, May 11, 1914. The roster, of fifteen sailors and four marines, was presented by the Secretary of the Navy, Mr. Daniels.]

Mr. Secretary:

I know that the feelings which characterize all who stand about me and the whole Nation at this hour are not feelings which can be suitably expressed in terms of attempted oratory or eloquence. They are things too deep for ordinary speech. For my own part, I have a singular mixture of feelings. The feeling that is uppermost is one of profound grief that these lads should have had to go to their death; and yet there is mixed with that grief a profound pride that they should have gone as they did, and, if I may say it out of my heart, a touch of envy of those who were permitted so quietly, so nobly, to do their duty. Have you thought of it, men? Here is the roster of the Navy-the list of the men, officers and enlisted men and marines-and suddenly there swim nineteen stars out of the list-men who have suddenly been lifted into a firmament of memory where we shall always see their names shine, not because they called upon us to admire them, but because they served us, without asking any questions and in the performance of a duty which is laid upon us as well as upon them.

Duty is not an uncommon thing, gentlemen. Men are performing it in the ordinary walks of life all around us all the time, and they are making great sacrifices to perform it. What gives men like these peculiar distinction is not merely that they did their duty, but that their duty had nothing to do with them or their own personal and peculiar interests. They did not give their lives for themselves. They gave their lives for us, because we called upon them as a Nation to perform an unexpected duty. That is the way in which men grow distinguished, and that is the only way, by serving somebody else than themselves. And what greater thing could you serve than a Nation such as this we love and are proud of? Are you sorry for these lads? Are you sorry for the way they will be remembered? Does it not quicken your pulses to think of the list of them? I hope to God none of you may join the list, but if you do you will join an immortal company.

So, while we are profoundly sorrowful, and while there goes out of our hearts a very deep and affectionate sympathy for the friends and relatives of these lads who for the rest of their lives shall mourn them, though with a touch of pride, we know why we do not go away from this occasion cast down, but with our heads lifted and our eyes on the future of this country, with absolute confidence of how it will be worked out. Not only upon the mere vague future of this country, but upon the immediate future. We have gone down to Mexico to serve mankind if we can find out the way. We do not want to fight the Mexicans. We want to serve the Mexicans if we can, because we know how we would like to be free, and how we would like to be served if there were friends standing by in such case ready to serve us. A war of aggression is not a war in which it is a proud thing to die, but a war of service is a thing in which it is a proud thing to die.

Notice how truly these men were of our blood. I mean of our American blood, which is not drawn from any one country, which is not drawn from any one stock, which is not drawn from any one language of the modern world; but free men everywhere have sent their sons and their brothers and their daughters to this country in order to make that great compounded Nation which consists of all the sturdy elements and of all the best elements of the whole globe. I listened again to this list of the dead with a profound interest because of the mixture of the names, for the names bear the marks of the several national stocks from which these men came. But they are not Irishmen or Germans or Frenchmen or Hebrews or Italians any more. They were not when they went to Vera Cruz; they were Americans, every one of them, and with no difference in their Americanism because of the stock from which they came. They were in a peculiar sense of our blood, and they proved it by showing that they were of our spirit-that no matter what their derivation, no matter where their people came from, they thought and wished and did the things that were American; and the flag under which they served was a flag in which all the blood of mankind is united to make a free Nation.

War, gentlemen, is only a sort of dramatic representation, a sort of dramatic symbol, of a thousand forms of duty. I never went into battle; I never was under fire; but I fancy that there are some things just as hard to do as to go under fire. I fancy that it is just as hard to do your duty when men are sneering at you as when they are shooting at you. When they shoot at you, they can only take your natural life; when they sneer at you, they can wound your living heart, and men who are brave enough, steadfast enough, steady in their principles enough, to go about their duty with regard to their fellow-men, no matter whether there are hisses or cheers, men who can do what Rudyard Kipling in one of his poems wrote, "Meet with triumph and disaster and treat those two impostors just the same," are men for a nation to be proud of. Morally speaking, disaster and triumph are impostors. The cheers of the moment are not what a man ought to think about, but the verdict of his conscience and of the consciences of mankind.

When I look at you, I feel as if I also and we all were enlisted men. Not enlisted in your particular branch of the service, but enlisted to serve the country, no matter what may come, even though we may sacrifice our lives in the arduous endeavor. We are expected to put the utmost energy of every power that we have into the service of our fellow-men, never sparing ourselves, not condescending to think of what is going to happen to ourselves, but ready, if need be, to go to the utter length of complete self-sacrifice.

As I stand and look at you to-day and think of these spirits that have gone from us, I know that the road is clearer for the future. These boys have shown us the way, and it is easier to walk on it because they have gone before and shown us how. May God grant to all of us that vision of patriotic service which here in solemnity and grief and pride is borne in upon our hearts and consciences!

Memorial Day Address at Arlington

[Delivered at the National Cemetery, Arlington, Va., May 30, 1914.]

Ladies and Gentlemen:

I have not come here to-day with a prepared address. The committee in charge of the exercises of the day have graciously excused me on the grounds of public obligations from preparing such an address, but I will not deny myself the privilege of joining with you in an expression of gratitude and admiration for the men who perished for the sake of the Union. They do not need our praise. They do not need that our admiration should sustain them. There is no immortality that is safer than theirs. We come not for their sakes but for our own, in order that we may drink at the same springs of inspiration from which they themselves selves drank.

A peculiar privilege came to the men who fought for the Union. There is no other civil war in history, ladies and gentlemen, the stings of which were removed before the men who did the fighting passed from the stage of life. So that we owe these men something more than a legal reëstablishment of the Union. We owe them the spiritual reëstablishment of the Union as well; for they not only reunited States, they reunited the spirits of men. That is their unique achievement, unexampled anywhere else in the annals of mankind, that the very men whom they overcame in battle join in praise and gratitude that the Union was saved. There is something peculiarly beautiful and peculiarly touching about that. Whenever a man who is still trying to devote himself to the service of the Nation comes into a presence like this, or into a place like this, his spirit must be peculiarly moved. A mandate is laid upon him which seems to speak from the very graves themselves. Those who serve this Nation, whether in peace or in war, should serve it without thought of themselves. I can never speak in praise of war, ladies and gentlemen; you would not desire me to do so. But there is this peculiar distinction belonging to the soldier, that he goes into an enterprise out of which he himself cannot get anything at all. He is giving everything that he hath, even his life, in order that others may live, not in order that he himself may obtain gain and prosperity. And just so soon as the tasks of peace are performed in the same spirit of self-sacrifice and devotion, peace societies will not be necessary. The very organization and spirit of society will be a guaranty of peace.

Therefore this peculiar thing comes about, that we can stand here and praise the memory of these soldiers in the interest of peace. They set us the example of self-sacrifice, which if followed in peace will make it unnecessary that men should follow war any more.

We are reputed to be somewhat careless in our discrimination between words in the use of the English language, and yet it is interesting to note that there are some words about which we are very careful. We bestow the adjective "great" somewhat indiscriminately. A man who has made conquest of his fellow-men for his own gain may display such genius in war, such uncommon qualities of organization and leadership that we may call him "great," but there is a word which we reserve for men of another kind and about which we are very careful; that is the word "noble." We never call a man "noble" who serves only himself; and if you will look about through all the nations of the world upon the statues that men have erected-upon the inscribed tablets where they have wished to keep alive the memory of the citizens whom they desire most to honor-you will find that almost without exception they have erected the statue to those who had a splendid surplus of energy and devotion to spend upon their fellow-men. Nobility exists in America without patent. We have no House of Lords, but we have a house of fame to which we elevate those who are the noble men of our race, who, forgetful of themselves, study and serve the public interest, who have the courage to face any number and any kind of adversary, to speak what in their hearts they believe to be the truth.

We admire physical courage, but we admire above all things else moral courage. I believe that soldiers will bear me out in saying that both come in time of battle. I take it that the moral courage comes in going into the battle, and the physical courage in staying in. There are battles which are just as hard to go into and just as hard to stay in as the battles of arms, and if the man will but stay and think never of himself there will come a time of grateful recollection when men will speak of him not only with admiration but with that which goes deeper, with affection and with reverence.

So that this flag calls upon us daily for service, and the more quiet and self-denying the service the greater the glory of the flag. We are dedicated to freedom, and that freedom means the freedom of the human spirit. All free spirits ought to congregate on an occasion like this to do homage to the greatness of America as illustrated by the greatness of her sons.

It has been a privilege, ladies and gentlemen, to come and say these simple words, which I am sure are merely putting your thought into language. I thank you for the opportunity to lay this little wreath of mine upon these consecrated graves.

Closing a Chapter

[Address in which President Wilson accepted the Monument in Memory of the Confederate Dead, at Arlington National Cemetery, June 4, 1914.].

Mr. Chairman, Mrs. McLaurin Stevens, Ladies and Gentlemen:

I assure you that I am profoundly aware of the solemn significance of the thing that has now taken place. The Daughters of the Confederacy have presented a memorial of their dead to the Government of the United States. I hope that you have noted the history of the conception of this idea. It was suggested by a President of the United States who had himself been a distinguished officer in the Union Army. It was authorized by an act of Congress of the United States. The corner-stone of the monument was laid by a President of the United States elevated to his position by the votes of the party which had chiefly prided itself upon sustaining the war for the Union, and who, while Secretary of War, had himself given authority to erect it. And, now, it has fallen to my lot to accept in the name of the great Government, which I am privileged for the time to represent, this emblem of a reunited people. I am not so much happy as proud to participate in this capacity on such an occasion, —proud that I should represent such a people. Am I mistaken, ladies and gentlemen, in supposing that nothing of this sort could have occurred in anything but a democracy? The people of a democracy are not related to their rulers as subjects are related to a government. They are themselves the sovereign authority, and as they are neighbors of each other, quickened by the same influences and moved by the same motives, they can understand each other. They are shot through with some of the deepest and profoundest instincts of human sympathy. They choose their governments; they select their rulers; they live their own life, and they will not have that life disturbed and discolored by fraternal misunderstandings. I know that a reuniting of spirits like this can take place more quickly in our time than in any other because men are now united by an easier transmission of those influences which make up the foundations of peace and of mutual understanding, but no process can work these effects unless there is a conducting medium. The conducting medium in this instance is the united heart of a great people. I am not going to detain you by trying to repeat any of the eloquent thoughts which have moved us this afternoon, for I rejoice in the simplicity of the task which is assigned to me. My privilege is this, ladies and gentlemen: To declare this chapter in the history of the United States closed and ended, and I bid you turn with me with your faces to the future, quickened by the memories of the past, but with nothing to do with the contests of the past, knowing, as we have shed our blood upon opposite sides, we now face and admire one another. I do not know how many years ago it was that the *Century Dictionary* was published, but I remember one day in the *Century Cyclopedia of Names* I had occasion to turn to the name of Robert E. Lee, and I found him there in that book published in New York City simply described as a great American general. The generosity of our judgments did not begin to-day. The generosity of our judgment was made up soon after this great struggle was over. Men came and sat together again in the Congress and united in all the efforts of peace and of government, and our solemn duty is to see that each one of us is in his own consciousness and in his own conduct a replica of this great reunited people. It is our duty and our privilege to be like the country we represent and, speaking no word of malice, no word of criticism even, stand shoulder to shoulder to lift the burdens of mankind in the future and show the paths of freedom to all the world.

Annapolis Commencement Address

[Delivered before the Graduating Class of the United States Naval Academy, Annapolis, Maryland, June 5, 1914.]

Mr. Superintendent, Young Gentlemen, Ladies and Gentlemen:
During the greater part of my life I have been associated with young men, and on occasions it seems to me without number have faced bodies of youngsters going out to take part in the activities of the world, but I have a consciousness of a different significance in this occasion from that which I have felt on other similar occasions. When I have faced the graduating classes at universities I have felt that I was facing a great conjecture. They were going out into all sorts of pursuits and with every degree of preparation for the particular thing they were expecting to do; some without any preparation at all, for they did not know what they expected to do. But in facing you I am facing men who are trained for a special thing. You know what you are going to do, and you are under the eye of the whole Nation in doing it. For you, gentlemen, are to be part of the power of the Government of the United States. There is a very deep and solemn significance in that fact, and I am sure that every one of you feels it. The moral is perfectly obvious. Be ready and fit for anything that you have to do. And keep ready and fit. Do not grow slack. Do not suppose that your education is over because you have received your diplomas from the academy. Your education has just begun. Moreover, you are to have a very peculiar privilege which not many of your predecessors have had. You are yourselves going to become teachers. You are going to teach those 50,000 fellow-countrymen of yours who are the enlisted men of the Navy. You are going to make them fitter to obey your orders and to serve the country. You are going to make them fitter to see what the orders mean in their outlook upon life and upon the service; and that is a great privilege, for out of you is going the energy and intelligence which are going to quicken the whole body of the United States Navy.

I congratulate you upon that prospect, but I want to ask you not to get the professional point of view. I would ask it of you if you were lawyers; I would ask it of you if you were merchants; I would ask it of you whatever you expected to be. Do not get the professional point of view. There is nothing narrower or more unserviceable than the professional point of view, to have the attitude toward life that it centers in your profession. It does not. Your profession is only one of the many activities which are meant to keep the world straight, and to keep the energy in its blood and in its muscle. We are all of us in this world, as I understand it, to set forward the affairs of the whole world, though we play a special part in that great function. The Navy goes all over the world, and I think it is to be congratulated upon having that sort of illustration of what the world is and what it contains; and inasmuch as you are going all over the world you ought to be the better able to see the relation that your country bears to the rest of the world.

It ought to be one of your thoughts all the time that you are sample Americans-not merely sample Navy men, not merely sample soldiers, but sample Americans-and that you have the point of view of America with regard to her Navy and her Army; that she is using them as the instruments of civilization, not as the instruments of aggression. The idea of America is to serve humanity, and every time you let the Stars and Stripes free to the wind you ought to realize that that is in itself a message that you are on an errand which other navies have sometimes tunes forgotten; not an errand of conquest, but an errand of service. I always have the same thought when I look at the flag of the United States, for I know something of the history of the struggle of mankind for liberty. When I look at that flag it seems to me as if the white stripes were strips of parchment upon which are written the rights of man, and the red stripes the streams of blood by which those rights have been made good. Then in the little blue firmament in the corner have swung out the stars of the States of the American Union. So it is, as it were, a sort of floating charter that has come down to us from Runnymede, when men said, "We will not have masters; we will be a people, and we will seek our own liberty."

You are not serving a government, gentlemen; you are serving a people. For we who for the time being constitute the Government are merely instruments for a little while in the hands of a great Nation which chooses whom it will to carry out its decrees and who invariably rejects the man who forgets the ideals which it intended him to serve. So that I hope that wherever you go you will have a generous, comprehending love of the people you come into contact with, and will come back and tell us, if you can, what service the United States can render to the remotest parts of the world; tell us where you see men suffering; tell us where you think advice will lift them up; tell us where you think that the counsel of statesmen may better the fortunes of unfortunate men; always having it in mind that you are champions of what is right and fair all 'round for the public welfare, no matter where you are, and that it is that you are ready to fight for and not merely on the drop of a hat or upon some slight punctilio, but that you are champions of your fellow-men, particularly of that great body one hundred million strong whom you represent in the United States.

What do you think is the most lasting impression that those boys down at Vera Cruz are going to leave? They have had to use some force —I pray God it may not be necessary for them to use any more-but do you think that the way they fought is going to be the most lasting impression? Have men not fought ever since the world began? Is there anything new in using force? The new things in the world are the things that are divorced from force. The things that show the moral compulsions of the human conscience, those are the things by which we have been building up civilization, not by force. And the lasting impression that those boys are going to leave is this, that they exercise self-control; that they are ready and diligent to make the place where they went fitter to live in than they found it; that they regarded other people's rights; that they did not strut and bluster, but went quietly, like self-respecting gentlemen, about their legitimate work. And the people of Vera Cruz, who feared the Americans and despised the Americans, are going to get a very different taste in their mouths about the whole thing when the boys of the Navy and the Army come away. Is that not something to be proud of, that you know how to use force like men of conscience and like gentlemen, serving your fellow-men and not trying to overcome them? Like that gallant gentleman who has so long borne the heats and perplexities and distresses of the situation in Vera Cruz-Admiral Fletcher. I mention him, because his service there has been longer and so much of the early perplexities fell upon him. I have been in almost daily communication with Admiral Fletcher, and I have tested his temper. I have tested his discretion. I know that he is a man with a touch of statesmanship about him, and he has grown bigger in my eye each day as I have read his dispatches, for he has sought always to serve the thing he was trying to do in the temper that we all recognize and love to believe is typically American.

I challenge you youngsters to go out with these conceptions, knowing that you are part of the Government and force of the United States and that men will judge us by you. I am not afraid of the verdict. I cannot look in your faces and doubt what it will be, but I want you to take these great engines of force out onto the seas like adventurers enlisted for the elevation of the spirit of the human race. For that is the only distinction that America has. Other nations have been strong, other nations have piled wealth as high as the sky, but they have come into disgrace because they used their force and their wealth for the oppression of mankind and their own aggrandizement; and America will not bring glory to herself, but disgrace, by following the beaten paths of history. We must strike out upon new paths, and we must count upon you gentlemen to be the explorers who will carry this spirit and spread this message all over the seas and in every port of the civilized world.

You see, therefore, why I said that when I faced you I felt there was a special significance. I am not present on an occasion when you are about to scatter on various errands. You are all going on the same errand, and I like to feel bound with you in one common organization for the glory of America. And her glory goes deeper than all the tinsel, goes deeper than the sound of guns and the clash of sabers; it goes down to the very foundations of those things that have made the spirit of men free and happy and content.

The Meaning of Liberty

[Address at Independence Hall, Philadelphia, July 4, 1914.]

Mr. Chairman and Fellow-Citizens:

We are assembled to celebrate the one hundred and thirty-eighth anniversary of the birth of the United States. I suppose that we can more vividly realize the circumstances of that birth standing on this historic spot than it would be possible to realize them anywhere else. The Declaration of Independence was written in Philadelphia; it was adopted in this historic building by which we stand. I have just had the privilege of sitting in the chair of the great man who presided over the deliberations of those who gave the declaration to the world. My hand rests at this moment upon the table upon which the declaration was signed. We can feel that we are almost in the visible and tangible presence of a great historic transaction.

Have you ever read the Declaration of Independence or attended with close comprehension to the real character of it when you have heard it read? If you have, you will know that it is not a Fourth of July oration. The Declaration of Independence was a document preliminary to war. It was a vital piece of practical business, not a piece of rhetoric; and if you will pass beyond those preliminary passages which we are accustomed to quote about the rights of men and read into the heart of the document you will see that it is very express and detailed, that it consists of a series of definite specifications concerning actual public business of the day. Not the business of our day, for the matter with which it deals is past, but the business of that first revolution by which the Nation was set up, the business of 1776. Its general statements, its general declarations cannot mean anything to us unless we append to it a similar specific body of particulars as to what we consider the essential business of our own day.

Liberty does not consist, my fellow-citizens, in mere general declarations of the rights of man. It consists in the translation of those declarations into definite action. Therefore, standing here where the declaration was adopted, reading its businesslike sentences, we ought to ask ourselves what there is in it for us. There is nothing in it for us unless we can translate it into the terms of our own conditions and of our own lives. We must reduce it to what the lawyers call a bill of particulars. It contains a bill of particulars, but the bill of particulars of 1776. If we would keep it alive, we must fill it with a bill of particulars of the year 1914.

The task to which we have constantly to readdress ourselves is the task of proving that we are worthy of the men who drew this great declaration and know what they would have done in our circumstances. Patriotism consists in some very practical things-practical in that they belong to the life of every day, that they wear no extraordinary distinction about them, that they are connected with commonplace duty. The way to be patriotic in America is not only to love America but to love the duty that lies nearest to our hand and know that in performing it we are serving our country. There are some gentlemen in Washington, for example, at this very moment who are showing themselves very patriotic in a way which does not attract wide attention but seems to belong to mere everyday obligations. The Members of the House and Senate who stay in hot Washington to maintain a quorum of the Houses and transact the all-important business of the Nation are doing an act of patriotism. I honor them for it, and I am glad to stay there and stick by them until the work is done.

It is patriotic, also, to learn what the facts of our national life are and to face them with candor. I have heard a great many facts stated about the present business condition of this country, for example —a great many allegations of fact, at any rate, but the allegations do not tally with one another. And yet I know that truth always matches with truth and when I find some insisting that everything is going wrong and others insisting that everything is going right, and when I know from a wide observation of the general circumstances of the country taken as a whole that things are going extremely well, I wonder what those who are crying out that things are wrong are trying to do. Are they trying to serve the country, or are they trying to serve something smaller than the country? Are they trying to put hope into the hearts of the men who work and toil every day, or are they trying to plant discouragement and despair in those hearts? And why do they cry that everything is wrong and yet do nothing to set it right? If they love America and anything is wrong amongst us, it is their business to put their hand with ours to the task of setting it right. When the facts are known and acknowledged, the duty of all patriotic men is to accept them in candor and to address themselves hopefully and confidently to the common counsel which is necessary to act upon them wisely and in universal concert.

I have had some experiences in the last fourteen months which have not been entirely reassuring. It was universally admitted, for example, my fellow-citizens, that the banking system of this country needed reorganization. We set the best minds that we could find to the task of discovering the best method of reorganization. But we met with hardly anything but criticism from the bankers of the country; we met with hardly anything but resistance from the majority of those at least who spoke at all concerning the matter. And yet so soon as that act was passed there was a universal chorus of applause, and the very men who had opposed the measure joined in that applause. If it was wrong the day before it was passed, why was it right the day after it was passed? Where had been the candor of criticism not only, but the concert of counsel which makes legislative action vigorous and safe and successful?

It is not patriotic to concert measures against one another; it is patriotic to concert measures for one another.

In one sense the Declaration of Independence has lost its significance. It has lost its significance as a declaration of national independence. Nobody outside of America believed when it was uttered that we could make good our independence; now nobody anywhere would dare to doubt that we are independent and can maintain our independence. As a declaration of independence, therefore, it is a mere historic document. Our independence is a fact so stupendous that it can be measured only by the size and energy and variety and wealth and power of one of the greatest nations in the world. But it is one thing to be independent and it is another thing to know what to do with your independence. It is one thing to come to your majority and another thing to know what you are going to do with your life and your energies; and one of the most serious questions for sober-minded men to address themselves to in the United States is this: What are we going to do with the influence and power of this great Nation? Are we going to play the old role of using that power for our aggrandizement and material benefit only? You know what that may mean. It may upon occasion mean that we shall use it to make the peoples of other nations suffer in the way in which we said it was intolerable to suffer when we uttered our Declaration of Independence.

The Department of State at Washington is constantly called upon to back up the commercial enterprises and the industrial enterprises of the United States in foreign countries, and it at one time went so far in that direction that all its diplomacy came to be designated as "dollar diplomacy." It was called upon to support every man who wanted to earn anything anywhere if he was an American. But there ought to be a limit to that. There is no man who is more interested than I am in carrying the enterprise of American business men to every quarter of the globe. I was interested in it long before I was suspected of being a politician. I have been preaching it year after year as the great thing that lay in the future for the United States, to show her wit and skill and enterprise and influence in every country in the world. But observe the limit to all that which is laid upon us perhaps more than upon any other nation in the world. We set this Nation up, at any rate we professed to set it up, to vindicate the rights of men. We did not name any differences between one race and another. We did not set up any barriers against any particular people. We opened our gates to all the world and said, "Let all men who wish to be free come to us and they will be welcome." We said, "This independence of ours is not a selfish thing for our own exclusive private use. It is for everybody to whom we can find the means of extending it." We cannot with that oath taken in our youth, we cannot with that great ideal set before us when we were a young people and numbered only a scant

3,000,000, take upon ourselves, now that we are 100,000,000 strong, any other conception of duty than we then entertained. If American enterprise in foreign countries, particularly in those foreign countries which are not strong enough to resist us, takes the shape of imposing upon and exploiting the mass of the people of that country it ought to be checked and not encouraged. I am willing to get anything for an American that money and enterprise can obtain except the suppression of the rights of other men. I will not help any man buy a power which he ought not to exercise over his fellow-beings.

You know, my fellow-countrymen, what a big question there is in Mexico. Eighty-five per cent of the Mexican people have never been allowed to have any genuine participation in their own Government or to exercise any substantial rights with regard to the very land they live upon. All the rights that men most desire have been exercised by the other fifteen per cent. Do you suppose that that circumstance is not sometimes in my thought? I know that the American people have a heart that will beat just as strong for those millions in Mexico as it will beat, or has beaten, for any other millions elsewhere in the world, and that when once they conceive what is at stake in Mexico they will know what ought to be done in Mexico. I hear a great deal said about the loss of property in Mexico and the loss of the lives of foreigners, and I deplore these things with all my heart. Undoubtedly, upon the conclusion of the present disturbed conditions in Mexico those who have been unjustly deprived of their property or in any wise unjustly put upon ought to be compensated. Men's individual rights have no doubt been invaded, and the invasion of those rights has been attended by many deplorable circumstances which ought sometime, in the proper way, to be accounted for. But back of it all is the struggle of a people to come into its own, and while we look upon the incidents in the foreground let us not forget the great tragic reality in the background which towers above the whole picture.

A patriotic American is a man who is not niggardly and selfish in the things that he enjoys that make for human liberty and the rights of man. He wants to share them with the whole world, and he is never so proud of the great flag under which he lives as when it comes to mean to other people as well as to himself a symbol of hope and liberty. I would be ashamed of this flag if it ever did anything outside America that we would not permit it to do inside of America.

The world is becoming more complicated every day, my fellow-citizens. No man ought to be foolish enough to think that he understands it all. And, therefore, I am glad that there are some simple things in the world. One of the simple things is principle. Honesty is a perfectly simple thing. It is hard for me to believe that in most circumstances when a man has a choice of ways he does not know which is the right way and which is the wrong way. No man who has chosen the wrong way ought even to come into Independence Square; it is holy ground which he ought not to tread upon. He ought not to come where immortal voices have uttered the great sentences of such a document as this Declaration of Independence upon which rests the liberty of a whole nation.

And so I say that it is patriotic sometimes to prefer the honor of the country to its material interest. Would you rather be deemed by all the nations of the world incapable of keeping your treaty obligations in order that you might have free tolls for American ships? The treaty under which we gave up that right may have been a mistaken treaty, but there was no mistake about its meaning.

When I have made a promise as a man I try to keep it, and I know of no other rule permissible to a nation. The most distinguished nation in the world is the nation that can and will keep its promises even to its own hurt. And I want to say parenthetically that I do not think anybody was hurt. I cannot be enthusiastic for subsidies to a monopoly, but let those who are enthusiastic for subsidies ask themselves whether they prefer subsidies to unsullied honor.

The most patriotic man, ladies and gentlemen, is sometimes the man who goes in the direction that he thinks right even when he sees half the world against him. It is the dictate of patriotism to sacrifice yourself if you think that that is the path of honor and of duty. Do not blame others if they do not agree with you. Do not die with bitterness in your heart because you did not convince the rest of the world, but die happy because you believe that you tried to serve your country by not selling your soul. Those were grim days, the days of 1776. Those gentlemen did not attach their names to the Declaration of Independence on this table expecting a holiday on the next day, and that 4th of July was not itself a holiday. They attached their signatures to that significant document knowing that if they failed it was certain that every one of them would hang for the failure. They were committing treason in the interest of the liberty of 3,000,000 people in America. All the rest of the world was against them and smiled with cynical incredulity at the audacious undertaking. Do you think that if they could see this great Nation now they would regret anything that they then did to draw the gaze of a hostile world upon them? Every idea must be started by somebody, and it is a lonely thing to start anything. Yet if it is in you, you must start it if you have a man's blood in you and if you love the country that you profess to be working for.

I am sometimes very much interested when I see gentlemen supposing that popularity is the way to success in America. The way to success in this great country, with its fair judgments, is to show that you are not afraid of anybody except God and his final verdict. If I did not believe that, I would not believe in democracy. If I did not believe that, I would not believe that people can govern themselves. If I did not believe that the moral judgment would be the last judgment, the final judgment, in the minds of men as well as the tribunal of God, I could not believe in popular government. But I do believe these things, and, therefore, I earnestly believe in the democracy not only of America but of every awakened people that wishes and intends to govern and control its own affairs.

It is very inspiring, my friends, to come to this that may be called the original fountain of independence and liberty in American and here drink draughts of patriotic feeling which seem to renew the very blood in one's veins. Down in Washington sometimes when the days are hot and the business presses intolerably and there are so many things to do that it does not seem possible to do anything in the way it ought to be done, it is always possible to lift one's thought above the task of the moment and, as it were, to realize that great thing of which we are all parts, the great body of American feeling and American principle. No man could do the work that has to be done in Washington if he allowed himself to be separated from that body of principle. He must make himself feel that he is a part of the people of the United States, that he is trying to think not only for them, but with them, and then he cannot feel lonely. He not only cannot feel lonely but he cannot feel afraid of anything.

My dream is that as the years go on and the world knows more and more of America it will also drink at these fountains of youth and renewal; that it also will turn to America for those moral inspirations which lie at the basis of all freedom; that the world will never fear America unless it feels that it is engaged in some enterprise which is inconsistent with the rights of humanity; and that America will come into the full light of the day when all shall know that she puts human rights above all other rights and that her flag is the flag not only of America but of humanity.

What other great people has devoted itself to this exalted ideal? To what other nation in the world can all eyes look for an instant sympathy that thrills the whole body politic when men anywhere are fighting for their rights? I do not know that there will ever be a declaration of independence and of grievances for mankind, but I believe that if any such document is ever drawn it will be drawn in the spirit of the American Declaration of Independence, and that America has lifted high the light which will shine unto all generations and guide the feet of mankind to the goal of justice and liberty and peace.

American Neutrality

[An appeal to the citizens of the Republic, requesting their assistance in maintaining a state of neutrality during the European War, August 20, 1914.]

My Fellow-Countrymen:
I suppose that every thoughtful man in America has asked himself, during these last troubled weeks, what influence the European war may exert upon the United States, and I take the liberty of addressing a few words to you in order to point out that it is entirely within our own choice what its effects upon us will be and to urge very earnestly upon you the sort of speech and conduct which will best safeguard the Nation against distress and disaster.

The effect of the war upon the United States will depend upon what American citizens say and do. Every man who really loves America will act and speak in the true spirit of neutrality, which is the spirit of impartiality and fairness and friendliness to all concerned. The spirit of the Nation in this critical matter will be determined largely by what individuals and society and those gathered in public meetings do and say, upon what newspapers and magazines contain, upon what ministers utter in their pulpits, and men proclaim as their opinions on the street.

The people of the United States are drawn from many nations, and chiefly from the nations now at war. It is natural and inevitable that there should be the utmost variety of sympathy and desire among them with regard to the issues and circumstances of the conflict. Some will wish one nation, others another, to succeed in the momentous struggle. It will be easy to excite passion and difficult to allay it. Those responsible for exciting it will assume a heavy responsibility, responsibility for no less a thing than that the people of the United States, whose love of their country and whose loyalty to its Government should unite them as Americans all, bound in honor and affection to think first of her and her interests, may be divided in camps of hostile opinion, hot against each other, involved in the war itself in impulse and opinion if not in action.

Such divisions among us would be fatal to our peace of mind and might seriously stand in the way of the proper performance of our duty as the one great nation at peace, the one people holding itself ready to play a part of impartial mediation and speak the counsels of peace and accommodation, not as a partisan, but as a friend.

I venture, therefore, my fellow countrymen, to speak a solemn word of warning to you against that deepest, most subtle, most essential breach of neutrality which may spring out of partisanship, out of passionately taking sides. The United States must be neutral in fact as well as in name during these days that are to try men's souls. We must be impartial in thought as well as in action, must put a curb upon our sentiments as well as upon every transaction that might be construed as a preference of one party to the struggle before another.

My thought is of America. I am speaking, I feel sure, the earnest wish and purpose of every thoughtful American that this great country of ours, which is, of course, the first in our thoughts and in our hearts, should show herself in this time of peculiar trial a Nation fit beyond others to exhibit the fine poise of undisturbed judgment, the dignity of self-control, the efficiency of dispassionate action; a Nation that neither sits in judgment upon others nor is disturbed in her own counsels and which keeps herself fit and free to do what is honest and disinterested and truly serviceable for the peace of the world.

Shall we not resolve to put upon ourselves the restraints which will bring to our people the happiness and the great and lasting influence for peace we covet for them?

Appeal for Additional Revenue

[Address delivered at a joint session of the two Houses of Congress, September 4, 1914.]

Gentlemen of the Congress:

I come to you to-day to discharge a duty which I wish with all my heart I might have been spared; but it is a very clear duty, and therefore I perform it without hesitation or apology. I come to ask very earnestly that additional revenue be provided for the Government.

During the month of August there was, as compared with the corresponding month of last year, a falling off of $10,629,538 in the revenues collected from customs. A continuation of this decrease in the same proportion throughout the current fiscal year would probably mean a loss of customs revenues of from sixty to one hundred millions. I need not tell you to what this falling off is due. It is due, in chief part, not to the reductions recently made in the customs duties, but to the great decrease in importations; and that is due to the extraordinary extent of the industrial area affected by the present war in Europe. Conditions have arisen which no man foresaw; they affect the whole world of commerce and economic production; and they must be faced and dealt with.

It would be very unwise to postpone dealing with them. Delay in such a matter and in the particular circumstances in which we now find ourselves as a nation might involve consequences of the most embarrassing and deplorable sort, for which I, for one, would not care to be responsible. It would be very dangerous in the present circumstances to create a moment's doubt as to the strength and sufficiency of the Treasury of the United States, its ability to assist, to steady, and sustain the financial operations of the country's business. If the Treasury is known, or even thought, to be weak, where will be our peace of mind? The whole industrial activity of the country would be chilled and demoralized. Just now the peculiarly difficult financial problems of the moment are being successfully dealt with, with great self-possession and good sense and very sound judgment; but they are only in process of being worked out. If the process of solution is to be completed, no one must be given reason to doubt the solidity and adequacy of the Treasury of the Government which stands behind the whole method by which our difficulties are being met and handled.

The Treasury itself could get along for a considerable period, no doubt, without immediate resort to new sources of taxation. But at what cost to the business of the community? Approximately $75,000,000, a large part of the present Treasury balance, is now on deposit with national banks distributed throughout the country. It is deposited, of course, on call. I need not point out to you what the probable consequences of inconvenience and distress and confusion would be if the diminishing income of the Treasury should make it necessary rapidly to withdraw these deposits. And yet without additional revenue that plainly might become necessary, and the time when it became necessary could not be controlled or determined by the convenience of the business of the country. It would have to be determined by the operations and necessities of the Treasury itself. Such risks are not necessary and ought not to be run. We cannot too scrupulously or carefully safeguard a financial situation which is at best, while war continues in Europe, difficult and abnormal. Hesitation and delay are the worst forms of bad policy under such conditions.

And we ought not to borrow. We ought to resort to taxation, however we may regret the necessity of putting additional temporary burdens on our people. To sell bonds would be to make a most untimely and unjustifiable demand on the money market; untimely, because this is manifestly not the time to withdraw working capital from other uses to pay the Government's bills; unjustifiable, because unnecessary. The country is able to pay any just and reasonable taxes without distress. And to every other form of borrowing, whether for long periods or, for short, there is the same objection. These are not the circumstances, this is at this particular moment and in this particular exigency not the market, to borrow large sums of money. What we are seeking is to ease and assist every financial transaction, not to add a single additional embarrassment to the situation. The people of this country are both intelligent and profoundly patriotic. They are ready to meet the present conditions in the right way and to support the Government with generous self-denial. They know and understand, and will be intolerant only of those who dodge responsibility or are not frank with them.

The occasion is not of our own making. We had no part in making it. But it is here. It affects us as directly and palpably almost as if we were participants in the circumstances which gave rise to it. We must accept the inevitable with calm judgment and unruffled spirits, like men accustomed to deal with the unexpected, habituated to take care of themselves, masters of their own affairs and their own fortunes. We shall pay the bill, though we did not deliberately incur it.

In order to meet every demand upon the Treasury without delay or peradventure and in order to keep the Treasury strong, unquestionably strong, and strong throughout the present anxieties, I respectfully urge that an additional revenue of $100,000,000 be raised through internal taxes devised in your wisdom to meet the emergency. The only suggestion I take the liberty of making is that such sources of revenue be chosen as will begin to yield at once and yield with a certain and constant flow.

I cannot close without expressing the confidence with which I approach a Congress, with regard to this or any other matter, which has shown so untiring a devotion to public duty, which has responded to the needs of the Nation throughout a long season despite inevitable fatigue and personal sacrifice, and so large a proportion of whose Members have devoted their whole time and energy to the business of the country.

The Opinion of the World

[Address before the American Bar Association, in Continental Hall, October 20, 1914.]

Mr. President, Gentlemen of the American Bar Association:

I am very deeply gratified by the greeting that your president has given me and by your response to it. My only strength lies in your confidence.

We stand now in a peculiar case. Our first thought, I suppose, as lawyers, is of international law, of those bonds of right and principle which draw the nations together and hold the community of the world to some standards of action. We know that we see in international law, as it were, the moral processes by which law itself came into existence. I know that as a lawyer I have myself at times felt that there was no real comparison between the law of a nation and the law of nations, because the latter lacked the sanction that gave the former strength and validity. And yet, if you look into the matter more closely, you will find that the two have the same foundations, and that those foundations are more evident and conspicuous in our day than they have ever been before.

The opinion of the world is the mistress of the world; and the processes of international law are the slow processes by which opinion works its will. What impresses me is the constant thought that that is the tribunal at the bar of which we all sit. I would call your attention, incidentally, to the circumstance that it does not observe the ordinary rules of evidence; which has sometimes suggested to me that the ordinary rules of evidence had shown some signs of growing antique. Everything, rumor included, is heard in this court, and the standard of judgment is not so much the character of the testimony as the character of the witness. The motives are disclosed, the purposes are conjectured, and that opinion is finally accepted which seems to be, not the best founded in law, perhaps, but the best founded in integrity of character and of morals. That is the process which is slowly working its will upon the world; and what we should be watchful of is not so much jealous interests as sound principles of action. The disinterested course is always the biggest course to pursue not only, but it is in the long run the most profitable course to pursue. If you can establish your character, you can establish your credit.

What I wanted to suggest to this association, in bidding them very hearty welcome to the city, is whether we sufficiently apply these same ideas to the body of municipal law which we seek to administer. Citations seem to play so much larger a role now than principle. There was a time when the thoughtful eye of the judge rested upon the changes of social circumstances and almost palpably saw the law arise out of human life. Have we got to a time when the only way to change law is by statute? The changing of law by statute seems to me like mending a garment with a patch, whereas law should grow by the life that is in it, not by the life that is outside of it.

I once said to a lawyer with whom I was discussing some question of precedent, and in whose presence I was venturing to doubt the rational validity, at any rate, of the particular precedents he cited, "After all, isn't our object justice?" And he said, "God forbid! We should be very much confused if we made that our standard. Our standard is to find out what the rule has been and how the rule that has been applies to the case that is." I should hate to think that the law was based entirely upon "has beens." I should hate to think that the law did not derive its impulse from looking forward rather than from looking backward, or, rather, that it did not derive its instruction from looking about and seeing what the circumstances of man actually are and what the impulses of justice necessarily are.

Understand me, gentlemen, I am not venturing in this presence to impeach the law. For the present, by the force of circumstances, I am in part the embodiment of the law, and it would be very awkward to disavow myself. But I do wish to make this intimation, that in this time of world change, in this time when we are going to find out just how, in what particulars, and to what extent the real facts of human life and the real moral judgments of mankind prevail, it is worth while looking inside our municipal law and seeing whether the judgments of the law are made square with the moral judgments of mankind. For I believe that we are custodians, not of commands, but of a spirit. We are custodians of the spirit of righteousness, of the spirit of equal-handed justice, of the spirit of hope which believes in the perfectibility of the law with the perfectibility of human life itself.

Public life, like private life, would be very dull and dry if it were not for this belief in the essential beauty of the human spirit and the belief that the human spirit could be translated into action and into ordinance. Not entire. You cannot go any faster than you can advance the average moral judgments of the mass, but you can go at least as fast as that, and you can see to it that you do not lag behind the average moral judgments of the mass. I have in my life dealt with all sorts and conditions of men, and I have found that the flame of moral judgment burned just as bright in the man of humble life and limited experience as in the scholar and the man of affairs. And I would like his voice always to be heard, not as a witness, not as speaking in his own case, but as if he were the voice of men in general, in our courts of justice, as well as the voice of the lawyers, remembering what the law has been. My hope is that, being stirred to the depths by the extraordinary circumstances of the time in which we live, we may recover from those depths something of a renewal of that vision of the law with which men may be supposed to have started out in the old days of the oracles, who communed with the intimations of divinity.

The Power of Christian Young Men

[Address at the Young Men's Christian Association's Celebration, Pittsburgh, October 24, 1914.]

Mr. President, Mr. Porter, Ladies and Gentlemen:
I feel almost as if I were a truant, being away from Washington to-day, but I thought that perhaps if I were absent the Congress would have the more leisure to adjourn. I do not ordinarily open my office at Washington on Saturday. Being a schoolmaster, I am accustomed to a Saturday holiday, and I thought I could not better spend a holiday than by showing at least something of the true direction of my affections; for by long association with the men who have worked for this organization I can say that it has enlisted my deep affection.

I am interested in it for various reasons. First of all, because it is an association of young men. I have had a good deal to do with young men in my time, and I have formed an impression of them which I believe to be contrary to the general impression. They are generally thought to be arch radicals. As a matter of fact, they are the most conservative people I have ever dealt with. Go to a college community and try to change the least custom of that little world and find how the conservatives will rush at you. Moreover, young men are embarrassed by having inherited their fathers' opinions. I have often said that the use of a university is to make young gentlemen as unlike their fathers as possible. I do not say that with the least disrespect for the fathers; but every man who is old enough to have a son in college is old enough to have become very seriously immersed in some particular business and is almost certain to have caught the point of view of that particular business. And it is very useful to his son to be taken out of that narrow circle, conducted to some high place where he may see the general map of the world and of the interests of mankind, and there shown how big the world is and how much of it his father may happen to have forgotten. It would be worth while for men, middle-aged and old, to detach themselves more frequently from the things that command their daily attention and to think of the sweeping tides of humanity.

Therefore I am interested in this association, because it is intended to bring young men together before any crust has formed over them, before they have been hardened to any particular occupation, before they have caught an inveterate point of view; while they still have a searchlight that they can swing and see what it reveals of all the circumstances of the hidden world.

I am the more interested in it because it is an association of young men who are Christians. I wonder if we attach sufficient importance to Christianity as a mere instrumentality in the life of mankind. For one, I am not fond of thinking of Christianity as the means of saving *individual* souls. I have always been very impatient of processes and institutions which said that their purpose was to put every man in the way of developing his character. My advice is: Do not think about your character. If you will think about what you ought to do for other people, your character will take care of itself. Character is a by-product, and any man who devotes himself to its cultivation in his own case will become a selfish prig. The only way your powers can become great is by exerting them outside the circle of your own narrow, special, selfish interests. And that is the reason of Christianity. Christ came into the world to save others, not to save himself; and no man is a true Christian who does not think constantly of how he can lift his brother, how he can assist his friend, how he can enlighten mankind, how he can make virtue the rule of conduct in the circle in which he lives. An association merely of young men might be an association that had its energies put forth in every direction, but an association of Christian young men is an association meant to put its shoulders under the world and lift it, so that other men may feel that they have companions in bearing the weight and heat of the day; that other men may know that there are those who care for them, who would go into places of difficulty and danger to rescue them, who regard themselves as their brother's keeper.

And, then, I am glad that it is an association. Every word of its title means an element of strength. Young men are strong. Christian young men are the strongest kind of young men, and when they associate themselves together they have the incomparable strength of organization. The Young Men's Christian Association once excited, perhaps it is not too much to say, the hostility of the organized churches of the Christian world, because the movement looked as if it were so non-sectarian, as if it were so outside the ecclesiastical field, that perhaps it was an effort to draw young men away from the churches and to substitute this organization for the great bodies of Christian people who joined themselves in the Christian denominations. But after a while it appeared that it was a great instrumentality that belonged to all the churches; that it was a common instrument for sending the light of Christianity out into the world in its most practical form, drawing young men who were strangers into places where they could have companionship that stimulated them and suggestions that kept them straight and occupations that amused them without vicious practice; and then, by surrounding themselves with an atmosphere of purity and of simplicity of life, catch something of a glimpse of the great ideal which Christ lifted when He was elevated upon the cross.

I remember hearing a very wise man say once, a man grown old in the service of a great church, that he had never taught his son religion dogmatically at any time; that he and the boy's mother had agreed that if the atmosphere of that home did not make a Christian of the boy, nothing that they could say would make a Christian of him. They knew that Christianity was catching, and if they did not have it, it would not be communicated. If they did have it, it would penetrate while the boy slept, almost; while he was unconscious of the sweet influences that were about him, while he reckoned nothing of instruction, but merely breathed into his lungs the wholesome air of a Christian home. That is the principle of the Young Men's Christian Association-to make a place where the atmosphere makes great ideals contagious. That is the reason that I said, though I had forgotten that I said it, what is quoted on the outer page of the program-that you can test a modern community by the degree of its interest in its Young Men's Christian Association. You can test whether it knows what road it wants to travel or not. You can test whether it is deeply interested in the spiritual and essential prosperity of its rising generation. I know of no test that can be more conclusively put to a community than that.

I want to suggest to the young men of this association that it is the duty of young men not only to combine for the things that are good, but to combine in a militant spirit. There is a fine passage in one of Milton's prose writings which I am sorry to say I cannot quote, but the meaning of which I can give you, and it is worth hearing.[68] He says that he has no patience with a cloistered virtue that does not go out and seek its adversary. Ah, how tired I am of the men who are merely on the defensive, who hedge themselves in, who perhaps enlarge the hedge enough to include their little family circle and ward off all the evil influences of the world from that loved and hallowed group. How tired I am of the men whose virtue is selfish because it is merely self-protective! And how much I wish that men by the hundred thousand might volunteer to go out and seek an adversary and subdue him!

I have had the fortune to take part in affairs of a considerable variety of sorts, and I have tried to hate as few persons as possible, but there is an exquisite combination of contempt and hate that I have for a particular kind of person, and that is the moral coward. I wish we could give all our cowards a perpetual vacation. Let them go off and sit on the side lines and see us play the game; and put them off the field if they interfere with the game. They do nothing but harm, and they do it by that most subtle and fatal thing of all, that of taking the momentum and the spirit and the forward dash out of things. A man who is virtuous and a coward has no marketable virtue about him. The virtue, I repeat, which is merely self-defensive is not serviceable even, I suspect, to himself. For how a man can swallow and not taste bad when he is a coward and thinking only of himself I cannot imagine.

Be militant! Be an organization that is going to do things! If you can find older men who will give you countenance and acceptable leadership, follow them; but if you cannot, organize separately and dispense with them. There are only two sorts of men worth associating with when something is to be done. Those are young men and men who never grow old. Now, if you find men who have grown old, about whom the crust has hardened, whose hinges are stiff, whose minds always have their eye over the shoulder thinking of things as they *were* done, do not have anything to do with them. It would not be Christian to exclude them from your organization, but merely use them to pad the roll. If you can find older men who will lead you acceptably and keep you in countenance, I am bound as an older man to advise you to follow them. But suit yourselves. Do not follow people that stand still. Just remind them that this is not a statical proposition; it is a movement, and if they cannot get a move on them they are not serviceable.

Life, gentlemen-the life of society, the life of the world-has constantly to be fed from the bottom. It has to be fed by those great sources of strength which are constantly rising in new generations. Red blood has to be pumped into it. New fiber has to be supplied. That is the reason I have always said that I believed in popular institutions. If you can guess beforehand whom your rulers are going to be, you can guess with a very great certainty that most of them will not be fit to rule. The beauty of popular institutions is that you do not know where the man is going to come from, and you do not care so he is the right man. You do not know whether he will come from the avenue or from the alley. You do not know whether he will come from the city or the farm. You do not know whether you will ever have heard that name before or not. Therefore you do not limit at any point your supply of new strength. You do not say it has got to come through the blood of a particular family or through the processes of a particular training, or by anything except the native impulse and genius of the man himself. The humblest hovel, therefore, may produce you your greatest man. A very humble hovel did produce you one of your greatest men. That is the process of life, this constant surging up of the new strength of unnamed, unrecognized, uncatalogued men who are just getting into the running, who are just coming up from the masses of the unrecognized multitude. You do not know when you will see above the level masses of the crowd some great stature lifted head and shoulders above the rest, shouldering its way, not violently but gently, to the front and saying, "Here am I; follow me." And his voice will be your voice, his thought will be your thought, and you will follow him as if you were following the best things in yourselves.

When I think of an association of Christian young men I wonder that it has not already turned the world upside down. I wonder, not that it has done so much, for it has done a great deal, but that it has done so little; and I can only conjecture that it does not realize its own strength. I can only imagine that it has not yet got its pace. I wish I could believe, and I do believe, that at seventy it is just reaching its majority, and that from this time on a dream greater even than George Williams[69] ever dreamed will be realized in the great accumulating momentum of Christian men throughout the world. For, gentlemen, this is an age in which the principles of men who utter public opinion dominate the world. It makes no difference what is done for the time being. After the struggle is over the jury will sit, and nobody can corrupt that jury.

At one time I tried to write history. I did not know enough to write it, but I knew from experience how hard it was to find an historian out, and I trusted I would not be found out. I used to have this comfortable thought as I saw men struggling in the public arena. I used to think to myself, "This is all very well and very interesting. You probably assess yourself in such and such a way. Those who are your partisans assess you thus and so. Those who are your opponents urge a different verdict. But it does not make very much difference, because after you are dead and gone some quiet historian will sit in a secluded room and tell mankind for the rest of time just what to think about you, and his verdict, not the verdict of your partisans and not the verdict of your opponents, will be the verdict of posterity." I say that I used to say that to myself. It very largely was not so. And yet it was true in this sense: If the historian really speaks the judgment of the succeeding generation, then he really speaks the judgment also of the generations that succeed it, and his assessment, made without the passion of the time, made without partisan feeling in the matter-in other circumstances, when the air is cool-is the judgment of mankind upon your actions.

Now, is it not very important that we who shall constitute a portion of the jury should get our best judgments to work and base them upon Christian forbearance and Christian principles, upon the idea that it is impossible by sophistication to establish that a thing that is wrong is right? And yet, while we are going to judge with the absolute standard of righteousness, we are going to judge with Christian feeling, being men of a like sort ourselves, suffering the same temptations, having the same weaknesses, knowing the same passions; and while we do not condemn, we are going to seek to say and to live the truth. What I am hoping for is that these seventy years have just been a running start, and that now there will be a great rush of Christian principle upon the strongholds of evil and of wrong in the world. Those strongholds are not as strong as they look. Almost every vicious man is afraid of society, and if you once open the door where he is, he will run. All you have to do is to fight, not with cannon but with light.

May I illustrate it in this way? The Government of the United States has just succeeded in concluding a large number of treaties with the leading nations of the world, the sum and substance of which is this, that whenever any trouble arises the light shall shine on it for a year before anything is done; and my prediction is that after the light has shone on it for a year it will not be necessary to do anything; that after we know what happened, then we will know who was right and who was wrong. I believe that light is the greatest sanitary influence in the world. That, I suppose, is scientific commonplace, because if you want to make a place wholesome the best instrument you can use is the sun; to let his rays in, let him search out all the miasma that may lurk there. So with moral light: It is the most wholesome and rectifying, as well as the most revealing, thing in the world, provided it be genuine moral light; not the light of inquisitiveness, not the light of the man who likes to turn up ugly things, not the light of the man who disturbs what is corrupt for the mere sake of the sensation that he creates by disturbing it, but the moral light, the light of the man who discloses it in order that all the sweet influences of the world may go in and make it better.

That, in my judgment, is what the Young Men's Christian Association can do. It can point out to its members the things that are wrong. It can guide the feet of those who are going astray; and when its members have realized the power of the Christian principle, then they will not be men if they do not unite to see that the rest of the world experiences the same emancipation and reaches the same happiness of release.

I believe in the Young Men's Christian Association because I believe in the progress of moral ideas in the world; and I do not know that I am sure of anything else. When you are after something and have formulated it and have done the very best thing you know how to do you have got to be sure for the time being that that is the thing to do. But you are a fool if in the back of your head you do not know it is possible that you are mistaken. All that you can claim is that that is the thing as you see it now and that you cannot stand still; that you must push forward the things that are right. It may turn out that you made mistakes, but what you do know is your direction, and you are sure you are moving in that way. I was once a college reformer, until discouraged, and I remember a classmate of mine saying, "Why, man, can't you let anything alone?" I said, "I let everything alone that you can show me is not itself moving in the wrong direction, but I am not going to let those things alone that I see are going downhill"; and I borrowed this illustration from an ingenious writer. He says, "If you have a post that is painted white and want to keep it white, you cannot let it alone; and if anybody says to you, 'Why don't you let that post alone,' you will say, 'Because I want it to stay white, and therefore I have got to paint it at least every second year.'" There isn't anything in this world that will not change if you absolutely let it alone, and therefore you have constantly to be attending to it to see that it is being taken care of in the right way and that, if it is part of the motive force of the world, it is moving in the right direction.

That means that eternal vigilance is the price, not only of liberty, but of a great many other things. It is the price of everything that is good. It is the price of one's own soul. It is the price of the souls of the people you love; and when it comes down to the final reckoning you have a standard that is immutable. What shall a man give in exchange for his own soul? Will he sell that? Will he consent to see another man sell his soul? Will he consent to see the conditions of his community such that men's souls are debauched and trodden underfoot in the mire? What shall he give in exchange for his own soul, or any other man's soul? And since the world, the world of affairs, the world of society, is nothing less and nothing more than all of us put together, it is a great enterprise for the salvation of the soul in this world as well as in the next. There is a text in Scripture that has always interested me profoundly. It says godliness is profitable in this life as well as in the life that is to come; and if you do not start it in this life, it will not reach the life that is to come. Your measurements, your directions, your whole momentum, have to be established before you reach the next world. This world is intended as the place in which we shall show that we know how to grow in the stature of manliness and of righteousness.

I have come here to bid Godspeed to the great work of the Young Men's Christian Association. I love to think of the gathering force of such things as this in the generations to come. If a man had to measure the accomplishments of society, the progress of reform, the speed of the world's betterment, by the few little things that happened in his own life, by the trifling things that he can contribute to accomplish, he would indeed feel that the cost was much greater than the result. But no man can look at the past of the history of this world without seeing a vision of the future of the history of this world; and when you think of the accumulated moral forces that have made one age better than another age in the progress of mankind, then you can open your eyes to the vision. You can see that age by age, though with a blind struggle in the dust of the road, though often mistaking the path and losing its way in the mire, mankind is yet-sometimes with bloody hands and battered knees-nevertheless struggling step after step up the slow stages to the day when he shall live in the full light which shines upon the uplands, where all the light that illumines mankind shines direct from the face of God.

A Message

[Returning to the House of Representatives without approval an act to regulate the immigration of aliens to and the residence of aliens in the United States.]

To the House of Representatives:

It is with unaffected regret that I find myself constrained by clear conviction to return this bill (H.R. 6060, "An act to regulate the immigration of aliens to and the residence of aliens in the United States") without my signature. Not only do I feel it to be a very serious matter to exercise the power of veto in any case, because it involves opposing the single judgment of the President to the judgment of a majority of both the Houses of the Congress, a step which no man who realizes his own liability to error can take without great hesitation, but also because this particular bill is in so many important respects admirable, well conceived, and desirable. Its enactment into law would undoubtedly enhance the efficiency and improve the methods of handling the important branch of the public service to which it relates. But candor and a sense of duty with regard to the responsibility so clearly imposed upon me by the Constitution in matters of legislation leave me no choice but to dissent.

In two particulars of vital consequence this bill embodies a radical departure from the traditional and long-established policy of this country, a policy in which our people have conceived the very character of their Government to be expressed, the very mission and spirit of the Nation in respect of its relations to the peoples of the world outside their borders. It seeks to all but close entirely the gates of asylum which have always been open to those who could find nowhere else the right and opportunity of constitutional agitation for what they conceived to be the natural and inalienable rights of men; and it excludes those to whom the opportunities of elementary education have been denied, without regard to their character, their purposes, or their natural capacity.

Restrictions like these, adopted earlier in our history as a Nation, would very materially have altered the course and cooled the humane ardors of our politics. The right of political asylum has brought to this country many a man of noble character and elevated purpose who was marked as an outlaw in his own less fortunate land, and who has yet become an ornament to our citizenship and to our public councils. The children and the compatriots of these illustrious Americans must stand amazed to see the representatives of their Nation now resolved, in the fullness of our national strength and at the maturity of our great institutions, to risk turning such men back from our shores without test of quality or purpose. It is difficult for me to believe that the full effect of this feature of the bill was realized when it was framed and adopted, and it is impossible for me to assent to it in the form in which it is here cast.

The literacy test and the tests and restrictions which accompany it constitute an even more radical change in the policy of the Nation. Hitherto we have generously kept our doors open to all who were not unfitted by reason of disease or incapacity for self-support or such personal records and antecedents as were likely to make them a menace to our peace and order or to the wholesome and essential relationships of life. In this bill it is proposed to turn away from tests of character and of quality and impose tests which exclude and restrict; for the new tests here embodied are not tests of quality or of character or of personal fitness, but tests of opportunity. Those who come seeking opportunity are not to be admitted unless they have already had one of the chief of the opportunities they seek, the opportunity of education. The object of such provisions is restriction, not selection.

If the people of this country have made up their minds to limit the number of immigrants by arbitrary tests and so reverse the policy of all the generations of Americans that have gone before them, it is their right to do so. I am their servant and have no license to stand in their way. But I do not believe that they have. I respectfully submit that no one can quote their mandate to that effect. Has any political party ever avowed a policy of restriction in this fundamental matter, gone to the country on it, and been commissioned to control its legislation? Does this bill rest upon the conscious and universal assent and desire of the American people? I doubt it. It is because I doubt it that I make bold to dissent from it. I am willing to abide by the verdict, but not until it has been rendered. Let the platforms of parties speak out upon this policy and the people pronounce their wish. The matter is too fundamental to be settled otherwise.

I have no pride of opinion in this question. I am not foolish enough to profess to know the wishes and ideals of America better than the body of her chosen representatives know them. I only want instruction direct from those whose fortunes, with ours and all men's, are involved.

Woodrow Wilson.
The White House, *28 January, 1915.*

Address Before the United States Chamber of Commerce

[Delivered in Washington, February 3, 1915.]

Mr. President, Ladies and Gentlemen:

I feel that it is hardly fair to you for me to come in in this casual fashion among a body of men who have been seriously discussing great questions, and it is hardly fair to me, because I come in cold, not having had the advantage of sharing the atmosphere of your deliberations and catching the feeling of your conference. Moreover, I hardly know just how to express my interest in the things you are undertaking. When a man stands outside an organization and speaks to it he is too apt to have the tone of outside commendation, as who should say, "I would desire to pat you on the back and say 'Good boys; you are doing well!'" I would a great deal rather have you receive me as if for the time being I were one of your own number.

Because the longer I occupy the office that I now occupy the more I regret any lines of separation; the more I deplore any feeling that one set of men has one set of interests and another set of men another set of interests; the more I feel the solidarity of the Nation-the impossibility of separating one interest from another without misconceiving it; the necessity that we should all understand one another, in order that we may understand ourselves.

There is an illustration which I have used a great many times. I will use it again, because it is the most serviceable to my own mind. We often speak of a man who cannot find his way in some jungle or some desert as having "lost himself." Did you never reflect that that is the only thing he has not lost? *He is there.* He has lost the rest of the world. He has no fixed point by which to steer. He does not know which is north, which is south, which is east, which is west; and if he did know, he is so confused that he would not know in which of those directions his goal lay. Therefore, following his heart, he walks in a great circle from right to left and comes back to where he started-to himself again. To my mind that is a picture of the world. If you have lost sight of other interests and do not know the relation of your own interests to those other interests, then you do not understand your own interests, and have lost yourself. What you want is orientation, relationship to the points of the compass; relationship to the other people in the world; vital connections which you have for the time being severed.

I am particularly glad to express my admiration for the kind of organization which you have drawn together. I have attended banquets of chambers of commerce in various parts of the country and have got the impression at each of those banquets that there was only one city in the country. It has seemed to me that those associations were meant in order to destroy men's perspective, in order to destroy their sense of relative proportions. Worst of all, if I may be permitted to say so, they were intended to boost something in particular. Boosting is a very unhandsome thing. Advancing enterprise is a very handsome thing, but to exaggerate local merits in order to create disproportion in the general development is not a particularly handsome thing or a particularly intelligent thing. A city cannot grow on the face of a great state like a mushroom on that one spot. Its roots are throughout the state, and unless the state it is in, or the region it draws from, can itself thrive and pulse with life as a whole, the city can have no healthy growth. You forget the wide rootages of everything when you boost some particular region. There are dangers which probably you all understand in the mere practice of advertisement. When a man begins to advertise himself there are certain points that are somewhat exaggerated, and I have noticed that men who exaggerate most, most quickly lose any proper conception of what their own proportions are. Therefore, these local centers of enthusiasm may be local centers of mistake if they are not very wisely guided and if they do not themselves realize their relations to the other centers of enthusiasm and of advancement.

The advantage about a Chamber of Commerce of the United States is that there is only one way to boost the United States, and that is by seeing to it that the conditions under which business is done throughout the whole country are the best possible conditions. There cannot be any disproportion about that. If you draw your sap and your vitality from all quarters, then the more sap and vitality there is in you the more there is in the commonwealth as a whole, and every time you lift at all you lift the whole level of manufacturing and mercantile enterprise. Moreover, the advantage of it is that you cannot boost the United States in that way without understanding the United States. You learn a great deal. I agreed with a colleague of mine in the Cabinet the other day that we had never attended in our lives before a school to compare with that we were now attending for the purpose of gaining a liberal education.

Of course, I learn a great many things that are not so, but the interesting thing about that is this: Things that are not so do not match. If you hear enough of them, you see there is no pattern whatever; it is a crazy quilt. Whereas, the truth always matches, piece by piece, with other parts of the truth. No man can lie consistently, and he cannot lie about everything if he talks to you long. I would guarantee that if enough liars talked to you, you would get the truth; because the parts that they did not invent would match one another, and the parts that they did invent would *not* match one another. Talk long enough, therefore, and see the connections clearly enough, and you can patch together the case as a whole. I had somewhat that experience about Mexico, and that was about the only way in which I learned anything that was true about it. For there had been vivid imaginations and many special interests which depicted things as they wished me to believe them to be.

Seriously, the task of this body is to match all the facts of business throughout the country and to see the vast and consistent pattern of it. That is the reason I think you are to be congratulated upon the fact that you cannot do this thing without common counsel. There isn't any man who knows enough to comprehend the United States. It is coöperative effort, necessarily. You cannot perform the functions of this Chamber of Commerce without drawing in not only a vast number of men, but men, and a number of men, from every region and section of the country. The minute this association falls into the hands, if it ever should, of men from a single section or men with a single set of interests most at heart, it will go to seed and die. Its strength must come from the uttermost parts of the land and must be compounded of brains and comprehensions of every sort. It is a very noble and handsome picture for the imagination, and I have asked myself before I came here to-day, what relation you could bear to the Government of the United States and what relation the Government could bear to you?

There are two aspects and activities of the Government with which you will naturally come into most direct contact. The first is the Government's power of inquiry, systematic and disinterested inquiry, and its power of scientific assistance. You get an illustration of the latter, for example, in the Department of Agriculture. Has it occurred to you, I wonder, that we are just upon the eve of a time when our Department of Agriculture will be of infinite importance to the whole world? There is a shortage of food in the world now. That shortage will be much more serious a few months from now than it is now. It is necessary that we should plant a great deal more; it is necessary that our lands should yield more per acre than they do now; it is necessary that there should not be a plow or a spade idle in this country if the world is to be fed. And the methods of our farmers must feed upon the scientific information to be derived from the State departments of agriculture, and from that taproot of all, the United States Department of Agriculture. The object and use of that department is to inform men of the latest developments and disclosures of science with regard to all the processes by which soils can be put to their proper use and their fertility made the greatest possible. Similarly with the Bureau of Standards. It is ready to supply those things by which you can set norms, you can set bases, for all the scientific processes of business.

I have a great admiration for the scientific parts of the Government of the United States, and it has amazed me that so few men have discovered them. Here in these departments are quiet men, trained to the highest degree of skill, serving for a petty remuneration along lines that are infinitely useful to mankind; and yet in some cases they waited to be discovered until this Chamber of Commerce of the United States was established. Coming to this city, officers of that association found that there were here things that were infinitely useful to them and with which the whole United States ought to be put into communication.

The Government of the United States is very properly a great instrumentality of inquiry and information. One thing we are just beginning to do that we ought to have done long ago: We ought long ago to have had our Bureau of Foreign and Domestic Commerce. We ought long ago to have sent the best eyes of the Government out into the world to see where the opportunities and openings of American commerce and American genius were to be found-men who were not sent out as the commercial agents of any particular set of business men in the United States, but who were eyes for the whole business community. I have been reading consular reports for twenty years. In what I came to regard as an evil day the Congressman from my district began to send me the consular reports, and they ate up more and more of my time. They are very interesting, but they are a good deal like what the old lady said of the dictionary, that it was very interesting but a little disconnected. You get a picture of the world as if a spotlight were being dotted about over the surface of it. Here you see a glimpse of this, and here you see a glimpse of that, and through the medium of some consuls you do not see anything at all. Because the consul has to have eyes and the consul has to know what he is looking for. A literary friend of mine said that he used to believe in the maxim that "everything comes to the man who waits," but he discovered after awhile by practical experience that it needed an additional clause, "provided he knows what he is waiting for." Unless you know what you are looking for and have trained eyes to see it when it comes your way, it may pass you unnoticed. We are just beginning to do, systematically and scientifically, what we ought long ago to have done, to employ the Government of the United States to survey the world in order that American commerce might be guided.

But there are other ways of using the Government of the United States, ways that have long been tried, though not always with conspicuous success or fortunate results. You can use the Government of the United States by influencing its legislation. That has been a very active industry, but it has not always been managed in the interest of the whole people. It is very instructive and useful for the Government of the United States to have such means as you are ready to supply for getting a sort of consensus of opinion which proceeds from no particular quarter and originates with no particular interest. Information is the very foundation of all right action in legislation.

I remember once, a good many years ago, I was attending one of the local chambers of commerce of the United States at a time when everybody was complaining that Congress was interfering with business. If you have heard that complaint recently and supposed that it was original with the men who made it, you have not lived as long as I have. It has been going on ever since I can remember. The complaint came most vigorously from men who were interested in large corporate development. I took the liberty to say to that body of men, whom I did not know, that I took it for granted that there were a great many lawyers among them, and that it was likely that the more prominent of those lawyers were the intimate advisors of the corporations of that region. I said that I had met a great many lawyers from whom the complaint had come most vigorously, not only that there was too much legislation with regard to corporations, but that it was ignorant legislation. I said, "Now, the responsibility is with you. If the legislation is mistaken, you are on the inside and know where the mistakes are being made. You know not only the innocent and right things that your corporations are doing, but you know the other things, too. Knowing how they are done, you can be expert advisors as to how the wrong things can be prevented. If, therefore, this thing is handled ignorantly, there is nobody to blame but yourselves." If we on the outside cannot understand the thing and cannot get advice from the inside, then we will have to do it with the flat hand and not with the touch of skill and discrimination. Isn't that true? Men on the inside of business know how business is conducted and they cannot complain if men on the outside make mistakes about business if they do not come from the inside and give the kind of advice which is necessary.

The trouble has been that when they came in the past-for I think the thing is changing very rapidly-they came with all their bristles out; they came on the defensive; they came to see, not what they could accomplish, but what they could prevent. They did not come to guide; they came to block. That is of no use whatever to the general body politic. What has got to pervade us like a great motive power is that we cannot, and must not, separate our interests from one another, but must pool our interests. A man who is trying to fight for his single hand is fighting against the community and not fighting with it. There are a great many dreadful things about war, as nobody needs to be told in this day of distress and of terror, but there is one thing about war which has a very splendid side, and that is the consciousness that a whole nation gets that they must all act as a unit for a common end. And when peace is as handsome as war there will be no war. When men, I mean, engage in the pursuits of peace in the same spirit of self-sacrifice and of conscious service of the community with which, at any rate, the common soldier engages in war, then shall there be wars no more. You have moved the vanguard for the United States in the purposes of this association just a little nearer that ideal. That is the reason I am here, because I believe it.

There is a specific matter about which I, for one, want your advice. Let me say, if I may say it without disrespect, that I do not think you are prepared to give it right away. You will have to make some rather extended inquiries before you are ready to give it. What I am thinking of is competition in foreign markets as between the merchants of different nations.

I speak of the subject with a certain degree of hesitation, because the thing farthest from my thought is taking advantage of nations now disabled from playing their full part in that competition, and seeking a sudden selfish advantage because they are for the time being disabled. Pray believe me that we ought to eliminate all that thought from our minds and consider this matter as if we and the other nations now at war were in the normal circumstances of commerce.

There is a normal circumstance of commerce in which we are apparently at a disadvantage. Our anti-trust laws are thought by some to make it illegal for merchants in the United States to form combinations for the purpose of strengthening themselves in taking advantage of the opportunities of foreign trade. That is a very serious matter for this reason: There are some corporations, and some firms for all I know, whose business is great enough and whose resources are abundant enough to enable them to establish selling agencies in foreign countries; to enable them to extend the long credits which in some cases are necessary in order to keep the trade they desire; to enable them, in other words, to organize their business in foreign territory in a way which the smaller man cannot afford to do. His business has not grown big enough to permit him to establish selling agencies. The export commission merchant, perhaps, taxes him a little too highly to make that an available competitive means of conducting and extending his business.

The question arises, therefore, how are the smaller merchants, how are the younger and weaker corporations going to get a foothold as against the combinations which are permitted and even encouraged by foreign governments in this field of competition? There are governments which, as you know, distinctly encourage the formation of great combinations in each particular field of commerce in order to maintain selling agencies and to extend long credits, and to use and maintain the machinery which is necessary for the extension of business; and American merchants feel that they are at a very considerable disadvantage in contending against that. The matter has been many times brought to my attention, and I have each time suspended judgment. I want to be shown this: I want to be shown how such a combination can be made and conducted in a way which will not close it against the use of everybody who wants to use it. A combination has a tendency to exclude new members. When a group of men get control of a good thing, they do not see any particular point in letting other people into the good thing. What I would like very much to be shown, therefore, is a method of coöperation which is not a method of combination. Not that the two words are mutually exclusive, but we have come to have a special meaning attached to the word "combination." Most of our combinations have a safety lock, and you have to know the combination to get in. I want to know how these coöperative methods can be adopted for the benefit of everybody who wants to use them, and I say frankly if I can be shown that, I am for them. If I cannot be shown that, I am against them. I hasten to add that I hopefully expect I *can* be shown that.

You, as I have just now intimated, probably cannot show it to me offhand, but by the methods which you have the means of using you certainly ought to be able to throw a vast deal of light on the subject. Because the minute you ask the small merchant, the small banker, the country man, how he looks upon these things and how he thinks they ought to be arranged in order that he can use them, if he is like some of the men in country districts whom I know, he will turn out to have had a good deal of thought upon that subject and to be able to make some very interesting suggestions whose intelligence and comprehensiveness will surprise some city gentlemen who think that only the cities understand the business of the country. As a matter of fact, you do not have time to think in a city. It takes time to think. You can get what you call opinions by contagion in a city and get them very quickly, but you do not always know where the germ came from. And you have no scientific laboratory method by which to determine whether it is a good germ or a bad germ.

There are thinking spaces in this country, and some of the thinking done is very solid thinking indeed, the thinking of the sort of men that we all love best, who think for themselves, who do not see things as they are told to see them, but look at them and see them independently; who, if they are told they are white when they are black, plainly say that they are black-men with eyes and with a courage back of those eyes to tell what they see. The country is full of those men. They have been singularly reticent sometimes, singularly silent, but the country is full of them. And what I rejoice in is that you have called them into the ranks. For your methods are bound to be democratic in spite of you. I do not mean democratic with a big "D," though I have a private conviction that you cannot be democratic with a small "d" long without becoming democratic with a big "D." Still that is just between ourselves. The point is that when we have a *consensus* of opinion, when we have this common counsel, then the legislative processes of this Government will be infinitely illuminated.

I used to wonder when I was Governor of one of the States of this great country where all the bills came from. Some of them had a very private complexion. I found upon inquiry-it was easy to find-that practically nine-tenths of the bills that were introduced had been handed to the members who introduced them by some constituent of theirs, had been drawn up by some lawyer whom they might or might not know, and were intended to do something that would be beneficial to a particular set of persons. I do not mean, necessarily, beneficial in a way that would be hurtful to the rest; they may have been perfectly honest, but they came out of cubby-holes all over the State. They did not come out of public places where men had got together and compared views. They were not the products of common counsel, but the products of private counsel, a very necessary process if there is no other, but a process which it would be a very happy thing to dispense with if we could get another. And the only other process is the process of common counsel.

Some of the happiest experiences of my life have been like this. We had once when I was president of a university to revise the whole course of study.[70] Courses of study are chronically in need of revision. A committee of, I believe, fourteen men was directed by the faculty of the university to report a revised curriculum. Naturally, the men who had the most ideas on the subject were picked out and, naturally, each man came with a very definite notion of the kind of revision he wanted, and one of the first discoveries we made was that no two of us wanted exactly the same revision. I went in there with all my war paint on to get the revision I wanted, and I dare say, though it was perhaps more skillfully concealed, the other men had their war paint on, too. We discussed the matter for six months. The result was a report which no one of us had conceived or foreseen, but with which we were all absolutely satisfied. There was not a man who had not learned in that committee more than he had ever known before about the subject, and who had not willingly revised his prepossessions; who was not proud to be a participant in a genuine piece of common counsel. I have had several experiences of that sort, and it has led me, whenever I confer, to hold my particular opinion provisionally, as my contribution to go into the final result but not to dominate the final result.

That is the ideal of a government like ours, and an interesting thing is that if you only talk about an idea that will not work long enough, everybody will see perfectly plainly that it will not work; whereas, if you do not talk about it, and do not have a great many people talk about it, you are in danger of having the people who handle it think that it will work. Many minds are necessary to compound a workable method of life in a various and populous country; and as I think about the whole thing and picture the purposes, the infinitely difficult and complex purposes which we must conceive and carry out, not only does it minister to my own modesty, I hope, of opinion, but it also fills me with a very great enthusiasm. It is a splendid thing to be part of a great wide-awake Nation. It is a splendid thing to know that your own strength is infinitely multiplied by the strength of other men who love the country as you do. It is a splendid thing to feel that the wholesome blood of a great country can be united in common purposes, and that by frankly looking one another in the face and taking counsel with one another, prejudices will drop away, handsome understandings will arise, a universal spirit of service will be engendered, and that with this increased sense of community of purpose will come a vastly enhanced individual power of achievement; for we will be lifted by the whole mass of which we constitute a part.

Have you never heard a great chorus of trained voices lift the voice of the prima donna as if it soared with easy grace above the whole melodious sound? It does not seem to come from the single throat that produces it. It seems as if it were the perfect accent and crown of the great chorus. So it ought to be with the statesman. So it ought to be with every man who tries to guide the counsels of a great nation. He should feel that his voice is lifted upon the chorus and that it is only the crown of the common theme.

To Naturalized Citizens

[Address delivered at Convention Hall, Philadelphia, May 10, 1915. The audience included four thousand newly naturalized citizens. This speech attracted great attention because in it no reference was made to the sinking of the "Lusitania," three days before.]

Mr. Mayor, Fellow-Citizens:
It warms my heart that you should give me such a reception; but it is not of myself that I wish to think to-night, but of those who have just become citizens of the United States.

This is the only country in the world which experiences this constant and repeated rebirth. Other countries depend upon the multiplication of their own native people. This country is constantly drinking strength out of new sources by the voluntary association with it of great bodies of strong men and forward-looking women out of other lands. And so by the gift of the free will of independent people it is being constantly renewed from generation to generation by the same process by which it was originally created. It is as if humanity had determined to see to it that this great Nation, founded for the benefit of humanity, should not lack for the allegiance of the people of the world.

You have just taken an oath of allegiance to the United States. Of allegiance to whom? Of allegiance to no one, unless it be God-certainly not of allegiance to those who temporarily represent this great Government. You have taken an oath of allegiance to a great ideal, to a great body of principles, to a great hope of the human race. You have said, "We are going to America not only to earn a living, not only to seek the things which it was more difficult to obtain where we were born, but to help forward the great enterprises of the human spirit-to let men know that everywhere in the world there are men who will cross strange oceans and go where a speech is spoken which is alien to them if they can but satisfy their quest for what their spirits crave; knowing that whatever the speech there is but one longing and utterance of the human heart, and that is for liberty and justice." And while you bring all countries with you, you come with a purpose of leaving all other countries behind you-bringing what is best of their spirit, but not looking over your shoulders and seeking to perpetuate what you intended to leave behind in them. I certainly would not be one even to suggest that a man cease to love the home of his birth and the nation of his origin-these things are very sacred and ought not to be put out of our hearts-but it is one thing to love the place where you were born and it is another thing to dedicate yourself to the place to which you go. You cannot dedicate yourself to America unless you become in every respect and with every purpose of your will thorough Americans. You cannot become thorough Americans if you think of yourselves in groups. America does not consist of groups. A man who thinks of himself as belonging to a particular national group in America has not yet become an American, and the man who goes among you to trade upon your nationality is no worthy son to live under the Stars and Stripes.

My urgent advice to you would be, not only always to think first of America, but always, also, to think first of humanity. You do not love humanity if you seek to divide humanity into jealous camps. Humanity can be welded together only by love, by sympathy, by justice, not by jealousy and hatred. I am sorry for the man who seeks to make personal capital out of the passions of his fellow-men. He has lost the touch and ideal of America, for America was created to unite mankind by those passions which lift and not by the passions which separate and debase. We came to America, either ourselves or in the persons of our ancestors, to better the ideals of men, to make them see finer things than they had seen before, to get rid of the things that divide and to make sure of the things that unite. It was but an historical accident no doubt that this great country was called the "United States"; yet I am very thankful that it has that word "United" in its title, and the man who seeks to divide man from man, group from group, interest from interest in this great Union is striking at its very heart.

It is a very interesting circumstance to me, in thinking of those of you who have just sworn allegiance to this great Government, that you were drawn across the ocean by some beckoning finger of hope, by some belief, by some vision of a new kind of justice, by some expectation of a better kind of life. No doubt you have been disappointed in some of us. Some of us are very disappointing. No doubt you have found that justice in the United States goes only with a pure heart and a right purpose as it does everywhere else in the world. No doubt what you found here did not seem touched for you, after all, with the complete beauty of the ideal which you had conceived beforehand. But remember this: If we had grown at all poor in the ideal, you brought some of it with you. A man does not go out to seek the thing that is not in him. A man does not hope for the thing that he does not believe in, and if some of us have forgotten what America believed in, you, at any rate, imported in your own hearts a renewal of the belief. That is the reason that I, for one, make you welcome. If I have in any degree forgotten what America was intended for, I will thank God if you will remind me. I was born in America. You dreamed dreams of what America was to be, and I hope you brought the dreams with you. No man that does not see visions will ever realize any high hope or undertake any high enterprise. Just because you brought dreams with you, America is more likely to realize dreams such as you brought. You are enriching us if you came expecting us to be better than we are.

See, my friends, what that means. It means that Americans must have a consciousness different from the consciousness of every other nation in the world. I am not saying this with even the slightest thought of criticism of other nations. You know how it is with a family. A family gets centered on itself if it is not careful and is less interested in the neighbors than it is in its own members. So a nation that is not constantly renewed out of new sources is apt to have the narrowness and prejudice of a family; whereas, America must have this consciousness, that on all sides it touches elbows and touches hearts with all the nations of mankind. The example of America must be a special example. The example of America must be the example not merely of peace because it will not fight, but of peace because peace is the healing and elevating influence of the world and strife is not. There is such a thing as a man being too proud to fight. There is such a thing as a nation being so right that it does not need to convince others by force that it is right.

You have come into this great Nation voluntarily seeking something that we have to give, and all that we have to give is this: We cannot exempt you from work. No man is exempt from work anywhere in the world. We cannot exempt you from the strife and the heartbreaking burden of the struggle of the day-that is common to mankind everywhere; we cannot exempt you from the loads that you must carry. We can only make them light by the spirit in which they are carried. That is the spirit of hope, it is the spirit of liberty, it is the spirit of justice.

When I was asked, therefore, by the Mayor and the committee that accompanied him to come up from Washington to meet this great company of newly admitted citizens, I could not decline the invitation. I ought not to be away from Washington, and yet I feel that it has renewed my spirit as an American to be here. In Washington men tell you so many things every day that are not so, and I like to come and stand in the presence of a great body of my fellow-citizens, whether they have been fellow-citizens a long time or a short time, and drink, as it were, out of the common fountains with them and go back feeling what you have so generously given me-the sense of your support and of the living vitality in your hearts of the great ideals which have made America the hope of the world.

Address at Milwaukee

[Between January 27 and February 3, 1916, President Wilson made a series of speeches in New York, Pittsburgh, Cleveland, Milwaukee, Chicago, Des Moines, Topeka, Kansas City, and St. Louis. The address made at Milwaukee, on January 31, has been chosen as representing the general tenor and spirit of the whole series.]

Mr. Chairman And Fellow-Citizens:

I need not inquire whether the citizens of Milwaukee and Wisconsin are interested in the subject of my errand. The presence of this great body in this vast hall sufficiently attests your interest, but I want at the outset to remove a misapprehension that I fear may exist in your mind. There is no sudden crisis; nothing new has happened; I am not out upon this errand because of any unexpected situation. I have come to confer with you upon a matter upon which it would, in any circumstances, be necessary for us to confer when all the rest of the world is on fire and our own house is not fireproof. Everywhere the atmosphere of the world is thrilling with the passion of a disturbance such as the world has never seen before, and it is wise, in the words just uttered by your chairman, that we should see that our own house is set in order and that everything is done to make certain that we shall not suffer by the general conflagration.

There were some dangers to which this Nation seemed at the outset of the war to be exposed, which, I think I can say with confidence, are now passed and overcome. America has drawn her blood and her strength out of almost all the nations of the world. It is true of a great many of us that there lies deep in our hearts the recollection of an origin which is not American. We are aware that our roots, our traditions, run back into other national soils. There are songs that stir us; there are some far-away historical recollections which engage our affections and stir our memories. We cannot forget our forbears; we cannot altogether ignore the fact of our essential blood relationship; and at the outset of this war it did look as if there were a division of domestic sentiment which might lead us to some errors of judgment and some errors of action; but I, for one, believe that that danger is passed. I never doubted that the danger was exaggerated, because I had learned long ago, and many of you will corroborate me by your experience, that it is not the men who are doing the talking always who represent the real sentiments of the Nation. I for my part always feel a serene confidence in waiting for the declaration of the principles and sentiments of the men who are not vociferous, do not go about seeking to make trouble, do their own thinking, attend to their own business, and love their own country.

I have at no time supposed that the men whose voices seemed to contain the threat of division amongst us were really uttering the sentiments even of those whom they pretended to represent. I for my part have no jealousy of family sentiment. I have no jealousy of that deep affection which runs back through long lineage. It would be a pity if we forget the fine things that our ancestors have done. But I also know the magic of America; I also know the great principles which thrill men in the singular body politic to which we belong in the United States. I know the impulses which have drawn men to our shores. They have not come idly; they have not come without conscious purpose to be free; they have not come without voluntary desire to unite themselves with the great nation on this side of the sea; and I know that whenever the test comes every man's heart will be first for America. It was principle and affection and ambition and hope that drew men to these shores, and they are not going to forget the errand upon which they came and allow America, the home of their refuge and hope, to suffer by any forgetfulness on their part. And so the trouble makers have shot their bolt, and it has been ineffectual. Some of them have been vociferous; all of them have been exceedingly irresponsible. Talk was cheap, and that was all it cost them. They did not have to do anything. But you will know without my telling you that the man whom for the time being you have charged with the duties of President of the United States must talk with a deep sense of responsibility, and he must remember, above all things else, the fine traditions of his office which some men seem to have forgotten. There is no precedent in American history for any action of aggression on the part of the United States or for any action which might mean that America is seeking to connect herself with the controversies on the other side of the water. Men who seek to provoke us to such action have forgotten the traditions of the United States, but it behooves those with whom you have entrusted office to remember the traditions of the United States and to see to it that the actions of the Government are made to square with those traditions.

But there are other dangers, my fellow-citizens, which are not past and which have not been overcome, and they are dangers which we cannot control. We can control irresponsible talkers amidst ourselves. All we have got to do is to encourage them to hire a hall and their folly will be abundantly advertised by themselves. But we cannot in this simple fashion control the dangers that surround us now and have surrounded us since this titanic struggle on the other side of the water began. I say on the other side of the water; you will ask me, "On the other side of which water," for this great struggle has extended to all quarters of the globe. There is no continent outside, I was about to say, of this Western Hemisphere which is not touched with it, but I recollected as I began the sentence that a part of our own continent was touched with it, because it involves our neighbors to the north in Canada. There is no part of the world, except South America, to which the direct influences of this struggle have not extended, so that now we are completely surrounded by this tremendous disturbance and you must realize what that involves.

Our thoughts are concentrated upon our own affairs and our own relations to the rest of the world, but the thoughts of the men who are engaged in this struggle are concentrated upon the struggle itself, and there is daily and hourly danger that they will feel themselves constrained to do things which are absolutely inconsistent with the rights of the United States. They are not thinking of us. I am not criticising them for not thinking of us. I dare say if I were in their place neither would I think of us. They believe that they are struggling for the lives and honor of their nations, and that if the United States puts its interests in the path of this great struggle, she ought to know beforehand that there is danger of very serious misunderstanding and difficulty. So that the very uncalculating, unpremeditated, one might almost say accidental, course of affairs may touch us to the quick at any moment, and I want you to realize that, standing in the midst of these difficulties, I feel that I am charged with a double duty of the utmost difficulty. In the first place, I know that you are depending upon me to keep this Nation out of the war. So far I have done so, and I pledge you my word that, God helping me, I will if it is possible. But you have laid another duty upon me. You have bidden me to see it that nothing stains or impairs the honor of the United States, and that is a matter not within my control; that depends upon what others do, not upon what the Government of the United States does. Therefore there may at any moment come a time when I cannot preserve both the honor and the peace of the United States. Do not exact of me an impossible and contradictory thing, but stand ready and insistent that everybody who represents you should stand ready to provide the necessary means for maintaining the honor of the United States.

I sometimes think that it is true that no people ever went to war with another people. Governments have gone to war with one another. Peoples, so far as I remember, have not, and this is a government of the people, and this people is not going to choose war. But we are not dealing with people; we are dealing with Governments. We are dealing with Governments now engaged in a great struggle, and therefore we do not know what a day or an hour will bring forth. All that we know is the character of our own duty. We do not want the question of peace and war, or the conduct of war, entrusted too entirely to our Government. We want war, if it must come, to be something that springs out of the sentiments and principles and actions of the people themselves; and it is on that account that I am counseling the Congress of the United States not to take the advice of those who recommend that we should have, and have very soon, a great standing Army, but, on the contrary, to see to it that the citizens of this country are so trained and that the military equipment is so sufficiently provided for them that when they choose they can take up arms and defend themselves.

The Constitution of the United States makes the President the Commander in Chief of the Army and Navy of the Nation, but I do not want a big Army subject to my personal command. If danger comes, I want to turn to you and the rest of my fellow-countrymen and say, "Men, are you ready?" and I know what the response will be. I know that there will spring up out of the body of the Nation a great host of free men, and I want those men not to be mere targets for shot and shell. I want them to know something of the arms they have in their hands. I want them to know something about how to guard against the diseases that creep into camps, where men are unaccustomed to live. I want them to know something of what the orders mean that they will be under when they enlist under arms for the Government of the United States. I want them to be men who can comprehend and easily and intelligently step into the duty of national defense. That is the reason that I am urging upon the Congress of the United States at any rate the beginnings of a system by which we may give a very considerable body of our fellow-citizens the necessary training.

I have not forgotten the great National Guard of this country, but in this country of 100,000,000 people there are only 129,000 men in the National Guard; and the National Guard, fine as it is, is not subject to the orders of the President of the United States. It is subject to the orders of the Governors of the several States, and the Constitution itself says that the President has no right to withdraw them from their States even, except in the case of actual invasion of the soil of the United States. I want the Congress of the United States to do a great deal for the National Guard, but I do not see how the Congress of the United States can put the National Guard at the disposal of the national authorities. Therefore it seems to me absolutely necessary that in addition to the National Guard there should be a considerable body of men with some training in the military art who will have pledged themselves to come at the call of the Nation.

I have been told by those who have a greater knack at guessing statistics than I have that there are probably several million men in the United States who, either in this country or in other countries from which they have come to the United States, have received training in arms. It may be; I do not know, and I suspect that they do not either, but even if it be true, these men are not subject to the call of the Federal Government. They would have to be found; they would have to be induced to enlist; they would have to be organized; their numbers are indefinite; and they would have to be equipped. Such are not the materials which we need. We want to know who these men are and where they are and to have everything ready for them if they should come to our assistance. For we have now got down, not to the sentiment of national defense, but to the business of national defense. It is a business proposition and it must be treated as such. And there are abundant precedents for the proposals which have been made to the Congress. Even that arch-Democrat, Thomas Jefferson, believed that there ought to be compulsory military training for the adult men of the Nation, because he believed, as every true believer in democracy believes, that it is upon the voluntary action of the men of a great Nation like this that it must depend for its military force.

There is another misapprehension that I want to remove from your minds: Do not think that I have come to talk to you about these things because I doubt whether they are going to be done or not. I do not doubt it for a moment, but I believe that when great things of this sort are going to be done the people of this country are entitled to know just what is being proposed. As a friend of mine says, I am not arguing with you; I am telling you. I am not trying to convert you to anything, because I know that in your hearts you are converted already, but I want you to know the motives of what is proposed and the character of what is proposed, in order that we should have only one attitude and counsel with regard to this great matter.

It is being very sedulously spread abroad in this country that the impulse back of all this is the desire of men who make the materials of warfare to get money out of the Treasury of the United States. I wish the people that say that could see meetings like this. Did you come here for that purpose? Did you come here because you are interested to see some of your fellow-citizens make money out of the present situation? Of course you did not. I am ready to admit that probably the equipment of those men whom we are training will have to be bought from somebody, and I know that if the equipment is bought, it will have to be paid for; and I dare say somebody will make some money out of it. It is also true, ladies and gentlemen, that there are men now, a great many men, in the belligerent countries who are growing rich out of the sale of the materials needed by the armies of those countries. If the Government itself does not manufacture everything that an army needs, somebody has got to make money out of it, and I for my part have been urging the Congress of the United States to make the necessary preparations by which the Government can manufacture armor plate and munitions, so that, being in the business itself and having the ability to manufacture all it needs, if it is put upon a business basis, it can at any rate keep the price that it pays within moderate and reasonable limits. The Government of the United States is not going to be imposed upon by anybody, and you may rest assured, therefore, that while I believe you prefer that private capital and private initiative should bestir themselves in these matters, it is also possible, and I assure you that it is most likely, that the Government of the United States will have adequate means of controlling this matter very thoroughly indeed. There need be no fear on that side. Let nobody suppose that this is a money-making agitation. I would for one be ashamed to be such a dupe as to be engaged in it if it had any suspicion of that about it, but I am not as innocent as I look; and I believe that I can say for my colleagues in Washington that they are just as watchful in such matters as you would desire them to be.

And there is another misapprehension that I do not wish you to entertain. Do not suppose that there is any new or sudden or recent inadequacy on the part of this Government in respect of preparation for national defense. I have heard some gentlemen say that we had no coast defenses worth talking about. Coast defenses are not nowadays advertised, you understand, and they are not visible to the naked eye, so that if you passed them and nothing exploded, you would not know they were there. The coast defenses of the United States, while not numerous enough, are equipped in the most modern and efficient fashion. You are told that there has been some sort of neglect about the Navy. There has not been any sort of neglect about the Navy. We have been slowly building up a Navy which in quality is second to no navy in the world. The only thing it lacks is quantity. In size it is the fourth navy in the world, though I have heard it said by some gentlemen in this very region that it was the second. In fighting force, though not in quality, it is reckoned by experts to be the fourth in rank in the world; and yet when I go on board those ships and see their equipment and talk with their officers I suspect that they could give an account of themselves which would raise them above the fourth class. It reminds me of that very quaint saying of the old darky preacher, "The Lord says unto Moses, come fourth, and he came fifth and lost the race." But I think this Navy would not come fourth in the race, but higher.

What we are proposing now is not the sudden creation of a Navy, for we have a splendid Navy, but the definite working out of a program by which within five years we shall bring the Navy to a fighting strength which otherwise might have taken eight or ten years; along exactly the same lines of development that have been followed and followed diligently and intelligently for at least a decade past. There is no sudden panic, there is no sudden change of plan; all that has happened is that we now see that we ought more rapidly and more thoroughly than ever before to do the things which have always been characteristic of America. For she has always been proud of her Navy and has always been addicted to the principle that her citizenship must do the fighting on land. We are working out American principle a little faster, because American pulses are beating a little faster, because the world is in a whirl, because there are incalculable elements of trouble abroad which we cannot control or alter. I would be derelict to the duty which you have laid upon me if I did not tell you that it was absolutely necessary to carry out our principles in this matter now and at once.

And yet all the time, my fellow-citizens, I believe that in these things we are merely interpreting the spirit of America. Who shall say what the spirit of America is? I have many times heard orators apostrophize this beautiful flag which is the emblem of the Nation. I have many times heard orators and philosophers speak of the spirit which was resident in America. I have always for my own part felt that it was an act of audacity to attempt to characterize anything of that kind, and when I have been outside of the country in foreign lands and have been asked if this, that, or the other was true of America I have habitually said, "Nothing stated in general terms is true of America, because it is the most variegated and varied and multiform land under the sun." Yet I know that if you turn away from the physical aspects of the country, if you turn away from the variety of the strains of blood that make up our great population, if you turn away from the great variations of occupation and of interest among our fellow-citizens, there is a spiritual unity in America. I know that there are some things which stir every heart in America, no matter what the racial derivation or the local environment, and one of the things that stirs every American is the love of individual liberty. We do not stand for occupations. We do not stand for material interests. We do not stand for any narrow conception even of political institutions; but we do stand for this, that we are banded together in America to see to it that no man shall serve any master who is not of his own choosing. And we have been very liberal and generous about this idea. We have seen great peoples, for the most part not of the same blood with ourselves, to the south of us build up polities in which this same idea pulsed and was regnant, this idea of free institutions and individual liberty, and when we have seen hands reached across the water from older political polities to interfere with the development of free institutions on the Western Hemisphere we have said: "No; we are the champions of the freedom of popular sovereignty wherever it displays or exercises itself throughout both Americas." We are the champions of a particular sort of freedom, the sort of freedom which is the only foundation and guarantee of peace.

Peace lies in the hearts of great industrial and agricultural populations, and we have arranged a government on this side of the water by which their preferences and their predilections and their interests are the mainsprings of government itself. And so when we prepare for national defense we prepare for national political integrity; we prepare to take care of the great ideals which gave birth to this Government; we are going back in spirit and in energy to those great first generations in America, when men banded themselves together, though they were but a handful upon a single coast of the Atlantic, to set up in the world the standards which have ever since floated everywhere that Americans asserted the power of their Government. As I came along the line of the railway to-day, I was touched to observe that everywhere, upon every railway station, upon every house, where a flag could be procured, some temporary standard had been raised from which there floated the stars and stripes. They seemed to have divined the errand upon which I had come, to remind you that we must subordinate every individual interest and every local interest to assert once more, if it should be necessary to assert them, the great principles for which that flag stands.

Do not deceive yourselves, ladies and gentlemen, as to where the colors of that flag came from. Those lines of red are lines of blood, nobly and unselfishly shed by men who loved the liberty of their fellow-men more than they loved their own lives and fortunes. God forbid that we should have to use the blood of America to freshen the color of that flag; but if it should ever be necessary again to assert the majesty and integrity of those ancient and honorable principles, that flag will be colored once more, and in being colored will be glorified and purified.

The Submarine Question

[Address delivered at a joint session of the two Houses of Congress, April 19, 1916.]

Gentlemen of the Congress:

A situation has arisen in the foreign relations of the country of which it is my plain duty to inform you very frankly.

It will be recalled that in February, 1915, the Imperial German Government announced its intention to treat the waters surrounding Great Britain and Ireland as embraced within the seat of war and to destroy all merchant ships owned by its enemies that might be found within any part of that portion of the high seas, and that it warned all vessels, of neutral as well as of belligerent ownership, to keep out of the waters it had thus proscribed or else enter them at their peril. The Government of the United States earnestly protested. It took the position that such a policy could not be pursued without the practical certainty of gross and palpable violations of the law of nations, particularly if submarine craft were to be employed as its instruments, inasmuch as the rules prescribed by that law, rules founded upon principles of humanity and established for the protection of the lives of non-combatants at sea, could not in the nature of the case be observed by such vessels. It based its protest on the ground that persons of neutral nationality and vessels of neutral ownership would be exposed to extreme and intolerable risks, and that no right to close any part of the high seas against their use or to expose them to such risks could lawfully be asserted by any belligerent government. The law of nations in these matters, upon which the Government of the United States based its protest, is not of recent origin or founded upon merely arbitrary principles set up by convention. It is based, on the contrary, upon manifest and imperative principles of humanity and has long been established with the approval and by the express assent of all civilized nations.

Notwithstanding the earnest protest of our Government, the Imperial German Government at once proceeded to carry out the policy it had announced. It expressed the hope that the dangers involved, at any rate the dangers to neutral vessels, would be reduced to a minimum by the instructions which it had issued to its submarine commanders, and assured the Government of the United States that it would take every possible precaution both to respect the rights of neutrals and to safeguard the lives of non-combatants.

What has actually happened in the year which has since elapsed has shown that those hopes were not justified, those assurances insusceptible of being fulfilled. In pursuance of the policy of submarine warfare against the commerce of its adversaries, thus announced and entered upon by the Imperial German Government in despite of the solemn protest of this Government, the commanders of German undersea vessels have attacked merchant ships with greater and greater activity, not only upon the high seas surrounding Great Britain and Ireland but wherever they could encounter them, in a way that has grown more and more ruthless, more and more indiscriminate as the months have gone by, less and less observant of restraints of any kind; and have delivered their attacks without compunction against vessels of every nationality and bound upon every sort of errand. Vessels of neutral ownership, even vessels of neutral ownership bound from neutral port to neutral port, have been destroyed along with vessels of belligerent ownership in constantly increasing numbers. Sometimes the merchantman attacked has been warned and summoned to surrender before being fired on or torpedoed; sometimes passengers or crews have been vouchsafed the poor security of being allowed to take to the ship's boats before she was sent to the bottom. But again and again no warning has been given, no escape even to the ship's boats allowed to those on board. What this Government foresaw must happen has happened. Tragedy has followed tragedy on the seas in such fashion, with such attendant circumstances, as to make it grossly evident that warfare of such a sort, if warfare it be, cannot be carried on without the most palpable violation of the dictates alike of right and of humanity. Whatever the disposition and intention of the Imperial German Government, it has manifestly proved impossible for it to keep such methods of attack upon the commerce of its enemies within the bounds set by either the reason or the heart of mankind.

In February of the present year the Imperial German Government informed this Government and the other neutral governments of the world that it had reason to believe that the Government of Great Britain had armed all merchant vessels of British ownership and had given them secret orders to attack any submarine of the enemy they might encounter upon the seas, and that the Imperial German Government felt justified in the circumstances in treating all armed merchantmen of belligerent ownership as auxiliary vessels of war, which it would have the right to destroy without warning. The law of nations has long recognized the right of merchantmen to carry arms for protection and to use them to repel attack, though to use them, in such circumstances, at their own risk; but the Imperial German Government claimed the right to set these understandings aside in circumstances which it deemed extraordinary. Even the terms in which it announced its purpose thus still further to relax the restraints it had previously professed its willingness and desire to put upon the operations of its submarines carried the plain implication that at least vessels which were not armed would still be exempt from destruction without warning and that personal safety would be accorded their passengers and crews; but even that limitation, if it was ever practicable to observe it, has in fact constituted no check at all upon the destruction of ships of every sort.

Again and again the Imperial German Government has given this Government its solemn assurances that at least passenger ships would not be thus dealt with, and yet it has again and again permitted its undersea commanders to disregard those assurances with entire impunity. Great liners like the *Lusitania* and the *Arabic* and mere ferryboats like the *Sussex* have been attacked without a moment's warning, sometimes before they had even become aware that they were in the presence of an armed vessel of the enemy, and the lives of non-combatants, passengers and crew, have been sacrificed wholesale, in a manner which the Government of the United States cannot but regard as wanton and without the slightest color of justification. No limit of any kind has in fact been set to the indiscriminate pursuit and destruction of merchantmen of all kinds and nationalities within the waters, constantly extending in area, where these operations have been carried on; and the roll of Americans who have lost their lives on ships thus attacked and destroyed has grown month by month until the ominous toll has mounted into the hundreds.

One of the latest and most shocking instances of this method of warfare was that of the destruction of the French cross-Channel steamer *Sussex*. It must stand forth, as the sinking of the steamer *Lusitania* did, as so singularly tragical and unjustifiable as to constitute a truly terrible example of the inhumanity of submarine warfare as the commanders of German vessels have for the past twelvemonth been conducting it. If this instance stood alone, some explanation, some disavowal by the German Government, some evidence of criminal mistake or wilful disobedience on the part of the commander of the vessel that fired the torpedo might be sought or entertained; but unhappily it does not stand alone. Recent events make the conclusion inevitable that it is only one instance, even though it be one of the most extreme and distressing instances, of the spirit and method of warfare which the Imperial German Government has mistakenly adopted, and which from the first exposed that Government to the reproach of thrusting all neutral rights aside in pursuit of its immediate objects.

The Government of the United States has been very patient. At every stage of this distressing experience of tragedy after tragedy in which its own citizens were involved it has sought to be restrained from any extreme course of action or of protest by a thoughtful consideration of the extraordinary circumstances of this unprecedented war, and actuated in all that it said or did by the sentiments of genuine friendship which the people of the United States have always entertained and continue to entertain towards the German nation. It has of course accepted the successive explanations and assurances of the Imperial German Government as given in entire sincerity and good faith, and has hoped, even against hope, that it would prove to be possible for the German Government so to order and control the acts of its naval commanders as to square its policy with the principles of humanity as embodied in the law of nations. It has been willing to wait until the significance of the facts became absolutely unmistakable and susceptible of but one interpretation.

That point has now unhappily been reached. The facts are susceptible of but one interpretation. The Imperial German Government has been unable to put any limits or restraints upon its warfare against either freight or passenger ships. It has therefore become painfully evident that the position which this Government took at the very outset is inevitable, namely, that the use of submarines for the destruction of an enemy's commerce is of necessity, because of the very character of the vessels employed and the very methods of attack which their employment of course involves, incompatible with the principles of humanity, the long established and incontrovertible rights of neutrals, and the sacred immunities of non-combatants.

I have deemed it my duty, therefore, to say to the Imperial German Government that if it is still its purpose to prosecute relentless and indiscriminate warfare against vessels of commerce by the use of submarines, notwithstanding the now demonstrated impossibility of conducting that warfare in accordance with what the Government of the United States must consider the sacred and indisputable rules of international law and the universally recognized dictates of humanity, the Government of the United States is at last forced to the conclusion that there is but one course it can pursue; and that unless the Imperial German Government should now immediately declare and effect an abandonment of its present methods of warfare against passenger and freight carrying vessels this Government can have no choice but to sever diplomatic relations with the Government of the German Empire altogether.

This decision I have arrived at with the keenest regret; the possibility of the action contemplated I am sure all thoughtful Americans will look forward to with unaffected reluctance. But we cannot forget that we are in some sort and by the force of circumstances the responsible spokesmen of the rights of humanity, and that we cannot remain silent while those rights seem in process of being swept utterly away in the maelstrom of this terrible war. We owe it to a due regard for our own rights as a nation, to our sense of duty as a representative of the rights of neutrals the world over, and to a just conception of the rights of mankind to take this stand now with the utmost solemnity and firmness.

I have taken it, and taken it in the confidence that it will meet with your approval and support. All sober-minded men must unite in hoping that the Imperial German Government, which has in other circumstances stood as the champion of all that we are now contending for in the interest of humanity, may recognize the justice of our demands and meet them in the spirit in which they are made.

American Principles

[Address delivered at the First Annual Assemblage of the League to Enforce Peace, May 27, 1916.]

When the invitation to be here to-night came to me, I was glad to accept it,—not because it offered me an opportunity to discuss the program of the League,—that you will, I am sure, not expect of me,—but because the desire of the whole world now turns eagerly, more and more eagerly, towards the hope of peace, and there is just reason why we should take our part in counsel upon this great theme. It is right that I, as spokesman of our Government, should attempt to give expression to what I believe to be the thought and purpose of the people of the United States in this vital matter.

This great war that broke so suddenly upon the world two years ago, and which has swept within its flame so great a part of the civilized world, has affected us very profoundly, and we are not only at liberty, it is perhaps our duty, to speak very frankly of it and of the great interests of civilization which it affects.

With its causes and its objects we are not concerned. The obscure fountains from which its stupendous flood has burst forth we are not interested to search for or explore. But so great a flood, spread far and wide to every quarter of the globe, has of necessity engulfed many a fair province of right that lies very near to us. Our own rights as a Nation, the liberties, the privileges, and the property of our people have been profoundly affected. We are not mere disconnected lookers-on. The longer the war lasts, the more deeply do we become concerned that it should be brought to an end and the world be permitted to resume its normal life and course again. And when it does come to an end we shall be as much concerned as the nations at war to see peace assume an aspect of permanence, give promise of days from which the anxiety of uncertainty shall be lifted, bring some assurance that peace and war shall always hereafter be reckoned part of the common interest of mankind. We are participants, whether we would or not, in the life of the world. The interests of all nations are our own also. We are partners with the rest. What affects mankind is inevitably our affair as well as the affair of the nations of Europe and of Asia.

One observation on the causes of the present war we are at liberty to make, and to make it may throw some light forward upon the future, as well as backward upon the past. It is plain that this war could have come only as it did, suddenly and out of secret counsels, without warning to the world, without discussion, without any of the deliberate movements of counsel with which it would seem natural to approach so stupendous a contest. It is probable that if it had been foreseen just what would happen, just what alliances would be formed, just what forces arrayed against one another, those who brought the great contest on would have been glad to substitute conference for force. If we ourselves had been afforded some opportunity to apprise the belligerents of the attitude which it would be our duty to take, of the policies and practices against which we would feel bound to use all our moral and economic strength, and in certain circumstances even our physical strength also, our own contribution to the counsel which might have averted the struggle would have been considered worth weighing and regarding.

And the lesson which the shock of being taken by surprise in a matter so deeply vital to all the nations of the world has made poignantly clear is, that the peace of the world must henceforth depend upon a new and more wholesome diplomacy. Only when the great nations of the world have reached some sort of agreement as to what they hold to be fundamental to their common interest, and as to some feasible method of acting in concert when any nation or group of nations seeks to disturb those fundamental things, can we feel that civilization is at last in a way of justifying its existence and claiming to be finally established. It is clear that nations must in the future be governed by the same high code of honor that we demand of individuals.

We must, indeed, in the very same breath with which we avow this conviction admit that we have ourselves upon occasion in the past been offenders against the law of diplomacy which we thus forecast; but our conviction is not the less clear, but rather the more clear, on that account. If this war has accomplished nothing else for the benefit of the world, it has at least disclosed a great moral necessity and set forward the thinking of the statesmen of the world by a whole age. Repeated utterances of the leading statesmen of most of the great nations now engaged in war have made it plain that their thought has come to this, that the principle of public right must henceforth take precedence over the individual interests of particular nations, and that the nations of the world must in some way band themselves together to see that that right prevails as against any sort of selfish aggression; that henceforth alliance must not be set up against alliance, understanding against understanding, but that there must be a common agreement for a common object, and that at the heart of that common object must lie the inviolable rights of peoples and of mankind. The nations of the world have become each other's neighbors. It is to their interest that they should understand each other. In order that they may understand each other, it is imperative that they should agree to coöperate in a common cause, and that they should so act that the guiding principle of that common cause shall be even-handed and impartial justice.

This is undoubtedly the thought of America. This is what we ourselves will say when there comes proper occasion to say it. In the dealings of nations with one another arbitrary force must be rejected and we must move forward to the thought of the modern world, the thought of which peace is the very atmosphere. That thought constitutes a chief part of the passionate conviction of America.

We believe these fundamental things: First, that every people has a right to choose the sovereignty under which they shall live. Like other nations, we have ourselves no doubt once and again offended against that principle when for a little while controlled by selfish passion, as our franker historians have been honorable enough to admit; but it has become more and more our rule of life and action. Second, that the small states of the world have a right to enjoy the same respect for their sovereignty and for their territorial integrity that great and powerful nations expect and insist upon. And, third, that the world has a right to be free from every disturbance of its peace that has its origin in aggression and disregard of the rights of peoples and nations.

So sincerely do we believe in these things that I am sure that I speak the mind and wish of the people of America when I say that the United States is willing to become a partner in any feasible association of nations formed in order to realize these objects and make them secure against violation.

There is nothing that the United States wants for itself that any other nation has. We are willing, on the contrary, to limit ourselves along with them to a prescribed course of duty and respect for the rights of others which will check any selfish passion of our own, as it will check any aggressive impulse of theirs.

If it should ever be our privilege to suggest or initiate a movement for peace among the nations now at war, I am sure that the people of the United States would wish their Government to move along these lines: First, such a settlement with regard to their own immediate interests as the belligerents may agree upon. We have nothing material of any kind to ask for ourselves, and are quite aware that we are in no sense or degree parties to the present quarrel. Our interest is only in peace and its future guarantees. Second, an universal association of the nations to maintain the inviolate security of the highway of the seas for the common and unhindered use of all the nations of the world, and to prevent any war begun either contrary to treaty covenants or without warning and full submission of the causes to the opinion of the world,—a virtual guarantee of territorial integrity and political independence.

But I did not come here, let me repeat, to discuss a program. I came only to avow a creed and give expression to the confidence I feel that the world is even now upon the eve of a great consummation, when some common force will be brought into existence which shall safeguard right as the first and most fundamental interest of all peoples and all governments, when coercion shall be summoned not to the service of political ambition or selfish hostility, but to the service of a common order, a common justice, and a common peace. God grant that the dawn of that day of frank dealing and of settled peace, concord, and coöperation may be near at hand!

The Demands of Railway Employees

[Address delivered at a joint session of the two Houses of Congress, August 29, 1916.]

Gentlemen of the Congress:

I have come to you to seek your assistance in dealing with a very grave situation which has arisen out of the demand of the employees of the railroads engaged in freight train service that they be granted an eight-hour working day, safeguarded by payment for an hour and a half of service for every hour of work beyond the eight.

The matter has been agitated for more than a year. The public has been made familiar with the demands of the men and the arguments urged in favor of them, and even more familiar with the objections of the railroads and their counter demand that certain privileges now enjoyed by their men and certain bases of payment worked out through many years of contest be reconsidered, especially in their relation to the adoption of an eight-hour day. The matter came some three weeks ago to a final issue and resulted in a complete deadlock between the parties. The means provided by law for the mediation of the controversy failed and the means of arbitration for which the law provides were rejected. The representatives of the railway executives proposed that the demands of the men be submitted in their entirety to arbitration, along with certain questions of readjustment as to pay and conditions of employment which seemed to them to be either closely associated with the demands or to call for reconsideration on their own merits; the men absolutely declined arbitration, especially if any of their established privileges were by that means to be drawn again in question. The law in the matter put no compulsion upon them. The four hundred thousand men from whom the demands proceeded had voted to strike if their demands were refused; the strike was imminent; it has since been set for the fourth of September next. It affects the men who man the freight trains on practically every railway in the country. The freight service throughout the United States must stand still until their places are filled, if, indeed, it should prove possible to fill them at all. Cities will be cut off from their food supplies, the whole commerce of the nation will be paralyzed, men of every sort and occupation will be thrown out of employment, countless thousands will in all likelihood be brought, it may be, to the very point of starvation, and a tragical national calamity brought on, to be added to the other distresses of the time, because no basis of accommodation or settlement has been found.

Just so soon as it became evident that mediation under the existing law had failed and that arbitration had been rendered impossible by the attitude of the men, I considered it my duty to confer with the representatives of both the railways and the brotherhoods, and myself offer mediation, not as an arbitrator, but merely as spokesman of the nation, in the interest of justice, indeed, and as a friend of both parties, but not as judge, only as the representative of one hundred millions of men, women, and children who would pay the price, the incalculable price, of loss and suffering should these few men insist upon approaching and concluding the matters in controversy between them merely as employers and employees, rather than as patriotic citizens of the United States looking before and after and accepting the larger responsibility which the public would put upon them.

It seemed to me, in considering the subject-matter of the controversy, that the whole spirit of the time and the preponderant evidence of recent economic experience spoke for the eight-hour day. It has been adjudged by the thought and experience of recent years a thing upon which society is justified in insisting as in the interest of health, efficiency, contentment, and a general increase of economic vigor. The whole presumption of modern experience would, it seemed to me, be in its favor, whether there was arbitration or not, and the debatable points to settle were those which arose out of the acceptance of the eight-hour day rather than those which affected its establishment. I, therefore, proposed that the eight-hour day be adopted by the railway managements and put into practice for the present as a substitute for the existing ten-hour basis of pay and service; that I should appoint, with the permission of the Congress, a small commission to observe the results of the change, carefully studying the figures of the altered operating costs, not only, but also the conditions of labor under which the men worked and the operation of their existing agreements with the railroads, with instructions to report the facts as they found them to the Congress at the earliest possible day, but without recommendation; and that, after the facts had been thus disclosed, an adjustment should in some orderly manner be sought of all the matters now left unadjusted between the railroad managers and the men.

These proposals were exactly in line, it is interesting to note, with the position taken by the Supreme Court of the United States when appealed to to protect certain litigants from the financial losses which they confidently expected if they should submit to the regulation of their charges and of their methods of service by public legislation. The Court has held that it would not undertake to form a judgment upon forecasts, but could base its action only upon actual experience; that it must be supplied with facts, not with calculations and opinions, however scientifically attempted. To undertake to arbitrate the question of the adoption of an eight-hour day in the light of results merely estimated and predicted would be to undertake an enterprise of conjecture. No wise man could undertake it, or, if he did undertake it, could feel assured of his conclusions.

I unhesitatingly offered the friendly services of the administration to the railway managers to see to it that justice was done the railroads in the outcome. I felt warranted in assuring them that no obstacle of law would be suffered to stand in the way of their increasing their revenues to meet the expenses resulting from the change so far as the development of their business and of their administrative efficiency did not prove adequate to meet them. The public and the representatives of the public, I felt justified in assuring them, were disposed to nothing but justice in such cases and were willing to serve those who served them.

The representatives of the brotherhoods accepted the plan; but the representatives of the railroads declined to accept it. In the face of what I cannot but regard as the practical certainty that they will be ultimately obliged to accept the eight-hour day by the concerted action of organized labor, backed by the favorable judgment of society, the representatives of the railway management have felt justified in declining a peaceful settlement which would engage all the forces of justice, public and private, on their side to take care of the event. They fear the hostile influence of shippers, who would be opposed to an increase of freight rates (for which, however, of course, the public itself would pay); they apparently feel no confidence that the Interstate Commerce Commission could withstand the objections that would be made. They do not care to rely upon the friendly assurances of the Congress or the President. They have thought it best that they should be forced to yield, if they must yield, not by counsel, but by the suffering of the country. While my conferences with them were in progress, and when to all outward appearance those conferences had come to a standstill, the representatives of the brotherhoods suddenly acted and set the strike for the fourth of September.

The railway managers based their decision to reject my counsel in this matter upon their conviction that they must at any cost to themselves or to the country stand firm for the principle of arbitration which the men had rejected. I based my counsel upon the indisputable fact that there was no means of obtaining arbitration. The law supplied none; earnest efforts at mediation had failed to influence the men in the least. To stand firm for the principle of arbitration and yet not get arbitration seemed to me futile, and something more than futile, because it involved incalculable distress to the country and consequences in some respects worse than those of war, and that in the midst of peace.

I yield to no man in firm adherence, alike of conviction and of purpose, to the principle of arbitration in industrial disputes; but matters have come to a sudden crisis in this particular dispute and the country had been caught unprovided with any practicable means of enforcing that conviction in practice (by whose fault we will not now stop to inquire). A situation had to be met whose elements and fixed conditions were indisputable. The practical and patriotic course to pursue, as it seemed to me, was to secure immediate peace by conceding the one thing in the demands of the men which society itself and any arbitrators who represented public sentiment were most likely to approve, and immediately lay the foundations for securing arbitration with regard to everything else involved. The event has confirmed that judgment.

I was seeking to compose the present in order to safeguard the future; for I wished an atmosphere of peace and friendly coöperation in which to take counsel with the representatives of the nation with regard to the best means for providing, so far as it might prove possible to provide, against the recurrence of such unhappy situations in the future,—the best and most practicable means of securing calm and fair arbitration of all industrial disputes in the days to come. This is assuredly the best way of vindicating a principle, namely, having failed to make certain of its observance in the present, to make certain of its observance in the future.

But I could only propose. I could not govern the will of others who took an entirely different view of the circumstances of the case, who even refused to admit the circumstances to be what they have turned out to be.

Having failed to bring the parties to this critical controversy to an accommodation, therefore, I turn to you, deeming it clearly our duty as public servants to leave nothing undone that we can do to safeguard the life and interests of the nation. In the spirit of such a purpose, I earnestly recommend the following legislation:

First, immediate provision for the enlargement and administrative reorganization of the Interstate Commerce Commission along the lines embodied in the bill recently passed by the House of Representatives and now awaiting action by the Senate; in order that the Commission may be enabled to deal with the many great and various duties now devolving upon it with a promptness and thoroughness which are with its present constitution and means of action practically impossible.

Second, the establishment of an eight-hour day as the legal basis alike of work and of wages in the employment of all railway employees who are actually engaged in the work of operating trains in interstate transportation.

Third, the authorization of the appointment by the President of a small body of men to observe the actual results in experience of the adoption of the eight-hour day in railway transportation alike for the men and for the railroads; its effects in the matter of operating costs, in the application of the existing practices and agreements to the new conditions, and in all other practical aspects, with the provision that the investigators shall report their conclusions to the Congress at the earliest possible date, but without recommendation as to legislative action; in order that the public may learn from an unprejudiced source just what actual developments have ensued.

Fourth, explicit approval by the Congress of the consideration by the Interstate Commerce Commission of an increase of freight rates to meet such additional expenditures by the railroads as may have been rendered necessary by the adoption of the eight-hour day and which have not been offset by administrative readjustments and economies, should the facts disclosed justify the increase.

Fifth, an amendment of the existing federal statute which provides for the mediation, conciliation, and arbitration of such controversies as the present by adding to it a provision that in case the methods of accommodation now provided for should fail, a full public investigation of the merits of every such dispute shall be instituted and completed before a strike or lockout may lawfully be attempted.

And, sixth, the lodgment in the hands of the Executive of the power, in case of military necessity, to take control of such portions and such rolling stock of the railways of the country as may be required for military use and to operate them for military purposes, with authority to draft into the military service of the United States such train crews and administrative officials as the circumstances require for their safe and efficient use.

This last suggestion I make because we cannot in any circumstances suffer the nation to be hampered in the essential matter of national defense. At the present moment circumstances render this duty particularly obvious. Almost the entire military force of the nation is stationed upon the Mexican border to guard our territory against hostile raids. It must be supplied, and steadily supplied, with whatever it needs for its maintenance and efficiency. If it should be necessary for purposes of national defense to transfer any portion of it upon short notice to some other part of the country, for reasons now unforeseen, ample means of transportation must be available, and available without delay. The power conferred in this matter should be carefully and explicitly limited to cases of military necessity, but in all such cases it should be clear and ample.

There is one other thing we should do if we are true champions of arbitration. We should make all arbitral awards judgments by record of a court of law in order that their interpretation and enforcement may lie, not with one of the parties to the arbitration, but with an impartial and authoritative tribunal.

These things I urge upon you, not in haste or merely as a means of meeting a present emergency, but as permanent and necessary additions to the law of the land, suggested, indeed, by circumstances we had hoped never to see, but imperative as well as just, if such emergencies are to be prevented in the future. I feel that no extended argument is needed to commend them to your favorable consideration. They demonstrate themselves. The time and the occasion only give emphasis to their importance. We need them now and we shall continue to need them.

Speech of Acceptance

[On being offered the nomination for President by the Democratic Party. Delivered at Shadow Lawn, Sea Girt, N.J., Saturday, September 2, 1916.]

Senator James, Gentlemen of the Notification Committee, Fellow-Citizens:

I cannot accept the leadership and responsibility which the National Democratic Convention has again, in such generous fashion, asked me to accept without first expressing my profound gratitude to the party for the trust it reposes in me after four years of fiery trial in the midst of affairs of unprecedented difficulty, and the keen sense of added responsibility with which this honor fills (I had almost said burdens) me as I think of the great issues of national life and policy involved in the present and immediate future conduct of our Government. I shall seek, as I have always sought, to justify the extraordinary confidence thus reposed in me by striving to purge my heart and purpose of every personal and of every misleading party motive and devoting every energy I have to the service of the nation as a whole, praying that I may continue to have the counsel and support of all forward-looking men at every turn of the difficult business.

For I do not doubt that the people of the United States will wish the Democratic Party to continue in control of the Government. They are not in the habit of rejecting those who have actually served them for those who are making doubtful and conjectural promises of service. Least of all are they likely to substitute those who promised to render them particular services and proved false to that promise for those who have actually rendered those very services.

Boasting is always an empty business, which pleases nobody but the boaster, and I have no disposition to boast of what the Democratic Party has accomplished. It has merely done its duty. It has merely fulfilled its explicit promises. But there can be no violation of good taste in calling attention to the manner in which those promises have been carried out or in adverting to the interesting fact that many of the things accomplished were what the opposition party had again and again promised to do but had left undone. Indeed that is manifestly part of the business of this year of reckoning and assessment. There is no means of judging the future except by assessing the past. Constructive action must be weighed against destructive comment and reaction. The Democrats either have or have not understood the varied interests of the country. The test is contained in the record.

What is that record? What were the Democrats called into power to do? What things had long waited to be done, and how did the Democrats do them? It is a record of extraordinary length and variety, rich in elements of many kinds, but consistent in principle throughout and susceptible of brief recital.

The Republican Party was put out of power because of failure, practical failure and moral failure; because it had served special interests and not the country at large; because, under the leadership of its preferred and established guides, of those who still make its choices, it had lost touch with the thoughts and the needs of the nation and was living in a past age and under a fixed illusion, the illusion of greatness. It had framed tariff laws based upon a fear of foreign trade, a fundamental doubt as to American skill, enterprise, and capacity, and a very tender regard for the profitable privileges of those who had gained control of domestic markets and domestic credits; and yet had enacted anti-trust laws which hampered the very things they meant to foster, which were stiff and inelastic, and in part unintelligible. It had permitted the country throughout the long period of its control to stagger from one financial crisis to another under the operation of a national banking law of its own framing which made stringency and panic certain and the control of the larger business operations of the country by the bankers of a few reserve centers inevitable; had made as if it meant to reform the law but had faint-heartedly failed in the attempt, because it could not bring itself to do the one thing necessary to make the reform genuine and effectual, namely, break up the control of small groups of bankers.

It had been oblivious, or indifferent, to the fact that the farmers, upon whom the country depends for its food and in the last analysis for its prosperity, were without standing in the matter of commercial credit, without the protection of standards in their market transactions, and without systematic knowledge of the markets themselves; that the laborers of the country, the great army of men who man the industries it was professing to father and promote, carried their labor as a mere commodity to market, were subject to restraint by novel and drastic process in the courts, were without assurance of compensation for industrial accidents, without federal assistance in accommodating labor disputes, and without national aid or advice in finding the places and the industries in which their labor was most needed. The country had no national system of road construction and development. Little intelligent attention was paid to the army, and not enough to the navy. The other republics of America distrusted us, because they found that we thought first of the profits of American investors and only as an afterthought of impartial justice and helpful friendship. Its policy was provincial in all things; its purposes were out of harmony with the temper and purpose of the people and the timely development of the nation's interests.

So things stood when the Democratic Party came into power. How do they stand now? Alike in the domestic field and in the wide field of the commerce of the world, American business and life and industry have been set free to move as they never moved before.

The tariff has been revised, not on the principle of repelling foreign trade, but upon the principle of encouraging it, upon something like a footing of equality with our own in respect of the terms of competition, and a Tariff Board has been created whose function it will be to keep the relations of American with foreign business and industry under constant observation, for the guidance alike of our business men and of our Congress. American energies are now directed towards the markets of the world.

The laws against trusts have been clarified by definition, with a view to making it plain that they were not directed against big business but only against unfair business and the pretense of competition where there was none; and a Trade Commission has been created with powers of guidance and accommodation which have relieved business men of unfounded fears and set them upon the road of hopeful and confident enterprise.

By the Federal Reserve Act the supply of currency at the disposal of active business has been rendered elastic, taking its volume, not from a fixed body of investment securities, but from the liquid assets of daily trade; and these assets are assessed and accepted, not by distant groups of bankers in control of unavailable reserves, but by bankers at the many centers of local exchange who are in touch with local conditions everywhere.

Effective measures have been taken for the re-creation of an American merchant marine and the revival of the American carrying trade indispensable to our emancipation from the control which foreigners have so long exercised over the opportunities, the routes, and the methods of our commerce with other countries.

The Interstate Commerce Commission is about to be reorganized to enable it to perform its great and important functions more promptly and more efficiently. We have created, extended and improved the service of the parcels post.

So much we have done for business. What other party has understood the task so well or executed it so intelligently and energetically? What other party has attempted it at all? The Republican leaders, apparently, know of no means of assisting business but "protection." How to stimulate it and put it upon a new footing of energy and enterprise they have not suggested.

For the farmers of the country we have virtually created commercial credit, by means of the Federal Reserve Act and the Rural Credits Act. They now have the standing of other business men in the money market. We have successfully regulated speculation in "futures" and established standards in the marketing of grains. By an intelligent Warehouse Act we have assisted to make the standard crops available as never before both for systematic marketing and as a security for loans from the banks. We have greatly added to the work of neighborhood demonstration on the farm itself of improved methods of cultivation, and, through the intelligent extension of the functions of the Department of Agriculture, have made it possible for the farmer to learn systematically where his best markets are and how to get at them.

The workingmen of America have been given a veritable emancipation, by the legal recognition of a man's labor as part of his life, and not a mere marketable commodity; by exempting labor organizations from processes of the courts which treated their members like fractional parts of mobs and not like accessible and responsible individuals; by releasing our seamen from involuntary servitude; by making adequate provision for compensation for industrial accidents; by providing suitable machinery for mediation and conciliation in industrial disputes; and by putting the Federal Department of Labor at the disposal of the workingman when in search of work.

We have effected the emancipation of the children of the country by releasing them from hurtful labor. We have instituted a system of national aid in the building of highroads such as the country has been feeling after for a century. We have sought to equalize taxation by means of an equitable income tax. We have taken the steps that ought to have been taken at the outset to open up the resources of Alaska. We have provided for national defense upon a scale never before seriously proposed upon the responsibility of an entire political party. We have driven the tariff lobby from cover and obliged it to substitute solid argument for private influence.

This extraordinary recital must sound like a platform, a list of sanguine promises; but it is not. It is a record of promises made four years ago and now actually redeemed in constructive legislation.

These things must profoundly disturb the thoughts and confound the plans of those who have made themselves believe that the Democratic Party neither understood nor was ready to assist the business of the country in the great enterprises which it is its evident and inevitable destiny to undertake and carry through. The breaking up of the lobby must especially disconcert them: for it was through the lobby that they sought and were sure they had found the heart of things. The game of privilege can be played successfully by no other means.

This record must equally astonish those who feared that the Democratic Party had not opened its heart to comprehend the demands of social justice. We have in four years come very near to carrying out the platform of the Progressive Party as well as our own; for we also are progressives.

There is one circumstance connected with this program which ought to be very plainly stated. It was resisted at every step by the interests which the Republican Party had catered to and fostered at the expense of the country, and these same interests are now earnestly praying for a reaction which will save their privileges, —for the restoration of their sworn friends to power before it is too late to recover what they have lost. They fought with particular desperation and infinite resourcefulness the reform of the banking and currency system, knowing that to be the citadel of their control; and most anxiously are they hoping and planning for the amendment of the Federal Reserve Act by the concentration of control in a single bank which the old familiar group of bankers can keep under their eye and direction. But while the "big men" who used to write the tariffs and command the assistance of the Treasury have been hostile, —all but a few with vision, —the average business man knows that he has been delivered, and that the fear that was once every day in his heart, that the men who controlled credit and directed enterprise from the committee rooms of Congress would crush him, is there no more, and will not return, —unless the party that consulted only the "big men" should return to power, —the party of masterly inactivity and cunning resourcefulness in standing pat to resist change.

The Republican Party is just the party that *cannot* meet the new conditions of a new age. It does not know the way and it does not wish new conditions. It tried to break away from the old leaders and could not. They still select its candidates and dictate its policy, still resist change, still hanker after the old conditions, still know no methods of encouraging business but the old methods. When it changes its leaders and its purposes and brings its ideas up to date it will have the right to ask the American people to give it power again; but not until then. A new age, an age of revolutionary change, needs new purposes and new ideas.

In foreign affairs we have been guided by principles clearly conceived and consistently lived up to. Perhaps they have not been fully comprehended because they have hitherto governed international affairs only in theory, not in practice. They are simple, obvious, easily stated, and fundamental to American ideals.

We have been neutral not only because it was the fixed and traditional policy of the United States to stand aloof from the politics of Europe and because we had had no part either of action or of policy in the influences which brought on the present war, but also because it was manifestly our duty to prevent, if it were possible, the indefinite extension of the fires of hate and desolation kindled by that terrible conflict and seek to serve mankind by reserving our strength and our resources for the anxious and difficult days of restoration and healing which must follow, when peace will have to build its house anew.

The rights of our own citizens of course became involved: that was inevitable. Where they did this was our guiding principle: that property rights can be vindicated by claims for damages and no modern nation can decline to arbitrate such claims; but the fundamental rights of humanity cannot be. The loss of life is irreparable. Neither can direct violations of a nation's sovereignty await vindication in suits for damages. The nation that violates these essential rights must expect to be checked and called to account by direct challenge and resistance. It at once makes the quarrel in part our own. These are plain principles and we have never lost sight of them or departed from them, whatever the stress or the perplexity of circumstance or the provocation to hasty resentment. The record is clear and consistent throughout and stands distinct and definite for anyone to judge who wishes to know the truth about it.

The seas were not broad enough to keep the infection of the conflict out of our own politics. The passions and intrigues of certain active groups and combinations of men amongst us who were born under foreign flags injected the poison of disloyalty into our own most critical affairs, laid violent hands upon many of our industries, and subjected us to the shame of divisions of sentiment and purpose in which America was contemned and forgotten. It is part of the business of this year of reckoning and settlement to speak plainly and act with unmistakable purpose in rebuke of these things, in order that they may be forever hereafter impossible. I am the candidate of a party, but I am above all things else an American citizen. I neither seek the favor nor fear the displeasure of that small alien element amongst us which puts loyalty to any foreign power before loyalty to the United States.

While Europe was at war our own continent, one of our own neighbors, was shaken by revolution. In that matter, too, principle was plain and it was imperative that we should live up to it if we were to deserve the trust of any real partisan of the right as free men see it. We have professed to believe, and we do believe, that the people of small and weak states have the right to expect to be dealt with exactly as the people of big and powerful states would be. We have acted upon that principle in dealing with the people of Mexico.

Our recent pursuit of bandits into Mexican territory was no violation of that principle. We ventured to enter Mexican territory only because there were no military forces in Mexico that could protect our border from hostile attack and our own people from violence, and we have committed there no single act of hostility or interference even with the sovereign authority of the Republic of Mexico herself. It was a plain case of the violation of our own sovereignty which could not wait to be vindicated by damages and for which there was no other remedy. The authorities of Mexico were powerless to prevent it.

Many serious wrongs against the property, many irreparable wrongs against the persons of Americans have been committed within the territory of Mexico herself during this confused revolution, wrongs which could not be effectually checked so long as there was no constituted power in Mexico which was in a position to check them. We could not act directly in that matter ourselves without denying Mexicans the right to any revolution at all which disturbed us and making the emancipation of her own people await our own interest and convenience.

For it is their emancipation that they are seeking,—blindly, it may be, and as yet ineffectually, but with profound and passionate purpose and within their unquestionable right, apply what true American principle you will, —any principle that an American would publicly avow. The people of Mexico have not been suffered to own their own country or direct their own institutions. Outsiders, men out of other nations and with interests too often alien to their own, have dictated what their privileges and opportunities should be and who should control their land, their lives, and their resources, —some of them Americans, pressing for things they could never have got in their own country. The Mexican people are entitled to attempt their liberty from such influences; and so long as I have anything to do with the action of our great Government I shall do everything in my power to prevent anyone standing in their way. I know that this is hard for some persons to understand; but it is not hard for the plain people of the United States to understand. It is hard doctrine only for those who wish to get something for themselves out of Mexico. There are men, and noble women, too, not a few, of our own people, thank God! whose fortunes are invested in great properties in Mexico who yet see the case with true vision and assess its issues with true American feeling. The rest can be left for the present out of the reckoning until this enslaved people has had its day of struggle towards the light. I have heard no one who was free from such influences propose interference by the United States with the internal affairs of Mexico. Certainly no friend of the Mexican people has proposed it.

The people of the United States are capable of great sympathies and a noble pity in dealing with problems of this kind. As their spokesman and representative, I have tried to act in the spirit they would wish me show. The people of Mexico are striving for the rights that are fundamental to life and happiness, —15,000,000 oppressed men, overburdened women, and pitiful children in virtual bondage in their own home of fertile lands and inexhaustible treasure! Some of the leaders of the revolution may often have been mistaken and violent and selfish, but the revolution itself was inevitable and is right. The unspeakable Huerta betrayed the very comrades he served, traitorously overthrew the government of which he was a trusted part, impudently spoke for the very forces that had driven his people to the rebellion with which he had pretended to sympathize. The men who overcame him and drove him out represent at least the fierce passion of reconstruction which lies at the very heart of liberty; and so long as they represent, however imperfectly, such a struggle for deliverance, I am ready to serve their ends when I can. So long as the power of recognition rests with me the Government of the United States will refuse to extend the hand of welcome to any one who obtains power in a sister republic by treachery and violence. No permanency can be given the affairs of any republic by a title based upon intrigue and assassination. I declared that to be the policy of this Administration within three weeks after I assumed the presidency. I here again vow it. I am more interested in the fortunes of oppressed men and pitiful women and children than in any property rights whatever. Mistakes I have no doubt made in this perplexing business, but not in purpose or object.

More is involved than the immediate destinies of Mexico and the relations of the United States with a distressed and distracted people. All America looks on. Test is now being made of us whether we be sincere lovers of popular liberty or not and are indeed to be trusted to respect national sovereignty among our weaker neighbors. We have undertaken these many years to play big brother to the republics of this hemisphere. This is the day of our test whether we mean, or have ever meant, to play that part for our own benefit wholly or also for theirs. Upon the outcome of that test (its outcome in their minds, not in ours) depends every relationship of the United States with Latin America, whether in politics or in commerce and enterprise. These are great issues and lie at the heart of the gravest tasks of the future, tasks both economic and political and very intimately inwrought with many of the most vital of the new issues of the politics of the world. The republics of America have in the last three years been drawing together in a new spirit of accommodation, mutual understanding, and cordial coöperation. Much of the politics of the world in the years to come will depend upon their relationships with one another. It is a barren and provincial statesmanship that loses sight of such things!

The future, the immediate future, will bring us squarely face to face with many great and exacting problems which will search us through and through whether we be able and ready to play the part in the world that we mean to play. It will not bring us into their presence slowly, gently, with ceremonious introduction, but suddenly and at once, the moment the war in Europe is over. They will be new problems, most of them; many will be old problems in a new setting and with new elements which we have never dealt with or reckoned the force and meaning of before. They will require for their solution new thinking, fresh courage and resourcefulness, and in some matters radical reconsiderations of policy. We must be ready to mobilize our resources alike of brains and of materials.

It is not a future to be afraid of. It is, rather, a future to stimulate and excite us to the display of the best powers that are in us. We may enter it with confidence when we are sure that we understand it,—and we have provided ourselves already with the means of understanding it.

Look first at what it will be necessary that the nations of the world should do to make the days to come tolerable and fit to live and work in; and then look at our part in what is to follow and our own duty of preparation. For we must be prepared both in resources and in policy.

There must be a just and settled peace, and we here in America must contribute the full force of our enthusiasm and of our authority as a nation to the organization of that peace upon world-wide foundations that cannot easily be shaken. No nation should be forced to take sides in any quarrel in which its own honor and integrity and the fortunes of its own people are not involved; but no nation can any longer remain neutral as against any wilful disturbance of the peace of the world. The effects of war can no longer be confined to the areas of battle. No nation stands wholly apart in interest when the life and interests of all nations are thrown into confusion and peril. If hopeful and generous enterprise is to be renewed, if the healing and helpful arts of life are indeed to be revived when peace comes again, a new atmosphere of justice and friendship must be generated by means the world has never tried before. The nations of the world must unite in joint guarantees that whatever is done to disturb the whole world's life must first be tested in the court of the whole world's opinion before it is attempted.

These are the new foundations the world must build for itself, and we must play our part in the reconstruction, generously and without too much thought of our separate interests. We must make ourselves ready to play it intelligently, vigorously, and well.

One of the contributions we must make to the world's peace is this: We must see to it that the people in our insular possessions are treated in their own lands as we would treat them here, and make the rule of the United States mean the same thing everywhere,—the same justice, the same consideration for the essential rights of men.

Besides contributing our ungrudging moral and practical support to the establishment of peace throughout the world we must actively and intelligently prepare ourselves to do our full service in the trade and industry which are to sustain and develop the life of the nations in the days to come.

We have already been provident in this great matter and supplied ourselves with the instrumentalities of prompt adjustment. We have created, in the Federal Trade Commission, a means of inquiry and of accommodation in the field of commerce which ought both to coördinate the enterprises of our traders and manufacturers and to remove the barriers of misunderstanding and of a too technical interpretation of the law. In the new Tariff Commission we have added another instrumentality of observation and adjustment which promises to be immediately serviceable. The Trade Commission substitutes counsel and accommodation for the harsher processes of legal restraint, and the Tariff Commission ought to substitute facts for prejudices and theories. Our exporters have for some time had the advantage of working in the new light thrown upon foreign markets and opportunities of trade by the intelligent inquiries and activities of the Bureau of Foreign and Domestic Commerce which the Democratic Congress so wisely created in 1912. The Tariff Commission completes the machinery by which we shall be enabled to open up our legislative policy to the facts as they develop.

We can no longer indulge our traditional provincialism. We are to play a leading part in the world drama whether we wish it or not. We shall lend, not borrow; act for ourselves, not imitate or follow; organize and initiate, not peep about merely to see where we may get in.

We have already formulated and agreed upon a policy of law which will explicitly remove the ban now supposed to rest upon coöperation amongst our exporters in seeking and securing their proper place in the markets of the world. The field will be free, the instrumentalities at hand. It will only remain for the masters of enterprise amongst us to act in energetic concert, and for the Government of the United States to insist upon the maintenance throughout the world of those conditions of fairness and of even-handed justice in the commercial dealings of the nations with one another upon which, after all, in the last analysis, the peace and ordered life of the world must ultimately depend.

At home also we must see to it that the men who plan and develop and direct our business enterprises shall enjoy definite and settled conditions of law, a policy accommodated to the freest progress. We have set the just and necessary limits. We have put all kinds of unfair competition under the ban and penalty of the law. We have barred monopoly. These fatal and ugly things being excluded, we must now quicken action and facilitate enterprise by every just means within our choice. There will be peace in the business world, and, with peace, revived confidence and life.

We ought both to husband and to develop our natural resources, our mines, our forests, our water power. I wish we could have made more progress than we have made in this vital matter; and I call once more, with the deepest earnestness and solicitude, upon the advocates of a careful and provident conservation, on the one hand, and the advocates of a free and inviting field for private capital, on the other, to get together in a spirit of genuine accommodation and agreement and set this great policy forward at once.

We must hearten and quicken the spirit and efficiency of labor throughout our whole industrial system by everywhere and in all occupations doing justice to the laborer, not only by paying a living wage but also by making all the conditions that surround labor what they ought to be. And we must do more than justice. We must safeguard life and promote health and safety in every occupation in which they are threatened or imperilled. That is more than justice, and better, because it is humanity and economy.

We must coördinate the railway systems of the country for national use, and must facilitate and promote their development with a view to that coördination and to their better adaptation as a whole to the life and trade and defense of the nation. The life and industry of the country can be free and unhampered only if these arteries are open, efficient, and complete.

Thus shall we stand ready to meet the future as circumstance and international policy effect their unfolding, whether the changes come slowly or come fast and without preface.

I have not spoken explicitly, Gentlemen, of the platform adopted at St. Louis; but it has been implicit in all that I have said. I have sought to interpret its spirit and meaning. The people of the United States do not need to be assured now that that platform is a definite pledge, a practical program. We have proved to them that our promises are made to be kept.

We hold very definite ideals. We believe that the energy and initiative of our people have been too narrowly coached and superintended; that they should be set free, as we have set them free, to disperse themselves throughout the nation; that they should not be concentrated in the hands of a few powerful guides and guardians, as our opponents have again and again, in effect if not in purpose, sought to concentrate them. We believe, moreover,—who that looks about him now with comprehending eye can fail to believe?—that the day of Little Americanism, with its narrow horizons, when methods of "protection" and industrial nursing were the chief study of our provincial statesmen, are past and gone and that a day of enterprise has at last dawned for the United States whose field is the wide world.

We hope to see the stimulus of that new day draw all America, the republics of both continents, on to a new life and energy and initiative in the great affairs of peace. We are Americans for Big America, and rejoice to look forward to the days in which America shall strive to stir the world without irritating it or drawing it on to new antagonisms, when the nations with which we deal shall at last come to see upon what deep foundations of humanity and justice our passion for peace rests, and when all mankind shall look upon our great people with a new sentiment of admiration, friendly rivalry and real affection, as upon a people who, though keen to succeed, seeks always to be at once generous and just and to whom humanity is dearer than profit or selfish power.

Upon this record and in the faith of this purpose we go to the country.

Lincoln's Beginnings

[Address delivered September 4, 1916, on the acceptance of a deed of gift to the Nation, by the Lincoln Farm Association, of the Lincoln Birthplace Farm, at Hodgenville, Kentucky.]

No more significant memorial could have been presented to the nation than this. It expresses so much of what is singular and noteworthy in the history of the country; it suggests so many of the things that we prize most highly in our life and in our system of government. How eloquent this little house within this shrine is of the vigor of democracy! There is nowhere in the land any home so remote, so humble, that it may not contain the power of mind and heart and conscience to which nations yield and history submits its processes. Nature pays no tribute to aristocracy, subscribes to no creed of caste, renders fealty to no monarch or master of any name or kind. Genius is no snob. It does not run after titles or seek by preference the high circles of society. It affects humble company as well as great. It pays no special tribute to universities or learned societies or conventional standards of greatness, but serenely chooses its own comrades, its own haunts, its own cradle even, and its own life of adventure and of training. Here is proof of it. This little hut was the cradle of one of the great sons of men, a man of singular, delightful, vital genius who presently emerged upon the great stage of the nation's history, gaunt, shy, ungainly, but dominant and majestic, a natural ruler of men, himself inevitably the central figure of the great plot. No man can explain this, but every man can see how it demonstrates the vigor of democracy, where every door is open, in every hamlet and countryside, in city and wilderness alike, for the ruler to emerge when he will and claim his leadership in the free life. Such are the authentic proofs of the validity and vitality of democracy.

Here, no less, hides the mystery of democracy. Who shall guess this secret of nature and providence and a free polity? Whatever the vigor and vitality of the stock from which he sprang, its mere vigor and soundness do not explain where this man got his great heart that seemed to comprehend all mankind in its catholic and benignant sympathy, the mind that sat enthroned behind those brooding, melancholy eyes, whose vision swept many an horizon which those about him dreamed not of,—that mind that comprehended what it had never seen, and understood the language of affairs with the ready ease of one to the manner born,—or that nature which seemed in its varied richness to be the familiar of men of every way of life. This is the sacred mystery of democracy, that its richest fruits spring up out of soils which no man has prepared and in circumstances amidst which they are the least expected. This is a place alike of mystery and of reassurance.

It is likely that in a society ordered otherwise than our own Lincoln could not have found himself or the path of fame and power upon which he walked serenely to his death. In this place it is right that we should remind ourselves of the solid and striking facts upon which our faith in democracy is founded. Many another man besides Lincoln has served the nation in its highest places of counsel and of action whose origins were as humble as his. Though the greatest example of the universal energy, richness, stimulation, and force of democracy, he is only one example among many. The permeating and all-pervasive virtue of the freedom which challenges us in America to make the most of every gift and power we possess every page of our history serves to emphasize and illustrate. Standing here in this place, it seems almost the whole of the stirring story.

Here Lincoln had his beginnings. Here the end and consummation of that great life seem remote and a bit incredible. And yet there was no break anywhere between beginning and end, no lack of natural sequence anywhere. Nothing really incredible happened. Lincoln was unaffectedly as much at home in the White House as he was here. Do you share with me the feeling, I wonder, that he was permanently at home nowhere? It seems to me that in the case of a man, —I would rather say of a spirit, —like Lincoln the question *where* he was is of little significance, that it is always *what* he was that really arrests our thought and takes hold of our imagination. It is the spirit always that is sovereign. Lincoln, like the rest of us, was put through the discipline of the world, —a very rough and exacting discipline for him, an indispensable discipline for every man who would know what he is about in the midst of the world's affairs; but his spirit got only its schooling there. It did not derive its character or its vision from the experiences which brought it to its full revelation. The test of every American must always be, not where he is, but what he is. That, also, is of the essence of democracy, and is the moral of which this place is most gravely expressive.

We would like to think of men like Lincoln and Washington as typical Americans, but no man can be typical who is so unusual as these great men were. It was typical of American life that it should produce such men with supreme indifference as to the manner in which it produced them, and as readily here in this hut as amidst the little circle of cultivated gentlemen to whom Virginia owed so much in leadership and example. And Lincoln and Washington were typical Americans in the use they made of their genius. But there will be few such men at best, and we will not look into the mystery of how and why they come. We will only keep the door open for them always, and a hearty welcome, —after we have recognized them.

I have read many biographies of Lincoln; I have sought out with the greatest interest the many intimate stories that are told of him, the narratives of nearby friends, the sketches at close quarters, in which those who had the privilege of being associated with him have tried to depict for us the very man himself "in his habit as he lived;" but I have nowhere found a real intimate of Lincoln's. I nowhere get the impression in any narrative or reminiscence that the writer had in fact penetrated to the heart of his mystery, or that any man could penetrate to the heart of it. That brooding spirit had no real familiars. I get the impression that it never spoke out in complete self-revelation, and that it could not reveal itself completely to anyone. It was a very lonely spirit that looked out from underneath those shaggy brows and comprehended men without fully communing with them, as if, in spite of all its genial efforts at comradeship, it dwelt apart, saw its visions of duty where no man looked on. There is a very holy and very terrible isolation for the conscience of every man who seeks to read the destiny in affairs for others as well as for himself, for a nation as well as for individuals. That privacy no man can intrude upon. That lonely search of the spirit for the right perhaps no man can assist. This strange child of the cabin kept company with invisible things, was born into no intimacy but that of its own silently assembling and deploying thoughts.

I have come here to-day, not to utter a eulogy on Lincoln; he stands in need of none, but to endeavor to interpret the meaning of this gift to the nation of the place of his birth and origin. Is not this an altar upon which we may forever keep alive the vestal fire of democracy as upon a shrine at which some of the deepest and most sacred hopes of mankind may from age to age be rekindled? For these hopes must constantly be rekindled, and only those who live can rekindle them. The only stuff that can retain the life-giving heat is the stuff of living hearts. And the hopes of mankind cannot be kept alive by words merely, by constitutions and doctrines of right and codes of liberty. The object of democracy is to transmute these into the life and action of society, the self-denial and self-sacrifice of heroic men and women willing to make their lives an embodiment of right and service and enlightened purpose. The commands of democracy are as imperative as its privileges and opportunities are wide and generous. Its compulsion is upon us. It will be great and lift a great light for the guidance of the nations only if we are great and carry that light high for the guidance of our own feet. We are not worthy to stand here unless we ourselves be in deed and in truth real democrats and servants of mankind, ready to give our very lives for the freedom and justice and spiritual exaltation of the great nation which shelters and nurtures us.

The Triumph of Women's Suffrage

[Address at the Suffrage Convention, Atlantic City, New Jersey, September 8, 1916.]

Madam President, Ladies of the Association:
I have found it a real privilege to be here to-night and to listen to the addresses which you have heard. Though you may not all of you believe it, I would a great deal rather hear somebody else speak than speak myself; but I should feel that I was omitting a duty if I did not address you to-night and say some of the things that have been in my thought as I realized the approach of this evening and the duty that would fall upon me.

The astonishing thing about the movement which you represent is, not that it has grown so slowly, but that it has grown so rapidly. No doubt for those who have been a long time in the struggle, like your honored president, it seems a long and arduous path that has been trodden, but when you think of the cumulating force of this movement in recent decades, you must agree with me that it is one of the most astonishing tides in modern history. Two generations ago, no doubt Madam President will agree with me in saying, it was a handful of women who were fighting this cause. Now it is a great multitude of women who are fighting it.

And there are some interesting historical connections which I would like to attempt to point out to you. One of the most striking facts about the history of the United States is that at the outset it was a lawyers' history. Almost all of the questions to which America addressed itself, say a hundred years ago, were legal questions, were questions of method, not questions of what you were going to do with your Government, but questions of how you were going to constitute your Government, —how you were going to balance the powers of the States and the Federal Government, how you were going to balance the claims of property against the processes of liberty, how you were going to make your governments up so as to balance the parts against each other so that the legislature would check the executive, and the executive the legislature, and the courts both of them put together. The whole conception of government when the United States became a Nation was a mechanical conception of government, and the mechanical conception of government which underlay it was the Newtonian theory of the universe. If you pick up the Federalist, some parts of it read like a treatise on astronomy instead of a treatise on government. They speak of the centrifugal and the centripetal forces, and locate the President somewhere in a rotating system. The whole thing is a calculation of power and an adjustment of parts. There was a time when nobody but a lawyer could know enough to run the Government of the United States, and a distinguished English publicist once remarked, speaking of the complexity of the American Government, that it was no proof of the excellence of the American Constitution that it had been successfully operated, because the Americans could run any constitution. But there have been a great many technical difficulties in running it.

And then something happened. A great question arose in this country which, though complicated with legal elements, was at bottom a human question, and nothing but a question of humanity. That was the slavery question. And is it not significant that it was then, and then for the first time, that women became prominent in politics in America? Not many women; those prominent in that day were so few that you can name them over in a brief catalogue, but, nevertheless, they then began to play a part in writing, not only, but in public speech, which was a very novel part for women to play in America. After the Civil War had settled some of what seemed to be the most difficult legal questions of our system, the life of the Nation began not only to unfold, but to accumulate. Life in the United States was a comparatively simple matter at the time of the Civil War. There was none of that underground struggle which is now so manifest to those who look only a little way beneath the surface. Stories such as Dr. Davis has told to-night were uncommon in those simpler days. The pressure of low wages, the agony of obscure and unremunerated toil, did not exist in America in anything like the same proportions that they exist now. And as our life has unfolded and accumulated, as the contacts of it have become hot, as the populations have assembled in the cities, and the cool spaces of the country have been supplanted by the feverish urban areas, the whole nature of our political questions has been altered. They have ceased to be legal questions. They have more and more become social questions, questions with regard to the relations of human beings to one another,—not merely their legal relations, but their moral and spiritual relations to one another. This has been most characteristic of American life in the last few decades, and as these questions have assumed greater and greater prominence, the movement which this association represents has gathered cumulative force. So that, if anybody asks himself, "What does this gathering force mean," if he knows anything about the history of the country, he knows that it means something that has not only come to stay, but has come with conquering power.

I get a little impatient sometimes about the discussion of the channels and methods by which it is to prevail. It is going to prevail, and that is a very superficial and ignorant view of it which attributes it to mere social unrest. It is not merely because the women are discontented. It is because the women have seen visions of duty, and that is something which we not only cannot resist, but, if we be true Americans, we do not wish to resist. America took its origin in visions of the human spirit, in aspirations for the deepest sort of liberty of the mind and of the heart, and as visions of that sort come up to the sight of those who are spiritually minded in America, America comes more and more into her birthright and into the perfection of her development.

So that what we have to realize in dealing with forces of this sort is that we are dealing with the substance of life itself. I have felt as I sat here to-night the wholesome contagion of the occasion. Almost every other time that I ever visited Atlantic City, I came to fight somebody. I hardly know how to conduct myself when I have not come to fight against anybody, but with somebody. I have come to suggest, among other things, that when the forces of nature are steadily working and the tide is rising to meet the moon, you need not be afraid that it will not come to its flood. We feel the tide; we rejoice in the strength of it; and we shall not quarrel in the long run as to the method of it. Because, when you are working with masses of men and organized bodies of opinion, you have got to carry the organized body along. The whole art and practice of government consists not in moving individuals, but in moving masses. It is all very well to run ahead and beckon, but, after all, you have got to wait for the body to follow. I have not come to ask you to be patient, because you have been, but I have come to congratulate you that there was a force behind you that will beyond any peradventure be triumphant, and for which you can afford a little while to wait.

The Terms of Peace

[Address to the Senate of the United States, delivered January 22, 1917.]

Gentlemen of the Senate:

On the eighteenth of December last I addressed an identic note to the governments of the nations now at war requesting them to state, more definitely than they had yet been stated by either group of belligerents, the terms upon which they would deem it possible to make peace. I spoke on behalf of humanity and of the rights of all neutral nations like our own, many of whose most vital interests the war puts in constant jeopardy. The Central Powers united in a reply which stated merely that they were ready to meet their antagonists in conference to discuss terms of peace. The Entente Powers have replied much more definitely and have stated, in general terms, indeed, but with sufficient definiteness to imply details, the arrangements, guarantees, and acts of reparation which they deem to be the indispensable conditions of a satisfactory settlement. We are that much nearer a definite discussion of the peace which shall end the present war. We are that much nearer the discussion of the international concert which must thereafter hold the world at peace. In every discussion of the peace that must end this war it is taken for granted that that peace must be followed by some definite concert of power which will make it virtually impossible that any such catastrophe should ever overwhelm us again. Every lover of mankind, every sane and thoughtful man must take that for granted.

I have sought this opportunity to address you because I thought that I owed it to you, as the council associated with me in the final determination of our international obligations, to disclose to you without reserve the thought and purpose that have been taking form in my mind in regard to the duty of our Government in the days to come when it will be necessary to lay afresh and upon a new plan the foundations of peace among the nations.

It is inconceivable that the people of the United States should play no part in that great enterprise. To take part in such a service will be the opportunity for which they have sought to prepare themselves by the very principles and purposes of their polity and the approved practices of their Government ever since the days when they set up a new nation in the high and honorable hope that it might in all that it was and did show mankind the way to liberty. They cannot in honor withhold the service to which they are now about to be challenged. They do not wish to withhold it. But they owe it to themselves and to the other nations of the world to state the conditions under which they will feel free to render it.

That service is nothing less than this, to add their authority and their power to the authority and force of other nations to guarantee peace and justice throughout the world. Such a settlement cannot now be long postponed. It is right that before it comes this Government should frankly formulate the conditions upon which it would feel justified in asking our people to approve its formal and solemn adherence to a League for Peace. I am here to attempt to state those conditions.

The present war must first be ended; but we owe it to candor and to a just regard for the opinion of mankind to say that, so far as our participation in guarantees of future peace is concerned, it makes a great deal of difference in what way and upon what terms it is ended. The treaties and agreements which bring it to an end must embody terms which will create a peace that is worth guaranteeing and preserving, a peace that will win the approval of mankind, not merely a peace that will serve the several interests and immediate aims of the nations engaged. We shall have no voice in determining what those terms shall be, but we shall, I feel sure, have a voice in determining whether they shall be made lasting or not by the guarantees of a universal covenant; and our judgment upon what is fundamental and essential as a condition precedent to permanency should be spoken now, not afterwards when it may be too late.

No covenant of coöperative peace that does not include the peoples of the New World can suffice to keep the future safe against war; and yet there is only one sort of peace that the peoples of America could join in guaranteeing. The elements of that peace must be elements that engage the confidence and satisfy the principles of the American governments, elements consistent with their political faith and with the practical convictions which the peoples of America have once for all embraced and undertaken to defend.

I do not mean to say that any American government would throw any obstacle in the way of any terms of peace the governments now at war might agree upon, or seek to upset them when made, whatever they might be. I only take it for granted that mere terms of peace between the belligerents will not satisfy even the belligerents themselves. Mere agreements may not make peace secure. It will be absolutely necessary that a force be created as a guarantor of the permanency of the settlement so much greater than the force of any nation now engaged or any alliance hitherto formed or projected that no nation, no probable combination of nations could face or withstand it. If the peace presently to be made is to endure, it must be a peace made secure by the organized major force of mankind.

The terms of the immediate peace agreed upon will determine whether it is a peace for which such a guarantee can be secured. The question upon which the whole future peace and policy of the world depends is this: Is the present war a struggle for a just and secure peace, or only for a new balance of power? If it be only a struggle for a new balance of power, who will guarantee, who can guarantee, the stable equilibrium of the new arrangement? Only a tranquil Europe can be a stable Europe. There must be, not a balance of power, but a community of power; not organized rivalries, but an organized common peace.

Fortunately we have received very explicit assurances on this point. The statesmen of both of the groups of nations now arrayed against one another have said, in terms that could not be misinterpreted, that it was no part of the purpose they had in mind to crush their antagonists. But the implications of these assurances may not be equally clear to all, —may not be the same on both sides of the water. I think it will be serviceable if I attempt to set forth what we understand them to be.

They imply, first of all, that it must be a peace without victory. It is not pleasant to say this. I beg that I may be permitted to put my own interpretation upon it and that it may be understood that no other interpretation was in my thought. I am seeking only to face realities and to face them without soft concealments. Victory would mean peace forced upon the loser, a victor's terms imposed upon the vanquished. It would be accepted in humiliation, under duress, at an intolerable sacrifice, and would leave a sting, a resentment, a bitter memory upon which terms of peace would rest, not permanently, but only as upon quicksand. Only a peace between equals can last. Only a peace the very principle of which is equality and a common participation in a common benefit. The right state of mind, the right feeling between nations, is as necessary for a lasting peace as is the just settlement of vexed questions of territory or of racial and national allegiance.

The equality of nations upon which peace must be founded if it is to last must be an equality of rights; the guarantees exchanged must neither recognize nor imply a difference between big nations and small, between those that are powerful and those that are weak. Right must be based upon the common strength, not upon the individual strength, of the nations upon whose concert peace will depend. Equality of territory or of resources there of course cannot be; nor any other sort of equality not gained in the ordinary peaceful and legitimate development of the peoples themselves. But no one asks or expects anything more than an equality of rights. Mankind is looking now for freedom of life, not for equipoises of power.

And there is a deeper thing involved than even equality of right among organized nations. No peace can last, or ought to last, which does not recognize and accept the principle that governments derive all their just powers from the consent of the governed, and that no right anywhere exists to hand peoples about from sovereignty to sovereignty as if they were property.

I take it for granted, for instance, if I may venture upon a single example, that statesmen everywhere are agreed that there should be a united, independent, and autonomous Poland, and that henceforth inviolable security of life, of worship, and of industrial and social development should be guaranteed to all peoples who have lived hitherto under the power of governments devoted to a faith and purpose hostile to their own.

I speak of this, not because of any desire to exalt an abstract political principle which has always been held very dear by those who have sought to build up liberty in America, but for the same reason that I have spoken of the other conditions of peace which seem to me clearly indispensable, —because I wish frankly to uncover realities. Any peace which does not recognize and accept this principle will inevitably be upset. It will not rest upon the affections or the convictions of mankind. The ferment of spirit of whole populations will fight subtly and constantly against it, and all the world will sympathize. The world can be at peace only if its life is stable, and there can be no stability where the will is in rebellion, where there is not tranquillity of spirit and a sense of justice, of freedom, and of right.

So far as practicable, moreover, every great people now struggling towards a full development of its resources and of its powers should be assured a direct outlet to the great highways of the sea. Where this cannot be done by the cession of territory, it can no doubt be done by the neutralization of direct rights of way under the general guarantee which will assure the peace itself. With a right comity of arrangement no nation need be shut away from free access to the open paths of the world's commerce.

And the paths of the sea must alike in law and in fact be free. The freedom of the seas is the *sine qua non* of peace, equality, and coöperation. No doubt a somewhat radical reconsideration of many of the rules of international practice hitherto thought to be established may be necessary in order to make the seas indeed free and common in practically all circumstances for the use of mankind, but the motive for such changes is convincing and compelling. There can be no trust or intimacy between the peoples of the world without them. The free, constant, unthreatened intercourse of nations is an essential part of the process of peace and of development. It need not be difficult either to define or to secure the freedom of the seas if the governments of the world sincerely desire to come to an agreement concerning it.

It is a problem closely connected with the limitation of naval armaments and the coöperation of the navies of the world in keeping the seas at once free and safe. And the question of limiting naval armaments opens the wider and perhaps more difficult question of the limitation of armies and of all programs of military preparation. Difficult and delicate as these questions are, they must be faced with the utmost candor and decided in a spirit of real accommodation if peace is to come with healing in its wings, and come to stay. Peace cannot be had without concession and sacrifice. There can be no sense of safety and equality among the nations if great preponderating armaments are henceforth to continue here and there to be built up and maintained. The statesmen of the world must plan for peace and nations must adjust and accommodate their policy to it as they have planned for war and made ready for pitiless contest and rivalry. The question of armaments, whether on land or sea, is the most immediately and intensely practical question connected with the future fortunes of nations and of mankind.

I have spoken upon these great matters without reserve and with the utmost explicitness because it has seemed to me to be necessary if the world's yearning desire for peace was anywhere to find free voice and utterance. Perhaps I am the only person in high authority amongst all the peoples of the world who is at liberty to speak and hold nothing back. I am speaking as an individual, and yet I am speaking also, of course, as the responsible head of a great government, and I feel confident that I have said what the people of the United States would wish me to say. May I not add that I hope and believe that I am in effect speaking for liberals and friends of humanity in every nation and of every program of liberty? I would fain believe that I am speaking for the silent mass of mankind everywhere who have as yet had no place or opportunity to speak their real hearts out concerning the death and ruin they see to have come already upon the persons and the homes they hold most dear.

And in holding out the expectation that the people and Government of the United States will join the other civilized nations of the world in guaranteeing the permanence of peace upon such terms as I have named I speak with the greater boldness and confidence because it is clear to every man who can think that there is in this promise no breach in either our traditions or our policy as a nation, but a fulfilment, rather, of all that we have professed or striven for.

I am proposing, as it were, that the nations should with one accord adopt the doctrine of President Monroe as the doctrine of the world: that no nation should seek to extend its polity over any other nation or people, but that every people should be left free to determine its own polity, its own way of development, unhindered, unthreatened, unafraid, the little along with the great and powerful.

I am proposing that all nations henceforth avoid entangling alliances which would draw them into competitions of power, catch them in a net of intrigue and selfish rivalry, and disturb their own affairs with influences intruded from without. There is no entangling alliance in a concert of power. When all unite to act in the same sense and with the same purpose all act in the common interest and are free to live their own lives under a common protection.

I am proposing government by the consent of the governed; that freedom of the seas which in international conference after conference representatives of the United States have urged with the eloquence of those who are the convinced disciples of liberty; and that moderation of armaments which makes of armies and navies a power for order merely, not an instrument of aggression or of selfish violence.

These are American principles, American policies. We could stand for no others. And they are also the principles and policies of forward looking men and women everywhere, of every modern nation, of every enlightened community. They are the principles of mankind and must prevail.

Meeting Germany's Challenge

[Address delivered at a joint session of the two Houses of Congress, February 3, 1917.]

Gentlemen of the Congress:

The Imperial German Government on the thirty-first of January announced to this Government and to the governments of the other neutral nations that on and after the first day of February, the present month, it would adopt a policy with regard to the use of submarines against all shipping seeking to pass through certain designated areas of the high seas to which it is clearly my duty to call your attention.

Let me remind the Congress that on the eighteenth of April last, in view of the sinking on the twenty-fourth of March of the cross-Channel passenger steamer *Sussex* by a German submarine, without summons or warning, and the consequent loss of the lives of several citizens of the United States who were passengers aboard her, this Government addressed a note to the Imperial German Government in which it made the following declaration:

"If it is still the purpose of the Imperial Government to prosecute relentless and indiscriminate warfare against vessels of commerce by the use of submarines without regard to what the Government of the United States must consider the sacred and indisputable rules of international law and the universally recognized dictates of humanity, the Government of the United States is at last forced to the conclusion that there is but one course it can pursue. Unless the Imperial Government should now immediately declare and effect an abandonment of its present methods of submarine warfare against passenger and freight-carrying vessels, the Government of the United States can have no choice but to sever diplomatic relations with the German Empire altogether."

In reply to this declaration the Imperial German Government gave this Government the following assurance:

"The German Government is prepared to do its utmost to confine the operations of war for the rest of its duration to the fighting forces of the belligerents, thereby also insuring the freedom of the seas, a principle upon which the German Government believes, now as before, to be in agreement with the Government of the United States.

"The German Government, guided by this idea, notifies the Government of the United States that the German naval forces have received the following orders: In accordance with the general principles of visit and search and destruction of merchant vessels recognized by international law, such vessels, both within and without the area declared as naval war zone, shall not be sunk without warning and without saving human lives, unless these ships attempt to escape or offer resistance.

"But," it added, "neutrals cannot expect that Germany, forced to fight for her existence, shall, for the sake of neutral interest, restrict the use of an effective weapon if her enemy is permitted to continue to apply at will methods of warfare violating the rules of international law. Such a demand would be incompatible with the character of neutrality, and the German Government is convinced that the Government of the United States does not think of making such a demand, knowing that the Government of the United States has repeatedly declared that it is determined to restore the principle of the freedom of the seas, from whatever quarter it has been violated."

To this the Government of the United States replied on the eighth of May, accepting, of course, the assurances given, but adding,

"The Government of the United States feels it necessary to state that it takes it for granted that the Imperial German Government does not intend to imply that the maintenance of its newly announced policy is in any way contingent upon the course or result of diplomatic negotiations between the Government of the United States and any other belligerent Government, notwithstanding the fact that certain passages in the Imperial Government's note of the fourth instant might appear to be susceptible of that construction. In order, however, to avoid any possible misunderstanding, the Government of the United States notifies the Imperial Government that it cannot for a moment entertain, much less discuss, a suggestion that respect by German naval authorities for the rights of citizens of the United States upon the high seas should in any way or in the slightest degree be made contingent upon the conduct of any other Government affecting the rights of neutrals and non-combatants. Responsibility in such matters is single, not joint; absolute, not relative."

To this note of the eighth of May the Imperial German Government made no reply.

On the thirty-first of January, the Wednesday of the present week, the German Ambassador handed to the Secretary of State, along with a formal note, a memorandum which contains the following statement:

"The Imperial Government, therefore, does not doubt that the Government of the United States will understand the situation thus forced upon Germany by the Entente-Allies' brutal methods of war and by their determination to destroy the Central Powers, and that the Government of the United States will further realize that the now openly disclosed intentions of the Entente-Allies give back to Germany the freedom of action which she reserved in her note addressed to the Government of the United States on May 4, 1916.

"Under these circumstances Germany will meet the illegal measures of her enemies by forcibly preventing after February 1, 1917, in a zone around Great Britain, France, Italy, and in the Eastern Mediterranean all navigation, that of neutrals included, from and to England and from and to France, etc., etc. All ships met within the zone will be sunk."

I think that you will agree with me that, in view of this declaration, which suddenly and without prior intimation of any kind deliberately withdraws the solemn assurance given in the Imperial Government's note of the fourth of May, 1916, this Government has no alternative consistent with the dignity and honor of the United States but to take the course which, in its note of the eighteenth of April, 1916, it announced that it would take in the event that the German Government did not declare and effect an abandonment of the methods of submarine warfare which it was then employing and to which it now purposes again to resort.

I have, therefore, directed the Secretary of State to announce to His Excellency the German Ambassador that all diplomatic relations between the United States and the German Empire are severed, and that the American Ambassador at Berlin will immediately be withdrawn; and, in accordance with this decision, to hand to His Excellency his passports.

Notwithstanding this unexpected action of the German Government, this sudden and deeply deplorable renunciation of its assurances, given this Government at one of the most critical moments of tension in the relations of the two governments, I refuse to believe that it is the intention of the German authorities to do in fact what they have warned us they will feel at liberty to do. I cannot bring myself to believe that they will indeed pay no regard to the ancient friendship between their people and our own or to the solemn obligations which have been exchanged between them and destroy American ships and take the lives of American citizens in the willful prosecution of the ruthless naval program they have announced their intention to adopt. Only actual overt acts on their part can make me believe it even now.

If this inveterate confidence on my part in the sobriety and prudent foresight of their purpose should unhappily prove unfounded; if American ships and American lives should in fact be sacrificed by their naval commanders in heedless contravention of the just and reasonable understandings of international law and the obvious dictates of humanity, I shall take the liberty of coming again before the Congress, to ask that authority be given me to use any means that may be necessary for the protection of our seamen and our people in the prosecution of their peaceful and legitimate errands on the high seas. I can do nothing less. I take it for granted that all neutral governments will take the same course.

We do not desire any hostile conflict with the Imperial German Government. We are the sincere friends of the German people and earnestly desire to remain at peace with the Government which speaks for them. We shall not believe that they are hostile to us unless and until we are obliged to believe it; and we purpose nothing more than the reasonable defense of the undoubted rights of our people. We wish to serve no selfish ends. We seek merely to stand true alike in thought and in action to the immemorial principles of our people which I sought to express in my address to the Senate only two weeks ago, —seek merely to vindicate our right to liberty and justice and an unmolested life. These are the bases of peace, not war. God grant we may not be challenged to defend them by acts of wilful injustice on the part of the Government of Germany!

Request for Authority

[Address delivered at a joint session of the two Houses of Congress, February 26, 1917.]

Gentlemen of the Congress:

I have again asked the privilege of addressing you because we are moving through critical times during which it seems to me to be my duty to keep in close touch with the Houses of Congress, so that neither counsel nor action shall run at cross purposes between us.

On the third of February I officially informed you of the sudden and unexpected action of the Imperial German Government in declaring its intention to disregard the promises it had made to this Government in April last and undertake immediate submarine operations against all commerce, whether of belligerents or of neutrals, that should seek to approach Great Britain and Ireland, the Atlantic coasts of Europe, or the harbors of the eastern Mediterranean, and to conduct those operations without regard to the established restrictions of international practice, without regard to any considerations of humanity even which might interfere with their object. That policy was forthwith put into practice. It has now been in active execution for nearly four weeks.

Its practical results are not yet fully disclosed. The commerce of other neutral nations is suffering severely, but not, perhaps, very much more severely than it was already suffering before the first of February, when the new policy of the Imperial Government was put into operation. We have asked the coöperation of the other neutral governments to prevent these depredations, but so far none of them has thought it wise to join us in any common course of action. Our own commerce has suffered, is suffering, rather in apprehension than in fact, rather because so many of our ships are timidly keeping to their home ports than because American ships have been sunk.

Two American vessels have been sunk, the *Housatonic* and the *Lyman M. Law*. The case of the *Housatonic,* which was carrying food-stuffs consigned to a London firm, was essentially like the case of the *Fry*, in which, it will be recalled, the German Government admitted its liability for damages, and the lives of the crew, as in the case of the *Fry*, were safeguarded with reasonable care. The case of the *Law*, which was carrying lemon-box staves to Palermo, disclosed a ruthlessness of method which deserves grave condemnation, but was accompanied by no circumstances which might not have been expected at any time in connection with the use of the submarine against merchantmen as the German Government has used it.

In sum, therefore, the situation we find ourselves in with regard to the actual conduct of the German submarine warfare against commerce and its effects upon our own ships and people is substantially the same that it was when I addressed you on the third of February, except for the tying up of our shipping in our own ports because of the unwillingness of our shipowners to risk their vessels at sea without insurance or adequate protection, and the very serious congestion of our commerce which has resulted, a congestion which is growing rapidly more and more serious every day. This in itself might presently accomplish, in effect, what the new German submarine orders were meant to accomplish, so far as we are concerned. We can only say, therefore, that the overt act which I have ventured to hope the German commanders would in fact avoid has not occurred.

But, while this is happily true, it must be admitted that there have been certain additional indications and expressions of purpose on the part of the German press and the German authorities which have increased rather than lessened the impression that, if our ships and our people are spared, it will be because of fortunate circumstances or because the commanders of the German submarines which they may happen to encounter exercise an unexpected discretion and restraint rather than because of the instructions under which those commanders are acting.

It would be foolish to deny that the situation is fraught with the gravest possibilities and dangers. No thoughtful man can fail to see that the necessity for definite action may come at any time, if we are in fact, and not in word merely, to defend our elementary rights as a neutral nation. It would be most imprudent to be unprepared.

I cannot in such circumstances be unmindful of the fact that the expiration of the term of the present Congress is immediately at hand, by constitutional limitation; and that it would in all likelihood require an unusual length of time to assemble and organize the Congress which is to succeed it. I feel that I ought, in view of that fact, to obtain from you full and immediate assurance of the authority which I may need at any moment to exercise. No doubt I already possess that authority without special warrant of law, by the plain implication of my constitutional duties and powers; but I prefer, in the present circumstances, not to act upon general implication. I wish to feel that the authority and the power of the Congress are behind me in whatever it may become necessary for me to do. We are jointly the servants of the people and must act together and in their spirit, so far as we can divine and interpret it.

No one doubts what it is our duty to do. We must defend our commerce and the lives of our people in the midst of the present trying circumstances, with discretion but with clear and steadfast purpose. Only the method and the extent remain to be chosen, upon the occasion, if occasion should indeed arise. Since it has unhappily proved impossible to safeguard our neutral rights by diplomatic means against the unwarranted infringements they are suffering at the hands of Germany, there may be no recourse but to *armed* neutrality, which we shall know how to maintain and for which there is abundant American precedent.

It is devoutly to be hoped that it will not be necessary to put armed force anywhere into action. The American people do not desire it, and our desire is not different from theirs. I am sure that they will understand the spirit in which I am now acting, the purpose I hold nearest my heart and would wish to exhibit in everything I do. I am anxious that the people of the nations at war also should understand and not mistrust us. I hope that I need give no further proofs and assurances than I have already given throughout nearly three years of anxious patience that I am the friend of peace and mean to preserve it for America so long as I am able. I am not now proposing or contemplating war or any steps that need lead to it. I merely request that you will accord me by your own vote and definite bestowal the means and the authority to safeguard in practice the right of a great people who are at peace and who are desirous of exercising none but the rights of peace to follow the pursuits of peace in quietness and good will, —rights recognized time out of mind by all the civilized nations of the world. No course of my choosing or of theirs will lead to war. War can come only by the wilful acts and aggressions of others.

You will understand why I can make no definite proposals or forecasts of action now and must ask for your supporting authority in the most general terms. The form in which action may become necessary cannot yet be foreseen. I believe that the people will be willing to trust me to act with restraint, with prudence, and in the true spirit of amity and good faith that they have themselves displayed throughout these trying months; and it is in that belief that I request that you will authorize me to supply our merchant ships with defensive arms, should that become necessary, and with the means of using them, and to employ any other instrumentalities or methods that may be necessary and adequate to protect our ships and our people in their legitimate and peaceful pursuits on the seas. I request also that you will grant me at the same time, along with the powers I ask, a sufficient credit to enable me to provide adequate means of protection where they are lacking, including adequate insurance against the present war risks.

I have spoken of our commerce and of the legitimate errands of our people on the seas, but you will not be misled as to my main thought, the thought that lies beneath these phrases and gives them dignity and weight. It is not of material interests merely that we are thinking. It is, rather, of fundamental human rights, chief of all the right of life itself. I am thinking, not only of the rights of Americans to go and come about their proper business by way of the sea, but also of something much deeper, much more fundamental than that. I am thinking of those rights of humanity without which there is no civilization. My theme is of those great principles of compassion and of protection which mankind has sought to throw about human lives, the lives of non-combatants, the lives of men who are peacefully at work keeping the industrial processes of the world quick and vital, the lives of women and children and of those who supply the labor which ministers to their sustenance. We are speaking of no selfish material rights but of rights which our hearts support and whose foundation is that righteous passion for justice upon which all law, all structures alike of family, of state, and of mankind must rest, as upon the ultimate base of our existence and our liberty. I cannot imagine any man with American principles at his heart hesitating to defend these things.

The Call to War

[Address delivered at a joint session of the two Houses of Congress, April 2, 1917.]

Gentlemen of the Congress:

I have called the Congress into extraordinary session because there are serious, very serious, choices of policy to be made, and made immediately, which it was neither right nor constitutionally permissible that I should assume the responsibility of making.

On the third of February last I officially laid before you the extraordinary announcement of the Imperial German Government that on and after the first day of February it was its purpose to put aside all restraints of law or of humanity and use its submarines to sink every vessel that sought to approach either the ports of Great Britain and Ireland or the western coasts of Europe or any of the ports controlled by the enemies of Germany within the Mediterranean. That had seemed to be the object of the German submarine warfare earlier in the war, but since April of last year the Imperial Government had somewhat restrained the commanders of its undersea craft in conformity with its promise then given to us that passenger boats should not be sunk and that due warning would be given to all other vessels which its submarines might seek to destroy, when no resistance was offered or escape attempted, and care taken that their crews were given at least a fair chance to save their lives in their open boats. The precautions taken were meager and haphazard enough, as was proved in distressing instance after instance in the progress of the cruel and unmanly business, but a certain degree of restraint was observed. The new policy has swept every restriction aside. Vessels of every kind, whatever their flag, their character, their cargo, their destination, their errand, have been ruthlessly sent to the bottom without warning and without thought of help or mercy for those on board, the vessels of friendly neutrals along with those of belligerents. Even hospital ships and ships carrying relief to the sorely bereaved and stricken people of Belgium, though the latter were provided with safe conduct through the proscribed areas by the German Government itself and were distinguished by unmistakable marks of identity, have been sunk with the same reckless lack of compassion or of principle.

I was for a little while unable to believe that such things would in fact be done by any government that had hitherto subscribed to the humane practices of civilized nations. International law had its origin in the attempt to set up some law which would be respected and observed upon the seas, where no nation had right of dominion and where lay the free highways of the world. By painful stage after stage has that law been built up, with meager enough results, indeed, after all was accomplished that could be accomplished, but always with a clear view, at least, of what the heart and conscience of mankind demanded. This minimum of right the German Government has swept aside under the plea of retaliation and necessity and because it had no weapons which it could use at sea except these which it is impossible to employ as it is employing them without throwing to the winds all scruples of humanity or of respect for the understandings that were supposed to underlie the intercourse of the world. I am not now thinking of the loss of property involved, immense and serious as that is, but only of the wanton and wholesale destruction of the lives of non-combatants, men, women, and children, engaged in pursuits which have always, even in the darkest periods of modern history, been deemed innocent and legitimate. Property can be paid for; the lives of peaceful and innocent people cannot be. The present German submarine warfare against commerce is a warfare against mankind.

It is a war against all nations. American ships have been sunk, American lives taken, in ways which it has stirred us very deeply to learn of, but the ships and people of other neutral and friendly nations have been sunk and overwhelmed in the waters in the same way. There has been no discrimination. The challenge is to all mankind. Each nation must decide for itself how it will meet it. The choice we make for ourselves must be made with a moderation of counsel and a temperateness of judgment befitting our character and our motives as a nation. We must put excited feeling away. Our motive will not be revenge or the victorious assertion of the physical might of the nation, but only the vindication of right, of human right, of which we are only a single champion.

When I addressed the Congress on the twenty-sixth of February last I thought that it would suffice to assert our neutral rights with arms, our right to use the seas against unlawful interference, our right to keep our people safe against unlawful violence. But armed neutrality, it now appears, is impracticable. Because submarines are in effect outlaws when used as the German submarines have been used against merchant shipping, it is impossible to defend ships against their attacks as the law of nations has assumed that merchantmen would defend themselves against privateers or cruisers, visible craft giving chase upon the open sea. It is common prudence in such circumstances, grim, necessity indeed, to endeavor to destroy them before they have shown their own intention. They must be dealt with upon sight, if dealt with at all. The German Government denies the right of neutrals to use arms at all within the areas of the sea which it has proscribed, even in the defense of rights which no modern publicist has ever before questioned their right to defend. The intimation is conveyed that the armed guards which we have placed on our merchant ships will be treated as beyond the pale of law and subject to be dealt with as pirates would be. Armed neutrality is ineffectual enough at best; in such circumstances and in the face of such pretensions it is worse than ineffectual: it is likely only to produce what it was meant to prevent; it is practically certain to draw us into the war without either the rights or the effectiveness of belligerents. There is one choice we cannot make, we are incapable of making: we will not choose the path of submission and suffer the most sacred rights of our nation and our people to be ignored or violated. The wrongs against which we now array ourselves are no common wrongs; they cut to the very roots of human life.

With a profound sense of the solemn and even tragic character of the step I am taking and of the grave responsibilities which it involves, but in unhesitating obedience to what I deem my constitutional duty, I advise that the Congress declare the recent course of the Imperial German Government to be in fact nothing less than war against the government and people of the United States; that it formally accept the status of belligerent which has thus been thrust upon it; and that it take immediate steps not only to put the country in a more thorough state of defense but also to exert all its power and employ all its resources to bring the Government of the German Empire to terms and end the war.

What this will involve is clear. It will involve the utmost practicable coöperation in counsel and action with the governments now at war with Germany, and, as incident to that, the extension to those governments of the most liberal financial credits, in order that our resources may so far as possible be added to theirs. It will involve the organization and mobilization of all the material resources of the country to supply the materials of war and serve the incidental needs of the nation in the most abundant and yet the most economical and efficient way possible. It will involve the immediate full equipment of the navy in all respects but particularly in supplying it with the best means of dealing with the enemy's submarines. It will involve the immediate addition to the armed forces of the United States already provided for by law in case of war at least 500,000 men, who should, in my opinion, be chosen upon the principle of universal liability to service, and also the authorization of subsequent additional increments of equal force so soon as they may be needed and can be handled in training. It will involve also, of course, the granting of adequate credits to the Government, sustained, I hope, so far as they can equitably be sustained by the present generation, by well conceived taxation.

I say sustained so far as may be equitable by taxation because it seems to me that it would be most unwise to base the credits which will now be necessary entirely on money borrowed. It is our duty, I most respectfully urge, to protect our people so far as we may against the very serious hardships and evils which would be likely to arise out of the inflation which would be produced by vast loans.

In carrying out the measures by which these things are to be accomplished we should keep constantly in mind the wisdom of interfering as little as possible in our own preparation and in the equipment of our own military forces with the duty,—for it will be a very practical duty,—of supplying the nations already at war with Germany with the materials which they can obtain only from us or by our assistance. They are in the field and we should help them in every way to be effective there.

I shall take the liberty of suggesting, through the several executive departments of the Government, for the consideration of your committees, measures for the accomplishment of the several objects I have mentioned. I hope that it will be your pleasure to deal with them as having been framed after very careful thought by the branch of the Government upon which the responsibility of conducting the war and safeguarding the nation will most directly fall.

While we do these things, these deeply momentous things, let us be very clear, and make very clear to all the world what our motives and our objects are. My own thought has not been driven from its habitual and normal course by the unhappy events of the last two months, and I do not believe that the thought of the nation has been altered or clouded by them. I have exactly the same things in mind now that I had in mind when I addressed the Senate on the twenty-second of January last; the same that I had in mind when I addressed the Congress on the third of February and on the twenty-sixth of February. Our object now, as then, is to vindicate the principles of peace and justice in the life of the world as against selfish, and autocratic power and to set up amongst the really free and self-governed peoples of the world such a concert of purpose and of action as will henceforth ensure the observance of those principles. Neutrality is no longer feasible or desirable where the peace of the world is involved and the freedom of its peoples, and the menace to that peace and freedom lies in the existence of autocratic governments backed by organized force which is controlled wholly by their will, not by the will of their people. We have seen the last of neutrality in such circumstances. We are at the beginning of an age in which it will be insisted that the same standards of conduct and of responsibility for wrong done shall be observed among nations and their governments that are observed among the individual citizens of civilized states.

We have no quarrel with the German people. We have no feeling towards them but one of sympathy and friendship. It was not upon their impulse that their government acted in entering this war. It was not with their previous knowledge or approval. It was a war determined upon as wars used to be determined upon in the old, unhappy days when peoples were nowhere consulted by their rulers and wars were provoked and waged in the interest of dynasties or of little groups of ambitious men who were accustomed to use their fellow-men as pawns and tools. Self-governed nations do not fill their neighbor states with spies or set the course of intrigue to bring about some critical posture of affairs which will give them an opportunity to strike and make conquest. Such designs can be successfully worked out only under cover and where no one has the right to ask questions. Cunningly contrived plans of deception or aggression, carried, it may be, from generation to generation, can be worked out and kept from the light only within the privacy of courts or behind the carefully guarded confidences of a narrow and privileged class. They are happily impossible where public opinion commands and insists upon full information concerning all the nation's affairs.

A steadfast concert for peace can never be maintained except by a partnership of democratic nations. No autocratic government could be trusted to keep faith within it or observe its covenants. It must be a league of honor, a partnership of opinion. Intrigue would eat its vitals away; the plottings of inner circles who could plan what they would and render account to no one would be a corruption seated at its very heart. Only free peoples can hold their purpose and their honor steady to a common end and prefer the interests of mankind to any narrow interest of their own.

Does not every American feel that assurance has been added to our hope for the future peace of the world by the wonderful and heartening things that have been happening within the last few weeks in Russia? Russia was known by those who knew it best to have been always in fact democratic at heart, in all the vital habits of her thought, in all the intimate relationships of her people that spoke their natural instinct, their habitual attitude towards life. The autocracy that crowned the summit of her political structure, long as it had stood and terrible as was the reality of its power, was not in fact Russian in origin, character, or purpose; and now it has been shaken off and the great, generous Russian people have been added in all their naïve majesty and might to the forces that are fighting for freedom in the world, for justice, and for peace. Here is a fit partner for a League of Honor.

One of the things that has served to convince us that the Prussian autocracy was not and could never be our friend is that from the very outset of the present war it has filled our unsuspecting communities and even our offices of government with spies and set criminal intrigues everywhere afoot against our national unity of counsel, our peace within and without, our industries and our commerce. Indeed it is now evident that its spies were here even before the war began; and it is unhappily not a matter of conjecture but a fact proved in our courts of justice that the intrigues which have more than once come perilously near to disturbing the peace and dislocating the industries of the country have been carried on at the instigation, with the support, and even under the personal direction of official agents of the Imperial Government accredited to the Government of the United States. Even in checking these things and trying to extirpate them we have sought to put the most generous interpretation possible upon them because we knew that their source lay, not in any hostile feeling or purpose of the German people towards us (who were, no doubt as ignorant of them as we ourselves were), but only in the selfish designs of a Government that did what it pleased and told its people nothing. But they have played their part in serving to convince us at last that that Government entertains no real friendship for us and means to act against our peace and security at its convenience. That it means to stir up enemies against us at our very doors the intercepted note to the German Minister at Mexico City is eloquent evidence.

We are accepting this challenge of hostile purpose because we know that in such a government, following such methods, we can never have a friend; and that in the presence of its organized power, always lying in wait to accomplish we know not what purpose, there can be no assured security for the democratic governments of the world. We are now about to accept gauge of battle with this natural foe to liberty and shall, if necessary, spend the whole force of the nation to check and nullify its pretensions and its power. We are glad, now that we see the facts with no veil of false pretense about them, to fight thus for the ultimate peace of the world and for the liberation of its peoples, the German peoples included: for the rights of nations great and small and the privilege of men everywhere to choose their way of life and of obedience. The world must be made safe for democracy. Its peace must be planted upon the tested foundations of political liberty. We have no selfish ends to serve. We desire no conquest, no dominion. We seek no indemnities for ourselves, no material compensation for the sacrifices we shall freely make. We are but one of the champions of the rights of mankind. We shall be satisfied when those rights have been made as secure as the faith and the freedom of nations can make them.

Just because we fight without rancor and without selfish object, seeking nothing for ourselves but what we shall wish to share with all free peoples, we shall, I feel confident, conduct our operations as belligerents without passion and ourselves observe with proud punctilio the principles of right and of fair play we profess to be fighting for.

I have said nothing of the governments allied with the Imperial Government of Germany because they have not made war upon us or challenged us to defend our right and our honor. The Austro-Hungarian Government has, indeed, avowed its unqualified endorsement and acceptance of the reckless and lawless submarine warfare adopted now without disguise by the Imperial German Government, and it has therefore not been possible for this Government to receive Count Tarnowski, the Ambassador recently accredited to this Government by the Imperial and Royal Government of Austria-Hungary; but that Government has not actually engaged in warfare against citizens of the United States on the seas, and I take the liberty, for the present at least, of postponing a discussion of our relations with the authorities at Vienna. We enter this war only where we are clearly forced into it because there are no other means of defending our rights.

It will be all the easier for us to conduct ourselves as belligerents in a high spirit of right and fairness because we act without animus, not in enmity towards a people or with the desire to bring any injury or disadvantage upon them, but only in armed opposition to an irresponsible government which has thrown aside all considerations of humanity and of right and is running amuck. We are, let me say again, the sincere friends of the German people, and shall desire nothing so much as the early reëstablishment of intimate relations of mutual advantage between us, —however hard it may be for them, for the time being, to believe that this is spoken from our hearts. We have borne with their present government through all these bitter months because of that friendship, —exercising a patience and forbearance which would otherwise have been impossible. We shall, happily, still have an opportunity to prove that friendship in our daily attitude and actions towards the millions of men and women of German birth and native sympathy who live amongst us and share our life, and we shall be proud to prove it towards all who are in fact loyal to their neighbors and to the Government in the hour of test. They are, most of them, as true and loyal Americans as if they had never known any other fealty or allegiance. They will be prompt to stand with us in rebuking and restraining the few who may be of a different mind and purpose. If there should be disloyalty, it will be dealt with with a firm hand of stern repression; but, if it lifts its head at all, it will lift it only here and there and without countenance except from a lawless and malignant few.

It is a distressing and oppressive duty, Gentlemen of the Congress, which I have performed in thus addressing you. There are, it may be, many months of fiery trial and sacrifice ahead of us. It is a fearful thing to lead this great peaceful people into war, into the most terrible and disastrous of all wars, civilization itself seeming to be in the balance. But the right is more precious than peace, and we shall fight for the things which we have always carried nearest our hearts, —for democracy, for the right of those who submit to authority to have a voice in their own governments, for the rights and liberties of small nations, for a universal dominion of right by such a concert of free peoples as shall bring peace and safety to all nations and make the world itself at last free. To such a task we can dedicate our lives and our fortunes, everything that we are and everything that we have, with the pride of those who know that the day has come when America is privileged to spend her blood and her might for the principles that gave her birth and happiness and the peace which she has treasured. God helping her, she can do no other.

To the Country

[President Wilson's Address to his Fellow-Countrymen, April 16, 1917.]

My Fellow-Countrymen:
The entrance of our own beloved country into the grim and terrible war for democracy and human rights which has shaken the world creates so many problems of national life and action which call for immediate consideration and settlement that I hope you will permit me to address to you a few words of earnest counsel and appeal with regard to them.

We are rapidly putting our navy upon an effective war footing and are about to create and equip a great army, but these are the simplest parts of the great task to which we have addressed ourselves. There is not a single selfish element, so far as I can see, in the cause we are fighting for. We are fighting for what we believe and wish to be the rights of mankind and for the future peace and security of the world. To do this great thing worthily and successfully we must devote ourselves to the service without regard to profit or material advantage and with an energy and intelligence that will rise to the level of the enterprise itself. We must realize to the full how great the task is and how many things, how many kinds and elements of capacity and service and self-sacrifice, it involves.

These, then, are the things we must do, and do well, besides fighting,—the things without which mere fighting would be fruitless:

We must supply abundant food for ourselves and for our armies and our seamen not only, but also for a large part of the nations with whom we have now made common cause, in whose support and by whose sides we shall be fighting.

We must supply ships by the hundreds out of our shipyards to carry to the other side of the sea, submarines or no submarines, what will every day be needed there, and abundant materials out of our fields and our mines and our factories with which not only to clothe and equip our own forces on land and sea but also to clothe and support our people for whom the gallant fellows under arms can no longer work, to help clothe and equip the armies with which we are coöperating in Europe, and to keep the looms and manufactories there in raw material; coal to keep the fires going in ships at sea and in the furnaces of hundreds of factories across the sea; steel out of which to make arms and ammunition both here and there; rails for worn-out railways back of the fighting fronts; locomotives and rolling stock to take the place of those every day going to pieces; mules, horses, cattle for labor and for military service; everything with which the people of England and France and Italy and Russia have usually supplied themselves but cannot now afford the men, the materials, or the machinery to make.

It is evident to every thinking man that our industries, on the farms, in the shipyards, in the mines, in the factories, must be made more prolific and more efficient than ever and that they must be more economically managed and better adapted to the particular requirements of our task than they have been; and what I want to say is that the men and the women who devote their thought and their energy to these things will be serving the country and conducting the fight for peace and freedom just as truly and just as effectively as the men on the battlefield or in the trenches. The industrial forces of the country, men and women alike, will be a great national, a great international, Service Army,—a notable and honored host engaged in the service of the nation and the world, the efficient friends and saviors of free men everywhere. Thousands, nay, hundreds of thousands, of men otherwise liable to military service will of right and of necessity be excused from that service and assigned to the fundamental, sustaining work of the fields and factories and mines, and they will be as much part of the great patriotic forces of the nation as the men under fire.

I take the liberty, therefore, of addressing this word to the farmers of the country and to all who work on the farms: The supreme need of our own nation and of the nations with which we are coöperating is an abundance of supplies, and especially of food-stuffs. The importance of an adequate food supply, especially for the present year, is superlative. Without abundant food, alike for the armies and the peoples now at war, the whole great enterprise upon which we have embarked will break down and fail. The world's food reserves are low. Not only during the present emergency but for some time after peace shall have come both our own people and a large proportion of the people of Europe must rely upon the harvests in America. Upon the farmers of this country, therefore, in large measure, rests the fate of the war and the fate of the nations. May the nation not count upon them to omit no step that will increase the production of their land or that will bring about the most effectual coöperation in the sale and distribution of their products? The time is short. It is of the most imperative importance that everything possible be done and done immediately to make sure of large harvests. I call upon young men and old alike and upon the able-bodied boys of the land to accept and act upon this duty-to turn in hosts to the farms and make certain that no pains and no labor is lacking in this great matter.

I particularly appeal to the farmers of the South to plant abundant food-stuffs as well as cotton. They can show their patriotism in no better or more convincing way than by resisting the great temptation of the present price of cotton and helping, helping upon a great scale, to feed the nation and the peoples everywhere who are fighting for their liberties and for our own. The variety of their crops will be the visible measure of their comprehension of their national duty.

The Government of the United States and the governments of the several States stand ready to coöperate. They will do everything possible to assist farmers in securing an adequate supply of seed, an adequate force of laborers when they are most needed, at harvest time, and the means of expediting shipments of fertilizers and farm machinery, as well as of the crops themselves when harvested. The course of trade shall be as unhampered as it is possible to make it and there shall be no unwarranted manipulation of the nation's food supply by those who handle it on its way to the consumer. This is our opportunity to demonstrate the efficiency of a great Democracy and we shall not fall short of it!

This let me say to the middlemen of every sort, whether they are handling our food-stuffs or our raw materials of manufacture or the products of our mills and factories: The eyes of the country will be especially upon you. This is your opportunity for signal service, efficient and disinterested. The country expects you, as it expects all others, to forego unusual profits, to organize and expedite shipments of supplies of every kind, but especially of food, with an eye to the service you are rendering and in the spirit of those who enlist in the ranks, for their people, not for themselves. I shall confidently expect you to deserve and win the confidence of people of every sort and station.

To the men who run the railways of the country, whether they be managers or operative employees, let me say that the railways are the arteries of the nation's life and that upon them rests the immense responsibility of seeing to it that those arteries suffer no obstruction of any kind, no inefficiency or slackened power. To the merchant let me suggest the motto, "Small profits and quick service"; and to the shipbuilder the thought that the life of the war depends upon him. The food and the war supplies must be carried across the seas no matter how many ships are sent to the bottom. The places of those that go down must be supplied and supplied at once. To the miner let me say that he stands where the farmer does: the work of the world waits on him. If he slackens or fails, armies and statesmen are helpless. He also is enlisted in the great Service Army. The manufacturer does not need to be told, I hope, that the nation looks to him to speed and perfect every process; and I want only to remind his employees that their service is absolutely indispensable and is counted on by every man who loves the country and its liberties.

Let me suggest, also, that everyone who creates or cultivates a garden helps, and helps greatly, to solve the problem of the feeding of the nations; and that every housewife who practices strict economy puts herself in the ranks of those who serve the nation. This is the time for America to correct her unpardonable fault of wastefulness and extravagance. Let every man and every woman assume the duty of careful, provident use and expenditure as a public duty, as a dictate of patriotism which no one can now expect ever to be excused or forgiven for ignoring.

In the hope that this statement of the needs of the nation and of the world in this hour of supreme crisis may stimulate those to whom it comes and remind all who need reminder of the solemn duties of a time such as the world has never seen before, I beg that all editors and publishers everywhere will give as prominent publication and as wide circulation as possible to this appeal. I venture to suggest, also, to all advertising agencies that they would perhaps render a very substantial and timely service to the country if they would give it widespread repetition. And I hope that clergymen will not think the theme of it an unworthy or inappropriate subject of comment and homily from their pulpits.

The supreme test of the nation has come. We must all speak, act, and serve together!

WOODROW WILSON.

The German Plot

[Speech in Washington Monument Grounds, June 14, 1917.]

We know now clearly, as we knew before we ourselves were engaged in the War, that we are not enemies of the German people, and they are not our enemies. They did not originate, or desire, this hideous war, or wish that we should be drawn into it, and we are vaguely conscious that we are fighting their cause, as they will some day see it themselves, as well as our own. They themselves are in the grip of the same sinister power that has stretched its ugly talons out and drawn blood from us.

The War was begun by the military masters of Germany, who have proved themselves to be also the masters of Austria-Hungary. These men never regarded nations as peoples of men, women, and children of like blood and frame as themselves, for whom Governments existed and in whom Governments had their life. They regarded them merely as serviceable organizations, which they could, either by force or intrigue, bend or corrupt to their own purpose. They regarded the smaller States, particularly, and those peoples, who could be overwhelmed by force, as their natural tools and instruments of domination.

Their purpose had long been avowed. The statesmen of other nations, to whom that purpose was incredible, paid little attention, and regarded what the German professors expounded in their class-rooms and the German writers set forth to the world as the goal of German policy as rather the dream of minds detached from practical affairs and the preposterous private conceptions of Germany's destiny than the actual plans of responsible rulers. But the rulers of Germany knew all the while what concrete plans, what well-advanced intrigue, lay at the back of what professors and writers were saying, and were glad to go forward unmolested, filling the thrones of the Balkan States with German princes, putting German officers at the service of Turkey, developing plans of sedition and rebellion in India and Egypt, and setting their fires in Persia.

The demands made by Austria upon Serbia were a mere single step in the plan which compassed Europe and Asia from Berlin to Bagdad. They hoped that these demands might not arouse Europe, but they meant to press them, whether they did or not. For they thought themselves ready for the final issue of arms. Their plan was to throw a belt of German military power and political control across the very center of Europe and beyond the Mediterranean into the heart of Asia, and Austria-Hungary was to be as much their tool and pawn as Serbia, Bulgaria, Turkey, or the ponderous States of the East. Austria-Hungary, indeed, was to become a part of the Central German Empire, absorbed and dominated by the same forces and influences that originally cemented the German States themselves.

The dream had its heart at Berlin. It could have had its heart nowhere else. It rejected entirely the idea of the solidarity of race. The choice of peoples played no part at all in the contemplated binding together of the racial and political units, which could keep together only by force. And they actually carried the greater part of that amazing plan into execution.

Look how things stand. Austria, at their mercy, has acted, not upon its own initiative or upon the choice of its own people, but at Berlin's dictation ever since the War began. Its people now desire peace, but they cannot have it until leave is granted from Berlin. The so-called Central Powers are, in fact, but a single Power. Serbia is at its mercy should its hand be but for a moment freed; Bulgaria consented to its will; Rumania is overrun by the Turkish armies, which the Germans trained into serving Germany, and the guns of the German warships lying in the harbor at Constantinople remind the Turkish statesmen every day that they have no choice but to take their orders from Berlin.

From Hamburg to the Persian Gulf the net is spread. Is it not easy to understand the eagerness for peace that has been manifested by Berlin ever since the snare was set and sprung?

"Peace, peace, peace" has been the talk of her Foreign Office for a year or more, not peace upon her own initiative, but upon the initiative of the nations over which she now deems herself to hold the advantage. A little of the talk has been public, but most of it has been private, through all sorts of channels. It has come to me in all sorts of guises, but never with the terms disclosed which the German Government would be willing to accept.

That Government has other valuable pawns in its hands besides those I have mentioned. It still holds a valuable part of France, though with a slowly relaxing grasp, and practically the whole of Belgium. Its armies press close on Russia and overrun Poland. It cannot go farther-it dare not go back. It wishes to close its bargain before it is too late and it has little left to offer for the pound of flesh it will demand. The military masters under whom Germany is bleeding see very clearly to what point fate has brought them: if they fall back or are forced back an inch, their power abroad and at home will fall to pieces. It is their power at home of which they are thinking now more than of their power abroad. It is that power which is trembling under their very feet.

Deep fear has entered their hearts. They have but one chance to perpetuate their military power, or even their controlling political influence. If they can secure peace now, with the immense advantage still in their hands, they will have justified themselves before the German people. They will have gained by force what they promised to gain by it-an immense expansion of German power and an immense enlargement of German industrial and commercial opportunities. Their prestige will be secure, and with their prestige their political power.

If they fail, their people will thrust them aside. A Government accountable to the people themselves will be set up in Germany, as has been the case in England, the United States, and France-in all great countries of modern times except Germany. If they succeed they are safe, and Germany and the world are undone. If they fail, Germany is saved and the world will be at peace. If they succeed, America will fall within the menace, and we, and all the rest of the world, must remain armed, as they will remain, and must make ready for the next step in their aggression. If they fail, the world may unite for peace and Germany may be of the union.

Do you not now understand the new intrigue for peace, and why the masters of Germany do not hesitate to use any agency that promises to effect their purpose, the deceit of nations? Their present particular aim is to deceive all those who, throughout the world, stand for the rights of peoples and the self-government of nations, for they see what immense strength the forces of justice and liberalism are gathering out of this war. They are employing Liberals in their enterprises. Let them once succeed, and these men, now their tools, will be ground to powder beneath the weight of the great military Empire; the Revolutionists of Russia will be cut off from all succour and the coöperation of Western Europe, and a counter-revolution will be fostered and supported; Germany herself will lose her chance of freedom, and all Europe will arm for the next final struggle.

The sinister intrigue is being no less actively conducted in this country than in Russia and in every country of Europe into which the agents and dupes of the Imperial German Government can get access. That Government has many spokesmen here, in places both high and low. They have learned discretion; they keep within the law. It is opinion they utter now, not sedition. They proclaim the liberal purposes of their masters, and they declare that this is a foreign war, which can touch America with no danger either to her lands or institutions. They set England at the center of the stage, and talk of her ambition to assert her economic dominion throughout the world. They appeal to our ancient tradition of isolation, and seek to undermine the Government with false professions of loyalty to its principles.

But they will make no headway. Falsehood betrays them in every accent. These facts are patent to all the world, and nowhere more plainly than in the United States, where we are accustomed to deal with facts, not sophistries; and the great fact that stands out above all the rest is that this is a peoples' war for freedom, justice and self-government among all the nations of the world, a war to make the world safe for the peoples who live upon it, the German people included, and that with us rests the choice to break through all these hypocrisies, the patent cheats and masks of brute force, and help set the world free, or else stand aside and let it be dominated through sheer weight of arms and the arbitrary choices of the self-constituted masters by the nation which can maintain the biggest armies, the most irresistible armaments, a power to which the world has afforded no parallel, in the face of which political freedom must wither and perish.

For us there was but one choice. We have made it, and woe be to that man, or that group of men, that seeks to stand in our way in this day of high resolution, when every principle we hold dearest is to be vindicated and made secure for the salvation of the nation. We are ready to plead at the bar of history, and our flag shall wear a new luster. Once more we shall make good with our lives and fortunes the great faith to which we are born, and a new glory shall shine in the face of our people.

Reply to the Pope

[This important and eloquent document, though signed by the Secretary of State, was of course authorized by the President, and indeed bears internal marks of being his own composition. The Pope had made a plea for peace, which was by our government deemed premature.]

AUGUST 27, 1917.

To His Holiness Benedictus XV, Pope:

In acknowledgment of the communication of Your Holiness to the belligerent peoples, dated August 1, 1917, the President of the United States requests me to transmit the following reply:

Every heart that has not been blinded and hardened by this terrible war must be touched by this moving appeal of His Holiness the Pope, must feel the dignity and force of the humane and generous motives which prompted it, and must fervently wish that we might take the path of peace he so persuasively points out. But it would be folly to take it if it does not in fact lead to the goal he proposes. Our response must be based upon the stern facts and upon nothing else. It is not a mere cessation of arms he desires; it is a stable and enduring peace. This agony must not be gone through with again, and it must be a matter of very sober judgment that will insure us against it.

His Holiness in substance proposes that we return to the status quo ante bellum, and that then there be a general condonation, disarmament, and a concert of nations based upon an acceptance of the principle of arbitration; that by a similar concert freedom of the seas be established; and that the territorial claims of France and Italy, the perplexing problems of the Balkan States, and the restitution of Poland be left to such conciliatory adjustments as may be possible in the new temper of such a peace, due regard being paid to the aspirations of the peoples whose political fortunes and affiliations will be involved.

It is manifest that no part of this program can be successfully carried out unless the restitution of the status quo ante furnishes a firm and satisfactory basis for it. The object of this war is to deliver the free peoples of the world from the menace and the actual power of a vast military establishment controlled by an irresponsible government which, having secretly planned to dominate the world, proceeded to carry the plan out without regard either to the sacred obligations of treaty or the long-established practices and long-cherished principles of international action and honor; which chose its own time for the war; delivered its blow fiercely and suddenly; stopped at no barrier either of law or of mercy; swept a whole continent within the tide of blood-not the blood of soldiers only, but the blood of innocent women and children also and of the helpless poor; and now stands balked but not defeated, the enemy of four-fifths of the world. This power is not the German people. It is the ruthless master of the German people. It is no business of ours how that great people came under its control or submitted with temporary zest to the domination of its purpose; but it is our business to see to it that the history of the rest of the world is no longer left to its handling.

To deal with such a power by way of peace upon the plan proposed by His Holiness the Pope would, so far as we can see, involve a recuperation of its strength and a renewal of its policy; would make it necessary to create a permanent hostile combination of nations against the German people who are its instruments; and would result in abandoning the newborn Russia to the intrigue, the manifold subtle interference, and the certain counter-revolution which would be attempted by all the malign influences to which the German Government has of late accustomed the world. Can peace be based upon a restitution of its power or upon any word of honor it could pledge in a treaty of settlement and accommodation?

Responsible statesmen must now everywhere see, if they never saw before, that no peace can rest securely upon political or economic restrictions meant to benefit some nations and cripple or embarrass others, upon vindictive action of any sort, or any kind of revenge or deliberate injury. The American people have suffered intolerable wrongs at the hands of the Imperial German Government, but they desire no reprisal upon the German people who have themselves suffered all things in this war which they did not choose. They believe that peace should rest upon the rights of peoples, not the rights of Governments-the rights of peoples great or small, weak or powerful-their equal right to freedom and security and self-government and to a participation upon fair terms in the economic opportunities of the world, the German people of course included if they will accept equality and not seek domination.

The test, therefore, of every plan of peace is this: Is it based upon the faith of all the peoples involved or merely upon the word of an ambitious and intriguing government on the one hand and of a group of free peoples on the other? This is a test which goes to the root of the matter; and it is the test which must be applied.

The purposes of the United States in this war are known to the whole world, to every people to whom the truth has been permitted to come. They do not need to be stated again. We seek no material advantage of any kind. We believe that the intolerable wrongs done in this war by the furious and brutal power of the Imperial German Government ought to be repaired, but not at the expense of the sovereignty of any people-rather a vindication of the sovereignty both of those that are weak and of those that are strong. Punitive damages, the dismemberment of empires, the establishment of selfish and exclusive economic leagues, we deem inexpedient and in the end worse than futile, no proper basis for a peace of any kind, least of all for an enduring peace. That must be based upon justice and fairness and the common rights of mankind.

We cannot take the word of the present rulers of Germany as a guaranty of anything that is to endure, unless explicitly supported by such conclusive evidence of the will and purpose of the German people themselves as the other peoples of the world would be justified in accepting. Without such guaranties treaties of settlement, agreements for disarmament, covenants to set up arbitration in the place of force, territorial adjustments, reconstitutions of small nations, if made with the German Government, no man, no nation could now depend on. We must await some new evidence of the purposes of the great peoples of the central powers. God grant it may be given soon and in a way to restore the confidence of all peoples everywhere in the faith of nations and the possibility of a covenanted peace.

Robert Lansing,
Secretary of State of the United States of America.

Labor Must be Free

[Address to the American Federation of Labor Convention, Buffalo, New York, November 12, 1917.]

Mr. President, Delegates of the American Federation of Labor, Ladies and Gentlemen:

I esteem it a great privilege and a real honor to be thus admitted to your public counsels. When your executive committee paid me the compliment of inviting me here I gladly accepted the invitation because it seems to me that this, above all other times in our history, is the time for common counsel, for the drawing together not only of the energies but of the minds of the Nation. I thought that it was a welcome opportunity for disclosing to you some of the thoughts that have been gathering in my mind during these last momentous months.

CRITICAL TIME IN HISTORY

I am introduced to you as the President of the United States, and yet I would be pleased if you would put the thought of the office into the background and regard me as one of your fellow-citizens who has come here to speak, not the words of authority, but the words of counsel; the words which men should speak to one another who wish to be frank in a moment more critical perhaps than the history of the world has ever yet known; a moment when it is every man's duty to forget himself, to forget his own interests, to fill himself with the nobility of a great national and world conception, and act upon a new platform elevated above the ordinary affairs of life and lifted to where men have views of the long destiny of mankind.

I think that in order to realize just what this moment of counsel is it is very desirable that we should remind ourselves just how this war came about and just what it is for. You can explain most wars very simply, but the explanation of this is not so simple. Its roots run deep into all the obscure soils of history, and in my view this is the last decisive issue between the old principle of power and the new principle of freedom.

WAR STARTED BY GERMANY

The war was started by Germany. Her authorities deny that they started it, but I am willing to let the statement I have just made await the verdict of history. And the thing that needs to be explained is why Germany started the war. Remember what the position of Germany in the world was-as enviable a position as any nation has ever occupied. The whole world stood at admiration of her wonderful intellectual and material achievements. All the intellectual men of the world went to school to her. As a university man I have been surrounded by men trained in Germany, men who had resorted to Germany because nowhere else could they get such thorough and searching training, particularly in the principles of science and the principles that underlie modern material achievement. Her men of science had made her industries perhaps the most competent industries of the world, and the label "Made in Germany" was a guarantee of good workmanship and of sound material. She had access to all the markets of the world, and every other nation who traded in those markets feared Germany because of her effective and almost irresistible competition. She had a "place in the sun."

GERMANY'S INDUSTRIAL GROWTH

Why was she not satisfied? What more did she want? There was nothing in the world of peace that she did not already have and have in abundance. We boast of the extraordinary pace of American advancement. We show with pride the statistics of the increase of our industries and of the population of our cities. Well, those statistics did not match the recent statistics of Germany. Her old cities took on youth and grew faster than any American cities ever grew. Her old industries opened their eyes and saw a new world and went out for its conquest. And yet the authorities of Germany were not satisfied.

You have one part of the answer to the question why she was not satisfied in her methods of competition. There is no important industry in Germany upon which the Government has not laid its hands, to direct it and, when necessity arose, control it; and you have only to ask any man whom you meet who is familiar with the conditions that prevailed before the war in the matter of national competition to find out the methods of competition which the German manufacturers and exporters used under the patronage and support of the Government of Germany. You will find that they were the same sorts of competition that we have tried to prevent by law within our own borders. If they could not sell their goods cheaper than we could sell ours at a profit to themselves they could get a subsidy from the Government which made it possible to sell them cheaper anyhow, and the conditions of competition were thus controlled in large measure by the German Government itself.

BERLIN-BAGDAD RAILWAY

But that did not satisfy the German Government. All the while there was lying behind its thought and in its dreams of the future a political control which would enable it in the long run to dominate the labor and the industry of the world. They were not content with success by superior achievement; they wanted success by authority. I suppose very few of you have thought much about the Berlin-to-Bagdad Railway. The Berlin-Bagdad Railway was constructed in order to run the threat of force down the flank of the industrial undertakings of half a dozen other countries; so that when German competition came in it would not be resisted too far, because there was always the possibility of getting German armies into the heart of that country quicker than any other armies could be got there.

Look at the map of Europe now! Germany is thrusting upon us again and again the discussion of peace talks,—about what? Talks about Belgium; talks about northern France; talks about Alsace-Lorraine. Well, those are deeply interesting subjects to us and to them, but they are not the heart of the matter. Take the map and look at it. Germany has absolute control of Austria-Hungary, practical control of the Balkan States, control of Turkey, control of Asia Minor. I saw a map in which the whole thing was printed in appropriate black the other day, and the black stretched all the way from Hamburg to Bagdad-the bulk of German power inserted into the heart of the world. If she can keep that, she has kept all that her dreams contemplated when the war began. If she can keep that, her power can disturb the world as long as she keeps it, always provided, for I feel bound to put this proviso in-always provided the present influences that control the German Government continue to control it. I believe that the spirit of freedom can get into the hearts of Germans and find as fine a welcome there as it can find in any other hearts, but the spirit of freedom does not suit the plans of the Pan-Germans. Power cannot be used with concentrated force against free peoples if it is used by free people.

PEACE RUMORS

You know how many intimations come to us from one of the central powers that it is more anxious for peace than the chief central power, and you know that it means that the people in that central power know that if the war ends as it stands they will in effect themselves be vassals of Germany, notwithstanding that their populations are compounded of all the peoples of that part of the world, and notwithstanding the fact that they do not wish in their pride and proper spirit of nationality to be so absorbed and dominated. Germany is determined that the political power of the world shall belong to her. There have been such ambitions before. They have been in part realized, but never before have those ambitions been based upon so exact and precise and scientific a plan of domination.

May I not say that it is amazing to me that any group of persons should be so ill-informed as to suppose, as some groups in Russia apparently suppose, that any reforms planned in the interest of the people can live in the presence of a Germany powerful enough to undermine or overthrow them by intrigue or force? Any body of free men that compounds with the present German Government is compounding for its own destruction. But that is not the whole of the story. Any man in America or anywhere else that supposes that the free industry and enterprise of the world can continue if the Pan-German plan is achieved and German power fastened upon the world is as fatuous as the dreamers in Russia. What I am opposed to is not the feeling of the pacifists, but their stupidity. My heart is with them, but my mind has a contempt for them. I want peace, but I know how to get it, and they do not.

COLONEL HOUSE'S MISSION

You will notice that I sent a friend of mine, Colonel House, to Europe, who is as great a lover of peace as any man in the world; but I didn't send him on a peace mission yet. I sent him to take part in a conference as to how the war was to be won, and he knows, as I know, that that is the way to get peace, if you want it for more than a few minutes.

All of this is a preface to the conference that I have referred to with regard to what we are going to do. If we are true friends of freedom, our own or anybody else's, we will see that the power of this country and the productivity of this country is raised to its absolute maximum, and that absolutely nobody is allowed to stand in the way of it. When I say that nobody is allowed to stand in the way I do not mean that they shall be prevented by the power of the Government but by the power of the American spirit. Our duty, if we are to do this great thing and show America to be what we believe her to be-the greatest hope and energy of the world-is to stand together night and day until the job is finished.

LABOR MUST BE FREE

While we are fighting for freedom we must see, among other things, that labor is free; and that means a number of interesting things. It means not only that we must do what we have declared our purpose to do, see that the conditions of labor are not rendered more onerous by the war, but also that we shall see to it that the instrumentalities by which the conditions of labor are improved are not blocked or checked. That we must do. That has been the matter about which I have taken pleasure in conferring from time to time with your president, Mr. Gompers; and if I may be permitted to do so, I want to express my admiration of his patriotic courage, his large vision, and his statesmanlike sense of what has to be done. I like to lay my mind alongside of a mind that knows how to pull in harness. The horses that kick over the traces will have to be put in corral.

Now, to stand together means that nobody must interrupt the processes of our energy if the interruption can possibly be avoided without the absolute invasion of freedom. To put it concretely, that means this: Nobody has a right to stop the processes of labor until all the methods of conciliation and settlement have been exhausted. And I might as well say right here that I am not talking to you alone. You sometimes stop the courses of labor, but there are others who do the same, and I believe I am speaking from my own experience not only, but from the experience of others when I say that you are reasonable in a larger number of cases than the capitalists. I am not saying these things to them personally yet, because I have not had a chance, but they have to be said, not in any spirit of criticism, but in order to clear the atmosphere and come down to business. Everybody on both sides has now got to transact business, and a settlement is never impossible when both sides want to do the square and right thing.

SETTLEMENT HARD TO AVOID

Moreover, a settlement is always hard to avoid when the parties can be brought face to face. I can differ from a man much more radically when he is not in the room than I can when he is in the room, because then the awkward thing is he can come back at me and answer what I say. It is always dangerous for a man to have the floor entirely to himself. Therefore, we must insist in every instance that the parties come into each other's presence and there discuss the issues between them, and not separately in places which have no communication with each other. I always like to remind myself of a delightful saying of an Englishman of the past generation, Charles Lamb. He stuttered a little bit, and once when he was with a group of friends he spoke very harshly of some man who was not present. One of his friends said: "Why, Charles, I didn't know that you knew so and so." "O-o-oh," he said, "I-I d-d-don't; I-I can't h-h-h hate a m-m-man I-I know." There is a great deal of human nature, of very pleasant human nature, in the saying. It is hard to hate a man you know. I may admit, parenthetically, that there are some politicians whose methods I do not at all believe in, but they are jolly good fellows, and if they only would not talk the wrong kind of politics to me, I would love to be with them.

NO SYMPATHY WITH MOB SPIRIT

So it is all along the line, in serious matters and things less serious. We are all of the same clay and spirit, and we can get together if we desire to get together. Therefore, my counsel to you is this: Let us show ourselves Americans by showing that we do not want to go off in separate camps or groups by ourselves, but that we want to coöperate with all other classes and all other groups in the common enterprise which is to release the spirits of the world from bondage. I would be willing to set that up as the final test of an American. That is the meaning of democracy. I have been very much distressed, my fellow-citizens, by some of the things that have happened recently. The mob spirit is displaying itself here and there in this country. I have no sympathy with what some men are saying, but I have no sympathy with the men who take their punishment into their own hands; and I want to say to every man who does join such a mob that I do not recognize him as worthy of the free institutions of the United States. There are some organizations in this country whose object is anarchy and the destruction of law, but I would not meet their efforts by making myself partner in destroying the law. I despise and hate their purposes as much as any man, but I respect the ancient processes of justice; and I would be too proud not to see them done justice, however wrong they are.

MUST OBEY COMMON COUNSEL

So I want to utter my earnest protest against any manifestation of the spirit of lawlessness anywhere or in any cause. Why, gentlemen, look what it means. We claim to be the greatest democratic people in the world, and democracy means first of all that we can govern ourselves. If our men have not self-control, then they are not capable of that great thing which we call democratic government. A man who takes the law into his own hands is not the right man to coöperate in any formation or development of law and institutions, and some of the processes by which the struggle between capital and labor is carried on are processes that come very near to taking the law into your own hands. I do not mean for a moment to compare them with what I have just been speaking of, but I want you to see that they are mere gradations in this manifestation of the unwillingness to coöperate, and that the fundamental lesson of the whole situation is that we must not only take common counsel, but that we must yield to and obey common counsel. Not all of the instrumentalities for this are at hand. I am hopeful that in the very near future new instrumentalities may be organized by which we can see to it that various things that are now going on ought not to go on. There are various processes of the dilution of labor and the unnecessary substitution of labor and the bidding in distant markets and unfairly upsetting the whole competition of labor which ought not to go on. I mean now on the part of employers, and we must interject some instrumentality of coöperation by which the fair thing will be done all around. I am hopeful that some such instrumentalities may be devised, but whether they are or not, we must use those that we have and upon every occasion where it is necessary have such an instrumentality originated upon that occasion.

So, my fellow-citizens, the reason I came away from Washington is that I sometimes get lonely down there. So many people come to Washington who know things that are not so, and so few people who know anything about what the people of the United States are thinking about. I have to come away and get reminded of the rest of the country. I have to come away and talk to men who are up against the real thing, and say to them, "I am with you if you are with me." And the only test of being with me is not to think about me personally at all, but merely to think of me as the expression for the time being of the power and dignity and hope of the United States.

The Call for War with Austria-Hungary

[Address delivered at a joint session of the two Houses of Congress, December 4, 1917.]

Gentlemen of the Congress:

Eight months have elapsed since I last had the honor of addressing you. They have been months crowded with events of immense and grave significance for us. I shall not undertake to retail or even to summarize those events. The practical particulars of the part we have played in them will be laid before you in the reports of the Executive Departments. I shall discuss only our present outlook upon these vast affairs, our present duties, and the immediate means of accomplishing the objects we shall hold always in view.

I shall not go back to debate the causes of the war. The intolerable wrongs done and planned against us by the sinister masters of Germany have long since become too grossly obvious and odious to every true American to need to be rehearsed. But I shall ask you to consider again and with a very grave scrutiny our objectives and the measures by which we mean to attain them; for the purpose of discussion here in this place is action, and our action must move straight towards definite ends. Our object is, of course, to win the war; and we shall not slacken or suffer ourselves to be diverted until it is won. But it is worth while asking and answering the question, When shall we consider the war won?

From one point of view it is not necessary to broach this fundamental matter. I do not doubt that the American people know what the war is about and what sort of an outcome they will regard as a realization of their purpose in it. As a nation we are united in spirit and intention. I pay little heed to those who tell me otherwise. I hear the voices of dissent,—who does not? I hear the criticism and the clamor of the noisily thoughtless and troublesome. I also see men here and there fling themselves in impotent disloyalty against the calm, indomitable power of the nation. I hear men debate peace who understand neither its nature not the way in which we may attain it with uplifted eyes and unbroken spirits. But I know that none of these speaks for the nation. They do not touch the heart of anything. They may safely be left to strut their uneasy hour and be forgotten.

But from another point of view I believe that it is necessary to say plainly what we here at the seat of action consider the war to be for and what part we mean to play in the settlement of its searching issues. We are the spokesmen of the American people and they have a right to know whether their purpose is ours. They desire peace by the overcoming of evil, by the defeat once for all of the sinister forces that interrupt peace and render it impossible, and they wish to know how closely our thought runs with theirs and what action we propose. They are impatient with those who desire peace by any sort of compromise,—deeply and indignantly impatient,—but they will be equally impatient with us if we do not make it plain to them what our objectives are and what we are planning for in seeking to make conquest of peace by arms.

I believe that I speak for them when I say two things: First, that this intolerable Thing of which the masters of Germany have shown us the ugly face, this menace of combined intrigue and force which we now see so clearly as the German power, a Thing without conscience or honor or capacity for covenanted peace, must be crushed and, if it be not utterly brought to an end, at least shut out from the friendly intercourse of the nations; and, second, that when this Thing and its power are indeed defeated and the time comes that we can discuss peace,—when the German people have spokesmen whose word we can believe and when those spokesmen are ready in the name of their people to accept the common judgment of the nations as to what shall henceforth be the bases of law and of covenant for the life of the world,—we shall be willing and glad to pay the full price for peace, and pay it ungrudgingly. We know what that price will be. It will be full, impartial justice,—justice done at every point and to every nation that the final settlement must affect, our enemies as well as our friends.

You catch, with me, the voices of humanity that are in the air. They grow daily more audible, more articulate, more persuasive, and they come from the hearts of men everywhere. They insist that the war shall not end in vindictive action of any kind; that no nation or people shall be robbed or punished because the irresponsible rulers of a single country have themselves done deep and abominable wrong. It is this thought that has been expressed in the formula "No annexations, no contributions, no punitive indemnities." Just because this crude formula expresses the instinctive judgment as to right of plain men everywhere it has been made diligent use of by the masters of German intrigue to lead the people of Russia astray-and the people of every other country their agents could reach, in order that a premature peace might be brought about before autocracy has been taught its final and convincing lesson, and the people of the world put in control of their own destinies.

But the fact that a wrong use has been made of a just idea is no reason why a right use should not be made of it. It ought to be brought under the patronage of its real friends. Let it be said again that autocracy must first be shown the utter futility of its claims to power or leadership in the modern world. It is impossible to apply any standard of justice so long as such forces are unchecked and undefeated as the present masters of Germany command. Not until that has been done can Right be set up as arbiter and peace-maker among the nations. But when that has been done,—as, God willing, it assuredly will be,—we shall at last be free to do an unprecedented thing, and this is the time to avow our purpose to do it. We shall be free to base peace on generosity and justice, to the exclusion of all selfish claims to advantage even on the part of the victors.

Let there be no misunderstanding. Our present and immediate task is to win the war, and nothing shall turn us aside from it until it is accomplished. Every power and resource we possess, whether of men, of money, or of materials, is being devoted and will continue to be devoted to that purpose until it is achieved. Those who desire to bring peace about before that purpose is achieved I counsel to carry their advice elsewhere. We will not entertain it. We shall regard the war as won only when the German people say to us, through properly accredited representatives, that they are ready to agree to a settlement based upon justice and the reparation of the wrongs their rulers have done. They have done a wrong to Belgium which must be repaired. They have established a power over other lands and peoples than their own,—over the great Empire of Austria-Hungary, over hitherto free Balkan states, over Turkey, and within Asia,—which must be relinquished.

Germany's success by skill, by industry, by knowledge, by enterprise we did not grudge or oppose, but admired, rather. She had built up for herself a real empire of trade and influence, secured by the peace of the world. We were content to abide the rivalries of manufacture, science, and commerce that were involved for us in her success and stand or fall as we had or did not have the brains and the initiative to surpass her. But at the moment when she had conspicuously won her triumphs of peace she threw them away, to establish in their stead what the world will no longer permit to be established, military and political domination by arms, by which to oust where she could not excel the rivals she most feared and hated. The peace we make must remedy that wrong. It must deliver the once fair lands and happy peoples of Belgium and northern France from the Prussian conquest and the Prussian menace, but it must also deliver the peoples of Austria-Hungary, the peoples of the Balkans, and the peoples of Turkey, alike in Europe and in Asia, from the impudent and alien dominion of the Prussian military and commercial autocracy.

We owe it, however, to ourselves to say that we do not wish in any way to impair or to rearrange the Austro-Hungarian Empire. It is no affair of ours what they do with their own life, either industrially or politically. We do not purpose or desire to dictate to them in any way. We only desire to see that their affairs are left in their own hands, in all matters, great or small. We shall hope to secure for the peoples of the Balkan peninsula and for the people of the Turkish Empire the right and opportunity to make their own lives safe, their own fortunes secure against oppression or injustice and from the dictation of foreign courts or parties.

And our attitude and purpose with regard to Germany herself are of a like kind. We intend no wrong against the German Empire, no interference with her internal affairs. We should deem either the one or the other absolutely unjustifiable, absolutely contrary to the principles we have professed to live by and to hold most sacred throughout our life as a nation.

The people of Germany are being told by the men whom they now permit to deceive them and to act as their masters that they are fighting for the very life and existence of their Empire, a war of desperate self-defense against deliberate aggression. Nothing could be more grossly or wantonly false, and we must seek by the utmost openness and candor as to our real aims to convince them of its falseness. We are in fact fighting for their emancipation from fear, along with our own, —from the fear as well as from the fact of unjust attack by neighbors or rivals or schemers after world empire. No one is threatening the existence or the independence or the peaceful enterprise of the German Empire.

The worst that can happen to the detriment of the German people is this, that if they should still, after the war is over, continue to be obliged to live under ambitious and intriguing masters interested to disturb the peace of the world, men or classes of men whom the other peoples of the world could not trust, it might be impossible to admit them to the partnership of nations which must henceforth guarantee the world's peace. That partnership must be a partnership of peoples, not a mere partnership of governments. It might be impossible, also, in such untoward circumstances, to admit Germany to the free economic intercourse which must inevitably spring out of the other partnerships of a real peace. But there would be no aggression in that; and such a situation, inevitable because of distrust, would in the very nature of things sooner or later cure itself, by processes which would assuredly set in.

The wrongs, the very deep wrongs, committed in this war will have to be righted. That of course. But they cannot and must not be righted by the commission of similar wrongs against Germany and her allies. The world will not permit the commission of similar wrongs as a means of reparation and settlement. Statesmen must by this time have learned that the opinion of the world is everywhere wide awake and fully comprehends the issues involved. No representative of any self-governed nation will dare disregard it by attempting any such covenants of selfishness and compromise as were entered into at the Congress of Vienna. The thought of the plain people here and everywhere throughout the world, the people who enjoy no privilege and have very simple and unsophisticated standards of right and wrong, is the air all governments must henceforth breathe if they would live. It is in the full disclosing light of that thought that all policies must be conceived and executed in this midday hour of the world's life. German rulers have been able to upset the peace of the world only because the German people were not suffered under their tutelage to share the comradeship of the other peoples of the world either in thought or in purpose. They were allowed to have no opinion of their own which might be set up as a rule of conduct for those who exercised authority over them. But the congress that concludes this war will feel the full strength of the tides that run now in the hearts and consciences of free men everywhere. Its conclusions will run with those tides.

All these things have been true from the very beginning of this stupendous war; and I cannot help thinking that if they had been made plain at the very outset the sympathy and enthusiasm of the Russian people might have been once for all enlisted on the side of the Allies, suspicion and distrust swept away, and a real and lasting union of purpose effected. Had they believed these things at the very moment of their revolution and had they been confirmed in that belief since, the sad reverses which have recently marked the progress of their affairs towards an ordered and stable government of free men might have been avoided. The Russian people have been poisoned by the very same falsehoods that have kept the German people in the dark, and the poison has been administered by the very same hands. The only possible antidote is the truth. It cannot be uttered too plainly or too often.

From every point of view, therefore, it has seemed to be my duty to speak these declarations of purpose, to add these specific interpretations to what I took the liberty of saying to the Senate in January. Our entrance into the war has not altered our attitude towards the settlement that must come when it is over. When I said in January that the nations of the world were entitled not only to free pathways upon the sea but also to assured and unmolested access to those pathways I was thinking, and I am thinking now, not of the smaller and weaker nations alone, which need our countenance and support, but also of the great and powerful nations, and of our present enemies as well as our present associates in the war. I was thinking, and am thinking now, of Austria herself, among the rest, as well as of Serbia and of Poland. Justice and equality of rights can be had only at a great price. We are seeking permanent, not temporary, foundations for the peace of the world and must seek them candidly and fearlessly. As always, the right will prove to be the expedient.

What shall we do, then, to push this great war of freedom and justice to its righteous conclusion? We must clear away with a thorough hand all impediments to success and we must make every adjustment of law that will facilitate the full and free use of our whole capacity and force as a fighting unit.

One very embarrassing obstacle that stands in our way is that we are at war with Germany but not with her allies. I therefore very earnestly recommend that the Congress immediately declare the United States in a state of war with Austria-Hungary. Does it seem strange to you that this should be the conclusion of the argument I have just addressed to you? It is not. It is in fact the inevitable logic of what I have said. Austria-Hungary is for the time being not her own mistress but simply the vassal of the German Government. We must face the facts as they are and act upon them without sentiment in this stern business. The government of Austria-Hungary is not acting upon its own initiative or in response to the wishes and feelings of its own peoples but as the instrument of another nation. We must meet its force with our own and regard the Central Powers as but one. The war can be successfully conducted in no other way. The same logic would lead also to a declaration of war against Turkey and Bulgaria. They also are the tools of Germany. But they are mere tools and do not yet stand in the direct path of our necessary action. We shall go wherever the necessities of this war carry us, but it seems to me that we should go only where immediate and practical considerations lead us and not heed any others.

The financial and military measures which must be adopted will suggest themselves as the war and its undertakings develop, but I will take the liberty of proposing to you certain other acts of legislation which seem to me to be needed for the support of the war and for the release of our whole force and energy.

It will be necessary to extend in certain particulars the legislation of the last session with regard to alien enemies; and also necessary, I believe, to create a very definite and particular control over the entrance and departure of all persons into and from the United States.

Legislation should be enacted defining as a criminal offense every wilful violation of the presidential proclamations relating to alien enemies promulgated under section 4067 of the Revised Statutes and providing appropriate punishments; and women as well as men should be included under the terms of the acts placing restraints upon alien enemies. It is likely that as time goes on many alien enemies will be willing to be fed and housed at the expense of the Government in the detention camps and it would be the purpose of the legislation I have suggested to confine offenders among them in penitentiaries and other similar institutions where they could be made to work as other criminals do.

Recent experience has convinced me that the Congress must go further in authorizing the Government to set limits to prices. The law of supply and demand, I am sorry to say, has been replaced by the law of unrestrained selfishness. While we have eliminated profiteering in several branches of industry it still runs impudently rampant in others. The farmers, for example, complain with a great deal of justice that, while the regulation of food prices restricts their incomes, no restraints are placed upon the prices of most of the things they must themselves purchase; and similar inequities obtain on all sides.

It is imperatively necessary that the consideration of the full use of the water power of the country and also the consideration of the systematic and yet economical development of such of the natural resources of the country as are still under the control of the federal government should be immediately resumed and affirmatively and constructively dealt with at the earliest possible moment. The pressing need of such legislation is daily becoming more obvious.

The legislation proposed at the last session with regard to regulated combinations among our exporters, in order to provide for our foreign trade a more effective organization and method of coöperation, ought by all means to be completed at this session.

And I beg that the members of the House of Representatives will permit me to express the opinion that it will be impossible to deal in any but a very wasteful and extravagant fashion with the enormous appropriations of the public moneys which must continue to be made, if the war is to be properly sustained, unless the House will consent to return to its former practice of initiating and preparing all appropriation bills through a single committee, in order that responsibility may be centered, expenditures standardized and made uniform, and waste and duplication as much as possible avoided.

Additional legislation may also become necessary before the present Congress again adjourns in order to effect the most efficient coördination and operation of the railway and other transportation systems of the country; but to that I shall, if circumstances should demand, call the attention of the Congress upon another occasion.

If I have overlooked anything that ought to be done for the more effective conduct of the war, your own counsels will supply the omission. What I am perfectly clear about is that in the present session of the Congress our whole attention and energy should be concentrated on the vigorous, rapid, and successful prosecution of the great task of winning the war.

We can do this with all the greater zeal and enthusiasm because we know that for us this is a war of high principle, debased by no selfish ambition of conquest or spoliation; because we know, and all the world knows, that we have been forced into it to save the very institutions we live under from corruption and destruction. The purposes of the Central Powers strike straight at the very heart of everything we believe in; their methods of warfare outrage every principle of humanity and of knightly honor; their intrigue has corrupted the very thought and spirit of many of our people; their sinister and secret diplomacy has sought to take our very territory away from us and disrupt the Union of the States. Our safety would be at an end, our honor forever sullied and brought into contempt were we to permit their triumph. They are striking at the very existence of democracy and liberty.

It is because it is for us a war of high, disinterested purpose, in which all the free peoples of the world are banded together for the vindication of right, a war for the preservation of our nation and of all that it has held dear of principle and of purpose, that we feel ourselves doubly constrained to propose for its outcome only that which is righteous and of irreproachable intention, for our foes as well as for our friends. The cause being just and holy, the settlement must be of like motive and quality. For this we can fight, but for nothing less noble or less worthy of our traditions. For this cause we entered the war and for this cause will we battle until the last gun is fired.

I have spoken plainly because this seems to me the time when it is most necessary to speak plainly, in order that all the world may know that even in the heat and ardor of the struggle and when our whole thought is of carrying the war through to its end we have not forgotten any ideal or principle for which the name of America has been held in honor among the nations and for which it has been our glory to contend in the great generations that went before us. A supreme moment of history has come. The eyes of the people have been opened and they see. The hand of God is laid upon the nations. He will show them favor, I devoutly believe, only if they rise to the clear heights of His own justice and mercy.

Government Administration of Railways

[Address delivered at a joint session of the two Houses of Congress, January 4, 1918.]

Gentlemen of the Congress:

I have asked the privilege of addressing you in order to report to you that on the twenty-eighth of December last, during the recess of the Congress, acting through the Secretary of War and under the authority conferred upon me by the Act of Congress approved August 29, 1916, I took possession and assumed control of the railway lines of the country and the systems of water transportation under their control. This step seemed to be imperatively necessary in the interest of the public welfare, in the presence of the great tasks of war with which we are now dealing. As our own experience develops difficulties and makes it clear what they are, I have deemed it my duty to remove those difficulties wherever I have the legal power to do so. To assume control of the vast railway systems of the country is, I realize, a very great responsibility, but to fail to do so in the existing circumstances would have been a much greater. I assumed the less responsibility rather than the weightier.

I am sure that I am speaking the mind of all thoughtful Americans when I say that it is our duty as the representatives of the nation to do everything that it is necessary to do to secure the complete mobilization of the whole resources of America by as rapid and effective means as can be found. Transportation supplies all the arteries of, mobilization. Unless it be under a single and unified direction, the whole process of the nation's action is embarrassed.

It was in the true spirit of America, and it was right, that we should first try to effect the necessary unification under the voluntary action of those who were in charge of the great railway properties; and we did try it. The directors of the railways responded to the need promptly and generously. The group of railway executives who were charged with the task of actual coördination and general direction performed their difficult duties with patriotic zeal and marked ability, as was to have been expected, and did, I believe, everything that it was possible for them to do in the circumstances. If I have taken the task out of their hands, it has not been because of any dereliction or failure on their part but only because there were some things which the Government can do and private management cannot. We shall continue to value most highly the advice and assistance of these gentlemen and I am sure we shall not find them withholding it.

It had become unmistakably plain that only under government administration can the entire equipment of the several systems of transportation be fully and unreservedly thrown into a common service without injurious discrimination against particular properties. Only under government administration can an absolutely unrestricted and unembarrassed common use be made of all tracks, terminals, terminal facilities and equipment of every kind. Only under that authority can new terminals be constructed and developed without regard to the requirements or limitations of particular roads. But under government administration all these things will be possible,—not instantly, but as fast as practical difficulties, which cannot be merely conjured away, give way before the new management.

The common administration will be carried out with as little disturbance of the present operating organizations and personnel of the railways as possible. Nothing will be altered or disturbed which it is not necessary to disturb. We are serving the public interest and safeguarding the public safety, but we are also regardful of the interest of those by whom these great properties are owned and glad to avail ourselves of the experience and trained ability of those who have been managing them. It is necessary that the transportation of troops and of war materials, of food and of fuel, and of everything that is necessary for the full mobilization of the energies and resources of the country, should be first considered, but it is clearly in the public interest also that the ordinary activities and the normal industrial and commercial life of the country should be interfered with and dislocated as little as possible, and the public may rest assured that the interest and convenience of the private shipper will be as carefully served and safeguarded as it is possible to serve and safeguard it in the present extraordinary circumstances.

While the present authority of the Executive suffices for all purposes of administration, and while of course all private interests must for the present give way to the public necessity, it is, I am sure you will agree with me, right and necessary that the owners and creditors of the railways, the holders of their stocks and bonds, should receive from the Government an unqualified guarantee that their properties will be maintained throughout the period of federal control in as good repair and as complete equipment as at present, and that the several roads will receive under federal management such compensation as is equitable and just alike to their owners and to the general public. I would suggest the average net railway operating income of the three years ending June 30, 1917. I earnestly recommend that these guarantees be given by appropriate legislation, and given as promptly as circumstances permit.

I need not point out the essential justice of such guarantees and their great influence and significance as elements in the present financial and industrial situation of the country. Indeed, one of the strong arguments for assuming control of the railroads at this time is the financial argument. It is necessary that the values of railway securities should be justly and fairly protected and that the large financial operations every year necessary in connection with the maintenance, operation and development of the roads should, during the period of the war, be wisely related to the financial operations of the Government. Our first duty is, of course, to conserve the common interest and the common safety and to make certain that nothing stands in the way of the successful prosecution of the great war for liberty and justice, but it is also an obligation of public conscience and of public honor that the private interests we disturb should be kept safe from unjust injury, and it is of the utmost consequence to the Government itself that all great financial operations should be stabilized and coördinated with the financial operations of the Government. No borrowing should run athwart the borrowings of the federal treasury, and no fundamental industrial values should anywhere be unnecessarily impaired. In the hands of many thousands of small investors in the country, as well as in national banks, in insurance companies, in savings banks, in trust companies, in financial agencies of every kind, railway securities, the sum total of which runs up to some ten or eleven thousand millions, constitute a vital part of the structure of credit, and the unquestioned solidity of that structure must be maintained.

The Secretary of War and I easily agreed that, in view of the many complex interests which must be safeguarded and harmonized, as well as because of his exceptional experience and ability in this new field of governmental action, the Honorable William G. McAdoo was the right man to assume direct administrative control of this new executive task. At our request, he consented to assume the authority and duties of organizer and Director General of the new Railway Administration. He has assumed those duties and his work is in active progress.

It is probably too much to expect that even under the unified railway administration which will now be possible sufficient economies can be effected in the operation of the railways to make it possible to add to their equipment and extend their operative facilities as much as the present extraordinary demands upon their use will render desirable without resorting to the national treasury for the funds. If it is not possible, it will, of course, be necessary to resort to the Congress for grants of money for that purpose. The Secretary of the Treasury will advise with your committees with regard to this very practical aspect of the matter. For the present, I suggest only the guarantees I have indicated and such appropriations as are necessary at the outset of this task. I take the liberty of expressing the hope that the Congress may grant these promptly and ungrudgingly. We are dealing with great matters and will, I am sure, deal with them greatly.

The Conditions of Peace

[Address delivered at a joint session of the two Houses of Congress, January 8, 1918.]

Gentlemen of the Congress:
Once more, as repeatedly before, the spokesmen of the Central Empires have indicated their desire to discuss the objects of the war and the possible bases of a general peace. Parleys have been in progress at Brest-Litovsk between Russian representatives and representatives of the Central Powers to which the attention of all the belligerents has been invited for the purpose of ascertaining whether it may be possible to extend these parleys into a general conference with regard to terms of peace and settlement. The Russian representatives presented not only a perfectly definite statement of the principles upon which they would be willing to conclude peace but also an equally definite program of the concrete application of those principles. The representatives of the Central Powers, on their part, presented an outline of settlement which, if much less definite, seemed susceptible of liberal interpretation until their specific program of practical terms was added. That program proposed no concessions at all either to the sovereignty of Russia or to the preferences of the populations with whose fortunes it dealt, but meant, in a word, that the Central Empires were to keep every foot of territory their armed forces had occupied, —every province, every city, every point of vantage, —as a permanent addition to their territories and their power. It is a reasonable conjecture that the general principles of settlement which they at first suggested originated with the more liberal statesmen of Germany and Austria, the men who have begun to feel the force of their own peoples' thought and purpose, while the concrete terms of actual settlement came from the military leaders who have no thought but to keep what they have got. The negotiations have been broken off. The Russian representatives were sincere and in earnest. They cannot entertain such proposals of conquest and domination.

The whole incident is full of significance. It is also full of perplexity. With whom are the Russian representatives dealing? For whom are the representatives of the Central Empires speaking? Are they speaking for the majorities of their respective parliaments or for the minority parties, that military and imperialistic minority which has so far dominated their whole policy and controlled the affairs of Turkey and of the Balkan states which have felt obliged to become their associates in this war? The Russian representatives have insisted, very justly, very wisely, and in the true spirit of modern democracy, that the conferences they have been holding with the Teutonic and Turkish statesmen should be held within open, not closed, doors, and all the world has been audience, as was desired. To whom have we been listening, then? To those who speak the spirit and intention of the Resolutions of the German Reichstag of the ninth of July last, the spirit and intention of the liberal leaders and parties of Germany, or to those who resist and defy that spirit and intention and insist upon conquest and subjugation? Or are we listening, in fact, to both, unreconciled and in open and hopeless contradiction? These are very serious and pregnant questions. Upon the answer to them depends the peace of the world.

But, whatever the results of the parleys at Brest-Litovsk, whatever the confusions of counsel and of purpose in the utterances of the spokesmen of the Central Empires, they have again attempted to acquaint the world with their objects in the war and have again challenged their adversaries to say what their objects are and what sort of settlement they would deem just and satisfactory. There is no good reason why that challenge should not be responded to, and responded to with the utmost candor. We did not wait for it. Not once, but again and again, we have laid our whole thought and purpose before the world, not in general terms only, but each time with sufficient definition to make it clear what sort of definitive terms of settlement must necessarily spring out of them. Within the last week Mr. Lloyd George has spoken with admirable candor and in admirable spirit for the people and Government of Great Britain. There is no confusion of counsel among the adversaries of the Central Powers, no uncertainty of principle, no vagueness of detail. The only secrecy of counsel, the only lack of fearless frankness, the only failure to make definite statement of the objects of the war, lies with Germany and her Allies. The issues of life and death hang upon these definitions. No statesman who has the least conception of his responsibility ought for a moment to permit himself to continue this tragical and appalling outpouring of blood and treasure unless he is sure beyond a peradventure that the objects of the vital sacrifice are part and parcel of the very life of society and that the people for whom he speaks think them right and imperative as he does.

There is, moreover, a voice calling for these definitions of principle and of purpose which is, it seems to me, more thrilling and more compelling than any of the many moving voices with which the troubled air of the world is filled. It is the voice of the Russian people. They are prostrate and all but helpless, it would seem, before the grim power of Germany, which has hitherto known no relenting and no pity. Their power, apparently, is shattered. And yet their soul is not subservient. They will not yield either in principle or in action. Their conception of what is right, of what it is humane and honorable for them to accept, has been stated with a frankness, a largeness of view, a generosity of spirit, and a universal human sympathy which must challenge the admiration of every friend of mankind; and they have refused to compound their ideals or desert others that they themselves may be safe. They call to us to say what it is that we desire, in what, if in anything, our purpose and our spirit differ from theirs; and I believe that the people of the United States would wish me to respond, with utter simplicity and frankness. Whether their present leaders believe it or not, it is our heartfelt desire and hope that some way may be opened whereby we may be privileged to assist the people of Russia to attain their utmost hope of liberty and ordered peace.

It will be our wish and purpose that the processes of peace, when they are begun, shall be absolutely open and that they shall involve and permit henceforth no secret understandings of any kind. The day of conquest and aggrandizement is gone by; so is also the day of secret covenants entered into in the interest of particular governments and likely at some unlooked-for moment to upset the peace of the world. It is this happy fact, now clear to the view of every public man whose thoughts do not still linger in an age that is dead and gone, which makes it possible for every nation whose purposes are consistent with justice and the peace of the world to avow now or at any other time the objects it has in view.

We entered this war because violations of right had occurred which touched us to the quick and made the life of our own people impossible unless they were corrected and the world secured once for all against their recurrence. What we demand in this war, therefore, is nothing peculiar to ourselves. It is that the world be made fit and safe to live in; and particularly that it be made safe for every peace-loving nation which, like our own, wishes to live its own life, determine its own institutions, be assured of justice and fair dealing by the other peoples of the world as against force and selfish aggression. All the peoples of the world are in effect partners in this interest, and for our own part we see very clearly that unless justice be done to others it will not be done to us. The program of the world's peace, therefore, is our program; and that program, the only possible program, as we see it, is this:

I. Open covenants of peace, openly arrived at, after which there shall be no private international understandings of any kind, but diplomacy shall proceed always frankly and in the public view.

II. Absolute freedom of navigation upon the seas, outside territorial waters, alike in peace and in war, except as the seas may be closed in whole or in part by international action for the enforcement of international covenants.

III. The removal, so far as possible, of all economic barriers and the establishment of an equality of trade conditions among all the nations consenting to the peace and associating themselves for its maintenance.

IV. Adequate guarantees given and taken that national armaments will be reduced to the lowest point consistent with domestic safety.

V. A free, open-minded, and absolutely impartial adjustment of all colonial claims, based upon a strict observance of the principle that in determining all such questions of sovereignty the interests of the populations concerned must have equal weight with the equitable claims of the government whose title is to be determined.

VI. The evacuation of all Russian territory and such a settlement of all questions affecting Russia as will secure the best and freest coöperation of the other nations of the world in obtaining for her an unhampered and unembarrassed opportunity for the independent determination of her own political development and national policy and assure her of a sincere welcome into the society of free nations under institutions of her own choosing; and, more than a welcome, assistance also of every kind that she may need and may herself desire. The treatment accorded Russia by her sister nations in the months to come will be the acid test of their good will, of their comprehension of her needs as distinguished from their own interests, and of their intelligent and unselfish sympathy.

VII. Belgium, the whole world will agree, must be evacuated and restored, without any attempt to limit the sovereignty which she enjoys in common with all other free nations. No other single act will serve as this will serve to restore confidence among the nations in the laws which they have themselves set and determined for the government of their relations with one another. Without this healing act the whole structure and validity of international law is forever impaired.

VIII. All French territory should be freed and the invaded portions restored, and the wrong done to France by Prussia in 1871 in the matter of Alsace-Lorraine, which has unsettled the peace of the world for nearly fifty years, should be righted, in order that peace may once more be made secure in the interest of all.

IX. A readjustment of the frontiers of Italy should be effected along clearly recognizable lines of nationality.

X. The peoples of Austria-Hungary, whose place among the nations we wish to see safeguarded and assured, should be accorded the freest opportunity of autonomous development.

XI. Rumania, Serbia, and Montenegro should be evacuated; occupied territories restored; Serbia accorded free and secure access to the sea; and the relations of the several Balkan states to one another determined by friendly counsel along historically established lines of allegiance and nationality; and international guarantees of the political and economic independence and territorial integrity of the several Balkan states should be entered into.

XII. The Turkish portions of the present Ottoman Empire should be assured a secure sovereignty, but the other nationalities which are now under Turkish rule should be assured an undoubted security of life and an absolutely unmolested opportunity of autonomous development and the Dardanelles should be permanently opened as a free passage to the ships and commerce of all nations under international guarantees.

XIII. An independent Polish state should be erected which should include the territories inhabited by indisputably Polish populations, which should be assured a free and secure access to the sea, and whose political and economic independence and territorial integrity should be guaranteed by international covenant.

XIV. A general association of nations must be formed under specific covenants for the purpose of affording mutual guarantees of political independence and territorial integrity to great and small states alike.

In regard to these essential rectifications of wrong and assertions of right we feel ourselves to be intimate partners of all the governments and peoples associated together against the Imperialists. We cannot be separated in interest or divided in purpose. We stand together until the end.

For such arrangements and covenants we are willing to fight and to continue to fight until they are achieved; but only because we wish the right to prevail and desire a just and stable peace such as can be secured only by removing the chief provocations to war, which this program does remove. We have no jealousy of German greatness, and there is nothing in this program that impairs it. We grudge her no achievement or distinction of learning or of pacific enterprise such as have made her record very bright and very enviable. We do not wish to injure her or to block in any way her legitimate influence or power. We do not wish to fight her either with arms or with hostile arrangements of trade if she is willing to associate herself with us and the other peace-loving nations of the world in covenants of justice and law and fair dealing. We wish her only to accept a place of equality among the peoples of the world,—the new world in which we now live,—instead of a place of mastery.

Neither do we presume to suggest to her any alteration or modification of her institutions. But it is necessary, we must frankly say, and necessary as a preliminary to any intelligent dealings with her on our part, that we should know whom her spokesmen speak for when they speak to us, whether for the Reichstag majority or for the military party and the men whose creed is imperial domination.

We have spoken now, surely, in terms too concrete to admit of any further doubt or question. An evident principle runs through the whole program I have outlined. It is the principle of justice to all peoples and nationalities, and their right to live on equal terms of liberty and safety with one another, whether they be strong or weak. Unless this principle be made its foundation no part of the structure of international justice can stand. The people of the United States could act upon no other principle; and to the vindication of this principle they are ready to devote their lives, their honor, and everything that they possess. The moral climax of this the culminating and final war for human liberty has come, and they are ready to put their own strength, their own highest purpose, their own integrity and devotion to the test.

Force to the Utmost

[Speech at the Opening of the Third Liberty Loan Campaign, delivered in the Fifth Regiment Armory, Baltimore, April 6, 1918.]

Fellow-Citizens:
This is the anniversary of our acceptance of Germany's challenge to fight for our right to live and be free, and for the sacred rights of freemen everywhere. The nation is awake. There is no need to call to it. We know what the war must cost, our utmost sacrifice, the lives of our fittest men, and, if need be, all that we possess.

The loan we are met to discuss is one of the least parts of what we are called upon to give and to do, though in itself imperative. The people of the whole country are alive to the necessity of it, and are ready to lend to the utmost, even where it involves a sharp skimping and daily sacrifice to lend out of meagre earnings. They will look with reprobation and contempt upon those who can and will not, upon those who demand a higher rate of interest, upon those who think of it as a mere commercial transaction. I have not come, therefore, to urge the loan. I have come only to give you, if I can, a more vivid conception of what it is for.

The reasons for this great war, the reason why it had to come, the need to fight it through, and the issues that hang upon its outcome, are more clearly disclosed now than ever before. It is easy to see just what this particular loan means, because the cause we are fighting for stands more sharply revealed than at any previous crisis of the momentous struggle. The man who knows least can now see plainly how the cause of justice stands, and what is the imperishable thing he is asked to invest in. Men in America may be more sure than they ever were before that the cause is their own, and that, if it should be lost, their own great nation's place and mission in the world would be lost with it.

I call you to witness, my fellow-countrymen, that at no stage of this terrible business have I judged the purposes of Germany intemperately. I should be ashamed in the presence of affairs so grave, so fraught with the destinies of mankind throughout all the world, to speak with truculence, to use the weak language of hatred or vindictive purpose. We must judge as we would be judged. I have sought to learn the objects Germany has in this war from the mouths of her own spokesmen, and to deal as frankly with them as I wished them to deal with me. I have laid bare our own ideals, our own purposes, without reserve or doubtful phrase, and have asked them to say as plainly what it is that they seek.

We have ourselves proposed no injustice, no aggression. We are ready, whenever the final reckoning is made, to be just to the German people, deal fairly with the German power, as with all others. There can be no difference between peoples in the final judgment, if it is indeed to be a righteous judgment. To propose anything but justice, even-handed and dispassionate justice, to Germany at any time, whatever the outcome of the war, would be to renounce and dishonor our own cause, for we ask nothing that we are not willing to accord.

It has been with this thought that I have sought to learn from those who spoke for Germany whether it was justice or dominion and the execution of their own will upon the other nations of the world that the German leaders were seeking. They have answered-answered in unmistakable terms. They have avowed that it was not justice, but dominion and the unhindered execution of their own will. The avowal has not come from Germany's statesmen. It has come from her military leaders, who are her real rulers. Her statesmen have said that they wished peace, and were ready to discuss its terms whenever their opponents were willing to sit down at the conference table with them. Her present Chancellor has said-in indefinite and uncertain terms, indeed, and in phrases that often seem to deny their own meaning, but with as much plainness as he thought prudent-that he believed that peace should be based upon the principles which we had declared would be our own in the final settlement.

At Brest-Litovsk her civilian delegates spoke in similar terms; professed their desire to conclude a fair peace and accord to the peoples with whose fortunes they were dealing the right to choose their own allegiances. But action accompanied and followed the profession. Their military masters, the men who act for Germany and exhibit her purpose in execution, proclaimed a very different conclusion. We can not mistake what they have done-in Russia, in Finland, in the Ukraine, in Rumania. The real test of their justice and fair play has come. From this we may judge the rest.

They are enjoying in Russia a cheap triumph in which no brave or gallant nation can long take pride. A great people, helpless by their own act, lies for the time at their mercy. Their fair professions are forgotten. They nowhere set up justice, but everywhere impose their power and exploit everything for their own use and aggrandizement, and the peoples of conquered provinces are invited to be free under their dominion!

Are we not justified in believing that they would do the same things at their western front if they were not there face to face with armies whom even their countless divisions cannot overcome? If, when they have felt their check to be final, they should propose favorable and equitable terms with regard to Belgium and France and Italy, could they blame us if we concluded that they did so only to assure themselves of a free hand in Russia and the East?

Their purpose is, undoubtedly, to make all the Slavic peoples, all the free and ambitious nations of the Baltic Peninsula, all the lands that Turkey has dominated and misruled, subject to their will and ambition, and build upon that dominion an empire of force upon which they fancy that they can then erect an empire of gain and commercial supremacy-an empire as hostile to the Americas as to the Europe which it will overawe-an empire which will ultimately master Persia, India, and the peoples of the Far East.

In such a program our ideals, the ideals of justice and humanity and liberty, the principle of the free self-determination of nations, upon which all the modern world insists, can play no part. They are rejected for the ideals of power, for the principle that the strong must rule the weak, that trade must follow the flag, whether those to whom it is taken welcome it or not, that the peoples of the world are to be made subject to the patronage and overlordship of those who have the power to enforce it.

That program once carried out, America and all who care or dare to stand with her must arm and prepare themselves to contest the mastery of the world —a mastery in which the rights of common men, the rights of women and of all who are weak, must for the time being be trodden underfoot and disregarded and the old, age-long struggle for freedom and right begin again at its beginning. Everything that America has lived for and loved and grown great to vindicate and bring to a glorious realization will have fallen in utter ruin and the gates of mercy once more pitilessly shut upon mankind!

The thing is preposterous and impossible; and yet is not that what the whole course and action of the German armies has meant wherever they have moved? I do not wish, even in this moment of utter disillusionment, to judge harshly or unrighteously. I judge only what the German arms have accomplished with unpitying thoroughness throughout every fair region they have touched.

What, then are we to do? For myself, I am ready, ready still, ready even now, to discuss a fair and just and honest peace at any time that it is sincerely purposed —a peace in which the strong and the weak shall fare alike. But the answer, when I proposed such a peace, came from the German commanders in Russia and I cannot mistake the meaning of the answer.

I accept the challenge. I know that you accept it. All the world shall know that you accept it. It shall appear in the utter sacrifice and self-forgetfulness with which we shall give all that we love and all that we have to redeem the world and make it fit for free men like ourselves to live in. This now is the meaning of all that we do. Let everything that we say, my fellow-countrymen, everything that we henceforth plan and accomplish, ring true to this response till the majesty and might of our concerted power shall fill the thought and utterly defeat the force of those who flout and misprize what we honor and hold dear.

Germany has once more said that force, and force alone, shall decide whether justice and peace shall reign in the affairs of men, whether right as America conceives it or dominion as she conceives it shall determine the destinies of mankind. There is, therefore, but one response possible from us: Force, force to the utmost, force without stint or limit, the righteous and triumphant force which shall make right the law of the world and cast every selfish dominion down in the dust.

Presidential Decisions

The State of War: The President's Proclamation of April 6, 1917.

Whereas the Congress of the United States in the exercise of the constitutional authority vested in them have resolved, by joint resolution of the Senate and House of Representatives bearing date this day "That the state of war between the United States and the Imperial German Government which has been thrust upon the United States is hereby formally declared";

Whereas it is provided by Section 4067 of the Revised Statutes, as follows:

> Whenever there is declared a war between the United States and any foreign nation or government, or any invasion or predatory incursion is perpetrated, attempted, or threatened against the territory of the United States, by any foreign nation or government, and the President makes public proclamation of the event, all natives, citizens, denizens, or subjects of a hostile nation or government, being males of the age of fourteen years and upwards, who shall be within the United States, and not actually naturalized, shall be liable to be apprehended, restrained, secured, and removed as alien enemies. The President is authorized, in any such event, by his proclamation thereof, or other public act, to direct the conduct to be observed, on the part of the United States, toward the aliens who become so liable; the manner and degree of the restraint to which they shall be subject, and in what cases, and upon what security their residence shall be permitted, and to provide for the removal of those who, not being permitted to reside within the United States, refuse or neglect to depart therefrom; and to establish any such regulations which are found necessary in the premises and for the public safety;

Whereas, by Sections 4068, 4069, and 4070 of the Revised Statutes, further provision is made relative to alien enemies;

Now, therefore, I, Woodrow Wilson, President of the United States of America, do hereby proclaim to all whom it may concern that a state of war exists between the United States and the Imperial German Government; and I do specially direct all officers, civil or military, of the United States that they exercise vigilance and zeal in the discharge of the duties incident to such a state of war; and I do, moreover, earnestly appeal to all American citizens that they, in loyal devotion to their country, dedicated from its foundation to the principles of liberty and justice, uphold the laws of the land, and give undivided and willing support to those measures which may be adopted by the constitutional authorities in prosecuting the war to a successful issue and in obtaining a secure and just peace;

And, acting under and by virtue of the authority vested in me by the Constitution of the United States and the said sections of the Revised Statutes, I do hereby further proclaim and direct that the conduct to be observed on the part of the United States toward all natives, citizens, denizens, or subjects of Germany, being males of the age of fourteen years and upwards, who shall be within the United States and not actually naturalized, who for the purpose of this proclamation and under such sections of the Revised Statutes are termed alien enemies, shall be as follows:

All alien enemies are enjoined to preserve the peace towards the United States and to refrain from crime against the public safety, and from violating the laws of the United States and of the States and Territories thereof, and to refrain from actual hostility or giving information, aid or comfort to the enemies of the United States, and to comply strictly with the regulations which are hereby or which may be from time to time promulgated by the President; and so long as they shall conduct themselves in accordance with law, they shall be undisturbed in the peaceful pursuit of their lives and occupations and be accorded the consideration due to all peaceful and law-abiding persons, except so far as restrictions may be necessary for their own protection and for the safety of the United States; and towards such alien enemies as conduct themselves in accordance with law, all citizens of the United States are enjoined to preserve the peace and to treat them with all such friendliness as may be compatible with loyalty and allegiance to the United States.

And all alien enemies who fail to conduct themselves as so enjoined, in addition to all other penalties prescribed by law, shall be liable to restraint, or to give security, or to remove and depart from the United States in the manner prescribed by Sections 4069 and 4070 of the Revised Statutes, and as prescribed in the regulations duly promulgated by the President;

And pursuant to the authority vested in me, I hereby declare and establish the following regulations, which I find necessary in the premises and for the public safety:

First. An alien enemy shall not have in his possession, at any time or place, any firearm, weapon or implement of war, or component part thereof, ammunition, maxim or other silencer, bomb or explosive or material used in the manufacture of explosives;

Second. An alien enemy shall not have in his possession at any time or place, or use or operate any aircraft or wireless apparatus, or any form of signalling device, or any form of cipher code, or any paper, document or book written or printed in cipher or in which there may be invisible writing;

Third. All property found in the possession of an alien enemy in violation of the foregoing regulations shall be subject to seizure by the United States;

Fourth. An alien enemy shall not approach or be found within one-half of a mile of any Federal or State fort, camp, arsenal, aircraft station, Government or naval vessel, navy yard, factory, or workshop for the manufacture of munitions of war or of any products for the use of the army or navy;

Fifth. An alien enemy shall not write, print, or publish any attack or threats against the Government or Congress of the United States, or either branch thereof, or against the measures or policy of the United States, or against the person or property of any person in the military, naval or civil service of the United States, or of the States or Territories, or of the District of Columbia, or of the municipal governments therein;

Sixth. An alien enemy shall not commit or abet any hostile acts against the United States, or give information, aid, or comfort to its enemies;

Seventh. An alien enemy shall not reside in or continue to reside in, to remain in, or enter any locality which the President may from time to time designate by Executive Order as a prohibited area in which residence by an alien enemy shall be found by him to constitute a danger to the public peace and safety of the United States, except by permit from the President and except under such limitations or restrictions as the President may prescribe;

Eighth. An alien enemy whom the President shall have reasonable cause to believe to be aiding or about to aid the enemy, or to be at large to the danger of the public peace or safety of the United States, or to have violated or to be about to violate any of these regulations, shall remove to any location designated by the President by Executive Order, and shall not remove therefrom without a permit, or shall depart from the United States if so required by the President;

Ninth. No alien enemy shall depart from the United States until he shall have received such permit as the President shall prescribe, or except under order of a court, judge, or justice, under Sections 4069 and 4070 of the Revised Statutes;

Tenth. No alien enemy shall land in or enter the United States, except under such restrictions and at such places as the President may prescribe;

Eleventh. If necessary to prevent violation of the regulations, all alien enemies will be obliged to register;

Twelfth. An alien enemy whom there may be reasonable cause to believe to be aiding or about to aid the enemy, or who may be at large to the danger of the public peace or safety, or who violates or attempts to violate, or of whom there is reasonable ground to believe that he is about to violate, any regulation duly promulgated by the President, or any criminal law of the United States, or of the States or Territories thereof, will be subject to summary arrest by the United States Marshal, or his deputy, or such other officer as the President shall designate, and to confinement in such penitentiary, prison, jail, military camp, or other place of detention as may be directed by the President.

This proclamation and the regulations herein contained shall extend and apply to all land and water, continental or insular, in any way within the jurisdiction of the United States.

Formal U.S. Declaration of War with Germany, 6 April 1917

Joint Resolution Declaring that a state of war exists between the Imperial German Government and the Government and the people of the United States and making provision to prosecute the same.

Whereas the Imperial German Government has committed repeated acts of war against the Government and the people of the United States of America; Therefore be it Resolved by the Senate and the House of Representatives of the United States of America in Congress Assembled, that the state of war between the United States and the Imperial German Government which has thus been thrust upon the United States is hereby formally declared; and that the President be, and he is hereby, authorized and directed to employ the entire naval and military forces of the United States and the resources of the Government to carry on war against the Imperial German Government; and to bring the conflict to a successful termination all of the resources of the country are hereby pledged by the Congress of the United States.

CHAMP CLARK
Speaker of the House of Representatives
THOS. R. MARSHALL
Vice President of the United States and President of the Senate
Approved, April 6, 1917
WOODROW WILSON

Biography of Woodrow Wilson

Woodrow Wilson
By Josephus Daniels

Woodrow Wilson is descended from a Scotch-Irish ancestry noted for its culture and its intensity of religious conviction. Some of his Scot forbears died for their faith. Immediately, he comes from a line of ministers and editors. William Duane, democrat and friend of Jefferson, had a hand in the training of James Wilson, grandfather of Woodrow Wilson, who came from County Down, Ireland, lured as a youth of twenty-two to the land of opportunity in the New World. Landing at Philadelphia in the year 1808, he quickly found a congenial task in the work rooms of Duane's militant "Daily Aurora." The joy of his new toil was enhanced by the fact that a fine Irish lass, who had sailed on the same ship with him, was watching him make his fortune; and within four years he was able to claim Ann Adams as his wife. The happy pair could not be disobedient to the enticing vision of the developing West, and in 1812 James Wilson founded the Western Herald at Steubenville, Ohio, and soon afterward the Pennsylvania Advocate at Pittsburg, Pennsylvania, and divided his time between the two newspapers.

As Providence would have it, Joseph Ruggles Wilson, youngest of seven sons and three daughters, was marked to be the scholar of the family. Trained by his parents, and especially by his mother, who was a Presbyterian of the "straitest sect," it was not surprising that he turned to the Gospel ministry as his calling. The stair steps in his education were the Steubenville Academy; Jefferson College, afterwards Washington and Jefferson College, where he took first honors; and a year each at Western Theological Seminary at Allegheny, Pennsylvania, and Princeton Seminary.

The Reverend Doctor Thomas Woodrow, English-descended but Scotch-born, some years before had left his church at Carlisle, England, to become a missionary in the New World, and had finally come to Chillicothe, Ohio. It came about that he sent his pretty and sprightly daughter, Janet, sometimes called Jessie, to the girls school at Steubenville at the same time that Joseph R. Wilson had returned to that place to teach for a couple of years in the male academy. Finding their tastes congenial and their ideals alike, these two were happily married on June 7, 1849, and after teaching rhetoric for a year at Jefferson College, and chemistry and the natural sciences for four years at Hampden Sidney College, Virginia, the young husband accepted a call to the pastorate of the Presbyterian church at Staunton, Virginia, in the year 1855, and moved there with his wife and two small daughters, Marian and Annie Josephine.

Staunton was the birthplace of Woodrow Wilson. As his father left there when he was two years old to accept a call to the important First Presbyterian church of Augusta, Georgia, he had no recollection of the home of his nativity in the beautiful valley of Virginia, but he will never for get the reception tendered him by citizens of that city upon the fifty-seventh anniversary of his birth, on December 28, 1912, when he was President-elect of the United States, and when he was quartered in the little room in the manse where he first saw the light.

Both at Augusta and at Columbia, South Carolina, where Doctor Wilson in 1870 accepted the chair of pastoral and evangelistic theology at the Southern Presbyterian Theological Seminary, Woodrow attended excellent private schools, but his real instructor was his father. Doctor Wilson was one of the brilliant leaders of the Presbyterian Church in the south. For forty years he was Stated Clerk of the Southern General Assembly. He was Moderator of the Assembly of 1879. Well-informed upon the news of the day and well-balanced and fair-minded, the father was keen to judge a new book, to analyze a political situation, to shatter a sham with irony, or to scorn a pretender. From him all the while the boy was unconsciously absorbing the ability to do the same things.

Wilson's decision as to his life purpose was formed suddenly. He had spent a year at Davidson College, North Carolina, an excellent institution with a strong faculty, and then a year at his new home in Wilmington, North Carolina, whither his father had been called from Columbia to the Presbyterian pastorate. In the early fall of 1875 he entered Princeton, then under the presidency of Doctor James McCosh. About three months had passed when young Wilson, while browsing in the library, took down a file of the Gentlemen's Magazine and turned to the series of articles entitled "Men and Manners in Parliament," written by "The Member for Chiltern Hundreds," the anonymous successor of Doctor Johnson. Wilson was captivated by these vivid reports of the parliamentary debates participated in by Gladstone, Disraeli, John Bright, Earl Granville, Sir William Vernon Harcourt and other figures in the public eye of England at that time. He eagerly devoured the entire series, and went on to the earnest study of English political history. He does not hesitate to confess that this was a turning point in his life and that no other circumstance did so much to make public life the purpose of his existence. In his senior year, Wilson embodied his conclusions in an article entitled "Cabinet Government in the United States," which was instantly accepted by the International Review and published in August, 1879. His criticism was that in Congress the important legislation was shaped in committee; and secrecy, he contended, is the atmosphere in which all corruption and evil flourish. To remedy the evil of committee government, which he attributed to lack of leaders, he devised a plan whereby Cabinet members should be entitled to a seat in Congress, and the right to participate in the debates, even if it were deemed advisable not to give them the right to vote. All through his later voluminous writings, Wilson clung to this theory and put the idea into practice, so far as he could, with marked effect, when he came to be the head of the nation, by personally appearing before joint meetings of both houses of Congress and reading his messages.

One effect of Wilson's selection of a career so early in his college course was to induce him to select all his studies with a view to it, and to reject as unsuited both to his tastes and his needs the rigid and inflexible curriculum then prescribed at Princeton. As illustrating how he reached for anything which would help him in his career, he went outside the campus to learn stenography so that he might the more easily make notes during his library work. This acquirement has proved an invaluable aid to him throughout his life, and all his public papers were originally prepared in the characters of the stenographic art. He was a famous and dreaded debater, belonging to Whig Hall, at Princeton, and it was conceded that he stood the best chance to win the Lynde Debate, an extemporaneous discussion participated in by three representatives from each of the two literary societies. But when in the preliminary trial in his society he drew out of the hat a slip labeled "Protection," requiring him to defend that side, he refused to participate in the debate at all, because he could not advocate what he did not believe.

Conceiving that the law guaranteed the surest promise of a useful career, Wilson took his law course at the University of Virginia. Meanwhile, however, he continued his studies of English government and contributed articles to the University Magazine on John Bright and Gladstone.

A year of rest with his parents at Wilmington followed his leaving college, and then young Wilson engaged in the practice of law at Atlanta, Georgia, but, after a waiting experience of eighteen months in which clients were slow in putting in an appearance, he decided that he would continue his studies in the science of government at Johns Hopkins University. They were mainly directed by Herbert B. Adams in history, and Richard T. Ely in political economy. A second year at Hopkins was spent as the holder of the Historical Fellowship. A brilliant composition at this time was a study of Adam Smith, while early in 1885 appeared his first important volume, "Congressional Government, a Study of Government by Committee." It was the first time a thorough consideration not only of the theory but of the actual working of the Constitution of the United States had ever been prepared in book form. It was the result of ten years of absorbing study. It met with immediate success, and Ambassador Bryce in the preface to his "American Commonwealth" acknowledges his indebtedness to the work. It brought him invitations to several college chairs, and, while still continuing his Hopkins studies, he accepted the place of associate in history and political economy at the new college for the higher education of women — Bryn Mawr. Mr. Wilson's course of lectures was one of the most popular in the college. In 1886 he took his Ph.D. from Johns Hopkins, his work on "Congressional Government" being accepted as his thesis, and one year later the University offered him a lectureship which took him to Baltimore once a week for twenty-five weeks.

Leaving Bryn Mawr, he was two years at Wesleyan University as professor of history and political economy, during which time he wrote "The State," and in 1890 he accepted an offer of the chair of jurisprudence and politics in Princeton University. After fifteen years the young professor who had received the inspiration for his life work in the Princeton Library was back on the campus of his Alma Mater as a member of the faculty. His lectures sprang into popularity here as well as with his earlier professorships. Princeton had never in all its brilliant history had a teacher who so captivated his classes. Upwards of four hundred students in all were in attendance, absorbing his carefully ascertained and impressively presented facts of history, or fascinated by his original views of current events. His teaching was enlightened by sprightly humor. He spoke with the greatest freedom, often with utter abandon, concerning modern events and those concerned in them, putting the students on their honor not to report him and none of them ever violated his confidences.

Twelve years went by. It was a period of development with Woodrow Wilson. His mind mellowed. There was a ripening into maturity. As he continued his studies along the line of his bent a number of new books came from his pen. They were: "The State," "Division and Reunion," "An Old Master," "Mere Literature" and "George Washington." Later still appeared his masterly "History of the American People." As he compared the conditions of government in this day with the ideals of government set up by the fathers of the Republic, and as he noted points of failure in the realization of these ideals, he was fired with a holy zeal to champion the cause of social justice.

In June, 1902, Woodrow Wilson was elected president of Princeton University. His thorough equipment, his proven capacity for leadership, his splendid scholarship, his eloquence and popularity as a speaker, his already widespread fame, his judgment and executive ability marked him as the man of the hour. His mettle had been tested in the faculty meetings when he had quickly made himself felt in his readiness in debate over the problems affecting the welfare of the campus and the college. His discernment, his preparedness for emergency, his loyalty, had been amply proven. He was the logical man for the place — this first layman in a list of presidents reaching back for one hundred and sixty years.

By his election a man who had no peer for genuine democracy was placed in supreme power in probably the most aristocratic educational institution in the United States. And this leaven of democracy mixed in with the fine flour of college aristocracy began soon to "work." After a year of quiet but earnest study of conditions from the new point of view of the presidency, Doctor Wilson initiated and carried through to rapid success certain reforms. After seeing to it that the actual scholarship and discipline corresponded properly to what they were scheduled in the catalogue to be, demanding genuine work to win a diploma and banishing the social pull that had theretofore existed, Doctor Wilson laid his hand to the revision of the course of study. Princeton must not only be a place of work, but of work which should be intelligent and calculated to put the worker in a position best to serve society in the twentieth century.

The new president next secured the preceptorial system. Out of one hundred and sixty-eight hours a week, fifteen hours a week in the classroom were not considered sufficient by President Wilson for the proper education of the students entrusted to Princeton's care. They were no longer to be allowed to drift aimlessly through the weeks and the years. The institution was to give better attention toward direction of their spare time. To this end preceptors were employed at a great expense — for the new system involved an annual cost of about one hundred thousand dollars — and they were to supply friendly companionship and have oversight of studies. The informal, personal contact of the students with these preceptors has been of infinite value. The new system proved its worth from the outset, and the eyes of the educational world were turned upon Princeton which was thus forging to the front with a forcefully constructive programme.

President Wilson next attempted a reorganization of the social life of the campus. For ten years he had been turning over in his mind a plan by which the exclusive clubs patronized by the wealthier of the upper classmen might be superseded by a number of "quadrangles," dormitories in which a certain number of men from each class together with several instructors should have their domicile. This would assure a commingling of all the students, the upper classmen demonstrating the value of the college training they were receiving and the lower classmen, through personal contact, receiving an impetus and inspiration for their further college career. As it was, Princeton had a dozen "swell" club-houses, to which only students possessed of large means could afford to belong. The aggregate value of these buildings and their elegant furnishings was upwards of a million dollars. The membership averaged about fifteen seniors and fifteen juniors each, the members of these two classes alone being eligible. Some three hundred or more other members of the senior and junior classes were excluded. Freshmen and especially sophomores engaged in fierce rivalry in their efforts to "make" a club. Their spirit was the dominant character-forming influence on the Princeton campus. It can readily be imagined how eagerly the democratic heart of President Wilson was throbbing in his desire to overthrow this pernicious system so alien to the American ideal.

A committee of seven trustees presented a report at the commencement of 1907, endorsing the President's plan for "the social co-ordination of the University" and the report was accepted. There were twenty-seven trustees. Twenty-five voted for the plan and one against. One member was absent. A circular outlining the plan was sent to the clubs and was read there by hundreds of returned alumni on the Friday night before commencement of the same year 1907. A cry of protest went up and continued through the year. The Alumni Weekly carried communications attacking the President for his high-handed attempts to "make a gentleman chum with a mucker," or to force men "to submit to dictation as to their table companions." The trustees, frightened by the noise the alumni had raised, on October 17 requested President Wilson to withdraw the proposition.

The Home of president Woodrow Wilson, Princeton, N. J., during his professorship. Built by Mr. & Mrs. Wilson

Yet another matter of serious controversy arose with the question of the establishment of a Graduate College. Bequests made for this purpose contained conditions which seemed to require of President Wilson that he should abrogate powers which he believed it his duty to exercise, and this he refused to do. It ended in Princeton getting her magnificent Graduate College — and losing her president. Mr. Wilson felt that he could be of no more service to Old Nassau. When therefore an opportunity to serve his fellow men came with the Democratic nomination to the governorship of New Jersey, he accepted it, and doubtless gladly, for it opened the avenues of statesmanship and public service for which his whole life had been an unconscious preparation.

New Jersey had begun to feel the effects of the great political reform movement sweeping the country and Democratic leaders knew that the state could not be won for their party unless a strong, clean man led the ticket. Woodrow Wilson's splendid campaign to make Princeton a truly American institution had caught the eye of the whole country. He had been a life long Democrat. New Jersey had within her borders the very man the party needed. The state was at the mercy of the big interests. Mr. Wilson hesitated to give his consent to consider the nomination, and was outspoken in the statement that he would make no promises and if elected he must be the accepted leader of his party. This latter condition he rightly regarded as essential to the carrying out of the reforms needed. When asked whether, if he were elected, he would refuse to listen to organization leaders and acknowledge the party organization, Mr. Wilson replied in this wise: "I have always been a believer in party organizations. If I were elected Governor I should be very glad to consult with the leaders of the Democratic organization. I should refuse to listen to no man but I should be especially glad to hear and duly consider the suggestions of the leaders of my party. If on my own independent investigation, I found that recommendations for appointment made to me by the organization leaders named the best possible men, I should naturally prefer, other things being equal, to appoint them, as the men pointed out by the combined counsels of the party." On July 15 he published a statement to the effect that he would accept the nomination if it were the desire "of a decided majority of the thoughtful Democrats of the State." He was enthusiastically nominated and made a brilliant campaign, convincing the people everywhere of his sincerity of purpose and of his freedom from leading strings. He was elected by 49,150 plurality, which marked a notable political revolution, for Taft had carried New Jersey before by a plurality of 82,000.

A primary for United States senator had been held the same day of the election of governor. Not dreaming that Democratic success would extend to the Legislature, the Democratic primary for senator had been allowed to go by default, or at least to take care of itself. The total Democratic vote was 73,000 and James E. Martine had received 54,000 of these. After a bitter fight, in which Governor Wilson showed he was the real leader of his party and able to cope successfully with the old politicians who did not know that a new day and a new leader had arrived, the Legislature elected Mr. Martine, who had led in the primary, giving him forty votes, while James Smith, Jr., who insisted upon becoming a candidate, when he had declared before election he would not run, received only four. It was a preliminary victory which greatly encouraged the new general and his soldiery for coming battles. For battles there must needs be, because not only was there Republican opposition to contend with but some of the old Democratic organization leaders could not soon forget the Governor's triumph in the defeat of their old leader. Governor Wilson found the Legislature to be constituted as follows: Senate: Republicans 12, Democrats 9; Assembly: Republicans 18, Democrats 42. The platform on which the party had won promised four vital reforms, a direct primary bill, a corrupt practices act, a public service commission with power to fix rates, and an employer's liability and workingmen's compensation law. Bitter opposition to these reforms developed, secretly even among some Democratic members who were supposed to be pledged to them. Few believed the Governor could force them through. When informed that it would be the end of the session before they could be reached, he replied that if that were the case an extra session would be called to pass them. He invited Republican as well as Democratic members to call upon him at his offices. If they did not come he sent for them. He won over some by his logical reasoning, others by his magnetic personality. To some who were extremely stubborn he proposed canvassing their own districts with them. Once in a message he intimated that he might be compelled to name publicly the balking members but as a matter of fact he never had to do so. He never made ugly threats but he often smilingly suggested that Jersey public opinion was back of his arguments.

In a legislative session of three months, in spite of the fact that the upper house of the legislature was of the opposite party to him, Governor Wilson fulfilled every demand of the people in securing this important legislation:

(1) The reform of the election laws was achieved by a Corrupt Practices Act, which makes it impossible for any corporation to contribute in any way towards the election of any candidate, and likewise makes the use of money on election-day unlawful and difficult; direct primaries for all elective state, county and municipal offices; direct primaries for United States senator and delegates to national conventions, with popular expression for choice for president; civil service tests for election officers and personal registration for all voters; non-partisan ballots in both primaries and elections.

(2) The better regulation of corporations was accomplished by a comprehensive Public Utilities Law, fixing the responsibility on officers of corporations for all violations, and vesting power in a commission to make rates and physical valuation of public service companies.

(3) Accidents to workingmen were provided for by a workmen's compensation law, providing for automatic payments for injuries or loss of life, in all industries, and doing away with the old fellow-servant responsibility of the common law.

(4) An act was passed enabling cities to adopt the commission form of government.

(5) A law was passed providing for the complete reorganization of the complicated state school system, whereby politics was eliminated.

(6) A law was passed regulating cold storage and other laws to purify the milk supply and to keep oysters from contamination.

Governor Wilson's extraordinary success in putting reforms through the New Jersey legislature gave him a strong lead for the Democratic nomination for the Presidency, and when the Democratic convention met at Baltimore on June 25, 1912, the New Jersey Executive was in a forward position as one of the people's favorites. Feeling that he was not the representative of progressive politics, the selection of Judge Parker as temporary chairman was earnestly opposed by Honorable William J. Bryan, who sent telegrams to every presidential candidate asking whether Parker was satisfactory for this position. To this telegram Wilson did not hesitate to reply without equivocation that he felt that the choice of Parker would be a mistake. That telegram, sent contrary to the dictates of the old political method of trimming, was a master stroke. It showed that Wilson was no opportunist, but was ready to declare his position when silence or straddling was recommended. Parker won, and it seemed at first as if those who opposed him were doomed to defeat. The deadlock, which lasted from June 25 until July 2, gave Bryan his opportunity, for it allowed the story of the fight that was being made for Wilson as the most militant leader of Progressive measures to find its way back to the uttermost corners of the country. The national Democracy was thrilled. The people began to telegraph their wishes to the delegates, and they strongly favored the nomination of Wilson. It is said that one hundred and ten thousand telegrams were received by delegates, Mr. Bryan himself receiving 1,112 signed by more than thirty thousand persons. Mr. Bryan became the leading spirit of the Convention and he threw his support to Governor Wilson, who made slow but steady gains until his final triumph. On the first ballot he received three hundred and twenty-four votes, and on the forty-sixth, which nominated, nine hundred and ninety.

Upon accepting the nomination for the presidency, Mr. Wilson thus succinctly summarized in his speech at Sea Girt the two great things he would undertake to do:

"There are two great things to do. One is to set up the rule of justice and of right in such matters as the tariff, the regulation of the trusts and the prevention of monopoly, the adaptation of our banking and currency laws to the varied uses to which our people must put them, the treatment of those who do the daily labor in our factories and mines and throughout all our great industrial and commercial undertakings, and the political life of the people of the Philippines, for whom we hold governmental power in trust for their service, not our own. The other, the additional duty, is the great task of protecting our people and our resources and of keeping open to the whole people the doors of opportunity through which they must, generation by generation, pass if they are to make conquest of their fortunes in health, in freedom, in peace and in contentment. In the performance of this second great duty we are face to face with questions of conservation and of development, questions of forests and water powers and mines and waterways, of the building of an adequate merchant marine, and the opening of every highway and facility and the setting up of every safeguard needed by a great, industrious, expanding nation."

In this speech Governor Wilson contended that representative government is nothing more nor less than an effort to give voice to the great, struggling body of the masses — the learned and the fortunate, as well as the uneducated — through spokesmen chosen out of every grade and class. He declared it to be a fact which it would be dangerous to ignore that, "We stand in the presence of an awakened nation — awake to the knowledge that she has lost certain cherished liberties and has wasted priceless resources which she had solemnly under taken to hold in trust for posterity and for all mankind; and she stands confronted with an occasion for constructive statesmanship such as has not arisen since the days in which the Government was set up." . . . "We are servants of the people, the whole people. The Nation has been unnecessarily, unreasonably at war within itself. Interest has clashed with interest when there were common principles of right and of fair dealing which might and should have bound them all together, not as rivals, but as partners. As the servants of all, we are bound to undertake the great duty of accommodation and adjustment."

The Nominee was outspoken in his conviction that the tariff should be revised. Said he:

"Tariff duties, as they have employed them, have not been a means of setting up an equitable system of protection. They have been, on the contrary, a method of fostering special privilege. They have made it easy to establish monopoly in our domestic markets. Trusts have owed their origin and their secure power to them. The economic freedom of our people, our prosperity in trade, our untrammeled energy in manufacture depend upon their reconsideration from top to bottom in an entirely different spirit. . . . It is obvious that the changes we make should be made only at such a rate and in such a way as will least interfere with the normal and healthful course of commerce and manufacture. But we shall not on that account act with timidity, as if we did not know our own minds, for we are certain of our ground and of our object. There should be an immediate revision, and it should be downward, unhesitatingly and steadily downward." . . .

President Wilson made an inspiring campaign, delivering a number of speeches at strategic centers in the various states. The triangular character of the race made it the most interesting in American history since Lincoln's time. Wilson got 6,293,454 of the popular vote; Roosevelt 4,119,538, and Taft 3,484,980, but the New Jersey Executive got an overwhelming majority in the Electoral College, the vote standing thus: Wilson 435, Roosevelt 88, and Taft 8.

The marrow of the man is his sincerity. His carrying out of every pledge made in New Jersey presaged his course as President. He kept the rudder true in his State in a storm that beat its fury upon the Commonwealth and threatened to divide and defeat his party, victorious for the first time in a dozen years. In his inaugural address, in which his sincere and genuine appeal to "all forward-looking men" fell upon ears that were glad to hear the pledge of the New Freedom he had come to inaugurate in our Republic, the new President showed that his campaign pledges were the sacred covenants between the new executive and the people.

His inaugural illustrated the truth that he was sailing by the chart which he himself had prepared in the campaign: After insisting that the change of government meant that the nation now sought to use the Democratic party to interpret a change in its own plans and point of view; after asserting that some old, familiar things have dropped their disguises and shown themselves alien and sinister, and that some new things have come to assume the aspect of things long believed in and familiar, he declared we had come to a work of restoration, and continued:

"We have itemized with some degree of particularity the things that ought to be altered and here are some of the chief items: A tariff which cuts us off from our proper part in the commerce of the world, violates the just principles of taxation, and makes the Government a facile instrument in the hands of private interests; a banking and currency system based upon the necessity of the Government to sell its bonds fifty years ago and perfectly adapted to concentrating cash and restricting credits; an industrial system which, take it on all sides, financial as well as administrative, holds capital in leading strings, restricts the liberties and limits the opportunities of labor, and exploits without renewing or conserving the natural resources of the country; a body of agricultural activities never yet given the efficiency of great business undertakings or served as it should be through the instrumentality of science taken directly to the farm, or afforded the facilities of credit best suited to its practical needs; water-courses undeveloped, waste places unreclaimed, forests untended, fast disappearing without plan or prospect of renewal, unregarded waste heaps at every mine. We have studied as perhaps no other nation has the most effective means of production, but we have not studied cost or economy as we should either as organizers of industry, as statesmen, or as individuals."

The inaugural address concluded with this appeal for co-operation in the great task upon which he was entering:

"This is not a day of triumph; it is a day of dedication. Here muster, not the forces of party, but the forces of humanity. Men's hearts wait upon us; men's lives hang in the balance; men's hopes call upon us to say what we will do. Who shall live up to the great trust? Who dares fail to try? I summon all honest men, all patriotic, all forward-looking men, to my side. God helping me, I will not fail them, if they will but counsel and sustain me!"

When the 63rd Congress was called in extraordinary session the President's proclamation did not limit the purpose to tariff reduction, as many party leaders desired, but it was primarily convened to revise and reduce the tariff. The previous Republican administration had revised but not reduced, and suffered a crushing defeat in the elections of 1910 and 1912. Wilson, moreover, had before his vision the mistakes of the late President Cleveland to aid him in determining to permit no new question or no reasonings to divert him from the paramount duty of responding to the double mandate of the voters to reduce the tariff and unfetter trade. His every utterance emphasized tariff as the first great reform to be carried out. He was in frequent conference with the leaders of the House, both before Congress assembled and when it convened. He led in the Nation in making and invoking public sentiment as he had successfully led when he was Governor of New Jersey. To emphasize his tariff program and impress the argument for genuine reduction, he astonished the country by going in person and reading his message to Congress, reviving an early custom which went into innocuous desuetude because Jefferson, who had no taste and little gift for public speaking, sent his message to be read by a clerk, instead of delivering it in person. There were those who declared this return to an old order suggested a king giving orders to Congress. They predicted that the innovation smacked of a return to Federalism. But on the day that Wilson entered the House to read his message every seat was occupied. Hundreds could not gain admission. Those who witnessed the contrast between the clear enunciation and impressive presentation of his convictions and recommendations, and the old humdrum reading, when clerks droned through a message, and the tense interest when the new leader enunciated his own views and the pledges of the majority party, rejoiced at the new freedom that ushered in the delivery in the flesh of a fresh message to the American people.

Wilson was in direct touch with Mr. Underwood and other members of the Ways and Means Committee and other leaders of the House in the preparation of the Underwood Bill. He did not shirk labor or responsibility, nor assume the duty resting upon others. But, in consonance with the duty which the leadership of the dominant party, to which he had been called, demanded, he helped to shape the character of the legislation on the schedules upon which there was the most difference of opinion. He freely discussed these schedules with those who had a claim upon his consideration of their views. The sugar people were the most active and earnest in trying to secure a reversal of the program of free sugar. They sought to impress the President with the view that a protective duty, which would bring in large revenue, should remain on sugar. He heard, he conferred, he debated, and declared that free sugar must be a part of the bill, and free sugar is in the Underwood-Simmons bill. The famous Schedule K, long called the key to the protection arch, had given so much trouble to the Democrats in the prior Congress that they had to be content to levy some tax on wool, much to the regret of the many who for more than a quarter of a century had been fighting for free wool. The advocates of a tariff on wool wished to enact the same wool schedule that passed the Sixty-second Congress, but the President stood firmly for free wool, as did nearly all the newly elected Congressmen, and free wool is in the bill. The old plan of permitting the beneficiaries of the tariff to write the tariff schedules, which put money in their purses, had come to an end. The President, with the overwhelming majority of his party in Congress, subordinated every local consideration to the passage of a tariff act drafted along the lines indicated in the pre-election promises of the President. In the tariff, as in important matters in which he was interested in New Jersey, he accepted no compromise. The Tariff act of 1913 owes much of its value to the wise and courageous President in the White House. To him is largely due the credit of a united party, with a narrow margin in the Senate, refusing to change in one jot or tittle the bill agreed upon in party council and approved by the Chief Executive. In 1894, with a like slender majority in the Senate, Mr. Cleveland was unable to lead his party in the famous tariff struggle. They divided and compromised so that, when the Senate finally passed a tariff bill which the House felt forced to accept, the President refused to sign it. He declared it to represent "party perfidy and party dishonor." But the Democratic party went into long exile as the result of party dissensions over tariff and currency legislation. There were those who predicted that history would repeat itself and that the Democratic Congress would so divide in 1913 as to invite another long exile such as the one that began in 1894 and lasted until 1912. To the President, in cordial co-operation with the leaders of his party in Congress, the historian will give the credit for the united action that insured tariff and currency legislation[71] without party dissension or serious financial disturbance.

It is well known that every revision of the tariff in the past half a century has been accompanied by a strong lobby of the interests which had commercial or industrial issues at stake. After the Underwood bill had gone to the Senate, President Wilson had occasion to inform the Senate that he had information that "a numerous, industrious and insidious lobby" was at work. The President's statement, which aroused the country, was, in full, as follows:

"I think that the public ought to know the extraordinary exertions being made by the lobby in Washington to gain recognition for certain alterations of the tariff bill. Washington has seldom seen so numerous, so industrious, or so insidious a lobby. The newspapers are being filled with paid advertisements calculated to mislead the judgment of public men not only, but also the public opinion of the country itself. There is every evidence that money without limit is being spent to sustain this lobby and to create an appearance of a pressure of public opinion antagonistic to some of the chief items of the tariff bill. It is of serious interest to the country that the people at large should have no lobby and be voiceless in these matters while great bodies of astute men seek to create an artificial opinion and to overcome the interests of the public for their private profit. It is thoroughly worth the while of the people of this country to take knowledge of this matter. Only public opinion can check and destroy it.

"The Government in all its branches ought to be relieved from this intolerable burden and this constant interruption to the calm progress of debate. I know that in this I am speaking for the members of the two Houses, who would rejoice as much as I would to be released from this unbearable situation."

The statement, at first, was received by a portion of the press and people with incredulity but, as the lobby investigating committee, headed by Senator Overman, proceeded with its work, it became plainly evident that the President was entirely correct in his charge and in his description of the nature of the lobby. Evidence adduced showed that the sugar-growing interests spent as much as $100,000 in agitation against free sugar, though there was no proof that this particular item was illegally expended. It was in evidence that more than 1,000,000 documents had been mailed under the franks of Congressmen in opposition to free sugar. In one quarter, charges were made that a long list of members of both branches of Congress had accepted money considerations in exchange for their influence in committees of Congress which had labor legislation in charge. Undue influence was exerted upon other members, it was alleged, by means of "business, political and sympathetic" reasons. It was proven that one shameless lobbyist had impersonated, over the long-distance telephone, several of the leading members of Congress and had offered in their name to influence pending legislation. Evidence was multiplied that strong bodies of men united to defeat members of Congress who opposed the legislation they desired, or sought to put laws on the statute books not favored by them. The trail of the lobbyist was found in a score of ways. The charge of the President of the existence of "a numerous, industrious and insidious lobby" was more than established by the evidence. The President was vindicated. The President's warning and the work of the lobby committee served to put Congress and the people on their guard, and history will doubtless record that the Underwood-Simmons tariff bill was freer from attack by this old enemy of tariff reduction than any other tariff measure passed for many years.

As soon as it became certain that a tariff bill, in accordance with the promises of the Baltimore platform, would pass the extra session, the President bent his energies toward co-operating with Congress to secure the passage of a currency reform measure. The bill, which was christened with the names of Representative Glass and Senator Owen, had the sanction of the Administration.

The President undertook to overcome the feeling of those members of the Senate that remaining in session through the hot summer in order to pass the tariff bill was sufficient achievement for one session and that the currency bill could go over to the regular session. With all the earnestness of his nature, the President urged that there would never be a more favorable opportunity to pass a currency reform measure than the present. He appeared personally before Congress in joint session for the second time and read his message on the currency. "When the work to be done is so pressing and so fraught with big consequence," he said, "we know that we are not at liberty to weigh against it any point of personal sacrifice." In making men free to employ individual initiative by removing the trammels of the protection tariff, the President held, there will be necessary some readjustments of purpose and point of view. Then will follow a period of expansion and new enterprise, and "it is for us to determine whether it shall be rapid and facile and of easy accomplishment. This it cannot be unless the resourceful business men who are to deal with the new circumstances are to have at hand and ready for use the instrumentalities and conveniences of free enterprise which independent men need when acting on their own initiative." One of the chief things business needs now is "the proper means by which readily to vitalize its credit, corporate and individual, and its originative brains. The tyrannies of business, big and little, lie within the field of credit. We know that. Shall we not act upon the knowledge? Do we not know how to act upon it? If a man cannot make his assets available at pleasure, his assets of capacity and character and resource, what satisfaction is it to him to see opportunity beckoning to him on every hand, when others have the keys of credit in their pockets and treat them as all but their own private possession?"

It is imperative, therefore, to act immediately and upon clear principles. "The country has sought and seen its path in this matter within the last few years — sees it more clearly now than it ever saw it before — much more clearly than when the last legislative proposals on the subject were made. We must have a currency, not rigid as now, but readily, elastically responsive to sound credit, the expanding and contracting credits of everyday transactions, the normal ebb and flow of personal and corporate dealings. Our banking laws must mobilize reserves; must not permit the concentration anywhere in a few hands of the monetary resources of the country or their use for speculative purposes in such volume as to hinder or impede or stand in the way of other more legitimate, more fruitful uses. And the control of the system of banking and of issue which our new laws are to set up must be public, not private, must be vested in the Government itself, so that the banks may be the instruments, not the masters, of business and of individual enterprise and initiative."

The Wilson administration, in its earliest stages, was called upon to consider diplomatic questions that at once gave the people a clear understanding of its foreign policy. With firmness and dignity, unmoved by jingoism or hesitation, the President made clear his determination to make friendliness and justice to other nations the duty and mission of the Republic. In his brief inaugural, Mr. Wilson did not touch upon foreign questions but confined himself to the few economic home problems that pressed for solution. He may have thought, as did most of the people, that no international complications would come up until the needed tariff and currency legislation had been enacted, and he doubtless hoped that not even a small cloud would appear upon the horizon to threaten our cordial and friendly relations with other nations. But there soon came rumors of threatened trouble in one or more Republics to the south of us. There seemed to be a feeling that, after a long period of Republican rule at Washington, the new Administration's induction into office would encourage self-imposed officials to seek to obtain the reins of government. What should the attitude of the Administration be toward our neighbor countries in Central and South America? The President deemed the answer to that question important enough to make a declaration that attracted world-wide attention. He said:

"One of the chief objects of my administration will be to cultivate the friendship and deserve the confidence of our sister republics of Central and South America, and to promote in every proper and honorable way the interests which are common to the peoples of the two continents. I earnestly desire the most cordial understanding and co-operation between the peoples and leaders of America and, therefore, deem it my duty to make this brief statement.

"Co-operation is possible only when supported at every turn by the orderly processes of just government based upon law, not upon arbitrary or irregular force. We hold, as I am sure all thoughtful leaders of republican government everywhere hold, that just government rests always upon the consent of the governed, and that there can be no freedom without order based upon law and upon the public conscience and approval. We shall look to make these principles the basis of mutual intercourse, respect and helpfulness between our sister republics and ourselves. We shall lend our influence of every kind to the realization of these principles in fact and practice, knowing that disorder, personal intrigues, and defiance of constitutional rights weaken and discredit government and injure none so much as the people who are unfortunate enough to have their common life and their common affairs so tainted and disturbed. We can have no sympathy with those who seek to seize the power of government to advance their own personal interests or ambition. We are the friends of peace, but we know that there can be no lasting or stable peace in such circumstances. As friends, therefore, we shall prefer those who act in the interest of peace and honor, who protect private rights, and respect the restraints of constitutional provision. Mutual respect seems to us the indispensable foundation of friendships between states, as between individuals.

"The United States has nothing to seek in Central and South America except the lasting interests of the peoples of the two continents, the security of governments intended for the people and for no special group or interest, and the development of personal and trade relationships between the two continents which shall redound to the profit and advantage of both and interfere with the rights and liberties of neither."

At the same time, the world was given to under stand that what is known as "dollar diplomacy" would not be countenanced by the Administration. During the Presidential campaign there had been much criticism of this policy and many had attributed to it a growing irritation in some of our sister republics.

The people of China had but latterly changed the form of their government into a republic, patterned after the United States. No great nation had recognized the Republic, and there was doubt whether it would maintain itself. The President determined not to join hands with other nations in a loan coupled with conditions that denied the government of China a free hand. He resolved also that as soon as the Chinese legislative branch was organized he would recognize the new Republic. The people of the United States rejoiced in the recognition, and shortly other nations followed. In extending the recognition of the greatest western Republic to the oldest nation that had put on the robes of self-government, the addresses by the new President of China and the American representative in China gave a thrill to all who believe that all governments derive their just powers from the consent of the governed. The words of President Wilson constitute the best expression of American thought. He wrote:

"The Government and people of the United States of America having abundantly testified their sympathy with the people of China upon their assumption of the attributes and powers of self-government deem it opportune at this time, when the representative National Assembly has met to discharge the high duty of setting the seal of full accomplishment upon the aspirations of the Chinese people, that I extend, in the name of my Government and of my countrymen, a greeting of welcome to the New China thus entering into the family of nations. In taking this step, I entertain the confident hope and expectation that in perfecting a republican form of government the Chinese nation will attain to the highest degree of development and well-being, and that under the new rule all the established obligations of China which passed to the Provisional Government will, in turn, pass to and be observed by the Government established by the Assembly."

Early in the history of the Administration, the Japanese Minister lodged a protest with the Department of State against the proposed passage of an anti-alien land law bill by the California Legislature. The claim of the Japanese Government was that such a measure would violate treaty rights. "To lease land for commercial purposes" is granted to Japanese subjects in our treaty with Japan. It was claimed by the California Legislature that the Japanese were increasing their leases and their ownership of lands, particularly agricultural lands, in California. President Wilson set himself to see that the treaty rights of Japan should be respected. In a telegram to Governor Johnson, of California, the President "very respectfully but most earnestly advised against" the use of the words "ineligible to citizenship," which were used in one or more of the bills pending. In a second telegram to Governor Johnson, he appealed to the Executive, the Legislature, and the people of California, "to act in the matter under consideration in a manner that cannot from any point of view be fairly challenged or called in question. If they deem it necessary to exclude all aliens who have not declared their intention to become citizens from the privilege of land ownership, they can do so along the lines already followed in the laws of many foreign countries including Japan itself. Invidious discrimination will inevitably draw in question the treaty obligations of the Government of the United States." The President added that he was "confident the people and the legislative authorities of California would generously respond the moment the matter was presented to them as a question of national policy and national honor."

Upon the receipt of a reply from Governor Johnson, President Wilson telegraphed to the Governor asking whether, on account of the difficulty from a distance of understanding fully the situation with regard to the sentiments and circumstances lying back of the pending proposition concerning the ownership of land in California, it would be agreeable to him and the Legislature to have the Secretary of State visit Sacramento for the purpose of counseling with the Governor and the members of the Legislature and co-operating in the framing of a law which would meet the views of the people of the State and yet leave untouched the international obligations of the United States.

Mr. Bryan went to California and conferred with the Governor and Legislature, but it soon be came clearly apparent that the Legislature was bent upon passing a law forbidding ownership of agricultural land by the Japanese.

Mr. Bryan's suggestions to the Legislature were the following:

1. Delay immediate action and permit the State Department to try to frame a new treaty with Japan.

2. Delay immediate action and appoint a legislative commission to investigate alien land ownership and act with President Wilson in gaining relief.

3. Enact a law similar to the Illinois statute, which allows all aliens to hold land six years.

4. Enact a law similar to the Federal statute in the District of Columbia, which applies to all aliens.

Mr. Bryan presented these suggestions with this happy statement: "Each State in the Union acts in a dual capacity. It is the guardian of local affairs of its people and in a sense the only guardian, and yet each State is a member of the Union and one of the sisterhood of States. Therefore, in acting upon questions of local conditions, the State always recognizes that it is its duty to share the responsibility with other States in actions affecting the nation's relations with foreign nations."

The Legislature passed an act that was regarded by Japan as a discrimination against that country. For a time there was a feeling that the friendly relations long existing between the two countries would be sundered. But the policy of the Federal Administration, couched in friendly and courteous terms, convinced the Japanese people of its genuine friendship and of its sincere desire to treat that country with justice and consideration. The tense feeling in both countries was relieved by the spirit of amity and justice shown in every act and note of the Wilson administration.

A second delicate diplomatic situation with which the President had to deal concerned Mexico. The Ambassador at Mexico City, Mr. Henry Lane Wilson, was an appointee of the previous Administration, and in his desire to have this country recognize the de facto Huerta government, which followed the Madero régime, he did not represent the views of President Wilson. Ambassador Wilson was summoned to Washington to confer with the President, but a variance of views developing between him and the Administration, his resignation was eventually accepted. The situation was one of grave difficulty. The President was constrained to send a personal representative to deal with it at first hand and for this delicate mission selected ex-Governor John Lind of Minnesota, who was sent to Mexico. He was sent as adviser of the United States Embassy at Mexico City, and he began his negotiations with the Huerta administration through the United States chargé d'affaires. General Huerta showed little inclination, however, to accept the good offices tendered by this country through Mr. Lind. At this juncture, President Wilson for the third time took the Congress and people of the United States into his counsels by appearing personally before the joint session of both houses and making public his purpose and plans in dealing with the Mexican situation and with the results that followed his efforts.

His address revealed how the Huerta provisional government had rejected the friendly offices of the United States, told of its effort to aid in the establishment of peace, and of a government which could be recognized by this nation, and which would be obeyed and respected by Mexico's own people. For the first time since Washington's administration, a President appeared before Congress to discuss foreign affairs. His cordial reception by members from all sides, and the endorsement of his course by a large majority of the members of Congress, the press, and of the people of the Union, showed how strongly public opinion was behind him in his efforts. He sounded a high note when he stated at the outset:

"The peace, prosperity and contentment of Mexico mean more, much more, to us than merely an enlarged field for our commerce and enterprise. They mean an enlargement of the field of self-government and the realization of the hopes and rights of a nation with whose best aspirations, so long suppressed and disappointed, we deeply sympathize. We shall yet prove to the Mexican people that we know how to serve them without first thinking how we shall serve ourselves."

May 19, 1913.

THE WHITE HOUSE
WASHINGTON

My dear General Wilson,

I wish most sincerely that it were possible for me to be present at the dedication of the Maine Monument. My thoughts will be very much with you that day, as will, I am sure, the thoughts of the whole country.

All Americans must look back to the tragedy of the Maine with the profoundest sentiments of sorrow for the fine men who then so tragically and unexpectedly lost their lives, and must always feel that to have been one of the turning points of our consciousness of what was involved in the struggle for human liberty.

Cordially and Sincerely Yours,
Woodrow Wilson

General James Grant Wilson

[*Fac-simile letter from President Woodrow Wilson to Gen. James Grant Wilson*]

Mr. Lind was sent with the following instructions:

"Press very earnestly upon the attention of those who are now exercising authority or wielding influence in Mexico the following considerations and advice:

"The Government of the United States does not stand in the same case with the other great governments of the world in respect of what is happening or what is likely to happen in Mexico. We offer our good offices, not only because of our genuine desire to play the part of a friend, but also because we are expected by the powers of the world to act as Mexico's nearest friend.

"We wish to act in these circumstances in the spirit of the most earnest and disinterested friendship. It is our purpose in whatever we do or propose in this perplexing and distressing situation not only to pay the most scrupulous regard to the sovereignty and independence of Mexico — that we take as a matter of course to which we are bound by every obligation of right and honor — but also to give every possible evidence that we act in the interest of Mexico alone, and not in the interest of any person or body of persons who may have personal or property claims in Mexico which they may feel that they have a right to press. We are seeking to counsel Mexico for her own good and in the interest of her own peace, and not for any other purpose whatever. The Government of the United States would deem itself discredited if it had any selfish or ulterior purpose in transactions where the peace, happiness, and prosperity of a whole people are involved. It is acting as its friendship for Mexico, not as any selfish interest, dictates.

"The present situation in Mexico is incompatible with the fulfillment of international obligations on the part of Mexico, with the civilized development of Mexico herself, and with the maintenance of tolerable political and economic conditions in Central America. It is upon no common occasion therefore that the United States offers her counsel and assistance. All America cries out for a settlement.

"A satisfactory settlement seems to us to be conditioned on —

"(a) An immediate cessation of fighting throughout Mexico, a definite armistice solemnly entered into and scrupulously observed;

"(b) Security given for an early and free election in which all will agree to take part;

"(c) The consent of General Huerta to bind himself not to be a candidate for election as president of the republic at this election; and

"(d) The agreement of all parties to abide by the results of the election and co-operate in the most loyal way in organizing and supporting the new administration."

The Mexican Government was to be assured that the United States wished to play any part in this settlement which it could play honorably and consistently. It pledged itself to recognize and assist an administration so set up. Could Mexico give the civilized world a good reason for rejecting these good offices?

Mr. Lind executed his delicate mission with singular tact, firmness and good judgment, but the proposals he submitted were rejected in a note of Foreign Minister Gamboa which was laid before the Congress in printed form. This rejection the President was constrained to believe was due to misinformation, first, as to the friendly spirit of the American people in this matter, and, second, because they did not believe that the present Administration spoke for the people of the United States. "The effect of this unfortunate misunderstanding on their part," he continued in his message, "is to leave them singularly isolated and without friends who can effectually aid them. So long as the misunderstanding continues, we can only await the time of their awakening to a realization of the actual facts. We cannot thrust our good offices upon them. The situation must be given a little more time to work itself out in the new circumstances; and I believe that only a little time will be necessary. For the circumstances are new. The rejection of our friendship makes them new and will inevitably bring its own alterations in the whole aspect of affairs. The actual situation of the authorities at Mexico City will presently be revealed." Meantime, "we can afford to exercise the self-restraint of a really great nation which realizes its own strength and scorns to misuse it." With increased activity on the part of contending factions in Mexico would come increased danger to non-combatants, and therefore the President earnestly urged all Americans to leave Mexico at once. We should assist them in getting away, but, at the same time, let every one who assumed authority know, in the most unequivocal way, "that we shall vigilantly watch the fortunes of those Americans who cannot get away and shall hold those responsible for their sufferings and losses to a definite reckoning." For the rest, the President would forbid the exportation of arms or munitions of war from the United States into any part of the Republic of Mexico. His policy of justice, patience and friendship in all dealings with Mexico won the approval of the whole world. This policy, dictated by neighborly regard and freedom from any spirit of aggression, has, it is believed, gone far to make for the enduring friendship of the neighboring republics when the present unhappy struggles in Mexico have given way to honorable peace.

Footnotes

1. These are Mr. Bagehot's words with reference to the British constitutional system. See his *English Constitution* (last American edition), p. 69.
2. *Works*, vol. vi., p. 467: "Letter to Jno. Taylor." The words and sentences omitted in the quotation contain Mr. Adams's opinions as to the value of the several balances, some of which he thinks of doubtful utility, and others of which he, without hesitation, pronounces altogether pernicious.
3. *Federalist*, No. 17.
4. Cooley's *Principles of Const. Law*, p. 143.
5. McMaster, *Hist. of the People of the U. S.*, vol. i., p. 564.
6. Lodge's *Alexander Hamilton* (Am. Statesmen Series), p. 85.
7. Lodge's *Alexander Hamilton*, p. 105.
8. Its final and most masterly exposition, by C. J. Marshall, may be seen in McCulloch v. Maryland, 4 Wheaton, 316.
9. The following passage from William Maclay's *Sketches of Debate in the First Senate of the United States* (pp. 292-3) illustrates how clearly the results of this were forecast by sagacious men from the first: "The system laid down by these gentlemen (the Federalists) was as follows, or rather the development of the designs of a certain party: The general power to carry the Constitution into effect by a constructive interpretation would extend to every case that Congress may deem necessary or expedient....The laws of the United States will be held paramount to all "state" laws, claims, and even constitutions. The supreme power is with the general government to decide in this, as in everything else, for the States have neglected to secure any umpire or mode of decision in case of difference between them. Nor is there any point in the Constitution for them to rally under. They may give an opinion, but the opinions of the general government must prevail....Any direct and open act would be termed usurpation. But whether the gradual influence and encroachments of the general government may not gradually swallow up the state governments, is another matter."
10. Pensacola Tel. Co. *v.* West. Union, 96 U. S. 1, 9. (Quoted by Judge Cooley in his *Principles of Constitutional Law*.)
11. 18 Stat., part 3, 336. See Ex parte Virginia, 100 U. S. 339.
12. Sect. 5515 Rev. Stats. See Ex parte Siebold, 100 U. S. 371. Equally extensive of federal powers is that "legal tender" decision (Juilliard *v.* Greenman) of March, 1884, which argues the existence of a right to issue an irredeemable paper currency from the Constitution's grant of other rights characteristic of sovereignty, and from the possession of a similar right by other governments. But this involves no restriction of state powers; and perhaps there ought to be offset against it that other decision (several cases, October, 1883), which denies constitutional sanction to the Civil Rights Act.
13. *Principles of Constitutional Law*, pp. 143, 144.
14. Marbury *v.* Madison, 1 Cranch, 137.
15. Cooley's *Principles*, p. 157.

16. For an incisive account of the whole affair, see an article Entitled "The Session," *No. Am. Review*, vol. cxi., pp. 48, 49.

17. 7 Wall. 506.

18. For a brilliant account of the senatorial history of these two treaties, see the article entitled "The Session," *No. Am. Rev.*, vol. cviii. (1869), p. 626 *et seq.*

19. In an article entitled "The Conduct of Business in Congress" (*North American Review*, vol. cxxviii. p. 113), to which I am indebted for many details of the sketch in the text.

20. No Committee is entitled, when called, to occupy more than the morning hours of two successive days with the measures which it has prepared; though if its second morning hour expire while the House is actually considering one of its bills, that single measure may hold over from morning hour to morning hour until it is disposed of.

21. Quoted from an exceedingly life-like and picturesque description of the House which appeared in the New York *Nation* for April 4, 1878.

22. *No. Am. Rev.*, vol. xxvi., p. 162.

23. *Id.*, the same article.

24. "Glances at Congress," *Dem. Rev.*, March, 1839.

25. *Autobiography*, pp. 264, 265.

26. *The National Budget, etc.* (English Citizen Series), p. 146. In what I have to say of the English system, I follow this volume, pp. 146-149, and another volume of the same admirable series, entitled *Central Government*, pp. 36-47, most of my quotations being from the latter.

27. See an article entitled "National Appropriations and Misappropriations," by the late President Garfield, *North American Review*, vol cxxviii. pp 578 *et seq.*

28. Senator Hoar's article, already several times quoted.

29. Adams's *John Randolph*. American Statesman Series, pp. 210, 211.

30. On one occasion "the House passed thirty-seven pension bills at one sitting. The Senate, on its part, by unanimous consent, took up and passed in about ten minutes seven bills providing for public buildings in different States, appropriating an aggregate of $1,200,000 in this short time. A recent House feat was one in which a bill, allowing 1,300 war claims in a lump, was passed. It contained one hundred and nineteen pages full of little claims, amounting in all to $291,000; and a member, in deprecating criticism on this disposition of them, said that the Committee had received ten huge bags full of such claims, which had been adjudicated by the Treasury officials, and it was a physical impossibility to examine them." —*N. Y. Sun*, 1881.

31. Congress, though constantly erecting new Committees, never gives up old ones, no matter how useless they may have become by subtraction of duties. Thus there is not only the superseded Committee on Public Expenditures but the Committee on Manufactures also, which, when a part of the one-time Committee on Commerce and Manufactures, had plenty to do, but which, since the creation of a distinct Committee on Commerce, has had nothing to do, having now, together with the Committees on Agriculture and Indian Affairs, no duties assigned to it by the rules. It remains to be seen whether the Committee on Commerce will suffer a like eclipse because of the gift of its principal duties to the new Committee on Rivers and Harbors.

32. See the report of this Committee, which was under the chairmanship of Senator Windom. An illustration of what the House Committees find by special effort may be seen in the revelations of the investigation of the expenses of the notorious "Star Route Trials" made by the Forty-eighth Congress's Committee on Expenditures in the department of Justice.

33. See General Garfield's article, already once quoted, *North American Review*, vol. cxxviii. p. 533.

34. *Essays on Parliamentary Reform.*

35. Green's *History of the English People*, vol. iv., pp. 202, 203.

36. "G. B." in N. Y. *Nation*, Nov. 30, 1882.

37. An attempt was once made to bring the previous question into the practices of the Senate, but it failed of success, and so that imperative form of cutting off all further discussion has fortunately never found a place there.

38. As regards all financial measures indeed committee supervision is specially thorough in the Senate. "All amendments to general appropriation bills reported from the Committees of the Senate, proposing new items of appropriation, shall, one day before they are offered, be referred to the Committee on Appropriations, and all general appropriation bills shall be referred to said Committee; and in like manner amendments to bills making appropriations for rivers and harbors shall be again referred to the Committee to which such bills shall be referred." —Senate Rule 30.

39. The twenty-nine Standing Committees of the Senate are, however, chosen by ballot, not appointed by the Vice-President, who is an appendage, not a member, of the Senate.

40. In the Birmingham Town Hall, November 3, 1882. I quote from the report of the *London Times*.

41. "No Senator shall speak more than twice, in any one debate, on the same day, without leave of the Senate." —Senate Rule 4.

42. These quotations from Bagehot are taken from various parts of the fifth chapter of his *English Constitution*.

43. These are the words of Lord Rosebery-testimony from the oldest and most celebrated second chamber that exists.

44. There seems to have been at one time a tendency towards a better practice. In 1813 the Senate sought to revive the early custom, in accordance with which the President delivered his messages in person, by requesting the attendance of the President to consult upon foreign affairs; but Mr. Madison declined.

45. *North American Review*, vol. 108, p. 625.

46. *English Constitution*, chap, viii., p. 293.

47. *Atlantic Monthly*, vol. xxv., p. 148.

48. Something like this has been actually proposed by Mr. Albert Stickney, in his interesting and incisive essay, *A True Republic*.

49. State, Treasury, War, Navy.

50. As quoted in *Macmillan's Magazine*, vol. vii., p. 67.

51. I quote from an excellent handbook, *The United States Government*, by Lamphere.

52. "In America the President cannot prevent any law from being passed, nor can he evade the obligation of enforcing it His sincere and zealous coöperation is no doubt useful, but it is not indispensable, in the carrying on of public affairs. All his important acts are directly or indirectly submitted to the legislature, and of his own free authority he can do but little. It is, therefore, his weakness, and not his power, which enables him to remain in opposition to Congress. In Europe, harmony must reign between the Crown and the other branches of the legislature, because a collision between them may prove serious; in America, this harmony is not indispensable, because such a collision is impossible." —De Tocqueville, i. p. 124.

53. *Westminster Review*, vol. lxvi., p. 193.

54. Tenure of Office Act, already discussed.

55. These "ifs" are abundantly supported by the executive acts of the war-time. The Constitution had then to stand aside that President Lincoln might be as prompt as the seeming necessities of the time.

56. *Central Government* (Eng. Citizen Series), II. D. Traill, p. 20.

57. Professor Sumner's *Andrew Jackson* (American Statesmen Series), p. 226. "Finally," adds Prof. S., "the methods and machinery of democratic republican self-government —caucuses, primaries, committees, and conventions-lend themselves perhaps more easily than any other methods and machinery to the uses of selfish cliques which seek political influence for interested purposes."

58. Bagehot: *Essay on Sir Robert Peel*, p. 24.

59. H. C. Lodge's *Alexander Hamilton* (Am. Statesmen Series), pp. 60, 61.

60. Bagehot, *Eng. Const.*, p. 293.

61. Bagehot, *Eng. Const.*, p. 296.

62. Green: *Hist. of the English People* (Harpers' ed.), iv., pp 58, 59.

63. *Statesman's Manual*, i. p. 244.

64. Mr. Dale, of Birmingham.

65. It had been the practice of our Presidents to send their Messages to Congress and not to read them in person.

66. The speech was made from a rostrum in the National Cemetery, on the battlefield.

67. General Victoriano Huerta had, on Feb. 18, deposed President Madero, and had been, on the 20th, elected President by the Mexican Congress. Three days later Madero was assassinated while in the custody of the new government. An army calling themselves Constitutionalists under General Villa, defeated the Mexican Federal forces in May. On August 20, Huerta declined the proposal of the United States government that he should cease to be a candidate for the Presidency.

68. In the *Areopagitica*: "I cannot praise a fugitive and cloistered virtue, unexercised and unbreathed, that never sallies out and sees her adversary, but slinks out of the race, where that immortal garland is to be run for, not without dust and heat."

69. Sir George Williams, 1821-1905, an English philanthropist, founder of the Young Men's Christian Association.

70. This was at Princeton, in 1902 and 1903.

71. The Tariff Bill was signed Oct. 3, 1913; the Currency Bill, Dec. 23, 1913.